Jorun Poettering
Migrating Merchants

Jorun Poettering

Migrating Merchants

Trade, Nation, and Religion in Seventeenth-Century
Hamburg and Portugal

Translated by
Kenneth Kronenberg

DE GRUYTER
OLDENBOURG

Revised version of "Handel, Nation und Religion. Kaufleute zwischen Hamburg und Portugal im 17. Jahrhundert", Vandenhoeck & Ruprecht: Göttingen 2013, translated by Kenneth Kronenburg.

The translation of this work was funded by Geisteswissenschaften International – Translation Funding for Work in the Humanities and Social Sciences from Germany, a joint initiative of the Fritz Thyssen Foundation, the German Federal Foreign Office, the collecting society VG WORT and the Börsenverein des Deutschen Buchhandels (German Publishers & Booksellers Association).

Printed with the support of the Marie Curie Alumni Association.

ISBN 978-3-11-046993-6
e-ISBN (PDF) 978-3-11-047210-3
e-ISBN (EPUB) 978-3-11-047001-7

Library of Congress Control Number: 2018951016

Bibliographic information published by the Deutsche Nationalbibliothek
The Deutsche Nationalbibliothek lists this publication in the Deutsche Nationalbibliografie; detailed bibliographic data are available on the Internet at http://dnb.dnb.de.

© 2019 Walter de Gruyter GmbH, Berlin/Boston
Typesetting: Integra Software Services Pvt. Ltd.
Printing and binding: CPI books GmbH, Leck
Cover image: Elias Galli "Ansicht von Hamburg von der Elbseite" © Museum für Hamburgische Geschichte/hamburgmuseum

www.degruyter.com

MIX
Papier aus verantwor-
tungsvollen Quellen
FSC
www.fsc.org
FSC® C083411

Contents

Part I: **The Political and Legal Context**

Part II: **Migration, Life, and Trade**

Part III: **Solidarity and Identity**

Figures and Tables

https://doi.org/10.1515/9783110472103-201

Introduction

In what is now the borough of Hamburg called Altona, there is an old Jewish cemetery that the city has recently proposed for UNESCO's list of World Heritage Sites in recognition of its outstanding cultural significance.[1] It contains a unique Portuguese-Jewish section established in 1611. With its richly ornamented grave slabs, lively figurative art, and elaborately composed elegies in several languages, the cemetery bespeaks prosperity. More particularly, it bespeaks the culture of the Portuguese Jews in Hamburg.

Many of these were merchants, well educated and widely traveled. As young men they might have spent apprenticeship years in Brazil, for example, and then moved on to Bordeaux, Livorno, or Antwerp before finally settling in Hamburg. Trade considerations influenced where they chose to settle, but their migration was not primarily motivated by economic concerns. It had far more to do with legal and social discrimination, and with the menacing presence of the Inquisition on the Iberian Peninsula. Believing Catholics for the most part, they differed very little from other Catholics in religious practice and way of life; but as *New Christians* (that is, descendants of baptized Jews) they were widely suspected of being clandestinely Jewish. And indeed, once in Lutheran Hamburg, most of the Portuguese New Christians did revert to the faith of their ancestors, and in so doing became a segregated group within the city community. Their main contact with the city's other inhabitants was by way of trade.

The Portuguese New Christians were not the only merchants who left their homelands in the seventeenth century to settle in other countries and conduct trade there. Hamburg merchants went out into the world, too, and many of them settled in Portugal. But unlike the New Christians, these people left their homes of their own accord, and were soon integrated into the host society. They learned the local language, married local women, and, if successful in business, became members of the local elite. They, too, often changed their religious identity. But again unlike the New Christians who converted to Judaism, they adopted the religious affiliation of the surrounding society: that is, Catholicism.

The history of the Portuguese Jews has been much researched, but that of the Hamburgers residing abroad is almost completely unknown. In this book I compare these two groups, and explain why the Hamburgers in Portugal behaved so differently from the Portuguese who settled in Hamburg. In particular, I examine how the two groups' different ways of integrating themselves into their new social contexts influenced their commercial activities. I will look too at the Netherlandish merchants who settled in Hamburg and Portugal, and pursued trade between both places. In their homeland they had been members of Reformed (sometimes called Calvinist, but see my note on terminology below),

https://doi.org/10.1515/9783110472103-001

Lutheran, or other Christian denominations, and in Hamburg most of them maintained these affiliations. In Portugal, however, like the Hamburgers who settled there, they adopted the Catholic faith and soon were little different from the local population.

Historians have generally ascribed behavioral differences among merchant groups to their cultures of origin. For this reason, many studies examine whole merchant diasporas whose widely distributed members were held together by common ethnic and/or religious bonds and cooperated closely in trade.[2] Jewish merchants, Portuguese or not, have been seen as salient examples of this phenomenon; so have Armenian, Greek, Chinese, Quaker, Scottish, and Basque merchant groups. Scholars studying merchant diasporas tend to analyze their mechanisms of networking and solidarity, and to emphasize their inner cohesion. They neglect, however, the way local conditions influenced individual settlements, and correspondingly how subgroups within a diaspora came to differ among themselves.

Specifically, historians have adduced three factors to explain the remarkable success in trade that is generally attributed to merchant diasporas: first, a "natural" loyalty and mutual support among the members, based on their common origins;[3] second, the social and political isolation of these merchants within the foreign societies in which they lived;[4] and finally, the diversity of their cultural experience, which imbued their trading practices with an innovative spirit.[5] But existing studies seldom examine to what extent these three factors were true, how much they contributed to the merchants' success, or even whether the foreign merchants were especially successful at all. And in fact, all of these claims are questionable. Do relatives and acquaintances never quarrel with and/or cheat one another? If they do, why should this not happen within an ethnic group or religious community? Might not the orientation of trade relations toward one's own group lead to limited trading opportunities just as easily as to greater profitability? Is it not possible that exclusion from social and political life was a detriment to mercantile success, rather than an advantage? And does "foreignness" necessarily lead to innovation, as opposed to insecurity, conservatism, or compliance with the host society's mores?

Economic historian Avner Greif was one of the first to research in depth how trading networks of ethnic minorities actually did enforce contract compliance and reduce commercial risk.[6] His studies of the Maghribi traders, a group of North African Jews of the eleventh and twelfth centuries, convinced him that merchants relied on each other not for social or ethical reasons, but out of rational self-interest. Lacking the backing of strong states, they had to monitor the integrity of their trading partners themselves, which they did by circulating letters containing comprehensive information about each other's mercantile practices. According to

Greif, it was understood that opportunistic behavior would be punished by exclusion from further business with the entire group. Thus regular communication discouraged dishonesty. But having demonstrated that commerce could indeed work under such conditions, Greif notes that a more successful approach was the one taken by the Genoese merchants of the time. They relied not on informal punishment by peers, but on a formalized, court-based and state-backed system for the enforcement of contracts. One reason this approach was more successful was that those institutions did not restrict the merchants' trade to members of their own group. Greif takes ethnic and religious homogeneity as a precondition for the reputation-based model of trade. But he gives no reason why the merchants' rational proceedings (on which he bases his exposition) would not work just as well among merchants from different groups of origin, as long as they remain in regular communication.

In this book I do not assume that there was anything intrinsically advantageous about membership in a merchant diaspora. Rather, I postulate that such membership was the result of limited integration and assimilation when foreign merchants moved into societies that were new to them. I ascribe the reasons for remaining foreign not primarily to the merchants themselves, but to external factors. I will show that the merchants adapted their behavior to the conditions they encountered. Where there were few barriers to their acceptance into the host society, they assimilated readily and gave up their status as a special group. But where they were met with resistance they banded together, defending their common interests and developing their group identity. In either case they made use of many different mechanisms to ensure contract compliance and reduce commercial risk, including private-order solutions and the state and city institutions available to them.

As I have said, the history of the Portuguese-Jewish merchants has received a lot of study. There are historical reasons for this. Over the centuries, Jewish commerce has served as a kind of benchmark for economists, both in discussions among themselves and in their communications with the public at large.[7] They have used (partly true and partly invented) descriptions of Jewish trade to illustrate positive and negative consequences of certain behaviors, thus making Jews "responsible" for economic and social developments of all kinds, including some that filled the public with dread and anxiety. As late as the early twentieth century, renowned scholars like Werner Sombart were explaining the entire economic modernization of Europe as a function of Jewish (specifically Portuguese-Jewish) commercial activities.[8]

Since the early 1980s, however, the Portuguese Jews have evoked a different kind of interest in historical researchers. Investigation has turned to questions of identity, and to their social, cultural, and intellectual life.[9] Only a few historians – most prominently Jonathan Israel – have continued to examine them primarily in terms of trade.[10] And Israel's writings remain largely faithful to conventional historiographic models. Like many of his predecessors, he ascribes to the Portuguese Jews a vanguard role in the economic development of Europe. He characterizes the Portuguese Jews as particularly mobile, especially well networked, and very cosmopolitan in their outlook. According to him, their trade networks were superior to those of other merchants, and their importing of goods (especially pepper, spices, and sugar) from Portugal's overseas territories opened up a new commercial sector in northern Europe that would be of crucial importance in the future. Hermann Kellenbenz advanced similar arguments several decades before Israel; his, however, were developed in the context of Nazi ideology. His research was funded in 1939 by the Research Department on the Jewish Question (Forschungsabteilung Judenfrage) of the anti-Semitic Reich Institute for the History of the New Germany (Reichsinstitut für Geschichte des neuen Deutschlands), and his results were published in 1958, probably in a much revised form. His monograph, *Sephardim an der unteren Elbe* (The Sephardim on the Lower Elbe), has up to now remained the most influential monograph on the history of the Portuguese Jews in Hamburg.[11]

Only recently have works appeared that take new approaches to Jewish economic history and come to new conclusions.[12] The most important of these is undoubtedly Francesca Trivellato's book on transcultural trade in the Portuguese-Jewish diaspora.[13] Trivellato calls into question the importance of ethnically homogeneous trade networks to the merchants' success, and shows that trust among merchants was not bound to any particular ethnic or religious solidarity. She argues that although common origins and kinship were useful in building trade networks, they were by no means necessary. Despite cultural limitations and religious prejudices, members of different ethnic and religious groups were able to develop the trust necessary for profitable economic cooperation. That is the assumption on which this book, too, is based.

Research about the non-Jewish merchant groups is much less developed. Whereas the limited integration of the Jews meant that they persisted over centuries as a recognizable, nameable, and describable group, merchants who assimilated quickly were not viewed as particularly interesting by those in their environment, nor did they themselves leave behind much evidence suggesting a significant sense of group identity. After a few generations, the Hamburgers and Netherlanders living abroad were only barely perceptible as such. As a result, few academic studies have examined the Netherlandish merchants out in the larger world, although in the seventeenth century they must have been just as numerous as the merchants of Portuguese-Jewish origin.[14] Even fewer studies have looked at merchants from Hamburg living abroad.[15]

Attention to the particularities of the prominent trading diasporas has tended to obscure the commonalities of their members with other merchants involved in long-distance trade. All of the merchants trading between Hamburg and Portugal were faced with the problem of establishing and maintaining sustainable trade relations between two distant places. All of them needed to surmount political, legal, and religious barriers. Almost all of them lived abroad for significant periods of time, and as a result were confronted with the experience of being foreigners. They had to learn to navigate new cities, master foreign languages, adapt to local trading customs, and find their place in unfamiliar social and religious environments. To the Hamburgers, Portuguese Catholicism was as strange as Hamburg Lutheranism was to the Portuguese. All merchants in foreign climes were forced to change their habits; only thus could the economic exchange take place that overcame cultural distance. However, the different groups altered their behavior in different ways.

As I will show, Portuguese merchants, whether living as New Christians in their homeland or as Jews abroad, had greater difficulties to contend with than other merchants. Whereas the latter were often privileged, the New Christians and Jews were discriminated against. While other merchants knew that they could count on a measure of support from the authorities back home, the New Christians and Jews could expect no such assistance. Nor could they earn access to the social or political elite of the countries where they settled, something the other merchants sometimes achieved. Portuguese merchants were also less mobile than other merchants. Because their migration often took the form of flight, they had not only to relocate their entire families, but also to come to terms with the fact that they might never return to their homeland. Their children and grandchildren, too, faced this definitive separation. Because of these highly restrictive circumstances, the Portuguese-Jewish merchants in Hamburg were in fact less successful in their commercial ventures with the Iberian Peninsula than the merchants who were free to travel there.

There is no doubt that the trade between Hamburg and Portugal that I examine in this book is only one example, and a very particular one, of the multifarious commercial activities pursued by the members of these three merchant diasporas. But it illustrates vividly the strategies that merchants developed in response to economic and political circumstances, legal frameworks, and social and religious influences. And for a number of reasons it is particularly well suited to a comparative study of these strategies, and of how they eventually came together in the distinctive ways in which the merchants constituted their commercial, ethnic, and religious groups.

First, the trade between Hamburg and Portugal was intense in the seventeenth century. Portugal was one of the most important commercial regions for merchants in Hamburg, and given the fact that Portugal was often at war with its other trading partners, Hamburg's neutrality was of major significance to merchants active there.

Second, Hamburgers, Portuguese, and Netherlanders were all substantially engaged in trade between Hamburg and Portugal. Merchants of all three groups migrated at approximately the same time, and in significant numbers, between the two places. Portuguese and Netherlandish merchants began to come to Hamburg in the 1580s, and continued to do so until about the mid-seventeenth century. Although the migration of merchants from Hamburg and the Netherlands to Portugal began earlier and continued later, it too intensified considerably after the 1580s.

Third, Hamburg and Portugal were profoundly different in political, economic, and religious organization. Hamburg was a largely independent city-state governed by a citizen oligarchy, most of whose members came from important merchant families. Portugal was a territorial state governed by a monarch who aspired to exclusive control over large areas of global trade; merchants there had little political power. Furthermore, in Portugal merchants had to deal with the Inquisition, whose complex interests were not always aligned with those of the Crown. In Hamburg, clerics wielded comparatively little power.

The different structures in these two locales shaped their different attitudes toward foreign merchants. Comparing the native merchants in each place with two different groups of foreign merchants enables us to distinguish between phenomena that were typical of foreigners generally, and those that were group-specific. To this end, I contrast the Portuguese in Hamburg and the Hamburgers in Portugal with the Netherlanders who migrated to both places. The inclusion of the Netherlanders allows us further to distinguish between membership in a foreign ethnic group and membership in a foreign religious faction. Unlike the two other groups, the Netherlanders before they emigrated had belonged to a variety of religious denominations (predominantly Reformed, Lutheran, and Catholic). Thus some of them entered Hamburg and Portugal as members of the religious majority, and some as part of a religious minority.

This book consists of three sections. In the first I examine the framework within which trade between Hamburg and Portugal took place, and which conditioned the migrations and lives of the merchants. I consider the wide-ranging political and economic interdependencies associated with Europe's opening to the Atlantic, the Portuguese overseas expansion, the Dutch War of Independence, and the Thirty Years' War. Exploration of these factors paves the way to an examination of policies regarding trade and aliens in both places, and their respective implementations. I analyze the foreign merchants' legal status in these places and also the creation of the foreign delegations that championed the mercantile concerns of the governments they represented. Finally, I explore the policies of the Portuguese Inquisition toward both local and foreign merchants, and its conflicts with the Crown in this regard.

In the second section I consider the merchants themselves, their lives, and their trade. After a description of the paths, causes, and consequences of their migrations, I take a closer look at the merchants' biographies. What were their social backgrounds? What kinds of education did they have? How well did they speak the languages of the countries to which they migrated? What public offices did they achieve? I then examine their assets and turnovers. Banking and customs data from Hamburg enable me to correct some persistent assumptions about the comparative success of the various ethnic groups, as well as their mercantile specializations. Finally, I describe the public infrastructures and services the merchants had at their disposal to overcome the many problems associated with long-distance commerce and their status as foreigners. These include the services of notaries and brokers, the postal system and newspapers, various means of insurance, and the use of bills of exchange for the transfer of capital.

The third section takes a closer look at social and business relationships among the merchants. I examine first how trust among merchants was generated, the significance of mercantile reputation, and the role religion played in this. I then examine the personal trade networks of the various merchant groups. How did they develop? What roles did kinship relations and ethnic or religious affiliation play? How flexible and resilient were the networks? I also consider alternative forms of mercantile organization, namely the Commercial Deputation in Hamburg and the Brazil Company in Portugal. I examine in particular the role of foreigners in these groups. Finally, I study the nation- and religion-bound communities of the foreign merchants, which not only reflected mercantile concerns, but fulfilled social, religious, and charitable functions as well.

As is usual with historical comparisons, the documentation upon which I base this study is vast but uneven. The different administrative structures in my two locales, and the variations among the three groups of merchants, mean that existing sources do not always provide comparable information. The Inquisition, in particular, left behind a rich store of biographical data for which there is no counterpart in Hamburg. On the other hand, a large amount of statistically analyzable material was preserved in Hamburg, while due to documentary losses in Portugal, hardly anything of that sort is available there. As to personal letters, I have those written by Hamburg mayor Johann Schulte to his son of the same name, a young merchant who was living in Lisbon; I have no such significant correspondences written by Netherlandish or Portuguese families with which to compare them. Similarly, the sources from the Portuguese-Jewish community in

Hamburg are far richer than the ones we possess about the communities of the Netherlanders and Hamburgers in Portugal. All in all, however, I have tried to reconstruct (insofar as possible) a balanced picture, and one that respects the complexity of the subject.

Finally, some notes about terminology. The word *nation* had a different meaning in the early modern period than it has today. Originally referring to ethnic (or cultural) groups – that is, to groups of people with similar customs who felt connected by actual or supposed shared origin – in the Middle Ages it was applied in particular to merchant communities that enjoyed special legal status in a city. Both of these meanings implied common origins, but in the latter case, membership in a nation was essentially defined by statute. Eventually the word also came to mean something closer to our modern understanding – that is, the inhabitants of a nation state – and was sometimes used in this way by the ruling authorities. Precise differences in meaning are spelled out in more detail over the course of the book.

While the term *Portuguese* designates all people from Portugal and of Portuguese descent, in this book it is relevant mostly, but not exclusively, to New Christians and Jews. I use *Portuguese Jews* to refer exclusively to Portuguese of Jewish faith; in general, either they or their ancestors had once been New Christians. I do not use the term *Sephardim* (which is employed in other studies), because the Portuguese Jews living in Hamburg and other towns of the Atlantic diaspora neither called themselves Sephardim nor were they called such by their host societies.[16] Also, it is important to keep in mind that while Portugal had been an independent kingdom since the High Middle Ages, during the *Iberian Union* (that is, from 1580 to 1640) it was governed by the Spanish king in personal union with Spain; while the meaning of the terms Portugal and Portuguese did not vary, the political context sometimes did.

In conformity with the historical sources I use the term *Netherlanders* to mean people who originated from any of the Seventeen Provinces of the Habsburg Netherlands, according to their mid-sixteenth-century boundaries: that is, the triangle delineated by Groningen in the north, Luxembourg in the south, and Artois in the west. By *Dutch* I mean only the Netherlanders of the seven northern provinces, the so-called *United Provinces* (or Dutch Republic) that declared independence from Spain in 1581. The independence of the United Provinces was formally recognized in the Peace of Westphalia of 1648; they form what we know today as the Netherlands, including the provinces of Holland and Zeeland. The southern provinces, which comprise most of modern Belgium and Luxemburg as well as parts of western Germany and northern France, remained under Spain's control well into the eighteenth century, and are referred to as the *Spanish Netherlands*. While the Spanish Netherlands were predominantly Catholic, most of the inhabitants of the United Provinces affiliated themselves with the Reformed Church. I use the term *Reformed* in preference to *Calvinist* because the Reformed themselves rejected that term, which had been coined by their opponents. Although their faith was influenced by John Calvin, other important reformers were involved in its foundation as well.[17]

The third group, the *Hamburgers*, were Germans from Hamburg, one of the great trading cities of the Holy Roman Empire; I distinguish them by that name from all other Germans for reasons of clarity, although the ruling authorities of the time (in Portugal, for instance) frequently did not. From the beginning of the ninth century through the beginning of the nineteenth, the empire played a central political role in Europe. Yet for all its historical importance, it was a singularly indeterminate entity. There was permanent uncertainty about its legal character, and the emperor held power to very different degrees over its diverse parts. Princes (*Landesherren*) ruled most of the several hundred territories of the empire, which in the early seventeenth century covered an area including what today would be Germany, the Czech Republic, Austria, Switzerland, Luxembourg, Belgium, and the Netherlands, as well as parts of France, Italy, and Poland. Scattered across that area were some 50 to 60 free imperial cities, which were subject only to the emperor. The empire was primarily a legal entity, connected by its feudal system, its shared laws, and the two imperial courts of last resort, the Reichshofrat and Reichskammergericht. Despite the empire's multiethnic composition, a growing sense of its German core led to its official denomination as "Holy Roman Empire of the German Nation" in 1512. Yet the link between the empire and the German nation (that is, the people who were ethnically and linguistically German), was never precisely defined. Hamburg, although not formally an imperial city until 1769, was in practice an autonomous, self-governing city-state of the empire.

Lastly, I have followed certain naming conventions. The names of Portuguese merchants, whether living in Portugal or Hamburg, are rendered in the modern Portuguese manner. The names of German and Netherlandish merchants are written in modern German, Dutch, or French if I draw predominantly on sources from Hamburg, and in Portuguese if I draw predominantly on sources from Portugal.[18] This decision reflects both the source documents and the merchants' varying degrees of assimilation. I have included life dates as necessary to distinguish among different bearers of one name. The names of rulers are rendered in the language of the countries they ruled; the kings who governed during the Iberian Union are therefore noted in accordance with the Spanish tradition: that is, as Felipe II (of Spain) rather than Filipe I (of Portugal); Felipe III (Spain) rather than Filipe II (of Portugal), and Felipe IV (of Spain) rather than Filipe III (of Portugal).

Part I: **The Political and Legal Context**

1 Economic and Political Trends

Merchants trading between Hamburg and Portugal in the seventeenth century worked against a backdrop of large-scale economic interdependencies, ever-shifting political alliances, and interstate hostilities that frequently broke out in open warfare. This chapter presents an overview of these relations within their European context, a context in which Spain and the United Provinces played especially important roles.

Portugal was dependent on northern Europe for its grain supplies, for ship-building materials, weaponry, and munitions, and also for access to the credit on which much of its overseas trade depended. Hamburg was especially well positioned to serve those needs. As an independent neutral city-state, its merchants could trade freely with all powers, even those engaged in hostilities. In return, expanding dye works in Hamburg profited greatly from the imports of dyes from Portugal, and sugar imports over the long term made the city one of the largest sugar-refining centers in Europe.

Salt for Grain

Trade relations between the north of the Holy Roman Empire and Portugal go far back into the Middle Ages.[1] They originated in the North Sea and Baltic regions' need for salt, which was used to preserve herring and other foodstuffs.[2] To satisfy this need, merchants made their way southward along the Atlantic coast, acquiring salt first from the Bay of Bourgneuf, near the mouth of the Loire, and then from the Bay of Biscay. By the end of the fourteenth century they were trading regularly with Lisbon and nearby Setúbal. Although the more expensive salt from the Lüneburg saltworks south of Hamburg was widely used as well, Setúbal remained for many centuries one of the most important sources of salt for northern Europe.

In exchange for salt, grain was transported to Portugal, where the supply was a serious concern and shortages were especially common in the Algarve, and later in Madeira.[3] Demand was high in Lisbon, too – not only to feed its inhabitants, but also to provision Portuguese vessels. On average, Portugal imported between 15 and 18 percent of its grain, and northern Germany, including the Baltic region, was one of its most important regions of origin.[4] Imports from northern Europe rose toward the end of the sixteenth century, when piracy increasingly disrupted the grain trade with the Levant, Morocco, Spain, Sicily, and other countries bordering the Mediterranean. Northern Europe also supplied Portugal with wood, metals, pitch, tar, cordage, and other shipbuilding materials. These had been in growing demand since the beginning of Portugal's overseas expansion and campaigns of conquest in the fifteenth century.

https://doi.org/10.1515/9783110472103-002

Portuguese Expansion

In 1415 Portugal captured Ceuta in northern Morocco, and with that its seafarers began making their way to ever more distant territories. In 1420 they reached Madeira; in 1427 the Azores; in 1458 the Cape Verde Islands. In 1482 they built Elmina Castle (São Jorge da Mina) on the coast of Guinea. In 1488 they rounded the Cape of Good Hope, and in 1498 they landed on the Malabar Coast of southwestern India. In 1500 they reached Brazil; in 1512 the Moluccas in the Pacific; in 1514 China; and in 1542 Japan. An intensive trade with the Indies developed; the royal fleet rounded the Cape annually, bringing pepper and other spices back to Europe. Chinese silks, porcelains, furnishings, and luxury items such as diamonds and other gemstones added even more lucrative trade. From Africa the Portuguese brought in dyes, ivory, slaves, and – above all – gold.

But of all this, little was consumed in Portugal proper; most made its way to European markets through the royal *feitoria* (trading post) in Antwerp. In return, Portugal acquired many of its own necessities from the north by way of that city. In 1549, however, the Portuguese Crown called the royal factor (*feitor*; that is, the king's representative at the head of the *feitoria*) back to Portugal for good, and so withdrew from active trade with northern Europe. The *feitoria* was kept up informally by Portuguese merchants residing in Antwerp until 1794, but once the Dutch in their struggle for independence started to blockade the mouth of the river Scheldt (first in the 1570s, and more intensively after the Spanish conquered Antwerp in 1585) the economic decline of that city began, and with it that of the *feitoria*.

By then the Portuguese trade in Asia was also running into difficulties.[5] Revolts against Portuguese rule broke out in many regions of southern and southeastern Asia. The Dutch and the English began to penetrate the Asian market, and Portugal had to struggle to maintain its dominance in those regions. Since the middle of the sixteenth century the Crown had been transferring the organization of trade and the equipping of vessels more and more to wealthy private parties (*contratadores*) by means of loan agreements (*contratos*). Nonetheless, by the turn of the seventeenth century Portugal's Asia trade had decreased to about a third of its high-water mark, and only two or three Portuguese ships were still plying the Cape route annually.

Thus it was the Atlantic trade that came to dominate Portugal's economic and political interests. Unlike the Asia trade, it was open to all Portuguese merchants except for the two areas in which the king retained monopoly rights: the trade in brazilwood, from which a precious red dye was produced, and the trade in slaves. But the sugar trade soon became far more important than the trade in brazilwood.[6] Sugarcane was first planted in the Azores and on São Tomé. Production in Brazil began in the 1530s, and after 1570 the number of sugar mills there increased rapidly, as did the number of vessels crossing the Atlantic. These did not sail in royal fleets, and were considerably smaller than the ships that plied the Cape route; furthermore, they did not put out only from Lisbon, but also from a number of less important ports in Portugal's north. This spread the profits of the overseas trade – and the merchandise it supplied – more widely across the country. Tobacco was another Brazilian crop that made its way to European markets in the seventeenth century, and it soon became the second most important Brazilian export.

Hamburg's Economic Ascendance

While Portuguese traders were extending their reach to new continents, northern German merchants were increasing their trade with Portugal.[7] Hamburg was in an especially advantageous position. It was closer to the Iberian Peninsula than the towns on the Baltic Sea, and unlike them was not subject to the toll levied by Denmark on ships passing through the Øresund, which reduced transport costs considerably. Another advantage was that while the Baltic froze over during the winter, the waterway from Hamburg generally remained open all year long. Nonetheless, the Baltic cities retained some importance in the Portugal trade.

As Portugal established itself as the fulcrum of a far-flung trading empire stretching from Lisbon to Africa, Asia, and the Americas, Hamburg was becoming the gateway to the central European hinterlands.[8] It acquired more and more importance as the transshipment port for English cloth, French and Spanish wines, and Portuguese salt and overseas products. The Elbe facilitated access to Leipzig, which in the seventeenth century was the site of Germany's leading trade fair. It became the largest port for the shipment of grain from the regions of Mark Brandenburg and Magdeburg, and it was connected by way of the Elbe and its tributaries to the copper-producing areas in the Harz region, Bohemia, and Hungary, and to the linen-weaving regions of Saxony, Silesia, and Bohemia. Hamburg also received linens and woolens from the area around Osnabrück, and horses, butter, cheese, and other agricultural products from Holstein. Last but not least, the Stecknitz Canal provided a narrow (that is, navigable only by barges) but direct connection to the still-important old trading city of Lübeck and to the Baltic Sea.

Hamburg was also a vital manufacturing and craft center in its own right. Beer brewing had a long history there. By about 1600 the preparation and dying of cloth had become the city's most important enterprise, and to this were added the bleaching of linen, the production of say (a cloth of fine texture resembling serge) and bombazine (a silk and worsted blend), and the production of velvet, stockings, and wigs as well as gold and silver wares. Sugar refineries sprang up, which (like the dye works) processed Portuguese raw materials. Finally, the area around Hamburg was home to a number of copper and iron mills; these produced metal products destined for the Portuguese territories overseas.

Trade between Hamburg and Portugal at the Beginning of the Seventeenth Century

The survival of several of the annual Hamburg Admiralty customs books (in which were listed customs payments, the goods to which they applied, and their destinations and origins of shipping) makes it possible to assess with relative precision the trade between Hamburg and Portugal in the first half of the seventeenth century (see appendix).[9] The earliest surviving records date from mid-April 1632 through mid-April 1633. Over that fiscal year, grain exports made up almost 70 percent (by value) of the city's total exports to Portugal. Textiles followed far behind, in particular bay (a light, flannel-like woolen or cotton cloth), say, buckram (a coarse linen cloth), and canvas. Other export goods and commodities included powder, copper and copper products, other metals and metal products, wax, hemp, flax, and miscellaneous household goods. Overall, a total of 82 different kinds of wares were exported, among them paper, mirrors, and trumpets.

Table 1: Hamburg's trade with Portugal, 1632/1633

	Exports				Imports		
	Absolute (in marks)	Percentage of exports	Percentage of total trade		Absolute (in marks)	Percentage of imports	Percentage of total trade
Grain	614,299	68.5%	46.6%	Spices	149,050	35.4%	11.3%
Textiles	64,575	7.2%	4.9%	Sugar	132,200	31.4%	10.0%
Weapons/munitions	36,429	4.1%	2.8%	Dyes/dye woods	69,269	16.5%	5.3%
Metals	30,300	3.4%	2.3%	Salt	27,713	6.6%	2.3%
Metal goods	24,317	2.7%	1.9%	Fruits/preserves	13,103	3.1%	1.0%
Wax	20,350	2.3%	1.5%	Other	29,550	7.0%	2.2%
Hemp/flax	14,513	1.6%	1.1%				
Finished goods	13,376	1.5%	1.0%				
Other	78,039	8.7%	5.9%				
Total	896,198	100.0%	68.0%	Total	420,885	100.0%	32.0%

Source: StAHH, Admiralitätskollegium, F3 Band 1 and 2; F4 Band 8 (see appendix).

Only 24 kinds of imports are listed in the Admiralty customs books, however, and these were almost exclusively raw materials. Fabrics, furnishings, and other luxury goods from Asia were apparently not yet being sold through Hamburg. But spices such as pepper, cinnamon, ginger, cardamom, and sugar, as well as dyes such as sumac and indigo, were imported in large quantities. The importation of salt was surprisingly small; according to the customs figures, it comprised less than 7 percent of the total value of imported goods.[10]

Wars, Alliances, and Trade Embargoes

This trade took place against a complicated and continuously changing political and military backdrop. Of the many hostilities that erupted during the seventeenth century, the Dutch War of Independence (also called the Eighty Years' War, 1568–1648), the Thirty Years' War (1618–1648), and the Portuguese Restoration War (1640–1668), which broke out when the Iberian Union (1580–1640) ended, had the greatest consequences for the trade between Hamburg and Portugal. The Thirty Years' War was the one that most heavily involved the Holy Roman Empire, but Hamburg was able to remain unaffected due to its strong fortifications and a mixture of diplomatic skill and luck. And in the struggles for Dutch and Portuguese independence, its avowed neutrality allowed it relatively free and unhindered trade with all involved powers.

Still, Hamburg was party to a number of alliances. The oldest and perhaps most important of these was the *Hansa* or *Hanseatic League*, which was in decline by then, but still consequential.[11] The Hansa began in the thirteenth century as a coalition of German merchants. It grew into, and flourished as, a network of towns with common interests in trade, first in the Baltic and North Sea regions and then increasingly farther afield. Representatives of the cities came together in occasional general meetings, called *diets* (*Hansetage*), which were held most often in Lübeck, and Hanseatic merchants met on a more informal basis in the *Kontore* (that is, the Hansa trading posts abroad).

For about three hundred years the Hansa concentrated its policies less on its own structure than on achieving and maintaining the broadest trading privileges it could. As a new political organizing principle of the early modern period began to take hold, however, this changed. The princes of the territories within the Holy Roman Empire and the rulers of the states around it began striving with increasing intensity to consolidate their dominions. Their governments organized political, legal, and economic frameworks to that end, and the privileges of the Hanseatic merchants were often constrained in favor of the new structures of statehood. In the second half of the century, therefore, the Hansa introduced a number of reforms aimed at strengthening its cohesion and tightening its organization.

It also tried to build new strategic alliances, and it engaged in negotiations with the southern German imperial cities, England, the United Provinces – and Spain.

In 1580 the Spanish king Felipe II, who already ruled over Castile, Aragon, Naples, Sicily, Milan, Franche-Comté, the Netherlands, and a large portion of the Americas, seized the Portuguese throne. During the ensuing Iberian Union, which lasted until 1640, Portugal was a part of Europe's largest economic power. Although there were few changes in the internal policies of the Portuguese kingdom, its interests in foreign relations were now subject to Spain's.

The union of the two kingdoms held a number of advantages for Portuguese merchants.[12] Among other things, the Portuguese received a virtual free hand in trade with Spain's American colonies. In particular, they gained direct access to American silver, which was crucial to their trade with India and important in procuring goods from the Baltic region.[13] However, for the population in general the union was detrimental, especially when in 1585 Felipe II placed a trade embargo on the recently seceded United Provinces; until then they had been one of Portugal's most important trading partners, and a major provider of its grain imports.

The Hamburgers profited from this embargo by taking over much of the former Dutch trade with Portugal. But acts of war exposed merchants and shipmasters from Hamburg to new risks. The Spanish authorities, for example, sometimes seized foreign vessels entering a Spanish or Portuguese port, and incorporated them into the royal fleet;[14] this is why a number of Hanseatic ships were involved when the Spanish Armada set sail against England in 1588. A year later, when English privateers under Francis Drake conducted a retaliatory raid against Spain, 60 Hanseatic ships were destroyed in the port of Lisbon. There were other disruptions of Hamburg's trade at England's hands. Queen Elizabeth I had empowered her subjects to stop Hanseatic vessels sailing for Spain or Portugal, and to seize not only weapons and munitions, but grain, wood, iron, copper, rope, flax, hemp, and canvas as well.[15] As the many complaints filed by the Hansa show, these policies led to numerous confrontations between English and Hanseatic shipmasters.[16] Furthermore, in 1586 the government of the United Provinces, which likewise sought to stop the importation of foodstuffs, war matériel, and maritime equipment to the Iberian Peninsula, emplaced ten warships at the mouth of the Elbe to control shipping out of Hamburg.[17] Hamburg's vessels were repeatedly captured, plundered, or damaged in consequence.

Despite these obstructions, trading continued among all parties concerned. Many of the merchants of the warring powers cooperated with each other, disregarding whatever bans the various governments had set in place. This was especially true of the Netherlandish merchants living in the United Provinces, who maintained their trade with the Iberian Peninsula despite the embargo. To avoid discovery, they often used Hanseatic vessels to transport their wares, or hoisted Hanseatic flags on their own vessels. The Netherlandish merchants who had settled in Hamburg supported these efforts. The Spanish Crown prohibited Hanseatic shipmasters headed to Spain or Portugal from taking Dutch goods on board, or even docking at Dutch ports. As proof of compliance, the shipmasters were asked to present bills of lading and certificates of origin for their merchandise when unloading in Iberian ports; even on return trips they were banned from docking in Dutch ports.[18] But the result was that the Hansa towns began issuing false certificates, helping the Netherlanders evade the Spanish proscriptions.

The Hansa's Treaties with Spain and the United Provinces

Spain itself was becoming increasingly dependent on grain, weapons, and other war matériel supplied by merchants from the north, and sought to solve this problem by allying with the Hansa. After sending two diplomatic delegations to Lübeck, in 1587 and 1589, Felipe II dispatched a third in 1597, with the purpose of establishing long-term cooperation. On condition that its merchants renounce their trade with the rebellious Netherlands, he offered the Hansa towns a sweeping defense alliance and a monopoly on trade with Iberian ports.[19] The Hansa, however, refused. Despite the losses suffered as a result of piracy and seizures, the business conducted by its merchants and shipmasters was apparently profitable enough without such an alliance. Maintaining good relations with the rebellious United Provinces seemed more important than the trade monopoly on offer.[20]

Only in 1603, when the Spanish Crown introduced an additional import duty of 30 percent on all wares, did the Hansa towns react and name the merchant Hans Kampferbeck as their agent. They charged him with representing their interests with the Spanish king, and with paving the way for a Hansa delegation to Spain (see chapter 4). The delegation arrived in Madrid in 1607 and negotiated a treaty between Spain and the Hansa that abolished the 30 percent duty and stipulated compensation for damages suffered by Hanseatic ships deployed in the Spanish wars.[21] It also affirmed the Hanseatic merchants' old privileges in Portugal and expanded them to Spain (see chapter 3). In exchange, the Hansa pledged to certify in good faith the origins of all wares being traded.[22] However, the Hanseatic-Spanish Treaty of 1607, which was intended as an alliance against the United Provinces, became irrelevant just two years later when Spain and the United Provinces entered upon the Twelve Years' Truce (1609–1621); during the years of the truce direct trade between Spain or Portugal and the United Provinces was possible once again, and the certification process became superfluous.

For Hamburg, the interruption of the Spanish embargo against the Dutch meant the loss of its profitable role as intermediary. This may have been one of the reasons why the Hansa entered into an alliance with the United Provinces in

1616.[23] The alliance provided for free trade and shipping for both powers in the North and Baltic Seas, and in all of their tributary rivers. It was aimed especially against Denmark, although the United Provinces were also hoping for Hansa assistance in their war against Spain. In practice, however, this alliance was as ineffective as the one between the Hansa and Spain. In 1620, when Denmark emplaced two warships in the lower Elbe, the United Provinces failed to provide the help that Hamburg asked for; they were in negotiation with their former adversary Denmark in hopes of winning its support in their battle against Spain.[24]

The truce between Spain and the United Provinces ended in 1621. After that, the Hansa supported neither the Dutch nor the Spanish. Hanseatic merchants continued to trade with both states, and Hamburg once again became, to its profit, the intermediary through which a considerable portion of the trade between Spain and the United Provinces was conducted. When in 1625 the United Provinces, England, and Denmark joined forces in the war against the Holy Roman Empire and Spain, Denmark again blockaded the mouth of the Elbe to prevent Hamburg's ships from trading with Spain, and its two allies did the same a year later.[25] Nonetheless, the United Provinces were well aware that their economy – and with it the newly constituted state itself – would suffer considerable damage if Dutch merchants were to withdraw completely from trade with the Iberian Peninsula. As a result, they were forced to cooperate with Hamburg, at least to some extent.

Spain's Almirantazgo Project

King Felipe IV assumed power on the Iberian Peninsula in 1621. Assisted by his influential favorite, the Count-Duke of Olivares, he sought to reinvigorate Spain's economy. Since one of the main problems was Spain's dependence on Dutch shipping to supply the Peninsula with goods from northern Europe, Olivares planned to equip Spain with an armed merchant fleet of its own, earmarked specifically for the North Sea and Baltic trade.[26] As a state-owned trading company along the lines of the Dutch East and West India Companies, the *Almirantazgo de los países septentrionales* (Admiralty of the Northern Countries) was to enjoy a monopoly in the trade between Spain, Portugal, the Spanish Netherlands, the North Sea, and the Baltic regions.[27] The necessary capital was to come from a combination of shipping seizures, fines, a 1 percent duty on all goods exported from Andalusia to the northern countries, and, most important, from investments by Flemish (that is, from the Spanish Netherlands) and Hanseatic merchants trading with the Iberian Peninsula.[28] According to this plan, Spain would control trade, and Hanseatic merchants could expect handsome profits. The company was officially established in 1624, but the Crown was unable to procure the requisite financing and it seems to have been active for only two years, after which a significant number of Flemish, Hanseatic, and Scandinavian seamen in the service of the Almirantazgo mutinied and went over to the Dutch.

Along with its trading project, the Almirantazgo had a second aim: the military destruction of Dutch trading preeminence in the North and Baltic Seas. According to Spanish sources, more than eight hundred Dutch vessels sailed two or three times a year to Norway and Archangelsk; a herring fleet of almost two thousand cutters also sailed north. This, not the trade with India, the Americas, and the Levant, was the Dutch economy's main artery.[29] The conquest of Denmark was critical to Olivares's goal, as it would give Spain a chokehold on traffic through the Øresund. At various times the Spanish government also considered the seizure of bases along the coast of the Holy Roman Empire, and even the occupation of Hamburg.[30]

The Almirantazgo's naval squadron was to be assembled in the Hansa towns.[31] Olivares sent emissaries to negotiate the leasing, building, and purchase of ships, the purchase of munitions, and port access. Holy Roman Emperor Ferdinand II encouraged the Almirantazgo project by granting Hamburg sovereignty over the lower Elbe.[32] Even so, the Hansa eventually declined Spain's offer to participate in the project. After Olivares had acquired twelve ships for the planned fleet, the Hansa Diet resolved in February 1628 not to provide any more.[33] At the next diet, the Hansa rejected all further investment in the Spanish project on the grounds that trade and shipping should remain free. Given the military alliances that had formed, the Hansa towns were once again disinclined to challenge the United Provinces (and their allies Denmark, Sweden, and England) by entering into too close a collaboration with Spain. With their withdrawal, this venture of the Almirantazgo fell apart, as the commercial one had previously.

Trade Developments up to the Mid-Seventeenth Century

Hamburg had been a major commercial crossroads and an important financial and communications center before the Thirty Years' War began, and the war only strengthened its position. Diplomats from all of the warring powers met there to gather or spread information, to raise funds, to organize war matériel and provisions, and eventually to prepare for the peace process. As a result, Hamburg was one of the few cities of the Holy Roman Empire that was not only spared destruction, but actually emerged from the hostilities with its political and economic standing enhanced.

Hamburg's sea trade also suffered very little from the war. Records of revenues from the Hamburg *Bakenzoll* and *Werkzoll* (duties levied for the upkeep of the navigation markers on the Elbe and the lighthouse at Neuwerk Island at its mouth) show that the traffic in goods increased between the beginning of the seventeenth century and the end of the Thirty Years' War in 1648.[34] After the Peace of Westphalia brought the war to a close, trade underwent a temporary period of stagnation, but there was another upswing toward the century's end. This general development was punctuated by a series of short-term economic swings, most of which can be traced back to specific events in the Thirty Years' War and other struggles among the European powers.[35] Natural occurrences such as droughts, heavy rains, exceptionally cold winters, and storms also impinged upon trade by influencing the availability of grain and like commodities.

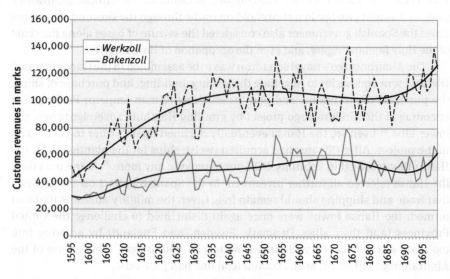

Figure 1: Development of Hamburg's long-distance trade
Source: StAHH Kämmerei I, Nr. 28, Band 1, 2, and 3.[36]

While trade in Hamburg grew more or less continuously, Iberian trade (and the Iberian economy) underwent a severe crisis between 1620 and 1630.[37] Up until then the Iberian Union had had a beneficial effect on the economies of both Spain and Portugal. But silver imports from Peru and Mexico decreased considerably, and by the end of the 1620s both Iberian countries faced a financial crisis. At the same time, Portugal lost a number of its holdings in Asia to the Dutch and the English. Brazil, the most valuable Portuguese colony, was seriously threatened when the Dutch conquered Recife in 1630 and took control of most of the sugar-growing region in the northeastern part of the colony. In 1632, the price of sugar, which until then had been rising, began to drop.[38] In 1637 Portugal lost access to African gold when the Dutch seized Elmina Castle, and during the 1640s it was deprived for a time of its colonies of Angola and São Tomé, its main sources of slaves for the plantations in Brazil.[39]

The Trade between Hamburg and Portugal
in the Mid-Seventeenth Century

In absolute terms, the value of Hamburg's imports from Portugal increased by a third between 1632/1633 and 1647/1648, and that of exports to Portugal by a sixth (see table 2). However, Portugal's percentage of Hamburg's overall trade declined. Between 1623 and 1633 Portuguese imports made up about 11 percent of Hamburg's import total, putting Portugal second among the city's trading partners.[40] At about the same time (the exact year we have is 1625), exports to Portugal made up about 10 percent of the city's export total, putting it in third place.[41] For the fiscal year 1647/1648, some 20 years later, exports to Portugal stood at only about 7 percent of the export total, placing it fourth.[42] No data are available for imports to Hamburg for that period. However, data do exist for the years 1642 to 1648 from Lisbon. With a share of 14 percent, Hamburg and Lübeck together counted as Lisbon's second greatest source of imports in these years; 9 percent came from Hamburg alone.[43]

Table 2: Hamburg's trade with Portugal, 1632/1633 and 1647/1648

	Imports to Hamburg (in marks)	Exports from Hamburg (in marks)	Total turnover (in marks)
April 1632–April 1633	420,885	896,198	1,317,083
February 1647–February 1648	556,829	1,042,019	1,598,848

Source: StAHH, Admiralitätskollegium, F3 Band 1, 2, and 8; F4 Band 8, 14, and 15 (see appendix).

Significant differences become apparent when comparing the goods traded between Hamburg and Portugal in 1647/1648 (see table 3) with those of 1632/1633 (see table 1). Grain, which had dominated Hamburg's exports to Portugal in the 1630s, dropped from nearly 70 percent to not quite 35 percent. This may have been the result of the changing status of the Dutch as grain exporters. In 1632/1633 the United Provinces were banned from trading with the Iberian Peninsula, but commerce resumed when Portugal seceded from Spain in 1640. On the other hand, the percentage of metal, weapons, and munitions exports from Hamburg increased considerably between 1632/1633 and 1647/1648. This increase occurred in large part because Portugal needed matériel for its Restoration War against Spain and to protect its overseas possessions.

Hamburg's imports changed too. In 1632/1633 spices had been the most significant import by value (35.4 percent), followed by sugar (31.4 percent), and dyes (16.5 percent). By 1647/1648 the overall share of sugar imports had more than

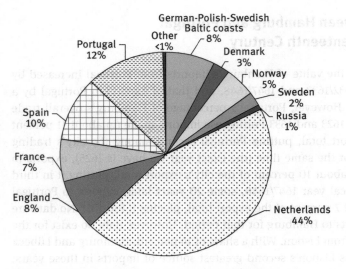

Figure 2: Regions of origin of Hamburg's imports, 1623–1633
Source: *Hamburger Schifferbücher*; see E. Baasch (1894).[44]

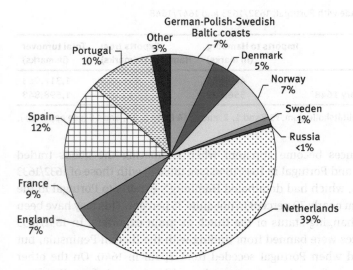

Figure 3: Destinations of Hamburg's exports, 1625
Source: *Hamburger Schifferbücher*; see E. Baasch (1894).[45]

doubled, to over 70 percent; the share of dye imports was approximately half what it had been; and spices had diminished to a quarter of previous levels. The increase in sugar imports was due mainly to the burgeoning Hamburg sugar industry, while the decrease in spice and dye imports may be traced to competition with

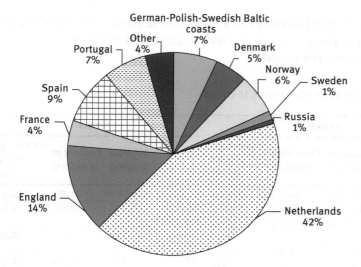

Figure 4: Destinations of Hamburg's exports, 1647/1648
Source: *Hamburger Schifferbücher*; see E. Baasch (1894).[46]

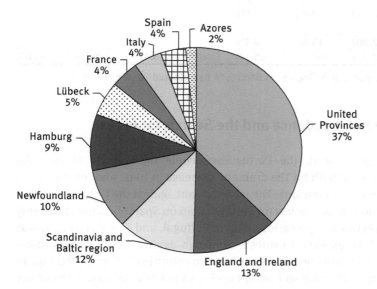

Figure 5: Regions of origin of Lisbon's imports, 1642–1648
Source: Ship visitation books of the Lisbon tribunal of the Inquisition; see V. Rau (1954).[47]

Dutch and English providers. This led to falling prices for those commodities on the world market, so that even if they had continued to be imported in the same quantity, their import value would have decreased. But it is also possible that

Hamburg was by then procuring those goods from Holland and England in addition to Portugal. The percentage of imported salt from Portugal also decreased, while that of tobacco increased.

Table 3: Hamburg's trade with Portugal, 1647/1648

	Exports				Imports		
	Absolute (in marks)	Percentage of exports	Percentage of total trade		Absolute (in marks)	Percentage of imports	Percentage of total trade
Grain	359,800	34.5%	22.5%	Sugar	400,076	71.9%	25.0%
Metals	207,363	19.9%	13.0%	Dyes/ dye woods	49,894	9.0%	3.1%
Weapons/ munitions	107,820	10.4%	6.7%	Drugs/ spices	48,852	8.8%	3.1%
Textiles	88,350	8.5%	5.5%				
Finished goods	59,672	5.7%	3.7%	Tobacco	27,700	5.0%	1.7%
				Other	30,307	5.4%	1.9%
Hemp/flax	52,576	5.1%	3.3%				
Metal products	24,431	2.3%	1.5%				
Other	142,007	13.6%	8.9%				
Total	1,042,019	100.0%	65.1%	Total	556,829	100.0%	34.8%

Source: StAHH, Admiralitätskollegium, F3 Band 8; F4 Band 14 and 15 (see appendix).

Portuguese Independence and the Search for Allies

As the 1630s progressed, the Portuguese people increasingly blamed the Spanish government both for the dramatic decrease in trade and for the loss of Portugal's overseas possessions. The trade boycott against the United Provinces had had a far more serious effect on Portugal than on Spain, because the supply of grain in Spain was less precarious than in Portugal, and Spain's economy was less dependent on exports. Olivares's campaign against Dutch traders therefore made for serious tensions between the two countries.[48] A grain shortage in 1637 and 1638 led to famine and violent uprisings in Portugal. And in December 1640 the Iberian Union suffered its death blow when disappointed aspirants to Olivares's patronage network called for Portuguese independence and proclaimed João IV of the House of Bragança the new Portuguese king. Their revolt was broadly supported by the populace, but Portugal still had to fight a long and debilitating war against Spain before that country finally recognized its independence in 1668.

Separation from Spain was a disadvantage for the many Portuguese merchants whose businesses were closely tied into the Spanish-American economic system.[49] Still, the change in government, and the war, produced new opportunities. João IV desperately needed weapons, munitions, provisions, and credit. He was trying to revive diplomatic relations with as many European powers as he could in order to win over allies in the fight against Spain. As a result, the Dutch and English governments were able to negotiate advantageous trade treaties with Portugal from which their merchants profited handsomely.[50]

Portugal's diplomatic relations with the Holy Roman Empire remained rather cool, however. The empire did not support Portugal's Restoration War because of its own densely intertwined dynastic ties with Spain, and the tension between the two monarchies was heightened by the affair of Duarte de Bragança, João IV's younger brother.[51] During the Thirty Years' War he had fought alongside Ferdinand III, emperor since 1637. But when the Portuguese revolt against Spain broke out, the emperor had him arrested; he died nine years later in a Habsburg prison. Only in 1687, when King Pedro II married the German princess Marie Sophie of Palatine-Neuburg, did the ensuing resentment come to an end.

Under those circumstances, João IV would not negotiate a trade treaty with the Holy Roman Empire. And the Hansa, which held its last diet in 1669, was rapidly losing importance. Nevertheless, João does appear to have made an "offer of friendship" (about which very little is known) to the Hansa towns in 1642.[52] Hamburg did not accept it, and instead sent almost two dozen fully-armed ships in support of Spain. When Portugal seized them off the Algarve coast with the intention of incorporating them into its fleet, Hamburg protested, declaring that they had not been warships but trading vessels, containing no cargo of any use in war. This was patently false, but the Portuguese king did release the ships, stating that Portugal did not need them and that in any case the Hansa towns had often supplied Portugal with weapons and munitions in the past. It seems clear that João IV attached great importance to good relations with Hamburg, and did not wish to jeopardize them.

In the same year, Felipe IV, the king of Spain, urged Ferdinand III to enjoin the Hansa towns from trading with Portugal, such that if Spain were to encounter Hanseatic vessels entering Portuguese ports, they might be viewed as hostile and be subject to seizure.[53] As part of the Peace of Westphalia, however, it was agreed that the Hansa towns would be permitted free trade with Spain's enemies as long as they refrained from supplying arms.[54] No further trade treaties were signed between Hamburg and Portugal during the seventeenth century, but in practice Hamburg merchants probably continued to enjoy the rights granted to them in the Treaty of 1607, which since then had become the standard for treaties between Portugal and other commercial powers.

Trade between Hamburg and Portugal at the Turn of the Eighteenth Century

Actual numbers illustrating the importance of the trade between Hamburg and Portugal become available again for several years at the end of the seventeenth century and the beginning of the eighteenth. For Portugal, Hamburg had receded in importance. If we compare Lisbon's imports of the 1640s with those of the late 1670s and early 1680s, we can see that the proportion of imports from Hamburg dropped from almost 9 percent to barely 6 percent.

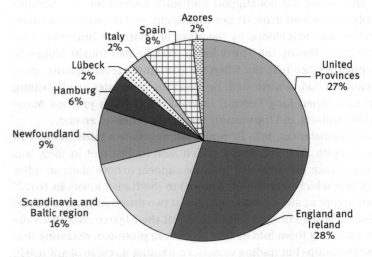

Figure 6: Regions of origin of Lisbon's imports, 1678 and 1682–1684
Source: Ship visitation books of the Lisbon tribunal of the Inquisition; see V. Rau (1954).[55]

In Hamburg, data exist for the years between 1702 and 1713.[56] In 1632/1633 and 1647/1648 the value of Hamburg's exports to Portugal had been approximately twice the value of its imports from there; at the beginning of the eighteenth century, the trade balance was almost in equilibrium. This change can be attributed to a drastic reduction in the grain trade. In 1632/1633, grain had comprised nearly 70 percent of exports, and in 1647/1648 it was (at almost 35 percent) still Hamburg's most important export commodity. By the beginning of the eighteenth century, however, grain's share of total exports to Portugal had dropped to only 6 percent. In part this was due to a decrease in grain availability resulting from the ravages of war, sinking productivity, and rising domestic demand in the regions of origin; in part it was due to the fact that Portugal was receiving more grain from England and the Netherlands.[57] The importance of trade with

Hamburg in weapons, munitions, and the metals needed for shipbuilding had also diminished since the end of the Portuguese wars. On the other hand, linen exports from Hamburg to Portugal had increased substantially. In 1647/1648 linen had comprised only about 1 percent of exports; in the early eighteenth century its share was more than 50 percent.[58] Linen production had expanded in Silesia, Lusatia, Bohemia, and Saxony after the middle of the seventeenth century, and remained important in Westphalia.[59]

Linen was now almost as large a component of the trade between Hamburg and Portugal as sugar, whose share of total imports, at about 68 percent, was now somewhat below mid-century levels. Sugar refining had become Hamburg's most important business; as the seventeenth century gave way to the eighteenth, there were more than 360 sugar refineries in the city, and about 8,000 inhabitants worked in these or in associated enterprises.[60] The value of the tobacco trade had also risen, and now comprised almost 14 percent of total imports from Portugal. The proportion of dyes had decreased, and spices, which in 1632/1633 had been Hamburg's most important imports, were now, like salt, a negligible contributor to import totals.

Table 4: Hamburg's trade with Portugal, 1702–1713

	Exports			Imports		
	Percentage of exports	Percentage of total trade		Percentage of imports	Percentage of total trade
Textiles	52.5%	27.0%	Sugar	68.3%	33.1%
Metals	15.2%	7.8%	Tobacco	13.7%	6.6%
Grain	6.1%	3.1%	Dyes/dye woods	6.9%	3.4%
Hemp/flax	3.8%	2.0%	Other	11.1%	5.4%
Finished goods	3.0%	1.6%			
Wood	2.8%	1.4%			
Other	16.5%	8.5%			
Total	100.0%	51.4%	Total	100.0%	48.5%

Source: Voluntary supplement to *Konvoigeld*; see E. Baasch (1929).[61]

While Hamburg continued to prosper, Portugal was visited by another deep economic crisis in the second half of the seventeenth century. The war with Spain was draining. Furthermore, since the 1640s the Brazilian sugar economy had been buffeted by strong competition from Dutch, French, and English sugar producers in the Caribbean. Sugar prices collapsed, and tobacco was now being grown in the Caribbean as well.[62] Spice prices also fell, and even such local products as wine and salt became harder to sell.[63] In addition, silver imports from South America again dropped considerably between 1670 and 1680, which affected not only the Spanish economy, but the Portuguese economy too.[64] It took until about 1690 for Portuguese trade to revive, at which point prices rose, and stocks that had accumulated in warehouses were sold. Sugar had become a mass consumer good, and the demand for wine and port also began to grow again. Finally, the onset of gold mining in Brazil catalyzed a long-term economic boom in Portugal. And Hamburg would remain, during the whole of the eighteenth century, one of the most important European transshipment centers for Portuguese goods.[65]

2 Alien Merchandise, Alien Merchants

The Kingdom of Portugal and the Hansa town of Hamburg were both independent and self-contained economic units. But Portugal was a territorial state ruled by a monarch who claimed exclusive trading rights over the kingdom's vast overseas possessions, while Hamburg was a city ruled by its citizens – many of them merchants – for whom the city's commercial alignment in the Hansa had long been of much greater importance than economic integration into the area that surrounded it. Both Portugal and Hamburg made use of protectionist trade policies in their efforts to ensure the livelihood of their people. However, the above-mentioned differences in their political and economic structures led them to pursue different strategies toward this goal. In both places provisioning of the population was a matter of crucial interest. Portuguese trade laws pursued that interest single-mindedly, often at the expense of its own merchants. But in Hamburg an equally compelling wish – to safeguard its assets – meant that the laws guaranteeing provisioning were structured to keep wealth in its own merchants' hands. In Portugal, therefore, regulations had to do with the merchandise that was traded. In Hamburg they were primarily directed at the merchants who did the trading, and were employed to privilege local traders over alien ones. In this chapter, therefore, I will examine the general attitudes toward merchandise and merchants in these two places, while in the next I will discuss in more detail the legal status of the specific merchant groups.

The Hamburg Constitution

To understand the trade regulations in Hamburg it is important to understand first how the city was governed. Hamburg, like most European towns of the time, was constituted as a body of citizens (*Bürger*; lit. burghers) with equal rights and duties. A council (*Rat*) of these citizens was supposed to work together with the citizenry at large (*Bürgerschaft*) to establish the town's laws, exercise jurisdiction, decide upon town expenditures, and secure town income by levying taxes and other duties. The Hamburg City Council was composed of about 24 members, and headed by four mayors (*Bürgermeister*) who wielded power in alternating pairs. In the late fifteenth century, a city law explicitly incorporated the citizenry into the political process by establishing an *Assembly of Citizens* (Erbgesessene Bürgerschaft) that included and represented all of Hamburg's propertied citizens and would be convened when required. The City Council, which at least in theory derived its powers from the citizens, was formally accountable to the Assembly, which had the right to participate in important decisions, such as declarations of

https://doi.org/10.1515/9783110472103-003

war and peace, contracts with foreign powers, and taxation. However, in practice the Council was so much more powerful that the will of the Assembly seldom prevailed.

When the Reformation was formally introduced in Hamburg in 1529, the citizens' assertion of their religious rights led to a reassertion of their right to participate in political matters, and they set up citizen boards (*bürgerliche Kollegien*) as instruments for parochial administration as well as for political negotiation with the Council. But in the long term the dominance of the City Council was not seriously challenged. The leading members of the citizen boards belonged to the same successful merchant families from which the Council recruited and were not in fundamental opposition to that body. And the Assembly of Citizens as a whole, which was dominated by artisans and small traders, still had only limited influence. At the beginning of the seventeenth century the Council audaciously declared that it was the city's sole ruling authority (*Obrigkeit*), claiming that its power derived not from the citizens but from God, and that citizens owed it obedience accordingly.[1] Still, the citizenry continued to strive for a redistribution of power between itself and the Council. This struggle remained a source of friction throughout the seventeenth century. In 1684 it broke out into open revolt and was permanently settled only with a constitutional reform in 1712.

Male inhabitants of Christian faith and sufficient age were admitted to citizenship upon the swearing of an oath, the payment of a fee, and registration in the citizen rolls (*Bürgerbücher*). All citizens were required to pay taxes, to serve in the town's defense, and to participate in the town's administration. They could be lawyers, merchants, craftsmen, shipmasters, brewers, innkeepers, grocers, and so on. But there were also many inhabitants of the city who were not citizens, and who shared neither the citizens' privileges nor their obligations. These included women, laborers, and domestics and other servants. And, as the sixteenth century drew to a close, the city found itself home to increasing numbers of *aliens*, that is, newcomers who came to Hamburg for business or other reasons, but did not acquire citizen status. There had always been aliens in Hamburg, but until then they had been transients, not residents.[2]

Staple Right, Customs, and Embargo Policies

The towns of the Middle Ages had been eager to defend their economic as well as their political independence. They were centers of trade and manufacture, and their governments took care to draw to them provisions, merchandise, and capital, and to retain the wealth that resulted. To this end they implemented so-called *alien laws* (in German euphemistically called *Gastrecht* or guest law), which were adopted to different extents all over Europe.[3] This body of laws – which we will explore further as we proceed – was based on the strict separation of citizen merchants from alien merchants, and granted the former considerable advantages over the latter.

The *staple right* was one of the chief ways that the benefits of trade were given into the hands of citizens. As we saw in chapter 1, Hamburg's economy was shaped by its role as intermediary in the movement of goods between the sea and the central European hinterlands accessed by the Elbe River. Hamburg's staple right, confirmed by the Holy Roman Emperor in 1482, established that no grain, flour, wine, or beer could pass through the city without first being unloaded there and offered for sale.[4] Grain was the most important of the goods to which this stricture applied. Until the end of the seventeenth century, alien (that is, non-citizen) merchants were forbidden to re-export any grain coming from the upper Elbe. Once it reached the city, they were required to offer half of it to Hamburg's citizens for three or four days on a retail basis, at a price set by the City Council. They were allowed to sell the rest at wholesale market price, but still exclusively to citizens. The staple right had two purposes: to ensure the provisioning of the population, and to enable citizens to profit from a lucrative intermediary trade.

As we saw in chapter 1, during the process of early modern state formation, most northern European towns lost a good deal of their political autonomy and became economically integrated into their surrounding territories. Hamburg, however, remained largely independent. Although (from the Danish perspective, at least) the city belonged to the Duchy of Holstein and was therefore subject to the king of Denmark, in practice Hamburg did not fall under the control of any territorial prince. It was subject only to the Holy Roman Emperor,[5] who made but sporadic attempts at an integrative economic policy.[6] Hamburg therefore kept the town-oriented economic policies that it had developed in the Middle Ages. In particular, it was able to maintain the staple right, which was reconfirmed by the emperor several times over the course of the seventeenth century.[7]

The situation in Portugal was quite different. By the mid-twelfth century, Portugal had already developed into a clearly demarcated territorial state. Almost simultaneous with its official founding in 1143, the new state had erected a chain of customs posts along its borders to oversee and tax the import and export of goods and capital.[8] These customs posts not only consolidated the borders, but also integrated the state into a social and economic unit and made it possible for its rulers to centralize power: they were the sites of the customs collections that filled the treasury coffers; they gave the king a means to ensure the provisioning of his country; and they served as contact points where the state connected with supraregional trade routes. With these functions, they framed the economic life of the Kingdom of Portugal.

As late as the seventeenth century, Portugal levied customs duties only on imports, not on exports. But according to the mercantilist principle of *ale-aldamento* (lit. customs declaration), which had been introduced in the mid-thirteenth century, every merchant was obliged to import within a year the same value in goods or money as he exported. Imports and exports were thus viewed as two halves of a single transaction. The two most important duties were the royal tithe (*dízima*) and the excise duty (*sisa*), each of which was set at 10 percent of the value of the imported goods.[9] The excise duty had originally been a sales tax, levied by the towns on goods brought in for consumption. By the seventeenth century, however, the excise duty was levied directly by the royal administration along with the tithe. Other duties included the *consulado*, a duty of 3 percent of the value of goods imported, which was introduced at the end of the sixteenth century to fund the protection of merchant ships from hostile forces.[10] In the seventeenth century, special duties on salt and tobacco were imposed. In total, import duties regularly exceeded 20 percent.

By contrast, duties in Hamburg in the first half of the seventeenth century totaled only about ½ percent of the value of the taxed goods, and in the second half 2½ percent, regardless (in most cases) of whether the goods were entering the city or leaving it (see table 5). Only on grain were additional duties (of less than ½ percent) charged.[11] These levies were much lower than the ones in Portugal because they were transit duties. If heavier customs duties had been imposed, merchants would have avoided the city and traded their wares more economically elsewhere.

The Portuguese Crown tried to attract certain goods and commodities that were unavailable or in short supply in the country by decreasing customs duties on them. This strategy affected the grain trade in particular. In 1504 King Manuel I lifted the tithe on the importation of wheat, barley, and zwieback into Lisbon and Setúbal because of an acute grain shortage; a year later he did the same for oats, rye, and meat. In 1516 all customs duties were lifted on the importation of these goods to Lisbon and environs. When Spain assumed sovereignty over Portugal in 1580 and Portugal was forced to enter the war against the United Provinces (from where much of the grain had previously been brought), customs duties on grain imports arriving by sea were discontinued throughout the country.[12] At times the government compromised on yet another basic principle to foster imports of grain; it permitted grain suppliers to export up to two-thirds of their profits in cash, although the export of gold and silver, both minted and unminted, was generally forbidden.[13]

Table 5: Hamburg customs duties

Customs duty	Affected goods	Amount of the duty
Werkzoll (*Werk* duty, *Werk* referring to the lighthouse on the island of Neuwerk)	All goods imported or exported by sea or land (Hamburg citizens were exempt from the *Werkzoll* on trade by land, which included trade on the upper Elbe)[14]	Originally an ad valorem duty; until 1621, approximately ¼ percent of the value of the goods, after 1622, about ⅜ percent
Bakenzoll (beacon duty)	All goods imported or exported by sea, except for grain	Like the *Werkzoll*
Kornzoll (grain duty)	Grain from the upper parts of the Elbe for export by sea	Originally an ad valorem duty; about 1/10 percent for rye, about 1/20 percent for wheat
Admiralitätszoll (Admiralty customs duty, after 1623)	All imported and exported goods to and from France, Spain, Portugal, the Mediterranean region, and more distant places	Originally an ad valorem duty; in about 1623, ¾ percent, and 1639/1640, ½ percent;[15] in about 1714 in trade with Spain, Portugal, the Mediterranean region and more distant places, ⅓ percent, in trade with France, ⅙ percent
Konvoigeld (convoy money, after 1662)	All imported and exported goods transported by sea	In trade with Spain, Portugal, the Mediterranean region, and more distant places, 1 percent, in trade with France, England, and Archangelsk, ½ percent
Schauenburger Zoll (Schauenburg duty)	All goods for export and transit goods[16]	Originally an ad valorem duty; about ⅛ percent of the value of the goods

Source: Compiled according to E. Pitz (1961) and C. Müller (1940), pp. 27–36.[17]

The 1587 Customs Code of Lisbon permanently exempted from duties not only wheat, barley, and rye, but also vegetables, meat, cheese and butter, books, weapons, gunpowder, horses, gold, and silver.[18] With the exception of gold, silver, and books, all of these were goods imported from Hamburg. According to old Hansa privileges and especially to the Hanseatic-Spanish Treaty of 1607 (see chapters 1 and 3), Hanseatic merchants were also exempted (either completely or by half) from customs duties on shipbuilding materials (masts, yards and planks, pitch, tar, rope, and such), metals (crude copper, brass, mercury, tin, and such), and munitions.[19] Because the *alealdamento* provided that no customs duties were to be levied on exported goods, this meant that Hanseatic merchants paid almost no duties at all in Portugal. It also meant that merchants from Hamburg enjoyed much more advantageous terms than merchants from Portugal when trading back and forth between the two places.

Moreover, the Portuguese merchants living in Portugal had to fund a considerably larger percentage of the state budget with their trade than did their colleagues living in Hamburg. In seventeenth-century Portugal about half of the state income was generated by customs revenues;[20] in Hamburg the figure was only about 20 percent.[21] In addition, Portuguese merchants were frequently called upon to pay high extraordinary levies in Portugal, from which alien merchants were very probably exempted.[22] In 1609, for example, merchants were dunned to outfit a fleet to defend Elmina Castle, the Portuguese trading outpost on the coast of Guinea.[23] The New Christian merchants in particular were frequently forced to pay special levies to the Crown (see chapter 5).

Regular taxes on the population as a whole did not exist in Portugal until after its independence from Spain in 1640. Only then did the government introduce a general income tax, the *décima*, which required for the first time that the nobility and the clergy as well as the commoners pay their share.[24] Intended to finance the war against Spain and highly dependent on agricultural proceeds, this tax fluctuated considerably in the income it realized. Yet it was maintained even after the end of the war, and as the seventeenth century came to a close it was bringing in about 12 percent of total state revenues.[25]

In Hamburg, by contrast, a regular property tax, the *Schoss*, had always been levied among the entire citizenry, and made up about 13 percent of total city revenues.[26] It amounted to about ¼ percent of a citizen's assets, and was assessed once a year by self-estimation and paid secretly into a tax box in the city hall. Many other duties were imposed on merchants and non-merchants alike, such that the burden of taxation was usually much more evenly distributed across the population in Hamburg than it was in Portugal. And alien merchants not only had to pay customs duties in Hamburg, but (unlike in Portugal) had to contribute their share to these other taxes as well.

The Hamburg Ban on Trade between Aliens, and the *Schragen* of 1604

As I have said, the point of alien laws was to keep goods and capital in the hands of a town's own citizens. That is why Hamburg's citizens could not enter into joint business partnerships with aliens, act as their *factors* (that is, as salaried local managers) or commission agents, or jointly own and outfit ships with them.[27] Another important law, the *Gasthandelsverbot* (lit. guest trading ban), forbade trade between aliens within a town: alien merchants were permitted to purchase goods only from citizens, and to sell goods to them alone. They were prohibited from trading with other alien merchants or with outside producers, consumers, or retailers. Thus by law no trade could be conducted in the city that did not include its citizens as intermediary merchants. Yet in Hamburg all these bans were infringed with increasing regularity as the sixteenth century wore on.[28]

The Hamburg City Council established new limits on trade when it enacted the *Schragen* (that is, administrative ordinance) of 1604.[29] The *Schragen* distinguished among three categories of goods. These were: "free goods or wares with which alien may trade with alien"; "citizens' goods, which alien may not trade with alien"; and "citizens' goods, which alien may not trade with alien, nor [citizen] with alien pennies [*Gastpfennige*]; and which no [citizen] factor may sell to aliens."[30]

The first category is clear enough; the difference between the second and third is less so. "Trading with alien pennies" referred to transactions conducted by citizens using alien assets. In other words, in the trade of third-category goods aliens were forbidden to cooperate with citizen merchants in any way; an alien could not even employ a citizen to trade the alien's goods for him, either in his own name (that is, on commission), or in the name of the alien (that is, as factor). The explicitness of this prohibition in the third category implies (by its absence in the second) that in the trade of second-category goods, also forbidden for direct trade between aliens, citizens *were* allowed to act as commissioners or factors. Up until 1604, such cooperation between citizens and aliens had been forbidden; the *Schragen* now opened the door to it.

The first category of goods, which could be traded freely by citizens and aliens alike, included "all goods that are brought here from foreign kingdoms and lands, and furthermore could be brought in the future, and which had not been customary in the city 30 and more years ago or had not been on offer and traded in such large numbers." The text of the *Schragen* specifies that "foreign kingdoms and lands" meant Italy, Spain, "and other like countries," among which Portugal was undoubtedly included. Many affected goods and wares are then enumerated, starting with products that originated overseas, namely: sugar and spices (such as pepper, cloves, nutmeg, mace, and ginger); exotic dyes (such as brazilwood, campeachy wood, and cochineal); gemstones, ivory, and ebony. Other goods specified in this category, however, were not particularly new or exotic, even though several of them were probably imported from foreign countries. These include gold, pearls, silk, velvet, velvet garments, grosgrain (a ribbed woolen or silk cloth), and fustian (a blend of cotton and linen). And, truly incongruously, the *Schragen* lists in this category a few commodities, like wax and flax, that had been traded within the Hansa for centuries. The second of the three categories (that is, the goods that were debarred from direct trade between aliens but could be traded with the intervention of a citizen commissioner or factor), included iron, lead, all types of munitions, oaken boards, shipbuilding supplies, and some dyed and undyed woolens and linens. The third category, still completely off-limits to trade between aliens, included salt, grain, and other basic foodstuffs (such as butter, cheese, herring and flounder) as well as French wine.

That the provisions of the *Schragen* were actually implemented, and that they influenced the merchants' selection of goods, is apparent in the repeated petitions of Netherlandish merchants settled in Hamburg to be allowed to trade with other aliens – especially in grain, as will be shown in chapter 3. The analysis of the Admiralty customs books that I present in chapter 9 offers additional confirmation. There the exclusion of alien merchants from free trade in certain products (in particular grain and wine) is clearly evidenced by the statistics.

As I have suggested, the criteria by which the commodities were categorized are not entirely clear. But on the whole, it seems that the goods that were reserved for the citizen merchants were those basic ones whose sale was essentially guaranteed, while aliens were given a free hand to trade in more speculative merchandise. Significantly, grain and salt, which had for a long time formed the backbone of the trade between Hamburg and Portugal and in the seventeenth century were still in great demand in Portugal and Hamburg respectively, belonged to the third category; that is, aliens were not allowed to buy them from, or sell them to, other aliens, even with a citizen factor or commissioner as intermediary. But the first category, in which aliens could trade freely, contained an array of luxury goods that were costly to obtain and might not be easily sold.[31] The large number of bankruptcies suffered by southern German firms trading overseas goods in Portugal in the first half of the sixteenth century had demonstrated all too clearly that trade in these goods was an especially risky venture.[32] The second category occupied a middle position with regard to turnover hazard. Aliens could trade these products with other aliens as long as they enlisted citizen factors or commissioners to act for them; thus the citizen intermediaries could profit from the sale of the goods without having first had to acquire them at their own expense.

But the strategic importance of the third category of goods – that is, the basic goods that sold easily – rested on more than just assured sales. As discussed above, on many goods in this category import duties in Portugal had been halved or entirely lifted. Not only could Hamburg citizens buy arriving grain and other foodstuffs such as butter and cheese advantageously from (alien) producers or providers; they could also send them to Portugal without being subject to customs duties there. Similar advantages extended to trade in wood, pitch, tar, rope, and munitions; these fell into the *Schragen*'s second category, were in heavy demand on the Iberian Peninsula, and so were exempt from import taxes there. Aliens in Hamburg, however, were forbidden to trade freely in any of the goods that were entirely exempt from customs duties in Portugal. And of the goods that were taxed at only half rate there, the *Schragen* permitted trade between aliens only in Hungarian copper and English pewter.[33]

When it came to trade with the Iberian Peninsula, therefore, the *Schragen* of 1604 disadvantaged aliens to a greater extent than a first glance would suggest. Where the most dependable trading goods were concerned, Hamburg citizens profited doubly (both in Hamburg and in Portugal) from their privileged position over the merchants from other places. Furthermore, the *Schragen* gave Hamburg merchants (even those who were risk-averse or without ready access to capital) a way to take advantage of new business opportunities by allowing them to participate as factors or commissioners in aliens' business. Yet despite the disadvantages under which the aliens operated, the partial liberalization of trade meant that they too could expand their economic opportunities. And because growing trade meant growing revenues from duties, the benefits of the *Schragen* accrued as well to the city as a whole.

The provisions of the *Schragen* of 1604 probably remained in effect until about 1653. After that year, the alien Netherlanders' group contracts were replaced by individual ones (see chapter 3), and these no longer contained the ban on trade between aliens.[34] At around the same time, in 1654, a new brokerage ordinance allowed brokers to arrange all kinds of business transactions between aliens. If the *Schragen* had still been valid, this would have been an infringement; and indeed, in the previous brokerage ordinance (of 1642) it had still been expressly forbidden.[35]

Portugal's Policy for Attracting Aliens

While Hamburg distinguished sharply between citizen merchants and alien merchants, in seventeenth-century Portugal it mattered much less where merchants came from. This had not always been so. Medieval laws had made special provisions regarding alien merchants, which in that case meant merchants who were not subjects of the Portuguese king. The fundamental codes of law of King Afonso V and King Manuel I, the *Ordenações Afonsinas* (ca. 1448) and the *Ordenações Manuelinas* (ca. 1513), still contained extensive sections on "alien merchants and how they are to sell and buy goods." For example, aliens were banned from entering into business partnerships with locals, something we also know from Hamburg.[36] Nevertheless, as far back as the fourteenth century, King Fernando I (1345–1383), to whom these regulations can be traced, seems to have been quite open to merchants from elsewhere in Europe. His chronicler, Fernão Lopes, reported that he granted privileges and liberties to many aliens residing in Lisbon.[37]

The Portuguese kings' receptiveness to foreigners was opposed by the *Cortes*, that is, the assembly of representatives of the estates of the realm (the clergy, the nobility, and the commoners). For example, in 1481, it held that aliens should not be permitted to reside in Portugal or its Atlantic islands without a special license from the king.[38] But such provisions ran counter to the economic policies of the Crown, and in such matters the Crown generally prevailed. Foreign merchants were badly needed, not only as providers of grain, but also of the capital, shipbuilding materials, and weapons that were required for the campaigns of conquest. Furthermore, the goods acquired overseas needed buyers, as Portugal itself was not a sufficiently large market. The king's willingness to integrate foreign merchants is evident in a new fundamental code of law. The provisions of the *Ordenações Manuelinas* regarding aliens no longer appear in the *Ordenações Filipinas*, which were completed in 1595 and published in 1603; "alien merchants" as a legal category no longer existed. From then on, unless they were specifically singled out in an individual letter of privilege or an intergovernmental treaty (see chapter 3), alien merchants in Portugal were largely on equal footing with local ones.[39]

Indeed, in their efforts to attract European merchants of substance, the Portuguese kings granted generous privileges and, especially in the fifteenth and early sixteenth centuries, sweeping licenses and contracts conferring the right to exploit specific overseas regions or commodities. From the High Middle Ages to the beginning of the seventeenth century, many of these went to Italians (the Genoese especially, but also to merchants from Piacenza, Milan, Florence, and Venice). Not wanting to become dependent on any individual trading house, cartel, or nation, however, the Crown had also granted privileges to French and English merchants since the fourteenth century, and to Netherlandish and German merchants since the fifteenth. Especially after Vasco da Gama's return from India in 1499, factors were dispatched to Lisbon by many large southern German trading firms, such as those of the Welser, Fugger, Imhof, Höchstetter, Vöhlin, Hörwart, and Ehinger families. Because these firms had access to the largest known silver and copper mines in Europe, they were able to advance both the credit and the merchandise that were needed in the new commerce with Africa and Asia.

One potent means that the Portuguese employed to attract foreign merchants, and one that reverberated for centuries in Hamburg in particular, was the *Português*, a much-sought-after coin of almost pure gold, which bore a high value symbolically as well as materially.[40] The *Português* was first minted in 1499, shortly after Vasco da Gama returned from his travel to India. It was adorned with the cross of the Order of Christ and the crown and shield of the royal coat of arms, and also with inscriptions promising fabulous opportunities for enrichment in the Portugal trade: *"In hoc signo vinces"* (In this sign you will conquer) and *"In commercii et navigatione Aethiopiae, Arabiae, Persiae, Indiae"* (In trade and navigation to Ethiopia, Arabia, Persia, and India). The coin quickly spread throughout Europe, along with the message it proclaimed. By the second half of the sixteenth century, a number of towns and principalities in the north of the Holy Roman Empire, including Hamburg, had begun minting coins of their own modeled on the *Português*, which they called *Portugaleser*. These too bore the cross of the Order of Christ, along with the inscription *"Nach Portugalis Schrot und Korn"* (According to Portuguese weight and fineness), the coat of arms of the city, and other place-specific inscriptions. *Portugaleser* became extraordinarily popular in Hamburg; the coins were used not only to cover large payments, but also given as gifts to mark elections, weddings, baptisms, and other important occasions. Over the course of the seventeenth century, they lost their commercial function and came to be used exclusively as commemorative coins. They continued to be minted, however, and were often decorated with trade symbols of the city, such as its bank, exchange, and convoy ships. In all of their various forms, they were a reminder of the potential for profit in the Portugal trade.

Despite this rich symbolism, by the early 1530s, almost all of the southern German trading houses that had sent factors to Lisbon had closed their Portuguese branches, and had either moved to Seville or gone bankrupt.[41] This was partly because the requisite silver for the Asia trade was now coming increasingly from America and the German silver was no longer needed, and partly because they had misjudged the trade risks of some of the new goods mentioned above. The Genoese bankers, however, continued to be important backers of the Crown, and Portuguese New Christians who had enriched themselves through the new overseas opportunities soon began to catch up. But the Portuguese kings still maintained their welcoming attitude toward German and other alien merchants.

This receptiveness took on a special quality after Portugal declared its independence from Spain in 1640. Within a month of his accession, King João IV decreed that the Treasury Council should call foreign merchants to the country, promise them friendly trade terms and favors, and invite them to import (in particular) weaponry, gunpowder, and munitions.[42] And once again, the king also had a great need for grain suppliers and for buyers of the goods from Portugal's overseas colonies as well as capital. Because the Portuguese economy was still closely intertwined with that of Spain, he feared the power of the Spanish Crown to place Portugal under economic pressure, and to win to its side the merchants who had hitherto been active in both countries.

Hamburg's Contentious Policy on Aliens

While in Portugal policies regarding alien merchants were based on the hope that they would bring capital and grain into the country, in Hamburg they were guided by the fear that alien merchants would take citizens' money, grain, and livelihoods away from them. That fear was widespread in the Assembly of Citizens. As we saw, the Portuguese Cortes – in some ways a counterpart of the Assembly of Citizens – were also skeptical of foreign merchants, but Hamburg's citizens had more leverage on the City Council than the Cortes had on the Crown.[43]

Still, when the Council's power in Hamburg expanded in the second half of the sixteenth century, an increasingly favorable attitude toward alien merchants developed. This resulted in a softening of the strict exclusion of aliens from the town economy, especially by loosening the ban on trade among them. And the City Council started to experiment with permitting the settlement of alien merchants in the city. As economic historian Oscar Gelderblom has pointed out, by that time many towns in the Netherlands had opened themselves and their commercial institutions up to alien merchants; this eventually turned into an outright competition among urban governments to attract aliens and increase trade.[44] Some Hamburg merchants had lived in those cities, and had seen the wealth that accrued to all parties, including the host towns, as a result of free trade. With the adoption of similar policies, the City Council joined in and participated in that competition.

However, the small traders and members of the artisan guilds, who made up the majority of the Assembly of Citizens, remained less open to the presence of foreigners, and the clergy in particular resisted the acceptance of people of other faiths.[45] In fact, most of the new resolutions adopted by the Hamburg City Council with regard to foreigners were pushed through against the opposition of much of the citizenry as well as against clerical resistance.

The first foreigners that the City Council allowed to settle in Hamburg were not merchants, but artisans. In 1530 the Hamburg Company of England Travelers (*Englandfahrergesellschaft*) successfully petitioned the Council to summon a cloth dresser and a cloth dyer from Antwerp to prepare and dye the English cloth that it imported.[46] The new enterprise in Hamburg was very successful, and as the cloth trade began to blossom other Netherlanders were soon also permitted to settle.

The first alien merchants were allowed to take up residence in Hamburg in 1567; they formed a branch of the Company of Merchant Adventurers.[47] Until 1563 the most important continental outpost of this English company had been in Antwerp, but Spanish obstruction prompted relocation. This proved even more favorable for Hamburg: *Werkzoll* revenues almost doubled, and the cloth finishing industry in Hamburg flourished.[48] Still, the agreement between the Merchant Adventurers and Hamburg was not renewed beyond its original ten-year term. After 1579 the English carried out their cloth trade from Emden, and after 1587 from Middelburg and Stade. This move was not to Hamburg's benefit. Not only was the cloth trade withdrawn from the city, but some inhabitants who had worked in cloth finishing or traded the cloth in the German hinterlands also left, following the English merchants to Stade, 35 kilometers downriver. Only in 1611 was the City Council able to bring the English Merchant Adventurers back to Hamburg.

The Hamburgers thus had had opportunity to learn that welcoming foreigners could lead to growth in trade, greater income from duties and taxes, and expanded profit opportunities in manufacturing and trading, as well as the leasing of houses, warehouses, and ships. In 1595, after the first Netherlandish and Portuguese merchants had already settled in Hamburg, a resolution of the City Council and the Assembly of Citizens stated that it was "abundantly clear what harm would follow ... if the foreigners were to be expelled."[49] Nonetheless, the authorization of alien settlement and the periodic renewal of settlement permissions remained a source of conflict between the City Council and the citizenry until the mid-seventeenth century – as we will see in the next chapter.

3 Legal Provisions and the Formation of Nations

In this chapter I will discuss the concrete rights accorded to alien merchants in Hamburg and Portugal, and, more broadly, the concept of *nation* as a group of merchants sharing the same legal status. Membership in a merchant nation was mainly conditioned by ethnic provenance; in the final analysis, however, it was defined by legal document. In Hamburg, the Netherlanders and the Portuguese entered upon a sequence of alien settlement contracts with the City Council. These contracts made clear the terms under which aliens were permitted to settle, but said little about their trading rights, which were addressed in the general laws that I described in chapter 2. Membership lists identified the individuals covered by the contracts. In Portugal, the formal distinction between local and alien merchants was far less rigid than it was in Hamburg, but special trade-related legislation – both in the individual privileges granted to the German merchants and, on a larger scale, in the Hanseatic-Spanish Treaty of 1607, was much more comprehensive, and much more advantageous for the aliens. This chapter explores the merchant nations as legal constructs; in the next I will take up the meaning of "nation" as it related to the appointment of consuls and diplomats. A third aspect of the concept, based on self-perception and religious identity within the diaspora groups, will be explored in the last section of the book.

The Legal Status of Alien Merchants in Hamburg

In the seventeenth century the legal status of aliens was regulated no more comprehensively or consistently than that of other social, corporate, or professional groups.[1] In theory, the *ius commune* (lit. common law, which was based on Roman law and applied to all people equally) took priority over the special rights governing specific groups. However, in legal practice the special rights were more adaptable, and therefore more effective. In the end, a complex negotiation process based on a multiplicity of legal sources often determined what law actually prevailed. That is why the legal status of alien merchants and other special groups cannot be adequately understood by looking only at the laws themselves. What really counted was how jurists applied them. A comprehensive understanding would require careful study of the legal proceedings and scholarly treatises of the time. That is a task well beyond the scope of this work, however, so I will limit my analysis here to the alien laws as they were legislated.[2]

The law applied to aliens in Hamburg derived from four sources: the *Stadtrecht* (the Hamburg town law); the *Burspraken* (a collection of provisions

https://doi.org/10.1515/9783110472103-004

and resolutions read aloud before the citizens about twice a year by the City Council); the *Rezesse* (agreements worked out between the Hamburg City Council and the Assembly of Citizens); and the alien contracts entered upon with individuals or with groups of persons according to their foreign origins.[3] The town law, which was reformed in 1603 and took effect in 1605, did not distinguish between locals and aliens; its preamble affirmed its validity for everyone, aliens included. The special legal status of aliens was defined mainly in the *Burspraken*, which in some points were complemented or modified by the *Rezesse*. These three were supplemented by the specific alien contracts. Historians working on the Portuguese and Netherlandish nations in Hamburg have largely ignored this plurality of legal sources and concentrated their attention on the alien contracts. For this reason they have tended to ignore the alien laws discussed in the previous chapter (most of which are part of the *Burspraken*).[4]

The *Burspraken* tell us that all aliens who wished to stay in Hamburg and engage in trade there for more than a few days had to become citizens.[5] Yet a Hamburg *Rezess* of 1579, implementing a statute of the Hansa, excluded foreigners, namely Netherlanders, English, Scots, French, "and others more" from becoming citizens.[6] This was why the City Council established specific contracts with foreigners who wanted to settle. I have already mentioned Hamburg's agreement with the Merchant Adventurers (see chapter 2). Other aliens were admitted on the basis of individual contracts that required them to pay taxes but exempted them from other civic obligations, such as administrative office or military service.[7] Aliens seeking such a contract, however, had to be "kin to our religion"; in other words, to be Christians.[8]

The exclusions of the *Rezess* of 1579 notwithstanding, a number of Netherlandish merchants did receive citizen rights before the turn of the seventeenth century.[9] But the formal citizenship criteria for merchants from outside the Holy Roman Empire continued to be contested for some years beyond that.[10] In 1605 the Council, which (as we saw in chapter 2) was always more hospitable to aliens than the Assembly of Citizens, advanced a proposal according to which "those who have lived here for several years, profess the Christian religion, are of honorable conduct and have no stain ... may without further specification of nation" be accepted as citizens at the "discretion" of the City Council.[11] Although the Assembly once again answered that the issue needed further thought before a definitive conclusion could be reached, this proposal probably reflects the common practice by which aliens were accepted as citizens in the opening decades of the seventeenth century. It should be noted that the profession of Lutheranism was not a condition of citizenship; Reformed Protestants were accepted, although with restricted political rights.[12]

The Collective Alien Contracts

Nor did religious persuasion matter in the first collective settlement contract, which was concluded between the City Council and the Netherlanders in 1605.[13] Religion is not mentioned at all in that contract, which applied to Lutheran and Reformed alike. The central issue underlying the negotiations was not Hamburg's refusal to accept Netherlanders or Reformed as citizens, but the refusal of many Netherlanders' to accept exclusive and permanent affiliation with Hamburg as a condition of citizenship. They preferred to remain mobile, so that they could easily return to their homeland or migrate to other places. As citizens they would have been required to remain in Hamburg for at least ten years, and to pay the city a tenth of their assets if they left later (*Abschoss*). The alien contract, however, allowed them to leave at any time upon payment of five times the annual property tax (*Schoss*). It also spared them the obligation of serving in the city administration and the militia, which further contributed to their mobility and saved them time and money.

The Portuguese negotiated their first collective settlement contract with the city in 1612.[14] They hoped in the beginning for a contract similar to the Netherlanders', but they did not achieve this goal.[15] Ultimately their chief success in the negotiation was to be allowed to settle in Hamburg as Jews, because up to that time Jews had not been admitted to the city. Although the Portuguese had come to Hamburg as Catholics, the Hamburgers soon suspected them of secretly adhering to Judaism, and in 1603 the Assembly of Citizens declared bluntly that those among the Portuguese who "profess the Jewish faith should be expelled and not tolerated here."[16] The Netherlanders negotiated their contract as an alternative to citizenship, but for the Portuguese it was an alternative to expulsion.

It is not clear when the Portuguese started to view and organize themselves as a predominantly Jewish community, but religious freedom was a central demand from their first known proposal for a settlement contract, advanced in about 1605. Their representatives urged that "the [same] freedom be given which those [Portuguese immigrants] in Holland had been granted, namely that in matters of religion they be treated with forbearance."[17] The Portuguese in Hamburg did not attain the same level of forbearance as their brethren in Amsterdam had; nonetheless it is striking that they were not subjected to the constraints customarily applied to Jews in the Holy Roman Empire. They were not required to wear identifying insignia, were not restricted to living in a particular quarter, and were not forbidden to hire Christian servants and domestics. It is true that they were not allowed to buy real estate, but neither were other aliens.[18] Although the contract included nominal bans on synagogues and circumcisions, the Portuguese were able to circumvent them by meeting privately in their homes and holding their services and ceremonies there, without any serious consequences. All told, the legal status of the Portuguese Jews in Hamburg was, if not equal, at least similar to that of other foreign merchant groups.

Still, the contracts entered into by the Netherlanders and by the Portuguese differed significantly in both form and content. The agreement with the Netherlanders is extensive, and identified in the text itself as a "contract"; that with the Portuguese is a much shorter collection of "articles." The contract with the Netherlanders begins with a detailed explanation of why they had come to Hamburg to settle, and of the circumstances of the agreement. By contrast, the articles pertaining to the Portuguese dispense with any elaboration and begin immediately with a list of briefly formulated demands regulating the religious and social behavior expected of Jews: "1. The nation shall behave peaceably and keep to itself. 2. Give no one annoyance. 3. Maintain no synagogue. 4. Not practice its religion in this city by holding meetings either in secret or in public, nor practice circumcision there."[19]

After a series of other provisos, Article 12 finally grants the Portuguese "that each of them, including his servants, will be protected, safeguarded, duly represented, and in no way hindered in his conscience because of his religion" on the condition that he pay all taxes as the articles provide. It is important to note that the Portuguese were protected only in their persons, while the contract with the Netherlanders guaranteed their property and their right of inheritance as well. These three rights – protection of person, of property, and of inheritance – had since the Middle Ages been fundamental components of settlement contracts with alien merchants.[20] And although the protection of property and inheritance were not mentioned in these articles or in subsequent contracts with the Portuguese, that does not mean that such rights were not accorded to them in practice; ultimately, like all aliens, the Portuguese had recourse to the town law. Nonetheless, the absence of clear and binding formulations in their contracts is evidence of their less secure legal status.

Duration of Contract Validity and Rate of Taxation

The series of contracts for the Portuguese were of shorter duration than those for the Netherlanders. The first contract signed by the Netherlanders guaranteed them a settlement of ten years, and the two later contracts, concluded in 1615 and 1639, extended to fifteen. The Portuguese contracts were less generous; the early ones, in 1612, 1617, and 1623, all differed from the Netherlander contracts in that the City Council had the right to terminate them at will, with one year's notice.[21] But the Portuguese, unlike the Netherlanders, could leave the city at any time without paying a multiple of the *Schoss* as a departure tax.[22] They did have to contend with the possibility of revocation, but with this insecurity came freedom of mobility. In fact there appears to have been a sort of revolving door between the Portuguese-Jewish communities in Hamburg, Glückstadt, and Amsterdam during much of the seventeenth century. This was clearly not what the City Council had had in mind; it held that "with respect to commerce, it is desirable that a considerable *Schoss* be established for 4 or 5 years." However, the Council was not able to come to an agreement about that with the Assembly of Citizens.[23]

The *Schoss* was also assessed differently in the contracts of the two groups.[24] In 1605 the Netherlanders pledged to pay a total of 5,172 marks for all the people covered by the contract, which came to an average of 40 marks per household. In 1639 they pledged to pay 15,000 marks, or 88 marks per household.[25] To this various and variable other charges were added, such as the excise, the *Matten* (milling tax), the *Grabengeld* (for fortifications, and formerly for moats), and the Turk tax (levied by the Holy Roman Empire to defend against the expanding Ottoman Empire). The Portuguese agreed to pay a total of 1,000 marks in 1612 and 2,000 marks in 1617, which came to averages of about 33 marks and 63 marks per household, respectively.[26] These payments too were subject to additional levies. Still, the Portuguese paid substantially lower taxes per capita than the Netherlanders. This was probably because they had fewer assets (see chapter 8); it was noted repeatedly in the contract negotiations that to impose the *Schoss* on the Portuguese would add almost nothing to the city's coffers, because they owned so little property. For that reason, the citizens' representatives originally proposed that the Portuguese pay an additional customs duty, the so-called Hundredth Penny (*Hundertster Pfennig*), instead of the *Schoss*, as their contribution to the city's treasury. However, the Portuguese were able to fend off this proposal.[27]

Legal "Belonging" and Protection in Foreign Lands

Under their Hamburg contracts, the Netherlanders retained the right to remain loyal to their "natural" rulers (that is, to the rulers of their homeland) and "not to damage them nor to ruin, weaken, or lessen their interests."[28] A number of Netherlanders in fact remained citizens of their home towns even while residing in Hamburg. For a small tax, residents of Antwerp and other towns could accept a *buitenpoorterschap* (*buiten* = away from home; *poorterschap* = citizen status), and let their citizen rights there go into temporary abeyance.[29]

Despite this, the Netherlanders benefited from Hamburg's protection even in foreign countries. Their contract states that they could count on the city's support while abroad if "a potentate, prince, or lord were to prosecute or cite them before the law."[30] And in fact the Hamburg City Council did repeatedly intercede on their behalf when such situations arose. For example, in 1605 goods belonging to the Netherlanders Dominicus van Uffeln and Jan van der Straeten, both of whom were "parties to" the Hamburg contract, were stolen from Hamburg ships, and the City Council complained to Archduke Alberto, the governor-general of the Spanish Netherlands.[31] As we will see later (p. 61), Netherlanders under contract also benefited from inclusion in the Treaty of 1607; like the Hamburgers, but unlike the Netherlanders living in the United Provinces, they could trade legally with Spain and Portugal. In many ways the Netherlanders enjoyed the advantages of citizenship in two places, without having to fulfill all of its obligations in either one.

The contracts with the Portuguese did not mention the right to continued loyalty to a "natural" ruler, or to protection in cases of action by foreign powers. Nevertheless, there is evidence that Portuguese merchants living in Hamburg also received aid and support from its City Council when away from home, if not always while in residence (see chapter 14). In 1648, for example, four Hamburg ships sailing for Lisbon were set upon by Spanish privateers. One of them sank, and from the other three all the goods belonging to Portuguese merchants were seized. The Hamburg City Council interceded with the Duke of Peñaranda de Duero on behalf of the Hamburg Portuguese. The Council maintained that according to the Peace of Westphalia, which in that same year had ended the Thirty Years' War, all Hanseatic merchants were to be permitted to trade with Portugal in all wares except for weapons and munitions. Although the owners of the seized merchandise were admittedly of Portuguese origin, they had resided in Hamburg for years and were to be treated accordingly. The City Council demanded that the ships and goods be returned, that restitution be paid for the sunken vessel, and that the perpetrators be punished.[32] It is not known whether these demands were honored.

Position in Trade

The Hamburg alien contracts contained only few trade-related additions to the alien laws presented in chapter 2. Although the scholarly literature has generally assumed that the Portuguese and the other merchants of the city had the same trading rights, this is a misunderstanding; the status of the Portuguese in trade was not equal to that of citizens.[33] Article 5 of the Portuguese contract of 1612, which is often cited in evidence of equality, reads literally: "Practice and pursue fair-minded and honest commerce in the same manner as our citizens and other residents."[34] But this wording does not mean that the Portuguese were *permitted* to ply their trade as other merchants did, but rather (as the context of the other articles makes clear) that they *must* do so. In other words, this was not a promise, but a disciplinary regulation. It required that the Portuguese behave in as upright and honest a manner when trading as the citizens of Hamburg and its other inhabitants. Similar formulations may be found in other sources, such as the City Council ruling of 1586, which instructed alien merchants:

> that you should prove upright and honest in your trade and doings and that likewise you behave in that same work and obligations, such that you may answer for them before the will of God. This the Honorable City Council urgently wishes to impress upon you, that each alien must conform to the *Bursprake*, in which it is sharply proclaimed that alien may not pursue trade with alien, and that he behave accordingly under penalty of law.[35]

Here the demand for rectitude and honesty in trade is linked with the ban on direct trade between aliens, and Article 5 of the Portuguese contract must be understood similarly. The alien laws, which distinguished aliens from citizens, applied to the Portuguese as well.

The 1605 Netherlander contract mentions the *Schragen* of 1604 explicitly, and reaffirms the ban on alien trade of the goods specified there.[36] The Netherlanders were not happy with this. In the contract negotiations they had attempted to procure the right to trade freely in some of the banned goods (especially grain, the most important commodity traded with the Iberian Peninsula). And a letter from the Netherlanders dated 1607 urged the City Council to drop a complaint against two of their members before the Imperial Chamber Court (Reichskammergericht). According to the letter, the grain in which these two merchants had traded had come from foreign countries and not from the environs of Hamburg, and therefore fell not into the category of goods and commodities reserved for citizens, but into the category of goods "brought here from foreign kingdoms and lands," which were free for everybody. The Netherlanders urged the Council to recognize this and act accordingly, or the consequences "would be harshly felt."[37] It is not known whether this appeal was successful, but their settlement contract of 1615 permitted the Netherlanders to trade with other aliens not only in the merchandise allowed in the *Schragen*, but also in grain from the lower Elbe, and in bay salt (that is, from France, Spain and Portugal), wool, and woolen cloth. The contract of 1639 added permission to trade in southern wines, and goods from Moscow.[38] However, trade in grain from the upper Elbe was always reserved for citizens.

We must assume that the *Schragen* of 1604 continued to apply fully to the Portuguese, since their contracts did not in any way curtail its restrictions on trade between aliens. The Netherlanders' contracts of 1615 and 1639, however, did permit trade of some of the previously banned goods. So by that time the contract Netherlanders as well as the citizens of Hamburg had an advantage over the Portuguese in the trade of such commodities as grain, salt, wine, wool, and woolen cloth.

Collective Contracts and the Formation of Nations

In the European commercial cities of the Middle Ages, the term *nation* had denoted associations of alien merchants of the same ethnic origin that had structured themselves as corporate bodies.[39] In early modern Hamburg, the English Merchant Adventurers came closest to this form of nation, in that their settlement contract recognized a governing board, independently framed bylaws, and autonomy in the exercise of jurisdiction (except in criminal matters).[40] Because the Merchant Adventurers lived in their own shared building, they were also separated spatially from the citizens of the city. Such arrangements were not adopted in the contracts of the Netherlandish and Portuguese settlers in Hamburg, however, although they, too, were designated as nations. Unlike the Merchant Adventurers, these immigrants had not arrived together, as a cohort. They came singly, in families, or in small groups, and their permission to settle was at first granted on an individual basis. Only after many of them had been living in Hamburg for some time was a common condition applied to them by the collective contracts. This condition was less restrictive than that of the Merchant Adventurers. Nevertheless, among the Netherlanders and Portuguese too it led to the emergence of a leadership, the development of internal rules founded on religious precepts, the monitoring and enforcement of these rules, and the formation of a specific group identity (see also chapters 14 and 15).

The group contracts enabled the City Council to simplify administration by delegating responsibility to the groups themselves, especially with regard to taxes, which the Netherlanders and Portuguese now paid collectively rather than as individuals. This strengthened the autonomy of the nations, which could decide by themselves how their taxes were to be divided up, and with that decision exert some influence on their composition.[41] That is why the otherwise rather conservative Hamburg Assembly of Citizens opposed bundling the aliens into collectives and sought to have them (the Netherlanders, at least) treated on an individual basis. During the negotiations around their third contract, the Assembly's representatives urged that "a special tax be made" for each of them. The Netherlanders, however, wished to continue to pay a lump sum as in previous contracts.[42] They pointed out that they themselves understood best "the condition of each," and so would be able to divide the total tax up appropriately, without having to resort to a relief fund to make up the difference for those whom the Council had taxed too high. The City Council acceded to the wishes of the Netherlanders, and was able to push this provision through against the opposition of the Assembly.

The negotiations over the contract and the partitioning of the tax promoted the development of a leadership within the Netherlandish nation. Its members came to serve as spokesmen during other negotiations as well. For example, the negotiators of the first contract acted as "representatives of the 130 united Netherlanders" in a lawsuit involving two contract members, Samuel Stockmann and Melchior Haßbeck, and represented "our interests, which are the same as theirs." The second Netherlander contract referred to a "committee of the nation" that at various times had maintained busy communication with the past and present mayors and with the deputies of the Assembly of Citizens. Similarly, the Portuguese contract implied the establishment of a leadership, which appears soon to have become identical with the board of the Portuguese-Jewish community (see chapter 14).[43] In other words, not only did the contracts encourage the formation of collectives among the aliens, they also led to the elaboration of internal organizational structures.

The last collective Netherlander contract was established in 1639. Once it expired, those who wished to continue enjoying their alien status had to register individually at the city hall and have their taxes set. A declaration from 1653 states that the Hamburg City Council "does not intend to negotiate with any body (*mit keinem corpore*), and has scrapped and canceled the respective authorization of the deputies."[44] Thus the *corpus* (that is, the corporate body) of the Netherlandish nation, which had defined itself as a political unit on the basis of a common contract, came to an end. The Portuguese nation, however, endured as a body with collective rights for many more years. Only in 1710 did the city group the Portuguese and the German Jews together under one set of rules, and the special legal status of both of them (as Jews) was not abolished until the second half of the nineteenth century.

The Formation of the Portuguese-Jewish Community

The collective contracts of the Portuguese created more than just a nation; they also supported the creation of the first Jewish community in Hamburg. Although the Portuguese were rumored to have pursued Judaism secretly in their homeland, and although some of them might have formally converted shortly upon their arrival, most of the Portuguese probably continued to live as Catholics in Hamburg during the first years of their stay (see chapter 14). While it was not a foregone conclusion that the City Council would accept Jews, its attitude toward them was much more receptive than that of the citizens at large and of the Lutheran clergy. The Council may have had an even greater interest in the settlement of Jews than of Catholics, and this may have been a further motivation for the Portuguese to convert to Judaism.

One possible reason for that greater interest is that in the conventional understanding of the time, Jews were supposed to be especially talented in matters of business and trade, and better able than other peoples to increase a city's wealth with the revenues they brought in (see chapter 11). But even more important was the fact that Jews, unlike Catholics, had no political power standing behind them. Portuguese Catholics in Hamburg would have had the emperor and the Spanish king as important intercessors. The negotiations surrounding the Treaty of 1607 (see chapter 1) made clear that the king intended to establish a Portuguese royal *feitoria* in Hamburg on the model of the former one in Antwerp. During much of the sixteenth century, that trading post had been the main European settlement of Portuguese merchants outside of Portugal. When the king's representatives tried to negotiate the foundation of a *feitoria* in Hamburg, they were determined that the Portuguese merchants living there should be able to achieve citizen rights and practice the Catholic religion in their homes.[45] This request was eventually rejected by the Hamburgers; nonetheless, it provides evidence that the city had had the opportunity to encourage the establishment of a Portuguese Catholic merchant nation if it had wanted one. The Hamburgers probably assumed that (even lacking a formal *feitoria*) the Spanish king would have cooperated with such a community, and possibly used it to gain influence over commercial and political developments in Hamburg. As Jews, the Portuguese were in a much weaker position; they had no powerful monarch behind them, and would be essentially dependent on Hamburg's ruling authority, the City Council. They would have been expected to be more submissive in their conduct and attitudes, and more modest in their demands. We may therefore interpret the Portuguese settlement contract of 1612, with its clear focus on the Jewish religion, as a means by which the City Council intended to take advantage of both the greater vulnerability and the greater loyalty of this group of immigrants.

Nation Membership in Hamburg

While the Portuguese settlement contracts probably extended to all of the Portuguese living in Hamburg, by no means were all of the Netherlanders living in the city included in the Netherlander contracts. It is not clear what conditions applicants had to meet to be included. The opening of the first contract states that it covered mainly war refugees from the southern Netherlands.[46] But the third contract also accepted seven "Germans and High Germans" who apparently wished to profit from the legal status that the contract provided.[47] Sons of the covered Netherlanders were also included in the contracts once they married or started their own businesses. However, the City Council rejected the Netherlanders' demand that daughters and their husbands be included, "because this is about commerce, and that is conducted by men and not by women."[48] That explanation makes clear that the contracts were aimed primarily at merchants, although we know that several manufacturers were covered as well.[49]

By contrast, the sons of Portuguese settlers who wanted to be accepted into the contract had to present themselves to the mayors as if they were new arrivals, despite the status of their parents. The pertinent provision states:

> If then the high and most wise City Council assesses their qualification such that it has no qualms about taking them under its protection and can come to an agreement with them about the *Schoss* and other matters, then such Portuguese arrivals shall enjoy the same freedom as those who already reside here, so long as they fulfill the above-cited articles.[50]

This shows that the City Council had the authority to decide whether or not a candidate might become a member of the city community, based on the individual's "qualification." However, the minute books of the Portuguese-Jewish community indicate that its board (see chapter 14) was also greatly involved in decisions about which Portuguese were permitted to settle in the city. A similar arrangement was probably in effect among the Netherlanders as well.

Lists were compiled of the aliens covered by each of the contracts. In the case of the Netherlanders, at first the whole group was designated by the number of names listed – as in the 1607 petition of the "representatives of the 130 united Netherlanders" to the City Council.[51] Presumably a more apt common designation was not yet available. With the second contract, however, and despite the fact that many Netherlanders remained outside it, the group that it covered was identified as the *Netherlandish nation*.[52] Corresponding lists of the Portuguese compiled for the city administration do exist, although they were not directly attached to the contracts as the Netherlandish lists were.[53]

The Legal Status of German Merchants in Portugal

In seventeenth-century Portugal there were no such group contracts or lists of alien merchants. Instead, beginning in the fifteenth century, German, Italian, English, French, and Netherlandish merchants were granted *privileges*. A privilege was a piece of special legislation favoring a specific individual or group, and was awarded by the grace of the king in the form of a *letter of privilege*. These letters were modeled one upon the other, but they were tailored to fit individual cases, and privileged merchants received similar but not necessarily identical rights. Some letters were valid for a limited time (usually fifteen years), while others were unlimited. However, after one final known letter granted to Netherlanders in 1509, letters of privilege seem to have been awarded exclusively to so-called "German merchants."[54] For most of the sixteenth century, they were listed in the books of the Royal Chancellery, but registrations suddenly stopped in 1588. We know that further letters of privilege were issued after that year, as we have examples of them, but they were no longer mentioned in the Chancellery books.[55] Nor is there any indication that they might have been listed elsewhere. It appears, therefore, that while the civic authorities in Hamburg knew exactly what aliens were living and trading in their city, and could monitor their activities (especially their compliance with the trade restrictions), the royal authorities in Portugal lacked this kind of overview. Nonetheless, because the privileged aliens in Portugal were far better off than the local merchants, it was in their own best interest to make certain that their special legal status be recognized and maintained.

The privileges awarded to "German merchants" evolved into a distinct legal instrument, the German Merchant Privilege (*privilégio de mercador alemão*). As we shall see, it was central to the status of many alien merchants in Portugal (not just Germans) in conjunction with the general laws set forth in the *Ordenações Manuelinas* (ca. 1513), in the *Ordenações Filipinas* (1603), and in the commercial treaties signed with foreign rulers. The letters of privilege provided comprehensive protection for the person and his property, guaranteed freedom of mobility and trade in the kingdom, granted exemptions from obligatory services and taxes, provided for reductions in customs duties and other trade concessions, and at times even permitted travel to India.[56] Among the key prerogatives of the people awarded this privilege was their "access to a special judge, the *juiz conservador dos alemães* (the Judge Conservator of the Germans). This judge was a royal official who ruled in accordance with Portuguese law, but handled cases much more expeditiously than the usual courts.

The bearers of the privilege were granted two other outstanding benefits: the rights of a *vizinho* of the city of Lisbon, and certain prerogatives that were generally reserved for the nobility. The term *vizinho* is often translated as *citizen*, although the legal status of a *vizinho* lay somewhere between that of citizen and inhabitant as the terms were defined in Hamburg.[57] As a rule, Hanseatic merchants living abroad who acquired citizen rights in another country had to renounce permanently their equivalent rights in the Hansa towns, thereby barring themselves from Hansa privileges.[58] But apparently the acquisition of *vizinhança* in

Portugal did not violate Hansa law; at any rate I found no traces of it ever having been discussed or punished. Hanseatic merchants who were granted a German Merchant Privilege in Portugal probably enjoyed a sort of dual citizenship much as the Netherlanders residing in Hamburg did (see pp. 48–49).[59]

The other prerogatives, ordinarily reserved for the nobility, included permission to ride horses and mules, carry firearms, and wear clothing made of or trimmed with silk.[60] Bearers of the German Merchant Privilege in Portugal therefore enjoyed social as well as legal advantages over most of their local confreres.[61] They were also better placed than the Portuguese and Netherlanders living in Hamburg, and not only because they were exempt from taxes and some of the customs duties.

From our perspective today, the structure of the letters of privilege is puzzling. The letter granted (though not registered) in 1639 to the Hamburg merchant Henrique Aires, for example, runs to 34 pages.[62] It makes no mention at all of the Treaty of 1607 between Spain and the Hansa, which contained a comprehensive and consistent list of the rights of Hanseatic merchants on the Iberian Peninsula (see chapter 1). Yet it quotes at great length letters of privilege that had been given to Germans in the fifteenth and sixteenth centuries but were now obsolete. Even privileges that had been given not to merchants, but to members of other professions, were recapitulated like this. The earliest privilege cited in many later letters (although not in Henrique Aires's) was that of a German shoemaker named Miguel Armão from the year 1452. Probably the repetition of these long series of privileges served a symbolic purpose; it bore witness to the antiquity and venerability of the institution. The details of a privilege's content were less important than the fact of having become privileged at all, and the privilege was a marker of the high social status of its bearer.

Individualization

The legal status of the alien merchants in Portugal, unlike that of the aliens in Hamburg, did not lead to the elaboration of corporate structures. The contracts in Hamburg were negotiated in protracted processes between the City Council and the aliens' representatives, but the privileges in Portugal were granted by the favor and grace of the king, and implied no obligation in return. Aliens in Portugal did not need representatives to press their interests. The bearers of privileges were exempt from taxation, so the merchants felt no need to organize for the purpose. Nor were violations of the law a group responsibility; the letters of privilege expressly state that there was no collective liability, and that the meting out of sanctions to individuals was the province of the special judge. Only in matters of inheritance did the letters of privilege imply the existence of a community among the aliens. When a bearer of the German Merchant Privilege died in Portugal and no other local representative of his firm could be found, his goods were to be inventoried by the judge and then entrusted to two merchants for safekeeping.[63] These two were to be chosen from among the deceased's social circle, and a few letters of privilege explicitly required that they belong to the same nation.

This legal individualization of alien merchants (as opposed to the group treatment in Hamburg) was consistent with the absolutist constitution of Portugal, where corporate structures were much more limited in scope than in the Holy Roman Empire. In general, privileged social groups in Portugal lacked internal organization, and their cohesion was considerably weaker than in Hamburg at that time.[64] Whereas the use of group contracts in Hamburg led to the segregation of aliens into corporate nations, privileging in Portugal promoted integration into the urban elite. Those who wished to benefit from the prerogatives available tried to acquire the German Merchant Privilege; however, possession of that privilege did not require affiliation with a legally defined German nation, or even that the possessor be ethnically German at all.

Nation Membership in Portugal

The group of all the merchants formally privileged under the German Merchant Privilege did not correspond to a nation in the ethnic sense. For one thing, not all Germans acquired the privilege;[65] conversely, many merchants who did were not German. In the sixteenth century, during which the letters of privilege were still registered in the Chancellery books, Netherlanders, French, Barcelonans, Burgalese, Venetians, and Genoese, along with at least fifteen Portuguese, acquired the German Merchant Privilege.[66] Among the Portuguese were such prominent traders as the New Christians Simão and André Rodrigues d'Évora, who together with their brother Manuel and other relatives played an important role in trade with Antwerp and Cologne.[67] Contrary to suggestions in the preface of a twentieth-century critical edition of one merchant's letter of privilege, a certain Duarte Fernandes was also probably not German, but Portuguese.[68] Although King Felipe II's confirmation of Fernandes's privilege refers to him as an *alemão privilegiado* (privileged German), another passage of the same document calls him *privilegiado de alemão* (privileged *as a* German). And the document originally issued by King Sebastião in 1578 states that Fernandes was to receive the privileges, graces, and freedoms that Sebastião's predecessors had granted to German merchants, *como se fora mercador alemão* (*as if he were* a German merchant). If we take this literally, he became a "German merchant" by being privileged as such.[69]

The German Merchant Privilege, therefore, developed into a legal designation independent of the origin of the person who bore it. The privilege was economically advantageous for all merchants active in trade with northern Europe, in that it reduced customs duties on many import goods from there, and gave access to the special judge and the other advantages. But it also conferred a social honor from which the New Christians especially benefited, as most other distinctions (especially ennoblement) were denied them because of their Jewish origins.[70]

Persons privileged as German merchants came from many different places, but to have been ethnically German, or originating from the Holy Roman Empire, may well have facilitated the acquisition of this privilege. The 1639 letter of Henrique Aires from Hamburg, for example, states that the goods he had brought through customs had increased the king's coffers, and that he had been born in Hamburg, which belonged to the Holy Roman Empire. For these two reasons, the argument went, he was entitled to the privileges that the kings had from time immemorial granted to Germans. Two witnesses (also Germans according to the document) declared that they were acquainted with Aires; they confirmed that his trade, especially in wood, yielded much in the way of customs revenues, and that he came from Hamburg. Five years after Aires, however, the Netherlandish merchant Duarte Sonnemans, a native of Delft, received the German Merchant Privilege with the sole justification that his trading activities had brought in much customs revenue.[71]

Contribution to the common good, especially by way of customs duties that accrued to the royal treasury, was an important support for acquiring the privilege. Nonetheless, it is important to remember that the privilege was an award, not a commitment. In Hamburg, the Portuguese paid with their taxes for their right to live and trade there, and would have been expelled if they failed in this obligation; in Portugal, all merchants had to do was obey the law. Certainly the king valued those who were active and successful in trade, but the granting of privilege implied no permanent obligation on the recipient's part.

The Hanseatic-Spanish Treaty of 1607 and Its Religious Implications

The Treaty of 1607 raised the German Merchant Privilege to the level of international law.[72] Rights that had previously been granted on an individual basis were now extended to all Hanseatic merchants, and their scope widened to cover Spain as well as Portugal. A series of provisions relating to the Dutch War of Independence (see chapter 2) supplemented the privilege.[73] The rights granted to Hanseatic merchants by this treaty extended well beyond those that

England and France had negotiated for their merchants in similar treaties only a few years before. Even though the treaty lost its immediate importance as a result of the Twelve Years' Truce (see chapter 1), it served as a precedent for the treaties, and the rights of alien merchants, subsequently negotiated in Portugal.[74]

The question of religion was not raised either in the individual privileges or in the Treaty of 1607. It was, however, important to the Hamburgers, because in the previous century Protestant merchants had repeatedly been arrested by the Inquisition. After a German named Joachim Stockmann was imprisoned for two years by the Inquisition in the early 1580s, a number of Hanseatic merchants refused to continue to travel to Portugal.[75] The first concession to the Lutherans was made in 1597, when the Spanish agreed not to question passengers on ships coming from German lands about their religion.[76] The treaty signed between Spain and England in 1604 went further. It guaranteed that English merchants would not be harassed on the mainland about their beliefs as long as no scandal arose from their behavior.[77] In 1607 the Hansa negotiators attempted to secure the same agreement for their people, but they did not succeed. The Spanish argued that unlike the English, Hanseatic merchants had been trading continuously with the kingdom without agreements over religion. They knew, so the argument went, how to behave on the Iberian Peninsula. They had always acted with discretion and seemliness. There had never been cause for prosecution on the grounds of their beliefs, and so it should remain.[78]

This argument is somewhat surprising, given that a number of Hanseatics had not long before been brought to trial by the Inquisition. A shipmaster from Lübeck named Johann Bolin was in the custody of the Inquisition in Seville at the very time that these statements were made, because two Protestant books had been discovered on his ship.[79] Nonetheless, with this declaration Spain indicated that it was prepared in principle to grant the Hanseatic Protestants the same rights as the English, although it was disinclined to put them in writing. Only in 1647, in the renewal of the Treaty of 1607 for Spain (now separated from Portugal), was there an explicit provision about religion: "the Hanseatic merchants and shipmasters will not be harassed or disturbed contrary to mercantile law in questions of conscience as long as they create no scandal."[80] Portugal, in its agreements with other states, had by this time taken the matter yet a step further. The 1641 treaty with the United Provinces was the first to deal with religion in positive terms rather than negative ones; that is, it stipulated not that merchants would *not* be harassed on account of their beliefs, but that the Dutch *would* have freedom of conscience, and be permitted to practice their religion freely in their homes and on their ships.[81] The same probably applied to merchants from Hamburg.

Thus the legal situation of Protestants in Portugal came to resemble that of the Reformed, Catholics, and Jews in Hamburg; they were not permitted to practice their religion publicly, but could do so in private. Despite the horrifying stories circulating throughout Europe about the policies of the Inquisition, merchants were well aware of this similarity. When in 1670 the Hamburg merchant João da Maya was interrogated by the Inquisition, he stated his belief that in Portugal, as in his homeland, he could confess whatever belief he deemed best, and that this freedom applied in particular to aliens from Protestant countries.[82] What da Maya did not know, however, or at least did not say, was that this policy did not apply to those who had officially converted to Catholicism in Portugal. Once converted, no apostasy was permitted. But even in that case, a Hanseatic or Netherlandish merchant who ran afoul of the Inquisition could count on being treated leniently (see chapter 5), and his home government might intercede if needed. There is evidence that the Hansa in a number of cases, and the United Provinces in many, attempted not only to protect their merchants, but also to recover goods confiscated by the Inquisition from their subjects.[83]

The Concept of Nation in the Treaty of 1607

The organization of the Hansa, and its membership, had long been confusing, especially to nonmembers. A declaration by the Portuguese king from 1517, customarily contained in the merchants' letters of privilege, states that although the "Easterling or Hanseatic" nation differed in name from the "German" nation, Hanseatic merchants had a claim to the same privileges as the Germans because the Hansa towns were imperial cities and their citizens were vassals of the Holy Roman Emperor. (*Easterling* was another word for *Hanseatic*, and referred especially to the Hansa towns east of the Netherlands.)[84] However, this declaration was an oversimplification, because not all Hansa towns were located within the territory of the empire, and of those that were, some (like Hamburg at that time) were not imperial cities, subject only to the emperor and not to any territorial prince. Furthermore, even within the empire itself there was no unanimity about which towns were Hansa towns or which cities were imperial cities.[85] The Treaty of 1607 addressed at least some of these issues, and in so doing enhanced to some degree the understanding of the Hanseatic nation on the Iberian Peninsula.

The treaty states that the Hansa towns and their inhabitants should be privileged, but excluded the towns in the United Provinces, among them such old Hansa towns as Kampen, Deventer, and Zwolle. It also specified that the privileges would not extend to towns that had recently left the Hansa, such as Stade, or that would leave it in the future.[86] But it did include Augsburg, Nuremberg,

Strasbourg, Ulm, and some other southern German cities that had never belonged to the Hansa, specifying that their inhabitants were to enjoy the same privileges as those of the Hansa towns.[87] The Hansa emissaries to the treaty process promised to clarify matters by providing a complete list of the towns affected by the treaty, but neither of the two lists included among the delegation documents in the Lübeck archive offers an up-to-date survey of the Hansa' towns.[88]

The Treaty of 1607 and the negotiations that preceded it also give us information about the civic status of the individuals who benefited from it. The Spanish version of the treaty uses seven different terms to designate the members of the towns who were to enjoy the privileges: *subditos, ciudadanos, vecinos, dependientes, naturales, moradores*, and *vasallos* (subjects, privileged citizens, simple citizens, dependents, natives, inhabitants, and vassals). This covered all the possible categories of "belonging" to a town. Most important, it included the Netherlanders and other aliens who resided in Hamburg but possessed no citizen rights. During the treaty negotiations, the Portuguese representatives had voiced concerns about the Netherlanders settled in Hamburg. According to the representatives, many citizens of the northern Netherlands – the "rebellious provinces" – who were barred from trade with Spain had moved to the Hansa towns, received *cartas de vizinhança* (lit. letters of citizenship, but probably also including the alien contracts), and were now conducting trade with Spain from there. To prevent fraud, the negotiators suggested that Netherlanders long settled in the Hansa towns should be permitted to continue trading so long as they used Hanseatic ships with Hanseatic crews and observed Hanseatic legal provisions; but that as long as no peace or truce had been concluded with the United Provinces, that privilege would not extend to Netherlanders recently settled in Hansa towns or settling there in the future.[89] This nuanced regulation was not included in the final text of the treaty, however. The Hansa negotiators apparently succeeded in asserting the interests of the Netherlanders covered by the alien contracts, and retained their advantageous conditions even for future immigrants. Thus, although the Netherlanders were not on an equal footing with Hamburg citizens in that city, the difference disappeared on the Iberian Peninsula.

4 Consulates and Residencies

As I described in the preceding chapter, alien nations were legal entities based on collective settlement contracts that the alien merchants negotiated with the ruling authorities in the places that hosted them. There were other meanings of nationhood, however. The merchants' home governments understood the term differently when appointing consuls, residents, and other diplomatic represent-atives to pursue their foreign policy interests. And their understanding was not necessarily congruent with the understanding of the host governments, which sought to redefine the responsibilities of diplomatic appointees to their own advantage. A major task of consuls and residents was to mediate between the ruling authorities of the home and host places, and to transact business for them. Only to a limited degree did they support the merchants of the nations they repre-sented; in Portugal, consuls repeatedly denounced merchants to the Inquisition, even Protestants who were theoretically under their protection.

The Establishment of the Hansa Consulate in Lisbon

Pursuant to the Hanseatic-Spanish Treaty of 1607, a Hansa consulate – one of the first consulates in the modern sense of the word – was founded in Lisbon.[1] The term *consul* is explained in Johann Heinrich Zedler's *Universallexikon* (published about a hundred years later, by which time the institution had become estab-lished):

> A *consul* is equivalent to a syndic, because the former serves an entire nation in the same way as the latter serves an entire *collegio* [city council] for the best of the republic; he resides in foreign places, but particularly in the large trading cities. ... Those who are employed in this function are mostly merchants, because their main task is to further the interests of the commerce of their nation. Their function consists approximately herein: that they 1) dispatch bills of exchange; 2) maintain the credit of their nation and support its merchants; 3) deliver the monies that one nation or republic or potentate owes to another; 4) give noti-fication of trafficking and bankruptcy of foreign nations that trade in a place to both the ministers of the prince or republic in which they reside as consul and to the republic and merchant company in their fatherland; 5) rule on the conflicts in their nation to the extent that they concern trade.[2]

According to Zedler, in other words, a consul functioned on three levels: he usually pursued the profession of merchant himself; he acted in the service of a council or potentate in the best interests of the nation (that is, the population of a city, prov-ince, or state) of which that council or potentate was the ruling authority; and he

https://doi.org/10.1515/9783110472103-005

supported the (local) merchants of that nation and settled their disputes. Although this is an early eighteenth-century definition, the conflicts of interest inherent in this constellation characterized the Hansa consulate in Lisbon throughout the entire seventeenth century.

The Hansa consulate grew out of two predecessor entities, the traditional consulates of the Mediterranean basin and the Hansa *Kontore*. The first consulates were established around 1100 along the Levantine coast, as foreign outposts of the Italian city-states and other trading cities such as Marseille, Montpellier, Barcelona, and Valencia. In time, they made up a dense network around the Mediterranean Sea. At first the consuls' most important task was to govern the cities' merchants abroad; after the turn of the seventeenth century, however, they increasingly came to represent the diplomatic interests of their home governments. The Hansa consulate in Lisbon was one of the first consulates whose home authority was not on the Mediterranean, and also one of the first to represent not a single city, but (in this case) an association of towns with state-like ambitions: the Hansa.

The Hansa *Kontore* were also trading outposts abroad. The most important were in Novgorod, Bergen, London, and Bruges (the latter later being moved to Antwerp), but there were many smaller ones about which we know much less. In general, all the Hanseatic merchants staying in a *Kontor* town had to live and work in the *Kontor*. The merchants elected aldermen (*Oldermänner, Älterleute*), often two at a time, who oversaw compliance with the *Kontor's* statutes, managed its finances, served as arbitrators or judges, and dealt with the local authorities.

Hansa representatives are documented in Lisbon from the middle of the fifteenth century.[3] The first known mention of a consul is from 1571, when the Hanseatic aldermen in that city and the representatives of the Netherlandish merchants were called to name a "consul of the Hansa towns of the Easterling nation as well as of several towns in the Netherlands that do business in Portugal and Lisbon."[4] The consulship was not a newly created position, however; it appears from this document that the post had been held until then by the recently deceased Andrea Núncio. The representatives of the Hanseatic and Netherlandish nations nominated as their new consul Ambrósio de Góis, the son of the renowned Portuguese humanist, chronicler, and diplomat Damião de Góis.[5]

His successor as consul in 1579 was the merchant Friedrich Plönnies (or Paulsen), who came from Lübeck. He is known to have represented Hansa interests in Lisbon as late as 1589, and in 1591 he continued to do so in Madrid.[6] Officially, however, he held the post for only a short while. When King Felipe II assumed sovereignty over Portugal in 1580, he combined the Hansa-Netherlands consulate with that of the southern German cities, and appointed as consul Hans Kleinhart, a merchant from Augsburg, who had been proposed by the German, Hanseatic and Netherlandish merchants.[7] Although this appointment was rejected by the Hansa at its diet in Lübeck, Kleinhart was not divested of the consulship. He probably held the office until the end of the decade, when his successor, Konrad Rot, also from Augsburg, took over the post, now called the Consul of the German Nation.[8] By that time the consul, like the Judge Conservator of the Germans (see chapter 3), appears not only to have been appointed by the king, but also to be working in his service and in Portugal's interests. The conflation of the Hanseatic, Netherlandish, and southern German merchants into a single "German nation" met the administrative needs of the Spanish-Portuguese authorities, but it ran counter to the Hansa's self-understanding and its aspiration to be treated as an independent entity.

The character of the trading post in Lisbon took on increasing importance in the diets of the Hansa starting in about the 1590s. The delegates intended to employ one Hansa-named consul each in Lisbon and Seville, and an agent in Madrid. They were to come from Hansa towns and represent Hansa interests exclusively, and their salaries were to be paid not by the Spanish king, but by the Hansa. This matter became all the more urgent in 1603, when Spain introduced a customs duty of 30 percent, aimed mainly at the Netherlanders (see chapter 1). England and France quickly freed themselves from it, and the Hansa too wanted to negotiate an exemption from the duty.

The Hansa assigned Hans Kampferbeck, in Lisbon, to be their mediator in this endeavor, and to prepare a Hansa mission to the royal court in Spain. Kampferbeck came from a Hanseatic merchant family that had been active in the Portugal trade out of Lübeck and Reval since the beginning of the sixteenth century.[9] He had lived on the Iberian Peninsula for many years, and was familiar with local mercantile practices. In 1605 he wrote a report for the Hansa discussing the state of Hanseatic trade in the Iberian ports, and especially the role of the German consul in Lisbon. He claimed that because Konrad Rot was a southern German, he had never bothered to represent Hansa interests. Furthermore, according to Kampferbeck, Rot had been ill for several years, and was being represented in office by a Dutchman named David Strenge, who was likely to become his successor. Kampferbeck maintained that only a born Hanseatic could convincingly represent Hansa interests – and then proposed himself as ideally suited for the task. Two years later, in fact, he would be installed as Hansa consul and successor of Konrad Rot.

In the negotiations leading up to the Treaty of 1607, the Hansa mission to Madrid achieved, at least on paper, two important successes: the choice of the Hansa consul, which until then had been made by the king at the request of the local Hanseatic aldermen, was given over to the Hansa itself; and the Hansa and

Netherlands consulates were separated.[10] Specifically, the Hansa was permitted to establish one or more of its own consuls in the kingdom to ensure (with the help of the judge for the Germans) that privileges and contracts would be maintained; and the Hansa's nominees would be confirmed, and supported in the execution of their office, by the king.[11] The "provisional ordinance" that established the consulate explicitly barred the Hansa consul from collaboration with the Netherlanders. He was required to be "partial to no alien, non-Hanseatic nation, nor to be of advantage to it; even less to accept another alien installation; nor to allow passage under the Hansa's name, for his own use and benefit, to other foreign ships or shipmasters, or to banned and unfree goods and wares that do not belong to the Hansa." The consul's oath confirmed these stipulations. To sail under a Hanseatic flag was forbidden to "Hollanders and Zeelanders, and to others from the United Provinces of the Netherlands"; the consul had to "keep a watchful eye," and, if he noted any violations, "duly report this to the royal officials and ministers." Clearly, the same oath that bound the consul to remain "loyal and faithful, also obedient and attentive" to the Hansa towns alone, and pledged him to promote "their honor and best interests," also made it obvious that one of his primary tasks would be aiding Spain's efforts to suppress Dutch trade and smuggling. That was the main reason why Spain agreed to separate the Hansa and Netherlands consulates.[12]

But the establishment of the consulate was also connected with internal reforms in the Hansa, which had begun in the second half of the sixteenth century (see chapter 1). In this context the separation from the Netherlands and the southern German cities may be understood as part of a renewal process out of which the Hansa hoped to gain a level of legitimacy matching that of the European states. The establishment of permanent foreign representation may be interpreted as a step toward modern statehood, as it was for more conventionally defined countries at that time.[13] But the fact that the consul was to be named and financed by the Hansa itself and not by the merchants living in the host country, and that it transferred to him some of the leadership functions that the aldermen had previously held, also meant that the merchants lost some of their traditional autonomy and would be more tightly bound to the home organization. The consul would monitor Hanseatic shipmasters, merchants, and merchant assistants and inform the authorities at home of any improper behavior. He would resolve disagreements between members of the Hansa in consultation with the local aldermen, but should anyone transgress the provisions of the Treaty of 1607, he was to report this to the judge for the Germans and "peremptorily insist on the execution of the designated punishment."[14]

In the deliberations leading up to the treaty, the establishment of a true Hansa *Kontor* or "freed residence" (*befreiete residentz*; that is, a privileged establishment subject to its own statutes and at least partly exempt from the law of the land) in Lisbon had been discussed as an alternative to a consulate. This would have meant a compound physically, legally, and socially separate from the city, as in Novgorod, Bergen, and London. In Antwerp, however, several of the wealthiest Hanseatic merchants had already renounced their Hansa privileges as the price of escape from the rigidly regulated *Kontor* life.[15] The representatives from Hamburg were among those most vehemently opposed to a *Kontor* in Lisbon, and their interest in establishing a consulate reflected the same attitude that had led Hamburg to open trade to aliens – that is, the Hamburgers had observed that it was more profitable to collaborate with traders from other countries than to restrict activity to their own community. Furthermore, as I explained in the previous chapter, Hamburg in its negotiations with Spain also considered the interests of the Netherlandish and other alien merchants residing in the city, so the treaty was applicable not only to Hanseatics but also to the aliens in Hansa towns. Integrating non-Hanseatic aliens, who had received permission to settle in Hamburg, into a Hansa *Kontor* might have raised objections from the other Hansa towns; a loosely organized Hanseatic nation dispersed across the city, and a consul who received instructions from the Hansa towns, would be easier to implement and accord better with the Hamburgers' ideas. The Hamburgers were in fact successful in the negotiations, and a consulate was established instead of a *Kontor*.

In the Service of the Hansa or of the Spanish King?

Barely two years after the Hansa consulate was established, Spain agreed to the Twelve Years' Truce with the United Provinces and lifted its trade boycott (see chapter 1). From the Spanish perspective, there was no longer any reason to separate the Hansa and Netherlands consulates, and soon both offices were again represented by a single individual. When Konrad Rot (whose obligation had been to the Netherlandish nation alone once Kampferbeck was installed as Hansa consul) died in 1610, Kampferbeck took on his functions as well. In 1612 he asked the king to confirm this award,[16] and with his official installation in 1614 he received, in addition to the Hansa consulate, "the consulship over the Hollanders, Netherlanders, and other northern places with trade to this place, in the same manner as [his] predecessor Konrad Rot had, with all force and power."[17] Although Kampferbeck wrote to Lübeck that this arrangement was "more honorable than profitable" to him, it is very doubtful that the Hansa was pleased with its consul's usurpation of the consulate of the Netherlands.

The United Provinces did not like the new arrangement either. As early as 1612 they had named Dietrich Rodenburg, who was living in Madrid, to be consul there, and Gregor Niederhoff to be Rodenburg's representative in Lisbon. But this did them no good. Kampferbeck reported to Lübeck: "When [Niederhoff] wished to assume that consulate, the authorities wanted to know upon whose orders this was occurring. As he was unable to name anyone, he was immediately arrested and taken to a galleon. It cost him considerable effort and favors to get free."[18] In the end, it was the Spanish Crown that made decisions about foreign representatives, and it is doubtful that the Hansa (despite its apparent success in the treaty negotiations) had any better standing with it than the United Provinces.

The merging of the two consular offices was not the only development that ran counter to Hansa interests. By the time Spain installed Kampferbeck officially, he had already been dismissed by the Hansa. His removal was probably the result of a salary dispute. Kampferbeck wrote to the Hansa towns as early as 1610, asking for pay due to him.[19] He must have gone bankrupt over the following year, because by early 1612 he had been imprisoned for his debts, and then released. The city of Lübeck, unhappy with this situation, wanted to dismiss him, but Hamburg at first rejected the plan, claiming insufficient cause. Hamburg argued that according to men who "knew that place [Lisbon]," Kampferbeck's arrest "would not damage his respect and reputation," and that because Hamburg entertained much more Spanish traffic than the other Hansa towns, it had the greater interest in who the consul should be; the other towns should not be permitted to outvote it.[20] In February 1613, however, the towns agreed to send Kampferbeck a "conditional letter of dismissal" that offered him a choice: accept a salary decrease to 600 ducats, or quit his post.[21] Kampferbeck took more than a year to respond. Shortly before his installation as consul by the king, he wrote to the Hansa that he was not prepared to serve for 600 ducats, whereupon he was dismissed.

The Hansa's justification for the salary decrease was a shortfall in trade and shipping. This was not Kampferbeck's fault; competition with the United Provinces had increased after the declaration of the Twelve Years' Truce with Spain. The Hansa had probably not benefited from the consulate as much as its delegates had hoped, and its continued existence and financing were even more in question now that Kampferbeck was also working for the Netherlanders. But although his obligations to the United Provinces clearly violated the provisional ordinance and his pledge to be "partial to no alien, non-Hanseatic nation, ... even less to accept another, alien installation," the Hansa did not accuse him of this. Hamburg insisted that the king and viceroy be informed that Kampferbeck was being dismissed because he was dissatisfied with his salary.[22] It is not clear whether Kampferbeck ever vacated his position in Lisbon, but in 1614 the Hansa named Hamburg merchant Peter Körner, who agreed to assume office for an annual salary of 600 ducats, to succeed him. Körner even received instructions and took the oath of office.[23] But then he disappears from the record. It is possible that the Spanish government refused to accept his credentials, as had happened two years earlier with the Netherlandish candidate Niederhoff. In any case, by 1621 at the latest, Hans Kampferbeck was consul again,[24] and as late as 1627 he negotiated a delivery of ship masts from Moscow in his role as Consul of the Germans in Lisbon.[25]

If the Lisbon consul's loyalty to the Hansa was shaky, the consuls in the smaller towns concerned themselves with Hansa interests even less. João Canjuel (or Consuel), who was born in Antwerp, held for many years the office of Consul of the Germans and Netherlanders in Évora, an important inland Portuguese trading town.[26] In 1627 he made an astonishing declaration to the Inquisition, considering the region and nation that he represented. According to him, the Hamburgers in Portugal were often erroneously taken for Germans. Hamburg, he argued, was not located in Germany (*Alemanha*) but in *Germania Inferior*, like most of the other Netherlandish states (*estados de Flandres*) that had previously been called Easterling (*estrelix*).[27] In his view, there was a clear difference between the Hanseatic and Netherlandish nations on the one hand and the German nation (from the south of the Holy Roman Empire) on the other. The inhabitants of the northern part were "rebellious" and "heretics," whereas the southern part was peopled by loyal Catholics. Hamburgers living in Portugal were as much to be suspected of seeking to harm Spanish-Portuguese economic interests as the inhabitants of the United Provinces.

Given his official status as Consul of the Germans and Netherlanders, Canjuel's ideas may seem surprising, but they were in accord with the Crown's intention to be watchful of the Hamburgers' habit of helping the Dutch in their illegal trade. And they were widespread among the population as a whole. Many Portuguese understood Hamburg to be located in the "Netherlandish"[28] or "rebellious" states.[29] This was consistent with their undifferentiated use of the word *flamengo*, which actually means "Flemish," but in an expanded sense designated "Netherlandish," and in practice often included "Hamburgish." Even in the minutes books of the Portuguese-Jewish community in Hamburg, the Hamburgers are invariably called *flamengos*, and the Portuguese merchant apprentices who came to Hamburg for training were expected to learn the *língua flamenga* (lit. Flemish tongue) there.[30]

After Kampferbeck died, Augustin Bredimus from the town of Trier succeeded him. Bredimus had worked as an interpreter for the Spanish captain-general in Lisbon in the 1620s, and in 1629 had rendered services to the Hansa in connection with the Almirantazgo project (see chapter 1). In 1632 he asked the Spanish Crown to transfer to him the Consulate of the German and Netherlandish Nation. Reportedly he submitted his request with a letter from the Hansa towns nominating him as their consul.[31] The official installation, however, probably did not take place until 1637, when Hamburg, Lübeck, and Danzig (Gdansk) finally agreed on his salary.[32] Bredimus was to receive 1,200 ducats annually when he resided in Lisbon and 2,000 when in Madrid. (This considerable increase over Körner's salary likely reflected the renewed growth of Hanseatic trade after the Twelve Years' Truce ended.) Payment was no longer disbursed from a common Hansa treasury; it was now covered on a percentage-of-trade basis by the cities that traded with Portugal, with Hamburg absorbing half the cost. In addition, the Hanseatic merchants in the Iberian Peninsula agreed to pay him $1/4$ percent of their trade revenue. Thus Bredimus's allegiance, like his predecessor's, was not given to any single authority or clearly delimited nation.

A German Consulate with Consuls from Hamburg

When Portugal became independent of Spain in 1640, Hansa-German and Netherlands representation there were once again separated. The United Provinces were now an ally of Portugal, which sought their support in its struggle against Spain. As a result they were permitted to establish their own independent consulate in Portugal, which in 1664 became a *residency* – that is, an establishment concerned more with the political aspects of diplomacy.[33] The German consulate also received a new consul just a few weeks after the accession of King João IV to the throne. The book of the Royal Chancellery states that "natives from Germany" (*naturais da Alemanha*) had selected Willem Heusch to represent their nation, and had requested that the king install him. João acceded to this request, trusting that Heusch would exercise the office "to the best of his nation and to the benefit of the king."[34] Heusch was a native of Hamburg and a member of the Netherlandish nation there. His father, Pieter Heusch, had been born in Antwerp in 1565 and emigrated to Hamburg, where he became very successful in the Iberia trade.[35] Willem Heusch's Netherlandish origin was apparently not an issue in Lisbon; it is not mentioned at all in Portuguese, Hansa, or Hamburg sources on the consulate. The Netherlander Heusch had become a Hamburger upon settling in Lisbon, and from then on, to the Hamburg and Portuguese authorities, "his nation" meant the German nation.

Heusch had bought the consulship. Two months before the revolt against Spain, he had already offered the future Portuguese king 30,000 reis for the post, which the king raised to 40,000 reis.[36] Like his predecessors, only after his official installation by the king did Heusch request confirmation by the Hansa, and this procedure once again stretched out over many years. At first Lübeck and Bremen were opposed, and there were the usual disagreements about compensation. In 1648 the Lübeck City Council proposed that Heusch continue in his activities, but without being officially appointed consul.[37] A year later Heusch apparently requested the title of Resident to which Lübeck responded that such a title had never been customary in the Hansa towns, and that the traditional title of German Consul should suffice.[38] This title did not actually conform to customary usage, however, since until then the Hansa (unlike the Portuguese authorities) had always called its consul a *Hansa* consul, and not a *German* consul.

Apparently Heusch did not meet the Hansa's expectations any more than had Kampferbeck or the other consuls, all of whom seem to have been more concerned with the king's interests (and their own) than with those of the Hansa. By 1658 the Lübeckers were thinking of discharging him.[39] The city was deterred only by the consideration that a new consul would not have the same access to the royal court that Heusch had. And he appears to have had very close relations with the court indeed, such that in 1649 he was able to induce the future Portuguese secretary of state, Gaspar de Faria Severim, to serve as his son's godfather.[40] As in the previous instances, Heusch's appointment as consul was a fait accompli, and the Hansa was not in a position to dismiss him on its own. In practice, it had no alternative but to accept the decision of the Portuguese king.

Upon Willem Heusch's death, his son Alexander succeeded him.[41] In 1669 the Portuguese regent, rather than appointing him Consul of the *German* Nation, made him (strangely enough) Consul of the *High German* Nation; this was perhaps meant to underscore the exclusion of the Netherlanders.[42] That Heusch had the authority to represent Hamburg is beyond doubt, because a year later he was confirmed as Consul of the *Hamburgish* Nation by that city's Admiralty board. In this instance the consul, who had been nominated by the local merchants and installed by the Portuguese Crown, was accepted by Hamburg alone, while the Hansa was sidelined completely in the nomination process.[43] Even so, it is doubtful that Heusch, who was born in Lisbon and may never have lived in Hamburg, met the city's expectations. In 1712 the Commercial Deputation (see chapter 13) complained to the City Council about the "miserable extenuations" spread by the consul, as a result of whose "negligence and weakness" the old privileges would "be lost and go to ruin." The consul, the complaint went, was not "capable of approaching the court with an offer or petition," and there was evidence that at a reception for the queen it had not been he, but a journeyman tailor, who had acted as spokesman for the Germans. Not only would trade not be well served by such a consul, but "the entire German nation" would reap "nothing but ridicule and shame" because of him.[44] The Commercial Deputation insisted that either he be replaced or that an assistant be assigned. Soon thereafter, the Germans in Lisbon appointed two merchants as assistants. Alexander Heusch died in 1726.

It was never entirely clear in the seventeenth century to what ruling authority at home – the Hansa, the Holy Roman Empire, or the city of Hamburg – the

German consuls in Lisbon offered their allegiance, while their commitment to the host authorities was frequently obvious. The Hansa was in decline; it was politically and economically weak. The empire had no economic policy of its own, and Hamburg had little power by itself. But the Spanish and Portuguese kings were not really interested in who dispatched the consuls. They wanted a reliable interlocutor to supply them with information relevant to their business interests and serve as mediator as needed, but they would not accommodate the Hansa's wishes for independence, representation, or political power.

Consuls as Businessmen

The consuls themselves were widely-networked businessmen who knew how to use the advantages that accrued from collaboration with the holders of power. This is why they accepted irregular remuneration, even while often deeming it inadequate. Those payments were only one source of income among many; the office itself opened up all kinds of other profitable business opportunities.

It was also risky, however. Konrad Rot is one of the best-known German businessmen of that time. Throughout his life he cultivated close ties with the royal households of Portugal and Spain. Born in about 1530, he had traveled to the Iberian Peninsula as a young man, provisioning the kings with Hanseatic goods. Later he was active in the Iberia trade from his base in Augsburg, and supplied copper to the Portuguese Crown. In 1575 he leased the European part of the royal pepper contract, assuming the sales of all Indian spices in Europe.[45] In return he granted King Sebastião a loan to finance his war in North Africa; most of this loan was to be delivered in the form of wood, tar, and other shipbuilding materials.[46] After Sebastião's death in 1578 Rot's contract for the distribution of spices in Europe was renewed and another one assigned, conceding to him the right of spice acquisition in Asia. Rot therefore controlled the entire Portuguese pepper and spice trade, while – because the two leasing contracts were formally separated – the Crown profited only from the difference between the buying and selling prices. This time, however, Rot had taken on too much. In 1580, heavily in debt, he fled Augsburg (evading his creditors by feigning suicide) and returned to the Iberian Peninsula. His pepper contract was not renewed by the newly crowned King Felipe II, although he did transfer the post of Master of the Royal Fisheries to Rot before appointing him Consul of the Germans in 1589 or 1590.

Hans Kampferbeck, too, had been active in the service of the Spanish Crown before his nomination as consul. Indeed, when he traveled to Lübeck in 1605 it was not on his own initiative, as he claimed, but at the behest of the king.[47] Even after taking the consular oath he continued to pursue trade in service to the

Crown, which was late in its payments and so contributed to his indebtedness.[48] It is not known precisely what led to the bankruptcy and imprisonment mentioned above. But apparently Kampferbeck too was active in the highly speculative pepper trade. He even tried to persuade the Crown to sell the Portuguese pepper exclusively through Hansa towns, which in return would supply shipbuilding material, weaponry, and provisions. According to contemporary estimates, about two-thirds of the pepper was consumed in Germany and other northern European lands. Netherlandish, English, and French imports were beginning to displace Portuguese imports from Hanseatic markets, and Kampferbeck intended to continue trade between Portugal and the Hansa under conditions beneficial to both sides. His proposal met with favor in Madrid, at least initially. The pepper was to be sold at any price that would edge out the competition; a contract with the Hansa was all that was needed. Why the plan was never executed is not known. It may be that relations between the Hamburgish and Netherlandish merchants were so close, and their interests so intertwined, that no such strategy could separate them. In any case, a few years later the Portuguese monopoly in the spice trade had collapsed; the Dutch East India Company, along with the English and the French, had stepped up its imports, and prices, now determined by the market, had dropped precipitously.[49]

Rot and Kampferbeck were not alone; there was a long list of German consuls who got into trouble with creditors. João Canjuel, the Consul of the Germans and Netherlanders in Évora, was also a businessman. He was active in the wool trade, and had for eight or nine years been in the service of the nobleman Diogo de Castro before being imprisoned for debt.[50] Willem Heusch was another businessman/consul who occasionally found himself in similar difficulties.[51]

In fact, insolvency was all too frequent among the German consuls, who were intimately involved in the kings' trading ventures and probably sometimes went into debt on their account. The selection of consuls appears to have had to do neither with an untarnished mercantile reputation nor with loyalty to a particular state, city, or nation, but rather with expansive networks including Portugal, the Hansa, and other ruling authorities abroad.

Consuls and Hanseatic Merchants

The fact that the consuls were supposedly representatives of the Hansa did not necessarily mean that the German or Hamburg merchants in Portugal received any substantial benefit from them. The 1607 provisional ordinance of the Hansa consuls makes only passing reference to the merchants' concerns. That the Hanseatic merchants in Lisbon did not feel adequately supported by their consul is evidenced, among other things, by the fact that they wanted to nominate in the early 1620s an additional agent, of their own choosing, to represent their interests at the Spanish court.[52] Rather than take this wish to Kampferbeck or the Hansa, they turned to the Holy Roman Emperor's envoy in Spain, Franz Christoph Khevenhüller. He agreed with their proposal, and so did the emperor himself. An imperial secretary, Carlos Gagino, was dispatched to Madrid to assume that responsibility, for which the merchants intended to pay him a percentage of their profits in compensation. Hans Kampferbeck failed to thwart this usurpation and so did the Hansa, which he had informed of the goings-on. His successor Augustin Bredimus, however, appears to have merged both offices in his person. As I have said, the merchants contributed to his remuneration (and that of succeeding consuls), which may have helped them to gain greater influence over the consuls' actions.

The consuls did not much intervene on behalf of the Hanseatic merchants in matters of faith. On the contrary, the consul João Canjuel denounced to the Inquisition a group of six Hamburg merchants living in Lisbon. He accused them of meeting regularly at the house of one of them, João Eggers, to read the Lutheran bible (see chapter 15). And he did so even though this was in principle legal; members of the Hansa were permitted freedom of conscience in the private sphere. Furthermore, Canjuel accused them of evading customs duties, of sending large sums of money to the "heretical lands," and of reporting to Hamburg by mail or ship everything that happened in Portugal – with regard not only to trade, but to the condition of the kingdom as a whole.[53] This is remarkable for two reasons: such reports were actually one of the duties of the consul himself; and the accusations bespeak quite an animus towards the Protestants whose interests he theoretically represented. Despite this attitude Canjuel held the post of consul for more than 14 years.[54] Diogo Timão, who served as Consul of the Germans and Netherlanders in Porto from 1629 to 1642, also worked for the Inquisition. It is known that he frequently seized books with "suspicious" contents, and arrested shipmasters at the behest of the Inquisition and held them captive in his house.[55]

Portuguese policies toward Protestants became more liberal during the second half of the seventeenth century. Lutheran services could now be held in the chapels of accredited diplomats in Lisbon and on foreign vessels lying at anchor.[56] It is not known, however, whether the Hamburgers took part in such services before the eighteenth century. The earliest known letter in which German merchants appealed for permission to attend a Lutheran service (in the home of the Swedish consul) dates from the year 1713. Their own consul, Alexander Heusch, gave them no support in this effort because, as stated in the letter, he was "partial to the inimical doctrine." Contrary to Hermann Kellenbenz's interpretation, this meant that Heusch, like his predecessors in office, favored Catholicism, not the Reformed faith.[57]

Early Representatives of Portugal in Hamburg

Given the structural differences between the Iberian kingdoms and the Hansa, it is not surprising that they handled the matter of representation differently. Instead of consuls, Spain and Portugal dispatched residents, commissioners, and agents. According to Zedler's *Universallexikon*, a *resident* was a diplomat who remained for a long time at the court of a potentate, and who was empowered to plead, solicit, and report in the interest of his principal. Zedler explicitly states that persons of noble birth were "seldom or never" chosen for such a position; residents were ordinarily "rich merchants in the trading cities, or even Jews, who are satisfied with the mere title without remuneration."[58] The term *commissioner* does not denote a firmly defined diplomatic office. According to Zedler, it generally meant a person "sent by a superior to specially administer a matter," and included envoys.[59] *Agents*, Zedler says, were used by sovereigns when dealing with people of "equal or lesser status" upon matters that were "not worth the cost" of maintaining a formal ministry; this type of agent, he says, was "mostly engaged in espionage."[60] In other words, these were all diplomatic officials of low rank, who were not expected to serve as advocates of the merchant nations. They had a single specified principal, whose affairs they represented and whom they supplied with intelligence. Especially in the trading cities, these posts were often held by wealthy merchants whose activities included high-profile business operations. Noble birth was not necessary (as it was in the higher diplomatic ranks), and indeed several sources suggest that financial negotiations would have been beneath the dignity of the aristocracy.[61]

The first Portuguese diplomats known to have gone to Hamburg went there on behalf of the Portuguese Crown. Gaspar Maciel, the Portuguese factor in Antwerp, went to Hamburg in 1572 to negotiate the release of a seized shipment of pepper. This was a complicated case that eventually gave rise to a suit before the Imperial Chamber Court, so he probably either resided in Hamburg for some time or traveled between there and Antwerp.[62] We may therefore assume that he became acquainted with local conditions, and that he reported to the Crown on economic circumstances in Hamburg and commercial opportunities for Portugal. Delegations sent by the Spanish government, which visited the Hansa towns in 1587, 1589, and 1597, surely also reported on trading conditions in Hamburg, and on the Portuguese New Christian merchants who by that time had settled there. Given that the hostilities between the Iberian states and the United Provinces and

England made Hamburg an especially important port for Spain's and Portugal's provisioning, cooperation with the members of the Portuguese nation living there would have been very much in the Crown's interest. However, we do not have knowledge of any such early contacts. On the contrary, at that time the Hamburg representatives of the pepper and brazilwood contracts were not Portuguese, but Netherlanders, Hamburgers, and members of other nations.[63]

The importance of the Hansa towns to the Spanish-Portuguese government is evident from its efforts, during the negotiation of the Treaty of 1607, to establish trading posts there along the lines of the former Portuguese *feitoria* in Antwerp.[64] The Portuguese *feitorias* were in many respects like the Hansa *Kontore*. But unlike the aldermen who directed the *Kontore*, the royal factors were official representatives of the king, by whom they were appointed and paid. The primary mission of the Antwerp *feitoria* had been to sell in Europe the goods imported from Africa, Asia, and America, and to raise the capital necessary for new ventures; it was officially closed in 1549, but it endured in an informal capacity.[65] In 1607 the Portuguese negotiators argued that the Hansa towns should succeed Antwerp as loci for *feitorias*. A royal representative would sell Portuguese goods there for the king. He and his agents and employees would enjoy the same rights as the Hansa town citizens (*vizinhos*), and be provided with houses, ships, and crates at the going prices, to ship the goods acquired in the north to the Iberian kingdoms.[66]

This proposal was not included in the Treaty of 1607, however. It may be that the Portuguese merchants living in Hamburg assumed the functions of the *feitoria* as private businessmen instead. During the second half of the seventeenth century, Portuguese Jews did serve as diplomatic representatives of the Spanish and Portuguese crowns in Hamburg, and negotiated trade on their behalf. Before that, we have only the controversy of 1609 regarding the avoidance of the Hundredth Penny (the proposed customs duty to be paid by the Portuguese in place of the *Schoss;* see chapter 3) to indicate that regular contact may have existed between the Portuguese living in Hamburg and the Spanish Crown. In that instance, the Hamburg Portuguese declared that they would "complain to the utmost" to His Royal Majesty in Spain if the Hundredth Penny were adopted, and "all manner of inconvenience might eventuate" from that for the city.[67] The Hamburg Portuguese apparently assumed that the Spanish Crown would intercede for them regarding this duty. It is not unreasonable to conclude from this that by this time the Portuguese were already acting as the Crown's trading agents. A year later, the Hamburg City Council warned the Assembly of Citizens that the Portuguese "seek to protect themselves against [the duty] with imperial mandates, and would dare to cause the arrest of goods and ships of the city even in Spain." Their threat was clearly taken seriously in Hamburg.[68]

This incident challenges Hermann Kellenbenz's claim that the Portuguese Jews in Hamburg were hiding from the Spanish authorities, concealing their true identities and trade connections behind German aliases. The Spanish Crown must have been well aware that some of the Portuguese living in Hamburg had converted to Judaism. During his stay in Lübeck in 1605, Hans Kampferbeck, the later Hansa consul, must have learned about the debate in Hamburg concerning the residence permission of the Portuguese, among whom were known to be Jews. Since Kampferbeck traveled to Germany in service to the Spanish king, he would surely have included this matter in his report.[69] Furthermore, there was a regular flow of information to Spain from Hamburg mayor Hieronymus Vogeler, who had been part of the delegation that visited Madrid in 1607 and afterward became a secret correspondent to the Spanish Crown.[70] Like the Hamburg merchants who had resided for some time on the Iberian Peninsula, Vogeler was likely well informed about the precarious position of the New Christians living in Portugal; but he undoubtedly also knew of any relations that the Spanish government might be maintaining with the Portuguese Jews living abroad. Thus the City Council was probably justified in its assessment of the Portuguese merchants' threat to seek support from the Spanish government over the matter of the Hundredth Penny.

The Representatives of the United Provinces in Hamburg

For the next several years we have no indication of further contact between the Spanish Crown and the Portuguese living in Hamburg. But in 1619 the seat of the permanent representative of the United Provinces to the Hansa towns (who had been named only two years earlier) was moved from Lübeck to Hamburg.[71] This may have been the first permanent residency in Hamburg; certainly it was one of the first. Its holder was Foppe van Aitzema, and he had a nephew, Lieuwe van Aitzema, who took up a similar post: as Hansa resident at The Hague. Their role in the development of trade between Hamburg and the United Provinces, and between Hamburg and the Iberian Peninsula, requires further investigation. At any rate, Foppe van Aitzema was probably not responsible for representing the concerns of the Netherlandish merchants who had migrated to Hamburg. By the time the Dutch resident was installed in Hamburg, the Netherlandish immigrants had already negotiated their second settlement contract and were well integrated into the economic life of the city. As a matter of fact, the members of the Netherlandish Reformed congregation in Hamburg turned to the United Provinces several times during the seventeenth century for support in matters of faith.[72] But it is not likely that they found any help in the Aitzemas, since Lieuwe at least was a harsh critic of the Reformed faith and of the religious controversies of the time in general.[73] Of far greater significance was the two residents' function as news correspondents. Lieuwe van Aitzema created a *nieuwsbureau,* an extremely efficient communications center through which he supplied many subscribers, including the Hansa towns, with the latest news.[74] He acquired much of his information by bribing officeholders, which sometimes worked against the interests of his clients.[75]

Spain's Representatives in Hamburg

The first official representative of Spain in the Hamburg region was also a Netherlander: Gabriel de Roy.[76] He had been one of the leading experts on Netherlandish and northern European trade at the Spanish court and a driving force behind the Almirantazgo project (see chapter 1); in 1627 the king sent him to the Baltic coast of Germany to organize the new armada, and to persuade the Hansa towns to cooperate with Spain in forming the trading company. In April 1628 the Holy Roman Emperor named him Commissioner-General of the Baltic and Oceanic Sea for this work. But as we have seen, de Roy failed in his mission. He next attempted to establish a network of Spanish agents in the German port cities and assign to them the monopoly on the right to certify the German origin of goods and ships. De Roy wanted to supervise this project himself, and in September 1628 Felipe IV named him inspector (*veedor*) for the northern German trade.[77] Hamburg and Lübeck, however, objected vehemently to this interference in their economic policies, and banned both de Roy and his subordinates from establishing a residency in their cities.[78] The cities were supported by the emperor, who at that moment was also trying to limit Spanish interference in his empire. Thus when de Roy started to issue certificates from the city of Glückstadt, the emperor prohibited it. In 1635 the emperor urged the authorities in Brussels, the capital of the Spanish Netherlands, to remove him completely; however, the inspector continued in his post for another ten years.

In 1645, after de Roy's death, Jacob Rosales was named representative of the Spanish Crown in Hamburg. He was not a direct subordinate of the king; the Spanish ambassador to the emperor paid for his services.[79] Rosales, who had been born Manuel Bocarro Francês in Lisbon, came to Hamburg in the late 1620s or early 1630s and converted to Judaism there. Unlike most of the other Portuguese in Hamburg, he earned his living not as a merchant but as a physician, and his patients in Portugal had included such high-ranking personages as Duke Teodósio de Bragança, father of the later King João IV. He was also active as an alchemist and political writer. In Hamburg he worked as a news correspondent for Spain and the Holy Roman Empire, and by 1639 was in official service in this capacity to the Spanish king. Two years later Rosales, who was reputedly of noble origin, received from the emperor the title of Count Palatine (*comitiva minor*), and a certificate freeing him of the "stain of Jewish ancestry." This rewarded him for his services to the imperial house and the Spanish kings.

But in practice, Rosales lacked the influence, money, and mercantile skill that the duties of a resident required. After Portugal declared its independence from Spain in 1640, he was ordered to stop the deliveries of weapons and ship-building material from Hamburg to Portugal, and to divert them to Spain. From 1647 on, he was also active in the military recruitment that the Spanish government in Brussels conducted in Hamburg and other coastal cities. The agent of the Portuguese Crown in Hamburg, Duarte Nunes da Costa, possessed the necessary funds and connections for tasks like these but Rosales did not, even though Sílvio del Monte, a Portuguese in Hamburg involved in the weapons and munitions trade, sometimes assisted him as financier. Rosales was officially confirmed in his post as resident in 1650 by the Spanish ambassador to Vienna, but shortly after that the Spanish government cut off his pay. Rosales made repeated efforts to have his expenses compensated, and then in 1652 wrote to the Spanish secretary of state that he could no longer pay his debts, and therefore had to sell his domicile and leave Hamburg. He moved by way of Amsterdam to Italy, where he died in the 1660s.

Portugal's Representatives in Hamburg

Portugal's independence from Spain had little effect on the self-perception of the Portuguese who lived in Hamburg. Kellenbenz claims that most of them took the side of Portugal, which led to conflicts between Rosales (as representative of the Spanish Crown) and the pro-Portugal elements of the community and culminated in an attack on Rosales's house in 1649. There is no convincing evidence that this act of aggression was due primarily to political loyalty to the new Portuguese monarchy. But it is likely that most merchants had more intensive contacts, both personal and commercial, with Portugal than with Spain. As we have seen, real controversies arose surrounding the German, Netherlandish, and Hanseatic nations and their legitimate representatives in Portugal. However, there was no comparable debate in Hamburg about membership in, or allegiance to, a Portuguese nation as distinct from a Spanish one. The residents and agents who acted from Hamburg on behalf of the Iberian kings did not represent the Portuguese nation in that city. They worked to serve the needs of the government that employed them – as long as they could derive benefit too.

Like Jacob Rosales, Duarte Nunes da Costa, Portugal's first official representative in Hamburg, was a Portuguese Jew.[80] The two of them had arrived in Hamburg at about the same time, but Nunes da Costa was a merchant, while Rosales was not. Before 1640, among his many other trading activities, he supplied the Spanish Crown with weapons, powder, and munitions.[81] But he supported the Portuguese side in the Restoration War. As early as June 1641 he was ennobled by the Portuguese king, and named his unofficial diplomatic agent in northern Germany; he was appointed formally three years later. From this position he continued to supply Portugal not only with weapons and munitions, but also with shipbuilding materials. He repeatedly lent large sums of money to the king and to Portuguese diplomats who passed through Hamburg. When the Portuguese Brazil Company (see chapter 13) was formed in 1649, he persuaded Duke Jacob of Courland to invest in the company, and sent three large, fully-armed ships to Portugal to establish its convoy. In 1650 he organized the recruitment and transport of 2,500 German soldiers, no longer needed in their homeland after the end of the Thirty Years' War, to defend the Portuguese border against Spain. In addition to the salary he received as an agent, after 1649 he also derived considerable revenue from the Brazil Company in his capacity as its agent in the Holy Roman Empire. But Nunes da Costa had no political power. For important matters of state, such as the negotiation of the Peace of Westphalia, Portugal sent high-ranking diplomats; da Costa's role was limited to receiving and housing them, furnishing them with the latest information, and supplying them with transport and money.[82]

Other duties included sending regular news reports to Portugal. The Ajuda Library in Lisbon holds letters in which Duarte and his sons report on political and diplomatic developments in northern Europe such as wars, peace treaties, weddings, births, deaths.[83] Hamburg was an ideal place in which to acquire such information, because Hamburg was where postal and newspaper networks crossed; it was also where the residents of the Holy Roman Empire, the United Provinces, Spain, Portugal, France, England, Sweden, Denmark, and Poland lived. There is little economic content in any of these letters, however, although Nunes da Costa would have been very well informed about trade and manufacturing, not to mention northern European economic developments. But in one letter held in the Portuguese Overseas Historical Archive, Nunes da Costa reported about the trade and smuggling conducted by Hamburg and Netherlandish merchants along the African coast at Mina and Guinea. He also reported that merchants on Dutch and other foreign vessels were transporting wine from Madeira to Barbados, and then returning directly from there to Hamburg instead of paying the required taxes in Madeira.[84]

Duarte's sons Manuel and Jorge Nunes da Costa were also active in the Brazil Company from their base in Hamburg, and were especially involved in recruiting cannoneers, ships' physicians, and other specialists to man its convoy vessels. They later assumed posts as official Portuguese representatives of the company in Hamburg.[85] In that function they were responsible, among other things, for selling Brazilian goods, especially large quantities of brazilwood, the sales of which appear to have sagged in northern Europe at the end of the 1660s. In exchange, they sent masts, powder, and munitions to Portugal, and also grain.[86] In 1656 Manuel had already been appointed his father's successor; he was confirmed as the Portuguese Crown's official agent after Duarte's death in 1664.[87] Like his father, Manuel did his work for the Portuguese government from Hamburg, while another brother, Jerónimo, took on the same duties in Amsterdam. They financed the shipping of goods, granted loans, and advanced money to recruit dyers and weavers from northern Europe and send them to Portugal to help develop the manufacturing industry there.[88] In 1687, when the Count of Vilar Maior arrived in the Holy Roman Empire to negotiate the marriage of the Portuguese king to Marie Sophie of Palatine-Neuburg, he was ordered to contact Manuel Nunes da Costa in Hamburg for support.[89]

Lending money to the Portuguese kings meant that the Nunes da Costa family frequently had to dip into its own private coffers. The residency itself was expensive, as it had to cover not only its household and its personnel, wagons, and clothing, but also the constant and costly hosting of guests that went with the position. But the members of that family did not go bankrupt as so many of the German consuls in Portugal did; apparently they were careful not to let their many official obligations distract them from their own interests.

Barely two years before Duarte Nunes da Costa's ennoblement, the Portuguese Inquisition brought him to trial in absentia, and eventually burnt him at the stake in effigy. He had been denounced for practicing Judaism, and had not appeared in Lisbon either to disprove the charge or to renounce his sins. But this did not keep the Portuguese king from continuing to work with him, and vice versa. It is curious that the Portuguese-Jewish diplomats, who risked discrimination and persecution in their homeland and were unlikely ever to be able to return, conducted themselves more loyally toward their employers, and were more financially responsible, than the Hansa consuls. But their loyalty was a matter of business. The Portuguese king opened up to them (as well as to their Hanseatic merchant colleagues) many lucrative trade opportunities, whereas Hamburg, the Hansa, and the Holy Roman Empire – having no overseas empire, no armed fleet and so on – had much less scope for making business partners of consuls and diplomats. The social prestige accorded to them as diplomats in Hamburg, not otherwise available to them as Jews, was another factor that motivated their commitment. The reliability and solidity of the Portuguese-Jewish diplomats contributed to the respect, and therefore the safety, of the entire Portuguese-Jewish community in Hamburg (see chapter 14).

What "loyalty" means when it comes to Jews is a long-debated issue. As Adam Sutcliffe has recently noted, their "patriotism" has received much positive attention in depictions from some Jewish authors, but he himself points out that the Portuguese Jews of the Atlantic diaspora were "exemplary non-patriots." Because their operations were transnational and engaged indifferently with the Portuguese, Spanish, Dutch, and English governments, their political loyalties were weak. Sutcliffe accounts it a special advantage that they felt bound to no political party and stood above the religious and political controversies of the day.[90] His opinion to the contrary, however, the Portuguese-Jewish residents' non-Jewish colleagues were no more steadfast or "patriotic" than they were. The Hansa consuls too were pragmatic and flexible in their loyalties, and often shifted allegiances between their home and host governments. The two groups differed primarily in that the Hamburgers benefited from greater support from their home city than did the Portuguese; despite this, the latter proved the more reliable.

5 The Inquisition and the State

The Inquisition was another key factor informing the very different conditions under which Portuguese, Hamburg, and Netherlandish merchants operated. The Spanish Inquisition's main concern was the suppression of "heresies," in particular those influenced by Protestantism. This was far less important to the Portuguese Inquisition; its main focus was the pursuit of New Christians, who were widely suspected of crypto-Jewish practices and beliefs. Merchants from Hamburg and the Netherlands were rarely investigated or brought to trial, but New Christian merchants were always at risk. Many critics of the Inquisition, and some historians, have suggested that the persecution of the Portuguese merchants destabilized the country's economy. This is a questionable assumption, however. There certainly did exist a complex interplay between the state, the Inquisition, and its victims, but I will argue that this took place within a relatively stable economic and political structure. In fact, at times the Inquisition was even a means of advancement for merchants.

Jews and New Christians

Jews had lived in Portugal for as long as we have historical records. There was a great increase in the Jewish population in 1492, however, when the Catholic monarchs of Spain, Fernando and Isabel, gave the Jews there an ultimatum: convert to Christianity or leave the country. Of the Jews who left, most went to Portugal. Estimates vary widely, but current research indicates that almost 30,000 Jews emigrated to Spain's neighbor on the Iberian Peninsula.[1] At that time, Portugal had almost one million inhabitants, of whom between 5 and 8 percent were Jews. With the newcomers, the proportion increased to 8 to 10 percent. But five years later, Judaism was banned in Portugal as well.

The impetus for this change was the marriage of King Manuel of Portugal to Isabel of Aragon and Castile (daughter of Fernando and Isabel of Spain), which was contingent upon Manuel's ending the Jewish presence in Portugal as it had previously been ended in Spain. Jews served important functions as craftsmen and shopkeepers in predominantly agrarian Portugal, however, and Manuel was unwilling to forgo their skills and services. To prevent their emigration he imposed a mass conversion, which only a few were able to avoid by flight. Manuel encouraged rapid assimilation of the baptized Jews, forbidding them to possess Hebrew books and expropriating their synagogues and cemeteries, but placing them in all other respects on an equal footing with the Old Christians. These

https://doi.org/10.1515/9783110472103-006

policies opened up entirely new opportunities for advancement to the former Jews. However, Manuel's plan was only partially successful. There were no longer any Jews in Portugal, but the former Jews, and their progeny, remained distinct from the rest of the population.

Many Portuguese viewed the converts and their descendents as Jews in a new guise. They doubted their religious sincerity and their political loyalty. They believed that in essence and nature the New Christians would always remain different from the Old Christians whose blood was "pure" – meaning (in this case), free of a supposed Judaic taint that was passed on inescapably from generation to generation, changes in professed religion notwithstanding. Jewish ancestry was equated with unreliability and cunning, with duplicity and arrogance. The old religious anti-Judaism was thus transformed into a modern racial anti-Judaism (or anti-Semitism). However, it was not until much later, after Portugal was united with Spain in 1580, that legal discrimination by statutes of purity of blood (*estatutos de limpeza de sangue*) was introduced. As in Spain, the statutes excluded New Christians from office in the ecclesiastic and civil administration.[2]

The Portuguese-Jewish philosopher Baruch Spinoza, whose parents left Portugal as New Christians and converted to Judaism in Amsterdam, commented on the differences between Spain and Portugal in his 1670 *Theologico-Political Treatise*:

> That they have been preserved in great measure by Gentile hatred, experience demonstrates. When the king of Spain formerly compelled the Jews to embrace the state religion or to go into exile, a large number of Jews accepted Catholicism. Now, as these renegades were admitted to all the native privileges of Spaniards, and deemed worthy of filling all honourable offices, it came to pass that they straightway became so intermingled with the Spaniards as to leave of themselves no relic or remembrance. But exactly the opposite happened to those whom the king of Portugal compelled to become Christians, for they always, though converted, lived apart, inasmuch as they were considered unworthy of any civic honours.[3]

Spinoza was not accurate in his assertions that in Spain converts "were admitted to all the native privileges of Spaniards," and that "no relic or remembrance" remained of the past Jewish presence. It is true, however, that after the 1530s the issue of the New Christians received considerably less attention in Spain than in Portugal. Only when the kingdoms were united and many Portuguese New Christians emigrated to Spain did the debate over the status of New Christians flare up again there for a time. In Portugal, on the other hand, the distinction between New Christians and Old Christians remained a critical one both to the ruling authorities and to the population at large; it endured as an important aspect of the social order until its formal abolition in 1773. As Spinoza implied, this ultimately helped Portuguese Judaism to survive.

The Inquisition and Its Victims

While the Portuguese state and society stigmatized New Christians, it was the Inquisition that actually persecuted them. In 1536, under pressure from the Spanish Crown and with the consent of the pope, King João III introduced the Inquisition into Portugal, along lines very similar to those in Spain. By about 1546, the Portuguese Inquisition was in full force throughout the country, with tribunals in Lisbon, Évora, and Coimbra.[4] According to the pope, its mission was to pursue heretics. But from the very beginning, both the Crown and some leading Old Christians aimed it at the New Christians.[5] About 32,000 trials were conducted between 1536 and 1767, the 230 years during which the institution operated in Portugal, and by far the most frequent charge was crypto-Judaism. At the tribunals in Coimbra and Évora, 83 percent and 84 percent of the trials respectively involved accusations of crypto-Judaism. In Lisbon, too, at least between 1540 and 1629, this was the most common allegation, at 68 percent. The percentage was lower in Lisbon because (due to its more cosmopolitan character) the city was home to a wider range of "heretical" beliefs and behaviors, and because Portugal's Atlantic possessions, including Brazil, were also under the jurisdiction of the Lisbon tribunal; there, too, a larger number of religious heterodoxies existed, especially among the recently converted indigenous peoples. In Spain, the Inquisition went after a different quarry. There, the accusation of *Judaizing* (practicing Judaism in secret) was leveled in only 10 percent of cases between 1540 and 1700. Most of the trials in Spain were for "heretical statements" (27 percent), then came Islamizing (24 percent). Only after these came the 10 percent of persons accused of Judaizing, followed by 8 percent each who were accused of Protestantism or of superstition.[6] And by the end of the sixteenth century the Spanish Inquisition was claiming far fewer victims than its Portuguese counterpart. Spain had a much larger population, but only 152 trials were held there per average year, compared to about 214 in Portugal. And while approximately 6 percent of those accused in Portugal were burned, only about 2 percent met that fate in Spain.[7]

Although accusations and trials in Portugal decreased over the years, they continued in significant number into the eighteenth century. Obviously the Inquisition did not succeed in eradicating the widespread belief in New Christian Judaizing. Nor would it have been likely to, given the methods it used to gather information. Rather than limiting itself to observed acts of religious transgression, the Portuguese Inquisition cast nets of suspicion over the relatives and business partners of the accused, spreading them ever more widely, so that the number of suspected Judaizers could only increase. A primary function of the Inquisition was to channel the social and religious sentiments of the population. Its apparently omniscient archives, the threat of denunciation, and the possibility of arrest, torture, and public burning asserted a constant, if sometimes latent, pressure on all New Christians. Indeed, many researchers have assumed that the Inquisition was attempting to control the population through this "pedagogy of fear." Recent publications, however, have pointed to a significant consensus between the Inquisition and large segments of the population.[8]

The Inquisition as "Marrano Factory"

The Portuguese Inquisition opposed the (frequently suggested) expulsion of all New Christians. Its mission, it declared, was to lead the misguided to Catholicism. But according to the Inquisition's opponents, accusations of Judaizing were rarely based on facts; both the accusations and the confessions were the result of arrest, torture, and violence.[9] The Inquisition, its opponents argued, was legitimizing its activities and its very existence by forcibly turning New Christians into Jews. Many of the accused learned what Judaism was only after they were charged and brought to trial. Some New Christians and Jews even came to this conclusion themselves, one more radical even than Spinoza's assumption of why Iberian Jewry survived. As the Portuguese Jew Fernão Álvares Melo, who was imprisoned by the Inquisition in Portugal before he arrived in Hamburg in 1622, wrote in the foreword of his translation of the Psalms into Spanish, which appeared in 1626:

> Not to our ancestors in Spain was the divine text referring when it said that the nations would say about us "surely a great and wise people is this," since they exercised such poor judgment in not teaching their children, that if the Blessed Lord had not permitted the Inquisition in that realm, a school where knowledge of Him is taught and the squandered blood is renewed, I do believe that to judge by its oblivion, by now knowledge of Him would have been completely lost.[10]

This idea became widespread in the eighteenth century and received attention once again when António José Saraiva's *Inquisição e Cristãos-Novos*, first published 1956, was translated into English in 2001 under the title *The Marrano Factory* (*marrano* being a pejorative expression for a New Christian who practiced Judaism in secret).[11] In Saraiva's interpretation, the Inquisition was an institution that developed out of the class struggle between the feudal elite (the clergy and the nobility) and the aspiring bourgeoisie. This bourgeoisie, goes his argument, consisted largely of former Jews who had been integrated and assimilated into society after their forced conversion; they became wealthy as a result of the extraordinary profits made possible by Portuguese expansion. Accusations of Judaizing, and the myth that Judaism could be inherited biologically, through "the blood," served the elites as a pretext for neutralizing a new contingent of competitors whose success was increasingly threatening. However, Saraiva continues, the resulting destruction of the merchant class increasingly placed the Portuguese economy under the domination of foreign powers, which eventually led to the country's decline.

More recent research has shown that many of Saraiva's claims are incorrect. In fact, the rise of mercantile capitalism was not incompatible with the persistence of the old privileged estates; there was no real conflict of interest between the New Christian businessmen and the higher nobility, the higher clergy, or the Crown. On the contrary, these were the groups most interested in the services provided by the New Christians, and who offered the few known instances of solidarity with them. Furthermore, at least in some regions, the most intensive persecution of New Christians was preceded by economic decline, which should therefore be viewed not only as a consequence of the Inquisition, but also as a cause of the emigration of many merchants.[12] Finally, there is no simple equation between the New Christians and the bourgeoisie or the merchant class; there was also a broad stratum of Old Christian Portuguese merchants, some of whom were very important.[13]

Despite the many incongruities in Saraiva's account, it is to his credit that he placed the Inquisition in a social context, thus challenging the exclusively political and religious approach to the topic that had predominated among historians until then. The first edition of his book met with virtually no response. The second, however, published in 1969, provoked vehement opposition. Saraiva was criticized not only for Marxist distortions of reality, but also for sloppy handling of the source material. In fact, Saraiva was not especially fond of archival work, and saw himself more as a venturesome essayist than as a historian. One leading critic was the French historian Israël S. Révah. He accused Saraiva of "utter incompetence," dismissed his book as "a demagogic diatribe against the Inquisition," and called libelous the claim that the Inquisition's activities were actually encouraging the very Judaism it intended to eradicate.[14] Révah himself was convinced that many New Christian families *had* retained their Jewish faith in secret after their forced baptism, and that the files of the Inquisition confirm this. However, over the course of the controversy, Révah increasingly came to be seen as a diligent but naïve scholar who failed to draw the appropriate conclusions from his scrupulous study of sources: that is, that the reports of crypto-Jewish practices among the New Christians in the trial documents might not be genuine.

The debate between defenders of the "Marrano factory" hypothesis and those who ascribe a high level of authenticity to the Inquisition protocols continues to this day. It is usually couched in terms of abstract "interests," "powers," and "forces," and often does not take into account that actual people were involved.

The inquisitors did manipulate and influence the New Christians, but they themselves were also manipulated and influenced – by members of the social elites, and also by merchants and people of lower rank. As Francisco Bethencourt has pointed out, the Inquisition was flexible; it formed alliances with different sectors of society and constantly adapted to new developments.[15]

The work of historian José Veiga Torres is crucial to a more dynamic perspective on the Inquisition. He followed its activities over most of the years of its existence, and was the first to analyze quantitatively not only the trials, but also the recruitment and social origins of the *familiars* (that is, the lay assistants of the Inquisition; see p. 98).[16] Joaquim Romero Magalhães drew attention to regional disparities in the Inquisition's activities. And Juan Ignacio Pulido Serrano has attempted to disentangle the intertwined relationships between the Inquisition, the Crown, and the New Christians, none of which were strictly self-contained bodies, but which were characterized by constantly evolving internal constellations of interests that ranged from the merely different to the diametrically opposed.[17] Yet despite all of this research, analysis of the Portuguese Inquisition remains much less comprehensive than that of its Spanish counterpart.[18]

Portugal's Economic Decline

That the Inquisition created Jews was not the only thesis current in the seventeenth century; another one was the belief in a causal connection between the persecution of New Christians, the takeover of trade by foreign merchants, and the decline of the Portuguese economy. The best-known proponent of this argument was the Jesuit priest and statesman António Vieira. In his opinion, the activities of the Inquisition had led to the takeover of trade by foreign merchants in Portugal. Vieira wrote:

> It is extraordinarily difficult to comprehend Portugal's reason of state in this regard: because being a kingdom based exclusively on trade that drives its own merchants to foreign kingdoms and permits foreign merchants in its own kingdom thus relinquishes to the foreigners all of the benefits and profits of trade, and nothing remains for us; because what the foreign merchants earn in other kingdoms remains there; and what the Portuguese merchants derive in our kingdom finds its way there as well.[19]

The Inquisition had also made the Portuguese merchants unreliable trading partners; there could be no guarantee that they were safe from arrest, and there was a perennial risk that goods consigned to them or under their control might be confiscated. According to Vieira, "the Portuguese living abroad, and many foreigners who recognize the benefits of our kingdom and our trade, do not send their money and their goods to our ports, because they do not believe that they are safe in the hands of our merchants."[20] The Portuguese diplomat Luís da Cunha took a similar tack. He held that by persecuting the New Christians, who were more capable traders and businessmen than anyone else, the Inquisition had made itself responsible for Portugal's economic decline. Foreign merchants placed no trust in Portuguese businessmen; they were generally suspected of Judaizing, which meant that foreign property in their keeping could be seized upon their arrest. As a consequence, foreigners, rather than working with the Portuguese, dug ever more deeply into the Portuguese economy, enriching themselves at Portugal's expense and then taking their profits elsewhere.[21]

Historians have often adopted this line of argument, taking over more or less uncritically its dubious stereotypes of Jewish trading prowess. Thus, for example, the historian L. M. E. Shaw wrote, "Between 1550 and 1750, Portugal lost its economic greatness and political standing in the world. By the latter date, her trade and commerce were almost entirely in the hands of foreign merchants. It can be argued that Portugal itself was to blame for this state of affairs, because of the impact of the Portuguese Inquisition on the economy of Portugal."[22] But although we owe Vieira (and other like-minded thinkers) many important insights into the social, economic, and political conditions in Portugal we should not forget that he himself was no neutral observer. He was a politician, a diplomat, and a gifted sermonizer; his writings were political in purpose, and the fact that he advocated for the New Christians does not mean that all of his arguments were pertinent.[23]

Positions less "enlightened" than Viera's are often glossed over by historians. But there were other reasons for the decline of the Portuguese economy than the persecution of the New Christians by the Inquisition, and observers at the time were not ignorant of this. Thus, for example, Inquisitor General Francisco de Castro defended his institution's actions in 1630, saying that it was an error to see a direct connection between the development of trade and the activities of the New Christians. He argued that only about 50 really wealthy New Christians had left Portugal, while Spain under the Catholic kings had expelled its entire Jewish population, and subsequently enjoyed an economic boom never before experienced. According to him, trade was not stagnant because New Christians were persecuted in Portugal, but because shipping between Portugal and the overseas colonies had been disrupted by war, piracy, and smuggling. He contended that lamentations over the decline of the Portuguese economy were being heard well before the New Christians had begun to leave the country, and that even if at some point all of the New Christians were to leave, there would still remain in Portugal (besides the foreign merchants) a sufficiency of Old Christians with enormous capital reserves.[24] Of course, Castro's argument, like Vieira's, was self-interested.

Nevertheless, he pointed not only to alternative reasons for the decline of trade, but also to a fact that continues to be overlooked: that the Portuguese mercantile class was not identical with the New Christians. By no means were all merchants New Christians, and not all New Christians were merchants. This equation of the two groups was not unusual in the seventeenth century, which led some later historians to adopt it in their work, but it is the product of an anti-Semitic cliché, and a common one.[25]

New Christians and Merchants

It is difficult to estimate the percentage of New Christians among the merchants (and vice versa). New Christian identity was transmitted by descent only in theory; in practice, it was determined by society at large and the Inquisition in particular. What really mattered was whether an individual's acquaintances (especially those from his place of birth) thought he was a New Christian, and whether the Inquisition thought their testimony credible. If so, he was considered a New Christian. However, since many of the people who were taken for New Christians were never prosecuted, their condition (that is, as Old Christian or New Christian) was seldom registered. And Old Christians were tried much more rarely still. Therefore it is difficult to arrive at any robust quantitative conclusions.

The only serious analysis of the New or Old Christian identity of the seventeenth-century Lisbon merchants relies exclusively on Inquisition trials, and is hampered accordingly. Its author, David Grant Smith, came to the conclusion that two-thirds to three-quarters of Portuguese merchants in the seventeenth century were New Christians, and the rest Old Christians.[26] We can only speculate on how much higher the number of Old Christians would have been if the merchants who never came to the attention of the Inquisition had been included. Significantly, foreign merchants are never mentioned in Smith's analysis. Although they definitely played a role in Portuguese commerce, they very rarely became targets of the Inquisition (see p. 96).

The occupations of New Christians also can be determined only to the extent that they came under Inquisition scrutiny, and not in any general sense. Among New Christians in the Évora tribunal's jurisdiction, craftsmen were the group most frequently accused (42 percent), while only 22 percent of the charged were merchants or bankers.[27] In the Algarve, between 1635 and 1640, 32 percent of the accused New Christians were merchants, followed by craftsmen at 30 percent. To date there has been no detailed analysis of trials in the Lisbon jurisdiction. According to the printed lists of the autos-da-fé (that is, the public exhibitions of penitents and condemned), which give us only a very approximate picture, over the entire period that the Inquisition was active in Portugal, about 60 percent of the sentenced were craftsmen and 20 percent merchants.[28] It is not clear, however, that the percentage of merchants reflected in Inquisition records can be generalized to their percentage among the New Christians as a whole. Joaquim Romero Magalhães's work, for example, hints at the possibility that the Inquisition persecuted merchants preferentially, to confiscate their property for its own purposes or to enrich the state treasury.[29] Yet the Inquisition might equally have preferred victims who (unlike the merchants) were of no particular importance to the state or to society, and therefore especially unprotected. Persecuting simple people, perhaps ones of dubious reputation, would have allowed the Inquisition to channel social desires for public humiliation and displays of power without having to fear any consequences.

Inquisition and State

Although the argument that the Inquisition caused the decline of the Portuguese economy must be rejected as too simple, it is nonetheless clear that the Inquisition did pose a threat to many merchants, that it was detrimental to their trade, and that it did encourage some of them to emigrate. Of the Portuguese merchants we know about, a great many had either been tried themselves by the Inquisition, or members of their families had been. Why did the state permit this? Why did the king not listen to advisors like António Vieira, who counseled greater tolerance toward the New Christians? Shaw claims that the king had lost control of the Inquisition: "It had become not a state within a state, but above the state, and the king in Portugal was no longer sovereign."[30]

Matters were more complicated than that, however. The Portuguese Inquisition had been established at the initiative of the Crown, and it became institutionalized, in many respects, against the resistance of the popes. It operated autonomously, but its activities were dependent on the king's support. Inquisitors general were installed by the pope, but the king retained the right to propose the candidates for the office. This led to a mixing of state and religious functions. Twenty inquisitors general held that position during the Inquisition's existence in Portugal; of them, fourteen held important secular political and administrative offices as well.[31] Several of the inquisitors general were members of the royal family. The later Cardinal-King Henrique combined the role of inquisitor general with that of regent, and, at the end of his life, with that of king. Archduke Alberto VII of Austria was simultaneously inquisitor general and viceroy of Portugal. Pedro de Castilho, too, was inquisitor general at the same time that he was viceroy. In other words, for long stretches of time there was no effective separation between the top-level administration of the Inquisition and that of the state, since individuals could and did hold office in both.

On the other hand, there were also inquisitors general who more or less openly opposed the secular government, such as the pro-Spanish Francisco de Castro, who after the 1640 declaration of independence entered into a conspiracy against the new Portuguese king.[32] The conspiracy was uncovered and Castro was imprisoned for two years, but the Crown was unable to unseat him as inquisitor general.

As a general rule, the Inquisition was dependent on the apparatus of the state, without which it could neither conduct trials nor enforce its judgments.[33] The death penalty in particular required the cooperation of secular tribunals, because canon law prohibited the clergy from participating directly in capital punishment. The Inquisition was also dependent on the Crown for financing, which came from regular church and state funds. It was the king who named the Inquisition's financial officials; they acted under the rule of the inquisitor general, but they confiscated the property of the accused under royal jurisdiction. Only a small portion of the proceeds from confiscations was designated for the Inquisition, to cover its expenses; the rest was due to the Crown. Much of the confiscation revenues, however, disappeared into the Inquisition's administration before being transferred. Inquisitional *visitators* (auditors or inspectors) repeatedly accused the institution of corruption. According to their reports, inquisitors appropriated without permission merchandise, valuables, books, and even real properties and houses belonging to the accused. It was rumored that they illegally trafficked in confiscated goods, and that in some cases they had business relationships with the accused. It therefore cannot be ruled out that the inquisitors' choice of prosecutions might have been motivated by interest in the victims' material assets.

However, the really prominent merchants who played major roles in the state were probably at far less risk than those of lower social status. The Inquisition's Rules of Procedure of 1640 provided that the *Council of the Inquisition* (Conselho Geral) be advised prior to the arrest of a merchant "with a large fortune,"[34] and the king may have been given notice as well. Special consideration was apparently given in such instances.[35] Nonetheless, occasionally a wealthy merchant banker favored by the king was arrested, shaking the economy of the entire state. Duarte da Silva, for example, one of the king's most important financiers, was arrested after Portugal declared its independence from Spain, when the Inquisition was openly opposing the new ruler. Shortly before his arrest in 1647, Silva had organized financing for the purchase of Portuguese warships in Amsterdam. His arrest led not only to the immediate cancellation of the financing, which prevented delivery of the ships; it also caused a panic on the Amsterdam Stock Exchange. Few people were willing to risk sending goods to Portugal out of fear that other

Portuguese businessmen would be arrested, too. The Portuguese-Jewish intellectual and diplomat Menasseh ben Israel, living in Amsterdam, wrote to Vicente Nogueira, the Portuguese agent in Rome, that after da Silva's arrest twelve important New Christian families had felt compelled to emigrate to Amsterdam and Hamburg, taking themselves and their money to a safer haven. He warned that although Portugal had the potential to be one of the wealthiest countries in the world, it would come to ruin if the Inquisition did not change course.[36] Nogueira forwarded Menasseh ben Israel's letter to the king, noting that he had received a similar letter from an Old Christian in Lisbon. That correspondent had written that da Silva's imprisonment had led to the resettlement of more than 200 Portuguese merchant houses to Spain.[37] Duarte da Silva was released from prison after five years. In 1661 he accompanied Princess Catarina de Bragança to England, where he was involved in negotiating and financing the dowry for her marriage to King Charles II. He did not return to Portugal.[38] His son, Isaac da Silva Solis, who accompanied him to England, later relocated to Hamburg, where he married the daughter of the Portuguese-Jewish businessman Duarte de Lima.[39]

Buying Freedom from Persecution

When he arrested Duarte da Silva, pro-Spanish inquisitor general Francisco de Castro may have intended to destabilize the country and so damage the new Portuguese king. Such confrontations, however, were rare; in general the Inquisition aligned itself with the economic and political interests of the Crown, and the Crown filled its empty treasury in part by selling freedom from Inquisition prosecution to New Christians.

The king was able to exempt individual New Christians from discrimination and prosecution by issuing them a royal document granting them the status of Old Christians, thereby lifting the "stain" of their birth. During the sixteenth century a number of wealthy merchants who had rendered service to the king benefited from this procedure.[40] Other distinctions that conferred privileged status, social prestige, and therefore also safety, included bestowal of the German Merchant Privilege (see chapter 3) or the title of cidadão (privileged citizen), ennoblement, and admission to a military order.[41] The king's acts not only honored past services rendered; they were also an attempt to secure the privileged person's loyalty in the future. Thus, for example, after Duarte da Silva was released from Inquisition custody, he was ennobled along with his brother-in-law, and two of his sons were named knights of the Order of Christ.[42]

There were also various forms of collective protection from the Inquisition's grasp. These included pardons and edicts of grace, which granted absolution for transgressions of faith committed in the past, exemptions from the seizure of goods, and permissions to leave the kingdom. The pope alone enjoyed the power to grant such a pardon, but it had to be requested by a sovereign, through his ambassadors in the Apostolic See. The largest transaction of this sort was the General Pardon of 1605 (see also chapters 6 and 14), for which the New Christians were assessed a payment of 1,700,000 cruzados to the Crown. That sum was intended to finance a fleet to force the Netherlanders and English out of the India trade, over which Portugal claimed exclusivity. In addition, the negotiators had paid a bribe of 50,000 cruzados to the duke of Lerma, the favorite and minister of Felipe III, and handouts of 50,000 to 60,000 cruzados to other intermediaries.[43]

Capital investments could also be protected from seizure by the Inquisition. For example, in 1628, when Felipe IV needed money for the war in Flanders, a group of New Christians negotiated a loan agreement with the king that guaranteed them immunity from confiscation not only of the capital that they made available, but also of the interest on that loan.[44] Another such attempt was made with the founding of the Brazil Company, which was established in 1649 on the model of the Dutch East and West India Companies (see chapter 13). To stimulate investment, the Crown prohibited the Inquisition from seizing investors' capital and merchandise (even that belonging to Portuguese living abroad as Jews).[45] However, the capital raised in this way was not nearly enough to finance the project.

Emigration and Border Controls

After protection from personal attack and from confiscation of goods, the right to emigrate was the third major concern of New Christian merchants. The Crown was intent on making emigration difficult, primarily for economic reasons. According to mercantilist thought, the highest goal of a ruler was to increase the population and wealth of his state. Emigrating New Christians would not only be a loss in themselves, but they would also try to take their property with them, in the form of gold and silver. And if, during the Iberian Union of 1580 to 1640, they had settled in Amsterdam or one of the other towns in the Netherlands' rebellious north, this would have harmed the monarchy even more by providing support to the enemy.

In 1577, for the first time in more than 50 years, New Christians were officially permitted to leave the country. But Cardinal-King Henrique nullified this decision two years later, and Felipe II affirmed the ban on emigration after his accession to power. To prevent preparations for clandestine emigration, the king also prohibited New Christians from selling real property, outstanding interest, or other such assets without a license. However, in 1601 Felipe III lifted the ban on emigration once again, in compensation for which the New Christians pledged to pay him 170,000 cruzados. Because the Spanish Inquisition was more restrained than the Inquisition in Portugal, and because of the trade possibilities offered to merchants in Seville and Madrid, the king hoped that many New Christians would relocate to Spain, which would have been very much in his interest.

After the General Pardon of 1605, New Christians who wanted to emigrate were required to present a license showing that they had paid their share of the pardon's costs. The licenses were valid only if they bore the signature of the king or the president of the king's advisory Council of State. But this provision was frequently violated, and so the king decreed the following year that all those who left the country without a proper license would forfeit any assets remaining in Portugal. In 1610 Felipe canceled completely the emigration provisions of 1601. His justification was that the New Christians had abused the privilege; by leaving the country for Protestant regions rather than Spain or the colonies they had transgressed against the Catholic faith, thereby imperiling both their own salvation and the welfare of the state.

But in fact only a minority of the emigrants had gone north. Most of them had moved to Spain. After the Spanish state declared itself bankrupt in 1627, leaving its Genoese bankers insolvent, the Crown profited from the services of the wealthy New Christian merchants and bankers who had settled in Seville and Madrid. As a result, in 1629 Felipe IV lifted the ban on emigration yet again, in exchange for a payment of 250,000 cruzados. He reasserted the terms of 1601, but this time with the proviso that the travelers could not take their property with them in the form of gold, silver, or other forbidden goods.[46] After this, no further restrictions on New Christian emigration appear to have been put in place.

The ports were the most important sites for monitoring compliance with emigration bans. The Inquisition did have employees in the ports, the so-called *visitadores*, but for a long time their duties were limited to confiscating Protestant books and similar objects from arriving vessels.[47] Only with the Inquisition Rules of Procedure of 1640 were they given additional authority to inspect ships from Protestant countries before they set sail, to look for refugees from the Inquisition, and for their property.[48] However, customs officials had precise information about the ships in port, as well as about their cargo and their passengers, and they often denounced refugees. In 1610, for example, Manuel Cardoso, Isabel Henriques, her Chinese domestic, and two small children were arrested by a customs official on the beach at São Bento near Lisbon as they tried to board the English trading vessel that was to take them to Antwerp.[49] I will return to this family in following chapters, in the context of their later resettlement in Hamburg.

Foreign consuls also played a key role in monitoring the ports. They knew the merchants who traded with the Protestant countries and the shipmasters who sailed there. For example, one Inquisition file states that Diogo Timão, who had been born in Hamburg and served as Consul of the German and Netherlandish Nation in Porto, always had precise and up-to-date information about the comings and goings in that port. This had helped him to intercept and arrest New Christians planning to board German or Netherlandish vessels. Furthermore, he had found much silver and gold, which they had attempted to take with them hidden in crates of sugar. According to the testimony, both the Inquisition and the king had profited greatly during the time in which this consul had monitored the port, reportedly by day and night.[50] That border controls functioned in the service of both Inquisition and state is evident here.

The ports were not only a critical point for emigrants, but also for Portuguese who wished to return to Portugal from Protestant countries. In principle, every Catholic who resided in a non-Catholic country without a "legitimate" reason, and who had inevitably come into contact with a foreign faith, was suspect.[51] If in addition he had been denounced for Judaizing or other heretical behavior (and possibly even sentenced in absentia), he could expect severe punishment upon his return. In any event, he was required to register with the Inquisition immediately.[52] Here, too, the consuls aided the Inquisition. In 1646 ten Portuguese Jews entered the port of Lisbon on a ship from what was then the Dutch colony of Pernambuco in northeastern Brazil, and the Inquisition attempted to determine whether they had been born in Portugal or in a Protestant country.[53] If born in Portugal, they would come under the jurisdiction of the Inquisition, because they would have been baptized Catholic and later renounced that faith. If, on the other hand, they had been born Jewish in another country, the Inquisition would not be authorized to bring them to trial. Of the ten Jews, several claimed to have been born in Hamburg, others in Amsterdam, and one in France. To determine their actual place of origin, the Netherlandish consul Pedro Corneles was brought in with some other Netherlanders to test how well they spoke Dutch. After talking with the prisoners, several of the Netherlanders maintained that while the accused spoke Dutch – some with a Hamburg or French accent – their Portuguese was considerably better. The accused countered that although they had grown up abroad, their parents had spoken Portuguese with them, so they felt more comfortable speaking that language. But in the end, a number of them admitted that they had been born in Portugal.

Portuguese Jews in the Diaspora

New Christians who succeeded in leaving the Iberian territories could not easily return lest they put themselves, or relatives and friends still in Portugal, at renewed risk. But at least they were safe from the inquisitors' grasp. Individuals could be denounced for transgressions committed abroad, and the Inquisition did indeed try people in absentia. But it did no actual harm to those outside of the Iberian territories. It did not seek to capture, arrest, or extradite them, or even to have them watched.[54] Inquisitors might, for instance, have sought to collaborate with the Jesuit mission in Altona (the Catholic congregation serving the Portuguese Catholics in Hamburg at the beginning of the seventeenth century; see chapter 14), collecting evidence against the defectors to Judaism that cost the Jesuits an important and wealthy portion of their community. But although the Inquisition was aware of this mission, there is no indication of any contact with it.

In its in-absentia trials, the Inquisition heard evidence from witnesses while the accused were not present to defend themselves or abjure their sins. If convicted, they would be burned in effigy in a public auto-da-fé.[55] Several Portuguese living in Hamburg were tried in this way.[56] It was extremely important to the Inquisition to be consistent in applying its methods. The statements of the denouncers and witnesses who appeared before it were always taken seriously and recorded in detail. The trials that resulted were rigorously prosecuted, even when the accused were beyond the Inquisition's reach. The intent was to demonstrate the omnipresence of the institution; its effect was aimed not only at the accused, but also at denouncers, witnesses, and society at large.

Foreign Protestants

The Inquisition had much less latitude in its dealings with the merchants who lived in Portugal but had come from Protestant countries. Neither the Crown nor the people wanted the Inquisition to apply to northern Europeans the vigorous steps it routinely took against New Christians. Northern Europeans were not viewed as fundamentally "different" the way the Jews and their descendants were, or the Moors and other non-European peoples. Scholarly writings from the sixteenth and seventeenth centuries treated the Arab presence on the Iberian Peninsula during the Middle Ages as a foreign rule. The Goths and Suevians, however, who had invaded the Peninsula before the Arabs, were considered forebears of the Iberian kings.[57] Consequently, the northern Europeans were able to rid themselves of their "foreignness" without lasting stigma by converting to and practicing the Catholic faith. Their blood was "pure."

Furthermore, the Crown did not permit the Inquisition to prosecute foreigners to the fullest. As discussed in previous chapters, it bent every effort to attract wealthy merchants from the north, and in negotiating the Treaty of 1607 with the Hansa had, at least informally, made concessions regarding religious tolerance (see chapter 3). From that time on, only those members of Hansa towns who had previously converted to Catholicism could be prosecuted. Protestants who had never converted, and who practiced their faith in private, were not seriously in danger. But even the number of trials of converted foreigners was extraordinarily low in Portugal. From 1536, the year the Portuguese Inquisition was founded, through 1700, it conducted only 971 trials involving foreigners. That is less than 5 percent of the total number of Inquisition trials during this period.[58] Only seven of the accused were burned. About a quarter of the foreigners were accused of Protestantism, the majority of them during the sixteenth century. There are only 26 known cases in which foreign merchants or merchant assistants were prosecuted. Six of these involved merchants from Hamburg in the seventeenth century. In contrast with the number of trials conducted against New Christians, this figure is vanishingly small.

Even when cases did come to trial, the Inquisition seldom pursued foreign merchants with the greatest possible severity. The Hamburg grain and wood trader Henrique Picht, for example, who had lived in Lisbon since he was 12 years old and converted to Catholicism there, admitted during his trial that he had briefly sympathized with Lutheranism during a return trip to Hamburg.[59] Since then, however, he had firmly committed himself to live and die as a Catholic, and asked for forgiveness. He was sentenced to grand excommunication and confiscation of property. But as a foreigner, according to the trial record, he did not have to undergo a public auto-da-fé, as the Inquisition feared that that would unleash an uproar among the other foreigners. He had only to don the raiment of the guilty during the reading of the sentence and his act of abjuration, and then he was free to take it off. For the salvation of his soul he was to be instructed in the Catholic faith.

In other instances, no trial whatever ensued. As previously mentioned, in 1627 the wealthy Hamburg merchant João Eggers was denounced to the Inquisition by João Canjuel, the Consul of the Germans and Netherlanders in Évora, and charged by him with espionage, smuggling, and practicing Lutheranism (see chapter 4). Despite several testimonies confirming his alleged religious transgressions, no trial documents regarding this denunciation are extant. Eggers, who apparently practiced his religion exclusively at home and caused no disturbance among the public, was protected by his status as a member of a Hansa town, and more generally as a foreigner.

But even if foreign Protestants were only minimally threatened by the Inquisition in the seventeenth century, they were still subject to its control. They were registered as soon as they arrived in Portugal. According to the Inquisition's 1613 Rules of Procedure, this applied especially to young people who had been sent by their parents to Portugal to learn the language and receive merchant training.

The rules required that the masters of the households in which these apprentices were placed be reliable. Every host had to register with the Inquisition when an apprentice arrived, lest he face a harsh penalty, and he was also responsible for registering a notification when the apprentice left.[60]

The Inquisition's 1648 Rules of Procedure further expanded this provision. When a vessel arrived from the "heretical countries," Inquisition *visitadores* were required to record the names and expected residences of all persons who intended to stay in the kingdom for any length of time.[61] They also had to inform all Protestants that they must not discuss religious matters with the locals, and that no public exercise of their religion, or denigration of the Catholic faith, would be tolerated.[62] Because foreigners assimilated so quickly – working as trading assistants in the households of Portuguese merchants, marrying Portuguese women, and even rising into the Portuguese upper class (see chapter 7) – they did in fact represent a danger to Catholic orthodoxy. Nonetheless, the Inquisition did little more than advise them of the regulations in effect.

Encouraging the Merchant Class

Foreign merchants who integrated well into Portuguese society and led a life that accorded with Inquisition precepts could become familiars (that is, as mentioned previously, prestigious lay officers of the Inquisition) in the same way as meritorious Portuguese Old Christians, by being judged worthy through the process of evaluation called *habilitation*. Familiars assisted Inquisition tribunals in their activities. To lend the Inquisition glory and prestige, they fulfilled ritual functions at autos-da-fé and other ceremonies.[63] In exchange, they benefited from the honor associated with the office. Aside from a good reputation, the most important criterion for this office was "purity of blood," and candidates were required to undergo the same kind of stringent examination for their Christian, Jewish, Moorish, or heathen origins, going back several generations, as occurred in trials. Once conferred, therefore, the title served as proof of pure blood. After the General Pardon of 1605, one of the times of greatest crisis for the Inquisition, the office was upgraded. Whereas previously craftsmen had been preferred for the post, it was now opened up to the social elites, especially to successful merchants. The title of familiar was soon a social distinction as much sought after as membership in a military order.[64]

In a quantitative analysis of the more than 20,000 extant habilitation proceedings filed by the Inquisition, José Veiga Torres found that in the last quarter of the seventeenth century there was a significant increase in their number, but that this was not accompanied by a corresponding increase in repression. In preceding decades there had been approximately 330 habilitations, as compared to 1,800 sentences. That is, about 6 individuals were sentenced by the Inquisition for each who was recognized officially as a familiar. From around 1675 until 1720, the number of habilitations increased to an average of about 1,100 per decade, while the number of sentences decreased to below 1,000. At that point, the ratio of familiars to victims was just over 1 to 1.[65]

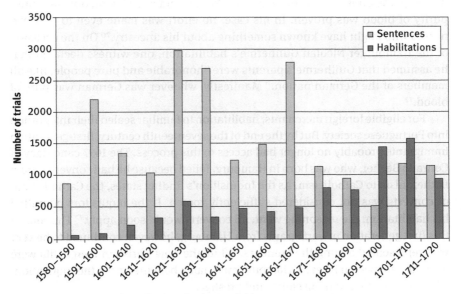

Figure 7: Sentences and habilitations by the Inquisition
Source: J. V. Torres (1994), p. 135.

There was a significant increase in the number of merchants among the familiars at the turn of the eighteenth century as well. In the years from 1580 to 1690, they accounted for about 13 percent; in the three subsequent decades that percentage approximately doubled.[66] The office of familiar implied a distinction that did not encroach upon the nobility, whose usages, at least in theory, were not consistent with trading activities. Saraiva's opinion that the Inquisition destroyed the merchant class can thus also be refuted, as the habilitations lent parts of the aspiring Old Christian merchant class social prestige, and thereby encouraged it.[67]

Foreign merchants sometimes achieved the office of familiar more easily even than high-ranking Portuguese. The latter were sometimes unable to furnish sufficient evidence of blood purity for the habilitation procedure.[68] For foreigners from the north, who generally had no documentation at all regarding their origin, the Inquisition was often prepared to forego such evidence. For example, in the case of the Hamburg-born consul Diogo Timão in Porto, none of the witnesses called by the Inquisition for his habilitation had known either his parents or his grandparents. Even the other Hamburgers there had known him only in Porto, and knew that he was from Hamburg only by hearsay. His Portuguese wife could document purity of blood, but not he. Yet that did not hinder his habilitation.[69] Similarly, during the habilitation of João Canjuel of Antwerp, the Consul of the Germans and Netherlanders in Évora, only his wife's purity of blood was proven. In his case, no effort was made even to find witnesses who might have known something about his ancestry.[70] On the occasion of the Hamburger Nicolau Guilherme's habilitation, one witness declared that he assumed that Guilherme's parents were "honorable and pure people, like all members of the German nation." Manifestly, whoever was German was pure of blood.[71]

For eligible foreign merchants, habilitation to familiar sealed their integration into Portuguese society. But by the end of the seventeenth century, first-generation immigrants probably no longer had access to this process. The 1697 candidacy of Conrado Becher, who was born in Hamburg, failed because he had converted from Lutheranism to Catholicism. As the Inquisition's finding states, the Catholic faith of converts was not considered sufficiently rooted. If the inquisitors permitted his habilitation, the reasoning went, all converts would soon apply.[72] The sons of this first generation of immigrants from Hamburg, however, continued to be very well represented among the familiars. While the New Christian merchants were generally suspect in its eyes, Hamburg merchants benefited from the Inquisition, which lavished upon them status and prestige.

Part II: **Migration, Life, and Trade**

6 Diaspora, Migration, and Mobility

The previous chapters dealt with the political and economic environment that conditioned the flow of trade and migration between Hamburg and Portugal. In this section I will look more closely at the merchants. Most of the Portuguese, and many Netherlanders, left their homelands as a result of the violence and persecution that constrained them greatly in their lives and in their commerce. Many of them had been well established in their home towns, and they took their wives and children with them, knowing that they might never be able to return. In contrast, the Hamburg merchants who emigrated did so of their own volition. Most of them traveled to Portugal alone, as adolescents or young men, to complete their training and lay the groundwork for later business ventures; very few women accompanied them. The trade networks that developed as a result of these different types of migration are the subject of chapter 12.

The Portuguese Diaspora

According to historian Jonathan Israel, the diaspora of the Portuguese Jews and New Christians was the largest merchant diaspora (see introduction) of the early modern period. It encompassed communities in France, Antwerp, Amsterdam, Hamburg, and London; Livorno, Venice, Salonika, Edirne, Istanbul, Izmir, Aleppo, and Alexandria; Tripoli, Algiers, Ceuta, Salé, Elmina (São Jorge da Mina), and Luanda; Recife, Buenos Aires, Potosí, Callao, Mexico, and the Caribbean Islands, and extended as far east as India, China, Indonesia, and the Philippines. According to Israel, it was the only merchant diaspora that "contrived for some two centuries to span in structurally crucial ways all the great religious blocs with exclusive claims (i.e., Catholicism, Protestantism, [Eastern] Orthodoxy and Islam), all the western maritime empires [the Venetian, Portuguese, Spanish, Dutch, English, French, and Ottoman] and all the continents [known at that time]."[1] Israel is convinced that the members of the diaspora viewed their common Jewish origin as a bond that united them and conferred a shared identity upon them, and that they sought social and trade relationships primarily among their own.

It is doubtful, however, that these widely dispersed Jews and New Christians really had as much in common as Israel assumes. Their social backgrounds and cultural experiences were very diverse. For example, many New Christians went to Brazil directly from Portugal, and some Portuguese Jews got there by way of Holland after northeast Brazil was conquered by the Dutch in 1630. These two groups tended to take different sides in the political and military conflict

https://doi.org/10.1515/9783110472103-007

between Portugal and the United Provinces, and they were religiously distinct as well. The Portuguese Jews from Holland founded a Jewish community in Recife, but the New Christians living there did not join it even though, now that they were under Dutch rule, they no longer had to fear persecution from the Inquisition.[2] The two groups did share a common ancestry, but their expectations and loyalties were very different. The New Christians who left Portugal to seek their fortunes in the overseas empire mingled with the Portuguese Old Christians they encountered there. To these they were bonded by language and culture, commonalities that emerged especially against the backdrop of the otherness of the indigenous peoples in the regions where they settled. There were often fewer commonalities with the Portuguese Jews whom the New Christians encountered in the diaspora.

Daniel Swetschinski offers a more differentiated picture than Israel. He identifies two major diasporas of Portuguese-Jewish origin that spread across the old world, which he traces back to two great waves of emigration.[3] These overlapped with an emigration to the overseas territories that, while less dense than the other two, continued longer and more steadily, and eventually came to include many more people. The first wave was the result of the decrees in Spain (1492) and Portugal (1497) that required that Jews either accept baptism or go into exile (see chapter 5). Many Jews who left Spain in 1492 relocated to Portugal, but, as we saw, five years later conversion was required there as well. This was a period of intensive violence; in 1506, for example, approximately 3,000 baptized Jews were killed in a massacre in Lisbon. In response to the omnipresent danger, many emigrants left the Iberian Peninsula precipitously and without preparation. They settled primarily along the Mediterranean coast – in North Africa, the Ottoman Empire, and Italy – and, because they had converted to Christianity only formally or not at all, in their exile they lived as Jews from the outset.

The second wave of emigration began in the late sixteenth century and continued through the first half of the seventeenth. Unlike the refugees of the first diaspora, the people of the second had been born and raised as Catholics, and their eventual return to Judaism would require a painstaking process of religious reacquaintance. Their departures were generally less precipitous. The violence after 1492 had been directed at the entire Jewish-New Christian population, but now the Inquisition was in place; it tended to target individual families, and its attacks could to some extent be anticipated and prepared for. Merchants who were wealthy and well established attempted not only to bring themselves to safety, but also to salvage their assets and maintain their social and business relationships. Where they resettled was determined not by the happenstance of what ship chanced to be leaving at the moment that they had to flee or other such coincidences, but by intent and by trade considerations.

One of the most important initial destinations for the Portuguese merchants of this second wave was Antwerp, where the New Christians were able to connect with the Portuguese *feitoria* (see chapters 1, 3, and 4). Italian trading centers, especially Venice and Livorno, had Portuguese settlements that had been founded during the first wave of emigration, and these too served as entry points for the new emigrants' future mercantile endeavors. Emigrants of lesser means often settled just across the Pyrenees in southwestern France; some of them stayed there permanently, and others only until they could garner sufficient resources to continue northward. In 1572 the Dutch began a blockade of the mouths of the Meuse and Scheldt rivers, and this markedly decreased trade through the port of Antwerp. Starting in the 1580s, therefore, the last major movement of emigrants spread out to cities that had the potential to supplant Antwerp as an international center of trade: Rouen, Middelburg, Rotterdam, Haarlem, Amsterdam, Cologne, Emden, and Hamburg. Jewish communities (both open and secret) developed in many of these cities, at least for a while. However, only in Hamburg and Amsterdam did lasting communities form.

The settlements of this second wave and their later offshoots in the Dutch, French, and English Atlantic colonies (that is, in Dutch Brazil, Surinam, the Caribbean Islands, and, later, New Amsterdam – today's New York), together with the Portuguese-Jewish community in London, comprised the Atlantic diaspora. They were in constant religious, personal, and material communication with each other. On the other hand, their connections with the first-wave Iberian Jewish communities in North Africa, and the eastern Mediterranean basin were relatively tenuous, and connections to the New Christians in the Portuguese and Spanish overseas territories were limited almost exclusively to business.

The Netherlandish Diaspora

A Netherlandish diaspora also took place in several waves during the sixteenth century and the beginning of the seventeenth. Antwerp's importance as an economic center had long been a powerful attraction. People came there from Flanders, Brabant, Hainaut, Tournai, Artois, Liège, and Limburg.[4] In the second quarter of the sixteenth century, however, an economic crisis coincided with the onset of the persecution of Protestants, and led to a first wave of emigration. Many left for Strasbourg, Frankfurt, and London, but also for towns close to the border in the Rhineland, such as Cleves, Wesel, Cologne, Aachen, Duisburg, and Emden. A second migratory peak occurred after the failed revolt against Spain in 1566 and the onset of the Duke of Alba's repressive "reign of terror" against supposed heretics and rebels the following year. Within five years between 30,000 and 60,000 Netherlanders left their homeland.[5] But the most important wave of emigration was the third, which reached its peak between 1580 and 1590. During this time, the cities in the southern Netherlands fell to Spain in rapid succession; in 1585, after a lengthy siege, Antwerp was conquered. The population of Antwerp decreased from almost 100,000 in 1567 to fewer than 42,000 in 1589.[6] Mechelen, Bruges, Ghent, Oudenaarde, Nieuwpoort, and Ostende all lost almost half their inhabitants. Many of them migrated to Amsterdam or other towns in the northern Netherlands, including Rotterdam, Gouda, Haarlem, Dordrecht, Enkhuizen, Leyden, Delft, Vlissingen, and Middelburg. Further important destinations of this third wave of emigration were the northern German towns of Hamburg, Altona, Stade, and Bremen.[7] Of the Netherlanders who emigrated to the Iberian Peninsula in flight from the war, most arrived between 1580 and 1620 as well.[8]

The departures of the first two waves of Netherlandish refugees were chaotic and hurried, like those of the New Christians who left Portugal early. In the third wave, which included most of the merchants who ended up in Hamburg and Portugal, the exodus was more orderly. The conqueror of Antwerp and governor of the Spanish Netherlands, Alessandro Farnese, gave the Protestants four years to convert to Catholicism or leave the country. During those four years they were permitted to sell their houses and properties and plan their resettlement. That meant that (like many of the last wave of Portuguese refugees) they could choose their new places of residence according to strategic economic criteria. While the poorer Netherlanders, who sought security above all, tended to settle just across the border, the more affluent merchants, and members of other more profitable or specialized professions, were interested in cities (even if distant) that offered them trade and financial opportunities. Their assets facilitated this long-distance travel. This is why the Netherlandish community in Hamburg, like the Portuguese one, was dominated by well-off merchants.

The de Hertoghe family, one of the wealthiest Netherlandish merchant families to settle in Hamburg, illustrates one migratory pattern.[9] The forebears of the de Hertoghes came from Brabant. Wouter de Hertoghe, the progenitor of the Hamburg branch of the family, settled in Antwerp as a merchant. He died in 1589 in Middelburg, where he had probably moved after the Spanish occupation of Antwerp. Of his four children, the eldest, Abraham, remained in Antwerp during the Spanish rule so that the family would continue to have a representative in its former base. He must have lived there as a Catholic, at least pro forma, until his death in 1607. The second-born, Cornelis de Hertoghe, relocated to Hamburg, where by 1585 at the latest he had become involved in the Iberia trade. He held a share of the Portuguese pepper contract, and was among the leading merchants of the city when he died in January 1612. Like all the other members of his family in Hamburg, he was a Lutheran. His sister Maria relocated to Rouen with her husband, who was also a merchant. Wouter de Hertoghe's youngest son Hans died before the Spanish occupation of Antwerp. Of Hans's three children, his son of the same name, born in 1567, settled in Hamburg after stays in various places in the southern Netherlands and northern France, including Brussels, Arras, and Rouen, where his uncle lived. His sister Anna's husband operated a trading business from Amsterdam and Frankfurt. A certain Paul de Hertoghe, who may have been related to the family, relocated from Brussels to Spain, where he lived in Medina del Campo, Bilbao, and San Sebastián.[10] The Spanish conquest of Antwerp thus led to the dispersal of de Hertoghe family members to many important port and trading cities – in Reformed and Lutheran as well as in Catholic regions – without severing the connection to their home base.

But this was only a small section of the Netherlandish diaspora, which, in its entirety, was probably at least as large as the New Christian-Jewish one that Israel sees as so widespread and so unprecedented. Netherlandish merchants were represented in almost all of the trading places frequented by New Christian and Jewish merchants, including the "great religious blocs" whose "spanning" he took to be unique to that community (see p. 103).[11] In the northern parts of the Holy Roman Empire in particular the Netherlanders settled in much larger numbers, and sometimes for far longer, than did the Portuguese, and they were present as well in all major Iberian port towns.[12] It is possible that the Netherlandish diaspora had more members globally than the New Christian-Jewish one, although the limitations of the extant data make comparison risky.[13] Historian Daviken Studnicki-Gizbert has estimated that the entire "Portuguese nation" (by which he means all Portuguese living outside of Portugal, including the Old Christians) comprised 20,000 persons in the seventeenth century.[14] Daniel Swetschinski has written that approximately 10,000 Portuguese New Christians migrated to Spain in the seventeenth century, and 6,000 crossed the Atlantic to Spanish America during the same period. Far fewer New Christians left Portugal for other destinations, including northern Europe. Estimates of the number of Netherlanders who emigrated between 1530 and 1630, by contrast, vary between 50,000 and 500,000; the current consensus is that the number of emigrants who left their country either permanently or temporarily was somewhat less than 100,000.[15]

Causes of Migration

Historians have taken two approaches to the question of why Netherlanders and Portuguese New Christians emigrated. One foregrounds violent persecution, religious discrimination, and the desire for religious freedom; the other focuses on economic motivations. Even though no immediate statistical connection can be confirmed between the number of victims of the Inquisition and the number of emigrants at any given time, the acute threat posed by the Inquisition was surely the most important factor impelling Portuguese merchants to leave their country.[16] In some instances, to this may be added the desire to practice Judaism; and the general discrimination that New Christians experienced on the Iberian Peninsula may have been a motive as well. Nonetheless, economic and trade considerations should not be underestimated. As previously mentioned, the emigration of New Christians from some regions of Portugal may have been a consequence of the economic decline in those areas rather than its cause (see chapter 5). Meanwhile, northern Europe was becoming increasingly important in world trade. To move there, or at least to send commercial representatives, met the business requirements of the time.

Religious persecution was widespread in the Netherlands as well, though its intensity was not comparable to the way New Christian families were targeted on the Iberian Peninsula. According to historian Heinz Schilling, in many cases Netherlandish merchants were forced to flee under circumstances inimical to their business interests.[17] But Oscar Gelderblom argues that religion was generally not the deciding factor in the merchants' decision to emigrate.[18] He points out in particular that the number of Lutherans from Antwerp who resettled to Amsterdam was not small, and that they could have simplified their lives considerably if they had relocated to the Lutheran stronghold of Hamburg, while many Reformed from Antwerp went there instead of settling in Reformed Amsterdam. A perhaps even more telling indication that freedom of religion was not the sole motive for the merchants' emigration is the fact that many Netherlanders emigrated to Portugal, Spain, and other Catholic regions. There may have been some who fled there because they were Catholics. João Canjuel, the Consul of the Germans and Netherlanders in Évora, for example, claimed that he had been driven out of Flanders and come to Portugal because of his Catholic faith.[19] All in all, however, far fewer Catholic merchants than Protestants emigrated, and most of the emigrants who settled in Portugal probably did so for the economic opportunities there.

Antwerp's decline and the gradual restructuring of international trade were important causes of the emigration from the Netherlands. Yet in defiance of these economic reasons for emigration, religious persecution became the central pillar of the Netherlanders' identity-building in exile, as it was among the Portuguese Jews and New Christians.[20]

The General Pardon of 1605

One group of New Christian merchants, who were closely associated through family and business relationships and eventually formed the core of the early

Portuguese settlement in Hamburg, illustrates the complex causes and conditions of Portuguese New Christian emigrations of the early seventeenth century. As we shall see, their migration was only partially a response to the Inquisition; as negotiators of the General Pardon of 1605 they also ran afoul of the Old Christian population, and even of many New Christians. The heads of this group were Rodrigo de Andrade and his wife's brother-in-law Henrique Dias Milão.

Rodrigo de Andrade came from a well-known banking family, the Rodrigues d'Évora; he was heir to a large estate in the diocese of Leiria and holder of important royal trade and tax contracts.[21] In 1600 he was one of a party of New Christians who went to Madrid to negotiate a pardon – the one that would eventually become the General Pardon of 1605 (see chapters 5 and 14) – and pursue other business dealings with the Crown. While he was in Spain, the Portuguese Inquisition arrested his wife Ana de Milão in Lisbon.[22] She was a New Christian too, about 60 years old, and she stood accused of preparing food in accordance with Jewish law, and of staring out an open window at the heavens instead of at a crucifix while praying. She had also expressed sympathy for several people who had been condemned to death by the Inquisition. But in all probability her arrest was motivated by her husband's participation in the pardon negotiations, which were heavily resisted by the inquisitors. The king, however, interceded on her behalf, and the pope threatened to excommunicate the inquisitors and halt the Portuguese Inquisition temporarily if Ana were not given a fair trial.[23] Shortly after the General Pardon was decreed she was released, having spent three years in prison. But in the meantime her husband had died in Rome, and there would be no respite from trouble for this family in the near future.

The fiercest opponents of the General Pardon, apart from the inquisitors themselves, were the Portuguese clergy, headed by the archbishops of Lisbon, Braga and Évora, the principal ecclesiastical dignitaries of the kingdom. The nobility and other sectors of the population were also strongly resistant. When the pardon was promulgated in January 1605, and more than 400 prisoners were released from Inquisition prisons, massive rioting occurred throughout the country. In Lisbon and Coimbra especially tumultuous rioting, including incidents of stoning, led to severe punishment of the leaders. Most of the priests who fanned the flames of riot at Mass, however, and the many students who supported them got off scot-free.[24]

Further unrest ensued when the board established to collect the 1,700,000 cruzados for which Rodrigo de Andrade had purchased the pardon began its work. The board compiled a list of about 6,000 solvent New Christians who were expected to contribute, establishing the amount that each had to pay according to his assets.[25] But many New Christians were not willing to pay their share. According to one witness report, the collection of monies was therefore accompanied by "the worst scandals and abuses." Manuel de Palácios, one of the people with primary responsibility for gathering the sum, who "had the best information, made no exceptions, and accepted no excuses for nonpayment," was murdered under unexplained circumstances.[26]

The causes of the New Christians' dissatisfaction were many. Some persons on the list denied that they were New Christians at all. Others claimed innocence of the charges for which they had been "pardoned," and refused to pay for other people's sins. Still others categorically rejected the agreements made in their name without their consent, and some New Christians were upset that people who in their eyes had indeed committed heresy were now being released from Inquisition prisons. New Christians who had never run afoul of the Inquisition derived no benefit whatsoever from the General Pardon of 1605, and the cost of it was not only financial; to be on the list at all meant to be officially identified and pinned down as a New Christian. For all of these reasons, Andrade and the others involved in the negotiation of the General Pardon were accused of having acted mainly for their own advantage (and this not totally without reason, see chapter 14).

Not only did resistance to the negotiations – and to the negotiators – develop on all sides; it endured long after the pardon was consummated. Andrade's activities were probably a factor in the arrest of Henrique Dias Milão and several members of his family immediately after the 1606 expiration of the Pardon's one-year period of grace (during which New Christians could confess their crimes with exemption from punishment). The Inquisition eventually released some of these prisoners, but Dias Milão himself, who like Andrade was a successful businessman and had trade connections in Angola, Brazil, and Mexico, was burned at the stake in an auto-da-fé three years later.[27] It was this triple threat – from the Inquisition, from the population at large, and from irate New Christians – that led the families of Rodrigo de Andrade and Henrique Dias Milão as well as those of Manuel de Palácios and of a number of their close business associates to leave, as they saw no possibility of maintaining their lives and businesses in Portugal.

One Inquisition document states that Andrade's children emigrated to Flanders, and that most of them died in poverty there.[28] In fact, however, while some family members did go to Antwerp, most emigrated to Hamburg, where they were very successful. Three of Andrade's four sons, Francisco, André, and Manuel, appear in the Hamburg Admiralty customs books; in 1632 Francisco booked the highest total turnover among the Portuguese. In 1647 his total was still the fifth highest. He died in 1648, and is buried in the Portuguese cemetery in Hamburg.[29] Andrade's daughter Branca fled to Antwerp, where she married Diogo Teixeira; he, after her death, married Ana de Andrade, Branca's niece and Rodrigo de Andrade's granddaughter. This couple too later settled in Hamburg. Diogo Teixeira became by far the wealthiest and most influential Portuguese businessman in that city (see chapter 8), and he and his wife are also buried in the Portuguese cemetery.[30]

Most of the family members of Henrique Dias Milão also made their way to Hamburg. In 1606, Henrique's son Paulo de Milão brought his sister Beatriz, Henrique's daughter, to Hamburg. There she married the merchant Álvaro Dinis, who had arrived just a year before, and already become successful in business.[31] Paulo then returned to Portugal, but a few weeks later he, his father, and several other members of his household were arrested by the Inquisition. As I have said, most of them were soon released and were eventually able to leave the country, with the exception of his father, who refused to abjure the Judaizing of which he stood accused. The flight of Paulo's other sister Isabel, which has already been mentioned (see chapter 5), was especially dramatic. After her father's burning in 1609, her mother instructed Manuel Cardoso, the son of an Old Christian merchant from the Azores, to bring Isabel, her Chinese servant, and two small children to Antwerp. He was to receive 20,000 reis for this service.[32] But as a New Christian, Isabel was not permitted to leave the country without the Inquisition's consent, and this was not likely to be forthcoming, given her family's history with the tribunal. Cardoso was an Old Christian, but he too needed Inquisition permission to leave, having previously been convicted of the Protestant heresy (see chapter 14). As I have said, just as the group was getting ready to board a boat that would take them to an English trading vessel and then to Antwerp, they were intercepted by a customs official and handed over to the Inquisition. But Isabel was finally able to flee; after some untraceable years we find her again in Hamburg, where she married Pedro de Palácios, the son of the Manuel de Palácios who had been murdered during the collection of money for the General Pardon.[33] Evidently he, as well as his brothers Duarte and Jácome, had also felt compelled to leave Portugal.[34] Isabel's mother, Guiomar Gomes, as well as her sister Ana de Milão, also lived in Hamburg,[35] and Paulo de Milão, her brother, who had returned to Portugal after escorting Beatriz to Hamburg, was living in Hamburg by 1612 at the latest, too.[36] He died in 1665, and like most of the others mentioned here is buried in the Portuguese cemetery in Altona.[37]

More than thirty years after the General Pardon, the Lisbon tribunal conducted a number of trials against Portuguese émigrés living in Hamburg. Various witnesses testified that the accused had been business contacts of Rodrigo de Andrade and Henrique Dias Milão, and had emigrated as a result of the events surrounding the General Pardon and Henrique's arrest.[38] All, according to the testimonies, had had reputations as good Christians, had attended church, had participated daily in the Mass, and had done pious deeds. That they practiced Judaism in secret is doubtful, and few members of the group were known to have been especially engaged with the Hamburg Jewish community. The children of

Rodrigo de Andrade and Henrique Dias Milão in particular appear not to have been very active in religious matters.[39] Everything indicates that they fled not for reasons of faith, but because they had been subject to the Inquisition's violence, and to serious threats from the Portuguese population at large.

The Portuguese and Netherlanders' Settlement in Hamburg

As detailed in chapter 1, Hamburg's economic growth began in the middle of the sixteenth century and continued well into the next, surviving (and even profiting from) the Thirty Years' War. This growth was accompanied by a surge in immigration. The population doubled between the mid-sixteenth century and the beginning of the seventeenth, from about 20,000 to 40,000. By 1643 it had risen to 56,000, and by about 1700 the city had approximately 70,000 inhabitants.[40] In a treatise written in 1628, Michael von Mentzel, who lived in Hamburg as the agent of Field Marshal Johann Tserclaes, Count of Tilly, estimated that only a third of Hamburg's inhabitants were native-born.[41] Although he held that most of the immigrants had come from outside the Holy Roman Empire, the truth is that the majority of new residents were drawn to Hamburg from the region around it – some from the immediate environs and some from a wider area with a radius of at least 125 miles. Merchants, however, often came from much farther afield; they were Rhinelanders, southern Germans, Balts, Scandinavians, Englishmen, Scots, Frenchmen, Italians, Spaniards, Portuguese, and Netherlanders. Even people from India were represented in Hamburg, according to one memorandum directed to the pope in 1603.[42]

Historian Martin Reißmann has shown that of the merchants who acquired citizen rights in Hamburg between 1623 and 1627, 62 percent had not been born there.[43] Even in the last three decades of the seventeenth century, long after the immigration occasioned by the Thirty Years' War had abated, 46 percent of the merchants who acquired citizenship were immigrants. To this number we must add the alien merchants who never did acquire citizen rights. In other words, migration was a common experience among Hamburg's merchants, and by no means restricted to the groups examined in this book.

Only for one year, 1619, do we have any detailed overall information about the origins of all of the merchants active in Hamburg. This is based on a unique document from the Bank of Hamburg. Because every person who wished to conduct a business transaction of 400 marks or more (see chapter 8) was required to run it through a bank account, we can match the account holders with the merchants active in large-scale trade in Hamburg at the time.[44] According to that document, in 1619 there were 540 accounts that belonged to 560 persons. Of these, 138 account holders were Netherlanders (25 percent) and 32 were Portuguese (6 percent).[45] In other words, in that year approximately one-third of the merchants active in Hamburg came either from the Netherlands or from Portugal. Foreigners from other countries were but few; most of the remaining merchants came either from Hamburg itself or were immigrants from the surrounding region.

In the first half of the century, both the Netherlandish and Portuguese merchant communities fluctuated widely in number. As the Lübeck City Council noted, many of the alien merchants in Hamburg resided there for a brief time only, "staying today, but soon moving elsewhere."[46] Like many other towns, Hamburg was often only one stop on a longer migratory route; merchants settled where there was peace and the economic and political conditions seemed advantageous. The Netherlander Cornelis le Brun, for example, originally came from Tournai. From there he moved to Wesel and then on to Bremen and Hamburg, before finally settling in Cologne.[47] François de Schott came from Antwerp, and spent time in Stade before moving on to Middelburg.[48] The Netherlander Antoni Engelbrecht lived in Emden and Lübeck before arriving in Hamburg. The Portuguese Duarte Nunes da Costa left his country in 1609, spent a scant two years in Madrid, then went to Saint-Jean-de-Luz and probably from there to Florence. He arrived in Amsterdam in 1621 and relocated to Glückstadt in 1626, finally settling in Hamburg in 1627.[49]

The fluctuation in the foreign merchant communities is also clearly evident in the changing number of people covered by the Netherlander contracts. 130 persons signed the settlement contract of 1605, but only 113 signed the second one, which was negotiated in 1615.[50] This decrease occurred partly because the great flow of emigration from the Netherlands had come to an end, and partly because, once the Twelve Years' Truce came into effect in 1609, many merchants went to Amsterdam and other cities in the United Provinces. As we saw in chapter 1, before the truce, when direct trade relations between the United Provinces and the Iberian Peninsula were severed, Dutch merchants had redirected their trade through neutral Hamburg, and at that time many merchants were attracted to the city. This was less true in 1615, when the truce was in effect. The third Netherlander contract, however, which was concluded in 1639, when war had resumed and Hamburg was once again playing its role as commercial intermediary, covered a total of 170 persons, considerably more than both contracts before.[51] The fluctuation shows up even more dramatically if we look at the individuals who signed the contracts. Only 15 persons were part of all three contracts: 69 signed the first and the second; 28 signed the second and the third; and 24 signed the first and the third, but not the second. Not all the individuals who disappeared from the contracts moved away, however. Some of them died; in later contracts only the names of their widows appear. And some of them became citizens.[52]

There were many more Netherlandish immigrants in total in Hamburg than the ones covered by the contracts. Historians estimate that about 2,000 Netherlanders lived in Hamburg and the neighboring towns of Stade and Altona shortly after the turn of the seventeenth century – that is, they accounted for nearly 5 percent of the entire population.[53] Only a fraction of them were merchants; most were employed in sugar refineries, as craftsmen in the textile trade, and in other such enterprises.[54] For the second half of the seventeenth century we lack data about the size of the Netherlandish community, probably because the fluctuation had calmed down and many Netherlanders had become so well integrated that they were no longer perceived as a separate group. The last known estimate is from 1653, when of all the Netherlanders said to be living in Hamburg, more than 400 were identified as merchants.[55]

Considerably fewer Portuguese merchants settled in Hamburg. Although in 1603 Hamburg citizens noted that Portuguese were arriving on a "daily" basis, in 1608 and 1609 only 20 Portuguese merchants paid *Werkzoll* (see chapters 1 and 2).[56] Very few Portuguese men pursued trades other than that of merchant at this time; therefore the Portuguese community as a whole, including family members, likely numbered about a hundred.[57]

The number of Portuguese living in Hamburg was probably also influenced by the truce between Spain and the United Provinces. As we have seen, in 1619 there were 32 Portuguese bank account holders, which is admittedly an increase in relation to the number of merchants just cited. But in 1623, two years after the truce ended, their number of account holders rose to 44.[58] And for a while the number of Portuguese merchants active in the city continued to rise; their peak number may have been reached around 1632, when a total of 57 of them paid Admiralty customs. In 1647, however, when war between Portugal and the United Provinces had ended, that number had decreased to 46 (although the trading region for which the duty had to be paid had been augmented; see chapter 2 and appendix).

By mid-century, the merchants engaged in long-distance trade may have made up only a small part of the Portuguese male adult population.[59] In 1652 an informer denounced to the Inquisition 1,212 members of the Portuguese-Jewish community in Hamburg. Assuming an average family size of five persons, this corresponds to as many as 250 families in the city at the time.[60] The discrepancy between this number and the 50 or so merchants implied by the Admiralty customs books can be explained either by assuming that the informer denounced many more Portuguese Jews than were actually living in Hamburg, or that the heads of a large number of Portuguese families were by then active in smaller businesses or other activities. It is also known that the number of Portuguese eking out only a precarious living in the city had risen. In any case, at about this time the total number of Portuguese in Hamburg began to decrease. In 1663, when the Italian count Galeazzo Gualdo visited Hamburg, he reported that Portuguese Jews were living in only 120 houses; in 1680, there were only about 60 Portuguese families left.[61]

The drop in population may have been helped by the increase in anti-Jewish violence in Hamburg, motivated in part by the large influx of German Jews that began at the end of the 1640s. Other cities now offered not only better economic opportunities but also more security and a richer cultural life that tempted those with the resources to pursue them. Many Portuguese moved to Amsterdam and London for these reasons; the more venturesome (or less fortunate, for lack of funds or other reasons) left for the Caribbean outposts of Curaçao, Jamaica, and Barbados, for Surinam on the Atlantic coast of South America, or for New Amsterdam (later New York).[62] In 1697, in the context of the escalating struggle for power between the City Council and an increasingly insubordinate citizenry, Hamburg downgraded the legal status of its Portuguese Jews and forced them to pay a high special tax. At that point the last group of wealthy families who had stayed in Hamburg despite the growing tensions there gave up their residences in the city and relocated to the safer and more congenial Amsterdam.[63] The heyday of the Hamburg Portuguese-Jewish community thus came to an end.

The Migration of the Netherlanders and Hamburgers to Portugal

While the Netherlanders' migrations to Hamburg and to Portugal were motivationally and structurally similar in many ways, the migration of the Hamburgers to Portugal was different. The Hamburgers did not leave their city for reason of violence, threat, discrimination, or religion. Nor did economic crisis play a role; personal interest was the only driver. The Hamburgers did not leave their homes in waves, either; their emigrations were a matter of individual initiative, and were spread out over a long period of time.

As we saw in chapter 2, German and Netherlandish merchants had been present in Portugal since the Middle Ages, and after Vasco da Gama's return from India, many of the large southern German trading firms founded branches in Portugal.[64] The northern Germans and Netherlanders left far fewer traces there than the southern Germans, however, whose family-owned firms had been established over generations, commanded substantial capital assets, and were able to assume the risks of the highly speculative India trade. The northern German and Netherlandish merchants tended to be involved in more workaday trading activities: sending grain, wood, shipbuilding materials, and munitions to Portugal, and bringing salt, wine, fruits, and, increasingly, sugar to the north.

It is difficult to estimate how many Hamburgers emigrated to Portugal. The kind of contractual, banking, and customs information that is available about immigrants to Hamburg does not exist for Lisbon. For the year 1605, historian Ernst Baasch compiled a list of 28 persons with German names who resided, or are known to have stayed for a time, in Lisbon and conducted business with Hamburg.[65] According to Eddy Stols, there were approximately 160 Netherlandish merchants in Lisbon between 1580 and 1620. Another dozen or so were present in Porto, Viana, and smaller Portuguese ports.[66] These estimates are not precise; they indicate, however, that there were almost as many German merchants in Lisbon as there were Portuguese merchants in Hamburg, while in both places there were more Netherlanders than either Germans or Portuguese respectively.

Like the Portuguese and Netherlanders in Hamburg, the Germans and Netherlanders in Portugal constituted only a small part of its foreign population. In his early seventeenth-century description of the city of Lisbon, Luís Mendes de Vasconcelos noted that there was hardly a nation whose members were not represented there. According to him, the conditions for foreign merchants were so good that none of them wanted to return to their homelands; that was why there were more foreigners than Portuguese in the city.[67] It might have seemed that way to him, but of the 100,000 inhabitants of Lisbon in 1551, probably only about 7,000 were in fact foreigners.[68] This is approximately the same percentage of foreigners as in Hamburg, even though the total population of Lisbon was about three times greater. Like Hamburg, Lisbon absorbed significant immigration from the region around it as well as from abroad. David Grant Smith determined the origins of 140 New Christian merchants who traded in Lisbon in the seventeenth century. Of these, 54 percent were born outside the Lisbon area, which closely approaches the regional immigration to Hamburg (see chapter 15).[69]

"Reduction" Registers as a Source on Immigration

For the second half of the seventeenth century, Inquisition registers give us an approximation of the number of Hamburgers who emigrated to Portugal and converted to Catholicism there. After 1641 the Lisbon tribunal systematically registered these conversions, which the Inquisition called "reductions [*reduções*] to the true faith." The tribunals in Évora and Coimbra began keeping registers somewhat later.[70] A convert gave the inquisitors his name, place of residence, nation, place of birth, marital status, age, original faith, profession, and the names and occupations of his parents. Information about when he arrived in Portugal and why he sought to convert was often also entered. Almost all of the converts registered in the files came from the Protestant countries of northern Europe. During the half-century between 1641 and 1691, 128 Hamburgers converted to Catholicism before the Lisbon tribunal – that is, about 20 percent of all converts listed in the Lisbon registers during that period. Another 23 converts came from the region immediately around Hamburg; for example from Stade, Glückstadt, or Lübeck. After the English, Irish, and Scots, who accounted for about 40 percent of the converts, those from Hamburg were the second largest group. "Germans," who were listed separately from the Hamburgers, comprised 10 percent of converts, Dutch 9 percent, and French 8 percent. These figures give an indication of the extraordinary importance of the Hamburg contingent in Lisbon; its members, unlike those of any of the other groups, all came from a single city, not from a country with many cities represented. There were far fewer Netherlandish immigrants; only 58 Dutch and four Flemings registered for reduction.

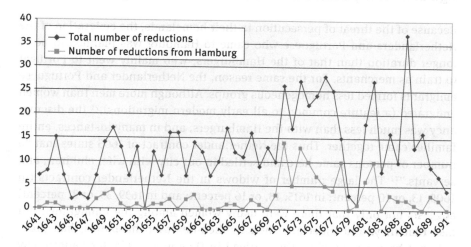

Figure 8: Conversions before the Lisbon tribunal of the Inquisition
Source: ANTT, TSO, Inquisição de Lisboa, livs. 708–715.

Conversions of Hamburgers reached their peak in the 1670s and early 1680s. Taking into account the information that many converts gave about the time of their arrival in Portugal, it is clear that immigration from Hamburg and environs was strongest between the mid-1660s and the mid-1670s, although it held steady at a lower rate both before and after. The Hamburg nation was much more homogeneous than the other nations. Almost all converts from Hamburg pursued mercantile interests in Portugal. About 95 percent were men, and 92 percent were single; only 76 percent and 62 percent of Netherlanders, respectively, were male and single. In addition, the Hamburgers tended to be very young: 60 percent of them converted before the age of 20, 28 percent between the ages of 20 and 30, and only 12 percent when they were over 30. The corresponding figures for Netherlanders are 32 percent, 40 percent, and 28 percent. Most of the Hamburgers worked as merchant apprentices or assistants, whereas the Netherlanders were represented in a much larger array of trades. Unlike the English but like the Netherlanders, the Hamburgers did not generally convert immediately upon their arrival in Lisbon, but only after a stay of between two and three years. In other words, these were not mere visitors. What remains unclear is how many of the Hamburgers and Netherlanders who moved to Lisbon did not convert. Because conversion was not obligatory, the total number of immigrants was probably much higher.

Age and Family Status of Immigrants in Hamburg

Because of the threat of persecution in their homelands, the emigration of the Netherlanders and Portuguese who came to Hamburg was planned to be of longer duration than that of the Hamburgers, who mainly went to Portugal to train as merchants. For the same reason, the Netherlander and Portuguese emigrants formed less homogeneous groups. Although more men than women emigrated (a feature common to all early modern migrations),[71] the discrepancy was much less than with the Hamburgers, and in many instances, entire families came together. Thus the Netherlander contract of 1605 states that "a number of persons came here and settled in our city with wife, children, and servants."[72] The large number of widows in the Netherlander contracts (in 1605, 13, or 10 percent; in 1615, 18, or 16 percent; and in 1639, 35, or 21 percent) suggests not only that there were many women among the immigrants, but also that they, and especially their by-then-deceased husbands, had probably not been young when they arrived in Hamburg. A similar pattern may be seen among the Portuguese who settled there. One of the earliest listings, from about 1612, shows that 75 Portuguese men and 45 women, among them 34 couples, lived in Hamburg.[73] Many of the single persons were young men, but there were also several older persons and nine widows. Younger children and servants, who were present in many households, were not mentioned individually in that list.

Most immigrant heads of household probably took their families with them at the outset, sometimes including unmarried sisters and nieces, or parents. The cloth dealer Pedro Francês, for example, left Portugal with his entire family.[74] In

Labastide, the first French town across the border from Spain, Francês disclosed to his children that he intended to live as a Jew. From there the group proceeded to Calais, where they joined up with several others who had been practicing Judaism secretly, and then Francês and most of his family continued on to Hamburg. In other cases, the family head went first and then returned to retrieve his wife and children, or a bride. Fulano Dias de Brito, for example, returned briefly from Hamburg to Lisbon. He married the daughter of a physician, and then took her with him to Hamburg. Others arrived in Hamburg single and later married there, such as the merchant Lopo Nunes, who married an Italian Jew.[75]

The Limited Mobility of the Netherlanders and Portuguese

Mobility, or the lack of it, was a defining difference between the migrants from Hamburg and those from Portugal and the Netherlands. The Portuguese and Netherlanders could not easily or safely return to their homelands, while those from Hamburg were free to do so at any time; they had left of their own volition, and there was nothing to stop them from going back. Even when the move to Portugal was permanent, they could still return to Hamburg for months at a time. Henrique Picht, for example, was sent to Lisbon when he was about 11. He lived there for 11 years before returning to Hamburg, where he stayed with his father for six months, and then returned to Lisbon.[76] Hamburgers in Portugal could also send their children to be educated in Hamburg, where they would find a home with relatives or acquaintances. The children then lived and worked there for some years, renewing old business contacts, before going back to Portugal.

This sort of flexibility was difficult, if not impossible, for individuals in the other two groups. They were not only emigrants; they were refugees. Return was risky, and they could not send their children back to be educated, either. It was easier for Netherlanders to return than for the Portuguese who had converted to Judaism and faced the menace of the Inquisition if they went back. But even the Netherlanders found it difficult to return home, as a correspondence conducted by Daniel and Andries Vermeulen testifies. The Vermeulens were a family of merchants from Antwerp with several members in Hamburg. Letters between Daniel in Leyden and his brother Andries in Bremen, written in about 1600, discuss the conditions that would have to be met for them to return: their recognition as free and equal citizens; a guarantee of religious freedom; an amnesty; and appropriate compensation for the losses they had suffered. In fact, in Daniel Vermeulen's estimation, these were precisely the conditions that would have to be fulfilled before the 100,000 other Netherlanders living outside the country would consider returning.[77]

For Jews residing in Hamburg who wanted to return to Portugal, the controls in the Iberian ports were a major obstacle. But even when they were able to make their way out of the harbors unrecognized, they were still in constant danger of denunciation. In pursuit of their business interests, they would have to seek out old acquaintances or make relationships with new business contacts. In so doing, they could hardly avoid disclosing that they lived in Hamburg, where it was well known that a Portuguese-Jewish community existed. In some instances Portuguese-Jewish businessmen requested royal immunity from arrest, and this allowed them to travel unhindered to Madrid or Lisbon. Gaspar Bocarro, for example, who had lived in Hamburg for several separate periods, visited the Portuguese ambassador to Amsterdam to apply for a return to Portugal and reconciliation with the Catholic Church.[78] But very few such applications were successful.[79] Another barrier to travel were bans imposed by the Jewish communities themselves. Yosef Kaplan has counted 82 instances between 1644 and 1724 in which Portuguese Jews sought forgiveness from the Portuguese-Jewish community board in Amsterdam because they had traveled to the "lands of idolatry" (*terras de idolatria*), that is, to Catholic countries in which the practice of Judaism was forbidden.[80] Many of these people lived at the margins of the Jewish community, which suggests that such a trip would have been completely off-limits for more devout Jews.

To maintain long-distance business connections over time, a merchant had to renew his relationships with the places he had left, either traveling himself or sending a trusted associate, apprentice, son, or nephew. For the Hamburgers who migrated to Portugal, this bidirectional mobility was a matter of course. It was harder for the Netherlanders, but still manageable. But for the Portuguese who emigrated to Hamburg, returning to the Iberian Peninsula was very difficult indeed. Sooner or later the trade connections to their old homeland would fail from lack of nurture. This is why long-term functional trading networks were seriously compromised for those merchants whose migration was compelled by expulsion. This issue will be taken up again in chapter 12.

7 Social Origins and Social Advancement

During the early modern period being a merchant was a prestigious occupation, yet it was an occupation open to almost anyone.[1] Even people of limited means could participate in larger business ventures using the possibilities afforded by commission trade and by making use of credit. This ease of entry, however, led to wide fluctuations within the merchant class, because in times of crisis only those with sufficient reserves, or access to additional funding, could survive. A merchant's fate could be altered at any time by political change, war, or natural disaster in Europe or overseas, to say nothing of the usual risks of doing business, such as the sudden insolvency of the other party to a trade or a misjudgment of the market. But even when blessed by both skill and fortune, a foreign merchant in Hamburg had little chance to climb the social ladder and find acceptance among the ruling class. This was not so in Portugal, which was an absolute monarchy where important positions and distinctions were awarded by the Crown; it was easier for successful foreign businessmen to attain them, and so rise into the ranks of the social elite.

Social Origins

The long-distance merchants varied greatly in social background. As we have seen in the preceding chapter, about half of those in Hamburg and Lisbon came from the regions around their respective cities. In general, they were not from the countryside, but from larger villages or towns. They usually arrived as adolescents or young single men, and completed an apprenticeship of several years under an established merchant. After that, a young merchant might be in a position to marry the daughter of a local resident (who was often a merchant too), and start his own business.[2] Those whose fathers or close relatives were already active in trading had considerable advantages over first-generation entrepreneurs. The relatives had access to capital that they could advance, bequeath, or (at least) offer as security for loans; they also had networks and consolidated business relationships that they could make available to the next generation.

In Hamburg, successful merchants and academics (especially jurists) were at the top of the social hierarchy. A prosperous merchant's son could hardly hope to climb any higher, even if he switched to another profession. This led to a high level of transgenerational continuity. Concrete data become available only in the early eighteenth century, but according to historian Martin Reißmann, of the merchants who were born in Hamburg and acquired the status of citizen in the years

https://doi.org/10.1515/9783110472103-008

1703 to 1711, between 65 and 85 percent came from families with a mercantile tradition.[3] In Portugal, on the other hand, successful Old Christian merchants tended to withdraw from active trading and seek to climb into the nobility, an ambition in which they often succeeded. But New Christian merchants, lacking the necessary "purity of blood" (see chapter 5) remained merchants even after achieving great wealth; society's highest levels were not open to them. In Lisbon, something over half (57 percent) of all merchants had fathers who had been merchants themselves. Looking at the New Christians alone, we see a continuity approaching that in Hamburg: about two-thirds of the fathers of New Christian merchants had been merchants.[4]

The social backgrounds of the foreign merchants in Hamburg are less well known than those of the locals. Although most of the Netherlandish refugees there had been active in trade before they left the Netherlands, some of them appear to have been of noble origin.[5] A few apparently became merchants only after their departure. Regarding Hans van Hemeren, for example, we read that "the Duke of Alba had caused [him] to enter the merchant trade, and [that he and his wife] had to forgo their considerable noble estates, which was why they found their way to Hamburg."[6] Abraham du Bois was another Netherlander who may have become a merchant only after emigrating; we read that he was forced to "leave his estates near Antwerp, in Brabant, because of religion." Hamburg officially rejected titles of nobility, and nobles were forbidden by law to acquire land or houses there.[7] But pragmatic ways were found around that prohibition, and it appears that the Netherlanders continued to value their titles; in 1641, for example, Peter Juncker had the emperor confirm the one he had borne in Flanders, and was granted an augmentation of his coat of arms. The van Uffeln family, to whom a grant of arms had been given in 1486 by Emperor Maximilian I and then augmented by Emperor Karl V, was likewise very conscious of this distinction.[8] The noble origins of Netherlandish merchants seem to have been an accepted social distinction in bourgeois Hamburg.

Some of the Portuguese who arrived in Hamburg emphasized their noble ancestry, too. This is rather surprising, because Jews and New Christians were theoretically barred from ennoblement on the Iberian Peninsula, and in most instances the claims cannot be corroborated. For example, in 1643 the businessman Diogo Teixeira had his noble credentials and coat of arms officially confirmed before he relocated from Antwerp. The Castro, Abendana, Aboab, and Mendes de Brito families also invoked noble origins. The Abas family was newly elevated to the nobility by Emperor Matthias in 1614; its members resided in Hamburg and Glückstadt.[9] As we have seen in chapter 4, Jacob Rosales, who lived in Hamburg, was granted the title of Count Palatine by the emperor in 1641. The similarities of the Portuguese and Netherlandish families in this regard suggest that reassertion of noble origins was a common pattern for migrants who had been driven from their homelands.

The Hamburgers who went to Portugal were mostly of less lofty background, according to the conversion registers of the Lisbon Inquisition tribunal (see chapter 6). The most frequent paternal occupation was seafarer (27 entries, or 38 percent), followed by merchant (21 entries, or 29 percent), craftsman (18 entries, or 25 percent), shopkeeper and innkeeper (4 entries, or 6 percent), notary and surgeon (one each). The registers are not always reliable, however. Johann Schulte (1662–1719), for example, son of the Hamburg mayor of the same name (Johann Schulte, 1621–1697), appears to have stated that his father was a merchant, although in reality he was a lawyer.[10] Still, the family names of the young Hamburgers make it clear that the large majority did not come from prominent merchant or City Council families; in this respect Johann Schulte the younger was an exception.

Although Hamburg claimed a high proportion of immigrants from the surrounding region, it appears that most of the people who left Hamburg for Portugal were the children not of these immigrants, but of native Hamburgers. It is possible that newly arrived persons did not send their sons to Lisbon because they did not have the contacts that long-established merchants and seamen had to fall back on. But it is also possible that for simplicity's sake, the new converts (regardless of the official question) gave their parents' place of residence, rather than their place of origin.

Education and Training

Before young merchant apprentices were sent from Hamburg out into the world, they received at least primary schooling. The city was home to many educational institutions. In 1668 the northern German author Conrad von Höveln wrote that there were in Hamburg "all kinds of arithmetic, bookkeeping, writing, and other schools, including children's schools," as well as "language instructors for the French, *Welsch* [Italian], and Spanish languages and the like."[11] The foreign apprentices who came to Hamburg for training also appear to have attended school there to learn German, reading, and writing. However, it was chiefly in merchants' offices that apprentices acquired the skills they needed to handle the bookkeeping, the instruments of credit and bills of exchange, the appraisal of merchandise, and all the other operations involved in buying and selling. It is not known whether apprentices from Hamburg attended school in Lisbon.

Because many of the Hamburg merchants and assistants who converted to Catholicism in Lisbon made statements specifying how long they had been in the country at the time of conversion, it is possible to estimate how old they were when they began their apprenticeships abroad. When they arrived in Lisbon, more than half of the Hamburgers were between 12 and 15 years old, about a third between 15 and 20, 3 percent between 20 and 25, and 9 percent older than that. Henrique Picht, for example, who was born in Hamburg in about 1593, was the son of a seaman, and just 11 years old when his father sent him to Lisbon.[12] There he was taken under the wing of Hamburger João Frins, who was active in the wheat and wood trades. Picht worked for him for a total of eleven years. Another Hamburger, João da Maya, was born in 1643; he was the son of a shipmaster, and arrived in Lisbon, at the age of 13.[13] After his time as apprentice and trading assistant to the Portuguese João Soares da Costa, he spent time in Hamburg, London, and Portsmouth, and then returned to Lisbon in 1665 or 1666, where he continued to be active as a merchant. João Frique is a third example.[14] He arrived in Lisbon in about 1657, at the age of 14. His father was one of the few who had not originally come from Hamburg. He had gone there from Hildesheim, and was a firemaster and blacksmith by profession. Frique's mother, however, was born in Hamburg. During his first two years in Lisbon, Frique lived with the Protestant merchant João Prus, after which he worked for four years as a clerk (*caixeiro*) under Gaspar Barneque, who had come from the Duchy of Mecklenburg. Like Picht, Frique returned to Hamburg for six months before settling permanently in Lisbon and establishing a business partnership. He died in 1694, and is buried in Lisbon in the Church of Saint Julian.

As previously mentioned, Johann Schulte, the mayor's son, was an exception among the Hamburg merchants who went to Portugal in their youth. He was already 18 years old when he arrived in Lisbon in 1680 to learn Portuguese, put the finishing touches on his training, build a network of trading contacts, and acquire working capital. It is probably because he had already completed an apprenticeship, possibly under one of his brothers-in-law in Hamburg, that he lived not in the home of a patron, but with a business associate, in their own house. It is very likely that he profited not only from his father's position, but also from the experiences and connections built up by his brother-in-law, Gerd Burmester, who had similarly lived in Portugal in his youth, and was now active in the Portugal trade from Hamburg. Schulte returned to Hamburg between 1685 and 1688, married there, and settled permanently in the city.

Merchants in Portugal too sent their children for training abroad. Manuel Cardoso, who originally came from Terceira Island in the Azores (and who, though an Old Christian, would later convert to Judaism in Hamburg), was sent by his parents to Exeter in 1599, when he was 14.[15] There he was to learn English to help his father in the woad trade. While in England, Cardoso lived with a business associate of his father; the two men had gotten to know each other through the Englishman's representative on Terceira. Cardoso attended school in Exeter for two years, and by the time the first was over had mastered the English language. Another Portuguese, the New Christian Luís Vaz Pimentel, was sent to live with relatives in Antwerp in 1606, at the age of 15, when he began his training.[16] João Aique, whose father was German, was born in Lisbon in 1612 and was sent to Hamburg to learn the *língua flamenga*, literally the Flemish language, but probably referring here to German or Low German (see chapter 4).[17] Aique lived in Hamburg for seven or eight years, during the first two of which he attended (and apparently lived at) a school. Then he worked for a little more than six years in the service of German or Netherlandish merchants (*mercadores flamengos*). João Hestorwege, whose father was German and whose mother was Portuguese, was also sent from Lisbon to Hamburg at 16 or so; he lived there for about four years and attended school.[18] The Lübeck merchant Diogo da Maya, who lived in Lisbon, sent not his son but his 12-year-old slave Julião to stay with his parents in Lübeck, so that he could go to school and learn German.[19] Julião da Maya remained in Lübeck for four years, returning to his master in Lisbon after Diogo's father's death in 1666. Portuguese who did not have relationships in other European countries generally sent their children to Brazil to train and build a business.[20]

Language

The Hamburg merchant apprentices learned Portuguese quickly. Those who converted to Catholicism in Portugal, generally two or three years after their arrival, often spoke it well enough by then that they did not require an interpreter. Converts from other occupational groups, and those who had spent less time in the country, were much more likely to use an interpreter's help to talk to the Inquisitors.[21] When Hamburgers married in Portugal, their brides were usually either Portuguese or women born in Portugal to a Portuguese mother and a foreign father. The language spoken within the families was probably Portuguese. As a result, the sons of Hamburgers born in Lisbon often spoke their fathers' language so haltingly that they had to be sent to a German town to learn it. Very much the same may be said of the Netherlanders living in Portugal.[22]

In Hamburg, the Netherlanders who spoke Flemish (as opposed to those who spoke French or its close relative Walloon) probably had little difficulty making themselves understood. As Conrad von Höveln regretfully stated, "the noble, heroic High German language" was little used in Hamburg, because "the merchant boys (who had traveled in Holland, and the many Brabanters, Hollanders, English, and the like, who reside in Hamburg) use Low German mixed up with Dutch."[23] The language of the northern Netherlanders apparently had the status of a lingua franca among the merchants in Hamburg.

Matters were quite different for the Portuguese living there. They tended not to adopt the prevailing language, and as knowledge of Portuguese was limited in Hamburg, misunderstandings were common. There is no information as to how well the Portuguese merchants of the first generation learned German, or whether they learned it at all. Almost without exception they married women belonging to the Portuguese-Jewish community, and well into the eighteenth century they continued to speak Portuguese (and occasionally Spanish) at home and within their community. In 1653 Johannes Müller, a pastor and senior of the Ministerium (the association of the city's Lutheran clergy) who was not well disposed toward the Jews, did write that most of the Portuguese had by then mastered German – so well that they could with little difficulty be converted to Christianity.[24] In legal proceedings, however, where mastery of the language was critical, the Portuguese merchants generally used interpreters.[25] For example, the Portuguese Jacob de Castro is mentioned as having worked as an interpreter for the merchants Duarte Nunes da Costa and Sílvio del Monte during an inheritance dispute.[26] From another trial document we learn that the merchant Manuel Rodrigues Isidro did not speak German, and made use of Ferdinando Nunes, who understood and spoke it well.[27] Rodrigues Isidro's servant also spoke German well and occasionally filled in as interpreter. That servant may have been Baltasar Álvares Nogueira, one of the very few Portuguese who married a German or Netherlandish woman (a *flamenga*).[28] In some instances, language deficiencies my even have kept Portuguese from participating in matters of legal importance. Thus, in a trial that took place in 1633, the Portuguese Jews, "because some of them do not understand the German language, quickly [stated] that they were in agreement."[29]

It is not clear why the Portuguese learned German so badly, or how they made themselves understood in the commercial life of Hamburg. They may have spoken one of the other Romance languages when speaking with other merchants and with members of the ruling elite; as Conrad von Höveln wrote, "it is praiseworthy that Hamburg's distinguished young men speak French, Spanish, and *Welsch*."[30] Diogo Teixeira seems to have taken for granted that mastering these languages in Hamburg was part of the general education of merchants and academics. In 1656 he initiated a suit against bank representatives who had overlooked abbreviations for "widow and heirs" on a remittance form that he had filled out in Portuguese.[31] The defendant objected that Teixeira had violated banking regulations by writing in Portuguese instead of German, so that the bank's bookkeepers had mistaken the abbreviations for titles. Teixeira responded that they understood Latin, French, and Italian, and should have known what the abbreviations stood for.

Residence

That merchants from Hamburg who chose to live and work in Portugal often spoke Portuguese fluently and married Portuguese women demonstrates how fully they became integrated into Portuguese society. The Portuguese living in Hamburg, however, became only poorly integrated into society there, and the Netherlanders only moderately. A similar contrast may be seen between the religious assimilation of the Hamburgers in Portugal and the religious segregation of the Portuguese and Reformed Netherlanders in Hamburg, which will be treated in detail in chapters 14 and 15. It is reflected also in the very different choices the three groups made about housing. Although merchants from all nations usually settled in the business centers of the cities where they worked, the Netherlanders and Portuguese in Hamburg tended to live with families of their own nation, while the young Hamburgers were often received into the households of local merchants.

The Portuguese Jews in Hamburg lived, like other merchants, in the center of the city, between the Alster and the port.[32] They did not have to confine themselves to a separate quarter – a freedom that Jews could not take for granted. But they were not permitted to acquire real estate, and they had to rent housing from Hamburg citizens, who often belonged to the mercantile and political elite of the city. Thus, at the turn of the seventeenth century, the most important Portuguese merchant in Hamburg, Rui Fernandes Cardoso, lived with his family and his brother and sister-in-law in a house that belonged to the von Spreckelsen family and was situated on the Burstah in the center of the city.[33] The von Spreckelsens were an old Hamburg merchant family that was active in trade with the Iberian Peninsula and Flanders; its members furnished the city with many City Councilors and mayors in the sixteenth and seventeenth centuries.[34] Other Portuguese lived in houses owned by the Arens, Elers, Petersen, Reder, Hoier, and Kentzler families, which also played important roles in the city's commercial and political life.[35] Single Portuguese men tended to join up with other Portuguese families.[36] We know of only one Portuguese who (at the beginning of the seventeenth century) lived "in a room in the house of people from Hamburg."[37]

Young Hamburgers who went to Lisbon did not usually move into quarters of their own until they had lived for several years with an employer. In some cases the employers were of German descent, but often they were Portuguese. Some young men neither married nor returned home after leaving their patrons; these were likely to join forces with other foreigners and live together in a shared house. Henrique Picht, for example, lived with an unmarried German merchant named Henrique Malhem,[38] and João Frique shared his house with a "heretic" (probably a Protestant), as the files of the Inquisition make clear.[39] Most of the merchants from Hamburg settled in Lisbon in the commercial districts of São Julião, São Nicolau, and Santa Maria Madalena. Some of them moved into houses vacated by New Christian merchants who had fled Portugal.[40]

Social Ascent in Hamburg

The difference in how foreigners were integrated in Hamburg and Portugal is seen most clearly in their access to government and administrative positions and to titles and privileges. In Hamburg, merchants weighed heavily in the political leadership. Even the lawyers who, as administration became professionalized increasingly took up posts in the City Council, came mostly from merchant families. In 1663 the City Council decreed that at least one of Hamburg's four mayors should not be an academic, but "be well knowledgeable in the merchant and sea trade."[41] Although craftsmen were in the majority in the Assembly of Citizens, merchants dominated the *citizen boards* (*bürgerliche Kollegien*), that is, the boards representing the parishes in their political negotiations with the Council.[42] Most important, the *Board of Senior Elders* (Oberaltenkollegium), the highest citizen board, was staffed from merchant families; it oversaw the administrative activities of the City Council, and monitored compliance with the laws. Merchants were also represented in the various administrative deputations. Offices in the Bank of Hamburg, in the Commercial Deputation (which represented Hamburgers active in maritime trade; see chapter 13), and in the Admiralty were filled exclusively by merchants.

The social prestige and status of a merchant in Hamburg depended on the administrative and political offices he assumed. These offices were open only to Lutheran citizens. Most merchants began to involve themselves in city administration shortly after acquiring citizen rights. A person might start out taking responsibility in relief work for the poor, or as a church warden (*Kirchgeschworener*). Then he could become an administrator of the *Bakenzoll* duty or the Admiralty customs (*Zollbürger*), of the City Treasury (*Kämmereibürger*), of the Bank (*Bankbürger*), or of the Commercial Deputation (*Commerzdeputierter*). Over time he might achieve the position of senior elder (*Oberalter*), city councilor (*Ratsmann*), or mayor (*Bürgermeister*). The term of office was always several years; in some cases people assumed more than one office at once. These were voluntary positions, and there was little if any remuneration; those who took on some of the higher offices had to have considerable assets to draw on.[43]

Merchants involved in the Portugal trade were consistently represented in Hamburg's prominent offices. The Beckmanns, for instance, were an old merchant family. They played an important role in the Iberia trade at the turn of the seventeenth century; a share in the pepper contract was one of their holdings. At one time the brothers Lukas and Barthold Beckmann were senior elder and mayor, respectively. After experience in several other positions, Lukas Beckmann's son Lukas became a city councilor. His brother Joachim became a treasury official and a senior elder.[44]

The close relations between the Hamburg City Council and the merchant families suggest that the political goals of the Council and the business interests of its members frequently aligned, intersected, and intermingled. Unearthing all these connections as they applied to the trade with the Iberian Peninsula would be an exhaustive study of its own, however, and I can give only a few hints here of the interplay between political office and personal interest. One is the case of Daniel and Heinrich von Bergen, who were active in the Portugal trade and brothers of Sebastian von Bergen, a later mayor. While Sebastian was still secretary of the City Council, he conducted for his brothers a correspondence in which they tried to obtain damages for several loads of grain that English privateers had intercepted on the way to Portugal.[45] Sebastian was in contact with a confidante of Archduke Alberto, the governor-general of the Spanish Netherlands and former viceroy of Portugal, and sent him economic and political information in the form of handwritten newsletters, hoping that this might to a mutually beneficial relationship.[46] During his time as city councilor, Sebastian also handled the first settlement negotiations with the Netherlandish and Portuguese merchant communities.[47]

As mayor of Hamburg, the above-mentioned Johann Schulte, whose son went to Lisbon as a young merchant, had both influence and sources of information that he may have used for his son's benefit. When the son, for instance, wanted to know why António de Freitas Branco appeared to be traveling to the Holy Roman Empire in the diplomatic service of the Portuguese Crown, his father turned for information to the Portuguese resident in Hamburg, Manuel Nunes da Costa. The resident disclosed to him Freitas Branco's entire itinerary, and shared his speculations that the trip was connected with the marriage of the princess of Portugal to the prince of Palatine-Neuburg (in fact the issue was the marriage of the widowed King Pedro II himself).[48] In another letter, Mayor Schulte mentioned that Consul Alexander Heusch in Portugal had every reason to act favorably toward his son, because Schulte himself had "shown him all manner of friendship and affection during his time at the Admiralty and had helped him to achieve the post he had requested."[49] That members of the mayor's family could occasionally evade the rules is demonstrated by a decision from Lübeck, which granted to Schulte's son-in-law, Gerd Burmester, free transit of iron, "because Burmester is married to Mayor Schulte's daughter."[50]

Jürgen Schröttering, who had originally come to the city as a poor orphan from the village of Wellingholzhausen near Osnabrück, was said to have been one of the three richest men in Hamburg when he died in 1631 (see chapter 8). He made his fortune importing salt from the Iberian Peninsula, taking it to be refined in Silesia, and exporting Hungarian copper back to the peninsula on his return there. Schöttering was elected senior elder, and his son Johann Schröttering, one of the most important Portugal merchants of the 1630s and 1640s, became mayor. Before that, the son had served as a treasury official, as overseer of the orphanage (*Waisenhausprovisor*), and as a city councilor. His older brother Dietrich had been a senior elder like their father Jürgen. Later, Johann's son Jürgen also held this office.[51] Clearly even impecunious newcomers could achieve great wealth as merchants, and by the second generation aspire to even the highest political offices. The percentage of immigrants in the city administration was large; among the high-ranking officials (in the Treasury, say, or the Bank, the Board of Senior Elders, or the City Council), more than a quarter were men whose fathers had not been citizens. But these were primarily immigrants from the surrounds of Hamburg, sometimes as far away as Osnabrück.

By law, Reformed Netherlanders in Hamburg could not hold office in the city administration. Lutheran Netherlanders with citizen status were permitted to hold office, but only one first-generation Netherlander, Peter Juncker – mentioned above in connection with the noble title that Emperor Ferdinand III confirmed for him in 1641 – actually achieved a higher-level post.[52] Juncker began his administrative career as an overseer of the orphanage; he then became a bank deputy and finally a senior elder. During this period, in 1632, Juncker had the second highest turnover in the Iberia trade of all merchants active in Hamburg. His son, Johann Baptista Juncker, who became first bank deputy, then judge in the lower court (*Niedergericht*; that is, the court of first instance), treasury official, and church warden at St. Catherine's, was also active in the Iberia trade. His turnovers were not comparable to his father's, but his brother Adrian took first place in turnover in the Iberia trade in 1647. Two other Netherlandish families, the Amsincks and the von Beselers, also held important political offices in the seventeenth century; they were both involved in the Iberia trade, although their turnovers were relatively low. Rudolf Amsinck, who belonged to the second Hamburg generation, rose to the level of city councilor in 1619, and for a time was the city's envoy to the United Provinces. His nephew Paul held a number of lower offices, became a church warden, was active in the lower court, and in 1681 was appointed a senior elder.[53] Nikolaus von Beseler was a third-generation Netherlander who also held several offices and was made a senior elder in 1680.[54]

Apart from these examples, Lutheran Netherlandish merchants assumed no political offices of importance in Hamburg during the seventeenth century. It is possible that they did not even aspire to such offices because of the expenditures of time and money involved. In fact, some historians claim that the Netherlandish immigrants were more successful than the average, having more resources for trading ventures precisely because they did not have any duties in the city administration.[55] Absent a detailed study we can only speculate, but it seems at least as plausible an argument that foreign merchants who had no access to these offices (either because they were of the Reformed faith or because they were outvoted by their German competitors) were at a long-term *dis*advantage. The many welfare projects in which the Netherlanders engaged – at an equal cost of time and money – may have partly compensated them for this disadvantage and at least gained them prestige. The Netherlanders Gillis de Greve and Simon von Petkum, for example, organized the building of an orphanage for children left parentless by an outbreak of plague. In 1600 the City Council and the Assembly of Citizens named Mayor Dietrich vom Holte as patron of the planned orphanage and city councilors Heinrich Sillem and Eberhard Esich as copatrons. Among the orphanage's eight overseers were two senior elders and de Greve and von Petkum.[56] In this way the two Netherlanders established ties to the top decision-makers of the city, which they might have expected would gain them some political influence. However, neither they nor their progeny assumed political office.[57]

Of the outstanding Portuguese entrepreneurs in Hamburg, the most important socially and politically were members of the Teixeira and Nunes da Costa families (see chapters 4 and 8). Both families were highly respected for their diplomatic activities and their role as bankers. However, they were never in any way integrated into the city oligarchy.

Of course, social mobility could go both ways. Mercantile pursuits not infrequently ended in bankruptcy for both native and foreign entrepreneurs. Once economically ruined, a merchant was unlikely to regain his footing in the commercial world. Vinzenz von Kampen, who came from one of the great Hamburg merchant families and lived in Cádiz, attempted suicide after massive business losses. He sought help from the church, but is said to have lost his reason in the end.[58] However, even to failed merchants there were a few avenues open that afforded a modicum of social respectability. If they had lost their means through no fault of their own, former merchants in Hamburg could, for example, find employment as commercial brokers, postmasters, or similar positions.[59]

Social Ascent in Portugal

There were no established routes to effective political participation for merchants in Portugal.[60] The *Cortes* (the assembly of representatives of the estates of the realm), which in the seventeenth century had little power anyway, were dominated by the nobility and the clergy, and were very hostile to New Christians. It would have been almost impossible for merchants to press for their interests in that body. Administrative offices of the monarchy, especially in the Council of State, the Overseas Council, and the Treasury were held almost exclusively by members of the nobility or the educated elite, as were posts in the Lisbon City Council. Only if they were elevated to the nobility could merchants hope to gain a political toehold. As a result, the merchants' political power corresponded not at all with their financial strength and economic importance to the state.

However, upward mobility was possible within the strongly differentiated merchant class itself. At the top of the hierarchy were the *contratadores*, the lessees of the very profitable crown contracts. In exchange for payments of money or for supplies of urgently needed raw materials, they received a license for monopolistic exploitation of a particular commodity (such as pepper or tobacco) or of a particular trading region (such as the Guinea trade). Profit margins could be in the 30 to 40 percent range.[61] Leases like this were often parceled out into subcontracts; to hold a contract, therefore, was to gain a powerful position within the merchant class. In addition, crown contracts often came with legal advantages. Like the bearers of the German Merchant Privilege, the contract holders had a judge of their own (*juiz conservador*) who was responsible for any legal issues that might arise from the contracts. For their services to the Crown, Old Christian *contratadores* were often granted ennoblements, admissions to the military orders, or appointments as familiars of the Inquisition.

But there were also smaller-scale crown contracts. As early as the first half of the seventeenth century, Hamburg merchants were entering into business dealings, often minor, with the Spanish-Portuguese Crown. In 1621, for example, a German merchant named João Vourquineque was contracted to supply a Portuguese fleet with 500 *quintais* (hundredweight) of copper.[62] A royal letter from the year 1625 mentions five ships from Hamburg that had supplied copper in fulfillment of a crown contract. The vessels were also laden with powder and lead.[63] In another letter from the same year, the king gave instructions to pay the German merchant Jacques Jacques, who lived in Lisbon, for a load of wood that he had delivered in 1619.[64] For 1626, a load of copper from Hamburg on the king's account is attested;[65] there is also mention of a ship having delivered tar, powder, copper, and lead from Hamburg to Portugal to outfit the king's India fleet.[66] The German consul Hans Kampferbeck was helpful in acquiring ships' masts from

Moscow in 1627.[67] Furthermore, the king repeatedly made use of Hamburg vessels in transporting troops across the Atlantic to reconquer northeastern Brazil from the Dutch.[68] In payment, the shipmasters were allowed to bring sugar and tropical fruits back to Portugal, a privilege otherwise forbidden to foreigners.

The Restoration War against Spain, which began in 1640, and the wars of reconquest of Portugal's Brazilian, African, and Asian assets, opened the Portuguese economy even wider to foreign entrepreneurs. Hamburg merchants advanced the necessary credit to the king, provided him with weapons, munitions, horses, and ships, and supplied his soldiers with grain. In return, they received monies from the taxes or other regular payments levied by the Crown, which made these transactions profitable and relatively secure.

Among the most successful Hamburg merchants in Portugal were Pedro Hasse and his son André. Pedro (Peter) was born in Hamburg in about 1620.[69] His father, who also bore the name Peter, was purportedly a Catholic merchant. Very little else is known about the family; the Admiralty customs books contain no such name. There is no indication that his parents, brothers (if he had any), or other relatives belonged to the city's elite. At about the age of 16, Pedro Hasse arrived in Lisbon, where he lived in the house of a German merchant. Later he opened his own business and worked for the Crown. With his son André, who was born in Lisbon, he was involved in outfitting the fleet used to retake northeastern Brazil. The Hasses advanced credit to the king and acquired ships, equipment, weapons, and horses from "the north," certainly by way of Hamburg. All in all, it seems that they were responsible for securing about 250 vessels for the Portuguese king between 1651 and 1690. For his services, André Hasse was accepted into the Order of Christ in 1671, and named a familiar of the Inquisition in 1675. He was furthermore made a knight of the royal household (*cavaleiro fidalgo*) in 1691; this status came with a monthly pension (*moradia*) and an allotment (*alqueire*) of barley a day (a medieval tradition, supposed to feed his horse). He was also named treasurer of a voluntary tax on sugar and other goods from Brazil (*Donativo dos Cruzados*). In 1699 he was named one of the four deputies of the Board of the Brazil Trade (see chapter 13), a post that came with a salary and a number of other privileges (*honras, graças, privilégios e franquezas*).

Pedro Hasse's wife was the Portugal-born daughter of the gem dealer and diamond contract holder André de Belém from Gelderland, in the northern Netherlands. His son André married first a Portuguese woman, and then a Swedish lady-in-waiting to the Portuguese queen. She was the daughter of Haquin (Håkan) Dreffling, who was said to be the captain-general of the Swedish provinces of Södermanland and Värmland.[70] The Hasses had a page from Hamburg in their service, which speaks both to their luxurious lifestyle and to their close connection with André's father's hometown. André's son, Pedro Hasse de Belém, inherited his father's knighthood and followed him in his office as treasurer of the Donativo dos Cruzados, which André had relinquished after assuming the office of deputy of the Board of the Brazil Trade. In 1706 Pedro Hasse de Belém married a maternal cousin, the daughter of Daniel Lossius, court councilor of the prince-bishop of Hildesheim and archbishop-elector of Cologne. Within three generations the Hasses had thus risen into not only Portuguese, but also European, high society.

Another northern German merchant who met with great success in Portugal was Diogo da Maya from Lübeck.[71] He arrived in Lisbon in the middle of the seventeenth century. He, too, was appointed a knight of the Order of Christ, and he received a patent of nobility in 1664 for the services that his father, Peter Meyer, also a merchant, had rendered to the Portuguese royal house: specifically, personal and financial support of the imprisoned Prince Duarte and of the Portuguese ambassadors and residents in the Hansa towns. In addition, he and his son Diogo had sent matériel to fortify Portugal's borders and outfit its army, and had advanced considerable credit to the Portuguese treasury, the repayment of which had been greatly delayed. As a result, Peter Meyer in Lübeck was granted an annual pension from a *commandery* (an income-yielding church property) belonging to the Order of Christ, which had apparently been abandoned when its previous holder moved back to Spain after the two Iberian kingdoms separated. The commandery itself was transferred to Meyer's son Diogo, who also received the title of Knight of the Order of Christ. There were other Meyers in Lisbon and Hamburg, some of whom held important positions, but no relationship to this Meyer/Maya family has been confirmed.[72] One of them was Joachim Meyer in Lisbon, whom Mayor Schulte mentioned several times in his letters as a "great benefactor" of his son.[73] The mayor regularly exchanged gifts with Joachim Meyer, which suggests that Joachim was an important personage in the German community in Lisbon.[74]

A final example of a successful Hamburg merchant family in Portugal is João Lamberto.[75] João was born in Hamburg and died in Lisbon before 1669. His father, of the same name, may possibly have migrated to Hamburg from the Netherlands, as a Johann Lambert is mentioned in the first Hamburg Netherlander contract. João married a Portuguese woman in Lisbon; he had two sons, Luís and Sebastião, and possibly another named Francisco. Luís became a Dominican monk, and Sebastião the superintendent of the royal frigate construction works in Brazil. Sebastião also served as a shipmaster in the fight against the Netherlanders in Pernambuco, and accompanied a delegation of emissaries to the Netherlands. He acquired ships and ship equipment and had 50 looms sent to Portugal, on which craftsmen from the north made sails. He was also involved in recruiting crews, and was overseer of the royal treasury (*provedor-mor da fazenda real*) in Bahia and administrator of the Board of the Brazil Trade. For his services he was named a knight of the Order of Christ, and elevated to the nobility in 1694.

8 Turnovers and Assets

As I have been describing, a merchant's social position and political influence were to a great extent determined by local conditions. Another important factor was his success in business, as measured (at least in part) by his turnover and by the assets he accumulated. As this chapter will show, the turnovers of the Netherlanders in Hamburg were far above the average there, while those of the Portuguese were somewhat lower than the Hamburgers'. About the merchants' assets we have few indications, but on that scale too some Netherlanders rated very high. Unfortunately, no quantitative sources equivalent to the ones in Hamburg are available for Portugal. Insight into the merchants' standards of living there can be gleaned only from descriptive sources, such as the inventories detailed in Inquisition trials. It is only about Hamburg that we have the sort of vivid accounts that allow us to picture the practical reality of these merchants' prosperity, how they displayed it to others, and the way that those others discerned it.

Trade Turnovers in Hamburg

The 1619 turnovers of the Hamburg merchants are recorded in a list compiled from the ledgers of the Bank of Hamburg, which had been founded by the City Council that same year.[1] It was one of a number of public *giro banks* (banks with the capacity to transfer money directly between accounts) established at the beginning of the modern era in Europe. The oldest, on the Iberian Peninsula in Barcelona, Valencia, and Girona, date from the fifteenth century; in the sixteenth century such banks could be found in several Italian cities and in Lyon. The first public giro bank in northern Europe was established in Amsterdam in 1609. It gave rise to a number of similar banks throughout the United Provinces, and provided the model for the Bank of Hamburg. Portugal also considered establishing a public bank. In 1622 the merchant and economist Duarte Gomes Solis proposed one in his *Discursos sobre los comercios de las dos Indias* (Discourses about the Trade with the Two Indies), but his suggestion was never acted upon. Another proposal made 20 years later by the Jesuit father and statesman António Vieira met the same fate.[2] In Portugal the primary purpose of such a bank would have been to create an additional source of credit for the Crown. The benefit to long-distance traders would have been less; they could rely just as well on private bankers.

Merchants, however, profited greatly from the founding of the Bank of Hamburg, because it stabilized currency and thus made their planning more reliable.[3] The political and economic upheavals of the seventeenth century had

https://doi.org/10.1515/9783110472103-009

plunged northern Europe into monetary chaos that was aggravated by coinage of inferior quality. Following the model of Amsterdam, the Bank of Hamburg introduced the *bank-mark* (*Mark Banco*) as a fictive currency against which all other currencies were valued. Furthermore, the bank held a monopoly in the city on clearing payments greater than 400 bank-marks. Thus all transactions exceeding that value (or, in the case of bills of exchange, exceeding 400 Lübeck marks [*Lübische Mark*], the prevalent currency in Hamburg at the time) had to be routed through the Bank of Hamburg. Any clearing outside the bank was punishable, and probably happened very seldom.[4] Profit was not the original motive of the Bank of Hamburg, as it had been with the never-realized projects in Portugal. Its board did soon add a credit section, however, the profits of which were reaped by the city.[5]

As I have said, a listing exists of account holders' turnovers in the year of the bank's founding. These show the amount of capital used by the merchants in trade, and because of the requirement that payments over 400 bank-marks be cleared through the bank, they are quite representative of the scope of the large-scale merchants' trading activity.

In 1619 a total of 540 parties held accounts at the Bank of Hamburg. Sixteen merchants held two or three accounts, one alone and the others with one or two business partners. Three accounts belonged to merchants jointly with unnamed associates; eight accounts belonged to groups of heirs, and two belonged to widows. The rest belonged to one merchant apiece. It is evident on examining the turnovers that a relatively small number of merchants moved a relatively large amount of capital (5 percent of the account holders transacted 36 percent of the total, and 10 percent more than half), while 80 percent accounted for only 27 percent of the total turnover.[6] Grouping the turnovers into five equal categories, we get the following distribution:

Table 6: Turnovers of account holders at the Bank of Hamburg, 1619

	Number of accounts	Percentage of accounts	Percentage of total turnover
More than 200,000 marks	10	1.9%	19.9%
150,000 to 200,000 marks	12	2.2%	12.1%
100,000 to 150,000 marks	20	3.7%	14.8%
50,000 to 100,000 marks	52	9.6%	22.6%
Less than 50,000 marks	446	82.6%	30.6%

Source: StAHH, Senat, Cl. VII Lit. Cb, Nr. 4, Vol. 1a, Nr. 1b.

The top three turnover categories were dominated by Netherlanders. They contributed six of the 10 merchants with transactions totaling more than 200,000 marks;

in the next two turnover categories, 9 and 14 Netherlandish merchants accounted for 75 percent and 70 percent of the account holders respectively. In the lowest category, comprising transactions of less than 50,000 marks, only 16 percent of the merchants were Netherlanders. The Portuguese, by contrast, were not represented in the two topmost categories at all. In the third and fourth they accounted for only two merchants each, while all other Portuguese were in the lowest category. Total turnover was distributed across the various nations as follows:

Table 7: Turnovers of account holders at the Bank of Hamburg by nation, 1619

	Netherlanders	Portuguese	Hamburgers	Regional immigrants	Origin unknown/other
Number of accounts	124	29	91	46	250
Percentage of accounts (a)	23.0%	5.4%	16.9%	8.5%	46.3%
Percentage of total turnover (b)	47.3%	4.5%	15.5%	4.6%	28.1%
Concentration index (b/a) x 100	207	83	92	54	61

Source: StAHH, Senat, Cl. VII Lit. Cb, Nr. 4, Vol. 1a, Nr. 1b (for allocation of the nations see appendix).

In short, almost half the total turnover in 1619 was in the hands of Netherlanders; the Portuguese held a mere 5 percent. If we examine the concentration of trade – that is, each nation's share of total turnover in relation to its share of the number of merchants involved – it is even clearer just how dominant a trading position the Netherlanders had in Hamburg. Their percentage of the total turnover was more than double the percentage of accounts in their holding. For the Portuguese, by contrast, the percentage of the total turnover was actually less than the percentage of account holders.[7]

Of the Netherlanders represented in these statistics, 55 were included in the Netherlanders' settlement contract and 69 were not. The concentration of trade was only slightly higher for those who had achieved citizen status than for those who lived and worked in Hamburg on a contractual basis. The religious affiliations of the Netherlanders were also more or less equally distributed: 68 merchants probably belonged to the Reformed congregation, and 56 were Lutherans (see appendix for more on these categories). The concentration of turnovers was the same for both. In other words, neither their legal status nor their religious affiliation was a determining factor in the Netherlanders' trading prowess.

Similar data regarding banking volumes are available for Amsterdam, and they make for a useful comparison. There the turnovers themselves have not survived, but they can be estimated based on the number of pages each account holder took up in the indexes to the ledgers.[8] Such information exists for eight of the years between 1609, the year the bank was founded, and 1627. From the beginning more accounts are listed in Amsterdam than in Hamburg. Already in 1609 there were 740 account holders, which number had increased to 1,230 by 1620. In Amsterdam, immigrants from the southern Netherlands made up an even greater percentage of the total number of merchants than Netherlanders did in Hamburg; and they also had the highest concentration of trade, although not nearly as high a concentration as in Hamburg. The percentage of Portuguese among the account holders, about 5 percent, was the same as in Hamburg, and their concentration of trade, like the Netherlanders', was less than that of their compatriots in Hamburg. In short, foreigners, and especially (southern) Netherlanders, were much more involved in Hamburg's commerce than in Amsterdam's.

Table 8: Turnovers of account holders at the Bank of Amsterdam by nation, 1609–1627

	Year	Southern Netherlanders	Portuguese	Other
Number of accounts	1609	267	22	451
	1610	269	27	420
	1611	260	31	419
	1612	275	50	439
	1615	313	61	498
	1620	364	121	745
	1625	364	78	892
	1627	367	94	890
Percentage of accounts (a)	1609	36.1%	3.0%	61.0%
	1610	37.6%	3.8%	58.7%
	1611	36.6%	4.4%	59.0%
	1612	36.0%	6.5%	57.5%
	1615	35.9%	7.0%	57.1%
	1620	29.6%	9.8%	60.6%
	1625	27.3%	5.9%	66.9%
	1627	27.2%	7.0%	65.9%
Percentage of total turnover (b)	1609	44.6%	2.1%	53.3%
	1610	48.3%	2.2%	49.6%
	1611	49.9%	2.6%	47.5%
	1612	48.9%	4.3%	46.8%
	1615	49.7%	4.2%	46.1%
	1620	42.8%	6.3%	50.9%
	1625	37.7%	4.1%	58.2%
	1627	36.6%	5.6%	57.8%

Table 8 (continued)

	Year	Southern Netherlanders	Portuguese	Other
Concentration index	1609	124	70	87
(b/a) x 100	1610	128	58	84
	1611	136	59	81
	1612	136	66	81
	1615	138	60	81
	1620	145	64	84
	1625	138	70	87
	1627	135	80	88
	Average	135	66	84

Source: C. Lesger (2006), p. 155.

Based on the Admiralty customs books a similar analysis may be performed for the Portugal trade in Hamburg. Here the total turnover was distributed differently among the nations. In both years the Netherlanders and the Portuguese were within 10 percentage points of each other, but the Netherlanders' share dropped from 30.2 percent in 1632 to 22.6 percent in 1647, while the share of the Portuguese increased from 23.5 percent in 1632 to 31.4 percent in 1647. This growth was accompanied by a rising concentration of trade, as the number of Portuguese merchants involved in the Portugal trade dropped from 47 in 1632 to 35 in 1647.

Table 9: Turnovers in the Portugal trade by nation, 1632/1633 and 1647/1648

		Netherlanders	Portuguese	Hamburgers	Regional immigrants	Origin unknown/ other
Number of merchants in Portugal trade	1632	46	47	37	30	38
	1647	35	35	33	13	70
Percentage of merchants in Portugal trade (a)	1632	23.2%	23.7%	18.7%	15.2%	19.2%
	1647	18.8%	18.8%	17.7%	7.0%	37.6%
Percentage of total turnover in Portugal trade (b)	1632	30.2%	23.5%	18.5%	18.7%	9.0%
	1647	22.6%	31.4%	17.6%	10.9%	17.5%
Concentration index (b/a) x 100	1632	130	99	99	123	47
	1647	120	167	99	156	47

Source: StAHH, Admiralitätskollegium, F3, Band 1, 2, and 8; F4, Band 8, 14, and 15 (see appendix).

Trade Turnovers and Migration

That Portuguese merchants should have participated more largely than others in the Portugal trade seems logical; after all, Portugal was their country of origin, where they still had many business contacts. So why were the overall turnovers of the Netherlanders so much higher than those of the local merchants? And why, to raise a secondary question, were the differences between Netherlanders and locals in Hamburg so much more pronounced than they were in Amsterdam?

First of all, it is likely that the assets held by the Netherlanders were more liquid than those of the local merchants. Because they were migrants, and not necessarily intending to settle in Hamburg forever, they were less likely to invest their capital in real estate or other fixed holdings; their assets remained easily accessible, and so lent themselves to investment in commerce. Second, most of the Netherlanders had probably been members of the mercantile elite in their home regions, while the backgrounds of the Hamburgers were more diverse. As we saw in chapter 5, the fact that the Netherlanders chose to settle in Hamburg shows that they were not concerned only with their safety; rather, these were ambitious merchants who either had capital of their own or were working with wealthy partners or principals.

The Portuguese, too, were likely members of the merchant elite in Portugal, but unlike the Netherlanders, many of them were able to take only a small fraction of their assets with them when they emigrated.[9] Prudence demanded that they not sell all of their properties and valuables in anticipation, lest it direct suspicion to an impending flight. This was especially true during the times when New Christians were required to acquire a license to sell real estate, outstanding interest, pensions, or other sources of income. In some cases the emigrants left their homes in a seemingly occupied state, taking only what was most important for survival.[10] Property left behind was often administered by family members or business associates, and if possible sold later on and the capital transferred northwards. Violante Correia, for example, a member of the Hamburg Portuguese community, listed in her 1659 will real estate still belonging to her that had been left behind in Portugal.[11]

But the Portuguese could not protect all of their assets. Refugees frequently lamented that between the Inquisition and the state they had been left destitute.[12] The previously-mentioned Andrade and Milão families, for example, disbursed some of their wealth during the negotiations for the General Pardon that precipitated their flight from the country. Furthermore, many members of those families were arrested; this made normal commercial dealings next to impossible, as did the fact that the Inquisition undoubtedly confiscated some of those families' assets. Flight itself must also have drained the émigrés' wealth. In 1610 the Hamburg City Council observed that the Portuguese possessed little property there, and so would yield the city little tax income.[13]

Having recognized that the Netherlanders chose Hamburg as much for reasons of mercantile ambition as for security, we can also answer the second question, about why the differences between them and the locals were more pronounced in Hamburg than in Amsterdam. Hamburg was farther away from the crisis-ridden southern Netherlands than Amsterdam was, and therefore more difficult to reach for the Netherlanders. As historian Oscar Gelderblom has shown, the merchants who moved from Antwerp to Amsterdam were primarily young people at the beginning of their careers who often did not possess much in the way of assets.[14] In Hamburg, however, the large number of widows in the Netherlander contracts (see chapter 6) would seem to indicate that many of the Netherlandish immigrants were older than that when they arrived. They were undoubtedly more established in their careers, and had likely accumulated more capital than had those who found their way only to Amsterdam. A second reason is that Amsterdam was just beginning to step out of the shadow of Antwerp, which even after 1585 remained an important trading and financial center, while Hamburg had already developed into an independent and increasingly important economic hub. It was the gateway between the Atlantic Ocean and central and eastern Europe, which at the end of the sixteenth century were being integrated into the world economy. Especially enterprising merchants who wanted to expand their businesses at this time thus might well have gravitated to Hamburg in preference to Amsterdam.

There is no indication, however, that local merchants were squeezed out by the immigrants. An economy can grow through the inclusion of new actors without displacing those who were there before. Hamburg experienced an extraordinary economic upswing along with the enormous spurt in population of the first half of the seventeenth century. The City Council, made up of members of old Hamburg merchant families, was especially keen to advocate for the acceptance of foreigners. To whatever extent these elite merchants withdrew from active trade as immigrants settled in the city and became successful, they did so not because they were pushed out, but of their own volition. Nor should the fact that a large number of Hamburg merchants showed low turnovers in the banking accounts be viewed as an indicator of the commercial decline of previously successful merchants. A merchant's ascent generally took place over time, whereas his decline usually occurred abruptly as a result of bankruptcy, which made further commerce, even at a low level, nearly impossible. The size of the merchant lower class therefore probably resulted from the ease with which commerce could be entered into, and not as a consequence of displacement by immigrants.

The Merchants' Assets

There are many indications that, along with their high turnovers, the Netherlanders enjoyed above-average prosperity.[15] According to the chronicler Friedrich Georg Buek, the three most prominent merchants in Hamburg in 1630 were two Netherlanders, (Hans?) de Hertoghe and (Jan?) de Greve, and Jürgen Schröttering, who had immigrated from nearby Osnabrück. While we do not have any estimates of the assets of the first two, we know that upon his death in the following year Schröttering is said to have left behind a fortune of about a million marks.[16] But two other Netherlanders, the brothers Rudolf and Arnold Amsinck, appear to have been nearly as wealthy. In 1634 they are said to have lost assets amounting to 700,000 marks in a storm surge, without suffering bankruptcy.[17]

Unfortunately there are no tax lists to give us an exact picture of each merchant's wealth. As I explained in chapter 2, Hamburg citizens paid an annual property tax (Schoss) of ¼ percent of their total assets. But no records of the individual contributions are available because they were calculated by the merchants themselves and paid in secret. Individual tax amounts are known only for aliens.[18] Nevertheless, we know that between 1586 and 1622 and between 1640 and 1650 the Netherlanders under contract paid between 10 and 15 percent of the total property taxes received by the city; the share paid by the Portuguese was under 5 percent.[19]

As we saw in chapter 3, the per capita tax of the Netherlanders under contract was considerably higher than that of the Portuguese, which suggests that their respective property was also much more extensive. And if we compare the taxes paid per capita in 1605 and 1639 by the Netherlanders listed in the contracts, it appears that this wealth was becoming more concentrated. Whereas in 1605 the 10 percent of contract members with the highest taxes paid 32 percent of the total, in 1639 their share had risen to 44 percent.

Table 10: Schoss payments by Netherlanders, 1605

	Number of contract parties	Percentage of contract parties	Percentage of total Netherlanders' Schoss
More than 120 marks	5	4%	15%
90 to 120 marks	12	9%	25%
60 to 90 marks	7	5%	10%
30 to 60 marks	34	26%	30%
Less than 30 marks	74	56%	20%

Source: StAHH, Niederländische Armenkasse, AI2, Stück 2.

Table 11: *Schoss* payments by Netherlanders, 1639

	Number of contract parties	Percentage of contract parties	Percentage of total Netherlanders' *Schoss*
More than 480 marks	5	3%	20%
360 to 480 marks	2	1%	6%
240 to 360 marks	6	4%	13%
120 to 240 marks	18	10%	19%
Less than 120 marks	143	82%	42%

Source: StAHH, Niederländische Armenkasse, AI2, Stück 3.

The only tax lists known for the Portuguese are two incomplete ones, from 1614 and 1616. They suggest that assets were more evenly distributed among them than among the Netherlanders. The 10 percent of Portuguese paying the highest taxes paid only 26 percent of the total taxes of the community.

Table 12: *Schoss* payments by Portuguese, 1614/1616

	Number of contract parties	Percentage of contract parties	Percentage of total Portuguese *Schoss*
More than 80 marks	1	4%	10%
60 to 80 marks	3	11%	24%
40 to 60 marks	4	15%	24%
20 to 40 marks	7	26%	26%
Less than 20 marks	12	44%	16%

Source: M. Grunwald (1902), pp. 35–36.[20]

We have available only one other compilation of property taxes of the Hamburg Portuguese in the seventeenth century, and that tells us about taxes paid not to the city, but to the Portuguese-Jewish community. In the year 1656 the taxes thus discharged were significantly less evenly distributed than those paid in 1616 and 1618. A few very wealthy Portuguese now stood out among their fellows. This was due to the arrival of some especially affluent New Christian bankers from Madrid and Antwerp in the 1640s. They had been protected by the Count-Duke of Olivares until his fall from power in 1643 (see chapter 1). By 1647 at the latest, when the state of Spain declared bankruptcy, they had left – some for Amsterdam and some for Hamburg – and apparently they succeeded in taking much of their fortunes with them.

Table 13: Community taxes paid by Portuguese, 1656

	Number of parties paying taxes	Percentage of parties paying taxes	Percentage of total tax revenues
More than 150 marks	2	2%	23%
100 to 150 marks	0	0%	0%
50 to 100 marks	8	7%	21%
25 to 50 marks	20	17%	27%
Less than 25 marks	86	74%	29%

Source: M. Grunwald (1902), p. 8.

Diogo Teixeira, his son Manuel, and João da Rocha Pinto were the wealthiest newcomers to Hamburg.[21] Diogo, born in Lisbon, had been active in trading in Antwerp since 1613. He settled in Hamburg in 1646 after a brief stay in Cologne. Like his son later, he was known in Hamburg as "the rich Jew." His assets were estimated at 300,000 guilders, or about 800,000 marks.[22] This was not as much as Jürgen Schröttering and the wealthiest Netherlanders were said to have owned in 1630, but within the Portuguese-Jewish community the Teixeiras were by far the most affluent. In 1656 father and son alone paid about one-third of the community taxes: Diogo 660 marks (23 percent of the total) and Manuel another 240 marks (9 percent).[23] Both Teixeiras were active as bankers and diplomats in Hamburg and provided various financial services, especially to the Portuguese government. They also conducted extensive business in weapons, copper, and iron. However, neither of them figured in the Admiralty customs books in 1647.

João da Rocha Pinto, who originally came from Porto, left Antwerp for Hamburg sometime between 1641 and 1645. He too appears to have been very wealthy, but although his name appears in the 1647 Admiralty customs books, his turnovers in the Iberia trade were relatively low.[24] Duarte Nunes da Costa, the resident of the Portuguese Crown and in fourth place in the 1656 taxation list, also paid only modest customs duties: in 1632 his total was not among the highest registered, and by 1647 it was among the lowest. Even adding the contributions of his sons Manuel and Jorge, who were also active in trade, his family's showing in the Admiralty customs books was not impressive. This indicates that by mid century affluent Portuguese were no longer engaging in regular commodity trade with the Iberian Peninsula, nor with France, the islands in the Caribbean, or the other regions for which Admiralty customs were levied at the time.

Unfortunately we do not know how exactly these affluent Portuguese invested their capital. They did not yet appear in the 1619 bank listing; the listing, however, suggests that by that time outstanding assets and outstanding turnovers tended to go together. Two of the three millionaire merchants of 1630 mentioned above, Jan de Greve and Hans de Hertoghe, were among the 10 percent of account holders with the highest turnovers. While Jürgen Schröttering, the third, was near the bottom, his son Johann was among the top 10 percent. The brothers Rudolf and Arnold Amsinck, who had the highest turnover of all account holders in 1619, were, as we have seen, known to be extremely wealthy too.

Bonds as an Indicator of Consolidated Assets

However, turnover was not the only indicator of affluence. Successful merchants often tried to consolidate some of their assets by investing them in real estate, public debt, or other bonds. Capital employed in this manner generated a regular income that could be used to buffer the family in case of economic crisis or the death of the head of the family. It also gave merchants the freedom to assume social or political positions. For citizens it opened the door to functions in the city administration; members of religious minorities were liberated for posts on their communities' boards (see chapters 7, 14, and 15). Active merchants of moderate assets who needed access to their money on short notice, or foreigners who might soon want to leave the city, were less likely to allocate their investments in such ways.

In Hamburg, aliens were excluded from owning real estate, but all inhabitants could acquire city treasury bonds (*Kammerbriefe*).[25] At the beginning of the seventeenth century, the annual interest rate for these bonds was 4½ or 5 percent; later it varied depending on the duration of the investment and the city's capital needs. The records of these bonds from 1601 to 1650 show us that the Netherlanders were again at the top: the largest lender to the city was Dominicus van Uffeln, who in 1620 alone bought three large bonds, one for 6,000 reichstalers over three years, one for 20,000 reichstalers over six years, and one for 8,000 reichstalers over one year. In 1622 he provided another loan amounting to 21,000 reichstalers. The Netherlander Jan de Greve was in second place. But only a single Portuguese appears as a lender: Duarte Peres Brandão, who in 1631 lent the city 416⅔ reichstalers over only six months. The wealthy new arrivals of the 1640s especially, whom we might have expected to look for investments outside of commodity trade, did not act as lenders to the city, at least up to 1650.

Most of the city bonds, however, were acquired by long-established citizens of Hamburg, frequently on behalf of their wives and sometimes of their children. A list for the year 1645 includes all the bonds owned at that time. And most of the owners either were not merchants at all, or were no longer active in trade.

At the top of the list was the lawyer Vincent Moller, with 53,200 marks. The sons of Ditmar Koel and several members of the Sillem and Spreckelsen families also had large investments in bonds. Prominent in the Iberia trade at the beginning of the century, by 1632 and 1647 these families no longer figured importantly in the Admiralty customs books.[26] Nor do other old City Council families with large numbers of bonds (such as the Mündens, vom Holtes, von der Fechtes, Scheles, Langermanns, Langenbecks, and Schaffshausens) seem to have been playing a significant role in trade by mid-seventeenth century.[27] The only exception was Johann Schröttering, the son of Jürgen (by then deceased). He was in second place, holding city bonds amounting to 33,600 marks. Schröttering was very active in commodity trading by this time, especially with Portugal. By keeping at least part of his capital out of commercial circulation and investing it in bonds he may have been paving the way for his withdrawal from active trading; in 1638 he had become a member of the City Council, and in 1667 would be elected mayor.

Representative Lifestyles in Hamburg

Even when they were extraordinarily large, the assets of long-established Hamburgers tended to draw less attention than those of the Netherlanders and Portuguese. People were not greatly surprised that the leading Hamburg families had accumulated fortunes over the generations. Wealthy foreigners – especially Jews – with their unfamiliar lifestyles were more remarkable to many observers. Like the Hamburgers, foreigners wished to assure other merchants of their creditworthiness by flaunting their affluence. And in most cases their lifestyles reflected their circumstances honestly, because sound business dealings required that all participants represent their financial capacities accurately. Those who lived above their means could count on unpleasant legal and social consequences in the case of bankruptcy, or if misleading financial characterizations led a colleague into trouble.

The Netherlanders in Hamburg were renowned for their extravagance; Netherlandish weddings were the epitome of ostentatious display.[28] The 1601 marriage of Rudolf Amsinck and Isabeau de Hertoghe, the daughter of Cornelis de Hertoghe, was celebrated with 200 guests over three whole days of the most exquisite feasts.[29] Rudolf and Arnold Amsinck owned several rural properties in Billwerder and in Curslack, near Hamburg. The Netherlander Dominicus van Uffeln (1545–1623) also lived very luxuriously.[30] In addition to a townhouse in the Kleine Reichenstraße, he owned an estate in the Duchy of Lauenburg, and the family acquired a country and summer residence in Billwerder. In 1631 his heirs commemorated him by donating a magnificent pulpit of white and black marble to the Church of St. Catherine, which a French legation secretary described in 1636 as the most beautiful that he had ever seen.[31] Dominicus van Uffeln's son, another Dominicus (1584–1656), acquired two other estates in addition to the one he inherited: one of them also located in the Duchy of Lauenburg, and the other in Mecklenburg. In 1645 Dominicus and his brother Jan offered the Danish king a loan of 200,000 to 300,000 reichstalers, to be forthcoming within five weeks, and then another 300,000 reichstalers within the next six months, with the island of Iceland pledged as security. This particular deal, however, was never consummated.[32] Another brother, Peter, owned two estates and parochial villages (that is, villages with their own permanent pastors) near Hamburg; he also bought two islands in the Elbe, Veddel and Grevenhof (today parts of Steinwerder).

The homes of the Netherlandish merchants were often extremely sumptuous; the Portugal trader Jan de l'Homel had his house decorated with ceiling paintings, perspective depictions, and grotesqueries by the Netherlandish painter and architect Hans Vredeman de Vries.[33] After all, they often entertained important guests. Cosimo de' Medici, the hereditary prince of the Grand Duchy of Tuscany, for example, stayed in the home of Johann Baptista Vrients in 1668, while those who accompanied him were housed by the merchants Arnold Beltgens and Philipp Verpoorten, who were related to Vrients and were also de' Medici's Hamburg bankers. In his report, the prince wrote that he had found all possible comforts. He specified that Beltgens and Verpoorten had placed their coaches at his disposal and presented him with some prized Portuguese oranges.[34]

For the Portuguese Jews it was even more important to project a clear picture of their circumstances, because it ensured respect in an environment that was largely hostile to them. The German Jews in Hamburg were generally poor, but affluent Portuguese Jews lived in magnificent homes, wore rich attire, traveled in coaches, and associated with the elite of Christian society.[35] This conduct, which was extraordinary for Jews in the Holy Roman Empire, attracted astonishment from the rest of the population, but also a certain amount of resentment and jealousy. The Portuguese Jews were repeatedly accused of excessive luxury in the polemics of Lutheran pastors; in 1650, the City Council admonished them to limit themselves, and behave in accordance with the general sumptuary and luxury regulations. The board of the Portuguese-Jewish community, aware of the sentiments in the city, repeatedly counseled restraint in clothing and celebration. But although these appeals convey the impression of excessive ostentation, their significance should not be overrated; the City Council directed the very same admonishments at the rest of the population.

The Teixeiras in particular cultivated a sumptuous lifestyle. Johann Balthasar Schupp, who arrived in Hamburg in 1649 to assume a post as pastor there, wrote a vivid account of the impression that Diogo Teixeira made on him the first time they met. He was,

> driven in a beautiful coach lined with satin. A servant in livery ran next to the coach. And when the coachman stopped, the servant, who as I hear was a Kristian, opened the coach with deep reverence and lifted an elderly man in a long silk robe out of it. I thought it must surely be the bishop or an ancient prince or count. I doffed my hat [and bowed] as low as if it had been for the Elector of Saxony, and asked a woman who this man was. The honest, pious woman answered with a smile: "He is a Jew; the one called 'the rich Jew.'" I could not have been more astonished.[36]

And the theologian Johann Jacob Schudt, who lived in Hamburg for a time, wrote about Diogo Teixeira's son:

> The so-called rich Jew Manuel Teixeira, who back in my time in 1684 and in subsequent years lived [in Hamburg], was the resident of Queen Kristina of Sweden, rode in a sumptuous carriage, behind and in front of which several and generally Christian servants stood, who served him with great reverence when he stepped in and out, and when he rode across Great New Market [Großneumarkt], the entire armed watch stood at attention. He resided in a splendid palace, and important gentlemen visited and played with him.[37]

Among his guests was Kristina after her 1654 abdication; in the early 1660s she repeatedly spent several weeks with the Teixeiras at their home on the Krayenkamp.[38] Others, too, praised their hospitality; in 1687, the Italian scholar Gregorio Leti published a report in which he wrote, "Resident Teixeira does great credit to the city, because he makes efforts to honor and flatter foreigners, and to treat the citizens of the city with great care and love, so that his magnificent house seems like a theater and an inn of courtesy."[39]

He was not alone among the Portuguese living luxuriously. Duarte Nunes da Costa, the resident of the Portuguese Crown (see chapter 4), also lived in a magnificent house on the Krayenkamp, which the German-Danish writer Conrad von Höveln characterized in his description of the city as an "earthly paradise."[40] In 1646 João da Rocha Pinto moved into a well-appointed house in the Wallstraße, next door to the de Hertoghes. A fountain, an aviary, and a summer house adorned his garden. He also owned a collection of paintings.[41] At least for a time, Rocha Pinto owned an estate in Herzhorn near Glückstadt.

From the very beginning, the Portuguese lived in ample homes in the center of the city.[42] Their households often included African servants or slaves. In 1612 "two Moors who were married to each other" lived in Miguel Dias's house.[43] The founder of the Portuguese-Jewish community, Álvaro Dinis, had a black employee or slave by the name of Filipa, and Paulo de Milão, one of Henrique Dias Milão's sons, took one with him to Danzig.[44] In 1680 Moisés Josua Henriques had at least four African slaves, and he recalled that his parents, who had lived in Glückstadt since the founding of the town in 1617, "had had Moors, [and] used them in their service or as needed."[45] Because Africans living in northern Germany have been almost completely ignored in the research on this area, it is not known whether Portuguese merchants alone had black employees or slaves, or whether Netherlanders and Hamburgers did as well. In Portuguese homes, they were fully integrated into the households, and usually practiced the same religion as their masters. If they were slaves, they were often freed when their masters died, in all probability becoming part of the growing marginalized underclass of the Portuguese-Jewish community which was dependent on the wealthy members and on religious charities (see chapter 14).

The lifestyles of the wealthy old Hamburg families and of the merchants drawn to the city from the surrounding region, were not by any means modest either, but as I have said, they evoked less astonishment. In 1668 von Höveln reported that "grand houses of gentlemen and distinguished citizens, mostly built in the new or Hollandish style, are abundant in Hamburg; they are outfitted inside with rooms plentiful and most comfortable, in which pictures, paintings, carvings, stonework table ornaments [*Tafelfloren*], candelabra, chandeliers, etc., may be seen."[46] In 1617 Jürgen Schröttering had a building constructed at Große Reichenstraße 49, known as the Red House, whose magnificent portal was built in the latest Netherlandish style and is today on display in the Museum of Hamburg History.[47] Conrad von Höveln also commented on the country homes outside the city: "Hardly a city in Germany can equal the multiplicity of beautiful pleasure gardens in Hamburg."[48] And the use of a coach, which drew so much attention to Teixeira, was anything but rare:

> Not only on Sundays and holidays, but daily during the spring, summer, and merry autumn days, one sees hundreds of carriages coming in during the evening, some from Altona, some from the Steintor [the main eastern gate], and these carriages are occupied by elegant and well-attired persons, who have been cavorting in the pleasure gardens in Hamm, Billwerder, Ottensen, Neumühlen, etc.[49]

And the Italian diplomat Galeazzo Gualdo Priorato, who traveled to Hamburg in 1663, had the following to say about the outskirts:

> Continuing on the way to Bergedorf one sees many charming small palaces, country houses, and pavilions with floral and fruit gardens, avenues, and sights so delightful that one would think one was viewing a play or a painting. The inhabitants of Hamburg of all classes, men and women, frequently ride out in coaches to these charming places for pleasure, in unbelievable numbers during the good season, especially on holidays. Not far from the Dammtor [the main northern gate] lies the village of Eppendorf, where there are also many houses and pleasure gardens.[50]

There were annual family celebrations, such as the so-called *Pfingsthöge* (Pentecost treat) thrown by the von Spreckelsens, during which several dozen family members were feasted for two full days, and although "all kinds of gorging or splurging, even all kinds of venison" were "strictly excluded from the statutory menu," dishes like oxmeat in mustard, veal, all manner of cold meat dishes, boiled salmon, fried foods, egg pudding with milk, butter, cheese, *Trundelkuchen* (a kind of cake or pie), sweet milk, and rice pudding with cinnamon and sugar were served up in abundance.[51] Johann Balthasar Schupp said of the hospitality of the Hamburgers in 1648:

> I spent time in the houses of many a citizen and saw such beautifully outfitted rooms, in which everything shone, in which so many beautiful artistic paintings hung, that my eyes could not get enough of them. I saw that private people held banquets and feastings and served up such delicacies, so many confections, such as I have hardly seen in princely courts when the children of princes are baptized or similar solemnities are held.[52]

But despite the magnificence described by these contemporaries, other observers asserted that Hamburgers avoided ostentatious display and cultivated simplicity. In 1663 the poet and scholar Christian Knorr von Rosenroth wrote about Hamburg:

> The sumptuary and luxury laws are mainly observed. And it is not permitted for a man or a woman of the people to wear their clothes decorated with gold or silver bands, or to wear a diamond ring. When the women appear in public, they mostly cover themselves with veils and black cowls, and in addition they wrap themselves in a black cloth (which they call rainwear), which serves as a coat. Ostentation is mostly absent at weddings, funerals, and baptisms. And thus life is in many ways adapted to the customs of the Hollanders, in accordance with trade, which prefers cash over jewelry and excessive expense, and so tends more to greed than to recklessness.[53]

This last quotation especially shows just how varied, subjective, and probably influenced by external factors were observers' impressions of, and ideas about, the lifestyles of merchants. They can give us but a very sketchy picture of the ways of life of foreigners and of locals.

Representative Lifestyles in Portugal

There are no statistically analyzable lists of turnovers, taxes, or assets for Portugal in general, or for Lisbon in particular, that compare to the material available for Hamburg. Nor are there such vivid accounts of the habits of the merchants in Portugal in the seventeenth century. According to historian Jorge Miguel Pedreira, who, it should be noted, concentrated his study on the eighteenth century, Lisbon merchants were exceptionally wealthy by international standards, although they did not necessarily make their wealth evident in displays of magnificence.[54] A grand house in Lisbon and a country residence (*quinta*), a coach with a mule team, and three or four servants would have sufficed to declare the social position of a successful merchant. Objects made of gold and silver, furnishings, clothing, household textiles, tableware, clocks, paintings, and other art objects might have given some additional clues to a merchant's financial status. But very wealthy merchants and well-to-do ones would have had very similar lifestyles. If any conclusion is admissible on such sparse information, it would seem that Lisbon's ways were not very different from Hamburg's.

Like the merchants who left Antwerp for Amsterdam, but unlike the better-established Netherlanders and Portuguese who went to Hamburg, most of the Hamburgers in Portugal arrived there without property. They were young, in training, and intent on laying the financial groundwork for later businesses. As shown in chapter 7, many of them were quite successful in that venture. The files of the Inquisition give a sense of the businesses, the stored merchandise, and the home furnishings of the few Hamburgers who were put on trial in Portugal. One of them was the merchant João da Maya. He had lived in Lisbon for thirteen years when his trial began.[55] According to his statement, the storeroom under his living quarters contained eleven or twelve crates of muscovado sugar and one of white sugar. In addition, he said, there were 53 rolls of tobacco, and 23 sacks plus 216 bundles of canvas. A closet in one of the upper stories contained about 300 knives and 9,000 or 10,000 small clay pots for smelting silver and gold, as well as four barrels of fishes' swim bladders (*grude de peixe*). In the desk were accounting books, in which were noted outstanding debts (his own and others'), mainly pertaining to goods he owned in Hamburg. He also possessed eleven large paintings of battle scenes, a sideboard with two drawers made of precious wood, a table with six chairs, six taborets covered in red calf leather with small metal fittings, and a medium-sized crate from India without drawers. Finally he listed a pinewood desk, a simple ebony bed without curtains, and a cashbox containing approximately 100,000 reis in coin. These furnishings were perhaps somewhat simpler than those Pedreira described as typical of a wealthy merchant in the eighteenth century. Nonetheless, they can be considered comfortable.

We do not have exact figures on the merchants' assets, and verbal descriptions tend to be biased. There are accounts highlighting the prosperity, if not magnificence, of the manners and homes of all three of the merchant groups studied in this book. But it is worth underlining that the wealth of the Portuguese Jews was very much noticed even though – with the exception of Diogo and Manuel Teixeira – they were not the most affluent of the merchants. These were Netherlanders, along with some newcomers from the regional surrounds like the Schrötterings, and some long-established Hamburgers.

9 Grain, Sugar, Wax, and Tobacco

Having presented the total trading turnovers and assets of the merchants, I will now consider the goods they traded, their specializations, and the ports where they exchanged their wares. To this end I analyze the customs books of the Hamburg Admiralty in light of the alien laws discussed in chapter 2. This analysis confirms the supposition made there that non-citizen Netherlanders and Portuguese were poorly represented as dealers in goods that were banned from direct trade between aliens. I also use the Admiralty customs books to challenge some claims prevalent in the research literature as to the most important commodities of the specific groups of merchants: that the Portuguese Jews dominated the sugar and spice trade, and that long-established Hamburgers were overrepresented in traditional Hamburg goods.

The Source

The foothold of quantitative methods in German-language historical scholarship has always been precarious.[1] This is exemplified by the work of Hermann Kellenbenz, who postulated the dominance of the Portuguese Jews in the Hamburg sugar and spice trade,[2] but eschewed rigorous statistical testing of his hypothesis.[3] Hamburg sources are plentiful, yet he failed to analyze them properly. He limited himself to excerpts from the *Werkzoll* registers for the years 1608/1609 and 1609/1610 that reflect only the trade of the Portuguese, and on that basis maintained that no conclusions could be drawn about how the scope of their business dealings compared with that of the local and Netherlandish merchants.[4] Yet the Portuguese share of overall trade may be calculated without difficulty based on the total revenues from the *Werkzoll* for the two years in question; in 1608/1609, their share was 3.3 percent, and in 1609/1610, 2.5 percent.[5] The only document he used to contrast the Portuguese with other merchants was a list from the year 1612 of "goods imported from Lisbon and other western ports, including those on the Mediterranean"; he cited this as evidence of the Portuguese Jews' "strong participation" in the sugar trade in Hamburg, even though it ignored exports altogether, and registered as imports only the wares of alien merchants, and not of citizens.[6]

There exists, however, a uniquely informative source on seventeenth-century trade, namely the Hamburg Admiralty customs books, of which Kellenbenz took no notice at all. The books log a duty introduced in 1623 to finance the Admiralty, which was responsible for safeguarding the city's shipping and trade (see chapter 13). It was levied on all goods imported to Hamburg from Spain, Portugal, and a few other regions, or exported from Hamburg to those places.[7] The scribes who worked in the customs

https://doi.org/10.1515/9783110472103-010

station in the city hall, mostly merchants themselves, compared the bills of each merchant's goods (made out by the shipmaster and submitted by the merchant or a representative) with the list submitted to the station by the officer at the *Niederbaum*, a floating customs barrier at the entrance of the inner harbor. If the figures were in agreement, the scribe collected the calculated duty and recorded the contents of the merchant's bills in the customs books.[8] Extant seventeenth-century records include the years 1632 through 1638, 1645, and 1647.[9] The ports of origin and destination of the ships and of their goods were recorded in a second series of customs books, which (with some interruptions) have survived for the years 1623 through 1651.[10] Together, these two series of books allow us to determine in detail which merchants shipped or received what goods to or from which ports on the Iberian Peninsula.

From the entries I developed a database into which I entered all the data from two complete customs years.[11] The database contains more than 6,200 units of merchandise, declared in about 4,000 customs procedures by 749 different merchants or trading companies over the course of 340 voyages. I then analyzed the data. Explanations of the calculations, and some notes on error estimation are compiled in the appendix. There I also discuss issues related to the assignment of nation, religious affiliation, and legal status to the merchants, which relies on information taken from other sources.

The analyzed data pertain to the first and the last full years of the seventeenth century for which we have complete customs books, namely the periods from April 1632 to April 1633 and from February 1647 to February 1648. During that first year, Portugal was part of the Spanish empire, and trade between the Iberian Peninsula and the United Provinces was officially banned. As a result, Hamburg functioned as a neutral alternative port for the Dutch merchants. By the second year, 1647, Portugal had regained its independence from Spain, and Hamburg had lost its intermediary position in the trade of the northern Netherlanders. Moreover, the Dutch had conquered northeastern Brazil and established trading settlements along the African and Asian coasts. This gave the United Provinces independent access to colonial wares, so that they could now compete much more directly with Portugal. In other words, very different trading conditions prevailed during the two analyzed years. This, and the fact that a decade and a half separates the two sets of data, enables us to draw certain conclusions about the development of trade during the first half of the seventeenth century.

It must be borne in mind, however, that the turnover of goods in the port of Hamburg reflects only part of the Hamburgers' total involvement in the Iberia trade. Some merchant ships were organized and financed by Hamburg merchants, but did not dock in Hamburg and so paid no duties there, sailing for instance directly between the Baltic Sea and the Iberian Peninsula. These voyages, of course, are not recorded in the Admiralty customs books.[12]

The Alien Merchants' Share of Trade

In both these years, 1632 and 1647, the Hamburg-based Netherlanders and Portuguese Jews together accounted for something more than half of all turnover in the trade between Hamburg and the Iberian Peninsula. The Netherlanders, whom I discuss first, were clearly in the stronger position. In 1632 their share of the Spain trade was 49.6 percent, and of the Portugal trade 30.2 percent. In 1647 their share of the Spain trade was 41.4 percent and of the Portugal trade 22.6 percent. Their absolute turnover in the Spain trade was approximately triple that of their Portugal trade in both years, and their per capita turnover in the trade with the Iberian Peninsula was 20,030 marks. The Netherlanders who were members of an alien contract (and thus not citizens) had a slightly higher turnover (23,210 marks). We should not, however, draw hasty conclusions about possible connections between business success and legal status. As I showed in chapter 8, there was no significant difference in the overall Hamburg trade between Netherlandish citizens and Netherlandish aliens.

Table 14: Turnovers in the Iberia trade by nation

		Turnovers in Iberia trade		Turnovers in Portugal trade		Turnovers in Spain trade	
		Absolute	Percentage	Absolute	Percentage	Absolute	Percentage
Hamburgers	1632	696,167	18.8%	244,235	18.5%	451,932	19.0%
	1647	825,773	21.8%	281,968	17.8%	543,805	24.6%
Regional immigrants	1632	517,115	14.0%	245,851	18.7%	271,264	11.4%
	1647	359,798	9.5%	173,513	10.9%	186,286	8.4%
Netherlanders	1632	1,578,717	42.7%	398,189	30.2%	1,180,529	49.6%
	1647	1,275,322	33.6%	360,785	22.7%	914,538	41.4%
Portuguese	1632	569,279	15.4%	309,955	23.5%	259,324	10.9%
	1647	680,161	17.9%	499,223	31.5%	180,938	8.2%
Partnerships of different nations	1632	118,687	3.2%	2,250	0.2%	116,437	4.9%
	1647	0	0%	0	0%	0	0%
Origin unknown	1632	201,858	5.5%	103,052	7.8%	98,806	4.2%
	1647	635,553	16.7%	268,638	16.9%	366,914	16.6%
Total[13]	1632	3,696,517		1,317,081		2,379,436	
	1647	3,796,664		1,586,827		2,209,837	

Source: StAHH, Admiralitätskollegium, F3, Band 1, 2, and 8; F4, Band 8, 14, and 15 (see appendix).

Table 15: Per capita turnovers in the Iberia trade by nation

		Number of merchants in Iberia trade	Per capita turnovers in Iberia trade[14]	Number of merchants in Portugal trade	Per capita turnovers in Portugal trade	Number of merchants in Spain trade	Per capita turnovers in Spain trade
Hamburgers	1632	53	13,135	37	6,601	37	12,214
	1647	60	13,763	33	8,544	42	12,948
Regional immigrants	1632	60	8,619	30	8,195	38	7,139
	1647	27	13,326	13	13,347	20	9,314
Netherlanders	1632	81	19,490	46	8,656	66	17,887
	1647	62	20,570	35	10,308	53	17,255
Portuguese	1632	57	9,987	47	6,595	39	6,649
	1647	43	15,818	35	14,264	19	9,523
Partnerships of different nations	1632	5	23,737	1	2,250	5	23,287
	1647	0	0	0	0	0	0
Origin unknown	1632	68	2,969	36	2,863	39	2,533
	1647	138	4,605	69	3,893	96	3,822
Total[15]	1632	326	11,339	198	6,652	226	10,528
	1647	338	11,233	186	8,531	237	9,324

Source: StAHH, Admiralitätskollegium, F3, Band 1, 2, and 8; F4, Band 8, 14, and 15 (see appendix).

While the share of the Netherlanders in the Iberia trade was lower than their share in the overall Hamburg trade (47.3 percent in 1619), the share of the Portuguese in the Iberia trade was considerably more than their share in the overall trade (4.5 percent in 1619) (see table 7). In 1632 their share in the Portugal trade was 23.5 percent, and in the Spain trade 10.9 percent. In 1647 their share in the Portugal trade was 31.4 percent; their share in the Spain trade was 8.2 percent. In absolute terms, in 1632 their turnovers in the Spain and Portugal trades were approximately equal; in 1647, however, their turnover in the Portugal trade was more than triple that in the Spain trade. In contrast to the Netherlanders, their share in the Iberia trade increased between 1632 and 1647, although the number of merchants involved decreased. In 1632 their per capita turnover in the Portugal trade had been the lowest among all the merchant groups; by 1647 it had more than doubled, and become the highest.

If we separate the merchants by religion, the average per capita turnover for the Portuguese Jews (12,878 marks) in trade with the Iberian Peninsula was about the same as that of the Reformed Netherlanders (12,626 marks), but lower than that of the Lutheran Netherlanders (14,227 marks).[16] Analysis of the Admiralty customs books therefore offers no support for the contention that either the Jews or the Reformed possessed greater business acumen than other merchants.

The Grain Trade

In 1632 grain was by far the most important commodity in the trade between Hamburg and Portugal, comprising almost half of the total turnover (46.6 percent). In 1647 its share had fallen to second place with 22.5 percent of total turnover, due to the substantial rise in sugar imports. Grain was one of the commodities in which direct trade between aliens was forbidden (see chapter 2). This did not mean that aliens were completely excluded from the grain trade; it meant only that they were not permitted to buy grain directly from producers or suppliers who did not have citizen rights in Hamburg. They were forced to use citizen middlemen if they wanted to acquire grain for export. As mentioned in chapter 3, this rule was loosened in 1615 for the Netherlanders under the alien contract. From then on they were permitted to trade in grain from the lower course of the Elbe without restrictions.

The consequences of the ban are seen clearly in the merchants' turnover figures. In 1632 two-thirds of the grain trade was handled by citizens (68.1 percent), and just under one-fifth by contract Netherlanders (18.1 percent). In 1647 the proportion controlled by Hamburg citizens was even higher; about three-quarters (75.8 percent) of the grain trade was now in their hands. This does not mean, however, that this trade was held by the old Hamburg families. In 1632 Netherlanders, both citizen and alien (35.3 percent), and merchants who had immigrated into the city from the surrounding region (35.1 percent) each accounted for a little more than a third of grain imports; the long-established Hamburgers, by contrast, accounted for only about a sixth (16.3 percent). The share taken by the Portuguese (7.3 percent) was even lower. In 1647 the regional immigrants were in first place (36.3 percent), followed by the Netherlanders (29.3 percent), the old Hamburgers (19.1 percent), and the Portuguese (12.6 percent). In other words, the grain trade was dominated by *new* citizens, and presumably one of the factors driving immigration into Hamburg from its surrounds was the desire of merchants to export grain from their home regions through the city, to which end they adopted citizen status there.

The Wine Trade

Although Hamburg seems to have imported no wine from Portugal during the first half of the seventeenth century, it did import a significant amount from Spain. In 1632 wine accounted for about a quarter (26.8 percent) of overall imports from Spain; in 1647 it made up more than half (54.7 percent). It was the other important commodity in the Iberia trade in which direct trade between aliens was completely banned.[17] As was to be expected, citizens predominated in this trade; the share of wine imports controlled by citizens in 1632 was 59.2 percent, and in 1647, 73.8 percent. Here again the established Hamburgers were not a dominant force; in 1632 their share of the wine trade was 15 percent, in 1647, 38 percent. By contrast, the Netherlanders imported 40.6 percent of the wine in 1632, and those who had immigrated from the region around Hamburg, 18.3 percent. In 1647 the Netherlanders accounted for 31.9 percent of wine imports; those who had immigrated from the surrounds 8.1 percent. In both years, the Portuguese were involved in only about 1 percent of the wine trade. The distribution of turnovers in the grain and wine trades shows that the alien laws were enforced in both, and that aliens were markedly disadvantaged in the Iberia trade.

The Sugar Trade

Sugar was another major commodity. In 1632 its share of the total turnover in the Hamburg-Portugal trade was only 10 percent; in 1647, however, that figure was 25 percent. Unlike the grain and wine trades, sugar was open to all merchants regardless of legal status. So it is hardly surprising that the Portuguese, who were disadvantaged in the trading of grain and wine, were in first place in the sugar trade, with about 40 percent of imports both in 1632 (41.3 percent) and in 1647 (39.3 percent). They did not dominate the trade, however, as is often claimed – at least not if "dominate" means to control half or more of it. In 1632 the Netherlanders were in second place (23 percent), followed closely by the Hamburgers (21.4 percent). In 1647 the Hamburgers (21.6 percent) were in second place, and the Netherlanders (16.2 percent) in third. The regional immigrants were significantly underrepresented; in 1632 their share was only 5.2 percent, and in 1647, 6.2 percent. They had probably not yet been able to build the requisite connections in Portugal.

The Spice Trade

Trade in spices made up 11.3 percent of total turnover in 1632, but dropped to an insignificant 3.1 percent in 1647. This was a category in which the Portuguese actually held a slight absolute majority in 1632. Their share of the total trade was 51.8 percent, followed by the Netherlanders (29.2 percent) and then the Hamburgers (7.1 percent). Other immigrants to the city were not involved in this trade. The list of spices imported included pepper, cinnamon, cardamom, galangal, cumin, turmeric, saffron, and some unidentifiables categorized only as "drugs." But not all spices were traded by all nations in the same proportions. In 1632 the Portuguese were hardly involved in trading pepper, which was dominated by the Netherlanders (50.8 percent). There is thus no evidence for the oft-cited "monopoly position" of the Portuguese Jews in the Hamburg pepper trade.[18] Ginger represents a curious special case. More than 90 percent of it came from Spain, while the other spices listed above were imported from Portugal. In 1632 ginger comprised 11 percent of total imports (more than sugar!); about half of it (52 percent) was imported by Netherlanders and 24 percent by Hamburgers. In 1647 its share of total imports was less than 1 percent.

Trade Conducted by the Portuguese Jews

The Portuguese share of the sugar and spice trades was significant, though not as great as Kellenbenz and others have claimed. Yet these commodities were not their most important goods in trade, at least not in 1632. Rather, it was wax and cloth that held first place that year. These commodities comprised 15.1 percent and 14.5 percent respectively of the Portuguese merchants' turnover, followed by spices at 11.9 percent and sugar at 9.9 percent. The Portuguese also exported grain (7.8 percent), weapons and munitions (4 percent), metalwares (3.7 percent), and metals (3.1 percent), while importing fruits and preserves (6.9 percent), olive oil (3.2 percent), and dyes (1.5 percent). Their balance of trade was near equal, with the total value of exports (56.4 percent) only slightly greater than that of imports. In 1647, sugar did indeed rank first; it represented a good fifth (23 percent) of the commodities traded by the Portuguese. But it was followed closely by exports of grain (19.6 percent), cloth (12.7 percent), metals (7.7 percent), weapons and munitions (6.1 percent), wax (5.4 percent), metalwares (2.3 percent), and hemp and flax (2.1 percent). Imports included spices (2.8 percent), tobacco (2.8 percent), and olive oil (1.1 percent). That year, exports (67.1 percent) considerably exceeded imports (32.9 percent).[19]

The Portuguese in Hamburg traded in a wide variety of commodities and goods. The highest percentage of Portuguese commercial activity involved goods that were defined in the *Schragen* of 1604 as freely tradable by aliens: namely sugar, spices, wax, and cloth. Nonetheless, grain, which came under the alien trade ban, played a considerable role too, at least in 1647, when it comprised 20 percent of their total turnover. Either the Portuguese, like the Netherlanders, had been permitted by then to trade freely in grain grown downriver from Hamburg (a possibility for which I have no evidence), or they paid the necessary surcharge to citizen middlemen. Munitions, metals, and metalwares, on the other hand, belonged to the second category; that is, the Portuguese had to make use of the services of a citizen factor or commission agent to trade in these wares (see chapter 2).

Trade Conducted by the Netherlanders

The Netherlanders, too, traded in a wide assortment of goods. In 1632 their trade with the Iberian Peninsula consisted of dyes (17.6 percent), wax (15 percent), grain (13.8 percent), wine and brandy (10 percent), spices (9.5 percent), cloth (7.8 percent) and other commodities. If we compare this with the trade conducted by the contract Netherlanders (that is, those who had no citizen status) alone, we see that the contract merchants account for a larger share of the goods open to the alien trade, and a lesser share of the goods excluded from it: the share of dyes traded by the contract Netherlanders was 25.2 percent, of wax 17.4 percent, and of spices 10.3 percent, while that of grain was only 12.4 percent. In 1647 non-specified goods held the top place in export share among all Netherlanders (19 percent).[20] Wax was a close second (18.7 percent); it now made up 30 percent of the commodities traded by the Netherlanders covered by contract, and it was followed at some distance by commodities banned for alien trade, namely grain (overall 9.5 percent, contract 7 percent) as well as wine and brandy (overall 8.9 percent, contract 3.1 percent). While the balance of trade was almost equal in 1632, in 1647 exports (72.3 percent) clearly exceeded imports in the Netherlanders' trade, even more than they did among the Portuguese.

Trade Conducted by the Hamburgers

Some scholars have argued that the local merchants wanted to retain control of the commodities in which they had traditionally dealt.[21] In Hamburg, these included grain, wine, and wax. However, the statistics show that the share of trade of the long-established Hamburg merchants in these commodities was not extraordinarily high. In 1632 they accounted for only 16 percent of the grain trade. Netherlanders and immigrants from surrounding regions played a much larger role, with about 35 percent each. In 1647 the Hamburgers controlled 28 percent. There was a similar pattern in the wine trade; in 1632 the established Hamburgers controlled only 15 percent of wine imports from the Iberian Peninsula, the new immigrants 18 percent, and the Netherlanders more than 40 percent. In 1647 the Hamburgers had a somewhat higher share in the wine trade, with 38 percent. In the wax trade too, the share of the established Hamburgers was not especially large in 1632; the Netherlanders dominated the trade with a 60 percent share, and the Portuguese controlled 22 percent. In 1647 the Hamburgers' share of the wax trade was a mere 8 percent, while that of the Netherlanders was 73 percent.

Of all the goods traded by the established Hamburg merchants, none that held first place in 1632 belonged to their palette of traditional commodities. Their trade was led instead by dyes and dyestuffs from the overseas regions. These included especially indigo (originally from Central America), sumac (from Africa, used for tanning and dyeing), St. Martin's wood (a red wood from the Antilles), campeachy wood (a blue wood from Central America), and brazilwood (a red wood from Brazil). They were used in Hamburg in the burgeoning production of textiles. Dyes and dyestuffs made up 17 percent of the turnover of the Hamburgers, and grain only 15 percent. The Hamburgers were by no means the conservative traders that portrayals of them frequently suggest. In fact, in 1632 they dominated the sumac imports, which came exclusively from Portugal, with 51 percent. In 1647 the picture was fundamentally different, however. Grain was now the undisputed leader in the Hamburgers' trade, at 21 percent of their turnover, followed by wine at 15 percent, and sugar at 10 percent. Dyes were down to 4 percent.

Specialization in Particular Commodities

Unlike other historians, Daniel Swetschinski assumes no link between particular commodities and merchant nations; he argues that specialization did not exist in long-distance trade during the early modern period.[22] According to him, any commodities that were bought or sold along a certain route were traded by all merchants active along this route. But as I have shown, the trade between Hamburg and Portugal was distorted by Hamburg's alien laws, with the effect that groups tended to focus on different commodities according to their legal status. Both Swetschinski's claim and the common counterclaim (asserting a connection between specific goods and specific nations) can be shown even more clearly to be false when we study individual merchants.

For instance, the Netherlandish merchant Antoni Lapistraet, who in 1632 held tenth place in turnover in the Iberia trade, booked 98 percent of his turnover in wax. The Portuguese Diogo Nunes Veiga, who in 1632 was seventeenth among the leading merchants, obtained 76 percent of his turnover from the wax trade. In the same year, the Netherlandish Dominicus & Jan van Uffeln Company, which was ninth in total turnover in the Iberia trade, dealt exclusively in indigo. Pieter Heusch, whose total turnover was almost as large, had a product palette consisting nearly exclusively of wheat (36 percent), rye (31 percent), and beans (18 percent). All of these merchants were significantly specialized (in that year, at least), and active only in one direction; that is, either from north to south or from south to north. Other merchants traded in both directions, but limited themselves to one main product each way. The Portuguese Manuel de Pina, for instance, derived 65 percent of his turnover from "drugs" and 12 percent from wax. Fifty percent of the turnover of the António & Diogo Saraiva Coronel Company was from wax and 19 percent from raisins; the Hamburger Gerd Burmester derived 72 percent from wheat and 16 percent from wine.

There were, however, also merchants who diversified more broadly. The one with the highest turnover in the Iberia trade in 1632, the Netherlander Ludwig von Dagen, had the following palette of goods:

Tobacco	25%
Miscellaneous merchandise	18%
(*Kaufmannschaft*)	
Rigging	10%
Tallow	7%
Wine	5%
Oil	4%
Buckram	4%
Wax	4%
Tar	2%
Sugar	2%
Lead	2%
Powder	2%
Raisins	2%
Copper	2%
Other	12%

Johann Schröttering, whose turnover in 1632 was in fifth place among merchants in the Iberia trade, also dealt in a very broad, though altogether different, array of goods.

Sumac	19%
Wheat	14%
Ginger	13%
Sugar	12%
Pepper	5%

Rice	5%
Oil	3%
Rye	2%
Flax	2%
Drugs	2%
Lemons	2%
Other	21%

In 1647 product specializations were no longer as pronounced as in 1632. Only among the grain dealers were there still merchants who dealt almost exclusively in a single branch of trade. Wilken Wrede, who was third in total turnover, derived 36 percent from wheat, 31 percent from rye, and 11 percent from barley. For Claus Martens, who was in tenth place, turnover consisted of 50 percent wheat and 27 percent rye. Daniel Schloier's heirs, in eleventh place, derived 47 percent from wheat, 18 percent from barley, and 11 percent from rye. But in 1647 there were also many merchants with well-diversified palettes of goods. The Netherlander Adrian Juncker, who was in first place in turnover that year, dealt in the following commodities:

Wheat	16%
Wax	14%
Rye	12%
Sugar	11%
Sumac	8%
Iron	6%
Beans	5%
Powder	4%
Steel	4%
Copper	4%
Hemp	3%
Cloth	2%
Barrel staves	2%
Tobacco	2%
Other	7%

The Portuguese Jew Manuel Rodrigues Isidro, who was in fifth place in 1647 in total turnover in the Iberia trade, also dealt in a wide array of commodities:

Sugar	25%
Steel	8%

Cinnamon	6%
Powder	6%
Sumac	5%
Buckram	4%
Household goods	3%
Pepper	3%
Cloth	3%
Tobacco	3%
Barrel staves	2%
Wool	2%
Ginger	2%
Oil	2%
Iron	2%
Tar	2%
Wine	2%
Other	20%

If we define as specialized a merchant who had a turnover of more than 2,500 marks per year (as was true of about half of the merchants in the Iberia trade in 1632 and 1647) and either derived 75 percent of his turnover from one type of commodity or 80 percent from two types, then 17 percent of the merchants may be classified as specialized in 1632 and 10 percent in 1647. However, no association whatsoever can be discerned between the nations they belonged to and the particular commodities in which they specialized.

Table 16: Specialized merchants

	1632		1647	
Hamburgers	8	15.1%	3	5.0%
Regional immigrants	2	3.3%	3	11.1%
Netherlanders	10	12.4%	4	6.5%
Portuguese	7	12.3%	3	7.0%
Origin unknown	3	4.4%	5	3.6%

Source: StAHH, Admiralitätskollegium, F3, Band 1, 2, and 8; F4, Band 8, 14, and 15 (see appendix).

When merchants did specialize in a single commodity, it was mostly grain or wax. Only in a few instances do we see specialization in dyes, spices, cloth, or other commodities. Grain and wax also held first place when merchants specialized in two commodities, followed by cloth, wine, and sugar.

The Formation of Monopolies

Commodities whose sale was not regulated by exclusive contracts with a ruling authority (like the pepper and brazilwood contracts of the Portuguese Crown) were seldom suitable for monopolization. This applies especially to bulk commodities such as grain, sugar, wine, and cloth. To search the Admiralty customs books for evidence of goods sold by just a single merchant, or a very few, is to encounter Ludwig von Dagen. In 1632 he dominated the Hamburg-Portugal trade in tobacco (78 percent), rigging (72 percent), tallow (81 percent), tar (76 percent), lead (100 percent), and fish oil (100 percent). The success of this Netherlander, who in 1632 claimed a share of more than 4 percent of the total turnover between Hamburg and the Iberian Peninsula (placing him in the top spot among all merchants), may well have resulted from his total or near monopolies in those goods. But in 1647 von Dagen's name was no longer mentioned in the records, and no other merchant had been able to pick up a monopoly position in his roster of goods. In 1632 the Netherlander Arnold van Haesdonck had a near monopoly in knives and blades. He was another of the most prominent merchants in Hamburg doing business with the Iberian Peninsula; his turnover was the eighth highest in 1632. The trade in knives and blades comprised only 17 percent of his total; nonetheless, he was responsible for 75 percent of the entire Hamburg turnover in these products in the Iberia trade. Van Haesdonck was still active in 1647; his 32-percent share of the knife and blade trade was still the largest at the time, but he no longer retained a greater than 50-percent share.

The Networks

The Admiralty customs books cannot give us a complete picture of the trade networks of merchants who were active in Hamburg. The number of ports in which they had trade contacts, however, may serve as an indicator for the networks' size. The two merchants who traded with the most places in Spain and Portugal in 1632 and 1647 were the Portuguese Duarte Esteves de Pina and the German Wilken Wrede, who was a newly immigrated citizen of Hamburg. Duarte Esteves de Pina imported goods from Lisbon, Porto, and Málaga while exporting to Lisbon, Porto, Málaga, Sanlúcar, Cádiz, San Sebastián, and Condado. Wilken Wrede received goods from Lisbon, Porto, and the Canary Islands while shipping to Lisbon, Porto, Málaga, Sanlúcar, Cádiz, and San Sebastián. If we calculate for those two years the average number of ports of call with which merchants of the various nations had trading contacts, the Netherlanders were at the top with an average of 2.5, the Portuguese in second place with 2.3, followed closely by the Hamburgers with 2.2, and finally the regional immigrants with 1.8. In other words, the documents indicate that foreign merchants had more extensive networks than local ones, with the Netherlanders somewhat more broadly networked than the Portuguese.

In an analysis of each of the two years separately, the Hamburgers, Netherlanders, and Portuguese shared first place in 1632 with an average of 2.3 ports of call on the Iberian Peninsula. In 1647, however, only the Netherlanders maintained this level. The number of ports at which the Hamburgers and Portuguese traded was now only 1.9, while for the immigrants from Hamburg's surrounds it was 1.8 in 1647 instead of the 1.5 it had been in 1632 – that is, almost the same as the Hamburgers and Portuguese. The fact that the average number of ports visited by the Netherlanders in the two years taken together (2.5) was higher than in the two years separately (2.3) shows that the networks of the Netherlanders were flexible.[23] In other words, although the average number of ports visited in 1632 was the same, the ports were not identical to those visited in 1647. This was not true for the Portuguese and the Hamburgers: they visited fewer ports of call in 1647 than in 1632, having been unable to replace the discontinued ports with others.

Table 17: Networking on the Iberian Peninsula

	Maximum contacts with places on the Iberian Peninsula		Average contacts with places on the Iberian Peninsula	
	1632	1647	1632	1647
Hamburgers	6	5	2.3	1.9
Regional immigrants	5	7	1.6	1.8
Netherlanders	6	6	2.3	2.3
Portuguese	6	6	2.3	1.9
Origin unknown	4	5	1.4	1.5
Total[24]	6	7	2.0	1.8

Source: StAHH, Admiralitätskollegium, F3, Band 1, 2, and 8; F4, Band 8, 14, and 15 (see appendix).

We can wonder whether the Portuguese and Hamburgers were able to compensate for their weakened networks in the Spain and Portugal trade by increasing trade relations with other regions. The Admiralty customs books can provide answers only with regard to the ports that were subject to the customs duties listed in them, and these were located in France, England, the Mediterranean, the Baltic region, and the Caribbean. They do not reflect trade with closer ports,

Table 18: Networking in the regions requiring payment of Admiralty customs duties

	Maximum contacts with places requiring payment of Admiralty customs duties		Average contacts with places requiring payment of Admiralty customs duties	
	1632	1647	1632	1647
Hamburgers	7	7	2.4	2.4
Regional immigrants	5	10	1.7	2.1
Netherlanders	8	13	2.4	3.1
Portuguese	7	8	2.5	2.1
Origin unknown	5	8	1.5	1.5
Total[25]	8	13	2.1	2.0

Source: StAHH, Admiralitätskollegium, F3, Band 1, 2, and 8; F4, Band 8, 14, and 15 (see appendix).

specifically those in the United Provinces. Analysis of these two years indicates that the Hamburgers were able to maintain their degree of networking among the ports that the Admiralty material covers. The average number of ports of call in both years was 2.4; that is, decreased contacts on the Iberian Peninsula were compensated for by expanded trade networks in other territories. This was not true for the Portuguese, however. For them, the average number of all ports of call registered in the Admiralty customs books in 1632 was 2.5; that is, a bit more than the average number of ports visited on the Iberian Peninsula. By 1647, however, that figure was down to 2.1. It appears that it is the decrease in networking with the Iberian Peninsula alone that is responsible for this diminution.

The Netherlanders, who realigned their trading networks in Spain and Portugal between 1632 and 1647, notably increased their networking throughout the region for which the Admiralty required customs payments; their average number of ports of call rose from 2.4 to 3.1, which meant that in 1647 they were trading in more ports than all other nations. The best-networked merchant was the Netherlander Michel Heusch, who had trading relations with 13 ports in 1647: Lisbon, Porto, Sanlúcar, Cádiz, Málaga, San Sebastián, Genoa, Venice, Sicily, Marseille, Rouen, London, and Danzig. The immigrants to Hamburg from its surrounding regions were the most poorly networked, presumably because most of them came from the interior and therefore had fewer trading contacts abroad than either the established Hamburgers, who could rely on their families' networks, or the foreigners who had immigrated from trading cities in the Netherlands or Portugal.

All of the nations included merchants who traded only with Portugal or only with Spain, and all included merchants who had business dealings with both countries. In particular, about 18 percent of the Portuguese traded only through Spanish ports and not at all through Portuguese ones. In other words, some Portuguese seemed to avoid trading with their country of origin. However, it is notable that the number of Portuguese trading exclusively with Portugal, which was 32 percent in 1632, rose to 56 percent in 1647. This does not mean that the absolute number of Portuguese trading exclusively with Portugal increased, but rather that the number of merchants trading exclusively with Spain decreased. This break in connections with Spanish ports was the primary cause of the reduction in Portuguese networking that I cited above.

Table 19: Trade relations with Portugal or Spain

	Trade relations with Portugal and Spain		Trade relations only with Portugal		Trade relations only with Spain	
	1632	1647	1632	1647	1632	1647
Hamburgers	39.6%	25.4%	30.2%	30.5%	30.2%	44.1%
Regional immigrants	13.3%	22.2%	36.7%	25.9%	50.0%	51.9%
Netherlanders	38.3%	41.9%	18.5%	14.5%	43.2%	43.5%
Portuguese	50.9%	25.6%	31.6%	55.8%	17.5%	18.6%
Origin unknown	10.4%	19.6%	43.3%	30.4%	46.3%	50.0%
Total[26]	30.2%	25.2%	30.8%	30.0%	39.1%	44.8%

Source: StAHH, Admiralitätskollegium, F3, Band 1, 2, and 8; F4, Band 8, 14, and 15 (see appendix).

The correspondents with whom the merchants networked, and the ways they limited or welcomed trade relations with other merchant nations than their own will be discussed in chapter 12.

10 The Cross-Border Infrastructure

Late sixteenth- and seventeenth-century long-distance trade and merchant mobility were very different from what they had been in the Middle Ages. Merchants were less dependent on their immediate social environments. Corporate bodies like the guilds, *Kontore* and *feitorias* had lost much of their importance. In their place new institutions and services arose that fostered individual enterprise: exchanges, brokers, and notaries; postal and news services; and innovations in insurance and financial transfer. Individual merchants of any nation or religion could take advantage of them. They facilitated migration, settlement, and supraregional trade in the face of Europe's political, legal, and religious fragmentation and the resulting wars. The law developed in step with these changes, responding with ever-growing sophistication, and greatly increasing merchants' security.[1] Many of the arrangements were introduced much earlier in Portugal than in Hamburg, consistent with its earlier accommodation of foreigners.

Exchanges and the Opening of Trade

Inscribed upon the building of the Antwerp Exchange (or Bourse), founded in 1531, was the pledge: *"In usum negotiatorum cujuscunque nationis ac linguae"* (For the use of merchants of all nations and languages).[2] These words would have been equally appropriate for the exchanges in Hamburg and Lisbon, because they too were inclusive spaces, open to all merchants for the conduct of business. Before Hamburg had an exchange of its own, where merchants met depended on which geography- or commodity-specific trading corporations they belonged to. After 1558, however, with the founding of the Exchange, there was a single place where all could gather. The City Council set aside a space for this purpose, close to the old harbor on Nikolaifleet (the St. Nicholas Canal) between the city hall and the nearby loading crane and scales that symbolized the city's commercial identity. At first it was just a paved square surrounded by a low wall with a gate at the front. A number of corporate bodies contributed to the paving and enclosure: the *Board of the Common Merchant* (Vorstand des Gemeinen Kaufmanns, that is, the board of the sea trading merchants; see chapter 13), which paid 40 marks; the merchant associations of the Flanders, England, and Scania Travelers (see chapter 13), which paid 10 marks each; the Hansa *Kontore* in London, Bruges, and Bergen, which together contributed slightly more than 34 marks; and the brewers' and shipmasters' corporations, which paid 10 marks each. But individuals contributed much more: 650 marks from 188 citizens, plus another

https://doi.org/10.1515/9783110472103-011

52 marks or so from 20 "traveling alien merchants."[3] The way the financing was distributed among these various groups and persons gives an indication of their respective positions in the city's commerce of the time, and points in particular to the increasing individualization of trade and the emerging openness to foreign participation. Between 1577 and 1583 the Hamburg Exchange erected its own building on the square, which featured an elegant hall of columns opening onto it. That was where merchants met from then on.

At about the same time as the wall was being built around Hamburg's new Exchange square, a part of the Rua Nova, later known as the Rua Nova dos Mercadores (lit. New Street of the Merchants), in Lisbon was being fenced in with iron grating to form the exchange there. This street, which connected the center of the city with the royal palace, was where the city's commercial life had concentrated since the thirteenth century at least. Wealthy merchants had their shops there in magnificent edifices that were three, four, and even five stories high. There were colonnades on both sides of the street, so that in Lisbon as in Hamburg the Exchange consisted of both an open-air space and a covered section with an arcade.[4] Locals and foreigners alike met there. As the chronicler and humanist Damião de Góis said of Lisbon's Rua Nova in 1554: "Every day merchants representing almost every people and region of the world flock together here, joined by great throngs of people enjoying the advantages of business at the port."[5]

The exchanges in Hamburg and Lisbon did not yet serve all the functions of the exchanges in Amsterdam and, later, London. Speculative trade in stocks and bonds was very limited in Hamburg and Lisbon. But there, too, trading had become more complex than the simple purchase and sale of commodities. In both the Hamburg Exchange and the exchange on the Rua Nova, the contents of ships were insured, freight contracts concluded, shareholdings negotiated, credits raised, payments made, and money exchange transactions accomplished. This concentration of functions made the exchanges the nerve centers of commerce, at which no merchant involved in wholesale or long-distance trade could fail to put in frequent appearances.

It was there also that the latest news was shared – much of it orally, although notices in written form were posted as well. In Hamburg, lists announced the postal schedule and departing vessels and convoys, and the City Council posted decrees of interest to merchants. When in 1692 several rolls of tobacco, presumably from ships sailing in from Lisbon, were fished out of the water at Ritzebüttel, an exclave of Hamburg at the mouth of the Elbe, the event was noted in a posting.[6] Those guilty of "malicious bankruptcies" (that is, bankruptcies entered upon with intent to defraud creditors) were named on the "black board."[7] On Lisbon's Rua Nova there was a board for public announcements too.[8] Much information important to trade was thus freely accessible to all merchants at the exchanges.

Brokers as Mediators between Nations

The institutionalization of exchanges also provided a context in which the scope and techniques of brokerage could develop.[9] As professional middlemen, brokers were especially helpful to foreign merchants, who might not be fluent in the local language, or familiar with local conditions. In Lisbon brokers had been licensed by the City Council as far back as the fourteenth century; in Hamburg this became customary only in the sixteenth. A comprehensive set of rules regulating the behavior of brokers was enacted in Lisbon in 1342, while in Hamburg the first such ordinance came into effect only in 1642, three hundred years later, and was revised several times within a few years. These ordinances required that brokers exercise honesty and confidentiality in their work, and forbade them from dealing with insolvent businessmen. Brokers also had to keep registers in which they entered all of the business deals in which they were engaged by date, name of buyer and seller, quantity and quality of merchandise, delivery date, and any other conditions. These registers could be used as evidence in lawsuits.

There were problems with the brokerage system in Lisbon, however. A broker was required to be employed in all business transactions, but the number of licensed brokers was officially limited to twelve. Some additional brokers did in fact acquire licenses, but not enough for the amount of business that had to be covered. And while brokers often delegated their role to proxies, these too were often unavailable when needed. The situation was made worse by the fact that since the beginning of the sixteenth century it had been customary for the Lisbon City Council to lease brokerage positions to the highest bidders or to assign them based on political considerations; would-be brokers did not have to present any proof of professional competence. Furthermore, only citizens of Lisbon deemed "honorable" (see chapter 11) were permitted to become brokers, and New Christians were explicitly excluded. This did not help to resolve the system's dysfunction. It only meant that merchants were repeatedly petitioning the authorities to release them from the onerous restriction to official brokers, and over time unlicensed brokers in great number became a feature of commerce in Lisbon. They came to be known as *zânganos* (lit. drones, but popularly "cutthroats"), and merchants from foreign nations especially, being more dependent on broker services than the Portuguese, made use of their services.

But even as brokers in Portugal facilitated trade, they posed a potential threat. They had detailed information about the merchants' business dealings, and so were in a position to do great harm. For example, one of the informers who denounced Ana de Milão, wife of Rodrigo de Andrade (who played a key role in the negotiations around the General Pardon of 1605; see chapter 6), to the Inquisition was a broker.[10]

The situation was different in Hamburg. There was no brokerage require-ment there; the number of licensed brokers was considerably larger; brokers were not required to be citizens; and most of them were well qualified. From the seventeenth century into the nineteenth, brokerage was probably the only public office in Hamburg that did not completely exclude Jews. At least in the beginning, however, Netherlandish brokers far outnumbered all others. In 1590 there were 22 licensed brokers in Hamburg, of whom 13 were Netherlanders, eight Hamburgers, and one a Portuguese. In 1606, the figures were 18, 12, and 1.[11] The large number of Netherlanders was probably not only a reflection of the Netherlanders' overall eco-nomic power, but also of the importance of the brokers' function as interpreters. In 1679 the number of licensed brokers permitted was 130 Christians and 20 Jews, but eventually these numbers were reduced to only 60 Christians and 10 Jews. As a practical matter, however, that was too few, and at the end of the seventeenth century Hamburg still employed 125 Christian and 20 Jewish brokers.

According to the brokerage ordinance established in 1679, merchants who had lost their assets through no fault of their own (that is, not through carelessness or dis-honesty) were permitted to become brokers.[12] They were especially qualified for the job, as they could rely on the knowledge and experience they had acquired in trade. As a listing from the year 1701 makes clear, brokers tended to specialize in certain areas, concentrating either on a particular type of commodity or on a particular trade-related service. The largest group of brokers, 19 in all, specialized in spices; 11 were experts in the sugar trade. Figures like these indicate both the economic impor-tance of Portuguese imports to Hamburg, and the importance of brokers' expertise to businesses like these. Except for insurance brokerage, which had 18 practitioners, the other areas of specialization were represented by fewer than ten brokers each.[13]

Although the number of licensed brokers in Hamburg was larger than in Lisbon, there were unlicensed brokers there, too: the so-called "interlopers" (*Beiläufer*). In 1660 the city introduced identification requirements to distinguish between them.[14] The brokers' insignia consisted of a round piece of copper that bore the coat of arms of the city on the front and the name of the broker on the back. From 1679 on, a list of all brokers was posted on the wall of the Exchange building in Hamburg, and another "black board" was instituted to name brokers who for various infractions had been expelled from the licensed ranks.

Notaries and the Strengthening of Legal Certainty

If it can be said that brokerage functioned better in Hamburg than in Lisbon in the seventeenth century, the situation was reversed with respect to notary services. Notaries, like brokers, furthered the development of commerce. Merchants made use of them when they concluded trade agreements, set up business partnerships or commission relationships, assigned powers of attorney, or issued freight contracts. Notaries also certified translations and letters of protest when deadlines were not met, goods were defective, or payment was late. By providing systematic written records of commercial contracts and transactions, which could be used to substantiate claims in cases of disagreement, the notaries produced safeguards against opportunistic behavior and thus strengthened the legal certainty of merchants – that is, the reliable enforcement of the laws under which they operated. Like brokers too, notaries often provided services in several languages. The notary office of Pieter Ruttens, one of several Netherlandish notaries active in Hamburg at the beginning of the seventeenth century, prepared documents in German, Dutch, Spanish, Portuguese, Italian, and Latin.[15]

Until the middle of the sixteenth century public notarization was a fairly marginal phenomenon in Hamburg. Notaries operated under the Imperial Notary Ordinance of 1512, which excluded Jews but demanded few formal qualifications. They were not organized into a self-governing corporate body, so the training and supervision customary in other professions were lacking. In Hamburg, charters issued by the City Council's scribes competed for evidentiary and probative value with documents provided by imperial notaries. And as it happened, the local court did not always accept notarial documents because of the dubious reputations of some imperial notaries; this could lead to considerable difficulties for merchants.[16]

The system of notaries in Portugal, by contrast, had been institutionalized and codified by the early thirteenth century at the latest, and by the seventeenth century seems to have been more functional than the one in Hamburg.[17] In Lisbon the notaries occupied their own building; it was close to the cathedral and known as the *Notary Court* (*paço dos tabeliães das notas*). The special judge for the Germans (see chapter 3) may also have been authorized to issue documents for German merchants in Lisbon. This possibility is suggested by a certified translation from the Ruttens notary office in Hamburg, which was drawn on a 1609 Portuguese notarial document issued by the Judge Conservator of the Germans Francisco Tavares de Sousa.[18]

Insurance and the Reduction of Risk at Sea

Maritime insurance (that is, policies individually purchased by the merchants to protect their goods, with compensation of damages guaranteed and enforced by the ruling authorities) was one of the most important kinds of contract mediated by brokers and drawn up by notaries.[19] During the Middle Ages maritime insurance had been a matter of pooled risk: all the merchants and shipmasters who plied a particular route paid into a common fund, from which monies were disbursed in case of loss. In Portugal, *bolsas comuns* (common purses) had served that function since the thirteenth century. In Hamburg, a similar pooling technique was employed by the traveler companies (*Fahrergesellschaften*; that is, the associations of long-distance merchants; see chapter 13). Another early form of risk reduction still important in the seventeenth century was *bottomry* (*câmbio a risco*), a loan arrangement in which the creditor assumed a part of the risk at sea in exchange for the payment of a premium and the pledging of the ship or freight; if the ship or its cargo should fail to reach its destination safely, the amount owed on the loan and the premium would be diminished in accordance with the extent of the loss. A third form of risk reduction, frequently used and very simple, was to divide goods among several ships.

Insurance contracts or policies in the modern sense became available in Lisbon at the end of the fifteenth century and in Hamburg at the end of the sixteenth. Insurers were mainly wealthy merchants who used the maritime insurance business as a profitable form of investment. In 1529 the king of Portugal introduced a new official, the insurance scribe, to keep records of insurance contracts and issue the certificates that pertained to them. Only he was authorized to perform this function, and by 1573 at the latest, the scribe's office was located in the *Insurance Chamber* (casa dos seguros) in the Rua Nova – that is, close to the Exchange. This was where all parties to insurance contracts met, and where insurers were vetted for their integrity. The Chamber also served as the court of first instance when legal disputes arose. In 1578 the post of insurance broker was created, which also came under the Insurance Chamber. No policy was complete without the insurance broker's signature. Like many other offices, this one was hereditary, much to the detriment of the Chamber's functioning over time. The insurance scribes and insurance brokers increasingly lost control of the contracting process, and foreign merchants in particular, represented by the English, Dutch, and French consuls, refused to subject themselves to the authority of the Chamber.[20]

In Hamburg, individual maritime insurance became available in the 1580s. At first this business was handled almost exclusively by immigrant Netherlandish merchants, and as late as the 1620s and 1630s foreign merchants continued to be prominent in it; more than half of the 60 known insurers were Netherlanders or Portuguese. Trade with the Iberian Peninsula was by far the most important factor in the insurance business, because the trips from Hamburg were frequent and long, the ships large, and the cargoes valuable. The almost constant state of war in the region posed its own threats, and so did pirates; Hamburg ships were frequently attacked by raiders from England, France, the Netherlands, the Ottoman Empire, and northern Africa (Tunis, Tripoli, and Algiers).

Even goods that were subject to embargo could be, and customarily were, insured; this practice was reflected in the policies by reference to goods "free or unfree."[21] As I have mentioned, in their efforts to evade war-related bans, shipmasters frequently employed false shipping certificates (see chapter 4), in which ship owners, ports of lading and destinations were described such that the ships and goods would appear neutral. The use of these false papers was tolerated in the insurance business; because the information on the policies often differed markedly from that on the certificates, policies began to include such clauses as: "If the certificates do not conform with the cargo on these policies, this will not prejudice or be impedimentary."[22] In this way, the policies offered protection geared to the specific needs of the merchants on the Iberia trade route.

In the 1620s and 1630s the insurance premium for the trip from Hamburg to the Iberian Peninsula was usually between 8 and 10 percent of the value of the goods, but premiums as high as 15 percent were sometimes negotiated.[23] The amount depended, among other things, on whether the ship was part of a convoy or sailing on its own. But wars and political events could also have an effect on premiums. Complaints that they were too high were common. As Hamburg mayor Johann Schulte wrote of Hamburg merchants in 1681, "they say as follows: If we have our wares insured the premium will consume the profit, but if we do not insure them we must fear that the capital will be lost altogether. That is why people have become almost timorous, especially as in recent years there has been so much damage at sea."[24] By no means were all shipments insured; for shorter trips merchants often bore the risk themselves.[25] But even the longer trips to Portugal were sometimes undertaken without insurance. In 1682 Schulte wrote to his son that his son-in-law Gerd Burmester had dispatched a ship from Warnemünde on the Baltic coast to Lisbon without insuring it and "therefore was all the happier that the ship had arrived safely."[26]

The Postal System and Communication over Long Distances

Advances in communication gave the Hamburg insurance business a substantial boost. Once regular mail connections were established, insurers could expect to receive information about important events within a more or less predictable timeframe. As a result they could estimate risk better and adapt their calculations accordingly, and when an accident or disaster occurred they could quickly and reliably acquire an assessment of the damage and its short- and long-term consequences.[27] Ruling authorities had been availing themselves of messengers for a long time before this, but the general public owed the ability to send and receive letters regularly to the initiative of merchants. In 1517, in

Hamburg, the newly founded Board of the Common Merchant began to manage a messenger service.[28] By about 1550 messengers' pay was being regulated, and based on the weight and stated value of what they carried and how far they carried it. Messengers were sworn in for the first time in 1570. In 1578, in a further effort to foster the reliability of the service, the *Börsenalte* (the elders responsible for administering the Exchange, who had by then taken over the functions of the Board of the Common Merchant; see chapter 13), issued the first ordinance pertaining to the messenger service, which specified that only "non-notorious and trusted persons" who could read and write could become messengers.[29]

By the beginning of the seventeenth century Hamburg had regular messenger connections with Antwerp, Amsterdam, and Copenhagen, and also with Lübeck, Lüneburg, Leipzig, Danzig, Emden, and Cologne. Connections with Frankfurt am Main and Nuremberg were mainly maintained by messengers from those cities.[30] After 1607 departure and arrival times were established for all routes, and in 1641 a postmaster was named. He dispatched and received all postal transmissions, collected the fees that were due, and posted notifications of mail that had come in. The merchants' servants picked this up and dropped off outgoing mail for dispatch. [31] In his 1668 description of Hamburg, Conrad von Höveln declared that "the postal system in Hamburg is very well organized,"[32] and in 1703 the Hamburg City Council called it "the soul of commerce, just as commerce is the soul of the city."[33] Because it was so important to the merchants, the Assembly of Citizens was convened "at all times on a Thursday, when no mail is dispatched and the merchants may appear in greater frequency."[34]

The public postal system in Portugal was established in 1520, about the same time as it was starting in Hamburg. By the second half of the sixteenth century there was a regular ordinary mail service (*ordinário*); other services introduced later included extraordinary mail (*extraordinário*), express mail (*a toda a diligência*), and relay mail (*pela posta*), which was intended primarily for letters being sent abroad.[35] The Portuguese postal system received a boost from King Felipe II's stay in Lisbon between 1580 to 1583. He needed regular and reliable connection with his territories in Spain, Italy and the Netherlands, with the imperial court in Vienna, and with other princely courts and trading centers in Europe, and so he integrated Lisbon into the existing Habsburg postal service. Soon the postmaster-general (*correio-mor*) in Lisbon had assistants throughout Portugal.[36]

Mail between Hamburg and the Iberian Peninsula traveled overland, first by way of Antwerp and later generally through Amsterdam.[37] Johann Schulte's letters to his son in Lisbon make it clear that in the early 1680s a letter ordinarily took between 40 and 50 days to cover the distance from Hamburg to Lisbon, but during the winter delivery might be considerably delayed.[38] On January 27, 1682, Schulte wrote his son:

> The roads are so deep and unusable that a traveling man can hardly pass, and as a result the mail is extremely slow and unreliable. Here we are missing 2 mails from Frankfurt, 2 from Antwerp, and 2 from Paris, as well as many others. Last Friday, the 20th of this month, we expected the Hispanic letters, but to date they have not arrived, which is caused by the bad roads.[39]

Only seldom do letters between Lisbon and Hamburg appear to have been sent *per mare* (that is, by sea), from which one may infer that, despite all inconveniences, the overland postal network functioned quite reliably.[40]

However, anyone who sent letters by post had to expect that they would be opened and read along the way. At the beginning of Felipe IV's reign, when the truce with the United Provinces had just ended, we read that the authorities opened "the letters of all merchants."[41] They were interested in people's business as well as in matters of religion. This at least is what we can infer from one of Schulte's letters, in which he advised his son "that you not write so freely about religion, because it may happen that a letter is intercepted, which would cause you inconvenience."[42]

Newspapers Cover Wars and Diplomatic Events

Largely thanks to the establishment of regular postal traffic, Hamburg became the leading newspaper city in the Holy Roman Empire.[43] The first printed periodical newspaper in Hamburg appeared in 1618 and was published by Johann Meyer.[44] Meyer was the owner of the Weißer Schwan Inn, which was close by the Exchange. The inn was a central meeting place for merchants, and a place where news was exchanged. At that time it also housed the mail depot for the Nuremberg messenger service and the office of the forwarding agent, and was thus ideally situated for the making of a newspaper.[45]

Unlike newspapers in Holland, which from early on printed detailed bills of lading of arriving ships,[46] German newspapers of the time contained no information that would have been directly useful to traders. Mostly they reported political and diplomatic news, and, especially, military events.[47] Troop movements, treaties, changes in government, and natural phenomena could certainly affect trade. But through their own networks of correspondents, merchants often had access to more pertinent sources of information than the newspapers could provide. As von Höveln wrote in 1668, subscribing to a newspaper seems to have been more of a hobby for merchants than a practical necessity:

The well-established newspaper houses are not to be forgotten. Two sorts of newspapers are printed in Hamburg: German and Dutch. Foreign, German, Swedish, Dutch, French, Latin and other news (for which the ambassadors, residents, and agents, as well as many postal correspondents and news printers, expend much to have the communications) arrive in the city in manuscript and in printed form. Some merchants are themselves devotees and subscribe to a few.[48]

This is why economic historian John McCusker's claim that newspapers considerably reduced the costs of doing business for seventeenth century merchants (because they were more regularly and reliably informed by newspapers than by conversations and letters) is not convincing with regard to Hamburg.[49] Only toward the end of the seventeenth century did Hamburg newspapers begin to develop importance for trade.[50] In 1671, for example, a listing of the exchange rates and prices of goods in the most important trading cities was printed for the first time in a newspaper. Georg Greflinger, the publisher, also started to include information on economic developments around the world in his newspaper from time to time: about the silver mines in Peru, for example, and comparative information on the condition of silver miners and craftsmen in Germany.[51]

The first periodical newspapers published in Portugal appeared in connection with the war for independence from Spain (1640–1668).[52] They focused even more exclusively than the Hamburg newspapers on military and diplomatic issues, and at the end of the war ceased publication. Not until the eighteenth century did a real periodical press develop in Portugal.[53]

Commodity Price and Exchange Rate Currents

Merchants also had access to lists of quotations called *currents* (*Kurante*), and these frequently updated listings of financial information were of greater service to them than the early newspapers.[54] *Exchange rate currents,* as one might expect, compiled the exchange rates of foreign currencies in a particular place, and *commodity price currents* the prices of goods. In general, the information in the currents reflected the quotations posted publicly in the local exchange. In Amsterdam printed exchange rate currents became available around 1585, and merchants could subscribe to them at a relatively low price.[55] In Hamburg, by contrast, for many years the exchange rates had to be filled out individually, by hand, on printed forms. The oldest extant example of one of these is from the year 1592.[56] Portugal apparently lacked both printed currents and the alternative forms, which we can infer from the fact that in the early 1680s Mayor Schulte was sending such forms to his son in Lisbon: "Spoke with Sieur Gerd Burmester about the price current. He's going to give me his copy, and I will have it printed here and send you a number of copies and leave the prices of goods blank."[57] By then in Hamburg currents were being published periodically in printed form by the broker Hermann Hermannsen. The Commercial Deputation, since 1665 the body that purportedly represented merchants active in maritime trade (see chapters 13), admitted "that such rate currents are not unserviceable for the merchant and commerce," and urged the City Council to swear Hermannsen in for his notational business, which would have given him an official imprimatur and made him accountable for his work.[58] However, his currents were not officially approved until the beginning of the eighteenth century.

Bills of Exchange and Cashless Transactions over Long Distances

The postal service did not only convey letters, newspapers, and currents of commodity prices and exchange rates; it also carried *bills of exchange*, which allowed merchants to transact payment without cash. This worked as follows: if a businessman in Hamburg wished to pay a colleague in Lisbon, he could issue a bill of exchange and mail it to his representative there, with instructions that the representative disburse the appropriate sum to the Lisbon merchant in his stead. Because a period of time elapsed between the bill's issuance and its due date, a bill of exchange could serve a credit function, with the interest on the credit hidden in the currency exchange rate.[59] Furthermore, bills of exchange were negotiable instruments, as they could be sold to other persons who were then authorized to redeem them. They thus offered a quick, safe, and flexible means for moving financial resources, and so contributed considerably to the speed with which capital circulated.

In Portugal bills of exchange had been used since the fifteenth century; by the sixteenth they were an established and legally sanctioned method of payment, although the government frequently stepped in to prevent speculation in currencies or usurious manipulations.[60] However, its interventions (such as fixing permissible interest rates and limiting the times during which bills could be traded) were not always appropriate; restrictions on the use of bills of exchange in 1570, for example, reduced their circulation so drastically that the measure was rescinded a few years later.

In the Hansa region for much of the sixteenth century only *promissory notes* were used.[61] These differed from bills of exchange in that they were not orders to pay money, but promises to do so. In practice, that meant that a payment could be made only by the debtor himself, and so it was not possible for a merchant to transfer money to a creditor in a different location. The use of bills of exchange in the Hansa area still appears to have been extraordinarily rare. The account books of the Hamburg merchant Jakob Schröder for the years 1553 and 1554 indicate that payments between Antwerp and Hamburg were still primarily executed by cash remittance, while transactions between Antwerp and London were conducted using bills of exchange.[62] When in the 1560s Richard Clough began scouting a new potential location for the English Merchant Adventurers, he asserted that only a few merchants in Hamburg transacted business with other places using bills of exchange, and that those were mostly foreigners who did not reside permanently in the city.[63] It took until 1605, when members of the City Council, together with "several persons from the Exchange," worked out the first Hamburg ordinance regulating bills of exchange, to create the legal framework for smooth cashless transactions.[64]

The importance of bills of exchange for merchants should not be overstated, however.[65] This instrument was used primarily when large sums of money were suddenly at stake. Transactions between two merchants who were constantly exchanging wares were often accomplished simply by a mutual balancing of debts in their respective account books.

Part III: **Solidarity and Identity**

11 Trust, Reputation, and Religion

A number of public institutions developed over the course of the sixteenth and seventeenth centuries that rendered trade more predictable and eased the way of merchants doing business as individuals in foreign countries. The importance of their communities of origin decreased, and so did that of the traditional merchant organizations to which they had given rise. This did not mean, however, that merchants completely abandoned either personal or collective forms of solidarity. Merchants still took business decisions in the context of their families, their ethnic and religious communities, and their commercial interest groups; these remained influential, and trust was crucial both to the business decisions and to the creation and maintenance of the social relationships that underlay them. This chapter will discuss how trust developed, how it functioned, and how ethnic and religious factors enlarged and limited it. It is important to note at the outset that a merchant's trust was not necessarily restricted by either his ethnicity or his religion, but could flourish across as well as within those boundaries. Subsequent chapters will introduce the various relationships that relied on trust among merchants; they included networks of trading correspondents, professional corporate bodies, and nations (as rooted in ethnic and religious commonality).

How Trust Works

Trust is as necessary in business as in most other human interactions. A buyer or seller provides something in advance; he offers the other a good of some sort – a commodity, capital, or even information – for which he expects compensation. But there is always the risk that the recipient will fail to honor that expectation, or will honor it inadequately. *Trust* is the interpersonal context in which such risk is evaluated and intuitively contained. Although in principle it is derived from available information and prior experience, it always retains an irrational component.[1]

Nonetheless, to trust or not is a decision for which a businessman is answerable to his associates and investors; he must make it on grounds that appear responsible to them. When rational grounds for trust are insufficient, he will likely resort to moral ones. But this will work only insofar as his colleagues share his values. If they do not, any misplacements of trust may be seen as a reflection of his own unreliability. Groups assess trustworthiness on the basis of their shared values, and embody that assessment in a code of conduct. When trust is broken, the code guides the group in sanctioning transgressions. A potential transgressor is discouraged not only by fear of punishment, but also by fear of the social stigma attached to

https://doi.org/10.1515/9783110472103-012

transgression, which might deter others from trusting him in the future. The rules of the group thus constrain both the judgment of the trusters and the behavior of the trusted; this is why trust ultimately reduces risk, despite its irrational elements.

In particular, trust discourages opportunistic behavior within the context of long-term relationships. People who know that they will encounter each other again are the ones with the most to lose from breaking trust. The more tightly woven the social fabric – that is, the more connections exist among the involved parties and the more these depend on mutual reliability – the better the conditions for the development of trust. Two parties who have transacted business in the past and demonstrated their trustworthiness to each other bring a greater degree of trust and commitment to a new venture than if they were engaging together for the first time. If they are simultaneously involved in dealings with other merchants of the same group, where a break in trust would have negative social and financial consequences, their motivation to avoid such breaks is greater still. Trust is consolidated all the more when business connections coexist with the links of family and friendship, or by cultural, religious, or political interests and dependencies.

The merchants who are the subject of this book lived within two value systems, one specific to their profession and the other to the segment of society in which they lived their private lives. In the former, trust was granted on the basis of a merchant's reputation in trade, as reflected in such values as honesty, integrity, reliability, good sense, and good will. His community in this value system was the community of the Exchange. Within his social group, however – the people from whom he would expect support and consolation, especially in times of illness, loss, or economic hardship – his trustworthiness depended on how he conducted his life, and on his commitment to the group's ethical principles. The two value systems overlapped. Merchants trading among their own people were squarely in the area of intersection, and that was the situation to which economic historian Avner Greif limited his studies of what he calls *private-order mechanisms* for enforcing contracts and reducing risk (see introduction).[2] But although that may have been the environment in which trust was most easily generated and social sanctions most easily brought to bear, the mechanisms that Greif discusses also operated among merchants of different origins and, as we will see in the following chapters, sometimes proved even more profitable there.

Credit as Mercantile Trust

Trust in business life was closely connected with the concept of *credit*, which in the seventeenth century meant something much closer to the word's Latin root, *credere* (to believe), than it does today. By 1733, Zedler's *Universallexikon* was defining credit as: "Good faith among human beings; that one person will entrust, lend, and give over his property to another in the hope that he will compensate and pay him for it." The entry continues: "A person has good credit, he stands in good credit with another, which means: one places trust in him."[3] It was in this sense that young Johann Schulte's parents were proud of his credit. His father wrote to tell him how happy they were that "you, praise God, advance in your profession and business, and are in such credit that goods amounting to many thousands are placed in and entrusted to your hands." His father observed in particular that he stood "in good credit" with his brother-in-law Gerd Burmester.[4]

A letter written about two years later gives us more precise information about how trust functioned among merchants. Young Schulte had gotten into business difficulties that had had a negative effect on his trading partners in Hamburg, especially Heinrich Burmester, his other brother-in-law. His father wrote him: "From your letter I have seen, though not gladly, the losses that have affected our friends; but because that woman was in full credit, our friends can impute nothing to you, nor do they do so." In the father's view it was manifestly "that woman" who had caused the losses, and because she herself had been in good credit, Schulte's son's business decision could not be faulted. In a different context, however, the father would not have trusted her, because "I see noted in your letter that the woman must have been loose and deceitful." Furthermore, although the mayor was well aware that his son-in-law had been seriously hurt by this incident, he gave no thought to helping him:

> I pity good Heinrich Burmester because, as I have heard, he was hit hard and his means cannot withstand large damages. ... Well, the wealthy God who still has so much to give shall [compensate] the friends and the good Heinrich Burmester for the damages that have accrued to them with his ample divine blessing ... mercifully protecting them from such treacherous people.[5]

The father's support here was a matter of mercantile principle, not of kinship or friendship. When his son expressed misgivings about letters he had received from business contacts that "do not sound for the best and as one would like," his father serenely advised him, "then tell them with few [words] that such is the way of the world."[6]

The *Universallexikon* stressed the importance of credit for trade: "If credit were abolished among merchants, all commerce would collapse."[7] To remain competitive, a merchant had to avoid anything that could harm his creditworthiness. In 1591 David de l'Homel, a Netherlandish merchant living in Hamburg, refused to pay a deposit or provide a guarantor for a sugar deal negotiated with Adam Hölscher. He said that he thanked God that he required no guarantor, "because all this time I have been known as honorable and of good credit." He was happy to pay immediately and in cash, but to pay a deposit would put him in ill repute with other merchants.[8] According to his understanding, if a merchant was deemed creditworthy, he needed give no security; indeed, to do so would damage his credit.

Once lost, credit was difficult to restore. The merchant Michael Schmidt, who in 1637 felt that Hartich von Spreckelsen had robbed him of his creditworthiness, sued him in Hamburg lower court and demanded compensation of 50,000 reichstaler, "which I had much rather done without and not won than suffer such great indignity." In addition, he published an account in which he attempted to prove his innocence. He felt forced to do so because,

> von Spreckelsen irresponsibly abused and grossly injured me and my much beloved family, and with that eventually caused people who had accepted my merchant's credit and promoted my livelihood to distance themselves from me, due to this publicly inflicted dishonor and subsequent false allegations. Thereby I was entirely deprived of my daily livelihood and plunged into utter perdition.[9]

It is not known whether by these means he managed to restore his credit.

Self-Representation, Recommendations, and Courtesies

Avoiding anything that might damage trust was one thing; the other was to actively build and consolidate it. Self-representation was extremely important in this regard. As I have indicated, people generally looked to a merchant's behavior and way of life in judging his business (see chapter 8). A successful merchant dressed with refinement and lived in a stately home in a prestigious location. But in Hamburg, as in Portugal, it was also important to avoid excessive luxury, and to give the impression of measured and rational behavior. In judging trustworthiness, potential creditors and business partners looked not only at a merchant's actual wealth, but also at how he husbanded it. Accordingly, in cases of bankruptcy, people distinguished sharply between malicious and innocent insolvencies. Willful, fraudulent, or frivolous ones were considered a crime to be prosecuted; innocent ones (also called unlucky or blameless) were caused by circumstances outside the merchant's control such as fire, storm, hail or enemy attack, and in those cases the person merited sympathy and charity. In one of his letters, Mayor Schulte wrote his son:

> Last Saturday young David Schulte, the son of the late Lorenz Schulte, fled on account of debt and withdrew to his garden in Ottensen [outside the city's jurisdiction]. He is truly a real malicious bankrupt, who as a result of excessive expenditures squandered and wasted his assets. He kept two pairs of beautiful carriage horses, went out for a drive every day, dominated [dined?] and feasted every day, so that upon such work no other wage could accrue.[10]

The mayor attributed David Schulte's bankruptcy on his wasteful lifestyle; he himself was to blame for his misfortune.

First contacts between businessmen could be made privately, but they were just as likely to occur in public spaces designated for this purpose, such as at the Exchange and its adjacent inns or coffeehouses, or the port or warehouses. As we saw in the last chapter, all merchants were welcome at these places, independent of nation or religion. All could freely enter into conversation; the Hamburg merchants João da Maya and João Frique, for example, both explicitly told the Inquisition in Lisbon that they spoke with everyone who offered to speak with them, whether they were Catholic or Protestant.[11] Mayor Schulte too advised his son to be broad-minded, participate in whatever was going on, and behave courteously in all situations. He should do this – always keeping an eye on his own benefit – even if he suspected that someone did not mean well by him. "My advice is that you give everyone good words and put on a good face; but you can always think and do what you believe to be advantageous. That is the way of the world."[12] At the beginning of his stay in Portugal, the younger Schulte had written his father that there were many in Lisbon who wished him ill, and that he believed that (Johann?) Frick (probably the João Frique above) and (Paul?) Amsinck were his greatest detractors. His father replied: "My son, who does not have detractors? The better one does, the more detractors one has." When these two gentlemen invite him to their homes, Mayor Schulte advised, Johann should not avoid them, but take the opportunity to pay them a visit. "You write that they wanted to sound you out about something; but you aren't a child such that they can ask you anything they please. You could have answered them as you wished, telling them what you wanted them to know."[13] Friendly conversations were essential in business transactions, even if a certain reserve was sometimes prudent.

Trust could also be created by third persons; in recommending merchants they considered trustworthy, they transferred their trust to others. Mayor Schulte recommended his son and his son's business companion to many Hamburg merchants, and asked acquaintances to recommend them as well. He wrote to Johann, for example: "As I found an apt opportunity to recommend you and your partner to Mr. Bümmelmann, he expressed praise and said that he would answer you by this mail."[14] Or: "Recently, Sieur Heinrich Burmester spoke at the Exchange with Sieur Peter Juncker and recommended your person; he expressed himself as willing, and added that he would like to be informed about some wares which may give profit in Lisbon."[15] There were also recommendations to merchants abroad: "Johann August Vossenholt misses no opportunity to recommend you to one and another, when there is an occasion, and he told me also that he had written on your behalf to Rouen."[16] Writing about a conversation with the brother of the future housemaster of the Steelyard (that is, the Hansa *Kontor* in London), the mayor declared, "when we came to speak of you and your business companion, he [the brother] wrote down both of your names and said that he would recommend you to him [the housemaster], to send you something on commission."[17]

Because the source material is so sparse, it is unclear to what extent such recommendations were forthcoming for persons belonging to ethnic or religious groups other than the recommender's own. The persons whom the mayor mentioned in his letters came from old Hamburg families (such as the Burmesters), or had immigrated to the city from the surrounding region (like the Dinschlags), or were Netherlanders (such as the Junckers and Heuschs). He did not explicitly mention the nation or the religion of any of these individuals, but none of the families he recommended were Portuguese Jews. From this it appears that Schulte's circle of trust quite naturally encompassed the locals and the Netherlanders, but not the Portuguese.

Once the initial contact had been made, positive experiences led to increased trust, and to further expansion of the business relationship. The mayor reported to his son that his son-in-law "was well-satisfied, and happy beyond all measure with the wares that you and your companion sent him on the recent ships." The previously mentioned (Henning?) Bümmelmann also "noted that he was very happy with your conduct, as well as with the transmitted invoices," for which reason he would now "place somewhat more in trade."[18] On the other hand, if experience with a particular merchant was poor, the consequences could be unpleasant. According to the mayor's son-in-law, the merchant (Jerónimo?) Wulf was a "scoundrel and coarse fellow." Schulte advised his son, therefore, "to avoid such objectionable company."[19]

The basic rule was: "One must do everything to remain in people's good graces, so that one's name and reputation might remain good."[20] Exchanges of greetings and courtesies, expressions of friendship, and gifts large and small were used to ensure good business relationships. For instance, young Johann Schulte's mother visited Bümmelmann's wife on the occasion of a death and expressed her condolences, which the wife "esteemed and received as a great honor." On that occasion, Schulte's mother also spoke of the good relationship between Bümmelmann and her son, and thanked her for her husband's kindness in having "done so much good and acted as a father toward you."[21] Daniel Dinschlag, whose son Johann Caspar also spent time in training in Lisbon, promised the mayor that he would "gladly be of service [to Johann] in one matter or another as needed," so long as young Schulte remained on amicable terms with Dinschlag's son.[22] Gifts were also frequently exchanged between Lisbon and Hamburg. The mayor was sent "apples of China" (that is, oranges), lemons, pine nuts, ham, and wine by his son and other merchants; he reciprocated, sending them beer from Zerbst, Rhine wine, smoked meat, ox tongue, and salmon from the Elbe. He also sent Johann "a small package containing the [periodical] *Curiose Nouvellen* and the wafers you wanted."[23]

The mayor seems to have calculated such gestures meticulously; he made sure to avoid remaining indebted to anyone, even to family members. Thus he asked his son not to send any more enclosures addressed to him in letters to his son-in-law Gerd Burmester, because the latter refused to accept the postage that was due, and the mayor desired "nothing for free."[24] On the other hand, when the Hansa consul in Lisbon, Alexander Heusch, enclosed a letter to his brother in Hamburg in a letter sent by young Johann Schulte, and the brother wanted to repay the father the cost of the postage, the mayor wrote his son that he "did not accept it, because it was a nothing, and the consul in question may perform acts of friendship for you in return."[25]

Correspondences

Regular letter contact did more than almost anything else to foster trust between and among merchants living and working in different places.[26] It could compensate for personal absence by allowing for the exchange of mercantile information, the offering of recommendations, and even the working out of misunderstandings. Letter writing was an essential part of mercantile networking, and apprentice merchants were instructed in the art. Mayor Schulte pointed out to his son the importance of business correspondence for trade: "Above all, pay close attention to your affairs and negotiations, and be diligent in your correspondence."[27]

The *Universallexikon* defined a correspondent as "he who exchanges letters with another. Among merchants, it is he who negotiates with another both in goods and in bills of exchange, and usually they call him their friend."[28] In other words, a merchant correspondent was someone with whom one engaged in both letters and trade, and the letters generally did contain both business and private matters. They reported on failed harvests, sunken ships, and successful business ventures as well as on personal news. In his letters, Mayor Schulte was concerned with his son's professional success and conveyed information to him about business partners and the economic situation in Hamburg. But the letters also addressed family matters, including advice about Johann's health from his mother, recommendations about appropriate religious behavior in Catholic Lisbon, and reports on the lengthy negotiations over young Schulte's planned marriage. A caring, stable and prosperous family enriched a merchant's profile, and promoted his success. And on a more general level, worries about the sick and needy were signs of loyalty and cohesion, which equally furthered the building of trust.

Reputation and Honorableness

For merchants, trustworthiness was intimately connected with *reputation*, which drew, as I have mentioned, on such attributes as integrity, honesty, good sense, good will, and reliability. These were qualities that any merchant could achieve regardless of his origins. But the granting of trust also depended on factors over which a merchant had little control; many of these were subsumed under the concept of *honorableness* (*Ehrbarkeit*), which derived from the prevalent notions of *honor*.[29] Different from reputation, honorableness was not so much an individual moral matter as a collective legal one. Traditionally, every estate or status group had its own honor and corresponding code of honor. There was a clerics' honor, a nobles' honor, and a citizens' honor; most professional groups had their own specific honors and codes of honor as well. *Merchants' honor*, which tended to overlap with citizens' honor, was one of these. Its code stipulated the attributes on which a merchant's reputation depended. But the sine qua non of honorableness was membership in the appropriate social estate, and such membership was usually acquired by birth. The merchants' honor was associated with citizen status. Individuals belonging to an estate other than the one associated with a given honor could rarely lay claim to that honor, and some groups were assigned a status below even the lowest estate, and accorded no honor whatsoever. These included serfs and the other unfree, members of the so-called dishonest professions (headsmen, flayers, gravediggers), Gypsies, Arabs – and Jews. For these people, in theory, there was no way of becoming honorable, and they were categorically excluded from many of the prerogatives of honor such as the holding of a fiefdom, or guild membership.

Over the long run, however, the borders between, and the hierarchies among, the status groups tended to change. It is in this context that historians today understand honor and honorableness: not as absolute static qualities, but as strategies of discourse and practice whereby certain groups delimited themselves against others.[30] Groups declared their own members honorable and excluded others by declaring them not so, thus establishing and perpetuating ideas about rank and value according to their own perceived social roles. The attribution of honor and honorableness was thus part of a complex system of social evaluation.

As I have said, the citizenry was a status group of its own, with its own honor and code of honor. In the early modern period it was a sector that was becoming ever more important to society, and its membership ever more self-confident. In Hamburg, as in most other cities, the city councilors occupied the top of the citizenry's scale of honorableness; their status was reflected in the way other citizens behaved toward them, and, especially, addressed them. Thus the City Council was always called the "Honorable Council" (*Ehrbarer Rat*), and its members were addressed as "Sir" (*Herr*). Honorableness was underscored by such devices as dress codes and sumptuary laws, which regulated what visual signifiers of status could be worn by whom.

In Portugal, as we have seen, a special deference extended to the bearers of the German Merchant Privilege, who were permitted to wear clothing made of or trimmed with silk, to bear arms, and to ride on horseback (see chapter 3).[31] In fact, in Portuguese society, Germans were viewed as honorable persons in themselves, and were accorded great respect independent of their reputation as merchants. On the occasion of the habilitation of Isabel Guilherme, for example, it was recorded that her father's parents, who lived in Altona, near Hamburg, were "honorable and pure-blooded people, like all members of the German nation."[32]

In both Portugal and Hamburg, on the other hand, the standing of people of Jewish origin was precarious. The New Christian António Bocarro declared that he chose not to go to Peru, where Jews could practice their faith in freedom, so as not to dishonor his family, which enjoyed a good reputation in Portugal.[33] In this declaration, honor and reputation are closely intertwined; apparently the family had managed to obscure doubts about its honorableness by maintaining a spotless reputation. This uncertain hold on respectability would have been lost, however, if Bocarro had sought out the company of outright Jews.

The purported lack of honor of the Jews was reflected in discriminatory language. Jewish merchants were often presented as arrogant and greedy. Thus Pedro Wrede and Jochim Schmidt wrote from Lisbon to Peter Burmester in Hamburg about their (Christian) business associate Hendrick Tonniessen: "He must be an impudent Jew that he could write such a letter to me without basis."[34] And the previously mentioned Michael Schmidt wrote in his conflict with Hartich von Spreckelsen "that it was permissible to take Christian interest but not Jewish usury of 10 [to] 12 percent."[35] Whether or not these correspondents meant their words literally, such negatively charged images of Jewish business practices presented Jews as a group of minor status, and potentially untrustworthy.

Yet even the conviction that Jews were devoid of honor gradually moderated. The Portuguese Jews in Hamburg in particular were able to revise the traditional picture. Compared with other Jewish communities of the Holy Roman Empire, they enjoyed much social respect (although not nearly as much as the Portuguese Jews in Amsterdam). By stressing their Iberian origins, their affluence, and their cosmopolitan and worldly outlook – in short, by strictly distinguishing themselves from German and Polish Jews – the Portuguese were able to confine to the Ashkenazic Jews a good portion of the lack of honor imputed elsewhere to Jews in general.[36] This effort was assisted by the especially confident behavior of outstanding members of the Portuguese-Jewish community. As I have noted, when Johann Balthasar Schupp first met Manuel Teixeira, he mistook him for "the bishop or an ancient prince or count," because Teixeira was driven in a coach and had servants who displayed reverence toward him (see chapter 8). Schupp deduced from this grandeur the honor to be accorded Teixeira: "I doffed my hat as low as if it had been for the Elector of Saxony." If Schupp had known that the man in the coach was a Jew, he might have behaved differently. This is an example of how practice (as well as discourse) concurred with certain expectations of honorableness – and how a counter-practice could modify them. And as a matter of fact, thanks to his diplomatic functions, Manuel Teixeira, like Duarte Nunes da Costa, was officially addressed as *Herr*, a courtesy otherwise reserved for city councilors.[37]

By 1665 at the latest (that is, when the influential Commercial Deputation was founded; see chapter 13), the title Honorable Merchant had edged out Common Merchant as a designation for the Hamburg merchant class. This change conveys the group's increased self-assurance as it established itself rhetorically on a par with the City Council. But while Common Merchant had been an inclusive term, Honorable Merchant may have been willfully chosen to exclude. As we will see, Jewish merchants had no access either to the Commercial Deputation or to the *Assemblies of the Honorable Merchant* (Versammlungen eines Ehrbaren Kaufmanns), which was the body that elected it. Here the socio-legal aspects of "honorableness," heavily contingent upon Christian birth, eclipsed the individual commercial reputations of the merchants. By falling in with the assumption that Jews lack honor, these institutions not only denied them full access to the fellowship and backing of their professional colleagues, but also demeaned their professional capacity and ultimately their trustworthiness.

Merchants' Ethics and Religion

Judgments about a merchant's reliability in business were also influenced to some degree by assumptions about his religious beliefs and his behavior with regard to them. The result was not necessarily distrust or rejection. Certain religious affiliations came to be associated with specific business practices, which in turn have been used to explain major tendencies in European economic development. Thus seventeenth-century scholars, politicians, and religious leaders debated the extent to which the economic decline of the Catholic countries of southern Europe, and the flourishing of the northern European economies, were associated with the social and moral characteristics of the religious cultures that characterized them.[38] Protestants especially tended to claim that their coreligionists were thriftier, more industrious, and more moderate than Catholics, who (because of their many holidays and their supposed devaluation of worldly success) were thought to have a rather lax work ethic and be inclined to indolence. English parliamentarian Slingsby Bethel, for example, argued in *The Present Interest of England Stated* (1671) that the Reformed thought idleness reprehensible, and that their success in business and trade grew along with their religious zeal; Catholics, on the other hand, were supposedly unsuited to business by nature. On these grounds he concluded that the Reformed should be tolerated in England because of the economic benefits they would bring with them, while Catholics should not.[39] Many rulers similarly welcomed Jews because of their reputed business prowess. It was argued that in their centuries of wandering and persecution they had become extraordinarily entrepreneurial, well-networked, and multilingual merchants who would not only increase local trade, but also contribute to the wealth and prosperity of the state through the taxes and customs duties they would pay. Such arguments were taken up even by the Portuguese Jews themselves, as in the *Discorso circa il stato de gl'hebrei et in particolar dimoranti nell'inclita città di Venetia* (Discourse on the State of the Jews and in Particular Those Living in the Illustrious City of Venice, 1638), written by the Rabbi Simone Luzzatto of Venice, and in the "Humble Addresses" written to Oliver Cromwell in 1655 by Rabbi Menasseh Ben Israel from Amsterdam.[40]

The debate over the connection between religion and economics has never really abated. At the turn of the twentieth century, it received renewed impetus from the works of Werner Sombart and Max Weber.[41] In Sombart's view, Jews, especially the Sephardic Jews, were responsible for the development of "modern capitalism." His arguments were quickly, and in my opinion thoroughly, refuted, although even today his work finds occasional mention.[42] Weber's understanding, that it was the Reformed who were most influential in these developments, still has many adherents. Weber assumed that the diligence and striving of the Reformed were motivated by their wish to ward off any doubt that they were indeed among the elect. But even a century of intensive research into such assumptions has failed to demonstrate that any faith has ever had specific effects on the business activities of the faithful as a group, or on the economic life of the regions in which they practiced their faith and their trade.[43] What can be shown, however, is that trading relationships have often broken through denominational boundaries, and that the trust necessary to do business has always existed among merchants of different religious groups.

12 Trading Networks, Family, and Nation

Trading networks were the scaffolding of long-distance trade. They connected merchants living in far-apart places and made possible the exchange of information as well as of merchandise. As I noted in the introduction, historians have generally supposed that merchants preferred to trade with members of their own ethnic or religious groups, since social sanctions, and the threat to withhold future business in the event of opportunistic or unscrupulous behavior, had the most power within such groups. But as I will show, there were other factors at play as well, and business relationships based on ethnic or religious homogeneity were not always advantageous. For this reason most merchants also did business with members of other nations and faiths. The Hamburgers and Netherlanders in Portugal often consolidated their interethnic trade relations through marriages across the boundaries of nation, but the Portuguese Jews in the diaspora married only among their own people. Their family connections to their old homeland were fragile, endangered concretely by the Inquisition and emotionally by the resentment of some of their New Christian kindred about their having adopted Judaism in exile. The result was that their networking opportunities were much more limited than those of the Hamburgers and Netherlanders.

Commission Relationships

"There are merchants [in Hamburg] who have correspondences in all of the major cities of Europe to which the Hamburg ships travel," observed the Italian diplomat Galeazzo Gualdo Priorato in 1663.[1] By "correspondence" he meant both the regular exchange of letters and the regular exchange of merchandise (see chapter 11), these being the two constituent elements of trading networks. The large sixteenth-century southern German firms trading with Portugal, such as the Fugger, Welser and Höchstetter houses, were hierarchical. They were mostly family enterprises; decisions were made by the head of the family, while his younger relatives and eventual heirs supervised and administered local managers (factors) who worked on salary and followed to their directives. Seventeenth-century enterprise functioned differently; it relied on the kinds of trading networks that Gualdo noted, and was less formal, less centralized, and less stratified. The networks were generally based on mutual commission relationships – that is, on relationships in which merchants in different places did business on each other's behalf in exchange for a percentage fee. This kind of horizontal structuring permitted multilateral cooperation among relatively independent, and sometimes changing, partners. It was

https://doi.org/10.1515/9783110472103-013

a much more flexible arrangement than the older one, and better able to respond to the rapid political, religious, and military changes that characterized the seventeenth century. If one correspondent dropped out of the network (for reason of arrest, for example, or flight, death, illness, or financial difficulty) there would likely be another who could replace him, and the network would continue to function.[2] Network maintenance still demanded constant attention, but specific members were not as indispensable as they had been in the past. On the other hand, as individuals became interchangeable, there was less economic incentive to support them in time of need. More liberty could mean less commitment.

So while it has often been assumed that the commitment among agents of a single nation was enough to make trade work, in fact there was no such guarantee of well-functioning collaboration. This is illustrated in an experience of Netherlander Andreas Snellinck, who lived in Hamburg. In 1604 he shipped 14 crates of English bay and say (light wool cloth) to Madeira, and consigned them to another Netherlander, Jan Willemsen Domann, who lived there.[3] Domann forwarded the shipment to Pernambuco, where it was to be transferred to Hans de Catter, or in his absence to Gaspar de Mere, both also Netherlanders. De Catter actually received Snellinck's woolens, but because he expected to be leaving the region soon, he handed them over to Gaspar de Mere, who was supposed to sell the material and send the proceeds back to Snellinck in Hamburg. However, as late as 1607, Snellinck reported to the notary Pieter Ruttens that he had still not received either the money owed him or an explanation for the delay. It appears that Gaspar de Mere never informed his correspondent in Hamburg about the fate of the shipment, nor had Hans de Catter investigated the matter.

In the notarial files I have examined, this case is one of the very few in which all of the merchants in an extended chain of trading correspondents were members of the same nation. Much more often the composition of trading networks was ethnically heterogeneous. The Beckmann family, for example, which furnished several members of the Hamburg City Council and played an important role in the city's Iberia trade at the turn of the seventeenth century, corresponded with Germans, Netherlanders, Spaniards, Italians, and possibly Frenchmen. Lukas Beckmann the elder worked as a commission agent on behalf of the Antwerp merchants François van der Willigen, Jan Boussemart, and Hieronymus and Balthazar Andrea; his trading correspondent in Burgos was García del Pezo. Barthold Beckmann the elder worked on behalf of the merchants Johann Jakob and Samuel Heuser, probably Germans, who lived in Genoa; his correspondents in Bilbao were the Netherlanders Johann von Eckeren and Louis de Boyleux from Cambrai, and in La Rochelle he corresponded with Wilhelm (von) Offenberg and David (de) Garin. In 1617 Barthold Beckmann the younger was represented by the Italian Abondio Somigliano at the Frankfurt Autumn Fair.[4] But in their trade with

Portugal the family did collaborate with a family member; according to a freight contract from the year 1605, the same Barthold had wheat and rye shipped to Faro in southern Portugal, where his brother Joachim would decide whether the shipmaster should unload the grain there or convey it elsewhere in the region.[5]

I found several instances where Hamburgers collaborated in trade with close relatives in Portugal.[6] It is rare, however, to find in the Hamburg notarial records Portuguese-Jewish merchants living in Hamburg who traded from that city with family members in Portugal. Nor did Kellenbenz, despite repeated contentions that kinship connections were "obvious" in the trading networks of the Portuguese Jews, cite much evidence to that effect.[7] The only Portuguese merchant in Hamburg who had both major turnovers in the Iberia trade (according to the Hamburg Admiralty customs books of 1632 and 1647) and trading correspondents with a family name that may have indicated kinship, was Duarte Esteves de Pina.[8] In Porto he collaborated with Diogo Henriques Pina until the latter's arrest by the Inquisition.[9] But after this experience he may have changed his mind about working with relatives; his next representative there was Domingos Faros da Fonseca, who by name seems not to have been one.[10] In the Canary Islands and Madeira, Duarte cooperated with João Teixeira, presumably not a relative either, while in Pernambuco he maintained business relations with Francisco Gomes Pina.[11] He had close relatives in Amsterdam with whom he did occasional business, although his official proxies, Francisco Lopes Rosa[12] and Henrique de Solis,[13] do not seem to have been related to him. Finally, he maintained a trading correspondence in Rouen with a certain Francisco Ramires de Pina.[14]

So business relationship did not necessarily imply kinship, but neither did kinship necessarily imply business relationship. Such was the case of two merchants bearing the same name, Manuel Rodrigues Isidro, who were uncle and nephew, and Baltasar Álvares Nogueira, another nephew of the former, and the brother of the latter.[15] The elder Manuel Rodrigues Isidro had lived in Madrid before moving north in 1608, probably first to Amsterdam and from there to Hamburg. He was active as a merchant in Hamburg in 1658, the year that his nephew of the same name in Lisbon was brought to trial before the Inquisition. The Hamburg Admiralty customs books indicate that in 1647 Manuel the elder had the third-highest turnover of all merchants in the Portugal trade. However, if one is to believe the information in the Inquisition files, Manuel the younger seems not to have done business with him. During the trial he gave detailed information about his various debtors and creditors. Among his trading correspondents in Hamburg he named André and Manuel Diques, both either Hamburgers or Netherlanders, for whom he had negotiated transactions in Bahia and Goa. He did not, however, name his uncle, nor his brother Baltasar Álvares Nogueira, who at the time worked as a clerk with his uncle in Hamburg. It may be that he was attempting to protect himself or his family by not naming them; however, it is also possible that he really did not trade with them. After all, he did name many Portuguese Jews in Amsterdam and London with whom he dealt, although admittedly none of them were relatives.

In many instances Portuguese Jews living in Hamburg cooperated with Hamburgers or Netherlanders in Portugal rather than with members of their own nation. In 1603, for example, Jorge Peres Brandão, who lived in Hamburg, had sugar sent to him from Lisbon by Jácomo Diriques, a merchant who was probably of German or Netherlandish origin.[16] In the 1620s Luís Pereira da Silva, who also lived in Hamburg, repeatedly received goods from the brothers Peter and Gerd Burmester in Lisbon, as well as from Christoph Meyer there.[17] The Burmester brothers were his proxies in Lisbon, and they cooperated with Portuguese Jews living in Amsterdam, too.[18] But of course they also worked with Hamburgers and Netherlanders. In 1624 Gerd Burmester and Christoph Meyer received goods from Hamburg that Gerd's brother Giese and his business partners, the Netherlanders Pieter Verpoorten and Carel Groenendael, had sent.[19]

When Portuguese Jews living in Hamburg or Amsterdam chose to rely on Hamburgers and Netherlanders in Portugal, the Inquisition was probably the main reason. To collaborate with family members or other New Christians would have meant risking their arrest and prosecution, as well as confiscation of goods in trade. Foreigners enjoyed far greater legal security in Portugal. It is also possible that the closest and most trustworthy relatives and acquaintances of many Portuguese Jews had already left Portugal themselves. But even in northern Europe, where there was no Inquisition to fear, we find many examples of collaboration between Portuguese Jews and members of other nations. According to a notarial deed, André Fernandes Cardoso and Ferdinand Vuijst (who lived in Hamburg) in cooperation with the above Peter Burmester (who had also moved to Hamburg by then) arranged in 1631 the delivery of eight crates of sugar and one crate of tobacco to Amsterdam.[20] They were a perfectly mixed group, ethnically and religiously; Cardoso was a Portuguese Jew, Burmester a Lutheran Hamburger, and Vuijst a Reformed Netherlander. In another instance, Pero Gomes de Lisboa and Jerónimo Henriques, two Portuguese-Jewish merchants living in Amsterdam, ordered that their proxy in Hamburg, the Netherlander Julius van den Moere, was to receive sugar and other goods, including cash, gold and silver coins, as well as diamonds and gems, all due to arrive in Hamburg from Lisbon, Porto, Viana, and other Portuguese ports.[21] In their power of attorney they explicitly stated that Duarte Fernandes Castanho, to whom their associates abroad may have had the goods consigned, had no rights to them. Whatever motivated the two, they apparently preferred to collaborate with the Netherlander van den Moere in Hamburg than with that member of their own nation.

Possibilities and Limitations of Quantitative Network Analysis

Individual examples, however, do not really tell us much about the general ethnic and religious composition of the merchant networks, because examples may be found for nearly every constellation. Quantitative analysis of the networks appears at first glance to promise a more accurate understanding of the dominant forms of merchant collaborations, and historians have repeatedly made statements about the composition of trading networks based on quantitative analysis.[22] It is my view, however, that in many cases the available data are inappropriate for that purpose. The assumption that Portuguese Jews and New Christians mainly traded among themselves has been supported, for example, by information gathered from Inquisition trial records.[23] But inquisitors demanding the names of an accused's business correspondents would have been less invested in uncovering his connections with Old Christians than with New Christians and Jews. As a result, uncritical analysis of Inquisition trials may easily lead us to overestimate contact between New Christian and Jewish traders.

Notarial files are somewhat better suited to the analysis of trading networks.[24] The notaries did not concentrate on particular groups. Their clients were New Christians and Old Christians; Portuguese, Hamburgers, and Netherlanders; Jews, Catholics, Lutherans, and Reformed. Furthermore, the notarial files contain information much more precise and reliable than the files of the Inquisition. They give particulars of the types and durations of business transactions, the amounts of money involved, and the roles played by individuals; these were, after all, legal documents that could be used in court to make claims or to contest the claims of others. Everyone had an interest in seeing that they were correct. Still, even notarial files pose a problem for quantitative network analysis in that there is no way to assess how completely the notaries documented the transactions that occurred, or the relative importance of documented versus undocumented transactions. As historian Oscar Gelderblom confirms, Antwerp and Amsterdam notaries registered only a fraction of the commercial and financial transactions made in those ports.[25] Certificates issued by a notary were especially necessary when other (informal) guarantees were lacking and merchants needed a legal instrument to ensure their rights. Alternative guarantees might include high levels of public awareness, as when there were especially prominent issues or parties engaged – when business was done with princes, for example. Moreover, in the Portuguese-Jewish community and others like it, well-functioning internal rules and sanctions may have generated contractual relations among the members that made the use of a notary superfluous. That, at least, is what Avner Greif seems to suggest. In short, the notarial files are not comprehensive records of trading activity either.[26]

Still, they are informative, and Jessica Vance Roitman conducted a statistical analysis of the notarial files in Amsterdam that is directly relevant to the issues raised in this book.[27] Roitman selected three outstanding Portuguese-Jewish merchants in that city and investigated their networks, comparing them with those of a randomly selected group of other Portuguese-Jewish merchants.[28] She did not make certain differentiations that might have been appropriate; she did not distinguish among more and less extensive relationships, for instance, giving the same weight to enduring partnerships with substantial shared capitalization as to short-term, less heavily capitalized alliances. She also weighted long-term powers of attorney the same as powers of attorney granted for a single transaction.[29] Nonetheless, her findings are worthy of note. She found that the Portuguese Jews in Amsterdam used notaries primarily to document transactions with non-Portuguese merchants, and only to a lesser extent those with other Portuguese. Of the 1,082 data sets that she analyzed on Portuguese trading operations, 74 percent involved non-Portuguese. For the data sets of the three prominent merchants, the figure was 86 percent, 76 percent, and 77 percent, respectively.[30] From this Roitman concludes not only that "intercultural" (that is, interethnic) trade was a common practice among Portuguese Jews, but also that the success of the merchants depended on the degree of interculturality of their trade. We may doubt that notarial data offer a perfectly representative image of their trade; even so, it is clear from this that the Portuguese Jews in Amsterdam were not at all an economically segregated group.

Business Partnerships and Training

The Portuguese Jews in Hamburg were likely as ethnically heterogeneous in their business relationships as Roitman's sample in Amsterdam. However, as I have said, it is important to recognize that these merchants engaged in more than one kind of business relationship, and in Hamburg ethnic heterogeneity was definitely not a feature of the *long-term trading partnerships*. These were close collaborations, often of unrestricted duration (as opposed to temporary alliances), in which most, if not all, of the partners' assets were wagered on their common venture. Of the shared bank accounts in Hamburg in 1619 (which we may suppose to have reflected such partnerships), very few involved members of different nations, and none whatever alliances between Jews and Christians. The same is true of joint payments of the Admiralty customs duties in 1632 and 1647.[31] In fact, most Hamburg long-term partnerships were family affairs. A son might enter into partnership with his father after concluding his training, or several brothers might take over the business of a deceased relative. Rudolf and

Arnold, the sons of the Netherlandish merchant Willem Amsinck, for example, began working for their father's partnership in Hamburg after they married, and eventually became partners themselves.[32] After the elder Amsinck's death in 1618 the two of them continued to run the partnership, which remained listed in the Admiralty customs books into the 1630s.

When the 18-year-old Johann Schulte arrived in Lisbon he immediately associated himself with a man by the name of Drinckherrn who was known to his family and who, according to the elder Schulte, would "love him like a brother" and "give him a hand with everything to the extent possible."[33] Within five months after the younger Schulte's arrival, the two associates appear to have entered into a fully-fledged trading partnership, whereupon the father wrote, "8 days ago I received your letter of May 31, from which I note that you and your associate have entered into a partnership contract [societät contract] for a duration of 5 years."[34] It does, however, seem to have been unusual for a young man to enter into that kind of partnership so quickly after his arrival, because the father noted in another letter that his son was doing much better than the son of his colleague Mayor Moller. Moller's son had been sent to Cádiz, where he had to work several years for an employer, whereas Schulte's son had gone to Lisbon and "immediately become his own master and taken up trading in God's name as a young man of 18."[35]

As I explained in chapter 7, the stay of most young merchants abroad started with an extended training period. During that time they often worked for, and lived in the houses of, business correspondents of their fathers, or of some family member. The names of many such employers of Hamburg apprentices in Portugal are known.[36] Sources are much scantier for foreign apprentices in Hamburg, but it is probable that both young Portuguese and young Netherlanders there, as well as the sons of Hamburgers who had settled in Portugal, were housed mostly with people of their own nation during their apprenticeships. As I have mentioned, the New Christian Baltasar Álvares Nogueira worked as a merchant assistant in Hamburg under his uncle Manuel Rodrigues Isidro. However, Nogueira's brother, who remained in Lisbon, took in not a young Portuguese from Hamburg, but a young Hamburger, João Bockol.[37] Once again, it may be assumed that otherwise the danger of being denounced to the Inquisition would have been too great both for the host and for his apprentice. As a result, the trading networks set up by the young Portuguese Jews, who were almost always taken in by other Portuguese in the diaspora, tended to be more ethnically and religiously homogeneous than those of the young Hamburgers, who could easily be housed by locals in Portugal.

After the Hamburger Henrique Picht had served his apprenticeship under his uncle in Lisbon, the two of them imported grain valued at 400,000 reis from

Hamburg in a temporary partnership (*em companhia de sociedade*) set up for this purpose.[38] This was typical; a merchant's first contracts and partnerships were often negotiated in the course of his apprenticeship. As a first step he could be permitted to take on some commissions of his own. Once his training was complete, his former employer might appoint him as a commission agent, enter into temporary partnership with him, or support him in other ventures. The continued support of erstwhile patrons was not without self-interest; it was important for them to retain the loyalty of former apprentices and business assistants once they had gone off on their own. Apprentices had access to their employers' account books; indeed, they were frequently charged with keeping them. During their employment they acquired knowledge of all aspects of the business: what goods their employers traded in and with whom; the underlying calculations by which such decisions were made; and the histories of successful and failed ventures. Bad blood between employers and their one-time apprentices or assistants could have nasty consequences. Furthermore, as I have suggested, New Christian and Jewish employers had to contend with the possibility of denunciation to the Inquisition. Heitor Mendes Bravo, for example, who worked as a bookkeeper for the merchant Manuel Pimentel in Amsterdam, later denounced him and many of his Portuguese-Jewish business correspondents, including some from Hamburg whom he had come to know on trips made on his employer's behalf.[39] In other words, good relationships with former apprentices were not only important to the business success of both, but they could also be a factor in personal safety.

Marriage, Family, and Business

Employers had yet another means of ensuring the loyalty of their former apprentices and assistants: marriage to a daughter or sister. Marriage contracts and the founding contracts of trading partnerships carried a similar legal status, as their adjacent positioning in the Hamburg town law of 1603/1605 makes clear. "Regarding honest engagement, marriage, and dowry" appears immediately after the section "Regarding partnerships or partnerships of merchants"[40] under the rubric "Regarding contracts and diverse transactions." Such a marriage offered many benefits to a young merchant. A father- and brothers-in-law would be ready collaborators and grant him entrée into their already established networks. A wife's dowry and inheritance were another important benefit. Before Rudolf Amsinck married, his father negotiated for two months with his bride's father, the Iberia merchant Cornelis de Hertoghe. According to Rudolf, the largest portion of the negotiated dowry was "in God's name invested on February 24, 1602 A.D. in the cloth and broadcloth trade which my father has in partnership with Liven van der Eggen."[41] In general, a dowry consolidated the assets that the young merchant had already accumulated himself; as Mayor Schulte noted, a young man had to put together "a good piece of money" in order to settle down permanently.[42]

Within-Group Marriages in Hamburg

In Hamburg, merchants generally married within their own ethnic and religious groups. This was true of both the old established Hamburg families and of the foreign nations. The extended Beckmann family, mentioned above, during the seventeenth century counted 14 daughters who married merchants, yet only three of them married men not from Hamburg.[43] The Hamburg merchant families that did not belong to the elite were somewhat more open, but they also clearly preferred families from Hamburg or the near vicinity over Netherlandish, not to mention Portuguese, families. Even the Lutherans among the first-generation Netherlanders were rarely the focus of Hamburgers' marital aspirations: only about 6 percent of first-generation Netherlanders' marriages included a partner of German origin.[44] In fact, until the third generation, most Lutheran Netherlanders in Hamburg married among their own.[45] Marriages between Lutheran and Reformed Netherlandish merchant families were very rare in Hamburg, although they appear to have been permitted by the Reformed Church at least.[46]

Endogamy was even more pronounced among the Portuguese who had converted to Judaism. According to community rules, both partners to a marriage had to be Jews and belong to the Portuguese nation – that is, to be of Portuguese or at least Iberian origin (thus excluding German and Polish Jews; see chapter 14). Of all the Portuguese living in Hamburg, only one is known to have married a *flamenga* (that is, a Hamburger or Netherlander; see chapter 4): Baltasar Álvares Nogueira, the nephew of Manuel Rodrigues Isidro.[47] Portuguese merchants who failed to find suitable wives within the Hamburg community sought them among the Portuguese Jews or New Christians of Amsterdam, Antwerp, Rouen, or London, and occasionally even farther afield.[48] In 1615, on the initiative of the Hamburg-based merchant Gonçalo Lopes Coutinho, a dowry society was established. The *Holy Society for the Dowering of Orphans and Poor Maidens* (Santa Companhia de Dotar Orfans e Donzelas Pobres) provided financial support for impoverished young women of Iberian-Jewish descent who converted to Judaism and married a Jew of the diaspora. Most of these women were New Christians in southern France who had recently crossed the border from the Iberian Peninsula; the funds they were given enabled them to travel north.[49]

That the Portuguese Jews married only within their own nation precluded many avenues for networking, and so limited the diversity of their trading opportunities. From the 1640s on, as the last great New Christian bankers in Madrid left the Iberian Peninsula, and Amsterdam was becoming the definitive economic and cultural center of Portuguese Jewry, the wealthiest families in the diaspora tended to confine their marriages even more. In principle, there may have been business advantages to endogamy at this level, since it concentrated economic and social capital within a small circle of families and thereby intensified business loyalties. But in practice, the Hamburg contingent of this oligarchy of merchant families consisted almost exclusively of members of the Teixeira and Nunes da Costa families.[50]

Intergroup Marriages in Portugal

It was different for the Hamburgish and Netherlandish merchants who married in Portugal. Marriages with Portuguese women were common even in the first generation. As we saw in chapter 6, converting to Catholicism was not difficult for Protestant immigrants. Most of them had converted by the time of their marriages; some few, however, appear to have viewed themselves as Catholics even without formal conversion.[51] This circumstance sometimes came to the attention of the Inquisition; for example, a young Hamburg wheat dealer by the name of David, who was 19 or 20 years old, was denounced by a (Catholic) cleric who served as confessor to the Germans, on the grounds that David, a Lutheran, had married a Catholic woman.[52]

The Netherlanders and Portuguese in Hamburg mostly arrived with their entire families, but Hamburgers usually went to Portugal as unmarried adolescents or young men. Because very few German women made the trip south, men who wished to marry there had to look to the local society.[53] Some Hamburg merchants who met with success in Portugal married the daughters of other Hamburg, German, or Netherlandish businessmen who had settled there. The businessman Pedro Pedrossen, who was born in Hamburg and to whom the king had rented a crown contract, married Luísa, the Porto-born daughter of Hamburg merchant Armão Piper.[54] Hamburger Pedro Hasse, also the holder of a contract, married Graça de Belém, the Lisbon-born daughter of diamond dealer André de Belém from Gelderland.[55] Consul Willem Heusch married a woman named Catarina Coler, who was born in Lisbon but whose maiden name indicates that her father was probably German or Netherlandish.[56] Heusch's own daughter Felicia married businessman Pedro da Maya de Thessen, who was born in Lübeck.[57] But many other merchants of Hamburg origin married women from Portuguese society.

Some Hanseatic merchants remained single, and this could be met with incomprehension. Thus João Canjuel, who denounced the Hamburg merchant

João Eggers (see chapters 4 and 15), pointed out that both the nearly 50-year-old Eggers and one of his "disciples" had never married. Two others among them had married New Christians, and a fourth had married a woman who was half Netherlandish and a quarter New Christian. These facts were seen by Canjuel as indicators of heresy.[58] In general, Old Christian merchants avoided marrying New Christians. To stave off the potential stigma attendant upon such a marriage they researched the ancestry of marriageable women. For example, the businessman Ricardo Henriques from Setúbal declared that he could vouch for the purity of blood of one of Willem Heusch's granddaughters; he explained that his own son had married her sister, and before consenting to that marriage he had acquired detailed information about the family of the bride.[59]

In summary, the Hamburg and Netherlandish merchants in Portugal became well networked with local merchants in part as a result of their marriages to local women. Religious discrepancies could be overcome by conversion, and ethnic differences mattered only if the wife was a New Christian. In Hamburg, by contrast, Netherlanders (in particular Reformed Netherlanders) and Portuguese Jews very rarely connected by marriage with the locals. Once again, it is evident that foreign merchants were able to integrate and assimilate much more easily in Portugal than in Hamburg.

Conversion as a Disruptive Force: Hamburgers and Old Christian Portuguese

A merchant's family was one of his primary sources of support. It was easier to trust people whom he already knew or who were at least known to his relatives. Nonetheless, kinship did not always mean solidarity. There has never been a time when families were not also potential loci of argument, exploitation, and even outright deceit. In one of his letters Mayor Schulte wrote, "I know of no family here in which misunderstanding and discord do not occasionally occur, even among sisters and brothers: the examples are legion, and I have no time to list them all specifically, nor describe them, because there are just too many examples of such."[60] The causes of such conflicts might have roots in personal or business matters, with the one not infrequently bleeding into the other. And in the families that traded between Hamburg and Portugal, a further factor has to be added to the usual bones of contention: migration, and the religious conversion that often went with it, had the potential to trigger and intensify conflicts at home.

Just choosing to migrate and work elsewhere could damage a young person's relationship of trust with family members left behind. In some cases, leaving home was tantamount to rebellion, or at least flight from the strictures of family. One example is that of the 17-year-old Hamburger Pedro Müller, who testified before the Inquisition that he had come to Portugal to escape his mother.[61] Among other things, he maintained, she had done everything in her power to force him to accept Lutheranism, whereas he, like his deceased father, had favored Catholicism. He had had many fights with her, including one over his request that she withdraw him from the Lutheran school he was attending. But when she finally agreed, she sent him to a Reformed school instead. He could hardly stand it there, he testified, and after two months he told her that he was quitting school and leaving the city to fend for himself out in the world, in freedom. He spent some time in Iceland, where he had a grandfather and some other relatives. However, in the end he decided to go to Portugal so he could live as a Catholic. Although Müller's report sounds as though it was tailored for the ears of the inquisitors, it is not unreasonable to assume that family conflicts did play a role in emigration from Hamburg or Portugal, and that family ties were sometimes severed in the wake of departure to a country with other religious affiliations.

Immigrants to Portugal frequently reported conflicts with their families after converting to Catholicism. The 26-year-old Hamburger João da Maya told the Inquisition that after living in Lisbon as a Catholic for five or six years he returned to Hamburg, where he informed his mother of his religious conversion, at which she became enraged and fought with him.[62] She seems then to have sent him to several Lutheran preachers so that they could convince him to renounce Catholicism. And in this they succeeded; he began practicing Lutheranism in Hamburg and promised his mother not to return to the Catholic faith. Once he returned to Lisbon, however, he did just that. He had considered appearing before the Inquisition earlier, he confessed, but had lacked the courage because of his promise to his mother. He had hesitated, too, lest his correspondents in Hamburg, having learned that he had reconverted, would no longer entrust him with commissions. This statement also seems colored by a desire to please the Inquisition, but it is plausible nonetheless. Conversion could lead to a break in business relationships; anyone who wavered in his self-representation, including his religious affiliation, risked losing credibility.

Hamburg was not the only place where conversion led to family strife. Manuel Cardoso, who has been mentioned several times (see chapters 5 and 6), was a Portuguese Old Christian who eventually converted to Judaism. In his autobiography he described how his father reacted when he learned that Manuel had converted to the Reformed faith during his apprenticeship in England.[63] When Manuel returned to his father's house in the Azores, his family celebrated with the usual feast. But on the following Saturday, just as he was about to go to bed, his father called him over, took him out onto the veranda overlooking the ocean, and asked whether he had ever said anything against the Catholic religion while abroad – because someone from the Inquisition had come to arrest him. His son should tell him if he were a thief, a murderer, or a bandit, because then he would give him money and a horse, and if he did not have one he would carry him on his own shoulders, because this is what fathers do for their sons and sons for their fathers. But if it were a question of faith, he would walk seven miles on foot, and personally fetch the wood for the stake. Manuel thanked his father for his good intentions, then turned his back on him and left him alone with his mother. After Manuel's arrest and confession that he was in fact an adherent of the Reformed faith, his father locked himself in his house, latching all the doors and windows as if he had been cursed, and forbade anyone from bringing a bed, food, or anything else from his house to his son's cell. The bare necessities were eventually provided by his grandmother. Unlike the other instances I have described, this was not a confession Cardoso delivered before the Inquisition, and therefore he had no need to legitimize himself with an eye toward absolution by Catholics. However, autobiography is not necessarily any more credible than confession; in this instance, it was a matter of self-justification as well as justification before his new Portuguese-Jewish community. Still, it is unlikely that he would have made up such a tale out of whole cloth; conversion was often a source of grief within families, both in the settlements of the diaspora and among those left behind.

Conversion as a Disruptive Force: New Christians and Jews

Old Christian Portuguese and Hamburg merchants feared being rejected or disinherited by their families and losing commissions from their colleagues if they converted. The situation was more complex for New Christians who converted to Judaism. Scholars have generally assumed that their different faiths did not cloud family or social relationships with other New Christians.[64] But if the New Christians who remained in Portugal were at all devout in their Catholicism, conflicts between them and the Portuguese-Jewish emigrants were likely. A family member who renounced the Catholic faith confirmed the view, widely held in Portuguese society, that New Christians were little more than clandestine Jews. Besides, this act posed a very real danger to his relatives, because it contributed to the suspicion that they too might be practicing Judaism in secret, and intending to leave the country.

There was also grave conflict sometimes when a Portuguese Jew returned to the Iberian Peninsula and reconverted to Catholicism there. That person's Jewish relatives in the diaspora were likely to suffer greatly. They lost not only a family member who might have been dear to them, but also a member of their community – the community of their new faith, acquired only recently and with much effort. In addition, there was the prospect that the reconvert might denounce family, friends, or acquaintances to the Inquisition. Diogo de Lima is one such example.[65] He was born in Hamburg to Portuguese-Jewish parents and raised as a Jew. At the age of about 18 he went to Lisbon, and was baptized there. As a member of the Hamburg community recounted later, his father reacted with open disgust when he learned of his son's apostasy.[66] A few years later Diogo appeared before the tribunal of the Inquisition and denounced his parents, his two older brothers (who had been born in Portugal), and a number of other members of the Hamburg community. He also named witnesses living in Lisbon who knew the Hamburg merchants and could confirm his statement. When asked why it had taken him so long to come forward with his denunciation, he declared that he had heard that goods belonging to the denounced persons had arrived in Lisbon from Hamburg. But, he continued, he was not intent on profiting from the seizure of these goods (as his denunciation gave him the right to do). Nor was he denouncing the members of his family out of hatred or ill will. He was acting solely out of religious zeal, and love of the truth. In 1644 Diogo de Lima denounced members of the Hamburg community again, but not long after that, he returned to Hamburg and converted to Lutheranism there.[67] The reasons for this are unknown. His father had died, and Diogo's conversion may have had to do with an intention to demand his portion of the estate.[68] But his brother Duarte no longer recognized him as a member of the family, and withheld his part of the inheritance. He did provide for an annual pension, but only on the condition that Diogo return to the Jewish fold. Diogo thereupon turned to the City Council and demanded that Jews be obliged to pay all estate claims made by former coreligionists who had converted to Lutheranism. He received support in this endeavor both from the City Council and the Hamburg clergy, but it seems that his efforts were unsuccessful. In 1669, 25 years after his father's death and nine years after his brother's, his claim had still not been settled.[69] But at least with the City Council's intercession he received an allowance, financed by the city treasury, sufficient to eke out an existence.

Stories like this account in part for the widely-held fear among the Portuguese Jews that their fellows might renounce Judaism and return to the Iberian Peninsula. Denial of inheritance or dowry was one of the most important forms of leverage applied by families against such decisions although, as the example of Diogo de Lima shows, it was not an infallible one.[70] The community board was also committed to preventing Jews from relapsing to Catholicism, and often forbade travel to Catholic countries. As I will show in chapter 14, in the long run, this ban was another detriment to the maintenance of trading relationships between Hamburg and Portugal.

13 Merchant Organizations

During the sixteenth century commercial practices developed that increased merchants' mobility and emancipated them from the corporate bodies that had been customary up to then (see chapter 10). Almost any merchant could, by means of a personal trading network, participate in long-distance trade on his own (see chapter 12). In the second half of the seventeenth century, however, the importance of corporate structures once again increased. Two commercial interest groups of major importance were the Commercial Deputation in Hamburg and the Brazil Company in Portugal. Merchants who were excluded from these organizations because they were foreigners or because they were Jewish either assimilated into the majority society and so became eligible to join the organizations that were not otherwise open to them, or formed supportive structures of their own within their respective nations. The two chapters that follow deal with the nations themselves; this one focuses on the corporate bodies that were strictly commercial, and on their importance as lobbying organizations for the merchants trading between Hamburg and Portugal.

Hamburg: Traveler Companies, the Common Merchant, and the Admiralty

During the Middle Ages, Hamburgers who engaged in long-distance trade organized themselves into so-called *traveler companies* (*Fahrergesellschaften*). The first such companies were made up of merchants trading with Flanders, England, and Scania respectively; they were followed somewhat later by companies for merchants trading with Iceland and Bergen.[1] These were not guilds in the narrow sense, but rather loose associations of people with similar commercial interests. They generally operated regionally, but the merchants who traded with a given region were not compelled to join, and merchants who traded with other regions were not excluded. Nor did every region with which Hamburg merchants traded have its own traveler company: Spain, Portugal, and the Mediterranean basin, for example, had none. Where the companies did exist, however, we can assume that they served their members for political, economic, and legal lobbying. They survived into the seventeenth century, but we know little about them so late in their history, except that their members by then came for the most part from the city's merchant elite. Of those accepted into the Company of Flanders Travelers between 1631 and 1700, almost half were city councilors, senior elders (*Oberalte*), or the sons of such officials.[2] As the membership lists make clear, recent citizens

https://doi.org/10.1515/9783110472103-014

who had come from abroad were seldom accepted, and merchants without citizen status were excluded from membership.

Until the year 1517, the sea-trading merchants in Hamburg, collectively known as the Common Merchant, had lacked any overall organization. In that year, however, the City Council permitted them to elect a board to represent their interests before local and foreign authorities.[3] The new board was also granted power to arbitrate commercial disputes pertaining to maritime trade. However, "in serious matters and those that concern the common good of the city" the two city councilors commissioned with customs issues (*Zollherren*) were to be called in to render a decision; it was made clear that "in all these matters the official authority of the Honorable Council would remain intact."[4] Furthermore, although the Board of the Common Merchant was to be composed entirely of merchants – specifically two aldermen (*Älterleute*) each from the companies of Flanders, England, and Scania travelers – the merchants were required to consult with the two customs councilors in their election. The new entity was established by written statute in 1523, but hardly anything is known about its activities after that, and disunity and other problems seem to have led to its formal dissolution in 1557, 40 years after its founding. One year later the Hamburg Exchange was founded (see chapter 10), and in about 1570, a new merchant board was established on the model of the old one, but this time with the primary task of overseeing the Exchange. The original board's assets, books, and other properties were handed over to the new aldermen, who came to be known after the beginning of the seventeenth century as exchange elders (*Börsenalte*).

After the Admiralty was founded in 1623, it assumed some of the functions that had previously resided with the Board of the Common Merchant.[5] The Admiralty was not a corporate merchant body, however, but a regulatory adjunct to the Hamburg City Council, in whose name all of its decisions were made. Though six deputies of the Admiralty board were merchants and two were shipmaster elders (*Schifferalte*; that is, the heads of the shipmasters' corporation), the other four (five as of 1687) were members of the City Council. We do not know how the first deputies were chosen, but we do know that from then on deputies recruited their own successors; the merchants at large were not consulted. The Admiralty had both administrative and judiciary functions in the safeguarding of trade and shipping.[6] To deter raids by pirates or foreign forces, it organized the arming of west-bound trading ships with cannons and munitions, and established admiralships (*Admiralschaften*; that is, associations of merchant ships for mutual protection under the leadership of a civilian admiral). To pay for this, the Admiralty established two levies: a customs duty upon the merchants (the one that we have encountered so often in this study), and a tonnage fee upon the shipmasters. Also for defensive purposes, in 1662 a convoy deputation was founded as an auxiliary to the Admiralty to manage the construction, arming, and maintenance of two convoy ships; from 1668 on these accompanied the trading vessels sailing to the Iberian Peninsula. A year after its founding, the Admiralty board also set up a public slave fund (*Sklavenkasse*) to gain the release of seamen who had been taken captive in North Africa.[7] But above all, the Admiralty assumed jurisdiction in all questions relating to maritime law, maritime trade law, and maritime insurance law. Neither nation nor religion had any legal relevance in the services that the Admiralty extended to merchants.[8]

Portugal: The Board of the Merchants' Commonweal and the Consulado

Since the Middle Ages the merchants' organization in Portugal had been the *Board of the Merchants' Commonweal* (Mesa do Bem Comum dos Mercadores).[9] Almost nothing is known about this body that in the eighteenth century, under the Marquis of Pombal, gave rise to the *Chamber of Commerce* (Junta do Comércio). Neither minutes nor other official writings have survived. In structure and function it may have been similar to the Hamburg Board of the Common Merchant, but it is unlikely that it had much autonomy. Its members were merchants engaged in long-distance and wholesale trade, but it probably also accommodated retailers and perhaps even members of other professions. Foreign merchants were most likely not permitted to join.

During the Iberian Union, however, a clearly defined Portuguese merchant association came into being. In 1592 King Felipe II founded the *Court and Board of the Consulate* (Tribunal e Mesa do Consulado). The Consulado was an organization along the lines of the merchant guilds in Burgos and Seville.[10] Its duties were similar to those of the Hamburg Admiralty; it had jurisdiction in merchant disputes involving matters relating to trade, insurance, and bills of exchange, and the responsibility to protect maritime shipping from raids and attacks. To this end it was supposed to build and outfit an armed fleet of at least twelve ships. Financing was to come from a levy of 3 percent on all goods imported from or exported to India, West Africa, Cape Verde, São Tomé, and Brazil.

In establishing the Consulado, the king recognized the long-distance merchants' claim to a privileged organization; it was not a corporate body in the strict sense, however, as it lacked self-governance. The Consulado did have a certain degree of independence, and it was not subordinate to the *House of India, Mina, and Guinea* (Casa da Índia, Mina e Guiné), the central state authority that oversaw administration and trade in the Portuguese overseas possessions. But while the founding edict of the Seville Consulado provided that its leading officers be elected by the merchants themselves, the Portuguese Consulado had no such provision, and it is likely that its leaders (its priors and consuls) were appointed by the king. In fact there are strong indications that Felipe established the Consulado primarily to shift the burden of defending maritime trade, which up to that time had been the responsibility of the state, to private entrepreneurs. Nothing is known about how foreign merchants were situated vis-à-vis the Consulado. Because those who were granted the German Merchant Privilege had their own judge, they may not have come under its jurisdiction.

While the Hamburg Admiralty was an enduring institution, the Consulado had only a short lifespan. In 1602, a mere ten years after its founding, it was dissolved by royal decree. Its jurisdiction was returned to the ordinary court of the realm (*juízo ordinário do reino*), and the power of disposition over money and ships was withdrawn too – although the 3 percent levy continued in effect. The reasons for the dissolution are unclear. It has been suggested that the board had enriched itself at the expense of poorer merchants.[11] Nevertheless, merchants in Lisbon, Porto, and Viana reacted to the dissolution with protests and revolts. Lisbon merchants periodically tried to revive the Consulado, but all efforts were in vain.

The Hamburg Commercial Deputation and its Membership

On January 19, 1665 the merchants in Hamburg introduced a new organizational framework for defending their interests: they founded the Commercial Deputation. According to the founding document,

> the merchants trading by sea here in Hamburg [declare] unanimously that seven persons from among them, six of them honorable merchants who have good trade and correspondence in the Baltic Sea as well as in the West [i.e., North] Sea and use insurances, and one shipmaster elder, shall be elected, to observe whatever is conducive to salutary commerce and convey most diligently the abuses and grievances that it may encounter to the Honorable Council, with which they shall cooperate to hinder those impediments in time and remedy them as well as possible.[12]

In 1674 the Commercial Deputation was well enough established to be recognized as a permanent institution by the Hamburg City Council and the Assembly of Citizens, and assigned a contribution from the convoy monies administered by the Admiralty to help defray its costs.[13] Unlike its predecessor, the Board of the Common Merchant, the Commercial Deputation became very powerful; it survives today as the Hamburg Chamber of Commerce.

According to its founding document, the Deputation was to represent all Hamburg merchants involved in maritime trade. In practice, however, it served only those merchants who had access to the Assemblies of the Honorable Merchant. The Honorable Merchant was the collective that succeeded the Common Merchant (see chapter 11). In 1668, at one of its first official conventions, it confirmed the empowerment of the Deputation to act in the interests of commerce, and promised to support its deputies faithfully in all matters.[14] A document to that effect was drafted and signed by all present. But it is clear in retrospect that from the very beginning some merchants were excluded from its assemblies: namely the English Merchant Adventurers – and the Jews.[15]

On the other hand, neither citizen status nor Lutheranism was a precondition for admission to the assemblies. Unlike in the traveler companies, Netherlanders and Hamburgers were equals in the Honorable Merchant, regardless of legal status or religious affiliation; on one occasion in 1694, at the behest of the City Council, only the citizens and members of "the Augsburg confession" (that is, Lutherans) were convened to an assembly, and there was an indignant outcry at the Exchange.[16] The members of the Commercial Deputation were not required to be Lutheran either, although they did have to be citizens.[17] Two of its six founding members were Netherlanders, Michel Heusch and Daniel le Conte, both of whom in time assumed the office of chairman.[18] Later members of the Commercial Deputation included the Netherlandish merchants Hinrich de Dobbeler, Adrian Boon, Valerius van Dalen, Paul Amsinck, Hinrich von Som, and Hans Hinrich von Dort. All in all, 16 percent of the deputies in the seventeenth century were Netherlanders. At least two of those named above, Le Conte and von Dort, were probably of the Reformed faith.

The Commercial Deputation and Hamburg Politics

The 1665 founding document of the Commercial Deputation defined its objective as the defense of "salutary commerce." Exactly what "salutary" meant was left to the deputies. According to historian Ernst Baasch, the Commercial Deputation was never willing to limit its functions to purely commercial and economic questions; from the outset it pressed strongly for its political interests too. In fact, as Baasch has argued, in the seventeenth century it had a "not inconsiderable influence on policies in Hamburg."[19] What this influence may have been regarding Portugal awaits further research. It seems certain, however, that Hamburg's relations with the Iberian Peninsula were one of its major concerns.

In principle, negotiations with other powers were conducted only by the City Council, but the Council worked closely with the Deputation in this matter. It is also known that the commercial deputies often discussed matters with diplomats on the quiet,[20] and occasionally foreign agents not accredited by the Council tried to enter into negotiations with it through the Deputation's intercession, a practice that the Council forbade.[21] Similarly, the Deputation was intent upon influencing the Hansa consulships. It worked to establish new consulates, recommended consuls, and, when necessary, complained about consuls in office.[22] The wide array of contacts that the Deputation had with officials abroad may be gauged, among other things, by the abundance of gifts it bestowed on diplomats, statesmen, consuls, and others.[23]

A matter of "salutary commerce", in which the Commercial Deputation is known to have become involved in the city itself, concerned Hamburg's Portuguese Jews. At the end of the seventeenth century, the Assembly of Citizens demanded that the Jews be assessed contributions beyond the usual levies, and the Commercial Deputation repeatedly asked the City Council to intercede on the Jews' behalf. This was not an act of disinterested solidarity. The deputies feared that new taxes might prompt the "large wholesalers and capitalists" among the Jews to move to the neighboring town of Altona, which, with the influx of their trade, would flourish at Hamburg's expense. They made very clear that they were speaking not "as patrons of the Jews, but as honest patriots who can well see that the Jews will not move across the Alps or Pyrenees Mountains, but rather as soon as they are gone from this city they will settle along these borders and begin their commerce in Altona, and establish large-scale trade there, to the great detriment of this city." The deputies emphasized that they were interested only in "what concerns the trade of the Exchange"; the "synagogues or religion" of the Jewish traders had "nothing to do with them."[24] They saw the *presence* of the Portuguese, who as Jews were excluded from the Honorable Merchant, as economically advantageous to themselves; the *interests* of these colleagues were not their concern.[25] Although the City Council agreed with the deputies that the Portuguese should be kept in the city, it was not able to prevail over the citizens in this matter. And in fact many Portuguese did leave the city as a result, although most of the wealthier ones left not for Altona, but for Amsterdam.

Another goal of the Commercial Deputation was to curtail conflicts. It tried to mediate in disputes among merchants, insurers, and shipmasters, and it asserted competency in matters that were actually the province of the Admiralty. It took to itself, for example, the nomination and appointment of *Dispacheure* (officials responsible for calculating shipping and sea damages) and *Taxadeure* (officials responsible for the sale of damaged goods), which until then had been the Admiralty's province. It drafted and revised the insurance, bankruptcy, and exchange laws, and it assumed responsibility for writing expert opinions or appraisals in lawsuits involving merchants.[26] By all these interventions it hoped to resolve conflicts internally and not have them become public. This was also the objective of a clause in certain insurance contracts discussed by the Deputation in 1700, which would have required the parties to accept the arbitration of other merchants – "good men" from among their own number. That is, disputes would be resolved without recourse to the Admiralty.[27]

The merchants' wish to protect and strengthen the reputation of the city of Hamburg by presenting it as a dependable place for secure and successful trading became explicit when the city was shaken by violent religious and political unrest in 1693 and 1694. On that occasion, the Honorable Merchant feared the turmoil would result in Hamburg's "commerce having a bad reputation outside the city," and the Commercial Deputation handed the City Council a detailed petition urging it to take sharp and energetic steps to halt the rioting. But this did little to quell the disturbances. Indeed, in January 1694 the Hamburg Exchange itself was drawn into the general tumult; the "common people" took to the streets armed "with cudgels and sticks" and prevented the merchants from convening.[28]

Lack of Representation by the Commercial Deputation

The 1665 founding document of the Commercial Deputation, as quoted above, states that the deputies were to inform the City Council of trade abuses or grievances, and cooperate with it in remedying them. In other words, the Deputation was not only supposed to represent the merchants' interests, but also to support the Council in an alliance that fostered the city's trade. And indeed, many of the deputies, being members of the merchant elite with (as the document affirmed) "good trade and correspondence," were closely entangled with the city oligarchy.

The first chairman of the Commercial Deputation was the Netherlander Michel Heusch, probably a brother of the Willem Heusch, who since 1641 had been the German consul in Lisbon. Willem's close relations with the Portuguese court, and the importance of his position during the Portuguese Restoration War, have already been discussed (see chapter 4). His relatives in Hamburg probably profited from them as well as he; in 1647 Michel Heusch accounted for the ninth highest turnover in the Portugal trade. In total he traded in thirteen ports on which Hamburg levied Admiralty customs duties. The Burmesters were another important merchant family active in both the Commercial Deputation and the Portugal trade. Gerd Burmester, Mayor Schulte's son-in-law, who had lived in Lisbon in his youth and in 1647 accounted for the second highest turnover among the Hamburg merchants trading with Portugal, was elected to the Commercial Deputation in 1676, although he withdrew the following year. Peter Burmester, probably his cousin, who had also spent time in Portugal as a young man, was a commercial deputy beginning in 1683, and chairman of the Deputation from 1687 to 1689.[29] Johann Schulte, the son of the mayor, became a member of the

Deputation in 1692, after his return to Hamburg. He served as its chairman in 1696 and 1697.[30]

To strengthen the connection between the Commercial Deputation and the Hamburg City Council, the deputies had asked as far back as 1665 that two councilors be assigned to them as adjuncts. In fact, three were named to assume this function, two of them merchants and the other a lawyer.[31] The adjuncts and the deputies probably had very similar interests. Johann Schröttering and Johann Eckhoff, both active in the Iberia trade, were the first two merchant adjuncts. In 1632 Schröttering had had the highest turnover of all Hamburg merchants trading in Portugal, and in 1647 he was in 13th place, and Eckhoff in 22nd. The first lawyer adjunct was Dietrich Moller, whose relationship with the Deputation also appears to have been very cordial. In 1680, when he was elected mayor, the Commercial Deputation honored him with 40 *Stübchen* of wine valued at 140 marks, "because back when he was with the honorable Commercial Deputation he made great efforts and served it laudably and very generously."[32]

Because the Council and the Deputation often pursued similar (if not identical) goals, the Council supported the convocations of the Assemblies of the Honorable Merchant, whose resolutions served as templates for the decisions of the Assembly of Citizens; it also encouraged merchants to participate in the Assembly of Citizens itself so that the concerns of the Commercial Deputation could be more successfully pushed through.[33] The Deputation too urged merchants to attend the conventions of the Assembly of Citizens so as to safeguard their rights and interests.[34]

But the merchants did not always agree with the commercial deputies, and many probably felt inadequately represented by them. As a matter of fact, the Honorable Merchant was rather seldom consulted, which may explain why, as time went on, many merchants simply ignored the invitations when Assemblies of the Honorable Merchant were called.[35] Even those who did appear often left before voting began.[36] Merchants received individual written invitations to the meetings, "so that no one may excuse himself by ignorance." Shortly before they began, the sergeant-at-arms at the Exchange (*Börsenknecht*) knocked several times with his stick to remind the merchants of this responsibility; if need be he went around with the minutes keeper and spoke to them individually. Even so, the assemblies often failed to achieve the quorum required to conduct business.[37] Because the merchants' presence at the assemblies and their participation in the election of deputies were important for legitimizing the Commercial Deputation, its first written regulations, drawn up in 1700, were almost exclusively concerned with ensuring regular attendance. Merchants who failed to comply were told that their interests would not be represented. The success of this threat was not impressive, however; between 1700 and 1747 only 277 persons undersigned the regulations.[38]

Among other things the merchants were dissatisfied with the way the deputies presented their issues to the City Council. In the early years, the merchants gave them specific petitions to be delivered to the Council, signed by all those who had been present at the relevant assembly. The Council, however, opposed this procedure. Handed a petition regarding Brandenburg privateers, in 1679 it declared "that this petition should be abandoned and that such [petitions] be withheld, as this and other petitions would not help the issue but rather add fuel to the fire, as much of their contents would be disseminated."[39] Problems should be resolved without fanfare through the appropriate institutional channel, and this, in the Council's view, was the Commercial Deputation.[40] In fact there is evidence that merchant groups did approach the deputies to discuss concerns, problems, and proposals, and to have the results of these discussions passed on to the City Council. But over time the Deputation acted more and more at its own discretion.

Although the Assemblies of the Honorable Merchant were usually convened by the Commercial Deputation at the behest of the deputies or the Hamburg City Council, in theory the merchants themselves could also summon an assembly. To do this they had to apply to the Deputation and specify the purpose of the meeting. Only once, in 1684, did the Honorable Merchant convene without the consent of the Deputation. On that occasion the merchants established a short-lived second representative body of eight delegates (selected from its membership) that challenged the Commercial Deputation for primacy. The City Council denied it recognition, and contested the resolutions of the assembly that the new delegates had convened. The Honorable Merchant dissolved the body in a subsequent assembly.[41]

Some of the merchants who were conspicuous by their absence at the assemblies openly debated the conditions of trade on the Hamburg Exchange, which was not at all what the deputies or the Council wanted. During one assembly a deputation chairman advised the merchants that "each may present his opinion adequately here and keep silent on the Exchange."[42] Still, in 1672 a few merchants turned directly to the City Council, without even informing the Deputation. The latter complained fervently about this, and the merchants placated the deputies with the assurance that it would not happen again.[43] Nevertheless, in 1699 the Honorable Merchant tried again to come as a whole before the presiding mayor of the city to negotiate a matter. The commercial deputies managed to prevent this, but with difficulty. Again the deputies advanced the objection that by congregating as a group the merchants were causing too much of a stir.[44]

All this meant that although the Portuguese Jews were excluded from the Honorable Merchant and its assemblies, that did not matter as much as we might have expected, since the Commercial Deputation often did not represent its members as they wished. In the Middle Ages membership in the relevant corporate bodies was essential to success in long-distance trade; in the seventeenth century, it appears, membership in the Honorable Merchant was not.

The Brazil Company and the Status of Foreigners

After the dissolution of the Consulado in 1602, the merchants in Portugal spent more than four decades largely unorganized and subject only to the centralizing pressures of an absolute monarchy. Any merchant who had concerns to voice had to bring them directly to the royal institutions. Some individual merchants took this step, and so did some groups claiming to represent merchant collectives. In 1626, for example, two petitions signed by "the merchants of the city of Lisbon" were taken up by the Council of State. The authors expressed concern that no warships had been outfitted to protect the Brazil fleet at sea and proposed, among other things, that vessels from Hamburg be used for that purpose. The Council of State supported in principle the outfitting of warships but rejected the proposal, regretting the lack of necessary funds.[45]

Merchant groups advanced the king several large loans in later attempts at such an enterprise.[46] By 1639, Felipe IV, as king of Spain and Portugal, owed them a total of about 400,000 ducats, and in the decades after the Restoration, merchants continued to lend money to the kings.[47] In part these monies came from duties that the merchants had imposed upon themselves, which implies the existence of some residual form of organization. In 1647, for instance, "the *comércio*" (lit. the trade, meaning here the collective of merchants) granted the Crown a credit of more than 200,000 cruzados for the military defense of Bahia. Because this was one of the main sugarcane-producing regions in Brazil, the credit was to be financed by extraordinary levies on the sugar trade collected by five elected representatives.[48] Likewise, in 1647, "the merchants of the city" of Lisbon decided to contribute to the building of a warehouse close to the customs house.[49] But the context in which such decisions were taken and by whom, and what the legal basis for the various imposts might have been, are not known. Nor is the role played by foreign businessmen. Probably the different groups were all loosely organized in the Board of the Merchants' Commonweal mentioned above.

It was not until 1649 that the Portuguese merchants succeeded in setting up a genuine trade organization: the *Brazil Company* (Companhia Geral do Comércio do Brasil; lit. General Brazil Trading Company). It was a joint-stock company chartered by the king and modeled on the Dutch West India Company. However, unlike its Dutch prototype, the Brazil Company had no state funding, and it was purely defensive in character. Its aim was not to promote further expansion or colonization overseas, but only to support trade with Brazil and take back its northeastern part from the Dutch, who had conquered it in 1630.[50] For this reason most of the merchants' capital went toward the building of a fleet of 36 warships, to accompany two annual convoys of trading vessels to and from Brazil and protect them from raids. In return for their investment, the king granted the company exclusive rights to supply Brazil with wine, dried cod, olive oil, and flour, and to import its brazilwood. The king, who was trying to attract New Christian investments especially, guaranteed that shareholder capital and goods would be exempt from seizure by the Inquisition. The company had its own judge (*juiz conservador*), and was led by an elected board composed of nine directors and seven councilors.

At first glance it would seem that the Brazil Company was a regionally limited company that had nothing to do with the trade with northern Europe. But the Brazil trade was so central to the Portuguese economy that it was in fact closely intertwined with all other sectors. Almost all Portuguese merchants were involved in it directly or indirectly, including those who traded with northern Europe. That did not mean, however, that the Brazil Company could claim to represent the interests of all merchants.

To understand this, it is worthwhile to look at its founding process and early development. The Crown's main concern, as in earlier such projects, was to raise money from private donors for the defense of Portuguese trade. For this purpose a meeting of "the merchants" was convened in November 1648, but (as in the 1647 conventions) it is not clear how they had been informed, or even who was included. One document, which may have come out of the meeting, gives some clues. It was drafted by the "elected representatives of the merchants" (*eleitos do comércio*) and signed by four of the nine eventual directors of the Brazil Company, two of whom belonged to the group of five merchants who had once before represented themselves as "elected" in connection with the credit of 1647 discussed above. In the 1648 document they declared their overall consent to the idea of the Brazil Company, but they also pointed out that as yet there was no consensus among the merchants at large – the *comércio* – and they recommended to the king that this be remedied before foundation. "The merchants" were convened at least twice more before an agreement with the king was reached and the Brazil Company was finally chartered. Opportunities did exist, therefore, for consultation with the larger merchant community. Nevertheless, it appears that the same merchant elite that advanced credits to the king and received crown contracts from him remained the driving force behind the company's founding and later development.

A claim has been made (and repeated in many studies) that the company was founded by and for New Christians, with the energetic support of the Jesuit father and statesman António Vieira. The exemption of New Christian investments from seizure by the Inquisition is often cited as evidence. That claim, however, is not accurate.[51] First of all, the New Christians were not the only ones to benefit from the asset-seizure exemption. The Brazil Company needed the New Christians' investments, and any impediments to them would have destabilized the entire undertaking; all shareholders profited from that protection. Second, while the company's first board did include eight New Christians, six other members were Old Christians; the origins of the remaining two could not be identified (which suggests that they too were Old Christians). Third, when the king tried to force all the New Christian merchants in Portugal to invest in the company, as the original shareholders (whose names and ethnic backgrounds are not known) urged him to do, many of them refused to comply. Finally, Vieira was not involved in the founding of the company. He was a supporter of the New Christians, and he believed that the Portuguese state had suffered considerably from their emigration and the attendant loss of their assets (see chapter 5). He also argued that the Crown should do everything in its power to get them, or at least their capital, to return to the kingdom. But as the Brazilian historian José Antônio Gonsalves de Mello has demonstrated, by the time the Brazil Company was founded in 1649, Vieira had given up on the company's main objective – to reconquer northeast Brazil from the Dutch.[52] On the contrary, he was attempting to negotiate a peace treaty with the United Provinces, and was prepared to cede Pernambuco to them permanently. Under those circumstances the Brazil Company no longer seemed relevant to him. However, a number of influential businessmen and political decision-makers in Portugal eventually prevailed against his efforts and, as it turned out, the Brazil Company did end up contributing greatly to the 1654 reconquest.

Furthermore, the company was from the beginning an international project, in which foreign investment was not only permitted but sought after. Like the New Christians, foreign Protestant investors too were protected from the Inquisition's asset seizures. According to historian Leonor Freire Costa, several of the company's business decisions in the late 1650s were heavily influenced by powerful Italian shareholders, although the total amount of their investment is not known. English merchants were also significantly involved in the activities of the Brazil Company. They worked closely with the inner circle of the company's management, and entered into partnerships such that the Portuguese handled the colonial part of the trade while the English took responsibility for marketing the goods on the European continent. We do not know if any Hamburgers participated actively in the company at this stage, but it is clear that they did benefit from the demand for ships, arms, and the other equipment needed to outfit the fleet (see chapters 4 and 7), as well as from the trade in the Brazilian goods that it made available.

In short, the Brazil Company was an association of Old and New Christian businessmen (and some participating foreign entrepreneurs) who were intent on integrating the overseas and European markets. As an economic lobbying group it sought to influence the political and military decisions of the Portuguese Crown. But its existence deepened the social split among the Portuguese merchants. Until the company was founded the Brazil trade had been open to all Portuguese; even merchants with little capital of their own could take an active hand. The company's monopoly power, however, was a severe blow to small and medium-sized merchants, because it forbade them to export local commodities such as olive oil and wine, and also because the requirement that ships going to Brazil sail in fleets concentrated the entire Atlantic trade in Lisbon while draining the smaller ports. Furthermore, the minimum investment for acquiring shares was 20 cruzados, which was felt to be dauntingly high. To be eligible for election to the board required an investment of 1,000 cruzados, but the threshold for the right to vote in board elections was even higher: 5,000 cruzados. The wealthy electors, therefore, likely exercised considerable influence over those they elected.

With the establishment of the Brazil Company the economic elite of royal contractors and creditors had created an influential institution to assert its interests. Shortly after the company's founding, pamphlets began to circulate accusing the Crown of favoring the wealthy upper class by squeezing small players out of the Brazil trade.[53] And even though the company did play a considerable role in the eventual reconquest of northeast Brazil, it encountered lasting resistance from the Council of State. In particular, the Council blamed the company for irregularities in conducting the convoys, leading to an inadequate supply of staples to Brazil. After the death of King João IV in 1658, its exemption from seizure and confiscation by the Inquisition and its monopoly on wine, dried cod, olive oil, flour were revoked. In essence that was the end of the Brazil Company. Although it remained a joint-stock company and existed formally until 1662, its only remaining function was the organization of convoys to Brazil. After that it was absorbed by the state under the name *Junta do Comércio do Brasil* (Board of the Brazil Trade) and reconstituted as a purely administrative entity.[54]

The most striking difference between the mercantile organizations in Hamburg and Portugal is the difference in their lifespans. The Hamburg Admiralty lasted for almost two hundred years, and the Commercial Deputation, in its current incarnation of the Hamburg Chamber of Commerce, has passed its 350th birthday. But the Consulado and the Brazil Company survived for only about ten years each. Merchants in Portugal were not able to acquire a position of power commensurate with their economic role, while the Hamburg Commercial

Deputation achieved a position of outstanding importance in the city's power structure. Through that institution, the Hamburg merchant elite was able, at least to some degree, to channel the interests of their less substantial colleagues such as to increase their own influence over commercial life. And as the composition of the Commercial Deputation makes clear, the Netherlanders were part of that elite, and the Portuguese Jews were not. In Portugal, by contrast, the Brazil Company was open to investment by any merchant, provided he was rich enough; foreigners seem to have had real influence, and even New Christian money was eagerly accepted.

14 The Portuguese Nation

The Portuguese-Jewish merchants in Hamburg, excluded from the traveler companies, the Honorable Merchant, and the Commercial Deputation, had to depend on their own people – the *Portuguese nation* (*nação portuguesa*) – for some of the services that those organizations provided to other merchants. Until now I have used that term in accordance with definitions imposed by the ruling authorities: that is, to refer either to the legally established body of Portuguese merchants in a given city (see chapter 3), or to the Portuguese population as a whole (see chapter 4). In this chapter I use it the way the Portuguese in Hamburg understood it: as a cultural reality referring to the Portuguese – New Christians and Jews – in the Atlantic diaspora (see chapter 6). This was a group that shared a common ethnic identity, a common set of beliefs about appropriate commercial behavior, and some common knowledge of each other's business practices. It resembled what Avner Greif calls a *coalition,* in that its mercantile activities were governed by reputation and depended upon a constant flow of information that allowed both for implicit contractual relations and for internal sanctions when breaches occurred.[1] According to Greif, those characteristics gave merchant groups an advantage in trade (see introduction and chapter 11); as we shall see, however, any advantage that they gave the Portuguese-Jewish merchants was not sufficient to make them more successful than their fellows of other nations. A clearly demarcated group, they remained burdened by diverse forms of discrimination from without, and there were internal constraints as well. Though the Portuguese-Jewish communities enforced few religious rules that interfered directly with trading practices, membership was still accompanied by disciplinary pressures that were not always beneficial to commerce and that tended to perpetuate their segregation from the majority society.

The Portuguese Nation and the Atlantic Diaspora

All of the foreign nations of the time constructed identities based on the shared ethnic origins, traditions, and languages that set them apart from their host societies. But the identity of the Portuguese abroad was more complex in character, as foreignness for them was not only a result of recent immigration. It was a much older experience, deeply felt even in their home country and rooted in their Jewish background. In Portugal, one of the most common designations for New Christians was "men of the nation" (*homens da nação*) or "people of the nation" (*gente da nação*), where "the nation" meant the most prominent "foreign" nation in the country: the

https://doi.org/10.1515/9783110472103-015

Hebrew nation. Its members had been born in Portugal or its overseas territories; they were linguistically, and mostly culturally, indistinguishable from the majority society. But they were distinct historically. And while membership in the Hebrew nation was theoretically a matter of ancestry, in practice it was determined as much by the testimony of "witnesses" as by genealogical research. Anyone who was held to be a New Christian by a sufficient number of persons and could not prove the absence of Jewish ancestry *was* a New Christian. To leave "the nation" by assimilating into Old Christian society was not an option. The New Christian exiles, whether or not they eventually chose Judaism, belonged to the Hebrew nation as well as to the Portuguese one. They came to call themselves "Hebrews of the Portuguese nation," or simply "the Portuguese nation," and not surprisingly, outsiders soon started to identify all Portuguese living outside of Portugal as Jews.[2]

Yet the reality was more complicated, and "Portuguese nation" did not always mean just one thing even to its own members. I confine myself here to the usage that predominated in Hamburg; there it referred to the Portuguese of the Atlantic diaspora (which was limited to western Europe until the Portuguese Jews followed the Dutch and English settlers into the areas they were beginning to occupy in the Americas; see chapter 6). This was the understanding recognized, for example, by the Holy Society for the Dowering of Orphans and Poor Maidens (see chapter 12), whose statutes limited eligibility to Portuguese and Spanish women of the Hebrew nation from "between Saint-Jean-de-Luz and Danzig, from France as well as from Flanders, England, and Germany."[3] It is important to note that in this case, and in general, membership in the Portuguese nation was determined not by Jewish religion, but by Jewish origin. The leaders of the Portuguese-Jewish communities undoubtedly strove to encourage the formal adoption of Judaism throughout the nation. Still, they remained willing to integrate heterodox members and accepted that in France, in the Spanish Netherlands, and even in England, New Christians could not openly embrace Jewish religious practice. What was essential was ancestry. "Purity of blood" was nearly as important in this new context as it was in Catholic Portugal and Spain – although, of course, the consequences were very different. And it was not just Jewish ancestry that mattered; there had to be Iberian ancestry as well. While Portuguese Jews were willing to disregard variations in religious observance, they distinguished sharply between themselves and Jews who were German or Polish in origin and therefore not, in their opinion, of their own people.

What all the members of the Portuguese nation did have in common was an emotional and intellectual preoccupation with Judaism. They came to terms with it in different ways, ranging from acceptance to indifference to rejection. But they had all absorbed the complex religious and ethnic associations, the intellectual and psychic conflicts, the everyday social discriminations, and the relentless fears that emerge in an environment of institutionalized persecution. The members of the Portuguese nation understood themselves as a community of fate, brought together by an experience of danger and crisis that distinguished them from others. This shared accident – persecution in, and exile from, the Iberian Peninsula – became the nation's founding myth. The New Christians who remained in Portugal or in Spain, or who settled in their overseas colonies, who never experienced the pain of exile or the resumption of Judaism, were excluded from this community, as were the Jews who had emigrated from the Iberian Peninsula to North Africa, the Ottoman Empire, or Italy by the early 1500s, and in consequence had never undergone Christianization or been subject to the Inquisition.

Among the settlements of the Portuguese nation intense personal, material, and intellectual exchanges took place: members visited among themselves and intermarried; congregations exchanged books, ritual objects, and religious officials. The Portuguese expatriates lived their entire social lives within the nation. Their relationships with the New Christians on the Iberian Peninsula and in the Iberian world outside of Europe were of a different sort. These were fostered not by community structures, but by family connections and business relationships that predated their exile.

The Nation prior to Emigration, and the General Pardon of 1605

Before their emigration from Portugal, the New Christians were not a unified group. There is no evidence of a sense of common bond among them, or of any common organizational structures. Most of what we know about them comes from their persecutors, who not only accused them indiscriminately of crypto-Judaism, but also assumed unity of purpose in its pursuit. Thus, for example, the archbishop of Évora warned his colleagues in Braga and Lisbon that New Christians, no matter how far apart, were in constant contact with each other.[4] Historians see this differently, however. Yosef Kaplan argues that there was a great heterogeneity among the group designated as New Christian on the Iberian Peninsula, which according to him included not only devout Catholics and crypto-Jews, but also deists, atheists, and members of various syncretistic sects.[5] Herman Prins Salomon, for his part, assumes that the New Christians in Portugal were largely assimilated into the rest of society, and that the variety of their beliefs as well as their sense of unity developed only in diaspora.[6]

The negotiations over the General Pardon of 1605 (see chapters 5 and 6) demonstrate the lack of coordination and solidarity among the New Christians. The fact that it was established at all has led some scholars to infer a well-organized New Christian political administration with a distinct leadership.[7] However, events seem to indicate otherwise. The initiator and leader of the negotiations was Lisbon businessman Heitor Mendes de Brito, who claimed to be acting on behalf of all New Christians.[8] He advanced significant sums of money toward the pardon, and until the very end he maintained contact with the negotiators at the Madrid and Valladolid seats of the Spanish court. Mendes de Brito's interest in the well-being of others had earned him the epithet "Father of the Afflicted" (*pai dos afligidos*). But he was also called "the Rich." He was extremely wealthy, and several of the New Christian businessmen with whom he had close relationships were too, holding key positions as tax collectors or as *contradores* (see chapters 1 and 7) in the India and Africa trade. Historian James Boyajian goes so far as to claim that the hefty payments that secured the General Pardon were intended to defend Portugal's access to Asia against the Dutch, and thus part of a strategy by Mendes de Brito and other Lisbon merchants to keep control of the India trade.[9] If this was so, however, the strategy was dramatically unsuccessful; in the end, most of the pardon's supporters derived little benefit from it, and for several it spelled financial ruin.[10]

Mendes de Brito and his co-negotiators had promised the Crown a substantial payment to petition the pope for the pardon, and they sought to distribute this cost over the New Christian population by assessing all solvent families for contributions. But many refused to comply with the assessment. The only New Christians who actually profited from the pardon were those who were already prisoners of the Inquisition or who were threatened with immediate arrest. Of the rest, many felt ill-served. A group of more than 50 prominent Portuguese New Christian businessmen, calling themselves "the substance of the merchants of this kingdom," submitted their objections to the king in a detailed memorandum.[11] They complained that the General Pardon harmed the reputation of honest New Christians by implying that they might all be Judaizers, while in fact they belonged, along with the Old Christians of the kingdom, to one shared mystical body. The authors decried the freeing of the Inquisition's prisoners as a scandal, opining that the accusations against them, and subsequent trials, might have been justified. They pointed out that although the negotiators had been accepted by both the Crown and the pope as official representatives, the New Christians themselves had never authorized the negotiators to speak for them; the New Christians had neither a "republic of their own" nor any governing body that could provide such authorization. The authors of the memorandum therefore vehemently condemned the initiators and negotiators of the General Pardon, suggesting that their motivation was primarily the release of their own kin from imprisonment, and the securing of their own property from confiscation by the Inquisition.[12]

These were serious accusations, which may not have been entirely without foundation. They demonstrate just how divided the New Christians, and especially the New Christian merchants, were. It is quite probable that the negotiators did represent only a small group around Heitor Mendes de Brito; and while he may have been a man of empathy in his own way, he might not have been able to distinguish between the interests of his acquaintances and those of the New Christians in general. For the Crown, however, it mattered little whether the negotiators represented the whole group or just a number of well-networked individuals, as long as they helped fill the empty coffers of the state.

Catholic Brotherhoods: Precedents for the Portuguese-Jewish Communities

Before emigrating, many New Christians had belonged to Catholic lay brotherhoods. The merchants Pedro and Miguel Francês, for example, served as church wardens (*mordomos*) of the Brotherhood of the Holy Sacrament in the Church of St. Julian before settling in Hamburg in the early 1630s and joining the Portuguese-Jewish community in that city.[13] Such brotherhoods, voluntary associations of men and women with common backgrounds or goals, experienced exceptional growth in the Iberian world in the sixteenth and seventeenth centuries. Many professional groups – merchants among them – had their own brotherhoods, to which they could turn for spiritual and material assistance. In addition to doctrinal instruction, sacramental services, and other devotional activities, the brotherhoods offered encouragement in charitable activities, a place for convivial gatherings, and a chance to make ties within the community. In brief, they crucially informed the identities of the social groups they served. The brotherhoods were usually attached to churches, where they had chapels with altars for their patron saints, but they enjoyed some degree of autonomy, having their own statutes and boards of governance. Although they tended to reproduce social inequalities by assigning leadership positions mostly to men of power and wealth and allowing them to arrogate important decisions to themselves, still they were an empowering force for most of their members.[14] As we will see, the Jewish communities that developed in diaspora shared many characteristics with the brotherhoods. Both allowed their members to combine the fulfillment of religious duties with the pursuit of socioeconomic interests, and both played fundamental roles in the forging of a group identity.

One mercantile brotherhood of special standing in Portugal was the Brotherhood of the Holy Spirit, which was closely connected with the Board of the Merchants' Commonweal in Lisbon, presented in chapter 13. But there were many other brotherhoods for merchants, who chose them according to their place of residence and their social status.[15] To date there have been no comprehensive studies of the importance of those brotherhoods for trade; Amândio Barros, however, has contributed an interesting piece on the mercantile Brotherhood of Our Lady of the Snows (also known as the Brotherhood of Our Lady of the Staircase) in Porto.[16] Its chapel was located in the Dominican monastery of that city (an important meeting place of the urban elite) with which the brotherhood concluded an agreement in 1556. It contained the extraordinary provision that the members of the brotherhood and their families would be granted asylum in the monastery in case of an emergency. In Barros's opinion, this would have enabled New Christian members who learned that arrest by the Inquisition was imminent to seek support at the monastery until they could make their way to a ship leaving the country.[17] This clause was apparently never put to the test, however.

Important trading centers in Catholic regions outside of Portugal – Seville, Cádiz, Huelva, Madrid, Granada, the Canary Islands, Rome, and Antwerp, for example – also had Portuguese brotherhoods with mercantile orientations.[18] They offered gathering places for Portuguese abroad, allowing the expatriates to meet others from their home country and to affirm their common identity by socializing and by participating together in religious ritual. In general these brotherhoods were led by wealthy businessmen who donated significant sums to their support; this sometimes ended up marginalizing the less well-to-do fellows. Several of King Felipe IV's Portuguese bankers belonged to the Portuguese brotherhood in Madrid, while the Portuguese brotherhood in Seville included businessmen with interests in the Iberian-Atlantic trade of that city and the institutions that controlled it. The brothers also looked after the local sick, poor, and imprisoned of their nation. In Seville, Madrid, and Rome they established organizations to provide dowries for poor and orphaned virgins so that they might get married. This concern for the disadvantaged was another area in which the brotherhoods and the Portuguese-Jewish communities throughout the diaspora were much alike.

The Catholic Congregation in Altona

When the first Portuguese arrived in Hamburg, most of them joined the Jesuit-led Catholic congregation in neighboring Altona. Soon after its founding (between 1589 and 1591) it had grown to well over a hundred members. Besides Portuguese, its many merchant members included Rhinelanders, Westphalians, Netherlanders, Italians and Spanish.[19] The driving force behind the congregation's founding was the Florentine merchant Alessandro della Rocca, who led the necessary negotiations with the territorial lord, the Count of Schauenburg, and engaged the first priest, a Jesuit from the Netherlands. In 1602 della Rocca acquired several pieces of land on which he built houses for the priests and their servants. However, in 1612 he had to leave Hamburg in a state of insolvency, which was a severe blow to the young flock; so was the fact that its priests were temporarily expelled by the count, and for some time pastoral services were only held intermittently.[20]

If we can give credence to some pertinent, if tendentious, mid-nineteenth-century descriptions, the Catholic congregation in Altona was greeted with great hostility not only by the Lutheran clergy and the "rabble" of Hamburg, but also by the city's ruling authorities.[21] It seems that the citizenry was publicly urged not to have business dealings with Catholics or rent them accommodations.[22] The City Council itself may have been involved in inciting the citizens to this belligerence; a *Rezess* of 1603 makes clear that it was prepared to expel those who went to Catholic Mass in Altona lest their "wicked examples" offend others.[23] This resonates with the statement of a German by the name of Heinrich Oher, who testified before the Inquisition in Lisbon that in 1609 he had witnessed Jesuits persecuted in Hamburg because they had opened a small Catholic church.[24] All this suggests that the anti-Catholic atmosphere in Hamburg may have weighed heavily in the decision of the Portuguese to renounce Catholicism. As I explained in chapter 3, the City Council seems to have been more disposed to accept Jews than Catholics in the city, if only because Jews would get no backing from Catholic powers. In fact representatives of the two most crucial such powers, the Holy Roman Empire and Spain, repeatedly complained to the city fathers that the Catholics in Hamburg were in a worse position than the Jews there, a charge that the Council denied, countering that the city protected equally the lives, property, and general well-being of both.[25]

It is not known how many Portuguese were once members of the Altona Catholic congregation, or exactly when they changed their religious allegiance. As early as 1603 some Portuguese were already said to be inclining towards Judaism,[26] and while many still clung to Catholicism as late as 1609, by that time they seem no longer to have been attending Mass regularly.[27] A letter written in 1612 in which the Catholics complained about property damage to the Jesuit holdings in Altona had only four Portuguese signatories.[28] By 1624 the Catholic congregation counted only one member from Portugal.[29] Finally a letter written in 1628 by the City Council to the emperor stated that the majority of the Catholics in Hamburg were of "no special quality" (that is, of few means), and modest in trade and livelihood.[30] By then, it seems, not only the Portuguese but also the numerous merchants from other nations had left the congregation.

The Portuguese-Jewish Community: Affiliation and Alternatives

By 1612, when Hamburg granted the Portuguese nation official recognition with the establishment of its first alien contract (see chapter 3), most Hamburgers probably already equated "Portuguese" with "Jews." This is consistent with the essentialist view of historians such as Israël S. Révah, who opined that when the Iberian Jews were baptized their Judaism remained within them, and that they would transform this "potential Judaism" into "real Judaism" as soon as they could.[31] According to Révah, the New Christians, who had yearned to be Jews while still on the Iberian Peninsula, directed all their ambition toward this goal once they had left for safer regions. He was not correct in this assumption, however; as we saw above, in 1612 there were still a few Portuguese officially advocating for the Catholic congregation in Altona, and Diogo de Lima, a Portuguese who was born in Hamburg in that same year (see chapter 12), reported that in his childhood only some of the Portuguese in Hamburg were Jewish, and that it was not until later that the others were circumcised.[32]

The community leaders probably exerted some pressure to win over to Judaism the newly arrived Portuguese. One of these leaders was Álvaro Dinis, a merchant who was central to the founding of the Hamburg community and its cemetery. He also served as a lay preacher to the congregation, and he addressed the resistance of the holdouts in two of his sermons, which were printed in Hamburg in 1629.[33] Families exerted pressure as well; Gaspar Bocarro testified before the Inquisition that when he arrived in Hamburg in the early 1630s, his brother would take him in only on the condition that he embrace Judaism.[34] So it seems clear that after the first New Christians became Jews and others began to follow them, a critical mass formed. The incentive to join the new Jewish community increased further once the Catholic congregation in Altona was no longer a serious alternative. Only as Jews could the Portuguese now hope to receive the recognition and support of their countrymen; all other alternatives increasingly meant social, political, and economic isolation in a foreign environment.

The memoir of Manuel Cardoso provides a description of one Hamburg merchant's religious evolution (see chapter 6).[35] Cardoso was an Old Christian by birth, but he was arrested by the Inquisition early in his life on the accusation that he had accepted the Reformed faith while in England, upon which his father disowned him. After his release he established a relationship with the family of his former cellmate, the New Christian Henrique Dias Milão, and was arrested again by the Inquisition, this time for helping some of that family to flee the country. In prison once more, he made the acquaintance of Josef bar Jacob, a Jew from Salonika, who taught him the rudiments of the Jewish religion. After his second release he followed Milão's family to Hamburg where, according to his report, they received him with open arms. Just four days after his arrival he had himself circumcised, underwent the prescribed ritual bath, and assumed the name Abraham Peregrino.

Since Cardoso had previously been an Old Christian, this was not a matter of reclaiming his "potential Judaism," as Révah put it. On the contrary, it was the Inquisition that brought him to the Jewish faith (see chapter 5). It had acquainted him intimately with the inhumane practices carried out in the name of Catholicism, destroyed his relationship with his family of origin, and brought him into close contact with a group of New Christians and a Jew. The requirements for acceptance by the Jewish community in Hamburg appear not to have been demanding; at the time of his circumcision he could hardly have known much about his new religion. It seems that in those early days of the community no formal instruction in, or examination about, the Jewish faith had yet been established. Even more notable, a New Christian background seems not to have been absolutely necessary.

We do not know to what degree Cardoso's report of his conversion is representative of the experience of others who came to affiliate with the Portuguese-Jewish community. As a former Old Christian, he certainly did not conform to the usual image of a Portuguese Jew. He was not, however, the only Old Christian Portuguese to become Jewish in Hamburg. Another was Fernando Almeida Pereira.[36] Unlike Cardoso, Pereira had not been persecuted by the Inquisition when in about 1620, at the age of 17 or so, he arrived in Hamburg. There he was persuaded to have himself circumcised, although (as he later explained to the Inquisition) by that time he had already decided to return to the Iberian Peninsula. A year and a half later he left Hamburg, and converted back to Catholicism in Venice.

As we have seen, remaining Catholic was not a promising option in Hamburg. Another alternative was to convert to Lutheranism. Acquiring the faith of the majority society was the path taken by many merchants from Hamburg and the Netherlands in Portugal – sometimes with considerable economic success, as we will see in chapter 15. But in fact only a very few Portuguese converted to Lutheranism. Certainly some of them really did cherish a wish to return to the faith of their ancestors. More generally, however, the Portuguese were probably not optimistic about ever being able to integrate fully into the host society in Hamburg, and may have felt that the more realistic alternative was to invest instead in the new community of Portuguese Jews, without whose support they would have little chance of achieving prosperity.

One of the Portuguese who did convert to Lutheranism was Manuel Álvares.[37] He was a well-to-do merchant, and one of the first of his countrymen to arrive in Hamburg. At the end of the sixteenth century, it was he among all the Portuguese who paid the most taxes into the city treasury.[38] At first he was active in Hamburg as a Catholic; he was one of the benefactors of the Altona Jesuit congregation, to which he entrusted both of his sons for their education.[39] In 1604, however, he converted to Lutheranism, and after his death his sons did the same. The reasons for his conversion are unknown, and Hamburg churchmen questioned its sincerity, accusing Álvares of having converted solely to ensure himself an honorable burial.[40] This was unlikely to have been the reason for the sons' conversions, however. Whatever their reasons, they seem not to have achieved any commercial success in Hamburg. It is not clear whether they were merchants at all, or whether they earned their livings in some other capacity or in some other place. Either way, we can learn nothing from the extant commercial records about the prosperity of any individuals (except Manuel) with the family name of Álvares.[41]

Duarte Rodrigues was another Portuguese who converted to Lutheranism; however, he converted not directly from Catholicism, but by way of Judaism.[42] Rodrigues was a merchant of modest fortune. In 1609, while he was still a Jew, his trade turnover in Hamburg was unexceptional, and at first, at least, he made part of his living as a broker.[43] He does not appear among the 1619 bank account holders, or in the 1632 Admiralty customs books. In 1633, at the age of 53, he became a Lutheran. His commercial fate does not seem to have changed much, and while his name does reappear in the 1647 Admiralty customs books, it still indicates a very low turnover. But his position vis-à-vis the Portuguese nation deteriorated. In 1669 Pastor Johannes Müller reported that the Portuguese Jews bent every effort to stop members of their community from adopting Lutheranism, and also to reclaim those who had already done so; he wrote that "the old Jew Rodericus lived in great fear that the Jews would catch him out and send him away. The seduction [to Judaism] also means that baptized Jews [converts to Lutheranism] have no peace from the unbaptized, but are pursued by them."[44] It is very possible that the Rodericus in question was Duarte Rodrigues. In the long run, according to historian Jutta Braden, the Jews in Hamburg most likely to convert to Lutheranism were the poor ones.[45] Many of them were encouraged by the missionary activities of the *Fund for Proselytes* (Proselytenkasse), a privately organized endowment for the conversion of Jews founded in 1667. For successful merchants conversion seems to have opened no doors; they rarely left Judaism.

Merchants as Community Leaders

Community structures developed quickly in Hamburg. The Assembly of Citizens took note of the new Jewish presence in the year 1603 (see chapter 3); the acquisition of the Jewish cemetery, which may be viewed as the final act of community foundation, took place in 1611. Nonetheless, adapting to the new religion was not an easy task for the Portuguese, because, heirs as they were to a truncated

Judaism, they had no tradition of Jewish scholarship or of lived Jewish values to fall back on. In the beginning the details of the new observance were foreign even to those who became the founders of the community. The requisite personnel – rabbis, cantors, teachers, and mohels – were recruited from among the Sephardic Jews of North Africa, the Ottoman Empire, and Italy, whose forebears had left the Iberian Peninsula in the late fifteenth century without ever having adopted the Christian faith. Still, the community built a specifically *Portuguese-Jewish* identity that differed from the established Sephardic and Ashkenazic models. The "New Jews" in Hamburg had been shaped spiritually and pragmatically by Iberian Catholicism, which now fused with Judaism in a unique amalgam. They continued to pattern their way of life on the practices of Christian society: they wore fashionable clothing instead of traditional garments; they went clean-shaven instead of bearded; they trafficked with non-Jews; and the discipline of Talmudic study gave way to a great value on secular education. And yet they embraced Judaism with ardor, and out of it constructed not only a new self-image but also a new way of being Jewish.

Until the end of the seventeenth century the resistance of Hamburg's citizenry prevented the establishment of a public synagogue. The Portuguese Jews met for services in the houses of successful merchants.[46] Two of the early hosts were Álvaro Dinis, mentioned above, and Rui Fernandes Cardoso; with a third colleague, André Faleiro, they were also responsible for the acquisition of the property for the Portuguese-Jewish cemetery.[47] The home of Duarte Esteves de Pina was another place of worship where, according to inquisition records, the Jewish faithful gathered to pray every morning, afternoon, and evening.[48] There was likely a lot of overlap between religious gatherings and those that served political purposes, as the hosts of the congregation were also the leaders of the community, and represented the nation in its dealings with the civil authorities. Cardoso and Dinis had already been acknowledged as leaders of the Portuguese in a 1606 letter to the emperor,[49] and when the settlement contract was renegotiated in 1617, Cardoso, Dinis, and Faleiro were among the seven deputies authorized by the community to negotiate in its name.[50] Since religious, social, political, and probably business activities were all facilitated by the same people – and likely in the same places – even community members to whom religious services meant little would not have wanted to miss them. That helps to explain why exclusion from services was an effective punishment for many kinds of transgressions (see chapter 11); it meant loss of access to the venue where the community's decisions were taken, and where much of its collective life took place. This gave individual members a strong incentive to honor their obligations.

During the second half of the century, members of the Nunes da Costa and Teixeira families became increasingly prominent as community leaders. The two family heads, Duarte and Diogo, had each made names for themselves as merchants and diplomats (see chapters 4 and 8), and they were both instrumental in the merger of the three earlier congregations into one in 1652. According to the statutes (*ascamot*) written in that year, the board (*mahamad*) of the newly established congregation consisted of seven persons (reduced to five in a 1659 amendment), and each year the current board elected the next one. Board members were likely to be chosen from the community's wealthiest and most influential families. Diogo and Manuel Teixeira served on the board 14 times for a total of 24 years (1653–1676), and members of the Nunes da Costa family 17 times over 25 years (1654–1678).[51] So the institution was oligarchic in character, and its leadership style was patriarchal. Diogo Teixeira, for example, financed the purchase of three houses on the Dreckwall (today the Alter Wall) for the establishment of a synagogue.[52] Duarte Nunes da Costa provided the congregation with ritual objects from his private holdings, including a sanctuary lamp (*ner tamid*) and a lectern for reading the Torah (*tevah*). The board also managed the social and charitable institutions of the community, and elected the superintendents of the school, the poor relief, a brotherhood for care of the sick, and several funds, among them one to bail out captives, one for the Holy Land and Jerusalem, and one for poor students.[53]

The Portuguese-Jewish Community and Trade

In other Jewish communities of the time, Jewish religious law (*halacha*) was profoundly important in the economic lives of their members; in Portuguese-Jewish communities, however, it played almost no role. According to historian Miriam Bodian, community leaders were less concerned with establishing a single "authentic" religious practice than with developing a group identity that could encompass diverse views of Judaism, and thereby secure the long-term survival of the community.[54] The Portuguese conducted their trade and treated their business partners in conformity with the norms and laws of the places where they lived. When in the mid-seventeenth-century Rabbi Menasseh ben Israel codified a set of rules and rituals for newly affiliated Jews, he built into them harsh condemnation for anyone who behaved unfairly in trade, whatever the religions of his business partners.[55] The board of the Hamburg Portuguese-Jewish community called on the Portuguese to conduct themselves in business "with the requisite honesty as prescribed by Judaism." Whoever failed to do so would be severely punished, "so that it not be said of the Portuguese Jews that they commit such wickedness, which is tantamount to a desecration of God's name."[56] No one should be permitted to settle in Hamburg "of whom it is not known how he conducts his business,

and that he would be of advantage and use to the commonweal [*a sua republica*]."
After all, "great harm could arise for our stay here, if the inhabitants of this city
were to be deceived, and to take offense as a result."[57]

But even though the community leaders paid little attention to the fine points
of religious prescription, and even though the Portuguese Jews enjoyed considerably more freedom than Jews in more traditional communities, religion could
nonetheless constrain their trade. As mentioned, the board forbade travel to
the "lands of idolatry," that is, to those Catholic countries where Judaism was
proscribed (see chapter 6). Not all merchants obeyed this ban, but all were disadvantaged by it: to obey was detrimental to the maintenance of their business
contacts on the Iberian Peninsula; not to obey was detrimental to their life in the
community at home.

Another limitation was the observance of the Jewish holy days. Jews observed
the Sabbath on Saturdays and forbore from work. They could not compensate for
this loss on Sundays, since that was the Christian Sabbath and the functions of
the exchange and the customs office were unavailable then. As a result, Christians
could work and do business six days a week, Jews only five. If we are to believe
the Englishman John Taylor, the day of rest was observed strictly by the Jews;
when he visited Hamburg in 1616, he noted them "in their execrable superstition
to be more devout and observant than these pedlars in their [Christian] profession; for on the Saturday, being the Jews' Sabbath, they neglect all human affairs,
and betake themselves irreligiously to their misbelieving faithless religion."[58]
The strictness with which the Portuguese Jews observed the day of rest was also
mentioned repeatedly in denunciations before the Portuguese Inquisition. Luís
Vaz Pimentel, a New Christian who had spent a month and a half in Hamburg,
testified before the Lisbon tribunal in 1613 that the Portuguese Jews there kept the
Sabbath, wore their best clothing on those days, did no work, transacted no business on the Exchange, and performed no other services.[59] Many other denouncers confirmed this, including the Old Christian António Gonçalves, a Portuguese
shipmaster who sailed frequently to Hamburg in the early 1630s. He reported that
the Jews in Hamburg went to the Exchange neither on Friday afternoons nor on
Saturdays.[60]

The community sanctioned members who failed to keep the Sabbath. Thus we
read in the minutes book that in 1659 Jacob Ulhoa and a colleague left a Sabbath
service during the period of voiced prayer (*tornada da amidá*) to assess a shipment of barley that had just come into the harbor and was feared to have become
wet.[61] They made their way back surreptitiously, hiding behind a wall, and had
returned to their places before the service ended. But their subterfuge eventually
came to light. Ulhoa had written an invoice for services rendered, and one of the
recipients complained to the board. Considering the matter, the board came to the

conclusion "that this made a mockery of our sacred law and our community." It then fined Ulhoa the amount of the invoice. In another instance, Daniel José de Vargas was given a warning: he had received wheat on the Sabbath "with considerable scandal," and this was not the first time he had broken the Sabbath.[62] If that were to happen again, the board said, it would forbid all community members to buy from him in the future. Josua Habilho was accused of having done business on the first day of Passover, and as a result of "such desecration of the holy day had provoked great displeasure."[63] He was punished with a fine of ten talers, a temporary ban on attending religious services, and exclusion from other activities of the congregation. To repeat this transgression would mean expulsion from the community.

Jewish Holy Days as Reflected in the Admiralty Customs Books

The Admiralty customs books make possible a statistical perspective on the observance of the Sabbath and other Jewish holy days. Counting entries for both Christian and Jewish merchants, there are only about half the number for Saturdays as for the other days of the week (with the exception of Sunday when, as mentioned above, customs duties were not collected).[64] If we analyze the listings according to the religion of the merchants involved, we find that in only a very few instances did Portuguese declare goods on Saturdays. In 1632 only six of the total of 120 Saturday customs entries involved Jewish merchants. In the 1647 book, only one Portuguese is entered among a total of 258 Saturday entries.[65] The other Jewish holy days may be analyzed in the same way.[66] Here, too, there were sporadic breaches of the work prohibitions: 15 instances in 1632, and nine in 1647. As a rule, however, the Portuguese in Hamburg seem to have observed the holy days according to Jewish law.

It should be noted that having to comply with the work prohibitions of two religions rather than just one did not lead to a decrease in the Jewish merchants' total turnover. The goods they did not declare on holy days they declared before or after them. For example, there are a large number of Jewish holy days in the month of Tishri, which in 1632 encompassed the 30 days from September 6 to October 5; in 1647 it extended from September 20 to October 19. Those two four-week periods included respectively a total of nine and ten Jewish holy days that did not fall on Saturday or Sunday. With few exceptions, the Portuguese paid no duties on those days.[67] Still, their turnovers during these spans were not significantly lower than they were during the rest of the year. In 1632 their percentage of total turnover over the month of Tishri was 15.2 percent; in 1647, 12.6 percent. Over the year as a whole their shares were 15.4 percent and 15.2 percent, respectively.

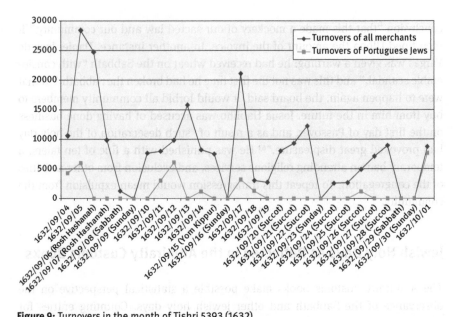

Figure 9: Turnovers in the month of Tishri 5393 (1632)
Source: StAHH, Admiralitätskollegium, F3, Band 1 and 2; F4, Band 8 (see appendix).

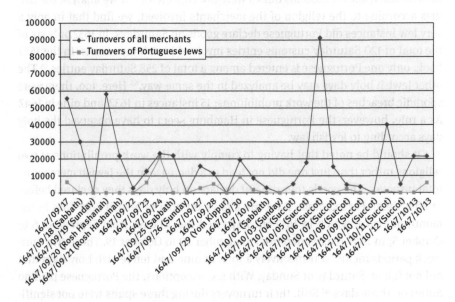

Figure 10: Turnovers in the month of Tishri 5408 (1647)
Source: StAHH, Admiralitätskollegium, F3, Band 8; F4, Band 14, and 15 (see appendix).

The Portuguese-Jewish Community as Protector

The legal and social discrimination that the Portuguese Jews suffered in their host society in Hamburg weighed more heavily than the disadvantages deriving from community norms and religious law. I have detailed some of the institutionalized manifestations of this already (see especially chapters 2 and 3), but there was also open aggression. In Hamburg at times Portuguese Jews were cursed, pelted with stones, or otherwise attacked in the streets.[68] Harassment occurred even on the Exchange. The board of the Portuguese-Jewish community complained to the City Council in 1649 that "not only the common rabble but other people as well are not ashamed to insult [us]," and that "seven members of our nation had their coats cut and desecrated in the most treacherous and underhanded manner at noon at the public Exchange."[69]

The settlement contracts alone did not suffice to guarantee the safety of the Portuguese. The community was engaged in a perennial process of negotiation with the authorities to secure its existence in the city. Its leaders reminded, admonished, and bribed the City Council in their efforts to create a tolerable situation. For example, representatives of the community complained to the Council and the senior elders after rioting interrupted the burial of Diogo Teixeira: bystanders had forcibly opened the coaches carrying the bereaved and had thrown snowballs and dirt at them. They felt seriously offended by this behavior, the spokesmen declared, and asked for assistance, "so that in the future we may pass through the streets freely and undisturbed." In support of the demand it was "further decided in the name of the community to send the city commander 12 loaves of the best rock sugar that is to be had, in addition to 40 pounds of the best white powdered sugar as a gift, and to express our thanks that he took care to send his soldiers to quell the mob."[70]

On their own, individuals would hardly have been able to defend themselves from a hostile population or press for their concerns. Only as a group did they have the power they needed to negotiate. This was the essential socioeconomic benefit of belonging to the community. Because the Hamburg City Council understood the economic advantages of retaining the Portuguese Jews, and feared their departure to neighboring cities like Altona, Stade, Glückstadt, or Emden, the members of the community were often successful in their efforts. In fact they used the threat of group departure in each of the negotiations around the alien contracts. In 1610 the Portuguese seriously considered leaving Hamburg for Stade.[71] In 1617 the heads of the families pledged that if the negotiations were not favorable, they would move to any country recommended by the community's delegates.[72] At the end of the 1640s the Portuguese Jews again threatened to leave in response to vituperative anti-Jewish remarks by the Hamburg clergy and the resultant hostility of the public; once again they were able to prevail upon the authorities to grant them protection.[73]

Community Statutes and Disciplinary Pressure

For its threats to be effective, the Portuguese nation in Hamburg had to speak with one voice, and, if need be, act in unity as well. This meant strict discipline and unconditional acquiescence to the decisions of the leadership. During the 1617 contract negotiations with the city, for example, the leaders resolved that should the Portuguese nation take the decision to leave Hamburg, any of its members who remained there, or returned, would be "amputated and excluded from the congregation of the children of Israel." That is, they would be expelled not only from the community of Hamburg Jews, but also, the threat seems to imply, from the community of Jews everywhere.[74] The community statutes written in 1652 were similarly stern: the community was to be ruled by a board with "absolute power and total authority," whose aim was not only to increase "the service of our Blessed God," but also, and especially, to act in "the service of our common good and preservation."[75] In its pursuit of these goals, the board demanded obedience without protest or appeal. Transgressors would be pressured to conform with all the punishments the board members might choose. Furthermore, the board had a free hand in such matters as finances, hiring and firing, and negotiations with the City Council. All this made sense against the background fear that if the community did not act collectively, the livelihood of each and every member would be threatened.

The board's internal jurisdiction was exercised not only over religious lapses and matters of marriage or inheritance but also, to a limited extent, over trade and business. One example is the lawsuit that Jacob Cohen Lobato and Salomão Gabai brought to the board over a cask of sugar. Although the board declared that it was not its purpose to get involved in lawsuits, it decided to attend to this case because Gabai was a visitor and wanted to leave the city.[76] Perhaps the Hamburg courts would have taken too long to act, or perhaps the board knew Gabai in a way that the city legal establishment did not. In other words, this seems to have been an attempt at facilitation and accommodation. For the most part the board seems to have handled simple cases and, when necessary, arranged for resolution by arbitration.[77]

More complicated cases, and those in which Christians were involved, were left to the city court (*joizo dos goim*).[78] Two other instances involving the above-mentioned broker Jacob Ulhoa illustrate how the board might hand jurisdiction over to city authorities. Salomão Cohen, who was in a dispute with Ulhoa, asked the board's permission to have the court force Ulhoa to open his account books. Even though this might redound to Ulhoa's detriment, Cohen argued, it was necessary to preserve his own rights, and to balance their accounts. After consultation, the board gave Cohen the necessary permission.[79] Not long after, the board allowed Abraham Israel Bravo, who accused Ulhoa of having harmed him in a barley deal he had brokered, to initiate a suit against Ulhoa in the city court.

The board granted permission with the proviso that "no scandal or disturbance be occasioned for our community."[80] A Portuguese who brought suit before the city court directly, however, bypassing the board, was viewed as one who informed against the community. Informing (*malsineria*) was a transgression punishable by excommunication, the most severe sanction available.[81] If possible, conflicts between Portuguese were to be resolved within their own ranks. The board also insisted that cases tried internally were to be kept secret from the city authorities.[82]

Punishments meted out within the community included: having to beg forgiveness before the congregation; exclusion from religious functions; fines; and rendition to the city authorities for confinement to prison or workhouse. Punishment could also include temporary or permanent banning or even total excommunication, as the community leaders had threatened in 1617. In the 30 years of the seventeenth century covered by the minutes book of the Hamburg community (1652–1681), at least 41 members were banned or excommunicated. Another 90 persons were temporarily forbidden to attend services.[83] This was a much greater number of bannings than in Amsterdam, where the Portuguese-Jewish community was much larger.[84] In all probability this reflected the particular precariousness of life in Hamburg.

Appearances, Welfare and Charity

The board made every effort to present a positive image of the Portuguese nation to the public at large.[85] It wanted to avoid alienating the city authorities (thereby risking expulsion), to offer the Lutheran clergy as little ammunition as possible, to minimize the danger of violent outbreaks, and to convince non-Jewish business partners of the community's trustworthiness. Some of the community's disciplinary rules were similar to those enacted by the city authorities, and included codes of dress and other limitations on luxuries and celebrations, and condemnations of idleness and loose morals.[86] When the board learned in 1660 that one community member had abused another at the Exchange with "words as scandalous as indecent," it punished him severely as an example to others.[87] Five years later the board reacted similarly when two Portuguese got into a loud argument at the Exchange and many non-Jews took offense.[88]

The community also tried to hide poor Jews from the public eye, and took rigorous steps to keep them from begging in the streets and so imposing on inhabitants. Only a limited number of poor were tolerated for any length of time within the community and supported financially by it. The majority of Jewish beggars, vagabonds, and other undesirables were not permitted to remain. The board usually gave them some travel money and pressured them to leave the city.[89] If they refused, they were turned over to the city authorities, who sent them to the workhouse to be put to work along with poor Christians.[90] Financial support was most forthcoming for those poor members of the community who were willing to emigrate overseas.[91] In 1658, for example, it was noted in the minutes book that:

> Abraham Senior Teixeira [Diogo Teixeira] has offered that all those who intend to emigrate to Serepique, a country newly discovered by the Hollanders [probably Essequibo in Guyana], are to be granted a travel allowance, the size of which will depend on the size of their family, under the condition that all who make use of this offer provide a security deposit guaranteeing that they not return to this city within three years.[92]

The community's impoverished could not usually afford such a security deposit, however, so the board provided the guarantee to Teixeira and made the emigrants sign a letter of commitment instead. This strategy encouraged many Portuguese Jews to leave for the Caribbean. We may note that Christians entertained similar concerns. A broadsheet from the year 1698 proposed to the Hamburg City Council that it send poor dwellers to the Netherlandish possessions in Africa, especially the Cape Colony.[93] In this way, as in others, the board of the Portuguese nation followed the agenda of the Hamburgers at the same time as it safeguarded the nation's reputation as a community of successful merchants.[94]

The Christian population also profited directly from the philanthropy of the Portuguese Jews. Several sources give evidence of charitable donations by Jews to Lutheran institutions. Álvaro Dinis, who was a leading founder not only of the community in Hamburg, but also of that in Glückstadt, willed the church in Glückstadt the sum of 20 lübisch marks "in God's honor and for the maintenance of church and school."[95] In 1649, two years after becoming a Jew, Diogo Teixeira donated 500 marks to the poor box of St. Michael's church in Hamburg.[96] When in 1660 the newly built St. Michael's had to be roofed, he acquired the necessary copper and refused repayment of the handsome sum (10,000 reichstalers) it had cost him.

The leaders of the Portuguese-Jewish community honored the commandments of their religion with such benefactions. They used them as well to underscore their own elevated position, to influence community life as they saw fit, and to ensure peaceable coexistence with the Christian majority society.[97] The concentration of power, careful coordination, and strict governance that we see in the board of the Portuguese nation in Hamburg were crucial determinants of the community's capacity not only to force its members to comply with each other's mercantile expectations, but also – and more importantly – to pressure authorities to grant it protection and justice. They were deployed to help the community's merchant members secure their position – that is, their trade, and thus their living – and in this they were successful up to a point. But the Portuguese

Jews still encountered disadvantages that other merchants, who did not have to struggle with persecution and discrimination, or submit to an ethnic and religious organization as autocratic as this one, did not. The Portuguese-Jewish community in Hamburg allowed the Iberian merchants to make a good living, but it could not provide for them a playing field for mercantile activities that was level with that of their non-Jewish compeers.

15 Netherlanders and Hamburgers

The Portuguese nation, with its complex structures and religious singularities, has been extensively researched and interpreted, often with controversial results. Not so the nations of the expatriate Netherlanders and Hamburgers, whose diasporas and settlements have so far met with much less interest among historians. Yet these groups deserve attention too, both on their own account and for the contrasts they offer with each other and with the Portuguese. There is no doubt that the Netherlanders led very different lives in Hamburg than they did in Portugal. In Hamburg, they, like the Portuguese Jews, remained a clearly recognizable group, especially those of the Reformed faith. In Portugal things were otherwise. There both Hamburgers and Netherlanders integrated easily into the majority society and many converted to Catholicism. The internal structures of their nations were much less critical to their commercial success than their personal networks and contacts with the country's economic elite. Unlike the Portuguese Jews, and to some degree the Netherlanders, in Hamburg, merchants in Portugal could afford to forego the benefits of corporate organization in favor of individual action.

The Netherlanders in Hamburg: What "Nation" Meant

As I have explained, the term *Netherlandish nation* had legal import in Hamburg; it denoted the persons covered by the Netherlander contracts (see chapter 3). In the early seventeenth century, however, and perhaps later on as well, many other immigrants of Netherlandish origin were also viewed (by themselves and by others) as members of the nation, even though they were not included in the contracts. This raises the question of whether they experienced a bond of nationhood independent of the city's determination, as the Portuguese did. Who were the members of the Netherlandish nation? What ethnic or cultural commonalities underpinned their sense of nationhood in Hamburg and abroad? And what forms of organization did they establish?

The Netherlanders came from the seventeen provinces of the sixteenth-century Habsburg Netherlands, which covered what we know today as the Netherlands, Belgium, Luxembourg, and northern France (see introduction). This was a region with a diverse population. The most important division was the one between the *Flemings*, who spoke Flemish, or other Low German dialects, and the *Walloons*, who spoke French or its Romance sibling Walloon. The expatriate Netherlanders perpetuated this split. By the end of the sixteenth century the Reformed congregation in the town of Stade was holding services in both Flemish and Walloon, and that pattern endured when the Reformed congregation of Altona was founded a little later.[1] The

https://doi.org/10.1515/9783110472103-016

Portuguese nation was far more uniform linguistically, even having absorbed some Spanish-speaking members. Unlike the two languages of the Netherlanders the closely related Iberian tongues were not an obstacle to communication.

The second important division was religious. The Hamburg Netherlanders included a good number of Mennonites and some Catholics, but the main split among the merchants active in trade with the Iberian Peninsula was between the Lutherans and the Reformed. The Reformed sought to legitimize their presence in Hamburg on the basis of the oppression they had suffered in their homeland. In a letter written to the Hamburg City Council in 1603, they explained that they had fled in order not "to remain under the tyranny of the Pope," and that they had "suffered singular persecution, left everything behind in property and blood, given all in order to remain of free conscience." In another passage they wrote that they had "fled Spanish tyranny."[2] The Lutheran Netherlanders, too, viewed the Catholics as adversaries. But this common enmity did not suffice to reconcile the two Protestant groups, who, before their immigration, had often "faced each other with weapons in hand," as nineteenth-century historian Wilhelm Sillem described it.[3] The Netherlanders' memory of religious persecution did not unify them in the way it marked and welded the Portuguese nation.[4]

Another difference between the Netherlanders and the Portuguese was that few of the Netherlandish immigrants intended to remain abroad for long. They hoped, during the first years of their exile at least, that the political, economic, and religious situation in their homeland would change in their favor, and that they would soon be able to return (see chapter 6). This did not encourage the development of a strong sense of unity. Emotional disengagement from the country of origin, a crucial factor in the forging of the diaspora identity of the Portuguese nation, was much less pronounced among the Netherlanders. Furthermore, the Netherlanders did not face the same hostility as the Portuguese in the places where they settled, another element that contributed to the creation of a shared Portuguese identity. Some Netherlanders were occasionally attacked in Hamburg, but that seems to have been not because they were Netherlanders, but because they were Reformed, and so harassment may have perpetuated the divisions among the Netherlandish groups instead of encouraging their transcendence as it did among the Portuguese.[5] And while the Hamburgers soon came to see all Portuguese as Jewish, they continued to distinguish among the various Netherlandish denominations

Internal Organization and the Netherlandish Relief Fund

The law in Hamburg fragmented the Netherlanders further, by dividing them into two major groups: contract Netherlanders and Netherlanders who had become citizens. The Portuguese, on the other hand, shared the single legal status conferred upon them by their alien contract, and this moved them to create corporate structures through which they could define common interests and negotiate in one voice with the City Council. As we saw in chapter 14, they used the threat of boycott – the possibility of leaving the city as a group – as a chief means of asserting their interests. The Netherlanders who were covered by the settlement contracts also organized themselves politically. They too named representatives to lobby for them and negotiate and sign the contracts in their name. Their leaders were such prominent merchants as Dominicus van Uffeln, Cornelis and Jan de Hertoghe, Jan de l'Homel, Abraham du Bois, and Pieter Heusch – all involved in the Iberia trade.[6] In these negotiations too the threat of boycott was used as leverage: for instance when they declared with regard to the second contract that they would collectively move to Stade if their demands were not met.[7] But they never made an effort to unite with Hamburg's citizen Netherlanders to further their mutual political aims.

The only institution in which the contract Netherlanders joined forces with the Netherlanders who had become citizens, and the Lutheran Netherlanders with the Reformed, was the *Netherlandish Relief Fund* (Niederländische Armen-Casse). This was founded in 1585 to support Netherlandish refugees, travelers, the poor, and the sick. Some studies imply that it was exclusively Lutheran, but this was not so – at least not in the beginning, when several Reformed Netherlanders (or Netherlanders from Reformed families) took part in the weekly collections for the poor.[8] It is possible, however, that these individuals later withdrew from the Fund; and it is true that the annual administrators who were responsible for proceeds and expenditures and took the most important decisions, were all Lutherans. Like the board of the Portuguese-Jewish community, the administration of the Netherlandish Relief Fund was oligarchic and shaped by the interests of prominent merchants. Among those who held office between 1585 and 1700, there were 16 de Hertoghes, 12 Berenbergs, and five each from the Heusch, Amsinck, van Overbeck, and Boschaert families.[9] Other influential merchant families whose members served as administrators of the Relief Fund were the van Uffelns, the de Greves, the Junckers, the van Haesdoncks, the Verpoortens, and the Rulants, all of whom are known to have been active in the Iberia trade. These families were thoroughly interconnected by marriage, and together they formed the leadership of the Lutheran Netherlandish community.

The Netherlandish Relief Fund was founded when the last great wave of refugees from the Netherlands was arriving in Hamburg (see chapter 6). The city responded to the influx with repressive provisions, and the Netherlandish merchants already in residence reacted in turn by trying to help compatriots in need. We may assume that, like the Portuguese, the Netherlanders considered it important to maintain the appearance of prosperity to ensure that their presence in the city would continue to be tolerated (see chapter 14). They would therefore have been pleased to see indigent newcomers leave Hamburg as quickly as possible. According to the first administrator's report, for the year 1586/1587, travel money was distributed to many Netherlanders who wished to continue on to Danzig.[10] A considerable portion of the fund's expenditures went to travelers' aid later, too.

Applicants for support from the Fund had to prove that they came from the Netherlands; a migrant could, for example, be vouched for by a person who was known to that year's administrator and believed to be trustworthy.[11] Over time, however, this criterion lost importance. Portuguese origin always remained a crucial factor for admission into the community of the Portuguese Jews, but after a generation or two the Netherlandish provenance of those who applied to the Netherlandish Relief Fund no longer mattered. At that point the only precondition was that people who sought support "work industriously, live honorably, and suffer hardship through no fault of their own."[12] The Relief Fund also cared for orphans and half-orphans by making it possible for them to get training.[13] The Fund's beneficiaries were thus likely to remain loyal, and a credit, to the Netherlandish community, as the donors wished.

The largest donations to the Netherlandish Relief Fund usually came from its administrators, several of whom were also involved in charitable endeavors for the general public:[14] the city orphanage, which was founded in 1604;[15] the workhouse and prison, founded in 1618;[16] and St. Job's Hospital. Others were active as wardens (*Kirchgeschworene*) at St. Peter's Church.[17] The city of Hamburg was very receptive to these charitable works, which were the Netherlanders' way of conveying to their hosts their good intentions and their gratitude.[18]

The Reformed Community

The religious affiliations of the Netherlanders, like those of the Portuguese, were not necessarily firmly established upon their arrival in Hamburg. For example, the minutes of the Walloon-Reformed congregation in Stade make reference to the fact that several new members had previously been Mennonites.[19] But with the exception of Dominicus van Uffeln, who apparently converted from Catholicism to Lutheranism, we know of no Netherlandish Iberia merchants in Hamburg who formally changed denomination.[20] In fact, we have only sparse information about the Netherlandish Lutherans as a religious subgroup. Apart from the Netherlandish Relief Fund (which, as we saw, integrated at least some Reformed members) they do not seem to have had any religious or charitable organization exclusive to them.

To be Lutheran was obviously an advantage in Hamburg, especially to those with political ambitions, because only Lutherans could hold office in the city administration and government (see chapter 7). But Lutheranism also provided one of the major platforms where issues essential to public life in the city were promoted. This was most obvious in the many functions taken by the churches. It is documented, for example, that the City Council's mandates and regulations were read out from their pulpits.[21] Furthermore, they were important meeting places, and business deals were sometimes negotiated in them. Paintings of churches in Amsterdam provide evidence of this, and church rooms there sometimes replaced the open Exchange, especially in inclement weather.[22] Things may have been similar in Hamburg. That a notary could meet the Portuguese merchant Gabriel Gomes (who was very probably a Jew) in the Church of Maria Magdalena shows that adherents of other religious creeds could also be found in Lutheran churches, if only to do business.[23] Still, they were places where Lutherans dominated, where merchants only of that denomination could perform pious acts by funding valuable works of art, and display at the same time their economic success for all to see. As previously mentioned, the heirs of Dominicus van Uffeln donated a magnificent pulpit of black marble and alabaster to the Church of St. Catherine, where he was buried (see chapter 8).[24] The secular and ecclesiastical spheres were closely intertwined; anyone who distanced himself from Lutheranism risked forfeiting participation in an important arena of public life.

Nonetheless, the Reformed Netherlander immigrants formed a clearly separate group that cultivated its own identity, both in Hamburg and elsewhere. They consciously practiced their segregation, for example, by excluding outsiders from the celebration of the Eucharist. Those who wished to take communion had to receive a special stamp or coin, to be redeemed at the communion table. Members of other Reformed congregations had to identify themselves to be admitted.[25]

Of all the foreign religious communities in Hamburg, it was probably the Reformed one that eventually became the most respected; but it was also the one most distrusted by the City Council, especially as the Reformed had by the end of the sixteenth century taken control of the government in several other cities, including Bremen and Emden.[26] Unlike the Portuguese Jews, who could practice their religion in their own homes, the Reformed were forbidden any form of religious practice in the city until 1648, when the Peace of Westphalia gave them permission to hold services in private residences.[27] Before that they had to go to church in neighboring towns: Stade from 1588 to 1601, and Altona after 1602, when most of them joined the newly formed congregation there. Yet the Hamburgers vehemently opposed their church attendance even in Altona, as they did that of the Catholics (see chapter 14). Both the clergy and the citizenry protested against what they called "walking out" (*Auslaufen*) to church. For a while the City Council acceded to their pressure, forcing landlords to terminate the tenancy agreements of persons who defiantly attended services, and fining churchgoers ten marks for each transgression.[28] But eventually the Council relented and compromised, much as it had with the Portuguese Jews.[29] The Lutheran clergy, however, continued to fulminate against the rival confession; in 1644 it was still swearing to oppose for all time the establishment of a Reformed church in Hamburg.[30]

Organizational Structure and Community Discipline

In its fight for survival and expansion in Europe, the Reformed Church had developed an organizational structure that helped it assert itself in hostile environments. The key institutions were its ecclesiastical councils: a system of local *consistories* (which governed congregations) and regional *synods* (whose participants were drawn from the consistories).[31] The synods made sure that no congregation went without a preacher, and offered congregations spiritual and financial support in emergencies. They resolved conflicts that were resistant to local resolution, and facilitated contact between Reformed communities – between Hamburg, for instance, and its counterparts in Emden, Aachen, Wesel, Cologne, and the smaller towns in the region. The communities of the Portuguese-Jewish diaspora also cooperated among themselves. But unlike the Reformed, they had no institutionalized structure for such collaboration; still, at least in some instances, they worked together over a much larger area extending from Hamburg, Glückstadt, and Amsterdam all the way to Recife, Surinam, and Curaçao.

The consistories resembled the boards of the Portuguese-Jewish communities in that they exercised both spiritual and (to some degree) secular power. The consistory in Stade included four lay elders, two lay deacons, and a minister.[32] The elders' and deacons' terms of office were generally two years. The elders, with the minister, were responsible for governing the congregation and for church discipline; the deacons administered alms and attended to the needs of destitute members and travelers. The elders imposed punishments similar to those meted out by the Portuguese-Jewish board: from reprimands, summonses, and fines to public apologies; and from minor bans (temporary exclusion from the Eucharist) through major bans (permanent exclusion from the congregation) to complete excommunication.[33] In theory only minor transgressions having to do with religious observance, church discipline, or general social behavior could be adjudicated within the congregation; anything involving "crime," as opposed to "sin," was turned over to the secular authorities.[34] In practice, however, these two spheres were difficult to separate. Like the Portuguese-Jewish boards that tried whenever possible to resolve disputes privately within the community, the Reformed consistories ensured that their deliberations and decisions were kept secret.[35]

The social control many Reformed communities exerted over their members appears to have been at least as strict as that evidenced in the Portuguese-Jewish communities. In some congregations it was common practice for elders to report weekly on the transgressions of members under their supervision; in other congregations all members were urged to denounce in writing any abuses that they observed.[36] In Hamburg, elders regularly visited all members of the congregation along with the minister. They instructed them in the Gospel, prepared them to celebrate the Eucharist – and reported any "scandals" to the consistory.[37] The elders also supervised the ministers. When in 1611 a Reformed minister in Hamburg caused trouble for the community by getting into a dispute with the Lutheran clergy, the consistory decreed that ministers would be required to subordinate themselves to its decisions. In particular, they were to write and publish no books without its consent.[38] In other matters too Reformed congregation leaders attempted to keep the attention of the Lutherans away from them and their religious practices. Weddings and baptisms were to be celebrated without ostentation.[39] Congregation members were to walk to religious services in inconspicuous small groups.[40] Here again, supporting the poor and the sick was an important means by which the Reformed protected their community from unwelcome notice.[41]

Whether the internal cohesion of the Hamburg Reformed would have been sufficient to push through a successful boycott is hard to say. There is no evidence that they ever contemplated a concerted move to leave Hamburg, as the Portuguese Jews did. When they considered resettling in Stade in 1602, they seem not to have formulated this intention as a threat against the City Council; they were simply reacting to the terminations of tenancy agreements that the Council had initiated.[42] In pressing their interests with the City Council, the Reformed made use of costly gifts and other emoluments rather than threats, and promised to remember their interlocutors in their Sunday prayers.[43] They also tried to gain the support of outside powers that were in sympathy with them: in particular the United Provinces; and after 1685, when Huguenots fleeing France arrived in Hamburg, the Elector Friedrich Wilhelm of Brandenburg.[44]

The Reformed Community and Its Merchants

Little research has been done to date on the social composition of the Hamburg consistories. It is known, however, that in other cities the elders were often recruited from among the congregation's wealthiest members. In many cases they were named by the consistory itself and the rest of the congregation only confirmed them.[45] In 1883 Wilhelm Sillem compiled a list of the elders and deacons of the Stade and Altona congregations up to 1618. As he wrote, these were men from among the communities' most distinguished families.[46] The elders included two negotiators of the first Netherlander contract, Jan de l'Homel and Nicolaes van der Willigen, as well as the merchant Antoni Lapistraet, who later stood out in the Portugal trade. It is hard to say, however, if power was as narrowly concentrated in this group of elders as it was in the board of the Portuguese-Jewish community.

As among the Portuguese, religious, social, and political ambitions were probably never completely uncoupled from the economic interests of the administrative elite, in this case the members of the consistories. Thus, for example, the five dates per year on which the Eucharist was celebrated – the high points of Reformed Church life – were coordinated so as not to conflict with the major trade fairs. If the fair in Frankfurt kept too many congregants away over Easter, the Eucharist was postponed.[47] This was a rather casual approach, compared with the strict observance of holy days by the Portuguese Jews (see chapter 14). But for both the Reformed and the Portuguese Jews, appearance of prosperity, avoidance of conflict, and a discreetly managed community were understood as prerequisites to tolerance in and by the city. By fulfilling them, the consistory secured the livelihoods of its members.

The Hamburgers in Portugal: Identity and Image

The Netherlandish nation in Hamburg is not easy to capture; little is known about its Lutheran segment, and even the Reformed community, with its internal administration and coherent presence, can be sketched only in outline. But the history of the Hamburgers and Netherlanders in Portugal is even more difficult to pin down, and in fact there are not many sources on which one could base an attempt to do so.[48] Unlike the Portuguese and the Netherlanders who settled in northern Europe after they were expelled from their homelands, the Hamburgers and Netherlanders who established themselves in Portugal of their own free will never wrote their own chronicles. They created no founding myth; nor did they look back on successfully surmounted crises or dramatic new beginnings. These lacks are consistent both with their weaker group identity and with their more complete integration and assimilation into the host society.

The Hamburg merchants in Portugal did not require a corporate organization. They did not have to assert themselves in the face of hostile authorities. No sources available from the sixteenth or seventeenth centuries suggest that they ever joined forces to press for their interests or to ensure their safety. While Portuguese and Netherlandish immigration to Hamburg was a recent phenomenon, merchants from the Hansa region had been living in Portugal since the Middle Ages. The king welcomed foreigners; at times he actively recruited them. They did not have to fight for the right to settle or for access to justice; in many respects Hamburgers and Netherlanders in Portugal were privileged even over their local counterparts, either by the German Merchant Privilege or by bilateral treaties (see chapter 3). There is little indication in extant sources that they were discriminated against by the local population; they seem to have been respected despite their Protestant backgrounds. They did not have to worry about projecting a socially acceptable image of their community. As we saw in chapter 5, even the Inquisition posed no real threat to them. Hamburgers and Netherlanders integrated themselves into Portuguese society sufficiently that if a merchant wished to improve his situation he could do so as an individual. He did not have to act in concert with his compatriots.

Nonetheless, the merchants from the Holy Roman Empire did experience something akin to a common bond. They were connected through joint consular representation (see chapter 4), and this cohesion was expressed, for example, on the occasion of royal entries into Lisbon.[49] In 1581, when Felipe II made his inaugural visit after assuming the Portuguese Crown, the city received him with a long series of triumphal arches representing the most important corporate bodies and social groups in the city. The triumphal arch of the Germans, erected along the wharf where the king was to alight, stood out in its magnificence. The Germans outdid themselves again in 1619, when Felipe III entered Lisbon, and in 1666 upon Afonso VI's entry. Probably the most grandiose triumphal arch of all was erected by the Germans in 1687 on the occasion of the marriage of Pedro II of Portugal to the German princess Marie Sophie of Palatine-Neuburg. Its hexagonal foundation accommodated eleven statues symbolizing key German cities: Heidelberg and Neuburg, the princess's cities of residence, and the trading cities of Lübeck, Hamburg, Bremen, Rostock, Wismar, Cologne, Nuremberg, Ulm, and Regensburg.[50] A statue of the emperor with all of his insignia sat on a throne protected by a canopy and surrounded by statues of his electors. Even though the triumphal arch was probably paid for largely by merchants from Hamburg, the monument represented them as members of the Holy Roman Empire, and posed the German emperor as their counterpart to the Portuguese king.

However, when the young Hamburg merchant apprentices who converted to Catholicism were asked what nation they belonged to, they did not identify as subjects of the empire.[51] With very few exceptions they claimed membership in the "Hamburgish nation," Hamburg being the only city in the files of the Inquisition to be listed as a nation in itself. Lübeckers, Frankfurters, Augsburgers,

Nurembergers, Westphalians, Brandenburgers, and Silesians all belonged to the "German nation"; Amsterdamers were part of the "Dutch nation."

Records of witness testimonies (given at the granting of the German Merchant Privilege, or at Inquisition trials and habilitation proceedings) offer information about another kind of bond among the foreign merchants in Portugal: that they came from the same place. When Henrique Aires was granted the German Merchant Privilege in 1639, witnesses testified that they knew him from Hamburg.[52] Even when, as in many cases, such witnesses did not actually know each other from their place of origin, but had first met in Portugal, the knowledge that they had come from the same city or country (or even more generally, from abroad) cemented their acquaintance. Jacques de Cramer, for instance, a Hamburger who had lived in Porto for many years, testified on the occasion of Diogo Timão's habilitation hearing that he had known him for about 16 years; Timão had told him that he also came from Hamburg, and they had therefore developed a friendship as compatriots.[53] Jacques de Pachter also testified to the bond between himself and Timão as fellow foreigners who had known each other for many years.

Other proceedings indicate that the prominent Hamburg and Netherlandish merchant families tended to congregate in the same Lisbon neighborhoods. Some of them had played there as children and grown up together. Pedro Hasse declared to the Inquisition that he had known Isabel Guilherme, the daughter of Altona native Nicolau Guilherme, since her childhood, when they had been neighbors in Lisbon.[54] Much of the social life of the northern European merchants probably took place within neighborhood contexts like these, where living and working together made for daily contact. But the neighborhoods were by no means ethnically restricted, and also led to acquaintanceships, business arrangements, friendships, and marriages with prominent Portuguese merchants.

The Catholic Brotherhoods of German Merchants

Besides encountering each other in their neighborhoods, Hamburgers often met to socialize at meetings of the Brotherhood of St. Bartholomew of the Germans, which was housed in one of the most important Catholic churches in Lisbon: the Church of St. Julian, in the heart of the city's commercial center.[55] The brotherhood's ministry was purely Catholic, and its clergy so deeply engaged in Church institutions that during the second half of the sixteenth century a chaplain of the brotherhood also served as a *visitador* for the Inquisition, searching German ships that entered the port of Lisbon for "heretical" books.[56] Yet it accepted many newly converted Catholics, and at least one of its administrators (*procuradores*) was secretly a Lutheran – at least he was denounced as one to the Inquisition.[57]

Sometime around 1650 the brothers even sought the patronage of the Swedish ambassador, Johann Friedrich von Friesendorff, a staunch Lutheran in whose embassy chapel German-language Lutheran services were held. Von Friesendorff, however, refused the "dangerous and highly prejudicial protection of the German St. Bartholomew chapel."[58]

Almost all of the brotherhood's files have been lost, so we do not know much about it.[59] We do know, however, that it was founded many years before the Reformation, and that it probably did not differ markedly from the Catholic brotherhoods in Hamburg in the fifteenth and early sixteenth centuries. Hamburgers knew what it was to come together under the patronage of a saint; the city had once had more than a hundred different brotherhoods under whose sponsorship citizens (merchants in particular) held religious services, buried their dead, organized memorial services, and administered charity. Over time their original spiritual purposes were pushed aside, and they became centers of ordinary conviviality. Even after the Reformation that tradition continued for a while; numerous brotherhoods retained the names of their old patron saints despite the change in creed.[60] All this is to say that organizations of this type were not totally unfamiliar to those who had grown up in Hamburg, and that it is not surprising that many of the Hamburgers who arrived in Lisbon as Lutherans eventually sought out the Brotherhood of St. Bartholomew. It was a social institution, and as such an important contact point for most Germans, whatever their faith.[61] As historian Heinrich Dormeier said of the religious brotherhoods in Lübeck, membership was probably a "ticket into city society for foreigners and new citizens."[62]

The Brotherhood of the Holy Cross and St. Andrew was another prestigious brotherhood of special significance to the Hamburgish and Netherlandish merchants. It was apparently led by Netherlanders, and its home was the church of the Dominican monastery, the other important church in the commercial center. It was home to other brotherhoods as well, among them the St. George Brotherhood, which welcomed English merchants; the Peter Martyr Brotherhood, for familiars of the Inquisition; and the Brotherhood of Jesus, whose members represented Lisbon's important citizenry and nobility.[63] Thus several groups of people of special interest to the northern European merchants were closely gathered in one place.

The Brotherhood of the Holy Cross, like the Brotherhood of St. Bartholomew, was permitted to bury its members in a special section of its home church.[64] That this was no small matter for the German merchants in Lisbon we can see from one of Mayor Johann Schulte's letters, in which he expressed his pleasure that Johann Bramfeld, whom he had known well in his youth, had "received an honest burial in St. Bartholomew Chapel."[65] The Brotherhood of the Holy Cross and St. Andrew was financed by dues paid by its members: merchants according to their turnover, and shipmasters according to their tonnage. As the seventeenth-century chronicler Luís de Sousa reported, it was extraordinarily wealthy, had a richly decorated chapel, and spared no expense when organizing its feasts.[66] But most praiseworthy in Sousa's eyes was the care that the brothers rendered to the needy members of their nation: the alms for the poor; the dowries for orphaned girls; the care for the sick; the free burials for the destitute. In such ways the brotherhoods served some of the same purposes for the Hamburgers and Netherlanders living in Lisbon that the Portuguese-Jewish and Reformed communities did for their members in Hamburg.

It appears that at times the consul of the Hamburg merchants (see chapter 4) held a post in the Brotherhood of St. Bartholomew. At least this was so in 1597, when Konrad Rot, the consul of the Germans and Netherlanders, convened the brothers to confirm him in his capacity as "judge of the brotherhood" (that is, the board member who exercised the organization's internal jurisdiction) for another two years.[67] And Alexander Heusch, who for many years in the second half of the seventeenth century served as consul of the German Nation, held the post of warden (*mordomo*) of the brotherhood together with young Johann Schulte in 1683/1684.[68] As in the foreign religious communities in Hamburg, political functions seem to have intertwined with religious and social duties.

Holding an office in the Brotherhood of St. Bartholomew was costly. When Mayor Schulte's son was named church warden, his father wrote to him: "As I gather from Sieur Heinrich Burmester, the expenses that you will have as a result of this commission will probably come to about 100 reichstalers, for which God, with his blessings, will richly recompense you in other ways." He added: "It seems to me that your associate should undertake to pay half of the expenses, and that these should be made good by the partnership." In other words, the mayor viewed his son's position in the brotherhood as a business investment, and thus proposed that his partner should take on some of the cost. We can assume that the office rewarded him with manifold contacts, business opportunities, and influence. Still, the younger Schulte's family seems to have been rather amused by the religious aspect of all this. His father wrote from Hamburg, "[On one of these holy days], Johann Pell was elected a church warden of St. Peter's Church. At supper, as the children were with us, your mother joked, saying that she had a son named Johann, who was also a church warden, at St. Bartholomew's Church in Lisbon, about which we all had a good laugh."[69]

Conversions to Catholicism

The religious life of the Hamburgers in Lisbon was complex; it appears that for many of them Lutheranism and Catholicism merged without engendering serious conflict. Yet while the Inquisition posed far less of a threat to the people of Lutheran background living on the Iberian Peninsula than to the New Christians there (see chapter 5), they too were harassed. Letters written home by Johann Schulte make clear that he felt some initial discomfort in the unfamiliar Catholic setting. In response to a letter sent about a month after his arrival in Portugal, his father wrote:

> I noticed in reading your letter that Lisbon and its inhabitants, both spiritual and worldly, do not yet appeal to you, and that you in your present state have not been able to find your footing, for which reason I feel a certain impatience on your part. ... But you must know that in this step [to live abroad] you have had many predecessors, there and in other places, who have experienced something similar, and for whom the great change in all things, including religious matters, felt very strange.

He then gave his son some concrete advice on how to deal with matters of religion:

> As far as religion is concerned, you would be wise to avoid as much as possible all hypocrisy and all occasions, and discuss or have discourse about religion with no one, not even with your business associate, but rather to read [the Bible] at opportune moments, and in the morning and evening to perform your prayers to God with devotion.[70]

The father's letter suggests an admission on his son's part that he had "already sinned once out of necessity when the consecrated host was borne," whereupon his "arms and legs shook."[71] His father responded that he should not be a "scared rabbit" and urged pragmatism:

> You report that there are many priests and many churches and monasteries in Lisbon. Of course! But regardless of how many there are, that shouldn't concern you. No matter how many priests there are, they won't bite you. Be patient. No one forces you to go to Mass and to church, and when at Easter time you receive a certificate [of confession] from a clergyman as if you had confessed and received communion, you do not have to bother about the clergy any further, and even when a priest appears with the consecrated host, you should use all caution and make a detour or repair to a house.[72]

A few months later it appears that the son had come to terms with the new religion. His father wrote that he was pleased to hear,

> that there are no difficulties on account of religion, and that you will avoid having disputes and keep these matters to yourself. All this pleases me greatly, and you will do well to continue, and not to say anything ill or belittling about the Catholic religion, and not speak about it in your house or in the presence of Sieur Drinckherrn [his son's associate], because people who have been Lutheran and converted to the Catholic religion do not wish to hear anything that is contemptuous or petty about the Catholic religion.[73]

In other words, a Lutheran merchant in Lisbon was well advised to read the Bible and pray at home; to talk about this with no one, not even with members of his own nation; and never under any circumstances to discuss questions of religion in public. He should respect the consecrated host, and he could even acquire a certificate at Easter as evidence that he had confessed and received holy communion.

In theory, as I have explained, Hansa merchants in Portugal were free to practice Lutheranism in their homes (see chapter 3). In practice, however, things were more complicated. Consider the case of the wealthy Hamburg merchant João Eggers (see chapters 4 and 5).[74] In 1627 he (along with five other Hamburgers) was denounced to the Inquisition by João Canjuel, the consul of the Germans and Netherlanders in Évora. Canjuel had been watching Eggers for a long time, and the grounds for the denunciation were that he and his confreres met regularly on Sunday mornings in Eggers's house, where they read the Lutheran Bible in German. Eggers had lived in Lisbon as a Lutheran for at least 15, and possibly more than 20, of his 50 or so years; he had never converted, was therefore in no danger of lapsing, and was not advertising his Protestant faith. Nonetheless, another German merchant, Heinrich Hoyer, also a long-time resident of Lisbon, supported Canjuel's denunciation, offering testimony that Eggers had invited him to take part in the Sunday meetings. Hoyer further maintained that he did not want to hear anything of it, had placed his hands over his ears, and had broken off all contact with Eggers because his mind was on redemption. Eggers was never brought to trial; at least I could not find any trial documents. But this story demonstrates clearly that a merchant known to be Lutheran risked not only denunciation, but also social and economic isolation.

The reduction registers of the Inquisition (see chapters 6 and 7) contain detailed information about the conversions of Hamburgers. Between 1641 and 1691, 130 of them officially became Catholics before the Inquisition tribunal in Lisbon alone. They averaged 21 years of age, and almost all of them were merchant apprentices or assistants. Most of them took this step two or three years after their arrival, having learned to speak Portuguese well enough that they no longer needed an interpreter. This indicates that decisions to convert were not made on the spur of the moment. Even Johann Schulte, originally so skeptical about his Catholic environment, converted about a year after his arrival in Lisbon.[75] On April 2, 1682 he requested an audience with the Inquisition, at which he declared that he had accepted Catholicism and would henceforth renounce the sect of Lutheranism. He testified that he was from Hamburg, 20 years old, and single; that his parents had raised him as a Protestant; but that in Portugal he had realized that this doctrine was false, and that he now condemned it wholeheartedly. He was persuaded of the dogma preached by the Holy Church of Rome, so he told the inquisitors, and he hoped to save his soul by following its teachings. He had therefore decided of his own free will to convert, being now completely convinced of the truth of the Catholic faith. He begged forgiveness and mercy for his errors, and hoped that the tribunal would accept him into the Roman Catholic community. The inquisitor responded that he should be grateful to God for his enlightenment, and that the church would gladly accept him, but that he must obey its commandments scrupulously, and in particular avoid any traffic with heretics. The conversion was finalized with the granting of a written certificate to the effect that he had confessed and received holy communion. Like many other Hamburg converts, Schulte received this certificate in the Chapel of St. Andrew in the Dominican monastery, and submitted it to the Inquisition for insertion into his conversion file.

Problems with the Inquisition

Not all Hamburgers who converted remained faithful to their new creed. Some of them returned to Protestantism during temporary stays in Hamburg, and then came into conflict with the Inquisition when they failed in their Catholic practice back in Portugal. João da Maya is one such case.[76] He testified before the tribunal in Lisbon that, although he was a Catholic with all his heart, he had, upon his return from Hamburg, lived as a Lutheran because he had feared that otherwise he would receive no further commissions from his Hamburg trading correspondents. He had assumed that in Portugal, as in his homeland, each person might follow the faith he deemed best, and that this was especially the case for foreigners coming from heretical countries. Even if Maya was embellishing the truth, his testimony makes clear the intricate connections between religious identification, trade interests, and the reality of the Inquisition. A change in religious affiliation could influence trust between business partners, as major changes in a person's presentation could hint at flightiness or unreliability. But Maya might also have known that the Inquisition, which strove not to imperil trade with the Protestant countries in the north (see chapter 5), was prepared to consider such arguments plausible and grant absolution.

The Hamburg merchant João Frique had a similar experience.[77] He testified before the Inquisition that he had returned to Hamburg for six months and had not told his relatives there about his conversion in Lisbon. His reasons, he stated, were that he needed their support in his business, and that he feared being disinherited. When he returned to Lisbon he began dealing with a Hamburg merchant of Lutheran faith, and because that man might have written to his relatives that he was a Catholic, he had lived his Catholicism in Lisbon only clandestinely. A priest confirmed that Frique had in fact performed most of the duties of a Catholic. We do not know what João da Maya and João Frique actually believed, or with whom or to what extent they dissimulated. Perhaps they even found aspects of both faiths attractive, adopting parts of one or the other depending on the situation. But apparently they were flexible enough to adapt them to their trading ventures.

Young Johann Schulte probably did not try to hide his conversion from his relatives back home. Although the issue was never broached directly in any of the mayor's letters, the passage quoted in chapter 10, in which he expressed concern about his son's writing too freely about religion (and which is dated just before the son's conversion) might relate to it.[78] It is possible that his son had told him of his intention to convert, and perhaps written that he would not take the change in creed seriously. The mayor may have been aware that conversion to Catholicism was common among Hamburgers in Lisbon; after all, his son-in-law Gerd Burmester had also spent time there in his youth. Certainly the family knew of their boy's conversion by the time the mayor congratulated him on being named church warden of the Brotherhood of St. Bartholomew.[79]

The Advantages of Conversion for a Merchant

We do not know how many of the Hamburgers living in Portugal converted: probably a lot of them; undoubtedly not all. Because Catholics alone were subject to persecution for heretical behavior and Protestants were protected, at least to some degree, in their private religious practices, the question arises why so many merchants and merchant assistants converted. The most obvious reason, it would seem, was the intention to settle in Portugal permanently and marry a Catholic woman, and in fact such motives can often be found in the conversion declarations of members of other nations. But they are less apparent among the Hamburgers. Most merchant assistants from Hamburg probably planned to return when their apprenticeships were over. In his letters to his son, Mayor Schulte reported on various merchants who, like Johann, had apprenticed in Lisbon and then returned to Hamburg. Right at the beginning of their correspondence he wrote: "If you believe that you have advanced so far in trade in two or three years that you think you could continue here with your trade to Lisbon, then you can inform me, and we can easily come to an agreement about your repatriation."[80] Soon after this letter, the family started the long process of negotiation for Johann's marriage to a bride in Hamburg. Permanent settlement in Lisbon, therefore, or marriage to a Portuguese woman, cannot have been the reason for Schulte's conversion.

Looking for reasons for conversion in the Inquisition files, we find several Hamburgers who testified that their local masters or business partners had persuaded them to convert; this hints at the importance of conversion for commerce.[81] The impressionability of youth may also have been a factor in some of these decisions; one young Hamburger said that he converted because most of the other people he knew from Hamburg had done so.[82] So might a desire to participate in the magnificent rituals of the Catholic Church, the need for a community of believers, or the eager presence of a small group of Catholic priests who spoke the converts' mother tongue. These latter often accompanied them when they testified before the Inquisition, and seem to have actively encouraged conversions.

Whatever their reasons, for the Hamburg apprentices acceptance into the Catholic Church opened up social and political possibilities. Conversion meant public assent to the conventions of the host society, and deliberate integration into it. It paved the way into social circles that were vital to the merchants, starting with the brotherhoods. It made possible the private, commercial, and political engagements that could further fledgling careers and facilitate access to credit, property, and privilege, as when Gaspar de Faria Severim, the *secretário das mercês* (state secretary for the administration of mercies) under King João IV and councilor of state under Afonso VI, agreed to stand godfather to Consul Willem Heusch's son Alexander (see chapter 5). Godfatherhood was an important relationship of support and sponsorship among Catholics, and as Alexander's godfather, Faria Severim was able to advance the Heusches' social fortunes greatly. Neither the relationship nor the advancement would have been possible if the family had remained Lutheran.[83] The importance of conversion was nowhere more apparent than when merchants underwent habilitation to become familiars of the Inquisition, or sought entry into a military order. As I have explained (see chapters 5 and 7), these were among the most important social distinctions a merchant could hope to achieve in Portugal. They attested to his preeminent economic and social status, and conferred upon him something akin to ennoblement. Foreigners often had trouble proving that their lineage was appropriate to their aspirations, as their ancestry could not always be adequately certified. But inquisitors treated them with leniency; while in theory proof of pure blood (that is, exclusively Christian ancestry; see chapter 5) was required, in practice, where Germans were concerned, they were charitable in their interpretations of the evidence. In many instances, familial ties to a cleric in Portugal were sufficient confirmation of a merchant's suitability. For example, in 1671 André Hasse's admission to the Order of Christ was partly justified on the grounds that his brother was a canon in the Cathedral of Lisbon.[84] Diogo Timão, the consul of the Germans and Netherlanders in Porto, was found eligible to serve as a familiar in 1642 because several of his children were clerics.[85] Isabel Guilherme was the daughter of a wealthy timber dealer from Altona who lived in Lisbon. When the purity of her blood was examined in the context of her husband's habilitation, the fact that two of her brothers were clergymen in Portugal became an important factor in his acceptance.[86] Willem Heusch also had a son and a brother-in-law who were friars in a religious order, which was why the habilitation of his descendants succeeded.[87] Once having been named a familiar of the Inquisition, a merchant could be accepted into the Peter Martyr Brotherhood. At the beginning of the seventeenth century it had opened itself up to the social elites, including even some members of the royal court, and by the final quarter of the century it had become a gathering place for the mercantile upper class.[88]

In sum, conversion promised social and mercantile advancement, and was essential for an individual's fullest integration into Portuguese society. While non-Lutheran merchants in Hamburg felt the need to join specific ethnic or religious communities so as to be able to assert themselves economically, the Hamburg merchants in Portugal were much less dependent on the help of compatriots to make their way in the economic life of the country. Hamburg's City Council, Lutheran clergy, and population in general all resisted the integration of foreigners; Portuguese society, however, with the support of the government and church institutions, integrated immigrants much more quickly and willingly. The occasional displays of nation-based identity evidenced by the Hamburgers in Portugal (as in the arches at the royal entries) may have been an expression of a particular self-understanding. It was not, however, a means to assert and maintain themselves against outside pressure. The Hamburgers living abroad never created any supraregional associations; among the German and Netherlandish brotherhoods on the Iberian Peninsula and abroad there seems to have been no networking, no sharing of personnel, and no organization for the overall administration of material aid. The Hamburgers and Netherlanders networked at an individual level, on the basis of family and business relationships. They did not form a diaspora identity in any way comparable to the lively long-distance exchange that characterized the Portuguese nation.

Conclusion

The merchants who plied the trade route between Hamburg and Portugal in the seventeenth century led lives marked profoundly by the experience of migration and foreignness. Merchants from Hamburg and the Netherlands moved to Portugal, and Portuguese and Netherlandish merchants moved to Hamburg. In Portugal foreign merchants were well received; the king had been dependent on them at least since the beginning of the overseas expansion in the fifteenth century, and he still needed them in the seventeenth. They provided foodstuffs, weaponry, munitions, shipbuilding materials, and copperware for Portuguese domestic consumption, war, conquest and trading ventures, and they were buyers of Portugal's imports from Africa, India, and Brazil. They were also an important source of funding for Portuguese enterprise. For this reason, qualified foreign merchants were often granted a legal status that was in some respects superior to that of their local colleagues. Merchants from Hamburg had an additional advantage: they belonged to a neutral city, and so could always trade freely with the Iberian kingdoms. Their colleagues from the United Provinces, England, France, and other countries, in contrast, were often constrained in their trade by embargoes and other impediments associated with the armed conflicts of the time.

Foreign merchants enjoyed a social prestige in Portugal that kept pace with their privileged legal status. Hamburgers often arrived in Portugal at a young age and with few assets, yet within a generation or two many of them managed to rise high on the social ladder. Their integration was facilitated by the Portuguese Church's openness toward other Europeans. The merchants' Lutheran faith was tolerated as long as it was practiced in private, and, more important, conversion to Catholicism was fairly uncomplicated; it was the gate opening the path to integration and the catalyst of advancement in Portuguese society. Once having converted, foreigners could join brotherhoods and be appointed as familiars of the Inquisition, accepted into military orders, and even granted titles of nobility.

Nearly all of these avenues to success and respectability were closed to the local New Christian merchants. Although they were Portuguese by birth, and their families had likely been Catholic for a century or even longer, they were suspected of never really having renounced Judaism. This suspicion produced both attitudes of chronic unwelcome and periodic clashes with the Inquisition, and came along with an array of discriminatory laws that hindered the New Christians' full participation in society. All this impelled many of them to leave the country.

The foreign merchants who settled in Hamburg were received far more ambivalently than their counterparts in Portugal. Hamburg at the turn of the seventeenth century was a largely independent city-state whose prosperity was

https://doi.org/10.1515/9783110472103-017

built on intermediary trade. It protected this trade with laws, medieval in character, that distinguished between aliens and citizens, and disadvantaged the former in their opportunities to pursue commerce in the city. Some Netherlandish merchants became citizens in Hamburg shortly after their arrival. But the legal status of the rest, and of the Portuguese merchants, was regulated by collective alien contracts and by alien laws. These included a ban on trade between aliens without a citizen intermediary (*Gasthandelsverbot*). Although the ban was lifted in 1604 on a variety of goods, it continued to restrict trade in some of the most crucial commodities; free trade in grain, wine, and salt remained limited to citizens of Hamburg until about 1653. Merchants' trade turnovers reflected this inequality. Citizens traded most heavily in the necessities that the ban reserved for them, while aliens concentrated on less crucial goods, such as wax and dyes (in the case of the Netherlanders) and wax, cloth, and sugar (in the case of the Portuguese).

Despite these disadvantages, foreigners, and especially the Netherlanders, played a powerful role in Hamburg long-distance trade. In 1619 the Netherlanders accounted for almost half of that trade, and the Portuguese for a bit less than 5 percent. In that year there were 138 Netherlandish merchants and 32 Portuguese merchants active in Hamburg (that is, about 25 percent and 6 percent respectively of the total merchant population). Furthermore, in 1632 and 1647 the Netherlanders and Portuguese together accounted for a good half of the value of the goods traded between Hamburg and the Iberian Peninsula. Each nation's share in the Portugal trade fluctuated between 20 and 30 percent. In the more extensive trade with Spain, however, the Netherlanders accounted for about 40 to 50 percent of total turnover, and the Portuguese for only about 10 percent.

Foreigners in Hamburg suffered other disadvantages, too. Jews could not become citizens. Christians could; but to be a Christian and a citizen was not enough to obtain administrative or government office in the city and the political influence that went with it. For that it was necessary to be a Lutheran, and the Lutheran clergy seems to have been disinclined to accept foreigners for conversion. While the alien contracts with the Portuguese stressed their Jewishness and contained disciplinary provisions specifically aimed at their religious identity, the Netherlander contracts were neutral in terms of religion and focused on their members' economic and social rights. In 1653 the Netherlander contracts ceased to be renewed, and the individual alien contracts that replaced them for those who did not seek citizen status conferred a higher degree of individual liberty. The city treated the Portuguese Jews very differently; by maintaining collective contracts it permanently established their distinctive corporate position.

Even those Lutheran Netherlanders who were in principle eligible for political office rarely found their way into the city's ruling circles until the end of the seventeenth century. In only a few instances did they achieve high office, and only very exceptionally did they marry into old city council families. Still, both Reformed and Lutheran Netherlanders became actively engaged in the Commercial Deputation, which, after its founding in 1665, helped greatly to integrate the Netherlandish merchants into Hamburg's economic organization. It did not, however, integrate the Portuguese Jews, as deputies were elected by the Honorable Merchant, a body that de facto, if not de jure, barred Jews from membership. In not recognizing Jewish merchants as equals, it gave the lie to its claim to represent (as well as regulate) all Hamburg long-distance merchants.

Local politics aside, however, in the seventeenth century the merchants' ethnic and religious backgrounds, and even their personal assets, mattered little in the Atlantic trade. Commerce was often conducted by way of reciprocal commissions in which merchant correspondents in different cities and of more or less equal status cooperated with each other. This permitted flexible networks that let merchants respond without delay to the exigent demands of the time: war, embargo, religious persecution, migration, and so on. When a correspondent was lost for any such reason, others were readily available, either in the same place or nearby. This flexibility was enhanced by some important innovations that promoted independent enterprise. The cities hosted ancillary supports such as multilingual brokers and notaries, financial and insurance facilities, public information services and a postal system. There also arose a legal substructure for sustaining individual merchants and safeguarding their goods, as well as the police and judicial machinery for enforcing it.

With arrangements like these at their disposal, none of the nations analyzed in this book functioned as segregated entities – at least not in business. Their trading networks were not homogeneous, either ethnically or religiously. Merchants acquired the trust and reputation critical in trade principally through compliance with established mercantile norms and through recommendations from trusted colleagues, not only of their own nations. Family bonds were of major importance too. Not only did they stabilize business relations over the long term, but they also brought with them such financial advantages as ready credit, the provision of guarantees, and the ability to acquire assets in the form of gifts, dowries, and inheritances. In Portugal, where conversion was relatively easy, many Hamburgers and Netherlanders married Portuguese women, so that the business relationships emerging from marriage often transcended the bounds of both nation and religion. In Hamburg, most merchants married within their own group, and trading relations tended to be somewhat narrower ethnically and religiously.

Still, family was not an infallible formula for success. Businesses based on family relationships could be destroyed by family conflicts, which were often triggered by migration and ensuing religious conversion. In this area too the experience of a merchant depended on the nation he belonged to. The conversion of a Hamburger or Netherlander to Catholicism might cause ripples of distrust among his family and trading partners at home. But for the Portuguese, the Inquisition made the consequences of conversion much more serious, even in Hamburg. Merchants who affiliated with a Jewish community in northern Europe exposed their relatives in Portugal to severe reputational, financial, and physical danger. This placed a serious strain on family relationships.

Conversely, the ongoing threat of the Inquisition on the Iberian Peninsula meant that New Christian businessmen there, whether of a merchant's own family or not, were riskier trading partners than Old Christians or foreign colleagues. A New Christian might be arrested or have to flee unexpectedly to avoid arrest by the Inquisition, and even if he managed to save himself, any goods entrusted to him would be seized. Because of this risk, even the Portuguese Jews in Hamburg sometimes preferred Hamburgers or Netherlanders to New Christians as their trading correspondents in Portugal. Jewish-New Christian trading networks were much more fragile, and therefore less competitive, than those among merchants of other nations.

Portuguese-Jewish merchants trading with the Iberian Peninsula were also less mobile than their Netherlandish and Hamburgish colleagues. Any travels to their old homeland exposed them to the Inquisition and put not only their own lives at risk, but also the lives of local family members and trading partners. Furthermore, such travels were forbidden by the boards of the Jewish communities in the diaspora, lest during their sojourns they be impeded in their practice of Judaism, or tempted to abandon it altogether. Once they had emigrated, therefore, the Portuguese could maintain old business contacts only with difficulty, and establishing new ones in their former home country was an even more daunting proposition. While the Hamburgers who settled in Portugal often sent their children back to their old homeland for training and to reinforce their trading contacts, the Portuguese living in Hamburg could not do the same. Sooner or later, inevitably, trading relationships between the Portuguese Jews and their colleagues on the Iberian Peninsula broke down.

Finally, the Iberian refugees were confronted with danger and discrimination even in Hamburg, where they received only limited protection from the City Council. They had no state to back them when negotiating with their hosts, or to intervene in the event of crisis. The Hamburgers in Portugal received this kind of support from their city of origin, and, at the beginning of the century, from the Hansa; in Portugal itself they had their consul to turn to. And as we have seen, some of the Netherlanders in Portugal were protected by Hamburg's institutions too: not only Netherlanders who had become citizens of Hamburg but even those who had only acquired alien status there. The Netherlanders had their own ruling authorities to call upon as well (except when relations between the states were strained by war), and in Hamburg especially the Reformed occasionally called for support by the government of the United Provinces.

Against the background of all these difficulties, the question arises why the Portuguese converted to Judaism in Hamburg, rather than simply remaining Catholic or converting to Lutheranism (as the Hamburgers and Netherlanders in Portugal converted to Catholicism). Surely the city of Hamburg was a factor, since it seems to have been more willing to welcome a vulnerable minority, one that would be modest in its demands and loyal to its benefactors, than one with a powerful political backing. But there was also, at least for some of the Portuguese Jews, the matter of desire. The Portuguese emigrants knew that their ancestors had been Jews, and this was a memory that most of them probably respected and valued. Their experience of discrimination and persecution by Christians and Christian institutions, especially the brutality of the Inquisition, may have further encouraged them to return to Judaism. A few convinced crypto-Jews among the early arrivals may have been sufficient to motivate and persuade waverers. And once the Portuguese-Jewish community was established, membership in it promised essential support to those who came later. Nothing, however, connected them to Lutheranism, and unlike the Inquisition in Portugal, which welcomed foreign Protestants into the bosom of the Catholic Church, the Lutheran clergy was not particularly receptive to converts. So it was to Judaism that they turned.

If we ask, as Herman Kellenbenz, Jonathan Israel, and so many others have done, what made the commerce of the Portuguese-Jewish merchants distinctive, we must come to conclusions different from theirs. It was not exceptional experience abroad or special linguistic skill. Nor was it outstanding economic success gained by any other means. All of the merchants who engaged in long-distance trade at that time possessed such experience and such skill. And the Netherlanders in Hamburg (perhaps the Hamburgers in Portugal, too, but we lack comparable data for them) were much more successful. As I explained, the Jews in Hamburg were less mobile than the other merchants, in that they had no way back to the Iberian Peninsula. Most of them spoke poorer German than the Hamburgers and Netherlanders in Portugal spoke Portuguese. Their networks covering the Iberian Peninsula were neither larger, more consolidated, nor more resilient than those of the other merchants. The Portuguese Jews did not differ from their Christian colleagues in ingenuity or adaptability, as Kellenbenz has proposed. Nor is there evidence that religious precepts had much effect on their commercial practices.

What really distinguished the Portuguese Jews from their Christian colleagues was their greater vulnerability and, linked to that, their commitment to strictly regulated communities. The leaders of those communities insisted on a disciplined solidarity that eventually enabled them to advocate effectively with the host authorities for their members' interests. But it also incurred the obligation to engage with great dedication in the social and religious life of their communities. The boards held extensive power over community members and maintained a strict social control; they did whatever they thought necessary to keep individuals in line lest they damage the collective reputation of the Portuguese Jews, and thus the host city's willingness to harbor them. They were especially intent on keeping internal conflicts out of the public eye and resolving them privately. Most of the Portuguese-Jewish merchants acquiesced to the absolute leadership claimed by their principals, because they understood that outside the Jewish communities their livelihoods and survival were endangered. This was true for most of the Portuguese-Jewish settlements in the Atlantic diaspora, but it seems to have been especially so in Hamburg.

The situation was fundamentally different for the Netherlandish and Hamburgish merchants living abroad. The Netherlanders evidenced no sense of solidarity comparable to that of the Portuguese nation, either in Hamburg or in their diaspora, comparable to that of the Portuguese nation. They too had known persecution – an experience that did become part of their identity – but the Netherlanders were considerably more heterogeneous than the Portuguese. They belonged to two different language groups and to at least two different religious persuasions; in Hamburg, even their legal status varied. And while the Lutheran Netherlanders did eventually integrate into the Hamburg society, the Reformed congregation, and the supraregional network of other Reformed congregations in which it was embedded, remained a separate group. Like the Portuguese-Jewish community, the community of Reformed Netherlanders was led by an economic elite that defined the parameters of acceptable behavior and administered the sanctions necessary to enforce them. As among the Portuguese Jews, the most severe punishment was excommunication. Yet in their trade, the Netherlandish Reformed were not constrained to the same extent as the Portuguese: not in Hamburg, where they had more opportunities open to them, and especially not in Portugal, where they were so much less obstructed by the Inquisition.

The common identity of the Hamburgers living in Portugal was even less developed than that of the Netherlanders in Hamburg. They had no history of suffering to bind them together or to explain their settlement in a foreign land. There was no pressure to organize in Portugal because they rarely had to assert their rights there. They were socially respected; they learned the language quickly; and many of them easily assumed the religious identification of the majority. In the half-century between 1641 and 1691, 130 merchants and merchant apprentices from Hamburg formally converted to Catholicism in Lisbon. Their children often spoke German so badly that they had to be sent to Hamburg to acquire fluency. The Hamburgers and Netherlanders living in Portugal also sought out social environments, like the Catholic lay brotherhoods, in which they could meet their compatriots. But membership in those associations was less a matter of self-defense than of advancement. A merchant could derive professional benefit by serving on their boards. Conversion and the possibilities it opened up paved the way to the most influential business circles in the kingdom.

Wherever they dwelled, the expatriates of all three nations lived with the fact of foreignness, an experience that fostered in them a wish for companionship and society among their own people. But the wish differed in intensity according to how much the host society opened to them its social resources, and also according to the way they wanted to live their nation's identity. The particularity of the Portuguese Jews was their permanent special status not as merchants, but as a social and religious group. They attracted more attention – from their contemporaries as well as from historians – not because there was anything special about them as merchants, but because they were less integrated and less assimilated into the culture in which they lived. Whereas other groups of foreign merchants melded into the surrounding society in one or two generations, the Portuguese-Jewish merchants retained their own identity, remaining clearly identifiable by their language, by their customs, and by their religion.

Appendix

Examining the Hamburg Admiralty customs books through the lenses of nation, religious affiliation, and legal status enables a nuanced view of seventeenth-century trade and, especially, of the merchants who engaged in it. I conducted such a study for two years for which we have complete customs books: from April 17, 1632 to April 16, 1633, and from February 22, 1647 to February 21, 1648 (see chapter 9). Since there are many potential sources of error in collecting and analyzing such data, the resulting figures should be viewed as approximations only. In this appendix I discuss my methodology and its most significant challenges.

Names and Identifications

In extracting and tabulating the names in my sources I standardized them in accordance with the conventions of modern spelling. It is important to note, however, that the information in the sources did not always permit me to make perfect distinctions between individuals. Sometimes a merchant bore the same name as his father, grandfather, or uncle; where generational suffixes such as "the elder" or "the younger" appear in the files, I have made use of them. Still, in many entries it was not clear to me which of two identically named merchants paid a given duty. I also may have erred at times in the interpretation of name variants, either by seeing identity where it does not exist, or by failing to recognize cases where name variants refer to a single individual. "Jürgen" is a common form of the name "Georg," for example, and I was unable to determine if the Jürgen Heintz covered by the Netherlander contract was the Georg Heintz entered in the customs books. The inconsistent use of multiple first and last names among the Portuguese poses difficulties as well. It was not clear to me, for example, whether Francisco de Andrade Rodrigues, Francisco de Andrade, Francisco Rodrigues, and Francisco Rodrigues de Andrade in the customs books refer to one person or several. Luís Dias might or might not be a variant of Luís Dias de Lima, and Manuel Rodrigues could be the same person as Manuel Rodrigues Isidro or Manuel Rodrigues Jorge.

In most cases of doubt I chose not to equate names, so the number of merchants included in the database is more likely too large than too small.

Classification by Nation

In my efforts to determine (insofar as possible) the nation, religious denomination, and legal status of the merchants named in the Admiralty customs books,

https://doi.org/10.1515/9783110472103-018

I made use of additional sources. I classified as "Hamburgers" all individuals who were listed in the citizens' rolls with the suffix *civis filius* (son of a citizen), and who belonged to no other nation. I classified as "regional immigrants" those who were citizens but *not* listed as *civis filius,* and who did not belong to any of the foreign nations. I also included the seven people who are listed as "Germans and High Germans" in the third Netherlander contract (see chapter 3), and all other merchants whose German origins are attested in research literature, in the "regional immigrants" category.[1]

Merchants who were covered by the Hamburg Netherlander contracts (with the exception of the seven "Germans and High Germans" mentioned above) and the administrators of the Netherlandish Relief Fund I classified as "Netherlanders."[2] An extensive biographical study by Wilhelm Sillem provided additional information for that category.[3] All persons who bore the same family name as a person of Netherlandish origin I also classified as Netherlanders, unless the family name was common in German too. I classified as "Portuguese" all those whose names appear in the membership lists of the Portuguese nation in Hamburg or of the Portuguese-Jewish community there, as well as those who bore names that were clearly Portuguese in origin.[4] There are also a few merchants who we know were *not* Hamburgers, Netherlanders, or Portuguese; Silvio Tensino and Abondio Somigliano, for example, were both Italian. When I had to make an educated guess about a person's nation I indicated the guess with a question mark.

This procedure allowed me to determine the nations of 79 percent of the merchants active in the Iberia trade in 1632, and 59 percent of those active in 1647. The others, most of whom were probably "Hamburgers," "regional immigrants," or staying in Hamburg only transiently, I classified as "origin unknown."

Table 20: Nations in the Iberia trade

	1632		1647	
	Number	**Percentage**	**Number**	**Percentage**
Hamburgers	53	16.3%	60	17.8%
Regional immigrants	60	18.4%	27	8.0%
Netherlanders	81	24.9%	62	18.3%
Netherlanders?	0	0.0%	5	1.5%
Portuguese	57	17.5%	43	12.7%
Portuguese?	1	0.3%	0	0.0%
English	0	0.0%	2	0.6%
Italians	1	0.3%	1	0.3%
Partnerships of different nations	5	1.5%	0	0.0%
Origin unknown	68	20.9%	138	40.8%
Total	326		338	

Classification by Religious Affiliation

It was more risky to classify the merchants by religious affiliation, because a person's affiliation could change. I could not take for granted a merchant's religion or denomination in 1632 or 1647, the years under consideration here, on the basis of its documentation at some other time. Nor could I necessarily assume that Hamburg citizens were Lutherans, because Reformed and Catholics could also become citizens (see chapter 3). Even to assume that all members of a merchant's family belonged to the same religion or denomination was chancy. Although I did occasionally resort to such extrapolations, I did so sparingly, and no critical arguments are based upon them.

Persons listed in the citizens' rolls I classified as "Lutheran" if no other religious affiliation was known to me. A person with the same family name as one classified as "Lutheran" I classified as "Lutheran?" if the family name was relatively uncommon and I knew of no other affiliation. I extracted the "Reformed" from the membership lists of the Stade and Altona Reformed congregations, and checked them against the names in Sillem's work.[5] I classified as "Jews" those Portuguese whose names appear in the only membership list (1617) of the Portuguese-Jewish community that survives from the first half of the seventeenth century, and also those known to have received Jewish burial.[6] Persons whose denomination I did not explicitly know, but who bore the same family name as a known member of the Reformed or Jewish community, I classified in the same religious category as their namesakes, again with a question mark. All other persons I classified as "religion unknown."

Table 21: Religious affiliations in the Iberia trade

	1632		1647	
	Number	**Percentage**	**Number**	**Percentage**
Lutherans	129	39.6%	105	31.1%
Lutherans?	23	7.1%	39	11.5%
Reformed	24	7.4%	16	4.7%
Reformed?	25	7.7%	36	10.7%
Jews	31	9.5%	27	8.0%
Jews?	26	8.0%	16	4.7%
Affiliation unknown	68	20.9%	99	29.3%
Total	326		338	

Classification by Legal Status

The sources that establish legal status are the clearest, yet that is the category in which we are left with the highest percentage of unclassifiable persons (45 percent in 1632 and 56 percent in 1647). I classified all persons listed in the citizens' rolls as "citizens." All persons listed in the Netherlander contracts who had not acquired citizen status prior to 1632 or 1647 I classified as "contract Netherlanders." It made little sense to differentiate legal status among the Portuguese, because the contract listings closest to 1632 (that is, the listings of 1616 and 1618) include very few of the Portuguese merchants active in the Iberia trade in that year (only 12 of 57); besides, it seems clear that none of the Portuguese acquired citizen status.

Table 22: Legal status in the Iberia trade

	1632		1647	
	Number	Percentage	Number	Percentage
Citizens	128	39.3%	114	33.7%
Citizens?	2	0.6%	2	0.6%
Contract Netherlanders	36	11.0%	26	7.7%
Merchant Adventurers	0	0.0%	2	0.6%
Status unknown/other	160	49.1%	194	57.4%
Total	326		338	

Standardization

I had to standardize the names and units of measurement of the merchants' wares before the data could be analyzed. The names posed few difficulties. Except for standardizing the spelling, in most cases I accepted them as they appeared in the customs files, and disregarded in my groupings any specific attributes that did not influence the level of duty assessed. For example, the files distinguished among common canvas, low canvas, coarse canvas, raw canvas, unbleached canvas, white canvas, Osnabrück canvas, Silesian canvas, and canvas (without specification). I pooled all these types together as *canvas*.[7] I also grouped wares with names that I understand to be synonymous under a single name; thus I subsumed linen (*Leinen*) under "canvas" (*Leinwand*), as they likely referred to the same thing. Similarly, I brought together indigo and anil (the shrub that yields it) under "indigo." If the wares on which duties were paid were not specified, I entered them as "unknown" in the database.[8]

I standardized measurements as they are used in the Admiralty customs books, which sometimes diverge from the equivalences attested in other sources. According to the standard reference by Ernst Pitz, for example, a cardel (*Quardeel*) of wine was the same quantity as two hogsheads (*Oxhoft*) of wine.[9] But because the customs books consistently placed the same duty on a cardel as on a hogshead, I used a conversion proportion of 1:1. In general I reduced measurements to the most frequently used unit.

Calculation of Value

Customs duties are calculated either by value or by quantity, in which latter case according to a tariff list. It is not entirely clear how the Hamburg Admiralty determined them. It appears that at first they were set by value (at 0.75 percent and 0.5 percent, according to documents from 1623 and 1639/1640, respectively).[10] But not long after 1623, a list of tariff rates seems to have been established as well. I have not found it, but the way the customs books are written very clearly suggests both its existence and its contents.[11] The books indicate that by 1632 only a few categories of merchandise were taxed by value, among them cloth, drugs, dyes, tobacco, and semi-fabricated wooden wares. The books also show that the duty to be paid on these wares in 1632 was 0.25 percent of value, and in 1647, 0.33 percent – that is, considerably less than the documents mentioned above (from 1623 and 1639/1640) indicate. Most wares, however, especially commodities such as grain, wax, wine, oil, ginger, and sugar, were subject to a fixed tariff. Because the customs books do not state the values of these substances, I have used in my analysis fictive values that would have yielded duties equal in amount to the duties paid on goods whose value is known. For example: the customs duties on a crate of sugar came to 6 shillings in 1632 and 8 shillings in 1647; its inferred (fictive) value would therefore be 150 marks (1 mark = 16 shillings; 1 shilling = 12 pennies) if the duties had been imposed at 0.25 percent and 0.33 percent, respectively.[12] Values calculated in this manner do not necessarily correspond to the market value on the day of assessment, but rather to the value of the good or commodity at the time that the tariff list was established (plus any other adjustments, such as politically motivated surcharges or reductions).[13]

Calculation Inaccuracies

Bookkeeping practices give rise to a major problem in evaluating the data. When duties were paid according to value, scribes often grouped several units of goods together, noting an overall value only. For example, on March 17, 1647, Claus

Schmidt shipped staves (*Pipensteven*) and clapboards (*Klappholz*, that is, oak or beech wood boards from which barrel staves were made) to Lisbon, having a total value of 600 marks. However, there is no way to determine the share of each in the overall value. On November 5, 1647, João da Rocha Pinto exported a crate of buckram (a coarse linen fabric), a crate of canvas, and a pack (*Packen*) of copper basins to Lisbon. Together his shipment was valued at 1,800 marks, but the value of each item was not noted separately. In such instances I approximated the value as follows: the staves that Claus Schmidt exported had a minimum value of 0 marks and a maximum of 600 marks; the same may be said of his clapboards. The buckram, canvas, and copper basins exported by João da Rocha Pinto each had a minimum value of 0 marks and a maximum of 1,800 marks.

In determining values of goods traded, I always calculated minimum and maximum values separately, and averaged them as late as possible. For example, the total value of all canvas exported from Hamburg in fiscal year 1632 was a minimum of 35,425 marks and a maximum of 224,025 marks. The reference value that I ultimately used was the average of the two, or 129,725 marks. This method can lead to considerable distortion; in this case, the error could theoretically be as large as 114 percent.[14] However, the enormous difference between the minimum and maximum in this illustration is an exception. It is the result of the extraordinarily large number of bookings involving canvas; and given such a large number it is probable that the value shifts even out in the end, eventually averaging close to the actual value.

For most of the other commodities traded at high frequency, such as grain, sugar, salt, wine, ginger, oil, powder, and tin, duties were based not on the value of the commodity, but on the quantity (measured in lasts, crates, pipes, sacks, and so on). In these cases the figures are accurate. For example, according to the customs books for fiscal year 1632, exactly 1,237.5 lasts of rye, corresponding to a total (fictive) value of 247,500 marks, were registered as having been exported to the Iberian Peninsula.[15] The error introduced by the imprecise bookkeeping on merchandise declared by value is therefore small in relation to the entire volume traded with the Iberian Peninsula. Using this method of calculation, the error for 1647 (minimum 3,195,318 marks; maximum 4,420,463 marks; yielding an average of 3,807,891 marks) would come at most to 17 percent, which is small in comparison with the potential 114 percent in that year for canvas exports alone.

Error Estimation

There is one way to estimate error that takes into account not only the distortions resulting from minimum and maximum limits, but also inaccurate conversions of measurement units, faulty derivations of good and commodity values, and mistakes in transcription and arithmetic introduced by customs scribes. This is to calculate the duties on goods (either by quantity, using individual duty tariffs, or by value, using the aforementioned approximations) and compare them against actual duties paid. A simple example: on November 27, 1632, Jochim Heusch paid 5 marks and 10 shillings duty on 10 butts (*Botten*) of Spanish wine and 100 small barrels of figs, which had been sent to him from Sanlúcar. If we calculate the duty on a quantity basis using the rates I established from the customs books (4 shillings per butt of wine and 6 pennies per barrel of figs), we come to the conclusion that he owed 5 marks and 10 shillings. In this case there is no discrepancy. If, however, an error had been made at any point in the assessment protocol – say a customs scribe had written down "10 small barrels of figs" instead of 100, but had him pay taxes for all 100 barrels and written down that correct sum – the tax predicted by quantity and rate would differ from the one actually paid and listed in the books.

To obtain an impression of the total error of my analysis, we can compare the total turnover as calculated by quantity or value of goods (as the data indicate) with the total turnover calculated by duty payment. For the year 1632, the discrepancy between the two totals comes to 14 percent (total turnover calculated by goods: 3,977,914 marks; total turnover calculated by duty: 3,448,725 marks); for the year 1647 the discrepancy is only 6 percent (total turnover calculated by goods: 5,558,018 marks; total turnover calculated by duty: 5,235,664 marks).[16] As the correct turnovers lie somewhere between the two values, the error is less than 14 percent and less than 6 percent for the two years, respectively.

Here too errors tend to be larger in small contexts than they are in big ones. If we look only at few bookings, the error will be greater than if we look at all bookings together. The following table, which lists the merchants with the highest turnovers in fiscal year 1647 (in each case based on the total trade for which Admiralty customs duties were paid) demonstrates this:

Table 23: Error estimation for individual merchants

Merchant	Total turnover by duty (in marks)	Total turnover by goods (in marks)	Discrepancy
Adrian Juncker	254,728	252,406	1%
Michel Heusch	221,719	227,707	3%
Wilken Wrede	157,003	155,738	1%
Duarte Esteves de Pina	141,216	134,150	5%
Gerd Burmester	131,288	132,538	1%
Cornelis de Hertoghe	114,572	202,603	56%
Johann Baptista Juncker	108,506	108,152	0%

(continued)

Table 23 (continued)

Merchant	Total turnover by duty (in marks)	Total turnover by goods (in marks)	Discrepancy
Manuel Rodrigues Isidro	106,097	102,229	4%
Lopo Nunes	105,900	107,375	1%
Daniel Brandes & Jeronimus Schnitker	96,263	101,303	5%
Johann Schröttering	95,025	107,849	13%
Claus Martens	91,191	96,975	6%

Notable is the case of Cornelis de Hertoghe, which shows an extreme discrepancy between the two values. The reason for this is that de Hertoghe traded in a large number of goods having discrepant minimum and maximum values (the turnover by goods shown in the table represents the average of a minimum of 51,053 marks and a maximum of 354,153 marks), which were bundled into relatively few, but large, customs duty entries. On May 4, 1647, for example, he paid customs duties on a shipment of goods amounting to the very high total value of 10,700 marks, which consisted of the following components:

- 2 barrels of bombazine
- 2 packs of Muscovy leather (used in shoes, furniture, coaches, and book covers)
- 2 barrels of general merchandise (*Kaufmannschaft*)
- 2 packs of canvas
- 2 barrels of manichords (clavichords)
- 1 barrel of goods manufactured in Nuremberg
- 1 barrel of uncut quills for writing (*Posen*).

We do not know how much each item contributed to the total, but we do know that in theory each could have been valued at between 0 and 10,700 marks, and the value of the entire shipment would therefore come to between 0 and 74,900 marks. I would register this as an average of 37,450 marks, resulting in a discrepancy of 26,750 marks, or 111 percent. De Hertoghe paid similar amounts of duty on shipments on September 17, 1647 (11,200 marks) and December 10, 1647 (10,700 marks; the sum is the same as the one above, but this is happenstance). It is essentially these three entries in the customs books that account for the great imprecision in calculating his total turnover. His main stock in trade was manufactured and luxury products, which were usually subject to customs duties calculated by value.[17] But his range of goods and trading volumes were exceptional. In most cases, as the above table shows, calculations are much more precise.

The Admiralty documentation is structured such that I could not use duty payments for the final data analysis, but only the turnover figures calculated by the quantity or value of goods. There are two sets of customs books; one specifies the goods each merchant declared on a certain day, the shipmasters with whom he sent or from whom he received these goods, and the amount of duties he paid. It does not, however, provide any information about the ports from which the goods came or to which they went, nor how duties were distributed over multiple shipments when paid all at once. This missing information must be established on the basis of the second set of books, which lists each shipmaster, its load of goods, and its port of destination or origin, but provides no information as to the merchants concerned or the duties paid. So I used the second set for the final analysis, having previously, with the help of the first set, identified the merchants who traded the goods with the respective ships (and the days on which they paid the duties).

Missing Information

Apart from the inaccuracies noted above, the data themselves pose some problems. The scribes did not always identify the merchandise on which customs duties were paid. In 1632, 250,637 marks worth fell into this unspecified category: about 7 percent of the turnover with the Iberian Peninsula. In 1647 that figure rose to 736,388 marks, just over 19 percent of that year's total turnover.[18] These may have been goods that were difficult to describe, bundles of multiple products, or articles that were intentionally left unspecified, because trading in them was illicit.

Smuggling, of course, introduced yet another source of distortion. From other studies of customs files we know that deliberate failures to declare goods were common. So was the disguising of more valuable types of merchandise as less valuable ones (similar in appearance or type of packing) to which lower duties applied: wheat masquerading as rye, for example, or pepper as raisins.[19] Such false declarations mean that actual quantities of higher-value goods were sometimes larger than those registered in the customs files; those of lower-value goods may sometimes have been smaller.

A final source of imprecision is that not all goods had to be declared. Gems, jewels, and minted and unminted precious metals were not subject to customs duties, and were therefore never registered. One commodity that was declared in surprisingly small quantities was brazilwood. Although it seems to have been of importance in the trade between Hamburg and Portugal,[20] none was entered in the Admiralty customs books in 1632, and in 1647 it was listed only at a value of 3,000 marks. It is possible that brazilwood and the other commodities on which the Portuguese king had a trading monopoly, and which would therefore have arrived in Hamburg by way of royal contractors, were exempt from duties. This might also explain the surprisingly low total duties registered for salt imports in the Admiralty customs books (see chapter 1). However, closer study is needed.

Acknowledgments

I would like to express my gratitude to everyone who helped make this book possible. My very special thanks go to my two academic advisors, Professor Horst Pietschmann and Professor Franklin Kopitzsch at the Historisches Seminar at the University of Hamburg. They complemented each other ideally, one as an expert in the history of the Iberian Peninsula, and the other in that of Hamburg. The different kinds of support that they offered were invaluable. I also thank Michael Studemund-Halévy, who inspired me to take up this exciting topic when he showed me around the Portuguese-Jewish cemetery in Hamburg-Altona.

I am also grateful for many helpful and inspiring discussions with my colleagues in Germany, namely Thomas Denk, Thomas Duve, Kilian Harrer, Frank Hatje, Ulrich Mücke, Sina Rauschenbach, Magnus Ressel, Esther Sahle, Klaus Weber, Thomas Weller, Florian Wieser, and, now back in France, Vincent Demont. Colleagues in Portugal not only provided much professional advice, but also guided me through the research institutions there. Thanks especially to Isabel Mendes Drumond Braga, Pedro Cardim, Leonor Freire Costa, Florbela Veiga Frade, Marília dos Santos Lopes, Susana Münch Miranda, Sandra Neves Silva, José Alberto Tavim, and last but not least Miriam Bodian (who happened to be working at the National Archive in Lisbon at the same time as I was).

My sincere gratitude also goes to the archivists and librarians who were so helpful in meeting my research needs and who provided me with many happy moments of enlightenment: Klaus-Joachim Lorenzen-Schmidt (State Archive of Hamburg) and Wiebke van Deylen (State and University Library of Hamburg), Rolf Hammel-Kiesow, Ulrich Simon, and Angela Schlegel (City Archive of Lübeck), Odete Martins and Paulo Tremoceiro (National Archive in Lisbon), Maria da Conceição Geada (Ajuda Library), Tiago Miranda (Overseas Historical Archive in Lisbon), and Erik Schmitz (City Archive of Amsterdam).

I owe particular thanks to Kenneth Kronenberg, who translated the book into English, for his great patience. And a specially warm word of gratitude goes to Eve Golden, who, while editing the manuscript with extraordinary dedication, taught me many lessons in language as well as in style. Finally I am grateful to Bettina Neuhoff and Suruthi Manogaran for patiently shepherding the book at De Gruyter.

This book would not have been possible without the financial support from the Friedrich Ebert Foundation during my first three years of research, and from the Gerda Henkel Foundation during the last year. The English translation was facilitated by Geisteswissenschaften International, and editing and publishing

https://doi.org/10.1515/9783110472103-019

were enabled with the help of LMU Mentoring (the mentoring program for highly qualified young women in research at Ludwig Maximilian University of Munich), and the Marie Curie Alumni Association.

Above all, my thanks go to my parents for their wise counsel and sympathetic ears, and especially to my mother, the most engaged and diligent of all proofreaders ever.

Jorun Poettering
Munich, June 2018

Notes

Introduction

1   Altona was an independent town from 1664 until 1938, when it was incorporated into Hamburg.

2   A. Cohen (1971); E. Bonacich (1973); P. D. Curtin (1984); F. Mauro (1990); S. Subrahmanyam (1996); a special issue of the journal *Annales* on "Réseaux marchands" (2003); I. B. McCabe et. al., eds. (2005); D. Hancock (2005); D. Studnicki-Gizbert (2007); R. L. Kagan and P. D. Morgan, eds. (2009); A. Crespo Solana (2010).

3   A characteristic formulation of this sort is for instance: "Intuitively, we understand that kinfolk and community members are less likely to cheat one another"; D. Studnicki-Gizbert (2009), p. 80.

4   According to Heinz Schilling (2009), p. 432, it was "the self-isolation, the desire for dogmatic and moral exclusivity, as well as the categorical recourse to the family, neighborhood, and community, which enabled the foreign colonies to develop an extraordinary economic, social, and cultural dynamism."

5   Thus, H. Schilling (2009), p. 417, speaks of a "powerful innovative push," which the "Sephardim" and "Calvinists" had supposedly unleashed wherever they settled. His claim that the Portuguese merchants in Hamburg had initiated the city's integration into southwestern European trade and especially the traffic with colonial merchandise, is incorrect, however. Hamburg merchants had been trading with Portugal since the Middle Ages, and their commerce intensified at the beginning of the sixteenth century due to the Portuguese expansion along the maritime routes to India. The first Portuguese settled in Hamburg only toward the end of the sixteenth century. See A. H. Marques (1959); I. Durrer (1953); L. Beutin (1933).

6   A. Greif (1993); A. Greif (2006); see also the discussion of his works in F. Trivellato (2009a).

7   For greater detail, see J. Karp (2008).

8   W. Sombart ([1911] 1913).

9   See, for example, Y. Kaplan (1989); Y. Kaplan (2000a); M. Bodian (1997); D. Swetschinski (2000); specifically about Hamburg, see M. Studemund-Halévy (1994b, 1997); M. Studemund-Halévy (2000); H. Wallenborn (2003).

10 J. I. Israel (1989); J. I. Israel (1983); J. I. Israel (1992); J. I. Israel (2002). For an assessment of Israel's approach, see also J. Karp (2007), pp. 252–253.

11 H. Kellenbenz (1958). Kellenbenz completed the manuscript in 1944. At the end of the war he personally burned most of the papers of his department, but saved his own work, with which he qualified as a professor. See H. Heiber (1966), pp. 456–457; C. Hoffmann (1995), p. 678.

12 J. Karp (2009); D. Penslar (2001); J. Karp (2008).

13 F. Trivellato (2009a); see also F. Trivellato (2003).

14 W. Brulez (1959); R. v. Roosbroeck (1974); H. Schilling (1972); E. Stols (1971); R. Baetens (1976); O. Gelderblom (2000); M. Gelder (2009). See J. Müller (2016) on Netherlandish exile memories. See chapter 6 for the extent and size of the two diasporas.

15 Recently, however, dealt with by K. Weber (2004) and M. Schulte Beerbühl (2007).

16 The term is adequate, however, for the Jews who lived on the Iberian Peninsula in the Middle Ages and emigrated to the lands around the Mediterranean at the turn of the

https://doi.org/10.1515/9783110472103-020

sixteenth century. In contrast with the Portuguese Jews, neither they nor their ancestors were ever Christianized, which is why the Judaism practiced by them differed considerably from that practiced by the Portuguese Jews. For greater detail, see M. Bodian (2008). The employment of *Sephardim* in regard to Portuguese Jews gained currency in particular owing to Kellenbenz's *Sephardim an der unteren Elbe*. See D. Swetschinski (2000), p. xii.

17 P. Benedict (2002), pp. xxii–xxiii; F. Graf (2009), p. 384.

18 Some native Hamburgers who were active in the Iberia trade even gave their names an Iberian form in Hamburg. Thus, for example, a certain Francisco Borstelmann appears in the Hamburg Admiralty customs books as well as in other connections only with a romanized given name. By contrast, the names of the Portuguese living in Hamburg, though mostly corrupted, were with few exceptions never Germanized. The Portuguese who converted to Judaism were given a Jewish name in addition. However, this name was usually reserved for religious contexts; in the trade they continued to use their Portuguese names. Portuguese who were born abroad as Jews, by contrast, used their Jewish names in trade as well.

Chapter 1

1 A. H. Marques (1959); I. Durrer (1953).

2 V. Rau (1984a); A. Agats (1904); P. Jeannin (1968); H. Bleeck (1985).

3 J. R. Magalhães (1997a), pp. 298–300.

4 V. M. Godinho (1968c), p. 22.

5 V. M. Godinho (1968a), p. 203; V. M. Godinho (1968e), p. 270; J. R. Magalhães (1997a), p. 312; J. Serrão (1998), p. 90.

6 J. L. de Azevedo (1978); F. Mauro (1960), pp. 501–502.

7 E. Kestner (1881).

8 M. North (2005); P. Kriedte (1996), p. 118; E. Baasch (1894); see also R. Ehrenberg (1893a); E. Baasch (1915); G. Schmoller (1884).

9 For greater detail, see chapter 3 and appendix.

10 Portuguese salt exports had slowed in the early seventeenth century when Margarita Island and the Araya Peninsula off the Caribbean coast of what is today Venezuela began to supply salt to Europe. In response, the Portuguese government at times mandated that at least one-third of the return freight on all Hanseatic merchant ships be salt. Sales were credited to the king, who also paid the shipping costs; see V. Rau (1984a); K. Reichard (1867). Whether this may have been associated with an exemption from customs in Hamburg or whether there were other consequences for registration in the Admiralty customs books is unknown. For more information on salt imports to Lübeck, see W. Vogel (1928/1929), p. 132.

11 It is generally viewed today as an association (*Gemeinschaft*) or "confederation of consent" rather than as a league (*Bund*), which would imply a more consolidated corporate body. P. Dollinger (1970), V. Henn (1998); R. Hammel-Kiesow (2004); G. Schmidt (2006); J. Wubs-Mrozewicz (2013).

12 J. R. Magalhães (1997b), pp. 477–478; V. M. Godinho (1968a).

13 M. North (1996b), pp. 185–195.

14 E. Kestner (1881), pp. 4–5; I. Durrer (1953), p. 71.

15 L. Beutin (1929), pp. 8–9, 21–22, 80, 82; Schildhauer et al. (1981), p. 213.

16 Beutin lists a number of incidents involving Hamburg's ships between the years 1598 and 1602 and again in 1610; L. Beutin (1929), pp. 21–22, 59.

17   K.-K. Weber (2002), pp. 54–57.
18   A. Domínguez Ortiz (1963), p. 90. For the certificates in question, see, for example, ANTT, Corpo Cronológico, parte 2, mç. 307, docs 101, 105, 106.
19   L. Beutin (1929), p. 20; E. Kestner (1881), p. 6.
20   On research discussions regarding the effectiveness of the trade restrictions, see K.-K. Weber (2002), pp. 64–66.
21   For the text of the treaty, see J. A. Abreu y Bertodano (1740), pp. 375–390.
22   The treaty was, however, never ratified by the Hansa; A. Girard (1932), p. 96; H. Kellenbenz (1954), p. 24.
23   For the text of the treaty, see H. Reincke (1939), pp. 198–213; in greater detail in J. C. Lünig (1714), pp. 142–145; see also K.-K. Weber (2002), p. 76.
24   H.-D. Loose (1963), p. 14; K.-K. Weber (2002), p. 85.
25   H.-D. Loose (1963), p. 24; H. Hitzigrath (1907), pp. 8–9.
26   J.-F. Schaub (2001), pp. 286–287.
27   Fr. Mareš (1880, 1881); A Gindely (1890); O. Schmitz (1903); H.-C. Messow (1935); A. Domínguez Ortiz (1963); R. Rodenas Vilar (1967); J. Alcalá-Zamora (1970); J. Alcalá-Zamora (1975), p. 181; J. I. Israel (1986), pp. 521–523; R. Grafe (1998).
28   J. I. Israel (1986), p. 523; H.-C. Messow (1935), p. 71.
29   E. Straub (1980), p. 289.
30   H.-C. Messow (1935), p. 12; E. Straub (1980), p. 304.
31   At first only 24 vessels were involved; later as many as 40 to 50 were mentioned.
32   In the future, no foreign warship should enter the river, no fortifications should be built along its shores, and no duties levied upon it without the consent of the Hamburg City Council. G. Rückleben (1969), p. 69.
33   Diets were the meetings, most often held in Lübeck, where Hansa merchants from various towns assembled to secure trading rights abroad. H.-C. Messow (1935), pp. 69, 86; E. Straub (1980), pp. 311–312; R. Rodenas Vilar (1967), p. 144.
34   The *Werkzoll* was levied on all incoming and outgoing goods and commodities whether by land or by sea. The citizens of Hamburg, however, were exempt from this duty for all incoming trade, which included trade on the upper Elbe. The *Bakenzoll* was levied on all incoming and outgoing goods traveling by sea, with the exception of grain; see E. Pitz (1961), p. 492.
35   For an interpretation of the various highs and lows of *Werkzoll* revenues, which approximate those of the *Bakenzoll*, see W. Vogel (1956), pp. 59–60.
36   The values up to and including 1620 were multiplied by a factor of 1.5, the 1621 value was multiplied by 1.6875 in order to compensate for the hidden duty increase of 50 percent that was enacted in 1621/1622 in connection with the preceding currency devaluation; see E. Pitz (1961), pp. XXII and XXV; W. Vogel (1956), p. 58.
37   V. M. Godinho (1968b), p. 12; A. M. Hespanha (1994), pp. 123–125.
38   V. M. Godinho (1968b), p. 12.
39   Hanseatic vessels played an important role in the defense of northeastern Brazil against the Dutch and later attempts at reconquest, which came to an end only in 1654. Some of them were purchased by the Crown, but often they were simply seized in order to transport war matériel and provisions to Brazil; R. Ehrenberg (1900), p. 121; AHU, Reino, cx. 8, pasta 26, doc. 4 and 5; BA, cód. 51-X-4, fl. 227v–232v. (December 25, 1632).
40   The Netherlands (including all 17 provinces, although trade was effectively concentrated almost completely in the United Provinces) were far ahead of Portugal with about 44 percent

of the imports; Spain, with about 10 percent, was in third place. As an exception, these figures relate not to the value of the merchandise but to their mass. The data were calculated from E. Baasch (1894).

41   Also, in terms of exports the Netherlands (almost 40 percent) and Spain (about 12 percent) were more important.

42   The Netherlands were still in first place at 42 percent, followed by England, whose share had almost doubled. Spain's share had also decreased, even though it was still ahead of Portugal at 9 percent.

43   The United Provinces' share of imports was about 37 percent. No data are available for this time regarding exports from Lisbon. These data also refer to the mass of the goods, not to their value. The data were calculated from V. Rau (1954).

44   For 1625 the number of vessels, including their load capacity, is available. For 1623, 1624, 1628, 1629, 1632, 1633, and 1647/1648 only the number of vessels is known; their approximate load capacity in lasts was calculated from that of 1625. The years always begin on January 1, except for 1647/1648, which refers to the fiscal year of St. Peter (February 22) 1647 to St. Peter 1648. The Netherlands include all 17 provinces, although effectively trade was concentrated almost completely in the United Provinces.

45   See note 44.

46   See note 44.

47   Although the cargo figures are incomplete (August 12, 1641 to January 4, 1649), according to Rau's estimate they are representative.

48   P. Cardim (1998); J.-F. Schaub (2001), pp. 292–313.

49   As a result, a few very wealthy merchants took part in a plot against João IV, which failed, however; V. M. Godinho (1968a), pp. 282–283.

50   Portugal concluded its two most important trade treaties with the United Provinces in 1641 and England in 1642. These were followed by treaties with England in 1654 and with the United Provinces in 1661; C. Roma du Bocage (1916), pp. 49–50, 91–92; E. Prestage (1925), p. 180.

51   Duarte was supposed to have taken a leading role in the uprising against Spain, possibly helped by his close contacts with Hamburg. While he was staying temporarily in Portugal in 1637, the Hansa had sent a mission to him, which had been financially supported by Hamburg. In October 1640 Duarte had requested that money be transferred to him for his passage from Hamburg to Portugal. Shortly thereafter he was arrested; J. Albrecht (1937); R. E. Horch (1983); J. S. Ribeiro (1876); J. F. Voigt (1912), p. 193; BA, cód. 51–IX–4, fl. 135–136 (October 17, 1640).

52   P. Coelho (1940), pp. 10–12 (September 27, 1642), 23–25 (December 28, 1642), 33–37 (February 16, 1643); BA, cód. 51–IX–8, fl. 62–62v., 63–65v. (November 6 and 22, 1642).

53   C. Menéndez Vives and C. Torroja Menéndez (1991), pp. 59–60.

54   Ibid., p. 88.

55   Although the cargo figures are incomplete (July 14, 1677 to January 5, 1683; January 21, 1683 to May 8, 1685), according to Rau's estimate they are representative.

56   E. Baasch (1929), pp. 89–144.

57   M. North (1996c), p. xiv. Grain exports from the Baltic region decreased from an average of 68,500 lasts per year for the period from 1600 to 1649 to 55,800 lasts per year for the span from 1650 to 1669, and then to 31,800 lasts per year for that between 1700 and 1749; P. Kriedte (1996), p. 121.

58   In 1647/1648, other textiles were exported to Portugal as well, especially buckram and bombazine. These were hardly exported at all between 1702 and 1713.

59 M. North (2005), p. 171; E. Wiskemann (1929), pp. 93–94.

60 C. Müller (1940), p. 22; E. Wiskemann (1929), p. 95

61 The figures relate to the documented totals for the years 1702 (possibly incomplete), 1703, 1704 (possibly incomplete), 1705 (possibly incomplete), 1706, 1709 (possibly incomplete), 1710 (possibly incomplete) and 1713. Because of the gaps, absolute figures are not displayed in the table. The figures presented by Karin Newman and cited elsewhere, which are based on the *Stader Elbzoll* (a duty charged on the Elbe at the town of Stade), represent only the trade conducted by aliens in Hamburg, but not that conducted by Hamburg citizens, because these were exempt from the duty. They are therefore not representative; K. Newman (1985).

62 V. M. Godinho (1968f), pp. 300–301.

63 J. V. Serrão (1998), p. 93; V. M. Godinho (1968f), p. 300; A. M. Faria (2005), p. 374.

64 V. M. Godinho (1968f), pp. 301–302.

65 J. M. Pedreira (1995), p. 331.

Chapter 2

1 In an oft-quoted pronouncement referring to the relationship between City Council and citizenry, Mayor Dietrich vom Holte stated in 1602: "Even if a ruling authority [*Obrigkeit*] is godless, tyrannical, and miserly, it is nonetheless improper for the subjects to revolt and oppose it; rather, the subjects should see therein a punishment from the Almighty which they have earned by their sin." [wenn schon eine Avericheit gottlos, tyrannisch und gitzich is, so gehoret dennoch den Underdanen nich, dat se scik darjegen uplehnen und thowedder setten, sundern scholen datsulve velmehr vor ene Straffe des Allmechtigen, so de Underdanen met erer Sünde verwirket hebben, erkennen]; cited in J. Bolland (1977), p. 29.

2 I use the word *alien* strictly in this legal sense, while I use *foreigner* when regarding the cultural difference.

3 E. F. Heckscher (1955), vol. 2, pp. 62, 75; H. Rachel (1910); O. Gönnenwein (1939); A. Schultze (1908); H. Thieme (1958); S. Jenks (1996); R. Sprandel (1984); N. Bulst (2008).

4 W. Naudé (1889), especially pp. 80–81, 85, 94; G. Schmoller (1884), J. F. Voigt (1916), pp. 75–77.

5 The ruling of the Imperial Chamber Court of 1618 formally established the imperial immediacy (*Reichsunmittelbarkeit*); see H. Reincke (1961).

6 Although Rudolf Häpke assumed the existence of an "economic will of the empire" for the sixteenth century, and believed that the Holy Roman Empire had an economic policy, his arguments are not persuasive; R. Häpke (1925b). Measures such as the ban on the importation of French manufactured products throughout the empire, which had been introduced at the end of the seventeenth century, were isolated cases; see I. Bog (1959).

7 Only around 1700 did Hamburg start to turn away from the staple trade, and to completely open up the transit traffic in grain by the middle of the eighteenth century.

8 On Portuguese customs duties, see M. A. Moreira (1992), pp. 11–49; A. M. Hespanha (1994), pp. 118–159; F. B. da Fonseca (1948/1949); F. B. da Fonseca (1954); M. G. Monteiro (1969); J. C. Pereira (2003); F. M. da Luz (1950).

9 Although these were ad valorem duties, in practice the amounts of the duties to be paid were determined using tariff tables. How the value of the goods was determined is unclear.

10 A. M. Hespanha (1994), p. 120.

11   R. Ehrenberg (1899), pp. 39–40. In the case of some duties Hamburg citizens could claim exemptions. They were exempt from the *Werkzoll* on all goods conveyed by land, and transport on the upper Elbe counted as land traffic. They were also freed from the *Stader Elbzoll*, that is duty on all goods passing on the Elbe levied by the town of Stade in Brunshausen. Before 1648 that duty was levied on goods being imported and exported by sea, after 1648 apparently only on imported goods. It was an ad valorem duty amounting to ¹⁄₁₆ percent with various exemptions. See C. Müller (1940); E. Pitz (1961), p. 491; E. Baasch (1915), vol. 1, pp. 521–522.

12   J. C. Pereira (2003), p. 83; J. R. Magalhães (1981), p. 299.

13   J. R. Magalhães (1981), p. 298.

14   E. Pitz (1961), p. 492.

15   In practice, however, in 1632 and 1647 a lower percentage of ¼ percent and ⅓ percent, respectively, was levied (see appendix).

16   This duty was administered by Hamburg. Half of it went to Hamburg, and until 1640 the other half to the count of Pinneberg; thereafter, 30 percent went to the king of Denmark and 20 percent to the duke of Schleswig-Holstein-Gottorf.

17   See also the brief overview in K. Zeiger (1936), pp. 28–29. The definition of the *Bakenzoll* given there is, however, incorrect. An excise duty was levied on imported wine, beer, and cattle, which was returned upon export.

18   J. Souza (1783), pp. 35–36 (Foral da Alfândega desta Cidade de Lisboa, October 15, 1587); see also F. M. da Luz (1950), p. 83. In order to prevent these goods from leaving the country again, the Crown supplemented the customs duty decrees by introducing export bans; see Ordenações Manuelinas ([ca. 1513] 1797), Liv. 5, Títs. 88, 96; Ordenações Filipinas ([1603] 1870), Liv. 5, Títs. 112, 113. Vegetables, meat, cheese, and butter as well as books were not affected by the export ban; however, skins and pelts, various cloths, flax, honey, wax, and tallow were.

19   J. Souza (1783), pp. 34–36 (Foral da Alfândega desta Cidade de Lisboa, October 15, 1587); Capítulos de Privilegios ... de 1607, in J. H. Abreu y Bertodano (1740), pp. 375–382, here p. 377; AHL, ASA, Externa, Hispanica 9, fl. 336–346; similarly in earlier privileges for German and Hanseatic merchants; see L. Silveira (1958), pp. 20–21, 34–35, 39–40.

20   Revenues from the import tithe and excise duty (1607: 27%, 1619: 23%, 1681: 24%); the *consulado* (1607: 8%, 1619: 11%, 1681: 7%); and the taxes on salt (1607: 6%, 1619: 6%, 1681: 5%) and tobacco (1681: 17%) made up 41% of Portugal's income without the overseas colonies in 1607, 40% in 1619, and 53% in 1681; see V. M. Godinho (1968d), pp. 56–60. There are significant inconsistencies between V. M. Godinho's and A. M. Hespanha's data, although they rely on much of the same documentation. The Godinho data used here are more complete and more compelling; A. M. Hespanha (1986), vol. 1, pp. 180–185.

21   This statement relates only to the first half of the seventeenth century. Revenues from the Admiralty customs are not included as they were administered separately; see J. F. Voigt (1912).

22   A. M. Hespanha (1998), pp. 195, 204–207. Approximately 18% of the extraordinary levies were collected from the merchants; indirectly, they probably also paid their share in the levies of the city of Lisbon (22%) and of the kingdom (23%). Hespanha does not count the high payments made by New Christians, without giving any reason for this. Nor does he give precise information about the time period under consideration.

23   A. M. Hespanha (1998), p. 199.

24   V. M. Godinho (1968d), p. 59; A. M. Hespanha (1994), pp. 141–142; A. M. Hespanha (1998), p. 208.

25   V. M. Godinho (1968d), pp. 59–60.
26   See J. F. Voigt (1912) for the share of the duties in the total city revenues of the first half of the century. It should be noted that some of the values in Zeiger differ considerably from these; see K. Zeiger (1936), pp. 74, 89, 107, 123.

	1601–1605	1606–1610	1611–1615	1616–1620	1621–1625	1626–1630
Customs duties	27.4%	31.2%	29.1%	21.8%	28.9%	15.1%
Regular *Schoss*	13.1%	14.9%	16.7%	15.6%	14.9%	8.4%
Extraordinary (direct) taxes	8.5%	1.5%	0.0%	12.7%	5.0%	15.9%
Sales taxes	19.7%	20.7%	22.9%	21.9%	23.7%	42.9%

	1631–1635	1636–1640	1641–1645	1646–1650	1601–1650
Customs duties	18.1%	19.9%	14.5%	18.3%	19.9%
Regular *Schoss*	9.2%	11.4%	11.8%	11.4%	11.7%
Extraordinary (direct) taxes	13.6%	9.9%	18.5%	16.1%	12.5%
Sales taxes	43.1%	39.6%	35.5%	33.7%	34.1%

27   For Hamburg, see, e.g., J. Bolland (1960), part 2, no. 134, art. 34 (1550) up to no. 146, art. 17 (1594) recurrently for commission trade; no. 125, art. 2 (1537) up to no. 145, art. 4 (1594) recurrently for business partnerships.
28   R. Ehrenberg (1885); S. Jenks (1996). The grain trade, however, which was especially important for the city's food supply, remained explicitly excluded from the easing of the trading ban. A resolution of 1595 read, "and as far as the grain trade is concerned, it shall remain with the citizens, and it shall not be permitted that aliens trade in grain with aliens." [Sonst wat de Kornkop belanget, desülwige werd billig by den Börgern gelaten und schall den Frembden mit Frembden solcken Kornhandel tho driwen nicht gestadet werden.]; cited in R. Ehrenberg (1885), p. 318.
29   The term *Schragen* probably derives from *Schra* (animal skin, parchment). The successive sets of rules regulating trade in the Hansa *Kontor* in Novgorod, dating back to the mid-thirteenth century, are contained in the Novgorod *Schragen* (plural of *Schra*). The *Alte Schrae*, the early fourteenth-century parchment book in which the town law of Soest, in Westphalia, was written, is the earliest documented city law in Germany. In sixteenth-century Hamburg this meaning probably blended with that of the board on which official notices were fixed.
30   The complete text of the *Schragen* of 1604 is contained in J.F. Blank (1763), part 1, pp. 491–493. The citations read in the original as follows: "Freye Güter sive Waaren, damit Gast mit Gast wol handeln mag"; "Bürgerliche Güter, damit Gast mit Gast nicht handeln mag"; "Bürgerliche Güter, damit Gast mit Gaste, auch mit Gaste Pfenningen nicht handeln, auch kein Factor an Fremde verkaufen mag"; "Alle Waaren, die aus fremden Königreichen und Ländern anhero gebracht und ferner könnten gebracht werden, und in dieser Stadt vor dreisig und mehren Jahren nicht gebräuchlich gewesen, oder in so grosser Anzahl nicht geführet oder verhandtieret seyn"; "und andere dergleichen Nationen".
31   If the sale of wax and flax were considered problematic in selling, too, at the turn of the seventeenth century, this would confirm my thesis.

32 J. Pohle (2000), pp. 255–268.

33 Not all goods on which customs duties were either nullified or reduced in Portugal were assigned to one of the three categories in the Hamburg *Schragen*. Among the unassigned goods that are known to have been exported to the Iberian Peninsula from Hamburg during the seventeenth century are weapons, horses, meat, vegetables, brass, and mercury.

34 StAHH, Senat, Cl. VII Lit. Cc No. 2 Vol. 1 Fasc. 2, fl. 69–70.

35 U. Beukemann (1912), pp. 473, 477. By 1763, a century later, the ban on trade between aliens was as good as forgotten. In a six-volume compendium of the laws of Hamburg, the *Schragen* is only mentioned as an "addendum," merely commenting that its implementation "had been attended by many difficulties, and as a result of increasing commerce in the city, which had also caused the number of aliens to multiply … its literal contents had passed out of memory." [bey der Ausübung mit vielen Schwierigkeiten vergesellschaftet gewesen, und bey zunehmendem *Commercio* der Stadt, wodurch auch die Zahl der Fremden sich vermehret, […], seinem buchstäblichen Inhalt nach, ganz aus dem Gedächtniß gekommen] J.F. Blank (1763), part 1, pp. 491–494.

36 Ordenações Afonsinas ([ca. 1448] 1792), liv. 4, tít. 2.

37 F. Lopes (1895), vol. 1, pp. 8–9.

38 Santarém (1924), pp. 201, 217, 223–224.

39 By contrast, alien merchants were not welcome in the Portuguese overseas territories. The Asian and African trade, on which the king held a monopoly, was generally denied to them as it was to most Portuguese merchants; see Ordenações Filipinas ([1603] 1870), liv. 5, tít. 107; Ordenações Manuelinas ([ca. 1513] 1797), liv. 5, títs. 81, 112. Aliens were permitted to travel to Brazil so long as they had been given special royal permission and pledged to sail from Portugal directly to their intended Brazilian port and then sail back to Portugal before returning to their home port. This provision amounted to compulsory stapling on a transcontinental scale. Just as all ships that sailed up the Elbe had to dock in Hamburg, all vessels crossing the Atlantic were forced to land in Portugal. However, unlike in Hamburg, the goods being carried did not have to be sold to local merchants; rather, Portugal instituted this provision for the sole purpose of receiving customs duties. Despite these restrictions, foreign shipmasters repeatedly returned directly to their home ports without making the detour to Lisbon. For this reason, in 1605 aliens were completely banned from sailing to the Portuguese overseas territories or to stay there. As in Hamburg, this required a clear distinction between locals (*naturais*) and aliens (*estrangeiros*). In contrast to the corresponding Spanish concepts, the Portuguese ideas about naturality and naturalization have rarely been researched. Presumably they were first introduced as legal categories under Felipe II; see the comment to Ordenações Filipinas ([1603] 1870), liv. 2, tít. 55. Aliens could be naturalized by an act of grace by the king, enabling them thereby to gain access to the overseas territories. But for European trade this probably did not gain them an advantage. One such naturalized Hamburger was Armão Piper, who was born in Hamburg in about 1608. From 1624 on he had been active as a merchant in Porto, later he married a Portuguese woman, and eventually had himself naturalized in 1653; see ANTT, Chancelaria de D. João IV, Doações, liv. 26, fl. 39v. For further information on Piper, see ANTT, TSO, Conselho Geral, Habilitações, Pedro, mç. 22, doc. 455; TSO, Conselho Geral, Habilitações, Diogo, mç. 2, doc. 83. Another Hamburger who became naturalized was Pedro Pedrossen, who had lived in Porto at least since 1664. He was a wealthy merchant who engaged in the contract trade, conducted extensive business

transactions, and owned several estates; see ANTT, TSO, Conselho Geral, Habilitações, Pedro, mç. 22, doc. 455.

40 J. J. A. Dias (1998), pp. 259–260; M. v. Bahrfeldt (1917); O. C. Gaedechens (1850), p. 3–5; J. Klefeker (1773), part 12, pp. 238–239. The *Portugaleser* continues to be awarded as a medal of honor by the Free and Hanseatic City of Hamburg.

41 Only the Welsers and the Fuggers remained active in Lisbon, with some interruptions, up to the end of the sixteenth century; see J. Pohle (2000), pp. 255–268; M. Häberlein (2016).

42 J. J. Silva (1856), vol. 1640–1647, p. 12.

43 O. Brunner (1963); R. Postel (1979); R. Postel (1980); R. Postel (1982); R. Postel (2006); F. Kopitzsch (1981).

44 O. Gelderblom (2013).

45 According to Rainer Postel, the craftsmen blamed the foreigners for negative developments in the economy out of a "sense of social inferiority." They rejected the technologies and ways of operating that these had newly introduced, whereas the "more socially consolidated classes," namely the merchants, proved "more open and willing to learn" in order to partake of the foreigners' success; R. Postel (1997), pp. 206–27.

46 R. Ehrenberg (1885), p. 294; G. H. Kirchenpauer (1841), p. 57.

47 W.-R. Baumann (1982); W. E. Lingelbach (1904); L. Beutin (1929), pp. 3–15; R. Postel (1998), pp. 181–183.

48 R. Ehrenberg (1896), p. 125.

49 "... männiglich bekannt, wat vor unheil daruth erfolgen und den tollen und gemeenen gude und ook intgemeen den Börgern unndt inwohnern affgahn würde, wen de Frembde schölen weggewiset werden"; cited in R. Ehrenberg (1885), p. 318.

Chapter 3

1 In his study of early modern special law, Thomas Duve wrote that it may "be understood only in the context of a special understanding of validity – and that it can be comprehended only distortedly from the perspective of the legalistic culture as seen through the historical perception of which we avail ourselves"; see T. Duve (2008), p. 8. According to Duve, all law that was not part of *ius commune* and that applied to certain legally distinguishable groups of persons or individuals was special law (*ius singulare*). Duve thus uses the term with a meaning different from that of Gotzmann and Wendehorst, who repeatedly pointed out that no special law was applied to the Jews in the Holy Roman Empire; see A. Gotzmann and S. Wendehorst (2007), pp. 4–5: "Even though there existed laws that surely applied exclusively to Jews as Jews and disadvantaged them in comparison to other population groups, the notion that the Jews in the Holy Roman Empire were subject to 'special law' is fundamentally false." (Our translations.)

2 For more on the state of the research regarding special legislation, see T. Duve (2008), pp. 12–19. Strangely, except for the older literature on the alien laws cited in the previous chapter, there have been barely any studies on special law applying to aliens or to alien merchants in the early modern period.

3 For the town law, see *Hamburger Stadtrecht* ([1605] 1978); for the *Rezesse*, see J. G. Gallois (1870), vols. 2 and 3. Many copies of the Netherlander contracts exist which differ from each other in minor details; see StAHH, Niederländische Armenkasse, AI2, Stück 2 (1605);

StAHH, Senat, Cl. VII Lit. Cc Nr. 2 Vol. 1 Fasc. 4, fl. 148–156v. (1615); StAHH, Niederländische Armenkasse, AI2, Stück 3 (1639). The Portuguese contracts are published in P. D. H. Reils (1847); for a detailed commentary, see J. Braden (2001).

4   These have been passed down in written form since the middle of the fourteenth century and were updated semiannually until the early seventeenth century. One of the earliest Hamburg *Burspraken* still extant, from 1453, already deals with alien rights; see J. Bolland (1960), part 2 no. 15, art. 1.

5   J. Bolland (1960), part 2, no. 126, art. 33; no. 145, art. 79; no. 145, art. 96; no. 146, art. 85.

6   N. A. Westphalen (1841), vol. 2, p. 382.

7   H. Kellenbenz (1958), p. 28, fn. 12.

8   J. Bolland (1960), part 2, no. 140, art. 72; no. 144, art. 28; no. 139, art. 78; no. 139, art. 81.

9   M. Reißmann (1975), p. 219.

10 A *Rezess* from the year 1603 states, "what sorts of people are to be accepted as citizens remains a matter of further consideration by the Council and the assembled citizens" [Was aber für Leute zu Bürgern sollen angenommen werden, steht noch zu zunerem Bedenken E. E. Rathes und der verordneten Bürger]; J. G. Gallois (1870), vol. 2, p. 1250.

11 "... diejenigen, welche einige Jahre hier gewohnt hatten, sich zur christlichen Religion bekennen, ehrbaren Wandels seien und keinen Makel an sich hatten ... ohne weitere specification der Nationalität"; J. G. Gallois (1870), vol. 2, p. 1279, 1281.

12 In his compilation of Hamburg's laws, Johann Klefeker stated that although non-Lutheran Christians were barred from assuming political office, they were not excluded from obtaining citizen rights: "although according to the fundamental laws which have been accepted, no one would be eligible for membership in the City Council, nor to take part in the citizen boards and deputations, nor in the Assembly of Citizens, nor even to serve as a city official other than one who professes the Evangelical-Lutheran faith; that notwithstanding, Roman-Catholic, Reformed, and even the Mennonites are not excluded from citizen rights and from the concomitant general advantages in their household and private business" [obzwar, nach einmal angenommenen Fundamental-Gesetzen, weder zum Raths-Stande, noch zu den bürgerlichen Collegiis und Deputationen, oder auch zur Versammlung der Erbgesessenen Bürgerschaft, ja nicht einmal zu den Stadt-Bedienungen, iemand fähig seyn kann, als der dem Evangelisch-Lutherischen Glaubens-Bekenntnisse zugethan ist; iedennoch darum die Römisch-Catholischen, Reformirtten, und auch die Mennonisten, vom Bürger-Rechte, und von den damit verbundenen allgemeinen Vortheilen in ihrem Hausstande und Privat-Gewerbe, nicht ausgeschlossen werden]; J. Klefeker (1766), part 2, p. 288. The scholarly research does not always present this correctly; Mirjam Litten, for example, has held that Lutheranism was a prerequisite for citizenship; see M. Litten (2003), pp. 247–248. As evidence, she cited the first paragraph of the *Rezess* of 1603, which, however, merely propagates the "fostering of the true Christian religion" [Beförderung der wahren christlichen Religion], but does not set forth the conditions for citizenship; see J. G. Gallois (1870), vol. 2, pp. 1230–1231.

13 StAHH, Niederländische Armenkasse, AI2, Stück 2 (1605).

14 P. D. H. Reils (1847), pp. 373–375.

15 Thus, in 1607 the Portuguese demanded "now to concede to us, too, their [the Netherlanders'] advantageous resolution" [auch unss dero [der Niederländer] grossgunstige resolution nunmher furderlichst hieruff wiederfahren zu lassen]; A. Cassuto (1931), p. 61. In 1611 the City Council proposed that "the Portuguese nation must finally enjoy all privileges and rights, general and special, in the same way as they are comprised in the Netherlander contract

and similar to the Netherlandish nation, and shall not be obstructed thereupon, and it will in return comply with all the points of practicing commerce and trade in conformance with the Netherlander contract" [Entlich soll die Portugiesische nation, aller und jeder privilegien, gerechtigkeitten, general und speciall, wie die nahmen haben mügen auf masse selbige, im Niederländischen vörtrage verfasset sein, der Niederländischen nation gleich, zu geniessen haben und darüber nicht beschweret weren, sie auch darkegen, sich in allen puncten mit verübung der commercien und handelungen, dem Niederländischen vertrage, zu conformiren schuldigk sein]; StAHH, Senat, Cl. VII Lit. Hf Nr. 5 Vol. 3a Fasc. 1, Stück 11; see also A. Cassuto (1931), pp. 61–62, and the proposals put forward shortly before the conclusion of the contract of 1612 that were significantly more far-reaching in StAHH, Senat, Cl. VII Lit. Hf Nr. 5 Vol. 3a Fasc. 1, Stücke 10, 11 and 12.

16 "... den jüdischen Glauben bekennen, sollen abgeschafft und allhier nicht geduldet werden"; P. D. H. Reils (1847), pp. 361–362.

17 "... die Freyheit zugeben welche Jene in Hollantt gegonnet wirdt, das man nemblich de Sachen die Religion betreffendt, sie gewehren lasse"; A. Cassuto (1931), p. 59.

18 The members covered by the Netherlander contract, however, were exempt from this ban. In practice, the ban on property ownership could be circumvented by a fiduciary transference to a citizen; J. Klefeker (1766), part 2, pp. 273, 279–280, 288, 291. The second Portuguese contract even officially granted the physician Rodrigo de Castro the right to retain a house that he had already acquired; see P. D. H. Reils (1847), p. 386.

19 "1. Soll sich die Nation friedlich und eingezogen verhalten. 2. Niemand Aergerniß geben. 3. Keine Synagoge halten. 4. Ihre Religion in dieser Stadt Bothmäßigkeit durch heim- und öffentliche Zusammenkünfte nicht exerciren, auch in derselben sich der Beschneidung nicht gebrauchen"; 12: "ein jeder sammt seinem gesinde geschützet, geschirmet, gebührlich vertreten und wegen der religion in seinem gewissen nicht beschweret werden"; P. D. H. Reils (1847), pp. 373–375.

20 Without the right of inheritance, the assets of a deceased merchant would, according to the right of escheat (*ius albinagii*), have gone to the city.

21 P. D. H. Reils (1847), pp. 373–375. Further contracts were concluded in 1650 and 1697.

22 Under the terms of the first contract, the Netherlanders had to pay five times the *Schoss* as a departure tax; under the third contract the simple *Schoss*; StAHH, Niederländische Armenkasse, AI2, Stück 2, fl. 4v; StAHH, Niederländische Armenkasse, AI2, Stück 3, fl. 3.

23 "... in Rücksicht auf die Commercia für wünschenswerth, das man sich für ein ansehnliches Schoß auf 4 oder 5 Jahr vergleiche"; P. D. H. Reils (1847), p. 365.

24 Reißmann doubts that the individual alien's payments could have come to ¼ percent of their assets, which was what citizens paid, and he believes that these payments were not proportional to their assets; see M. Reißmann (1975), pp. 129–131.

25 The first contract nominally included 130 persons, in some copies 132 are listed. The contract of 1639 included between 169 and 174 persons, counting the heads of household; see also M. Reißmann (1975), p. 130.

26 There were approximately 30 households in 1612; in 1619, 32 Portuguese parties opened an account in the newly founded bank (see Chapter 6).

27 A. Cassuto (1931), pp. 60–61.

28 "... in nichtes ... präjudiciren, noch deroselben habendes interes vernichten, schwechen oder ringern"; StAHH, Niederländische Armenkasse, AI2, Stück 2, fl. 2–2v. (1605); also StAHH, Senat, Cl. VII Lit. Cc Nr. 2 Vol. 1 Fasc. 4, fl. 151 (1614); StAHH, Niederländische Armenkasse, AI2, Stück 3, fl. 2 (1639).

29 J. Verbeemen (1957), pp. 81–82, 204–205. A similar provision seems to have been in effect in some German towns, for instance in Augsburg; see StAHH, Senat, Cl. VII Lit. Cc Nr. 2 Vol. 2 Fasc. 1. Several of the Netherlanders included in the Hamburg contract were registered as *buitenpoorter* in the Antwerp citizens' rolls. These included Jan de Greve, Guilliam Staes, and Baltazar van Dortmont. Gillis de Greve and his wife Maria van Haesdonck were also *buitenpoorter* in Antwerp; Gillis nonetheless acquired civic rights in Hamburg; see FelixArchief Antwerpen, Poortersboeken Inv. 029. According to a report of the Hamburg secretary of the English Merchant Adventurers, more than 400 Netherlandish merchants, subjects of the States General, lived in Hamburg in 1653; see H. Hitzigrath (1907), pp. 46–47.

30 "… einiger potentat, fürst oder herr [sie] mit recht belangen oder citiren würde"; StAHH, Niederländische Armenkasse, AI2, Stück 3, fl. 5 (1639); StAHH, Niederländische Armenkasse, AI2, Stück 4, fl. 3v. (1650).

31 AHL, Nachlass Hagedorn, Packen 9–1, fl. 134 (StAHH, Senat, Cl. VIII, Nr. XXXI, 4). On Bernhard Hagedorn see D. Schäfer (1914); R. Häpke (1925a).

32 "… qui origine dicuntur esse Lusitani"; AHL, Nachlass Hagedorn, Packen 9–1, fl. 416–417 (StAHH, Senat, Cl. VI Nr. 6 Vol. 3b Fasc. 1).

33 Incorrect indications, for example in J. Braden (2001), p. 111; H. Kellenbenz (1958), p. 31.

34 "Aufrichtige, redliche kaufmannshandtierung, unseren bürgern und anderen einwohnern gleich, üben und treiben"; P. D. H. Reils (1847), p. 373.

35 "… dat gy ock in juwen handel und wandel uprichtig und redlich willen schicken und ertögen, … und jow sonst in solcken und derglicken tostüren und unplichten dermalen verholden, alse gy sulckes vor Gott willen tho verantworten weten. … Wie den e. e. rath jow wil ernstes flietes erinnern, dat en jeder fremder sick der burspraeke erinnere, dewile darinne jahrlickes werd afgekündiget, dat gast mit gast nicht handeln schal, derselben sick by wilköhrlicher strafe gemete verholde"; C. Ziegra (1767), no. 34, pp. 126–129.

36 StAHH, Niederländische Armenkasse, AI2, Stück 2, fl. 5–5v. Mirjam Litten is mistaken when she writes that, "the Netherlandish community had received citizen freedom of trade," and that the City Council had succeeded in "the unlimited economic integration of the wealthy aliens"; M. Litten (2003), p. 251. (Our translation.)

37 "… die aus fremden königreichen und landen anhero gebracht"; "habenden authoritet bei deroselben bürgern unnd weddeherrn woll effectuiren … keineswegs zu unglimpffen vermercken"; StAHH, Senat, Cl. VII Lit. Cc Nr. 2 Vol. 2 Fasc. 1.

38 Not all goods were categorized consistently. Thus, for example, wax and flax appear in the list of goods that aliens could trade freely since 1604; nonetheless, the Netherlanders were permitted to trade in these goods in the contract of 1639. On the other hand, the Netherlanders were forbidden to trade in white English cloth in 1615 and 1639, an item that was permitted by the *Schragen* of 1604.

39 University members also organized themselves into nations.

40 The contract of 1618, which largely resembles the prior contracts of 1567 and 1611, consists of 51 articles. This is far more than either the Netherlander or Portuguese contracts contained. Detailed provisions regulated trade and commission trade, the loading and unloading of ships, the hiring and payment of servants, measurers, packers, and carriers. The Merchant Adventurers were exempt from the real estate tax as well as from quay, anchorage, and crane fees. They were not required to pay the usual taxes and tolls, but were subject to special taxation. No citizen and no alien was permitted to transport goods that belonged to an Englishman from Hamburg to England or from England to Hamburg. In exchange, they

were obligated not to dock at any port on the Elbe other than Hamburg, and in addition to persuade their government that this restriction should be honored by their compatriots as well; see W. E. Lingelbach (1904), pp. 269–272.

41 The Netherlanders feared that if they did not themselves establish the amount of their taxes, the Council "would give those to whom it feels dislike hard conditions and raise their taxes ad libitum, thus driving them out indirectly" [man [der Rat] denen, so man ungeneigt, schwere conditiones gebe, ihr tax nach belieben hoch setzen, und also per indirectum von hinnen vertrieben warden]; StAHH, Senat, Cl. VII Lit. Cc Nr. 2 Vol. 1 Fasc. 4, fl. 256v. (July 8, 1638).

42 "... eines jeden condition"; StAHH, Senat, Cl. VII Lit. Cc Nr. 2 Vol. 1 Fasc. 4, fl. 254v. and 257v. (July 7, 1638).

43 To the extent possible, the Portuguese, much like the Netherlanders, tried to resolve disciplinary matters and issues of civil law such as marriage, family matters, and inheritance issues within the nation (see Chapters 14 and 15). In some instances, the board of the Portuguese-Jewish community even worked out trade conflicts. Only in serious cases did it resort to the jurisdiction and laws of the city and imperial courts; see, for example, StAHH, Senat, Cl. VII Lit. Hf Nr. 5 Vol. 3a Fasc. 1, Stück 11; A. Cassuto (1931), pp. 61–62, as well as the minutes books of the Portuguese-Jewish community.

44 "... mit keinem corpore zu tractiren gemeinet, auch die deswegen den deputirten ertheilte vollmacht cassiret und aufgehoben hat"; StAHH, Niederländische Armenkasse, AI2, Stück 8, fl. 2 (1653).

45 When using the word *vizinho* it is not totally clear whether the documents really refer to citizen rights or to the rights of inhabitants with permanent settlement permission; see note 57. AHL, ASA, Externa, Hispanica 9, fl. 37v., 339; see also BA, cód. 51-VIII-18, n. 341, fl. 147–148v.

46 StAHH, Niederländische Armenkasse, AI2, Stück 2.

47 StAHH, Niederländische Armenkasse, AI2, Stück 3. High Germans probably referred to Upper Germans (*Oberdeutsche*), that is, the German-speaking people from south of the Main River.

48 "... dan alhie siehet es auff die commercia, die werden von männern und nicht von frauen getrieben"; StAHH, Senat, Cl. VII Lit. Cc Nr. 2 Vol. 1 Fasc. 4, fl. 255v. (July 8, 1638).

49 In connection with calculations regarding the city's revenues from the contract, mentioned are also "the many families depending on them due to their manufactures and services" [die von ihnen wegen der manufacturen in großer anzahl dependirenden familien und diensten]; see StAHH, Senat, Cl. VII Lit. Cc Nr. 2 Vol. 1 Fasc. 4, fl. 259v. (July 19, 1638).

50 "Da dann ein hoch- und wohlweiser Rath deren Qualification also beschaffen befindet, daß sie dieselbe in Schutz zu nehmen kein Bedenken tragen, Ihr Hoch- und Wohlweisen auch mit denselben sich wegen des Schosses und sonsten vergleichen können, so sollen solche ankommenden Portugiesen, woferne sie sich obigen Artikeln bequemen werden, dieselbe Freiheit, welche den jetzt allhie Residirenden hierin gegeben, auch genießen"; P. D. F. Reils (1847), pp. 373–375; see also StAHH, Senat, Cl. VII Lit. Hf Nr. 5 Vol. 3a Fasc. 4, fl. 1–2 (February 19, 1612).

51 StAHH, Senat, Cl. VII Lit. Cc Nr. 2 Vol. 2 Fasc. 1.

52 See, for example, StAHH, Senat, Cl. VII Lit. Cc Nr. 2 Vol. 1 Fasc. 4, fl. 148.

53 The list that is chronologically closest to the contract of 1612 is titled "*Rolla* of the Portuguese nation or *Nomina* of all Portuguese residing and living here" [*Rolla* der portugiesischen Nation oder *Nomina* der sämmtlichen allhie residirenden und wohnenden Portugiesen]; it does not refer to the contract. See P. D. F. Reils (1847), pp. 376–379; A. Cassuto (1931), pp. 63–69; see also StAHH, Senat, Cl. VII Lit. Hf Nr. 5 Vol. 3a Fasc. 4, fl. 2v–3v. In contrast to the

lists of the Netherlanders, those of the Portuguese often include the activities and residences as well as the composition of the households along with the names.

54 J. P. Cassel (1771); J. Denucé (1909); V. Ribeiro (1917); L. Silveira (1958); H. Kellenbenz (1960); M. V. do Amaral (1965); V. Rau (1984c); J. Pohle (2000).

55 The privilege granted to Duarte Fernandes in 1589 is the earliest known privilege not registered in the Chancellery books. No privileges granted to German merchants are to be found in the *Registo Geral das Mercês*, in which the honorary titles and favors granted by the kings since 1639 were listed; ANTT, *Registo Geral de Mercês*. In addition to the letter of privilege granted to Duarte Fernandes, after 1580 such letters were given to merchants, including Duarte Sonnemans, Geraldo Hugues, Jacques Lourenço, Sebastião Lamberto, José Fernandes Jol, Gaspar de Mere, Jacques Biquer, and Henrique Aires. Those granted to Duarte Fernandes (1589) and Duarte Sonnemans (1644) have been edited; see L. Silveira (1958); V. Ribeiro (1917); J. Denucé (1909); BNL, Manuscritos Reservados, cód. 11392.

56 The trade benefits included, among other things, freedom of pricing (with the exception of pepper, which had to be bought at established prices), permission to re-export unsold goods and unspent money, and permission to use one's own scales for home use.

57 A *vizinho* of a town was everyone who was free-born there, who had been manumitted from slavery or servitude in the town or had lived there for several years and married a local woman, owned most of his property there or held an office; Ordenações Manuelinas ([ca. 1513] 1797), liv. 2, tít. 56. Apart from that, there was a privileged form of citizenship, that of the *cidadão*, from whose ranks the communal administrations were recruited. The *cidadão* enjoyed most of the privileges of the lesser nobility and lived accordingly. Persons working in the mechanical trades (crafts) were excluded just as were those who could not prove the "purity of their blood" (i.e., Jews, Muslims, non-Europeans and their progeny; see also Chapter 5). It was possible to become a *cidadão*: as the child of a *cidadão*; if the king granted that privilege; by exercising functions in the local government; by marrying the daughter of a *cidadão*; or by university degree; see M. F. B. Bicalho (2003). For an example of a *carta de cidadão*, see F. V. Frade (2006), p. 341; see also F. da Silva (1988), pp. 296–301. In terms of constitutional law, however, the status of *vizinho* was the determining factor, because *naturalidade* – that is, citizenship of the state – was derived from *vizinhança*: see A. M. Hespanha (2005), p. 16. This also seems to have been the case, at least initially, with the privileged German merchants; see L. Silveira (1958), pp. 36–38. The Portuguese draft of the Treaty of 1607, thus states with regard to the *vizinhança* of Hanseatic merchants, "they shall be taken as *vizinhos* of the city of Lisbon and enjoy the privileges that were conceded to them, but not as *naturais*" [Que sejão tidos por vezinhos da cidade de Lisboa, e como esses gozem dos privilegios que les estão conçedidos, mas não como naturaes]; AHL, ASA, Externa, Hispanica 9, fl. 337v., 343v.

58 In the view of the Hansa, not only were non-Hanseatic merchants to be excluded from admission to its towns, but the integration of Hanseatic merchants in foreign cities should be discouraged as well (see pp. 45, 55). At the end of the sixteenth century, the Hansa syndic Heinrich Sudermann still demanded that the Hanseatic merchants who had married and resided in Antwerp for a long time and who worked together with non-Hanseatic merchants should leave Antwerp and transfer their residence to one of the Hansa towns. Their business was to be continued by an unmarried Hanseatic factor; see R. Hammel-Kiesow (2004), p. 107; E. Daenell (1906), vol. 2, pp. 407–408.

59 Because the Germans were granted all the rights of a *vizinho*, some of the authorities were against exempting them from city levies. However, the king ruled in 1511 that because of

their privileges the Germans should not suffer any damages, they should enjoy both the privileges of aliens and the rights of locals; see L. Silveira (1958), pp. 36–38.

60 L. Silveira (1958), pp. 18, 31–32, 39–40.

61 As early as 1503, it was noted that the privileges and freedoms that were accorded to the Germans were not enjoyed by the country's own subjects; see L. Silveira (1958), p. 19.

62 BNL, Manuscritos Reservados, cód. 11392. A booklet from the year 1653, today housed in Lübeck, was much more serviceable to merchants, giving "the Hanseatic merchant and shipmaster all useful and necessary information" [dem hansischen kauffman und schiffer zu nutz und nothwendiger information]. In 106 folio pages written in German it lists all of the provisions in Spain affecting Hanseatic merchants, and it does so systematically rather than chronologically. In each case it cites the appropriate legal source, referencing in particular the treaties of 1607 and 1648; AHL, ASA, Externa, Hispanica 18.

63 L. Silveira (1958), pp. 31–32.

64 A. M. Hespanha (1994), p. 322.

65 It seems that the merchants turned to the royal officials not only to obtain individual privileges but also to enjoy the benefits of the collective privileges whereupon a letter of privilege was issued in their name. This seems to be indicated in the texts of some letters of privilege.

66 M. V. do Amaral (1965), pp. 53–59; F. V. Frade (2006), p. 351.

67 F. V. Frade (2006), pp. 270–295.

68 L. Silveira (1958).

69 Although the name Duarte Fernandes was common in Portugal, this person may have been the same as the Duarte Fernandes who was born in Porto in 1541, settled in Amsterdam in 1598, and converted to Judaism there. Together with his seven sons, who resided for shorter or longer periods of time in Lisbon, Madrid, Antwerp, Amsterdam, Hamburg, Florence, and Livorno, he built up a well-functioning trade network. In about 1620 he moved to Hamburg, where he died in 1623. Even prior to 1614, he was in the service of the Spanish Crown, which he supplied with information from Amsterdam; see D. M. Swetschinski (2000), p. 108; M. Studemund-Halévy (2000), pp. 458–459. The possessor of the privilege also worked for the king; he received his privilege, among other things, for his services as a royal page.

70 For the distinctions conferred on New Christians, see F. V. Frade (2006), pp. 49–52, 316. Consequently, the concept of the Judge Conservator of the Germans, the *juiz conservador dos alemães*, was expanded to *e (outros) privilegiados*: that is, "and (other) privileged persons," as it appears in the *Ordenações Filipinas* and other places; Ordenações Filipinas ([1603] 1870), liv. 1, tít. 49; see also L. Silveira (1958), p. 11; A. M. Hespanha (1986), vol. 1, p. 472.

71 J. Denucé (1909), p. 377.

72 J. C. Lünig (1714), pp. 153–191. A German translation is also printed there, although only in a version from 1647, when the treaty between Spain and the Hansa was renewed in the context of negotiations for the Peace of Westphalia. The collection of treaties published by José Antonio de Abreu y Bertodano contains both versions (1607 and 1647); J. A. Abreu y Bertodano (1740), pp. 375–390. No Portuguese version of the treaty is known. For Portuguese preliminary discussion of the treaty, see, however, the letters written to the king by Pedro de Castilho, the Portuguese viceroy, dated March 10, 1607, BA, cód. 51-VIII-18, n. 341, fl. 147–148v. as well as that dated July 21, 1607, BA, cód. 51-VIII-18, n. 547, fl. 220v–221. A Portuguese draft of the treaty, including a contemporary German translation, is held in Lübeck; AHL, ASA, Externa, Hispanica 9, fl. 336–346. This draft has little in common with the contemporaneous

Spanish draft; its contents, however, were clearly included in the final treaty. It may be assumed that the Portuguese version of the Treaty of 1607 corresponded in most points to the Spanish version. In place of Seville as the central hub of trade, the Portuguese version probably cited Lisbon. In addition, the customs regulations were probably adapted to their own practice. In the Portuguese draft in Lübeck, the regular import levies came to the usual 10 percent excise (*sisa*) and 10 percent import tithe (*dízima*). In the final Spanish version of the treaty, however, the regular customs duty was an 8 percent *alcabala* (like the Portuguese *sisa* actually a sales tax) and a 5 percent *almojarifazgo* (general import duty). If the Portuguese duties for Hanseatic merchants had been decreased from 20 percent to 13 percent, this would have been a successful negotiation that would surely have been mentioned elsewhere. It is more probable that the rates established for Spain and Portugal actually differed.

73　The Spanish side pledged not only to maintain the privileges, but also to rescind a number of barriers to trade, in exchange for which the Hanseatic negotiators pledged to cooperate in the blockade of the Netherlandish-Spanish trade. The office of the Hansa consul was created at that time, too (see chapter 4).

74　See A. Girard (1932), pp. 96, 106, 109.

75　I. Durrer (1953), p. 68.

76　F. Bethencourt (1996), p. 181; W. Thomas (2001a), p. 298.

77　F. G. Davenport ([1917] 1967), vol. 1, pp. 246–247.

78　AHL, ASA, Externa, Hispanica 9, fl. 138–138v., 142v., 285.

79　AHL, ASA, Externa, Hispanica 9, fl. 35.

80　"... que por la dicha causa de la conciencia no sean molestados, ni inquietados, contra el derecho del Comercio, mientras no dieren escandalo à los demàs." J. A. Abreu y Bertodano (1740), p. 66, art. 14. Similar formulations appear in the Spanish-English peace treaty of 1630 and in many later treaties as well; see C. Roma du Bocage (1916), p. 200.

81　"The subjects and inhabitants of these Provinces who are Christians may use and enjoy liberty of conscience privately in their homes, and free execise of their religion on their ships" [Os subditos e moradores destas Provincias que são christãos, uzem e gozem de liberdade de consciençia privadamente em suas casas, e dentro de suas naos de livre exerciçio de sua Religião]; cited in C. Roma du Bocage (1916), p. 200; see also pp. 93–94, 180.

82　ANTT, TSO, Inquisição de Lisboa, proc. 10451, fl. 42v.

83　AHL, ASA, Externa, Hispanica 9, fl. 35; J. I. Israel (1978).

84　L. Silveira (1958), p. 13.

85　Volker Henn has written on this point that "as difficult as it is to describe adequately the legal nature of the Hansa using the concepts of constitutional law, determining who ultimately belonged to the Hansa is just as difficult. Here, too, it acted with caution. Whatever the circumstance, it avoided giving precise information about who, i.e., in the main which towns, were members of the Hansa and to which merchants privileges were consequently permitted"; V. Henn (1998), p. 17. (Our translation.)

86　J. A. Abreu y Bertodano (1740), p. 389.

87　J. A. Abreu y Bertodano (1740), pp. 389–390.

88　In particular, they still contain Stade, which had been excluded from the Hansa in 1601; AHL, ASA, Externa, Hispanica 9, fl. 75, 411–411v.

89　AHL, ASA, Externa, Hispanica 9, fl. 340v–341.

Chapter 4

1 L. Beutin (1928); G. Fink (1931), H. Kellenbenz (1954), pp. 21–23, 291; see also J. Ulbert (2006) pp. 10–16.

2 "*Consul*, hat Gleichheit mit dem *Syndico*, weil er einer gantzen Nation, gleichwie jener einem gantzen *Collegio*, zum Dienst und Besten der Republic, in auswaertigen Orten, sonderlich aber in den grossen Handels-Staedten sich aufhaelt. ... Diejenigen, welche zu dieser *function emploiret*, sind meistens KauffLeute, weil sie hauptsaechlich das *Interesse* derer *Negotien* ihrer Nation befoerdern sollen. Deren Amt ungefehr darinnen bestehet: daß sie (1) die Wechsel-Brieffe wohl befoerdern, (2) den Credit ihrer Nation erhalten, und ihre Kauff-Leute unterstuetzen, (3) die Gelder, so eine Nation oder Republic auch Potentate dem andern auszuzahlen hat, liefern, (4) So wohl denen *Ministris* des Fuersten oder Republic, in welcher sie als Consul leben, als auch der Republic und Kauffmanns-*Compagnie* ihres Vaterlandes *Avis* geben von den *Trafiquen*, und dem *Concurs* der fremden Nationen; welche Handel an einem Orte treiben. (5) Die unter ihrer Nation entstandene Differentien, so weit sie die Handlung *concerniren, decidiren*"; J. H. Zedler (1733), vol. 6, cols. 1105–1106.

3 J. Pohle (2000), pp. 33, 270; I. Durrer (1953), p. 70.

4 "... consul van den henze steden oostersche natie ende eenige steden van herwertsover [den Niederlanden] Portugal ende Lisbona frequenterende"; R. Häpke (1923), no. 670, p. 266.

5 "... eenige anderen aldaer residerende." Widely traveled, Damião de Góis had also visited Danzig, and in 1567 he had been named Danzig's permanent agent in Lisbon. Kellenbenz is mistaken in considering him a Netherlander; H. Kellenbenz (1954), p. 291.

6 I. Durrer (1953), pp. 70, 81.

7 P. D. Braga (1998), p. 235.

8 On Konrad Rot, see also R. Hildebrandt (1970/1971).

9 H. Kellenbenz (1954), pp. 21–23. Kellenbenz did not provide solid evidence for his place of origin; see W. Pelus-Kaplan (1981), p. 29.

10 The Portuguese viceroy had explicitly protested against the concessions shortly before; BA, cód. 51-VIII-18, n. 326, fl. 141v.; n. 341, fl. 147–148v.

11 J. A. Abreu y Bertodano (1740), pp. 381–382.

12 "... keiner frembden, ausserhansischen nation zugethan sein, noch sich daran vorwandt machen, vielweiniger eine andere frembde bestallung annehmen, noch auch umb seines privatnutzens und vortheils willen andere frembde schiffe oder schiffere, noch verbotne und unfreye gueter und wahren, so in die hanse nicht gehoren, unter deroselben nahmen durchpassiern lassen"; "Holl- oder Seelander, noch andere so aus den unyrten provincien der Niederlanden"; "ein wachendes auge haben"; "dessen ichtwas erstahen und vormerken wurde, den koniglichen officianten und ministris geburlich vormelden"; "treu und hold, auch gehorsam und gewertig sein"; "ihre ehr und bestes"; AHL, ASA, Externa, Hispanica 9, fl. 405–407.

13 In fact, both England and France were attempting to establish consulates in Lisbon at the same time, see J.-F. Labourdette (1988), p. 141; AHL, Nachlass Hagedorn, Packen 9-1, fl. 199v–200 (StAHH, Senat, Cl. VI Nr. 7 Vol. 4a Fasc. 1).

14 "... auf die execution der aufgesetzten straff hart tringen"; AHL, ASA, Externa, Hispanica 9, fl. 405–407.

15 P. Dollinger (1970), p. 339; R. Hammel-Kiesow (2004), pp. 106–107.

16 BA, cód. 51-VIII-9, fl. 103.

17 AHL, Nachlass Hagedorn, Packen 9-1, fl. 198–198v (StAHH, Senat, Cl. VI Nr. 7 Vol. 4a Fasc. 1).

18 "Da er sich aber gedachts consulats anmassen wollen," so reported Kampferbeck, "hat die obrigkeit von ihme zu wissen begert, auss wess befellich solches geschehe. Weil er aber nichts aufzulegen gehabt, hat man ihn alssobalt gefengklich auf eine gallion legen lassen, warvon er sich mit keiner geringen mühe und favor entledigen müssen." AHL, Nachlass Hagedorn, Packen 9–1, fl. 199v (StAHH, Senat, Cl. VI Nr. 7 Vol. 4a Fasc. 1).

19 AHL, Nachlass Hagedorn, Packen 9–1, fl. 163 (StAHH, Senat, Cl. VI Nr. 1a Vol. 1 Fasc. 10).

20 "... dess ortss gelegenheit bekandt"; "seinem respect und fam nachtheilich sey"; AHL, Nachlass Hagedorn, Packen 9–1, fl. 171 (StAHH, Senat, Cl. VI Nr. 1a Vol. 1 Fasc. 10).

21 "... conditionirtes losskundigungsschreiben"; AHL, Nachlass Hagedorn, Packen 9–1, fl. 197 (StAHH, Senat, Cl. VI Nr. 7 Vol. 4a Fasc. 1).

22 AHL, Nachlass Hagedorn, Packen 9–1, fl. 205 (StAHH, Senat, Cl. VI Nr. 1a Vol. 1 Fasc. 10).

23 AHL, Nachlass Hagedorn, Packen 9–1, fl. 204 (StAHH, Senat, Cl. VI Nr. 7 Vol. 4a Fasc. 1).

24 H. Kellenbenz (1954), p. 290.

25 AHU, Códice do Conselho da Fazenda, n. 37, fl. 50 v.

26 BA, cód. 51-VIII-21, fl. 151; ANTT, TSO, Conselho Geral, Habilitações, João, mç. 1, n. 36.

27 ANTT, TSO, Inquisição de Lisboa, liv. 212, fl. 19–28v.

28 ANTT, Inquisição de Coimbra, proc. 2425.

29 ANTT, TSO, Inquisição de Lisboa, proc. 11448, fl. 15.

30 ANTT, TSO, Inquisição de Lisboa, proc. 3922.

31 ANTT, Corpo Cronológico, parte 1, mç. 118, n. 165.

32 Bredimus was still waiting to be installed at the beginning of 1637; see AHL, Nachlass Hagedorn, Packen 9–1, fl. 350–375 (StAHH, Senat, Cl. VII, Lit. Ca, Nr. 2 Vol. 1b; Cl. VI Nr. 6, Vol. 5a Fasc. 1). Bredimus also held the office of Imperial Consul-General. He was ennobled in 1635, probably in connection with this function; BA, cód. 51-IX-8, fl. 250–251v; see also R. Häpke (1925b), p. 173.

33 E. Prestage (1925), p. 234.

34 His predecessor, probably Augustin Bredimus, had died in Madrid, according to the entry in the Chancellery book; ANTT, Chancelaria de D. João IV, Doações, liv. 13 [Mf. 926], fl. 5v. See also BA, cód. 51-IX-15, fl. 157v.

35 C. Amsinck (1894), part 2, pp. cix–cxviii.

36 BA, cód. 51-IX-15, fl. 157v.

37 AHL, Nachlass Hagedorn, Packen 9–1, fl. 405–407 (StAHH, Senat, Cl. VI Nr. 1a Fasc. 10).

38 AHL, Nachlass Hagedorn, Packen 9–1, fl. 419 (StAHH, Senat, Cl. VI Nr. 7 Vol. 4a Fasc. 1).

39 AHL, Nachlass Hagedorn, Packen 9–1, fl. 521 (StAHH, Senat, Cl. VI Nr. 1a Vol. 1 Fasc. 10).

40 ANTT, Freguesia de Santa Catarina do Monte Sinai, Lisboa, liv. 5B, fl. 7v. Gaspar de Faria Severim was still *secretário das mercês* (State Secretary for the Administration of Mercies) at the time of the baptism. He was the nephew of the renowned poet Manuel Severim de Faria.

41 C. Amsinck (1894), part 2, pp. cxxvi–cxxvii; AHL, Nachlass Hagedorn, Packen 9–1, fl. 857–860 (StAHH, Senat, Cl. VII, Lit. Ca, Nr. 1 Vol. 4a, p. 171–173).

42 C. Amsinck (1894), part 2, pp. cxxvi–cxxvii; AHL, Nachlass Hagedorn, Packen 9–1, fl. 857–860 (StAHH, Senat, Cl. VII, Lit. Ca, Nr. 1 Vol. 4a, p. 171–173).

43 In addition Alexander Heusch, at least temporarily, also seems to have represented the kingdoms of Sweden and Denmark. This caused some uncertainties at first, because the Danish king had appointed another candidate before Heusch eventually came into office; see ANTT, Chancelaria de D. Afonso VI, liv. 31, fl. 59v.; ANTT, Chancelaria de D. Afonso VI, liv. 47, fl. 331v. Alexander's brother Luís Heusch became the Polish consul in Lisbon at the beginning of the eighteenth century. See H. Kellenbenz (1958), p. 183.

44 "... elenden Beschönigungen"; "Negligence und Schwachheit"; "verloren und zu trümmern gehen"; "capable, etwas bey Hofe anzutragen"; "die gantze teutsche Nation"; "nichts als Spott und Schande zu gewarten"; cited in E. Baasch (1915), vol. 1, p. 428.

45 On the pepper trade, see H. Kellenbenz (1956a).

46 For the precise composition of the loan, see R. Hildebrandt (1970/1971), p. 35.

47 H. Kellenbenz (1954), p. 21.

48 In 1612 the king ordered payment of 1,238 milreis to Kampferbeck; AHU, Reino, cx. 1, pasta 112. In 1614 Kampferbeck asked that a decree be issued against his imminent arrest until the state had paid the money it owed him; BA, cód. 51-VIII-21, fl. 159v. For more on this, see also AHL, Nachlass Hagedorn, Packen 9–1, fl. 182–187 (StAHH, Senat, Cl. VI Nr. 7 Vol. 4a Fasc. 1).

49 H. Kellenbenz (1956a), pp. 7, 24–27.

50 ANTT, TSO, Conselho Geral, Habilitações, João, mç. 1, doc. 36.

51 When Joachim van Wicquefort consigned to Heusch a shipment of a hundred tons of powder destined for Portugal on behalf of Amalie Elisabeth, the regent of Hesse-Kassel, the munitions intended for the Portuguese Crown were seized and delivered to Heusch's longest-standing creditors. AHU, Reino, cx. 11A, pasta 12, doc. 4.

52 H. Kellenbenz (1954), p. 27.

53 ANTT, TSO, Inquisição de Lisboa, liv. 212, fls. 19–28v.

54 Earliest mention was on December 26, 1613; BA, cód. 51-VIII-21, fl. 151; last mention May 6, 1627; ANTT, TSO, Inquisição de Lisboa, liv. 212, fls. 19–28v.

55 ANTT, TSO, Conselho Geral, Habilitações, Diogo, mç. 2, doc. 83.

56 P. W. Gennrich (1936); H. Kellenbenz (1950).

57 H. Kellenbenz (1950), p. 33. Heusch's relatives in Hamburg were not Reformed but Lutheran, and Alexander, who was born in Lisbon, had a Portuguese mother, had been baptized there, and was therefore almost assuredly Catholic (see also chapter 15).

58 "... diejenigen Personen, welche mit einer solchen Gewalt geschickt werden, daß sie lange an dem Hof eines Potentaten verbleiben, und ohne Unterscheid daselbst verschiedene Angelegenheiten ihres Principals, als suppliciren, sollicitiren, erinnern, Nachricht geben, und sein übriges Interesse beobachten. ... Man nimmt zu solchen Chargen selten oder gar niemahln Leute von adelicher Geburt, oder solche, welche an dem Hofe ihres Principalen eine den Cavalliers gebührende Stelle bekleiden, sondern meistens nur in den Handels-Städten reiche Kaufleute, oder auch wohl gar Juden, die sich mit dem blossen Titul ohne Besoldung begnügen lassen"; J. H. Zedler (1742), vol. 31, cols. 715–716. "Resident" is also mentioned under the term *Abgesandter* (emissary, envoy), but with a slightly different definition: "Among the envoys are also residents, who are nothing but ordinary envoys. ... In particular, attention is paid to whether such a resident is a minister and attends to matters of state, or whether he is only occupied with solicitation. If the first, he may be treated somewhat better than an agent; in the latter case, however, he will be viewed as a mere agent – that is, not as an envoy, but as a person who takes care of his employer's affairs. ... They have no accreditation, but only letters of recommendation: they do not enjoy the safety of international rights: are not received in audiences, but must present their matters to the person who ordinarily receives these, such as the secretary of state etc." [Unter die *Envoyés* gehören nun auch die *Residenten*, welche nichts anders als *ordinair Envoyés* seyn. ... Insonderheit pfleget man darauf Acht zu haben, ob ein solcher *Resident* ein *Minister* sey, und Staats-Geschäffte unter Händen habe, oder ob er sich nur mit sollicitiren bemühe. Ist jenes, so lässet man ihm etwas besser als einen *Agenten* tractiren; im letzern Fall aber wird er vor einen blossen *Agenten* angesehen, das ist, nicht vor einen Gesandten, sondern vor

eine solche Person, die sich lasset angelegen seyn, das seines Herren Sachen gefertiget werden mögen. ... Sie haben keine *Creditive*, sondern nur *Recommendations*-Schreiben: geniesen die Sicherheit des Völcker-Rechts nicht: bekommen keine *Audienzen*, sondern müssen ihre Sachen bey demjenigen, der sonst dergleichen annimmt, als beym Staats-*Secretair* & c. vorbringen]; J. H. Zedler (1732), vol. 1, col. 120.

59 J. H. Zedler (1733), vol. 6, cols. 833–834.

60 "... souveraine bey ihres gleichen und geringern ihre Agenten [halten], wenn sie etwas zu verrichten haben, welches derer Unkosten nicht werth wäre, einen formalen Ministre alldort zu haben; und diese Art derer Agenten sind meistentheils mit zu espioniren abgeordnet"; J. H. Zedler (1732), vol. 1, cols. 769–770.

61 P. Cardim (2002), pp. 59–60.

62 H. Kellenbenz (1958), p. 26; see also F. V. Frade (2006), p. 288.

63 H. Kellenbenz (1954), p. 227; E. Stols (1973), p. 41; see, however, GA, Not. Arch. 98/28, 28v. They were not themselves the lessees, but were in the service of the Portuguese and Italian contract holders who had settled in Lisbon and Antwerp. The Hamburg representatives were the Netherlanders Dominicus van Uffeln, Gillis de Greve, and Cornelis de Hertoghe; the Hamburgers Bartholomäus and Lukas Beckmann; the southern German Martin Entzisberger; and the Italian Alessandro della Rocca; see M. Kalus (2010), pp. 205–238; H. Kellenbenz (1956a).

64 On the Portuguese *feitorias*, see A. H. Marques (1962); V. Rau (1984b); H. Pohl (1977).

65 In some instances royal factors are attested later as well; see H. Pohl (1977), p. 44.

66 "And that in the same way his majesty will be allowed to set up *feitorias* in some of the Hansa towns which seem convenient to him, like the one the Portuguese kings who preceded his majesty had had in Flanders for some years, providing the said *feitorias* with ministers whom he approves and takes into his service, to whom merchandise of any sort will be remitted, so that they may sell and trade it on account of his royal treasury. And the towns in which the *feitorias* will be located will have to concede to the factors and their agents and servants the same privileges and exemptions that are granted to their *vizinhos*, and they [the towns] have to provide houses, crates and ships (which they [the factors, agents and servants] have to pay for at the ordinary prices) so that they may trade in said merchandise and other that they might buy in the said regions to be sent to these kingdoms of Spain" [E que da mesma maneira podera sua magestade mandar assentar casas de feitoria em algumas das çidades ansiaticas, que lhe bem pareçer, como a tiveraõ os reys de Portugal antecessores de sua magestade alguns anos em Flandes, provendo as dittas casas de feitoria dos ministros que lhe aprouver aos quaes se remetteraõ as mercadorias de toda sorte que sua magestade ouver por seu serviço para que se vendaõ e comerçeem por conta de sua real fazenda. E aos feitores, e seus agents e criados convenha e haõ de conceder as çidades, nas em que as feitorias estiverem, os mesmos privilegios, e izensois conçedidas aos vezinhos della, e lhes haõ de dar casas, trouxas e navios (pagando o elles polos preços ordenarios) para effeito de comercearem as dittas mercadurias, e as mais que comprarem nas dittas partes para enviarem a estes reynos de Hespanha]; AHL, ASA, Externa, Hispanica 9, fl. 339–339v.

67 "... zum hochsten beschweren"; "allerhandt ungelegenheit erfolgen könte"; StAHH, Senat, Cl. VII Lit. La Nr. 1 Vol. 4e.

68 "... dawider mit kaiserlichen Mandaten sich zu schützen, ja auch wohl in Hispanien auf dieser Stadt Güter und Schiffe Arrest auszubringen sich unterstehen würden"; P. D. H. Reils (1847), pp. 367–368.

69 H. Kellenbenz (1954), p. 21.

70 H. Kellenbenz (1954), p. 347.
71 K.-K. Weber (2002), p. 62; C. F. Wurm (1855), p. 47; see also G. Das (1920); G. v. d. Plaat (2003).
72 R. v. Roosbroeck (1964), pp. 53, 72–73; see also P. Benedict (2002), p. 291.
73 H. H. Rowen (1987), p. 178. Both the uncle and nephew converted to Catholicism on their deathbeds.
74 He had subscribers in Germany, Sweden, Denmark, Venice, England, and France; G. v.d. Plaat (2003), pp. 33–35.
75 H. H. Rowen (1987), p. 171; see also G. v.d. Plaat (2003).
76 J. I. Israel (1986).
77 J. I. Israel (1986), pp. 533–536.
78 In 1629 de Roy turned to the Danish king to ask that he might employ an agent in Glückstadt who might at the same time certify the trade from Hamburg and Bremen. In 1630 Spain established the post of a Spanish commissioner in Glückstadt, which Gabriel de Roy assumed in 1632, although he only settled there in 1640; AHL, ASA, Externa, Hispanica 17; see also J. I. Israel (1986), p. 542; E. M. Kiecksee (1952), pp. 37, 42; G. Köhn (1974), p. 54.
79 H. Kellenbenz (1956b); M. Studemund-Halévy and S. Silva (2004).
80 J. I. Israel (1987).
81 In addition, he was the banker and postal agent of Duarte de Bragança, the brother of the later Portuguese king João IV, for whom he advocated until Duarte's death in 1649.
82 P. Cardim (2004).
83 BA, ms. av. 54-XIII-7, n. 5; 54-XIII-8, ns. 244, 257; 54-XI-29, ns. 162–162a, 171–172, 189, 191–199, 201–203, 206–210, 258.
84 E. M. Lobo (1963), pp. 74–75.
85 BA, cód. 51-VIII-26, fl. 95.
86 BA, ms. av. 54-XIII-8, ns. 244, 257 (October 10, 1666); ms. av. 54-XI-29, ns. 193 (September 23, 1667/9), 162, 171, 203 (January 31, 1668), 189, 196 (July 1, 1668), 210 (January 8, 1669).
87 ANTT, RGM, D. Afonso VI, liv. 4, fl.267–267v.
88 A. M. Faria (2005), p. 325.
89 E. Brazão (1979), p. 147.
90 A. Sutcliffe (2009), p. 28; A. Sutcliffe (2007), pp. 435–436.

Chapter 5

1 M. J. Tavares (1982), pp. 74, 252–257. Contemporary figures were considerably higher; Abraham Zacuto, for example, estimated the number at 120,000; according to the chronicle of André Bernaldez, 93,000 Jews were involved; see H. P. Salomon (1982), p. 14.
2 Mass conversions of Jews began considerably earlier in Spain than in Portugal; accordingly they penetrated the urban elites earlier as well, from where the Spanish purity of blood laws largely originated; see F. Bethencourt (2009), pp. 323–330.
3 B. de Spinoza ([1670] 1883), chapter 3, pp. 55–56.
4 The Inquisition's activities were suspended between 1674 and 1682.
5 F. Bethencourt (2000), p. 99; G. Marcocci (2011).
6 F. Bethencourt (2000), pp. 278–288.
7 Ibid., pp. 274–275.
8 W. Thomas (2001b), pp. 30–50.

9   F. Bethencourt (2000); H. P. Salomon (1971).
10 "No ablaua con nuestros padres en Espanha el diuino texto quando dixo que dirían las gentes por nosotros, 'deçierto gente grande y sabia la ésta', pues tan mal gouierno tuuieron en no ensenhar sus hijos, que a no primitir en aquel reino el D[io] B[endito] la inquiçiçión, escuela adó se ensenha su conosimiento y se renueua la perdida sangre, creo bien que según su oluido, ya de todo fuera perdido su conosimiento"; cited in H. P. Salomon (1982), p. 293; English translation (with one minor error) ibid., p. 167.
11 A. J. Saraiva (1956); A. J. Saraiva (2011).
12 This has been demonstrated especially for the Algarve; see J. R. Magalhães (1993), p. 373.
13 F. Bethencourt (1993).
14 These quotations come from an interview that he gave in May 1971 to the *Diáro de Lisboa*; cited in F. Bethencourt (1993), p. 125; and in English translation in A. J. Saraiva (2011), p. 235.
15 F. Bethencourt (1993), p. 132.
16 J. V. Torres (1978); J. V. Torres (1986); J. V. Torres (1994).
17 J. R. Magalhães (1981); J. R. Magalhães (1987); J. R. Magalhães (1993); F. Bethencourt (1996); J. I. Pulido Serrano (2007).
18 See G. Marcocci (2010).
19 "Verdadeiramente é dificultosíssima de entender a razão de estado de Portugal nesta parte; porque, sendo um reino todo fundado no comércio, os seus mercadores portugueses lançaos para reinos estranhos, e os mercadores estrangeiros admiteos dentro de si, com que o proveito e interesses da negociação vem a ser todos deles, e nada nosso; porque o que os mercadores estrangeiros ganham nos reinos estranhos lá fica, e o que os mercadores estrangeiros ganham neste para lá vai"; A. Vieira (1951), p. 59.
20 "Da mesma maneira os portugueses ausentes de Portugal e muitos estrangeiros, que reconhecem as utilidades do nosso Reino e comércio, não mandam o seu dinheiro e mercadorias a nossos portos, por as não terem por seguras nas mãos dos nossos mercadores"; A. Vieira (1951), p. 65.
21 L. M. E. Shaw (1989), p. 428; J. R. Magalhães (1993), p. 382.
22 L. M. E. Shaw (1989), p. 415.
23 For a critical view of Vieira's tolerance, see S. B. Schwartz (2003).
24 A. B. Coelho (1987), vol. 2, pp. 195–197.
25 See, for example, F. Mauro (1958).
26 D. G. Smith (1975), p. 19.
27 Over the period from 1536 to 1668.
28 All figures from F. Bethencourt (1996), p. 282.
29 J. R. Magalhães (1993), p. 380.
30 L. M. E. Shaw (1989), p. 421.
31 F. Bethencourt (1996), pp. 109–110.
32 J. L. de Azevedo (1989), pp. 240–241.
33 F. Bethencourt (2000), pp. 96, 114; F. Bethencourt (1996) pp. 171, 173, 297–301.
34 Rules of Procedure of 1640, Liv. 2, Tít. 4, § 5, in J. E. Franco and P. de Assunção (2004), p. 299.
35 This is well documented in the case of Spain, where wealthy Portuguese New Christians held influential positions as bankers to the Crown; see B. López Belinchón (2000).
36 BA, cód. 51-X-16, fl. 203 (April 17, 1648).
37 BA, cód. 51-X-16, fl. 202–202v (May 11, 1648).
38 J. L. de Azevedo (1989), pp. 265–266, 281–282.
39 P. A. d'Azevedo (1910), p. 197; M. Studemund-Halévy (2000), p. 817.

40 F. Bethencourt (1996), pp. 266–267, 291.
41 F. Olival (1991).
42 D. G. Smith (1975), pp. 80–81.
43 J. I. Pulido Serrano (2007), pp. 47–76.
44 A. B. Coelho (2001), p. 144.
45 V. M. Godinho (1968a), p. 289.
46 J. A. de Figueiredo (1790), p. 194; J. J. Silva (1854), vol. 1603–1612, pp. 185, 286–288; J. J. Silva (1855), vol. 1627–1633, pp. 158–159.
47 Rules of Procedure of 1613, Tít. 1, Cap. II; Rules of Procedure of 1640, Liv. 1, Tít. 12, in J. E. Franco and P. de Assunção (2004), pp. 151–152, 273–275. See also M. D. Domingos (1993).
48 Rules of Procedure of 1640, Liv. 1, Tít. 12, § 10 in J. E. Franco and P. de Assunção (2004), p. 275.
49 ANTT, TSO, Inquisição de Lisboa, procs. 319, 319–1.
50 ANTT, TSO, Conselho Geral, Habilitações, Diogo, mç. 2, doc. 83.
51 Rules of Procedure of 1640, Liv. 3, Tít. 10, § 2 in J. E. Franco and P. de Assunção (2004), p. 357.
52 Rules of Procedure of 1613, Tít. 4, Caps. 15, 16; Rules of Procedure of 1640, Liv. 3, Tít. 23, §1, 2 in J. E. Franco and P. de Assunção (2004), pp. 164, 377.
53 ANTT, TSO, Inquisição de Lisboa, proc. 11362.
54 The position of the Portuguese Inquisition in relation to Spain and Spanish America was somewhat different than toward the Protestant countries. It repeatedly demanded extradition of suspected New Christians from Spain and made efforts to exchange information regularly with the Spanish Inquisition. Nonetheless, very few extraditions took place; see J. R. Magalhães (1987); J. E. Franco and P. de Assunção (2004), p. 54.
55 If persons to be accused could not be found, a warrant of arrest was issued. If they did not report to the Inquisition within a certain time period, where they were to justify the absence and prove their innocence or confess their sins, they were additionally accused of rebellion; see the warrants of arrest for Pedro Francês, Miguel Francês, and Duarte Nunes da Costa in ANTT, TSO, Inquisição de Lisboa, proc. 11448, fl. 30.
56 The following persons living in Hamburg were sentenced and burned in absentia in Lisbon in 1638: Henrique de Lima (ANTT, TSO, Inquisição de Lisboa, proc. 3922); Duarte de Lima (proc. 7195); Miguel Francês (proc. 9173); Pedro Francês (proc. 11448); João Francês (proc. 12215); Rodrigo de Andrade (proc. 12212); Diogo Nunes Veiga (proc. 7193); Duarte Nunes da Costa (proc. 7192); Luís Dias de Lemos (proc. 7119); Simão Gomes de Paz (proc. 9892).
57 See, for example, B. De Brito (1609), part 2, section "Ao catholico e sempre augusto rey Dom Phelippe III."
58 P. D. Braga (2001), pp. 262, 371.
59 ANTT, Inquisição de Lisboa, proc. 12387.
60 Rules of Procedure of 1613, Tít. 5, Cap. 17, in J. E. Franco and P. de Assunção (2004), p. 181.
61 Rules of Procedure of 1640, Liv. 1, Tít. 12, § 9, in J. E. Franco and P. de Assunção (2004), pp. 181, 275.
62 Rules of Procedure of 1640, Liv. 1, Tít. 12, § 5, in J. E. Franco and P. de Assunção (2004), p. 274.
63 F. Bethencourt (1996), pp. 47–52; G. Cerrillo Cruz (2000), p. 12.
64 F. Bethencourt (1996), pp. 91–92.
65 J. V. Torres (1994), p. 130.
66 Ibid., p. 133.
67 According to José Veiga Torres, the Inquisition became a "legitimizing body for the social promotion of the merchant bourgeoisie," so the subtitle of his essay; J. V. Torres (1994).
68 An example of this is the diplomat Duarte Ribeiro de Macedo; see A. M. Faria (2005), p. 416.

69   ANTT, TSO, Conselho Geral, Habilitações, Diogo, mç. 2, doc. 83.
70   ANTT, TSO, Conselho Geral, Habilitações, João, mç. 1, n. 36.
71   "... que era gente honrada e limpa como são todos os da nação alemaa"; ANTT, TSO, Conselho Geral, Habilitações, João, mç. 11, doc. 338.
72   ANTT, TSO, Conselho Geral, Habilitações Incompletas, mç. 27, doc. 1131.

Chapter 6

1   J. I. Israel (2005), p. 10.
2   J. A. G. de Mello (1996); see also Kellenbenz's (1966) essay, which has been partly refuted by Mello; also B. N. Teensma (1988).
3   D. Swetschinski (2000), pp. 54–101.
4   O. Gelderblom (2000), pp. 42, 44, 62–63.
5   A. Pettegree (1994), p. 449.
6   M. Carlier (1994), p. 358.
7   R. v. Roosbroeck (1974).
8   J. Everaert (1995), pp. 347–348; E. Stols (1973), pp. 11, 52–54.
9   J. Zunckel (1997), pp. 224–2026; H. Kellenbenz (1954), pp. 207–208.
10   E. Stols (1971), part 2, p. 36.
11   Thus, Wilfrid Brulez described the diaspora of the Flemings as the largest mercantile diaspora in Europe during the early modern period, it having further included many ports outside of Europe; see W. Brulez (1960), p. 284.
12   W. Brulez (1960), p. 284; E. Stols (1973), pp. 226–228; E. Stols (1997), p. 120; E. Stols (1988), p. 46.
13   The estimates relate not only to different time periods, they were also made by different researchers employing different methods.
14   D. Studnicki-Gizbert (2007), p. 41. According to Vitorino Magalhães Godinho's estimates, between 300,000 and 360,000 people emigrated from Portugal between 1580 and 1640, and another 150,000 between 1640 and 1700; see V. M. Godinho (1978), pp. 8–9.
15   H. Schilling (1994), p. 179. In a more recent work, Schilling cites a figure between 100,000 and 150,000; H. Schilling (2009), p. 412. It is estimated that the number of people who left the southern Netherlands to settle in the northern Netherlands was between 60,000 and 150,000, although the studies on which the second figure is based are contested; see O. Gelderblom (2000), p. 22.
16   D. Swetschinski (2000), p. 69.
17   H. Schilling (2009), p. 21.
18   O. Gelderblom (2000), pp. 72–74. Clé Lesger also presumed strategic trade considerations for the emigration of Antwerpers and their settlement in Amsterdam; C. Lesger (2006), pp. 156–157.
19   ANTT, CG, Habilitações, João, mç. 1, doc. 36.
20   J. Müller (2016).
21   H. P. Salomon (1982), p. 42; see also J. I. Pulido Serrano (2006b), p. 357.
22   ANTT, TSO, Inquisição de Lisboa, procs. 14409, 16420.
23   The pope's letter is reprinted in H. P. Salomon (1982), p. 203.
24   J. L. de Azevedo (1989), pp. 162–163; A. B. Coelho (2001), pp. 133–134; J. I. Pulido Serrano (2007), p. 72.

25 C. B. Stuczynski (2007); J. I. Pulido Serrano (2006b), pp. 366, 370.
26 "... cauzando grauissimos escandalos e inconunientes"; "que como pessoa de mais authoridade, e conheçimento, não exetuou nimguem, nem admitio causa que os releuasse de pagar, o qual foj morto sem se saber por quem"; A. B. Coelho (1987), vol. 2, pp. 199, 206.
27 A. B. Coelho (2001), pp. 117–123.
28 A. B. Coelho (1987), vol. 2, p. 207.
29 M. Studemund-Halévy (2000), p. 248.
30 Ibid., pp. 790–795, 809–810.
31 According to *Werkzoll* registers, a good fourth of the trade volume realized by the Portuguese was carried out by him; StAHH, Senat, Cl. VII Eb Nr. 11 Vol. 6. See also ANTT, TSO, Inquisição de Lisboa, proc. 3338.
32 ANTT, TSO, Inquisição de Lisboa, procs. 319, 319–1; B. N. Teensma (1976).
33 M. Studemund-Halévy (2000), p. 734.
34 His name appears for the first time in 1608 in the Hamburg *Werkzoll* registers; StAHH, Senat, Cl. VII Eb Nr. 11 Bd. 6. In 1619 he shared a bank account with his brother Duarte, who later moved to Amsterdam, and as late as 1632 and 1647 he was represented with considerable turnovers in the Admiralty customs books. He died in Hamburg in 1664. See M. Studemund-Halévy (2000), p. 734. In 1623 Jácome had a bank account of his own at the Bank of Hamburg, but he does not appear in the Admiralty customs books.
35 ANTT, TSO, Inquisição de Lisboa, proc. 6677.
36 A. Cassuto (1931), p. 67.
37 M. Studemund-Halévy (2000), p. 201. Manuel Cardoso was apparently another brother, not to be confused with the already cited Old Christian Manuel Cardoso, who was a close friend of the family. He had spent many years in Brazil, where, among other things, he had had a share in the brazilwood contract. In around 1610 he lived in London, in 1616 he was active in Amsterdam, and he finally settled in Hamburg; see H. Kellenbenz (1958), p. 118; H. P. Salomon (1982), p. 49; A. B. Coelho (2001), pp. 117–123. The other Manuel Cardoso also spent time in Hamburg, where he converted to Judaism (see chapter 14). Finally, there are indications that Henrique Dias Milão's children António and Leonor lived in Hamburg, while two others, Gomes Rodrigues and Fernão Lopes de Milão, established themselves in Amsterdam; H. P. Salomon (1982), p. 50. See also Heitor Mendes Bravo's denunciation of Hamburg community members (between 1612 and 1617), ANTT, TSO, Inquisição de Lisboa, proc. 12493.
38 Thus, it was stated that Henrique de Lima and his sons Duarte de Lima and Rodrigo de Andrade had left Portugal in 1606 along with Lopo Nunes, Diogo Nunes Veiga, Diogo Carlos, António Saraiva, João Francês, Pedro Francês, and Miguel Francês after Henrique Dias Milão was arrested. One witness believed that Henrique de Lima's son Rodrigo de Andrade, who was living in Hamburg, had been the lead negotiator for the General Pardon because he had the same name; see ANTT, TSO, Inquisição de Lisboa, proc. 3922, 11448, and 12212. Not all of the Portuguese named arrived in Hamburg immediately after the General Pardon of 1605 or the arrest of Henrique Dias Milão. The 1608 *Werkzoll* register gives evidence only of Henrique de Lima, Diogo Carlos, and João Francês. Some may have come at this time, but been too young to be active in trade themselves; see ANTT, TSO, Inquisição de Lisboa, proc. 11448; StAHH, Senat, Cl. VII Eb Nr. 11 Vol. 6.
39 See the pertinent entries in M. Studemund-Halévy (2000).
40 H. Mauersberg (1960), p. 47. By contrast, Heinrich Reincke estimates the population in 1600 at 36,000 to 40,000, in 1620 at 45,000 to 54,000, in 1680 at 50,000 to 60,000; H. Reincke (1951), pp. 172–173.

41   A. Heskel (1935), pp. 48–49.
42   F. Wagner (1894), p. 634.
43   M. Reißmann (1975), p. 214
44   Nuremberg had a similar banking requirement, whose noncompliance was successfully pursued; L. F. Peters (1994), pp. 39–42, also p. 47. Another estimate of the number of merchants active in Hamburg may be gleaned from the Admiralty customs books. A total of 57 Portuguese and 85 Netherlandish parties appear in the customs books during the accounting year of 1632. It should be noted that by far not all merchants who paid Admiralty customs in 1632 had a bank account in 1619. Of the 339 parties obliged to pay Admiralty customs, only 63 had bank accounts, that is, barely 20 percent. Even though the two samples are a good 10 years apart this finding is astonishing. Because at this point the Admiralty customs were levied almost entirely on goods being traded with the Iberian Peninsula, the total number of Netherlandish merchants must have amounted to far more than 85. The number of Portuguese parties recorded in the Admiralty customs books decreased between the accounting years 1632 and 1647; it was then only 46, whereas the number of Netherlanders rose slightly to 90, and the total number of merchants to 492. By then, some of the shipping in the Baltic Sea, along with that along the English, Flemish, and French Atlantic coast, and to Barbados was also subject to the Admiralty customs duty (see chapter 2 and appendix).
45   Here I mean of presumable Portuguese or Netherlandish origin. For more on assignment to the various nations, see the explanations in the appendix.
46   "... mehrenteils nur residieren und heut alda, bald aber anderswo hinziehen"; cited in E. Baasch (1907), pp. 118–119.
47   R. v. Roosbroeck (1974), p. 13, 21.
48   J. V. Roitman (2009), p. 171.
49   J. I. Israel (1987).
50   The first contract nominally included 130 persons, but in some copies 132 are listed. StAHH, Niederländische Armenkasse, AI2, Stück 2, fl. 1; StAHH, Senat, Cl. VII Lit. Cc Nr. 2 Vol. 1 Fasc. 4b, fl. 6–11.
51   With the exception of seven "Germans and high Germans" (*teutsche und hochteutsche*) mentioned explicitly in the contract, the approximately 170 persons were Netherlanders; StAHH, Niederländische Armenkasse, AI2. See also M. Reißmann (1975), p. 130.
52   M. Reißmann (1975), p. 215.
53   R. v. Roosbroeck (1964), p. 75; H. Schilling (1972), p. 77; J. Whaley (1985), p. 113. By contrast, Heinrich Reincke held, somewhat adventurously, that almost a quarter of Hamburg's population had immigrated from the Netherlands during the decades after 1585, which he estimates to have been about 10,000 persons; H. Reincke (1951), pp. 172–173, 192.
54   W. Sillem (1883); O. Beneke (1875); R. v. Roosbroeck (1974).
55   This probably imprecise figure comes from a report by Thomas Skinner, the secretary to the English Merchant Adventurers; see H. Hitzigrath (1907), pp. 46–47.
56   P. D. Reils, pp. 361–362; StAHH, Senat, Cl. VII Eb Nr. 11 Bd. 6.
57   However, among the first immigrants was the physician Rodrigo de Castro; several Portuguese brokers, too, came early. Households included servants and maidservants; see A. Cassuto (1931).
58   StAHH, Senat, Cl. VII Lit. Cb Nr. 4 Bd. 1a Nr. 1b. With minor errors as well in H. Kellenbenz (1958), pp. 255–258.

59 In Amsterdam, during the second half of the seventeenth century, approximately 80 percent of the economically active Portuguese still participated in trade; see D. M. Swetschinski (2000), pp. 102–103.

60 For more on these and subsequent figures, see M. Studemund-Halévy (2000), pp. 46–47, 66, 69; J. Braden (2001), p. 203. For comparison the number of Portuguese in Amsterdam: in the 1650s, 1,825–1,925; 1660s, 2,000–2,100; 1670s, 2,200–2,325; 1680s, 3,275–3,475; 1690s, 3,000–3,175; D. M. Swetschinski (2000), p. 91.

61 J. Braden (2001), pp. 203, 218–233, 262–276, 308–339.

62 D. M. Swetschinski (2000), pp. 75–96, 126–130; Y. Kaplan (1992), p. 271; J. I. Israel (1983), pp. 389–390.

63 J. Braden (2001), pp. 298–299, 328.

64 V. Rau (1984c); V. Rau (1968b); H. V. Livermore (1954).

65 Of these, probably only a portion came from Hamburg; E. Baasch (1894), p. 315.

66 Stol's method of sampling the data was to compile names from various sources, as a result of which he certainly missed a number of merchants. On the other hand, he also counted some Low Germans and Hamburgers among the *flamengos* (lit. Flemings). For example, he himself admitted that João Hulscher was a German and not a Netherlander; João van Heque, alias Banique, whom he also listed, was probably a German as well; see ANTT, TSO, Inquisição de Lisboa, proc. 3922, 12212, 11448, 7119. Finally, there was probably a relatively wide fluctuation in Lisbon as it was in Hamburg, which would lead to further distortion in the calculation; E. Stols (1970), pp. 52–54.

67 L. M. de Vasconcelos ([1608] 1990), pp. 127, 182.

68 M. V. Amaral (1965), p. 16. Lisbon had approximately 123,000 inhabitants in 1617; after 1640 there were 165,000; see J. R. Magalhães (1997a), p. 298; J. P. Ferro (1996), p. 12; V. M. Godinho (1968c), p. 22.

69 Of the 110 fathers whose origins are known, 74 percent came from outside Lisbon, and of the 69 grandfathers, 90 percent; see D. G. Smith (1975), pp. 20, 34–42. There are no reliable estimates regarding the total number of merchants in Lisbon. For the reign of King João IV (1640–1656), David Grant Smith arrived at the surprisingly low number of about 200 merchants (*mercadores*) who were involved exclusively or primarily in the wholesale trade and overseas traffic; D. G. Smith (1975), pp. 14–15. However, for his estimate he mainly drew on Inquisition trial documents, which of course capture only a portion of the merchants active in Lisbon. Avowedly he did reference other sources, especially a list compiled by Nicolau d'Oliveira, but he misinterpreted it; N. d'Oliveira ([1620] 1804). Smith assumed that it captured all of the merchants active in Lisbon at this time, while in fact it only contains those who had been "examined," i.e., those organized into a guild. As a result the merchants are missing who dealt in Atlantic products, especially sugar, but also grain traders, salt traders, and many others. In comparison to Hamburg, where there were a total of 560 bank account holders in 1619, who may more or less be equated with the number of merchants, the figure of 200 merchants in Lisbon would be very low. The number of merchants captured in the Admiralty customs books, which came to 339 parties in 1632 and 492 parties in 1647, shows that, even though these figures cover only a portion of the long-distance trade, a total of 560 merchants or more in Hamburg is not unreasonable.

70 ANTT, TSO, Inquisição de Lisboa, livs. 708–715; TSO, Inquisição de Coimbra, livs. 744, 613; TSO, Inquisição de Évora, liv. 562.

71 J.-P. Poussou (1994), p. 27.

72 "... etliche persohnen mit weib, kinndern unnd gesinde anhero begeben, in diese unnser stad niedergesezett"; StAHH, Niederländische Armenkasse, AI2, Stück 2, fl. 1.

73 P. D. H. Reils (1847), pp. 376–380.
74 ANTT, TSO, Inquisição de Lisboa, procs. 11448, 7276.
75 ANTT, TSO, Inquisição de Lisboa, proc. 3922.
76 ANTT, TSO, Inquisição de Lisboa, proc. 12212.
77 R. v. Roosbroeck (1974), pp. 21, 51. In the same vein, see the letters by Johann Thijs mentioned in J. Müller (2016).
78 I. S. Révah (1957), p. 84.
79 J. I. Israel (1978); for a successful case, see D. M. Swetschinski (1975), p. 164. Former New Christians traveled quite frequently between southern France and Spain for trade purposes; see N. Muchnik (2007); D. Graizbord (2004).
80 Y. Kaplan (1985).

Chapter 7

1 Not all branches of trade were freely accessible to everyone; only wholesale and long-distance trade had no guild restrictions. In Hamburg, cloth merchants, who specialized in the retail sale of imported cloth, and grocers who retailed manufactured products and consumer goods from outside Europe, were organized into corporations with formalized entry requirements and limited membership, to which aliens had no access. In Portugal, too, in addition to independent merchants there were corporately organized traders. A listing of members of "examined tradesmen" (*oficiais examinados*) in Lisbon from the year 1620 lists 88 textile dealers (*fanqueiros*), 38 silk thread dealers, 33 dealers in silk fabric, 36 cloth dealers (*mercadores de panos*), 15 leather dealers, 10 linen dealers, 18 dealers of drugs, 17 dealers of porcelain and other goods from India, 6 dealers of goods from Venice, 24 dealers of small goods from Flanders (nails, fittings, brushes, knives, etc.), and 18 dealers in oil, honey, figs, raisins, and resin; see N. d'Oliveira ([1620] 1804), pp. 173–186.

2 M. Reißmann (1975), pp. 227–228; D. G. Smith (1975), p. 28.

3 M. Reißmann (1975), pp. 255–259, 276.

4 D. G. Smith (1975), p. viii.

5 W. Sillem (1883) pp. 504–505.

6 "... des Duc de Alba Verfolgungen ... verursachet, den Caufhandel anzunehmen und ihre ansehnliche adeliche Güter ... verlohren gehen [lassen zu] müßen, daher sie sich nach Hamburg begeben"; cited in M. Reißmann (1975), p. 221.

7 According to the Hamburg town law reformed in 1603/1605, "no knight or knight-like person" [kein Ritter oder Rittermässige Persone] was allowed to live in the city or its region, and this ban was confirmed numerous times over the course of the century; *Hamburger Stadtrecht* ([1605] 1978), p. 8; see also N. A. Westphalen (1841), vol. 2, pp. 381–382. Nonetheless, several Hamburg families had themselves been ennobled, including the vom Holte, von Kampen, Anckelmann, and von Spreckelsen families. Supposedly they made no use of their title within the city limits; rather, its purpose seems to have been to elevate their status in delegations to princely courts; see P. E. Schramm (1969), p. 88; O. Beneke (1886), p. 52.

8 P. E. Schramm (1969), pp. 87, 91.

9 M. Studemund-Halévy (2005); H. Kellenbenz (1958), pp. 35, 341.

10 ANTT, TSO, Inquisição de Lisboa, liv. 713, fl. 280.

11 "... allerhand Rechne-, Buchhalter-, Schreibschulen und Sculehaltereien samt Kinder-Lären"; "Sprachmäistren zum Franschen, Wälschen und Spanischen s. dergl."; K. v. Hövelen (1668), p. 129.

12 ANTT, TSO, Inquisição de Lisboa, proc. 12212.

13 ANTT, TSO, Inquisição de Lisboa, proc. 10451.

14 ANTT, TSO, Inquisição de Lisboa, proc. 10442.

15 ANTT, TSO, Inquisição de Lisboa, procs. 319, 319–1; B. N. Teensma (1976), p. 7.

16 ANTT, TSO, Inquisição de Lisboa, proc. 3922.

17 Ibid.

18 ANTT, TSO, Inquisição de Lisboa, proc. 8089.

19 ANTT, TSO, Inquisição de Lisboa, proc. 10449.

20 In 1610 the French seafarer François Pyrard de Laval reported that the Portuguese who went to Brazil for training often returned with great wealth after a stay of nine or 10 years. Poor emigrants tended to settle there permanently and quickly integrate into colonial society. It is estimated that fewer than 10 percent returned; V. M. Godinho (1978), pp. 18–19.

21 An interpreter was present at only 28 percent of the reductions of Hamburgers.

22 See also E. Stols (1970), pp. 229–232.

23 "... die ädele hoch-deutsche Heldensprache"; "die Kaufbursche (um Das Sie in Holland gereiset und auch Brabander, Holländer, Englische und dergl[eichen] Vile in Hamburg Säshaft) Niederdeutsch gebrauchen und Holländisch meist untermischen"; K. v. Hövelen (1668), p. 132.

24 J. Braden (2001), p. 259.

25 Portuguese living in Hamburg were not the only foreigners who needed interpreters; the Italian Silvio Tensino used his son for the purpose; AHL, Nachlass Hagedorn, Packen 11–3, fl. 124 (StAHH, Reichskammergericht, B 93).

26 AHL, Nachlass Hagedorn, Packen 11–3, fl. 530–567 (StAHH, Reichskammergericht, F 34).

27 AHL, Nachlass Hagedorn, Packen 11–3, fl. 466 (StAHH, Reichskammergericht, D 11).

28 ANTT, TSO, Inquisição de Lisboa, proc. 6707, fl. 117.

29 "... weilln sie theils der Teutschen sprache nicht wol erfahren, ganz kurz ziemlich übereinstimmend"; AHL, Nachlass Hagedorn, Packen 11–3, fl 653–783 (StAHH, Reichskammergericht, H 127).

30 "... stehet doch zu rümen das Hamburgs Fürnäme Junge Manschaft Französisch, Spanisch, Wälsch rädet"; K. v. Hövelen (1668), p. 132.

31 AHL, Nachlass Hagedorn, Packen 12–4, fl. 517–525 (StAHH, Reichskammergericht, T 7).

32 These included at the Dreckwall (today Alter Wall), Mönkedamm, Burstah, in the Reichenstraße, and at the Rödingsmarkt and the Herrlichkeit; see A. Cassuto (1931), pp. 64–69; P. D. H. Reils (1847), pp. 381–387. The Netherlanders also lived in this area, as an undated listing, probably from 1644, indicates. According to this list, the Netherlanders who were liable for paying defense taxes lived at the following places: 32 in St. Nikolai parish, 14 in St. Petri, 24 in St. Katharinen, and 16 in St. Jakobi; A. Nikolajczyk (2006), pp. 35–36.

33 A. Cassuto (1931), p. 64; M. Studemund-Halévy (2000), pp. 208–210; H. Kellenbenz (1954), pp. 244–245; H. Kellenbenz (1958), pp. 111, 114–115, 128–129, 255–256, 478; O. Beneke (1886), pp. 51–56.

34 F. G. Buek (1840), pp. 21–23, 222–226; M. Reißmann (1975), pp. 162–163, 238, 378, 380; H. Kellenbenz (1954), p. 124.

35 StAHH, Senat, Cl. VII Lit. La Nr. 1 Vol. 4e, Konventsprotokoll; see A. Cassuto (1931), pp. 64–65; M. Reißmann (1975), pp. 92, 374–375, 377, 380–381; H. Kellenbenz (1954), pp. 109, 117–119, 126, 157.

36 There is evidence that some single Reformed Netherlanders were taken in by their Reformed compatriots; W. Sillem (1883) pp. 555–556.

37 "... bei Hamburger Volk im Hause auf einer Cammer"; P. D. H. Reils (1847), p. 379.

38 ANTT, TSO, Inquisição de Lisboa, proc. 12212.

39 ANTT, TSO, Inquisição de Lisboa, proc. 10442.

40 L. F. Costa (2002), vol. 1, p. 124. Unfortunately the author provides no source.

41 "... des Kauff- und See-Handels woll kundig seyn"; cited in M. Reißmann (1975), p. 345.

42 Ibid, pp. 347, 350, 353, 365.

43 Ibid., pp. 349, 356, 361, 364–366

44 F. G. Buek (1840), pp. 71–73; F. G. Buek (1857), pp. 31–32, 43–44, 93.

45 F. G. Buek (1840), pp. 68–69; H. Kellenbenz (1954), pp. 288, 345.

46 In 1601, for example, he wrote: "In Holland and the Provinces everything is calm at the moment. The navigation of the Hansa towns to Spain is not hindered[?] any more, but is in motion. From Brazil there arrived on the Elbe many Hamburg vessels loaded with sugar." [In Holland und denen Provincien ist itzo alles stille. Die Navigationes der Anzestetter uf Hispania werden durch die Holländere nicht mehr voessieret etc., sondern gehen im Schwange. Auß Brasilia seind anhero uff den Elbstrom viele Hamburgische Schiffe mit Sukker angelanget]; cited in H. Reincke (1958), pp. 208–209.

47 H. Reincke (1955).

48 E. Merck (1856), p. 238. See also S. M. Miranda (2011).

49 "... der Zeit auff der *Admiralität* allhie auch Ihm ... freundtschafft und *affection* erwiesen und zu der verlangten *Charge* ... befodern helffen"; E. Merck (1856), p. 123, as well as pp. 45, 68, 153.

50 "... weil der Burmester des Herrn Bürgermeister Schulzens zu Hamburg Tochtermann ist"; cited in E. Baasch (1907), pp. 134–135.

51 F. G. Buek (1840), pp. 99–103; F. G. Buek (1857), pp. 74, 97–98, 101, 123. Joachim Lemmermann was another Hamburg mayor who was prominent in the Portugal trade. He, too, was the son of an important merchant, Johann Lemmermann, and spent ten years abroad. After his father's death, Johann took over his business relationships on the Iberian Peninsula. He was elected to the citizen board of St. Petri, became a judge in the lower court and member of the Commercial Deputation, senior elder, and city councilor, before being elected mayor in 1684; F. G. Buek (1840), pp. 132–134.

52 M. Reißmann (1975), pp. 235–236; F. G. Buek (1857), pp. 79–81.

53 A. Nikolajczyk (2006), p. 29; F. G. Buek (1857), pp. 153–154; A. Schuback (1820), p. 40.

54 F. G. Buek (1857), p. 151.

55 H. Schilling (2009), pp. 432–433

56 F. G. Buek (1840), p. 60.

57 Simon von Petkum had already been named treasury citizen in 1599. After that, the two names no longer appear among the city's high officials.

58 AHL, Nachlass Hagedorn, Packen 12–4, fl. 48–144 (StAHH, Reichskammergericht, K 5).

59 U. Beukemann (1912), pp. 494–495; R. Postel (1992), p. 22.

60 D. G. Smith (1975), pp. 177–180.

61 A. Domínguez Ortiz (1996), p. 23.

62 AHU, Reino, cx. 5, pasta 19, doc. 3 (April 12.–15, 1621).

63 AHU, Reino, cx. 5, pasta 55, doc. 4 (September 18, 1625).

64 AHU, Reino, cx. 5, pasta 72, doc. 4 (September 26, 1625).

65 AHU, Reino, cx. 5A, pasta 2, doc. 5 (February 23, 1626).

66 AHU, Reino, cx. 38, pasta 30, doc. 1 (February 13, 1626).
67 AHU, Códice do Conselho da Fazenda, n. 37, fl. 50v (June 12, 1627).
68 AHU, Reino, cx. 8, pasta 26, doc. 4 (August 18, 1635); cx. 8, pasta 26, doc. 5 (August 25, 1635); cx. 8, pasta 22, doc. 5 (August 27, 1635).
69 ANTT, RGM, D. Pedro II, liv. 7, fl. 80v; RGM, D. Pedro II, liv. 10, fl. 293; RGM, D. João V, liv. 7, fl. 571v; ANTT, Habilitação da Ordem de Christo, letra A, mç. 45, doc. 72; ANTT, TSO, Conselho Geral, Habilitações, André, mç. 3, doc. 57; TSO, Conselho Geral, Habilitações, Pedro, mç. 12, doc. 299; TSO, Conselho Geral, Habilitações, João, mç. 11, doc. 338; ANTT, TSO, Inquisição de Lisboa, liv. 713, fl. 307.
70 He was probably identical with the navy captain Johann Månsson Dreffling who operated in that capacity during the 1670s and early 1680s. However, although he became a nobleman he did not govern the counties of Södermanland and Värmland. He was only an acknowledged and well rewarded military officer. Thanks to Jan Mispelaere for this information.
71 ANTT, TSO, Inquisição de Lisboa, proc. 10449; TSO, Conselho Geral, Habilitações, Teodósio, mç. 1, doc. 10; TSO, Conselho Geral, Habilitações, Diogo, mç. 8, doc. 196; TSO, Conselho Geral, Habilitações, André, mç. 3, doc. 57; ANTT, RGM, Ordens, liv. 5, fl. 238.
72 The brothers Hans, Heinrich, Hermann, and Paul Meyer, who were from Lübeck and traveled to Spain, were members of a grocer company there at the end of the sixteenth century; P. Jeannin (1975), p. 22. In Hamburg, several Meyers and also de Meijers paid Admiralty customs duties, although none of them large amounts. They included Berend, Daniel, Heinrich, Joachim, Johann, Lüder, and Markus Meyer and Cornelis and Johann de Meijer. A certain Christoph Meyer was elected senior elder in 1700; F. G. Buek (1857), p. 183. In addition, a certain João da Maya lived in Lisbon at the end of the seventeenth century, having arrived in Lisbon from Hamburg in 1656. He had a brother in Hamburg, Diogo da Maya (Jakob Meyer), who was also a merchant. Their father was likewise named Diogo da Maya and was a shipmaster in Hamburg; ANTT, TSO, Inquisição de Lisboa, proc. 10451. Finally, there was also a Pedro da Maya de Thessen in Lisbon, who originally came from Lübeck; ANTT, TSO, Conselho Geral, Habilitações, Diogo, mç. 8, doc. 196.
73 E. Merck (1856), pp. 19, 73, 153, 167, 187, 226, 248.
74 Ibid., pp. 158, 167, 241.
75 ANTT, TSO, Inquisição de Lisboa, proc. 10295; ANTT, RGM, D. Pedro II, liv. 8, fl. 458v.

Chapter 8

1 Although the actual bank registers and documents were lost in the 1842 Great Hamburg Fire, excerpts by Otto Christian Gaedechens, Jr. from 1826, which contain all account holders for the year 1619, including their turnovers, survived the fire; StAHH, Senat, Cl. VII Lit. Cb Nr. 4, Vol. 1a Nr. 1b.
2 D. Peres (1971), p. 33.
3 H. Sieveking (1933); L. F. Peters (1994), pp. 39–88.
4 As Lambert Peters has shown for the Bank of Nuremberg, which was founded two years later, even financial dealings with close family members or compatriots were not transacted directly but through the bank; L. F. Peters (1994), p. 42; see also C. Lesger (2006), p. 280.
5 For bank profits, see J. F. Voigt (1892), pp. 292–293.
6 If we limit consideration to the Portugal trade, we find a similar distribution. In 1632, the 5% of Portugal traders with the highest turnovers were responsible for 36% of the turnover

with Portugal; the 10% with the highest turnovers for 53%; and the 80% of merchants with the lowest turnovers were involved in 26% of the total turnover. The concentration of turnover among merchants was considerably higher in 1647: by then, the 5% of merchants with the highest turnovers accounted for almost half of the total (47%); the 10% of merchants with the highest turnovers were responsible for 66%, and the 80% with the lowest turnovers had only 20% of the total. This concentration of the largest share of the turnover on a small group of merchants and the simultaneous large base of relatively unimportant merchants was replicated in the different foreign nations. Among the Netherlanders, 10% of the merchants were responsible for 41% of the turnover, while 80% only did 36% of the total turnover. Among the Portuguese, the top of 10% of merchants shared 45% of the turnover, while the share of the 80% of merchants with the lowest turnovers was only 37%; StAHH, Admiralitatskollegium, F3 Band 1, 2 and 8; F4 Band 8, 14 and 15 (see appendix).

7   The concentration of turnovers is commensurate with the per capita turnovers: Netherlanders, 62,319 marks; Portuguese 25,279 marks; Hamburgers 27,789 marks; immigrants from surrounding areas 16,255 marks; unknown/other 18,403 marks.

8   Clé Lesger has argued convincingly on the reliability of this approach; C. Lesger (2006), p. 279–282.

9   H. Schilling (2009), p. 26.

10   Thus, for example, Manuel Álvares Pinto wrote the following about his family's planned flight from Antwerp to Cologne in 1646: "And the houses in Antwerp were left with the usual outfittings and ornaments on the outside, understanding that jewelry, gold and silver, tapestries and other valuables had been sent to Holland secretly with such precautions that only some of the most loyal servants, who later came with us, knew about them." [E se deixauao as cazas de Anueres no esterior dellas con o fato e ornamentos que tinhao, suposto que secretam[en]te joyas, ouro e prata, tapisarias e o mais de valor se auia mandado p[ar]a Olanda, con tanto precato que sso alguos dos criados mais leais, e que despois vierao connosco, o souberao]; H. P. Salomon (1975), p. 54.

11   M. Grunwald (1902), p. 7.

12   See, for example, a statement from a group of Portuguese in Amsterdam from the year 1623 containing a request for tax exemption, in E. M. Koen (1989), no. 2825 (February 24, 1623).

13   The occasion for this statement was the discussions around the departure tithe, a tax on assets due when a person moved away from Hamburg; P. D. H. Reils (1847), pp. 367–368. Nor were the Portuguese merchants in Amsterdam especially prosperous during the first half of the century; see D. M. Swetschinski (2000), p. 109; A. M. Dias (1936).

14   O. Gelderblom (2000), pp. 38–39, 61–68.

15   Proposals were made to the emperor several times to impose forced loans or special taxes on them to finance wars; see R. Häpke (1925b), pp. 184–185; H. Kellenbenz (1955), p. 290.

16   F. G. Buek (1840), p. 100. According to M. Reißmann (1975), p. 140, the two Netherlanders were Gillis de Greve and Antoni de Hertoghe; however, the first names cited here accord with the prominence of the account holders, the property tax payments, and the information contained in H. Kellenbenz (1954), pp. 201–203, 207–209.

17   M. Reißmann (1975), p. 140.

18   See chapter 3, note 24.

19   For an analysis of the figures, see K. Zeiger (1936). The share of the Netherlanders decreased after 1622, and in 1629 disappeared completely. However, there were considerable back payments after the signing of the third contract in 1639. Payments made by the Portuguese were recorded disparately in the account books of the City Treasury.

20 In the 1614 list, payments are entered for only 12 of 25 persons; in the 1616 list, for only 15 of 34 persons. Because for the 15 names common to both lists a payment is indicated in only one list, the second list was probably a supplement to the first. But even if both lists are combined, entries are missing for 16 persons, among them several economically important members of the community. Overall, their payments come to a total of only 799 marks (391 marks in 1614, 408 marks in 1616), while the contract specified payments of 1,000 marks. The table includes only those persons for whom the amount of payment is known for one of the two years.

21 M. Studemund-Halévy (2000), pp. 790–795.

22 H. Kellenbenz (1955), p. 296. Conversion according to M. Reißmann (1975), p. 135.

23 The next highest of the 17 contributors gave only 96 marks; M. Grunwald (1902), p. 36.

24 He does not appear in the tax list of 1656, because he had already died; M. Studemund-Halévy (2000), pp. 762–763.

25 J. F. Voigt (1912). See also K.-J. Lorenzen-Schmidt (1979), p. 24 for more information on the local bond market. Wills could also give us insight into the composition of total assets. Wills have survived for both Hamburg and Portugal, some in the case of Hamburg, many in that of Portugal, and it would surely pay to analyze them systematically. However, it is difficult to extract usable information about the total assets of merchants because they do not contain absolute totals, but only descriptions of shares. Nonetheless, Martin Reißmann evaluated all available wills of Hamburg merchants and supplemented the data with legacy lists from legal proceedings, although he considered them to be partially unreliable. Reißmann's data are a relatively undifferentiated lot, and, as he himself has stated, the classification system he used for different classes of assets is anything but satisfactory; M. Reißmann (1975), pp. 137–138, 147–149.

26 In 1619 Johann and Hartich von Spreckelsen were in 63rd place in terms of turnovers. Dietmar Koel, the elder, was in 102nd place, other members of his family had even lower turnovers.

27 Their family names are mentioned among the account holders with very low turnovers, if at all.

28 A. Fuchs (1921), p. 137.

29 C. Amsinck (1886), part 1, pp. 50–54.

30 J. M. Lappenberg (1851), pp. 274–276; R. Hauschild-Thiessen (1974), p. 35.

31 H. Schwindrazheim (1930), pp. 140–141.

32 H.-D. Loose (1968), pp. 144–145.

33 H. A. Lier (1896).

34 H. Geisenheimer (1912), pp. 24–27, 44–45.

35 M. Studemund-Halévy (2002), pp. 158, 160.

36 "... gefahren in einer schönen mit Sammet gefütterten Kutschen. Neben der Kutschen lieff ein Diener in Liverey gekleidet. Und als der Kutscher still hielte, machte der Diener, welcher ich höre, ein Christ gewesen, nach tiefer *Reverenz* die Kutschen auf und hob einen alten Mann heraus, welcher einen langen seydenen Talar anhatte. Ich dachte, es müsse entweder der Bischoff oder ein abgelebter Fürst oder Graf seyn. Ich zohe meinen Huth ab so tieff als wenn es der Churfürst von Sachsen wäre und sagte zu einer Frauen, wer ist doch der Herr? Die ehrliche fromme Frau antwortete mit lachendem Munde: Er ist ein Jude, allein er wird genennet der reiche Jude. Ich könnte mich nicht genug darüber verwundern"; cited in J. J. Schudt ([1714] 1922), p. 375.

37 "Der sogenandte reiche Jude Manuel Texera, der zu meiner Zeit anno 1684 und folgenden Jahren lebte, war der Königin in Schweden Christina Resident, fuhr in einer kostbahren

Carosse, darauf hinten und vorne einige und gemeiniglich Christliche Diener stunden, welche mit grosser *Reverenz* bey dem Ein- und Aussteigen ihn bedienten, fuhr er über den grossen Neuen Marckt, so stunde ihm die gantze Haupt-Wache im Gewehr, er wohnte in einem fürtrefflichen Pallast, große Herren gaben ihm *Visiten* und spielten mit ihm"; J. J. Schudt ([1714] 1922), p. 374.

38 M. Studemund-Halévy (2002), p. 161

39 "Der Herr Resident Teixeira macht der Stadt große Ehre, weil er sich bemüht, die Fremden zu ehren und ihnen zu schmeicheln und die Bürger der Stadt mit großer Vorsicht und Liebe zu behandeln, sodass einem sein prächtiges Haus wie ein Theater und ein Gasthaus der Höflichkeit dünkt"; cited in M. Studemund-Halévy (2002), pp. 173–174.

40 M. Studemund-Halévy (2000), pp. 379–384.

41 Ibid., pp. 762–763; AHL, Nachlass Hagedorn, Packen 11–3, fl. 530–567 (StAHH, Reichskammergericht, F 34).

42 See also J. G. Gallois (1870), vol. 2, p. 1282, according to which the citizens complained that the Portuguese Jews lived in "big houses" but paid hardly any taxes.

43 "... 2 Mohren welche einander gefreyet." Another "*malate*" (probably a mulatto) lived with his wife and children "outside before the gate" [Draussen furm Thore]; see A Cassuto (1931), p. 69.

44 B. N. Teensma (1976), p. 14.

45 "... Mohren gehabt, in ihren Diensten gebraucht oder nach Belieben damit geschaltet"; cited in M. Studemund-Halévy (2000), pp. 665–667.

46 "Gar statliche Herren und Fürnämer Bürger-Häuser meistenteils nach Neuer oder auch Holländischer Art gebauet finden sich in Hamburg überflüssig, die Inwändig dan auf das bekwämligste mit Zimmern zu Gnüge versähen und auf das Reinligste mit Bildern,Gemälden, Snizwärken, Steinernen Tafelfloren, Kronen, Armleuchtern u.s.w. sich schauen lassen mügen"; K. v. Hövelen (1668), p. 64-65.

47 H. Schwindrazheim (1930), pp. 180–181.

48 "Kaume wird eine Stadt in Deutschland an Vihlheit der so Schönen umligenden Lustgarten Hamburg gleichen"; K. v. Hövelen (1668), p. 134.

49 "Nicht nur auf Sontags- und Feierfäst-Zeit, sondren auch sonst Täglich im Frühling, Sommer und Lustigen Herbst-Tagen sihet man etliche Hundert Carossen teils von Altona, teils vom Steintohre zu Abends herein kommen, welche Carossen mit Vohrnämen Wolausgepuzten sich auf den Lusthöfen im Ham, Bilwarder, Ottensen, Neumülen u.s.w. verlustirten Personen besäzet sind"; ibid., p. 123.

50 "Continuandosi la strada verso il sudetto Berghendorff, si mira vna quantità di Palazzotti, case, e casini leggiadramente posti gli vni dietro a gli altri, con giardini, horti, passeggi, e prospettiue così vaghe, che sembra vna scena, ò girarchia. In questi luoghi, delitiosi e puliti sogliono i Cittadini di quando in quando, ne tempi fuori dell'inuerno trasferirsi huomini, e donne a ricreatione, in modo tale, che particolarmente ne giorni di festa si vede moltitudine incredibile di persone d'ogni qualità ad vscire per diuertirsi con gran numero di carrozze. Fuori della porta di Duntar vi è vn'altro Borgo chiamato Ependorff, doue pur sono case, e giardini di delitie"; G. Gualdo Priorato (1674), p. 106.

51 "... alles Schlemmen und Prassen, sogar jede Art von Wildpret, ... von dem statuarischen Speisezettel streng ausgeschlossen"; O. Beneke (1886), p. 53.

52 "Ich kam in manches Bürgers Hauß und sahe so schöne ausgebutzte Sähl, darinnen alles glänzte, darinn so manche schöne künstliche Schilderey hing, daß meine Augen sich nicht genugsam darinn kunten ersättigen. Ich sahe, daß *privat*-Leute *Panquetten* und Gastereyen hielten, und solche köstliche *Tractamenten*, so vielerley *Confect* aufftragen liessen, daß ich

dergleichen an Fürstlichen Höfen nicht gesehen habe, wann Fürstliche Kindtaufen und dergleichen Solennitäten sind gehalten worden"; cited in W. Beutin (1994), p. 145.
53 "Die Kleider- und Luxusordnungen werden meist beobachtet. Und es ist nicht gestattet, daß ein Mann oder eine Frau aus dem Volke ihre Kleider mit Gold- oder Silberbändern schmücken oder einen Diamant im Ringe tragen. Wenn die Frauen in der Öffentlichkeit erscheinen, verhüllen sie sich meist mit Binden und schwarzen Kapuzen und außerdem wickeln sie sich in ein schwarzes Tuch (das sie Regenkleid nennen) ein, das ihnen als Mantel dient. Hochzeiten, Begräbnisse und Taufen entbehren meist des Prunkes. Und so ist das Leben in vielen Dingen den Bräuchen der Holländer gemäß gestaltet, nämlich nach den Ordnungen des Handels, der bares Geld dem Schmuck und übermäßigem Aufwand vorzuziehen heißt und so eher zur Habsucht neigt, als zum Übermut"; A. Fuchs (1921), pp. 135–137.
54 J. M. Pedreira (1995), pp. 294–317.
55 ANTT, TSO, Inquisição de Lisboa, proc. 10451, fl. 33–34.

Chapter 9

1 H. Kaelble (1990).
2 H. Kellenbenz (1958), p. 452.
3 In the introduction to his *Unternehmerkräfte im Hamburger Spanien- und Portugalhandel*, Kellenbenz shows little sympathy for historians who wish to derive "primarily factual contiguities" from the sources and work with pertinent statistics. This remark was specially aimed at Ernst Baasch; H. Kellenbenz (1954), pp. 11–13.
4 H. Kellenbenz (1958), p. 111.
5 During the first year, the Portuguese together paid 1,902 marks; during the second 1,179 marks. Kellenbenz's figures are slightly different. Total receipts came to 57,885 marks and 46,863 marks; StAHH, Kämmerei I Nr. 28, Bd. 1, 2, and 3; these figures had already been calculated at Kellenbenz's time in K. Zeiger (1936).
6 H. Kellenbenz (1958), pp. 111, 478. He also used a 1605 register of the certificates issued for the Spanish authorities, which supposedly gave a "good overview" of trade and the merchants involved in it. Of the 110 persons named there, only one was a Portuguese. Kellenbenz explained this by saying that the Portuguese Jews traded under false names; however, he gave no evidence for this claim; ibid., p. 110.
7 In 1632 the affected regions included the Iberian Peninsula, France, and the North (especially Gothenburg); in 1647 also the Baltic coast (Danzig, Elbing, Königsberg), England, the southern Netherlands, France, Italy, and the Caribbean (Barbados).
8 E. Pitz (1961), pp. XXII–XXXII; O.-E. Krawehl (2001), p. 10.
9 StAHH, Admiralitätskollegium, F3, Bd. 1 to 8.
10 StAHH, Admiralitätskollegium, F4, Bd. 1 to 15.
11 A critical edition of the Hamburg Admiralty customs books from the eighteenth century was undertaken within the framework of a major project funded by the German Research Foundation (DFG), which resulted in a book titled *Hamburger Handelsstatistiken im 18. Jahrhundert*, finally published in 1997. Although the project was meant to provide a "service for varied future research," neither the underlying digital database nor its structure (which could have been taken as a model for the present evaluation) were ever made public; see A. Kunz (1997); J. Schneider et al. (2001); K. Weber (2000).

12　Such voyages may be found in the notarial files; see for Amsterdam C. Lesger (2006), pp. 200–202; D. M. Swetschinski (2000), p. 123.

13　This includes an insignificant number of unclear cases and the Italians and English.

14　Trading companies are counted as a single "head."

15　See note 13.

16　Here are also taken into account those merchants for whom there is no explicit evidence but a well-founded reason to assign the religious denomination (see the detailed explanations in the appendix).

17　Salt, which had been quite important in the Iberia trade, also fell under the alien trading ban; however, as already indicated (see chapter 1, note 10) there were irregularities in recording the salt trade in the Admiralty customs books. Among these is that a great many of the salt importers cannot be found in the citizen rolls, nor can they have been Portuguese or contract Netherlanders. Their legal status is unclear in most cases. A quantitative analysis would therefore serve no purpose.

18　See, for example, R. Postel (1992), p. 24.

19　Not all goods subject to customs duties were specified, which is why the sums of the shares are lower than the total imports and exports.

20　These may either have been varied or difficult-to-describe commodities, or commodities prohibited for trade which were therefore not specified.

21　For example, R. Ehrenberg (1885), p. 319.

22　D. M. Swetschinski (2000), p. 105.

23　This applies only to the entire group, not necessarily to the individual merchants.

24　In addition to the merchants listed, this includes an insignificant number of Italians, English, mixed trading companies, and unclear cases.

25　See note 24.

26　See note 24.

Chapter 10

1　Among other things, such legislation regulated mercantile rights, commercial partnerships, commissions, maritime trade and freight, brokerage, maritime insurance, bonds and shares, bills of exchange, and bankruptcy; see S. Lammel (1976).

2　G. H. Kirchenpauer (1841); L. Gelder and M. Fischer (1991), pp. 11–14; D. Justino (1994).

3　"20 reisende frembde Kaufleute"; G. H. Kirchenpauer (1841), p. 5. The Exchange building, which was erected about 20 years later, was, however, financed exclusively by cloth merchants.

4　It is not clear when the term *bolsa* (i.e., bourse, exchange) came to mean the particular place. In the Middle Ages the term was used in the sense of maritime insurance; since the fifteenth century also in the sense of the common fund of the brokers. At the latest since the seventeenth century the word has been used in its current meaning of exchange; D. Justino (1994), pp. 26–27.

5　D. de Góis ([1554] 1996), p. 27.

6　AHL, Nachlass Hagedorn, Packen 9–1, fl. 557 (Blank, Mandatensammlung I, p. 162, 163); fl. 688 (StAHH, Senat, Cl. VII, Lit. La, Nr. 3, Vol. 2c).

7　E. Baasch (1915), vol. 1, pp. 706–711, 516.

8　D. Justino (1994), p. 8.

9   D. Justino (1994), pp. 6–20; U. Beukemann (1912).

10   ANTT, TSO, Inquisição de Lisboa, proc. 14409, fl. 4.

11   R. Ehrenberg (1885), p. 313; H. Kellenbenz (1954), pp. 280–281; H. Kellenbenz (1958), pp. 200–201.

12   U. Beukemann (1912), p. 485.

13   Other specializations included fats, iron, fish oil, pitch, and tar (9); money (9); wine (8); grain (8); bills of exchange (6); pelts and leather (5); chartering and sale of ships (4); linen (4); silk, cotton, and woolen fabrics (3); houses and estates (3); and wooden goods (1). In addition there were 22 Portuguese Jews whose specializations, if any, are unknown; see U. Beukemann (1912), p. 561.

14   Brokers in Lisbon held identity papers (*cartas dos corretores*) as early as 1342.

15   GA, Archief 5075, inv. no. 619X (page numbers given for this book refer to the digitized microfilm version; the original source is unpaginated); H. Kellenbenz (1954), p. 284; W. Sillem (1883), p. 554. Ruttens is the only Hamburg notary from this time whose files have survived. In 1610 he went to Amsterdam and continued his work there, taking with him his Hamburg archives. For the background, see W. Sillem (1883), p. 532; H. Kellenbenz (1954), p. 284.

16   S. Bachmann (2017); R. Postel (2001), pp. 10–12; H. Schultze-von Lasaulx (1961), pp. 12–36.

17   S. A. Gomes (2005).

18   GA, Archief 5075, inv. no. 619X, MF, pp. 439–440. Documents of the Judges Conservators of the Germans from the seventeenth century have not survived.

19   Maritime insurance law was codified neither in Portugal nor in Hamburg; it is probable that the regulations current in the Antwerp Exchange were used in both places; see A. H. Marques (1977), p. 99; G. A. Kiesselbach (1901), pp. 110, 131–133. In Hamburg, in case of damages, the insured party gave a detailed accounting to a notary who was appointed for the purpose and confirmed by the City Council. He then calculated the amount of the damages. Originally these notaries were Netherlandish jurists, and until about 1605 the office was held by the aforementioned Pieter Ruttens. When his successor, also a Netherlander, died in 1611, the City Council attempted to find an expert replacement in Antwerp or Amsterdam. Apparently the Council had no success, because eventually Pieter Heusch acquired the office, although he was not a notary but a merchant. From 1639 onward a "dispatcher" (*Dispacheur*), who was proposed by the merchants and nominated by the Admiralty, was given the task; G. A. Kiesselbach (1901), pp. 122, 130–131. If the damages eventuated in a lawsuit, the case was decided in the first instance by a court of arbitration consisting of three expert arbitrators selected for the particular case; G. A. Kiesselbach (1901), pp. 121–122. These arbitrators were not necessarily citizens, as is evident from an arbitration that began in the early 1650s. Although whether a Jew could serve as arbitrator was controversial, it did occur repeatedly; G. A. Kiesselbach (1901), p. 24. If no agreement could be reached through arbitration within three months, the case went to the court of the Admiralty for a ruling; see G. A. Kiesselbach (1901), p. 129.

20   A. H. Marques (1977), pp. 21–37, 69–89, 110, 250; F. Espinosa (1972); C. Amsinck (1894), p. 466. The significance of Portuguese insurers in trips between Hamburg and the Iberian Peninsula in the seventeenth century is unclear. Almost all of the ships were of northern European origin, especially Hanseatic, Dutch, and Danish vessels which probably were generally insured in Hamburg or Amsterdam.

21   "... frei oder unfrei"; G. A. Kiesselbach (1901), p. 125.

22   "... so de Conossemente niet Conforme diese Policen luden, sol solches niet prejuditzeren oder hinderlick sin"; G. A. Kiesselbach (1901), pp. 125–126.

23 G. A. Kiesselbach (1901), pp. 32, 41.

24 "Sie sagen so; laßen wyr Unsere wahren versichern, so nimpt die praemie den vortheil weg, laßen wyr aber nicht versicheren, müßen wyr in den Sorgen stehen, daß daß Capital gar auff den Lauff gehe und werden die Leute fast zaghafft, nachdemahl eine Zeithero So viel Schade zur See geschehen"; E. Merck (1856), p. 64.

25 G. A. Kiesselbach (1901), pp. 26–27.

26 E. Merck (1856), p. 95.

27 G. A. Kiesselbach (1901), pp. 15, 16, 20, 22, 24, 38.

28 The City Council, however, exercised ultimate supervision and conducted the negotiations with the imperial authorities, the magistrates of the imperial cities, and foreign governments; see R. Postel (1992), pp. 21–22; G. Ahrens (1962); E. Maack (1935); see also W. Behringer (1990); Behringer (2003).

29 G. Ahrens (1962), p. 35.

30 In addition to the Hamburg messenger service, there was also the postal service of the Princely House of Thurn and Taxis, which was privileged by the emperor. It had had an office in Hamburg since 1616, along with the post offices of various imperial princes of the surrounding region. Nonetheless, the messenger service was for many years able to compete, and for merchants it remained the most important connection between Hamburg and Amsterdam.

31 E. Baasch (1915), vol. 1, pp. 514, 516.

32 "Das Postwäsen ist in Hamburg sehr Wol ingerichtet"; K. v. Hövelen (1668), p. 133.

33 "... die Seele des Commercii, gleich als das Commercium die Seele der Stadt"; E. Baasch (1915), vol. 1, p. 438.

34 "... allemal auf einen Donnerstag, da keine Posten abgehen und die Kaufleute in mehrerer Frequenz erscheinen können"; Windischgrätzscher Rezess of 1674, art. 19; E. Baasch (1915), vol. 1, p. 717.

35 Letters were first sent to Spain. From there, since the beginning of the sixteenth century, the mail continued by way of the postal service operated by the Taxis family and financed by the Spanish Crown, which connected Spain with France, the Burgundian-Netherlandish provinces, southern Germany, the Habsburg residence in Innsbruck, the Habsburg lands along the Danube, and Italy; see G. Ferreira (1964), p. 72; E. C. Cardoso (1999); M. Dallmeier (1990), pp. 24–25; A. Koch (1955).

36 In the sixteenth century, the postmaster-general was still named by the king. In 1606, Felipe III leased the position for the extraordinarily large sum of 70,000 cruzados to Luís Gomes da Mata, a descendent of the influential Gomes d'Elvas merchant and banking family. For the next 200 years his family held this very lucrative position. As in Hamburg, where the messenger service had since the middle of the seventeenth century been leased out to citizens who bid the highest and could in turn sublease the position, leasing had considerable negative long-term effects on mail transport in Portugal.

37 E. Baasch (1915), vol. 1, p. 483.

38 E. Merck (1856), pp. 12, 13, 89, 226. I assume that the notation of dates in Lisbon followed the New Style and those in Hamburg the Old Style. If time was of the essence, a letter could be sent by express mail, in which case it took only about a month from one city to reach the other. Thus, in 1681 the mayor wrote his son: "In reference to your letter, I was amazed that it took so short a time to arrive, such that you wrote it on January 3 and I received it on February 4. Whereupon Sieur Gerd Burmester said that this letter had been sent by *expressen* (as you confirm in your letter), which rarely happens, and

otherwise takes many more days to arrive" [Nun, auff Deinen Brieff zu kommen, so habe Mich verwundert das derselbe in so kurtzer Zeit, als da Du denselben den 3ten *January* geschrieben und er Mirh den 4 *Febr.* eingereichet worden, übergekommen, darauff sagte S[ieu]r Gerdt Burm[mester] das dieser Brieff mit einem *expressen* (wie Du den auch in Deinem Schreiben meldest) sei übergekommen, welches selten geschehe und sonsten Sie etliche tage später über kemen]; E. Merck (1856), p. 13. Somewhat later he reported: "Your letter from Lisbon using the *ordinari* was 5 weeks and 3 days old, but this letter of May 10, sent by *extraordinari*, was only 4 weeks and 3 days old, which is an entire 8 days difference" [Deine Schreiben aus Lisabon bei der *ordinari* sein alt 5 wochen und 3 tage, dieses Schreiben aber vom 10 May bei der *extraordinari* war nur 4 wochen und 3 tage alt, das es also gantzer 8 tage *differiret*]; E. Merck (1856), p. 39. According to Jürgen Schlimper, in 1650 an event that took place in Spain or Portugal took about 60 days to appear in a German newspaper; J. Schlimper (1999), p. 174.

39   "Die Wege sind so tieff und unbrauchbar, daß der reisende Man kaum passiren kann und gehen die Posten dahero auch gar langsahm und unrichtig. Allhie mangeln Unß 2 Posten von Franckfurt, 2 von Antwerpen und 2 von Pariß auch mehr andere; am verschienen Freytag, alß 20ten dieseß waren wyr die Hispanischen Brieffe vermuhten, allein biß dato sein sie noch nicht angekommen, welcheß die bösen Wege causiren"; E. Merck (1856), p. 66.

40   E. Merck (1856), p. 29.

41   H. Kellenbenz (1954), p. 26.

42   "... das Du nicht so frey von der *Religion* schriebest, den es möchte ohngefehr ein brief aufgefangen werden und würdestu ungelegenheit haben"; E. Merck (1856), p. 89.

43   H. Böning (2007), p. 123.

44   Earlier, Meyer and his father-in-law Hans Schrenck had published a so-called *"geschriebene Zeitung."* These newsletters, sold since the sixteenth century, were handwritten periodicals, which, among other things, drew their information from merchant correspondences. The best-known are the so-called Fugger newsletters; see C. Prange (1978), pp. 46–47; H. Bode (1908), pp. 24–25. Letters written by merchants were deemed of lower interest than private correspondence between business partners because an informational head start was almost as important as the information itself.

45   C. Prange (1978), p. 74; H. Reincke (1958), pp. 210–214. Because of the Exchange's importance as a news exchange, the later newspaper publishers Georg Greflinger, Thomas von Wiering, and Nicolaus Spieringk also had their offices in the immediate vicinity of the Exchange; C. Prange (1978), p. 144.

46   M. Morineau (1985); H. Bode (1908), p. 32. In Hamburg, such information long remained subject to secrecy; see E. Baasch (1902), pp. 122–126.

47   A remark by Mayor Schulte to his son speaks for the quality of the diplomatic reports in the newspapers: "Don't write me anything about the Prince of Savoy, especially since I learn everything much better from the *Gazetten*" [Von dem Printzen von Savoja schreib Mihr nur nichtß, zu mahlen Ich auß den Gazetten alleß beßer erfahre]; E. Merck (1856), p. 125.

48   "Die wol eingerichtete Avisen-Häuser und Zeitungsbuden sind Hie nicht zuvergässen, gestalt in Hamburg zweierlei, Deutsche und Holländische, gedruckt wärden u. s. w. Ausländische, Deutsche, Swedische, Holländische, Franzsche, Latinische s. a. m. Novellen (Worauf die Ambassadeurs, Residenten und Agenten samt etlichen Posthalteren und Zeitungdrükker, um die Correspondenz zu haben, Viles wänden) kommen so wol Schriftlich als Gedrükket ein. Manghe Kaufherren selbsten sind Libhaber Einige mit zuhalten"; K. v. Hövelen (1668), p. 134.

49 J. J. McCusker (2002), pp. 70–71. The newspapers in the comprehensive collection of the Bremen State and University Library contain almost no information that would have been of immediate use to a merchant. The statistical analysis conducted by Jürgen Wilke on the *Wöchentliche Zeitung auß mehrerley örther* found that in 1622 as in 1674 only about 2 percent of the information was business-related. The same was true of other newspapers; J. Wilke (1984), pp. 130, 152, 207, 213.

50 C. Prange (1978), p. 157.

51 C. Prange (1978), pp. 153–156.

52 *Gazetas da Restauração* (1641–1648), *Gazeta de Lisboa* (1641–1642?), *Le Mercure Portugais* (1643), *Mercurius Ibernicus* (1645), and between 1663 and 1667 the *Mercúrio Português*; see E. G. Dias (2006).

53 A. Belo (2001).

54 J. J. McCusker and C. Gravesteijn (1991), p. 22.

55 H. Bode (1908), pp. 9–13; C. Lesger (2006), p. 233.

56 A. H. Marques (1987).

57 "Mit S[ieu]r Gerdt Burm[ester] habe wegen der Pryß Courante geredet, der will Mihr sein exemplar geben und will Ich selbige allhie dan drücken laßen und Dir etzliche exemplaria übersenden, auch die Prysen der wahren in blanco lassen"; E. Merck (1856), p. 83.

58 "... das solche Cours-Zettuln nicht undienlich vor den Kaufmann und Commertien weren"; E. Baasch (1915), vol. 1, p. 308.

59 The use of bills of exchange also circumvented the Christian ban on lending money for interest; see also F. Irsigler (2008), pp. 67–68.

60 D. Justino (1994), pp. 29–33; V. Rau (1984d); D. Peres (1971), pp. 29–32.

61 M. Neumann (1863); M. North (1996a); M. North (2000), pp. 32–33, 91–92.

62 R. Ehrenberg (1889), p. 151.

63 R. Ehrenberg (1896), p. 67; M. North (1991), p. 8.

64 M. Neumann (1863), p. 181.

65 For the relatively rare use of bills of exchange in Nuremberg, Amsterdam, and other places, see the evidence in L. F. Peters (1994), pp. 114–117.

Chapter 11

1 N. Luhmann (1968); U. Frevert (2003); S. Gorißen (2003); C. Hillen (2007). I disagree with Timothy Guinnane, who argues that the concept of trust is superfluous. He ignores the irrational part of trust and overestimates the belief in the factuality of information; T. Guinnane (2005). A similar critique applies to A. Greif (1993).

2 A. Greif (1993); A. Greif (2006).

3 "Treu und Glauben unter den Menschen, daß einer dem andern sein Gut anvertrauet, hinborgt und übergiebt, in der Hoffnung, daß er ihn dafür vergnugen und bezahlen werde"; "Der Mensch hat guten *Credit*, er stehet bey ihm in gutem *Credit*, das ist: man setzt ein Vertrauen auf ihn." At the same time "giving credit" also meant "giving someone a loan" [einem auf Borg geben] and that was "as hard to separate from the merchants as heat from fire" [so wenig von der Kauffmannschafft als die Hitze von den Feuer, zu trennen]. In other words, on the one hand credit defined the trustworthiness of a merchant; on the other, it also meant the business transaction that was negotiated on the basis of trust, i.e., the consignment of goods in the expectation of monetary compensation. In its definition of credit,

Zedler's *Universallexikon* did not, however, mention the lending of money for interest; J. H. Zedler (1733), vol. 6, col. 1559.

4 "Du Gott Lob in Deinem Beruff und Handlung *avançirest* und in dem *credit* bist, daß Dir auff viel tausende sich belauffende Güter unter handen gethan und anvertrawet werden"; "in guten *credit*"; E. Merck (1856), p. 95.

5 "Auß Deinem Schreiben ... habe Ich zwar ungern ersehen den Schaden, welcher die Freunde getroffen, allein weil daß Weib in vollen *credit* gewesen, so können die Freunde Dir auch nichtß *imputiren*, welcheß Sie auch nicht thuen"; "Ich habe auch auß Deinem Schreiben angemercket, daß daß Weib ein loseß Betrieglicheß weib muß gewesen sein"; "Ich bedawre den guten Henrich Burmester, welchem eß, wie Ich vernemme waß hart getroffen hat, deßen Mittele aber keinen großen Schaden ertragen können. ... Nun der reiche Gott, der noch viel unvorgeben hat, wolle den Freunden und auch dem guten Henr[ich] Burm[ester] diesen Ihnen zugewachsenen Schaden mit seinem Göttlichen Segen reichlich wiederumb ... für Solch und dergleichen Betrieglichen Menschen in Gnaden bewaren"; ibid., pp. 202–203.

6 "... nicht allemahl zum Besten und nach gefallen lauten"; "Nun berichte hierauff mit wenigen, daß solcheß alleß der Weldt lauff sei"; ibid., p. 216.

7 "Wenn der *Credit* unter den Kauffleuten aufgehoben ware, so würde zugleich alles Commercium darnieder liegen"; "Mangel an *Credit* viele die gern was rechtschaffenes thun wolten, in das Unvermögen setzet,daß sie ihre nützlichen *Concepte* in der Geburt ersticken, und sich nur nach ihrer kurtzen Decke strecken mussen"; J. H. Zedler (1733), vol. 6, col. 1559.

8 "... godtlob keine burgen notigk, aldieweile ich nemichlichen in ehren und mit guten credit bekant"; AHL, Nachlass Hagedorn, Packen 9–1, fl. 31–41 (StAHH, Senat, Cl. VIII, N. XXXI, Nr. 3a, fl. 123–125).

9 "... welche ich viel lieber wolte entberet und nicht gewonnen, als solchen grossen Schimpff erlitten haben"; "der von Sprekelsen mir und die vielgeliebten meinigen unverantwortlicher weise beschimpffet, groeblich Injuriret und darmit entlich so viel verursachet, daß die Leute, so meinen kauffmans Credit erhalten und meine Nahrung befuerdert, wegen diesen mir offentlich zugefuegten schimpff und folgend falschen ansprengen von mir abgetretten, dadurch ich dann gaentzlich meiner taeglichen Nahrung entsetzet und ins eusserste Verderben gestuertzet"; M. Schmidt (1638).

10 "So ist auch am verschienen Sonnabendt der Junge David Schulte deß sehl. Lorentz Schulten Sohn schulde halber außgetreten und Sich nacher Ottenßen auff seinen Garten *retiriret.* Dieser ist woll ein rechter Muhtwilliger *Bancrottirer,* welcher durch übermeßigeß Haushalten daß seinige verschlampampet und verbraßet hat. Er hielt 2 paar schöne Wagenpferde, fuhr alle tage auß, *dominirte* und Bancketirte alle tage, also daß auff solche arbeit kein ander Lohn erfolgen könnte"; E. Merck (1856), p. 127.

11 "He spoke with all kinds of people who offered to speak with him" [Fallava com toda sorte de gente que se offerecia fallar com elle]; ANTT, TSO, Inquisição de Lisboa, proc. 10451; "he dealt with all sorts of people, both Catholics as well as heretics" [tratava com toda a sorte de gente assi catholicos, como hereges]; ANTT, TSO, Inquisição de Lisboa, proc. 10442.

12 "Mein Raht ist, Du gebest einem jedtweden ... gute Wordte und machest gute *minen,* kanst doch bei Dir gedencken und thuen, waß Dir zuträglich sein mag, daß ist der Weldt lauff"; E. Merck (1856), pp. 73–74.

13 "Mein Sohn, wer hat keine Mißgönner? je beßer eß einem gehet, je mehr Mißgönner hat man"; "Du schreibest, das Sie Dich wurden haben etwaß abfragen wollen: aber Du bist kein Kindt, daß Sie Dihr hetten konnen was abfragen, besonderß hettestu Ihnen ja nur können andtwordten waß Du gewoldt und Sie wißen sollen"; ibid., pp. 22–23.

14   "... da Ich dan bequeme gelegenheit gehabt Dich und deinen *confrater* dem Hrn.
     Bümmelman zu *recommendiren*, derselbe rühmte Mihr sehr woll herauß, sagte auch, daß er
     bei dieser Post Euch andtwordten wollte"; ibid., p. 24.

15   "Dieser tage hat S[ieu]r Henr[rich] Buermeister ... an der Börse mit S[ieu]r Peter Juncker ge-
     redet und Deine Person *recommendiret*, der Sich den auch sehr woll hat erkleret, dabei aber
     gesaget, man möchte Ihm nur nahmkündig machen einige wahren, worauff nach Lißabon
     etwaß zu gewinnen"; ibid., p. 46.

16   "*Joh. Aug. Vossenholt* ermangelt auch nicht bei *occasie* bei einem und andern Dich zu *recom-
     mendiren*, sagt Mihr auch, daß er auff *Roan* Deinenthalben geschrieben habe"; ibid., p. 47.

17   "... wie wyr von Dich und Deinen *compagnonen* zu reden kamen, schrieb er ewer beider
     nahmen auff und sagt er wollte Euch an Ihn *recommendiren*, Euch etwaß in *commissis*
     zusenden"; ibid., p. 5.

18   "... über die maßen wollzufrieden und vergnüget were mit denen wahren, welche Du und
     Dein *confrater* Ihm mit neulichen Schiffen gesandt hettet"; "vermerckte, daß er mit ewer
     conduite, auch übergesandte Rechnungen wollvergnüget"; "waß mehr in der Handlung
     thuen"; ibid., p. 181.

19   "Lumpen und ungeschliffener kerl"; "solche wiederwertige *Compagnien*"; ibid., p. 129.

20   "Alleß muß man thuen umb der Leute Gewogenheit Beizubehalten und daß man in einem
     guten *praedicat* und Ruhm bleiben müge"; ibid., p. 223.

21   "... alß eine große Ehre hat *aestimiret* und auffgenommen"; "so viel guteß und wie ein Vatter
     bei Dir thete"; ibid., p. 180.

22   "... gerne in einem und andern nach begehren zu willn sein"; ibid., p. 16.

23   "... ein klein Päckchen worin die *curiosen nouvellen* und begehrte *oblaten* sein"; ibid.,
     pp. 86, 167, 241.

24   "... begehre nichtß umbsonst"; ibid., p. 59.

25   "... selbigeß von Ihm nicht genommen, anerwogen eß ein pagatel und besagter Consul Dir
     anderwertß einige Freundtschafft hinwiederumb dafür leisten kann"; ibid., p. 52.

26   Therefore F. Trivellato (2009a), A. Greif (1993) and others studied the problem of trust
     among merchants on the basis of merchant letters.

27   "Auff Deine *affaires* und *negotia* gib vor allen Dingen gute acht und unterhalte die *corre-
     spondentz* fleißig"; E. Merck (1856), p. 38.

28   "... der mit einem andern Briefe wechselt. Bey den Kaufleuten ist es derjenige, welcher mit
     einem anders so wohl in Waaren als Wechsel negotiiret, und welchen sie meistentheils nur
     ihren Freund nennen"; J. H. Zedler (1733), vol. 6, col. 1370.

29   F. Zunkel (1975); D. Burkhart (2006), pp. 11–43.

30   J. Nowosadtko (1994); S. Backmann and H.-J. Künast (1998), p. 14–15.

31   At the beginning of the negotiations around the second settlement contract, the Nether-
     landers living in Hamburg demanded that they be excluded from the restrictions of the
     Hamburg sumptuary laws, but were not successful; see A. Nikolajczyk (2006), p. 38.

32   "... that they were honorable and pure people as are all those of the German nation" [que era
     gente honrada e limpa como são todos os da nação alemaa]; ANTT, TSO, Conselho Geral,
     Habilitações, João, mç. 11, doc. 338.

33   P. A. d'Azevedo (1910), p. 186.

34   "Het moet een onverschaemen Juden sein, dat hij sonder fundamento solchen breef aen my
     schrifft"; AHL, Nachlass Hagedorn, Packen 11–3, fl. 186–265 (StAHH, Reichskammergericht,
     B 96).

35 "... daß es zugelassen sey, das man Christliche Interesse, aber keinen Juden-Wucher, als 10 [bis] 12 vons hundert nemen muege"; M. Schmidt (1638). In Hamburg, Jews, like all other businessmen, were subject to the same legally established maximum interest rate of 6 percent.

36 On the status of the *tudescos* (German Jews) and the Portuguese Jews' instrumentalization of their Iberian origins, see M. Studemund-Halévy (2000), pp. 41–43; Y. Kaplan (2000b); Y. Kaplan (2001).

37 Duarte Nunes da Costa was noted with this title in the Admiralty customs books; see, e.g., StAHH, Admiralitätskollegium, F4, Vol. 3, fl. 297. Manuel Teixeira was given this title in Mayor Schulte's letters; E. Merck (1856), p. 90.

38 See F. W. Graf (2004).

39 P. Benedict (2002), p. 538.

40 D. J. Penslar (2001), pp. 64–65; C. B. Stuczynski (2000). See also Manuel Martins Dormido's application for acceptance written to Cromwell in which he requested permission to live in London with his family. He argued that if England accepted the New Christians who had been driven out of Spain and Portugal, it would become the wealthiest, most populous, and most magnificent country in the world; A. M. Faria (2005), pp. 418–419.

41 M. Weber ([1904/1905] 1958); W. Sombart ([1911] 1913).

42 L. Brentano (1916), pp. 158–199; N. Z. Davis (1997), pp. 56–60.

43 Among other things, the hypothesis has been investigated with respect to biconfessional cities like Augsburg and Nîmes, as well as the United Provinces; see P. Benedict (2001); J. de Vries and A. van der Woude (1997). Friedrich Wilhelm Graf has advanced the thesis that religious and confessional discourses relating to business success should be understood as the expression of a perception of crisis by an insecure cultural elite, based on an experience of blocked development or relative underdevelopment. For this reason only consistent historicization of the discourses conducted in the eighteenth and nineteenth centuries could be productive; F. W. Graf (2004), p. 254; see also Y. Y. Lifshitz (2004), pp. 35–47; D. J. Penslar (2001), pp. 52–55; P. Benedict (2002), p. 539.

Chapter 12

1 "Qui vi sono mercanti, che hanno corrispondenza in tutte le Città principali d'Europa, doue i Vascelii Hamburghesi nauigano"; G. Gualdo Priorato (1674), p. 99.

2 See D. Hancock (2005) for characteristics and problems of trading networks and W. Schmidt-Rimpler (1915) for the development of the commission trade.

3 GA, Archief 5075, inv. no. 619X, MF, p. 262.

4 H. Kellenbenz (1954), pp. 111–113 (the family tree printed there is incorrect, as Barthold the younger and Joachim were brothers), 265, 297, 303.

5 GA, Archief 5075, inv. no. 619X, MF, pp. 372, 374.

6 See the many examples in H. Kellenbenz (1954), pp. 288–289.

7 For example in H. Kellenbenz (1954), p. 292.

8 GA, Not. Arch. 151, blz. 183; Not. Arch. 628, blz. 338–340; Not. Arch. 611A, blz. 267; Not. Arch. 380, blz. 729; Not. Arch. 645, blz. 799; Not. Arch. 942/933. According to the Hamburg Admiralty customs books, he was the Portuguese with the second largest turnover in trade with the Iberian Peninsula. After his death in 1644 his widow and children continued the

partnership he had founded, and in 1647 they were actually the Portuguese merchants who paid the highest amount of customs to the Admiralty.

9   GA, Not. Arch. 151, blz. 183–185.
10 GA, Not. Arch. 645, blz. 799.
11 GA, Not. Arch. 151, blz. 183–185.
12 GA, Not. Arch. 628, blz. 125, 126, 338–340.
13 GA, Not. Arch. 642, blz. 130, 141–142.
14 GA, Not. Arch. 151, blz. 183–185.
15 ANTT, TSO, Inquisição de Lisboa, proc. 6707; M. Studemund-Halévy (2000), p. 262. The year of death (1642) cited in Studemund-Halévy is incorrect, or else there were two different persons in Hamburg with that name.
16 GA, Archief 5075, inv. no. 619X, MF, p. 105.
17 GA, Not. Arch. 645B, blz. 1424–1427; Not. Arch. 646A, blz. 58, 59.
18 GA, Not. Arch. 645B, blz. 1424–1427; Not. Arch. 645, blz. 846.
19 H. Kellenbenz (1954), pp. 115, 234.
20 GA, Not. Arch. 665 (20), blz. 45–45v.
21 Koen, Not. Rec., SR 23, Nr. 2784; Koen, Not. Rec., SR 23, Nr. 2793; GA, Not. Arch. 629, blz. 32v–33v.
22 E.g. S. Wasserman and K. Faust (1994).
23 E.g. M. Kalus (2010).
24 Because of the comprehensive holdings and the detailed indexing of the notarial files in Amsterdam, the merchants who were active there are given special attention in historical research. Between 5 and 8 percent of the files in the Amsterdam city archive are accessible by way of a card index system comprising approximately 2 million cards with personal, professional, subject, and place indexes for the period between 1578 and 1800. In addition, a project supported by the Portuguese-Jewish community compiled all of the files in which Portuguese are mentioned before 1639, and published them in the form of English-language registers in the *Studia Rosenthaliana*. Although there exist notarial holdings of some significance from the seventeenth century in Portugal, scholars have up to now ignored these when examining the Portugal trade, opting instead to use the Amsterdam files; see, for example C. Antunes (2004). For Hamburg, with the exception of the notarial files kept by Pieter Ruttens cited in the present book, no other such files have survived from the seventeenth century. This is also the reason why H. Kellenbenz used the Amsterdam files in his *Sephardim an der unteren Elbe* (1958).
25 O. Gelderblom (2013), p. 94.
26 Account books would be a more reliable set of sources for investigating trading networks. In contrast to notarial files, which contain only isolated transactions, account books give us an integral picture of the nature of personal trading networks. Unfortunately, such books from the seventeenth century are lacking for both Hamburg and Portugal.
27 For this purpose Roitman used the Amsterdam card index system, the registers in the *Studia Rosenthaliana* (see also n. 24), and an edition of Amsterdam shipping contracts for the Baltic region; P. H. Winkelman (1977–1983). Roitman processed 608 records for the first three merchants cited; 709 records for the rest.
28 J. V. Roitman (2009), pp. 93–94. It is not clear, however, whether these merchants really were leading members of the community. The members of the Nunes da Costa family, for example, who undoubtedly disposed over an extraordinarily extensive and well-frequented network, do not appear in the Amsterdam notarial files nearly as often as the three merchants cited by Roitman. In Daniel Swetschinski's opinion, the business of at least one of them, Manuel Rodrigues Veiga, was not one of the "truly great firms"; nor does he

count the other two merchants as having belonged to the elite; D. M. Swetschinski (1981), p. 66.

29 J. V. Roitman (2009), p. 162.

30 Ibid., 232. The figures given here were calculated from her somewhat more complex data.

31 StAHH, Senat, Cl. VII Lit. Cb no. 4, vol. 1a no. 1b; StAHH, Admiralitätskollegium, F3 vols. 1, 2, and 8.

32 C. Amsinck (1886), part 1, pp. 35–37, 50–57.

33 "… als seinen Bruder lieben"; "in allen nach müglichkeit an die Handt gehen"; E. Merck (1856), pp. 14–15.

34 "Vor 8 tagen ist Mihr Dein Schreiben vom 31ten May wolgeliefert, worauß Ich … ersehen, … daß Du mit Deinem compagnon einen societät contract auff 5 Jahr geschloßen"; ibid., p. 41.

35 "… alß ein junger Mensch von 18 Jahren so fort [sein] eigen Herr geworden und [hätte seinen] Handel im nahmen Gotteß angefangen"; ibid., p. 15.

36 According to Inquisition registers, the following Hamburg merchant apprentices were housed with relatives or compatriots in Lisbon: Vicente Wulf was an assistant to his brother Jerónimo Wulf; Paulo Becker lived with his brother Guilherme Becker; João Christovão Frique worked for his uncle João Frique; João and Reinaldo Bockol lived at various times with their uncle João Bockol and worked for him as assistants; Jerónimo Eding was a shop assistant for Gaspar Verver, a Hamburger; Pedro Hagen and Nicolau Postel also worked for employers from Hamburg; ANTT, TSO, Inquisição de Lisboa, liv. 711, fl. 226, 359; liv. 712, fl. 84, 118, 172, 190; liv. 713, fl. 49, 227; liv. 715, fl. 13. Young Hamburgers who worked as shop assistants for Portuguese merchants included Julião Flecão, who worked for Vicente Pinel; António Volters, for Domingo Soares; Pedro Blanque, for Estevão de Azevedo; João Sudermann, for Rodrigo Machado de Siqueira; Pedro Rippe, for Dinis Simões Borralho; Gaspar Brocquman, for João Caldeira; João Buque, for António Rodrigues Lima; and Jacques da Maya, for Vicente de Bastos; ANTT, TSO, Inquisição de Lisboa, liv. 710, fl. 1, 66; liv. 711, fl. 194, 484, unpaginated; liv. 712, fl. 230; liv. 713, fl. 304; liv. 714, fl. 58.

37 ANTT, TSO, Inquisição de Lisboa, proc. 6707.

38 ANTT, TSO, Inquisição de Lisboa, proc. 12387.

39 J. A. Tavim (2009), p. 379.

40 "Von Contracten und allerley handtierungen," "Von ehrlicher Vertrawung, Verheyrahtung und Brautschatz," and "Von Gesellschaft oder Mascopey"; in Hamburger Stadtrecht ([1605] 1978) part 2, chapters 10 and 11.

41 "In Gottes Nhamen mit minen Vatter in den tuch oder lakenhandel in Compagnie von Liven van der Eighenen Ao. 1602 d. 24. Februarij eingelecht"; C. Amsinck (1886), part 1, p. 54.

42 "… ein gut stück geldes"; E. Merck (1856), p. 130.

43 M. Reißmann (1975), pp. 238–239.

44 See the survey by A. Nikolajczyk (2006), p. 37. One of the few exceptions was the Netherlandish de Greve merchant family of which several first-generation immigrants married into important Hamburg families, namely the Beckmann, Sillem, and Rodenburg families; H. Kellenbenz (1954), pp. 111, 128, 136, 141.

45 M. Reißmann (1975), p. 330; W. Sillem (1883), p. 514.

46 W. Sillem (1883), p. 555; StAHH, Deutsch-Evangelisch-Reformierte Gemeinde, II A b 1, May 19, 1606. In the known instances, Lutheran-Netherlandish merchants married Reformed-Netherlandish merchants' daughters: Pieter Heusch married Marie van Meere, and in his second marriage Eva le Petit; his brother Gerard Heusch married Anna van Meere; and Peter Juncker married Anna Maria van der Straeten; H. Kellenbenz (1954), pp. 2010, 2013; W. Sillem (1883), pp. 516, 518–519.

47 ANTT, TSO, Inquisição de Lisboa, proc. 6707, fl. 117.

48 Between 1630 and 1699, 107 Hamburg Portuguese married in Amsterdam; D. M. Swetschinski (1981), p. 68.

49 D. M. Swetschinski (1981), pp. 178–181; M. Bodian (1987); I. S. Révah (1963).

50 D. M. Swetschinski (1981), pp. 160–161, 194, 252–253; Y. Kaplan (1993), p. 139.

51 Nikolaus Postel, one of the few Hamburgers who converted only after his marriage, declared before the inquisitors that he had lived as a Catholic since his arrival in Lisbon 17 years earlier, but had not registered with the Inquisition until then. He was 32 years old when he converted; his wife's name was Mariana de Sousa; ANTT, TSO, Inquisição de Lisboa, liv. 711, fl. 359, 375.

52 ANTT, TSO, Inquisição de Lisboa, liv. 210, fls. 331. The accusation apparently did not lead to a trial, at least as far as I have been able to ascertain.

53 One of the exceptions was Catarina Brotesser, who converted to Catholicism in 1649 at the age of 37. She had lived in Portugal for four or five years and was supposedly married to a Lutheran; ANTT, TSO, Inquisição de Lisboa, liv. 708, fl. 201. Anna Francina from Hamburg converted to Catholicism in 1686 and was married to a man whose name indicates a German origin, Arnaldo Molder; ANTT, TSO, Inquisição de Lisboa, liv. 714, fl. 72. The Hamburg merchant Cornelius Classen moved to Porto together with his wife Katharina Elisabeth née Stockfleth; M. Reißmann (1975), p. 247. Most of the Hamburgers who later returned to Hamburg remained single while in Portugal and married only after their return. Only Dietrich Gotthard Schlebusch is known to have married in Lisbon and brought his Portuguese wife with him to Hamburg, where he became a citizen in 1698. His children Vicente and Sebastiana Maria are entered in the church registers of the Hamburg Catholic community. M. Reißmann (1975), p. 245.

54 ANTT, TSO, Conselho Geral, Habilitações, Pedro, mç. 22, doc. 455.

55 ANTT, TSO, Conselho Geral, Habilitações, André, mç. 3, doc. 57.

56 ANTT, TSO, Conselho Geral, Habilitações, Teodósio, mç. 1, doc. 10.

57 ANTT, TSO, Conselho Geral, Habilitações, Teodósio, mç. 1, doc. 10; TSO, Conselho Geral, Habilitações, Diogo, mç. 8, doc. 196.

58 ANTT, TSO, Inquisição de Lisboa, liv. 212, fls. 19–28v.

59 ANTT, TSO, Conselho Geral, Habilitações, Teodósio, mç. 1, doc. 10.

60 "Ich kenne keine Familie alhie, da nicht zuweilen einige Mißverstendnus und Mißhelligkeiten ja auch unter Schwester und Brüdern zuweilen vorkommen sollten: exempla sunt odiosa, und habe keine Zeit solche in specie zu referiren, noch anzuziehen, den deren exempla gar zu viel sein"; E. Merck (1856), pp. 222–223.

61 ANTT, TSO, Inquisição de Lisboa, proc. 4718.

62 ANTT, TSO, Inquisição de Lisboa, proc. 10451.

63 B. N. Teensma (1976), pp. 8–9.

64 See, for example, Y. Kaplan (1993), p. 132.

65 The denunciation appears in a number of trials; it is printed in P. A. d'Azevedo (1910), pp. 191–192. See also ANTT, TSO, Inquisição de Lisboa, proc. 3922, proc. 12212, proc. 7276, proc. 11448.

66 ANTT, TSO, Inquisição de Lisboa, proc. 7276. However, in his confession Miguel Francês confuses Diogo/Jacob de Lima with his brother Elias.

67 J. Braden (2001), pp. 259–260, 512–513.

68 M. Studemund-Halévy (2000), p. 561. Kellenbenz was probably wrong about the year of death; see H. Kellenbenz (1958), p. 302.

69   M. Studemund-Halévy (2000), pp. 558–559.
70   M. Grunwald (1902), p. 7; Y. Kaplan (1993), pp. 133–134.

Chapter 13

1   M. Reißmann (1975), pp. 156–212; J. Bolland (1951); K. Friedland (1960).
2   Nonetheless, in 1675 three members of the Netherlandish de Hertoghe family and one member of the Mahieu family were accepted into the Company of England Travelers; M. Reißmann (1975), p. 209.
3   R. Postel (1992), pp. 9–21; see also G. H. Kirchenpauer (1841), pp. 13–28.
4   "... in swaren saken,unde wor dem gemenen besten düsser Stadt ane gelegen"; "dat ehnes Erssamen Rades behorliche overicheit in düssen allen unvorletzt blive"; cited in E.-C. Frentz (1985), pp. 282–283.
5   E. Baasch (1915), vol. 1, pp. 7–9.
6   E.-C. Frentz (1985); R. Postel (1992), pp. 23–31; E. Baasch (1899), p. 3.
7   Another slave fund, the *Casse der Stück von Achten* (Fund of the Pieces of Eight), had existed since 1622 under the leadership of the shipmaster elders. For more on the slave funds, see M. Ressel (2013).
8   This led to temporary differences between the Admiralty and segments of the citizenry; see G. Rückleben (1969), p. 6.
9   It was also called the Mesa do Espírito Santo dos Homens de Negócio (Board of the Holy Spirit of the Merchants); see E. M. Lobo (1965); E. M. Lobo (1963), pp. 35–36; D. G. Smith (1975), p. 164; J. M. Pedreira (1995), p. 447; E. de Lima (1958), p. 35.
10   E. M. Lobo (1963), pp. 37–49; D. G. Smith (1975), pp. 161–163.
11   D. G. Smith (1975), pp. 162–163.
12   "... alhie zu Hamburg zur See handelnde Kaufleute einhellig, daß sieben personen ihres mittels, als 6 aus den Erb. Kaufleuten, die da guten Handel und Correspondence sowoll umb die Ost- als West-See trieben, auch der Assecurantz sich bedienten, und einen Schiffer-Alten, möchten erwehlet werden, welche da alles und jedes, was dem heilsamen Commercio diensamb beobachteten, die drangsal und beschwerden, so demselben zustoßen mochten, E. Hochw. Rahte fleißigst hinterbrächten und cooperirten, daß solche in Zeiten gewehret oder bestmüglich geremediirt werden möchten"; cited in E. Baasch (1915), vol. 1, pp. 1–2
13   Ibid., p. 13.
14   Ibid., p. 6.
15   Ibid., p. 218; E. Baasch (1899), p. 33.
16   E. Baasch (1915), vol. 1, p. 332; E. Baasch (1899), p. 36.
17   E. Baasch (1915), vol. 1, p. 544.
18   Ibid., p. 216.
19   Ibid., p. 16.
20   For example, in 1695 there was some negotiation between the Commercial Deputation and the Spanish resident over certifications demanded by his government; ibid., p. 420.
21   Ibid., p. 421.
22   Ibid., pp. 425–426. In 1669, when Alexander Heusch succeeded his father as consul in Lisbon, he was installed by the Admiralty without any interference by the Commercial Deputation.

23 Ibid., pp. 639–641.

24 "... große Negotianten und Capitalisten"; "als Juden-Patronen, sondern als ehrliche Patrioten, die woll sehen, daß die Juden nicht über die Alpes oders Pireneische Gebirge hinüber ziehen, sondern, sobald sie aus dieser Stadt sind, ihren Fuß alsofort wieder auf diese Grenzen niederlassen, zu Altona ihr Commercium anfangen und daselbst eine grose Handlung zum grosen Nachteil dieser Stadt stabiliren werden"; "was die Handlung der Börse angienge, da sie, was ihre Synagogen oder Religio betreffend, damit nichts zu thun hetten"; cited in ibid., pp. 218–219.

25 Much the same held true for the members of the English Court. Only when the Commercial Deputation required support in negotiations with England did its members seek contact with English merchants; otherwise, they were extremely reluctant to do so; ibid., p. 217.

26 Ibid., pp. 271–274 (*Dispacheur*), 277 (*Taxadeur*), 181–183, 190, 199 (laws), 645–646 (expert opinions).

27 Ibid., pp. 183, 203.

28 "... das Commercium in schlechten Ruf ausserhalb der Stadt"; "erschien einmal das gemeine Volk in armis mit Prügeln und Stecken"; cited in ibid, p. 718.

29 For more on the Burmesters' family relationships, see C. Amsinck (1891), part 2, pp. LXXXII–LXXXIX.

30 E. Baasch (1915), vol. 2, pp. 899–904.

31 Ibid., vol. 1, p. 572.

32 "... weyl er bey seyner Zeyt das er bey dem löblichen Commertio gewesen, viel muehe gehabt und demselben ruemlich und sehr generoes mit vorgestanden"; cited in ibid., p. 635.

33 Ibid., pp. 717, 721; E. Baasch (1899), p. 12.

34 E. Baasch (1915), vol. 1, p. 720.

35 E. Baasch (1899), pp. 2–3, 7–8.

36 E. Baasch (1915), vol. 1, p. 544.

37 "... damit sich Niemand mit der ignorantz zu entschuldigen"; cited in E. Baasch (1899), pp. 13–17.

38 Ibid., p. 26.

39 "... daß mit dieser Supplic woll möchte nachgelassen sein, und man solche zurückgehalten haben, maßen solche und dergleichen Suppliquen diese Sache nicht heben wollten, sondern were nur gleich, wan man Olie ins Feuer gösse, allermassen allerhand davon spargiret [verbreitet] würde"; "also hinfüro mit dergleichen einzuhalten"; cited in ibid., pp. 9–10.

40 E. Baasch (1915), vol. 1, p. 682.

41 E. Baasch (1899), p. 11; E. Baasch (1915), vol. 1, pp. 558–560.

42 "... jeder seine Meinung hübsch hier sagen und auf der Börse schweigen"; cited in E. Baasch (1899), p. 24.

43 E. Baasch (1915), vol. 1, p. 11.

44 Ibid., p. 723; E. Baasch (1899), pp. 5–6, 10.

45 D. G. Smith (1975), pp. 165–167.

46 Ibid., p. 176.

47 That is, in the years 1644, 1647, 1656, and 1668; see E. F. de Oliveira (1982), vol. 4, pp. 372, 571; vol. 5, p. 81; vol. 7, pp. 101–103; E. M. Lobo (1963), pp. 67, 87.

48 L. F. Costa (2005), p. 110.

49 D. G. Smith (1975), p. 164.

50 Unless otherwise indicated, the information on the Brazil Company was taken from L. F. Costa (2002), vol. 1, pp. 477–587. There were other trading companies in Portugal during the sixteenth and seventeenth centuries; however, relatively few of them were successful, and they cannot be viewed as autonomous, large-scale merchant organizations operating globally. These included the Companhia Portuguesa das Índias Orientais (founded in 1587), Companhia para a Navegação e Comércio da Índia (1619), Companhia da Índia Oriental e Comércios Ultramarinos (1624), Companhia de Cacheu e Rios (Guinea) (1656), Companhia de Cabo Verde e de Cacheu (1680), Companhia do Pará e Maranhão (1682), and the Companhia do Reino do Oriente e de Moçambique (1687).

51 J. L. de Azevedo (1989); J. L. de Azevedo (1931); C. R. Boxer (1949); I. S. Révah (1975). However, see L. F. Costa (2004).

52 J. A. G. de Mello (2000).

53 L. F. Costa (2002), vol. 1, p. 521.

54 In 1663 it received statutes to that effect, which were reformed in 1672; L. F. Costa (2002), vol. 1, p. 587; A. N. Faria (2005), p. 404.

Chapter 14

1 A. Greif (1993), p. 525.

2 Researchers attach different meanings to the term Portuguese nation. See, for example, the extraordinarily broad definition of Daviken Studnicki-Gizbert, for whom the New Christian origin plays only a very subordinate role; D. Studnicki-Gizbert (2007), pp. 5–11.

3 "... desde Jam de Lus ate Danzque por hũa e outra parte, assim de França como de Flandes, Inglaterra e Alemanha"; I. S. Révah (1963), p. 653; See also M. Bodian (1987).

4 "... because among themselves, howsoever distant they sojourn, they keep company with each other and all together understand themselves" [porque elles entre sy por mais distantes que estejão tem companhia entre sy, e todos juntos se entendem]; cited in J. Marques (1993), pp. 180–181.

5 Y. Kaplan (1993), p. 132.

6 H. P. Salomon (1982), pp. 36–40.

7 C. B. Stuczynski (2007), for example, speaks of such an administration.

8 The following statements are based almost exclusively on J. I. Pulido Serrano (2006b); see also C. B. Stuczynski (2007); A. B. Coelho (2001); J. Marques (1993); A. A. M. de Almeida (1986), pp. 885–898.

9 J. C. Boyajian (1993), pp. 91–93.

10 J. I. Pulido Serrano (2006b) p. 361.

11 Ibid. pp. 367–369.

12 In fact, several close relatives of the negotiators were in prison (see chapter 6). In addition, Heitor Mendes de Brito, whose brothers lived openly as Jews in Venice and Salonika, repeatedly ran into difficulties with the Inquisition.

13 ANTT, TSO, Inquisição de Lisboa, proc. 11448.

14 P. Penteado (2000a), pp. 460–463; P. Penteado (2000b), pp. 331–332.

15 The *Ordenações Filipinas* speak of "Hospitals and brotherhoods which the merchants have in Santo Espírito and São Francisco" [Hospitaes e Confrarias, que os Mercadores tem em Sancto Spririto e S. Francisco]; Ordenações Filipinas ([1603] 1870), Liv. 1, Tít. 52, § 14.

16 A. J. Barros (2003).

17 However, after the *Ordenações Filipinas* were published in 1603, the churches were forbid-
    den to grant asylum to "Jews, Moors, or other infidels": "And if any Jew, Moor, or other
    infidel escape to the church, asking for shelter there, he will not enjoy immunity because
    the Church does not defend those who do not live according to its Rule nor obey to its
    commandments" [E se algum Judeu, ou Mouro, ou outro infiel fugir para a Igreja, acoutan-
    do-se a ella, não será per ella defendido, nem gozará de sua immunidade, porque a Igreja
    não defende os que não vivem debaixo de sua Lei, nem obedecem a seus mandamentos];
    Ordenações Filipinas ([1603] 1870) Liv. 2, Tít. 5, § 1.

18 J. I. Pulido Serrano (2006a).

19 C. Linkemeyer (1931), pp. 202–209; J. Whaley (1985), p. 48.

20 P. Schmidt-Eppendorf (2004), p. 411.

21 L. B. Dreves (1850), pp. 34, 37–38; A. Pieper (1886), pp. 17–21.

22 L. B. Dreves (1850), pp. 37–38.

23 "... mit ehren bösen Exempeln andern ferner tho ärgern sick würden gelüsten laten"; cited
    in L. B. Dreves (1850), p. 35.

24 ANTT, TSO, Inquisição de Lisboa, liv. 212, fls. 21–21v.

25 R. Ehrenberg (1893b), pp. 47, 54.

26 P. D. H. Reils (1847), pp. 361–362.

27 R. Ehrenberg (1893b), p. 5.

28 Namely Paulo de Barros de Bessa, G. Lopes, Gaspar Gomes, and Manuel Valmonte; see
    R. Ehrenberg (1893b), p. 39. A certain Gabriel Lopes was an important member of the Jewish
    community a little later; the other three are unknown as Jews in Hamburg.

29 A. Pieper (1886), p. 17.

30 L. B. Dreves (1850), p. 43.

31 I. S. Révah (1960), pp. 55–56; see also H. P. Salomon (1982), p. 35.

32 P. A. d'Azevedo (1910), p. 194.

33 H. P. Salomon (1982), pp. 49–50.

34 I. S. Révah (1957), p. 79.

35 B. N. Teensma (1976).

36 M. Studemund-Halévy (2005).

37 Fernando Salvador, whose place of origin is unknown, embraced the Reformed faith in
    Hamburg and married into a Netherlandish-Reformed family. Additionally, Wilhelm Sillem
    lists the following Hamburg residents who were members of the Reformed congregation
    in Stade and had Portuguese names: Luís Peres, Virgínio de Barra, and Filipe Segueiro.
    According to Kellenbenz, António Anselmo, who was also mentioned, was a Netherlander;
    H. Kellenbenz (1954), p. 242; W. Sillem (83), pp. 544–545.

38 H. Kellenbenz (1958), pp. 250–251.

39 H. Kellenbenz (1954), p. 266; R. Ehrenberg (1893b), pp. 34–35.

40 J. Braden (2001), p. 101.

41 In 1619 two bank accounts were held under the name Álvares: Rodrigo Álvares and Diogo
    Álvares Vargas. Both had moderate turnovers; the first names of Manuel Álvares's two sons
    are not known. For 1632 no merchants bearing this surname appear in the Admiralty cus-
    toms books; in 1647, a certain João Álvares had very low turnovers.

42 ANTT, TSO, Inquisição de Lisboa, proc. 3020; see also A. Leoni and H. P. Salomon (2001), p. 282.

43 H. Kellenbenz (1958), p. 200.

44 "Der alte Jude Rodericus stund in grosser Furcht, die Jüden würden ihn ertappen und wegschicken. Zur Seduction gehörte auch, daß die getaufften Juden für andere Ungetaufften keinen Friede haben, sondern werden von ihnen verfolget"; cited in J. Braden (2001), pp. 269, 516–517.

45 Ibid., pp. 260–261; J. Braden (2005); J. Braden (2016), pp. 280–285; W. Treue (2000).

46 Synagogues were hosted in the houses of Rui Fernandes Cardoso, Álvaro Dinis, Rodrigo Peres Brandão, António Faleiro, Duarte Esteves de Pina, Henrique de Lima, and his son Duarte de Lima; see C. Roth (1930), p. 230; A. Leoni and H. P. Salomon (2001), p. 267. Almost all of the persons named were among the economically most active members of the community between March 1608 and February 1610. Rui Fernandes Cardoso and Álvaro Dinis together accounted for more than half of the *Werkzoll* paid by the Portuguese. No comparable figures have survived for Rodrigo Peres Brandão, but in 1619 and subsequent years his brother João Francês Brandão along with António Faleiro were among the Portuguese with the highest turnovers at the Bank of Hamburg. In 1619 the two of them together accounted for almost 30 percent of the total turnover of the Portuguese. In 1632 the Admiralty customs books indicate that Duarte Esteves de Pina was in second place among the Portuguese in terms of total turnover, and in 1647 in first place. In that year he accounted for almost one-fifth (18 percent) of the total turnover of the Portuguese. Henrique and Duarte de Lima each had only relatively small turnovers. Although Duarte de Lima was active in the jewelry and credit businesses at the courts in Copenhagen and Gottorf, in 1656 he seems to have had only moderate assets, as can be inferred from the list of community taxes in the minutes book; H. Kellenbenz (1958), pp. 119, 277–278, 302.

47 A. Leoni and H. P. Salomon (2001), p. 267.

48 P. A. d'Azevedo (1910), p. 192.

49 R. Häpke (1925b), pp. 184–185.

50 A. Leoni and H. P. Salomon (2001).

51 B.-Z. Ornan Pinkus (1994), pp. 12–13.

52 Even though this did not lead to the founding of an official synagogue, these, and later other houses, were purchased to provide meeting places; I. Cassuto (1910), p. 285 (25th of Av 5419); see also J. Braden (2001), pp. 262–276.

53 J. I. Israel (1987), pp. 33–34; B.-Z. Ornan Pinkus (1994), pp. 29–34.

54 M. Bodian (2008), p. 76.

55 F. Trivellato (2009b), p. 259.

56 I. Cassuto (1916), pp. 36–37 (7th of Av 5427).

57 Ibid. p. 39 (27 Elul 5427).

58 J. Taylor (1888), p. 136.

59 ANTT, TSO, Inquisição de Lisboa, proc. 3922.

60 ANTT, TSO, Inquisição de Lisboa, proc. 3922.

61 I. Cassuto (1910), pp. 265–268 (28th of Adar and the 6th of Nisan 5419).

62 StAHH, Jüdische Gemeinden 993, vol. 1, p. 176 (1st of Shevat 5420).

63 I. Cassuto (1912), pp. 247–248 (25th of Nisan 5424).

64 In sporadic instances there are entries even on Sundays. 1632/1633: Monday through Friday, an average of 18.2 percent of weekly customs duties events per day; Saturday, 7.5 percent; Sunday, 1.7 percent; 1647/1648: Monday through Friday, an average of 17.8 percent per day; Saturday, 10.7 percent; Sunday, 0.2 percent. Among the Sunday entries, in 1632/1633 the

number of Jews was fairly high (8 of 27 entries); in 1647/1648, however, there were none (0 of 6 entries).

65 The Jews who broke the Sabbath during those two years were Duarte Esteves de Pina, Duarte Nunes da Costa, Gonçalo Cardoso, Diogo Nunes Veiga, Manuel Rodrigues, Francisco Vaz (de Castro), and João Castro (presumed to have been Jewish)

66

Jewish holy days	Jewish calendar	Julian calendar 1632/1633	Julian calendar 1647/1648
Passover	15th–22nd of Nisan	March 16–23, 1633	April 10–17, 1647
Lag baOmer	18th of Iyyar	April 29, 1632	May 13, 1647
Shavuot	6th–7th of Sivan	May 16–17, 1632	May 30–31, 1647
Tisha B'Av	9th or 10th of Av	July 17, 1632	August 1, 1647
Rosh Hashanah	1st–2nd of Tishri	September 6–7, 1632	September 20–21, 1647
Yom Kippur	10 Tishri	September 15, 1632	September 29, 1647
Succot and Simchat Torah	15th–23rd of Tishri	September 20–28, 1632	October 4–12, 1647
Hanukkah	25th of Kislev–2nd of Tevet	November 28– December 5, 1632	December 12–18, 1647
Purim	14th of Adar	February 14, 1633	March 11, 1647

67 In 1632 two Jews (Diogo Nunes Veiga and Gabriel Lopes) paid customs duties during the nine-day festival of Succot. In 1647 customs duties were paid by three Jews and a Portuguese who was probably also a Jew (Manuel Rodrigues Isidro, João Francês Brandão, Rodrigo Peres Brandão, and Gonçalo Brandão).

68 The many examples of harassment of Portuguese Jews will not be detailed here; see, for example, G. Böhm (1994); B. Schmidt (2007); J. Braden (2001).

69 "… nicht allein der gemeine Pöbel, sondern auch andere Leute sich finden, die sie zu beschimpfen keine Scheu haben"; "sieben von unserer Nation in der öffentlichen Börsen Mittagszeit, die Mäntel tückischer und hinterlistiger Weise zerschnitten und schamsiret"; cited in G. Böhm (1994), p. 97.

70 I. Cassuto (1916), p. 1 ([5426]).

71 J. Braden (2003), p. 7.

72 A. Leoni and H. P. Salomon (2001).

73 J. Braden (2003), pp. 19–20; J. Braden (2001), pp. 218–225.

74 "E qualquer pessoa de entre nós que aqui ficar ou, depois de saído, tornar a vir fazer sua residência em esta terra, sera contada por desmembrada e excluída da congregação de filhos de Israel"; cited in A. Leoni and H. P. Salomon (2001), p. 287.

75 After the unification of the three Hamburg congregations into a single congregation a new minutes book was opened, starting with the record of the constitution; B.-Z. Ornan Pinkus (1994), pp. 4–5; see also Y. Kaplan (1997), pp. 66–67. "absoluto poder E autoridade plena"; "para aumento do servisso del Dio Bendito"; "ão servisso de Nossos beim Jeral e conservansa nossa"; M. Studemund-Halévy (1994a), p. 37.

76 I. Cassuto (1910), pp. 245, 247 (14th, 21st of Cheshvan 5419).

77 Some of the high-ranking community members attempted to influence the proceedings. Thus, in 1661 the merchant Jorge Nunes da Costa attempted to convince the board to have Jacob Baruch sign a declaration that would make it easier for Nunes da Costa

to withdraw an insurance sum; StAHH, Jüdische Gemeinden 993, vol. 1, p. 214 (7th of Cheshvan 5422).

78 See, for example, I. Cassuto (1909), p. 169 (29th of Nisan 5416) or pp. 178–180 (17th, 24th, 28th of Tamuz, 16th of Av 5416).

79 I. Cassuto (1910), p. 272 (11th of Iyyar 5419).

80 I. Cassuto (1910), pp. 259–261 (3rd, 7th of Adar 5419) and 275 (11th of Sivan 5419).

81 I. Cassuto (1909), pp. 164–166 (24th of Adar 5416).

82 See, for example, I. Cassuto (1912), p. 236 (6th of Iyyar 5423).

83 Y. Kaplan (1997), p. 85.

84 Ibid., pp. 70–71. Most of the bans, however, were of short duration, a few days or weeks.

85 Ibid id., pp. 69–70.

86 See, for example I. Cassuto (1912), p. 236 (19th of Sivan 5423).

87 "... palavras tam escandalosas como indesentes"; StAHH, Jüdische Gemeinden 993, vol. 1, p. 183 (7th of Iyyar 5420).

88 StAHH, Jüdische Gemeinden 993, vol. 1, p. 267 [271] (24th of Cheshvan 5425).

89 Y. Kaplan (1997), pp. 66–67. For the general policy for expelling foreigners, see, for example, I. Cassuto (1909), p. 167 (9th of Nisan 5416).

90 Y. Kaplan (1997), p. 68.

91 See, for example I. Cassuto (1912), p. 237 (27th of Sivan 5423) or p. 246 (23rd of Adar 5424).

92 I. Cassuto (1910), pp. 234–235 (25th of Nisan 5418). See also R. Cohen (1982).

93 What became of the project has not been researched; see A. Wohlwill (1894).

94 See also M. Bodian (2008), p. 75.

95 "... tho Gottes Ehren und tho Underholdung Kerken und Scholen"; cited in D. Detlefsen (1906), p. 193.

96 J. F. Voigt (1912), p. 224.

97 Y. Y. Lifshitz (2004), pp. 51–56; for the general social significance of charitable activities, see M. Leeuwen (1994).

Chapter 15

1 R. v. Roosbroeck (1964), p. 67; P. Piper (1893), p. 5. In the Altona congregation, sermons were soon held in German as well; by mid century, German-speaking congregation members were in the majority. At about the same time conflicts erupted between the Flemish-speaking and Walloon-speaking parts of the community. However, only after the revocation of the Edict of Nantes in 1685, when a group of about 900 French Huguenots arrived in Hamburg, did the congregation split into a (Flemish-)German and a French part; see R. Hermes (1934), pp. 13–14, 51–52, 68, 76–77; R. v. Roosbroeck (1964), p. 71; J. Whaley (1985), pp. 123–124.

2 "... unter der Tirannie des Papstes zu bleiben"; "seltsame Verfolgung gelitten haben, in Gut und Blut und alles verlassen haben, und alles gegeben, um in unserem Gewissen frei zu bleiben"; "voor de Spaensche tyrannie gevlucht zijn"; cited in R. v. Roosbroeck (1964), pp. 73–74.

3 W. Sillem (1883), p. 482; see also J. Müller (2016), pp. 104–106.

4 For the Netherlanders' exile memories see J. Müller (2016).

5 For legislation against undifferentiated xenophobia, see J. Bolland (1960), part 2, no. 147, art. 6, "Frömbden nationen schal men nich naroopen" (1623); no. 145, art. 84, "Frembden nationen alhir nicht nachzuschreien" (after 1594, corrections up to 1646).

6   For 1605: StAHH, Niederländische Armenkasse, AI2, Stück 2, fl. 6v. See also the imperial report of 1606 in which Jochim van Meere, Dominicus van Uffeln, Jan de l'Homel, and Peter van der Straeten are named as the leaders of the Netherlanders in Hamburg and Jan de Schott, Jacob de Greve, and Arnoult Pels are identified as the leaders of the Netherlanders in Stade; R. Häpke (1925b), pp. 184–185. For 1639: StAHH, Senat, Cl. VII Lit. Cc Nr. 2 Vol. 1 Fasc. 4, fl. 261v. See also StAHH, Senat, Cl. VII Lit. Cc Nr. 2 Vol. 1 Fasc. 4, fl. 272; StAHH, Niederländische Armenkasse, AI2, Stück 3, fl. 5v; StAHH, Niederländische Armenkasse, AI2, Stück 8, fl. 1. Abraham du Bois was in third place with regard to turnover in the Iberia trade, and was thus the most important Iberia trader of all the Netherlanders covered by the contract. Dominicus van Uffeln and Jan van Uffeln were tied in 15th place in terms of turnover; Cornelis de Hertoghe in 10th place.

7   H. Schilling (1972), p. 79.

8   This was the case with the sugar merchant Jan de l'Homel, who in 1588 was one of the first deacons of the Walloon-Reformed congregation in Stade and became an elder in 1592; it was also true of the merchant Louis de Behout, who in 1590 took part in the Eucharist of the Reformed congregation in Stade, and in 1612 held the meeting in his home that elected the preacher for the congregation in Altona; see W. Sillem (1883), pp. 517–518. Others who either themselves or whose family members made weekly alms collections for the Reformed congregation included Hans Baten, Guillaume le Petit, Martin des Champs, François van Coninxloe, Peter and Jan van der Straeten, Hans van der Wyle, Thomas de Coymans, Guilliam, Jacob Staes, Willem de Barry, and Gottfried Gertsen; see W. Sillem (1883), pp. 505–523. Curiously, the Reformed are not mentioned even once in Renate Hauschild-Thiessen's comprehensive monograph on the institution, nor did she mention explicitly the limitation of her work to members of the Lutheran denomination; R. Hauschild-Thiessen (1974). Similar observations apply to an older work by O. C. Gaedechens (1880). Robert van Roosbroeck, on the other hand, expressly states that some Reformed belonged to the circle of contributors to the Relief Fund; R. v. Roosbroeck (1964), p. 64.

9   R. Hauschild-Thiessen (1974), pp. 273–296.

10   R. v. Roosbroeck (1964), p. 63; R. Hauschild-Thiessen (1974), p. 31.

11   Hauschild-Thiessen (1974), p. 35. According to Gaedechens, Lutheranism was a prerequisite for support; O. C. Gaedechens (1880), p. 14.

12   "… fleißig arbeiten, in allen Ehren leben und ohne ihre Schuld Not leiden"; R. Hauschild-Thiessen (1974), pp. 27, 30.

13   Girls could often work in the households of the directors of the Relief Fund and would receive a dowry when they married; boys were apprenticed in a craft; see R. Hauschild-Thiessen (1974), p. 30.

14   Ibid., pp. 18, 20, 25, 35, 38–40, 54; W. Sillem (1883), p. 554.

15   Dominicus van Uffeln, Cornelis de Hertoghe, Gillis de Greve, Willem Amsinck, and Paul and Hans Berenberg.

16   Willem Amsinck, along with Guilliam van der Aa, Jasper van Dortmont, and Heinrich Herinks.

17   Willem Amsinck, Cornelis de Hertoghe, his son Hans de Hertoghe, Gillis de Greve, and Heinrich Herinks.

18   For general information on the functions of charity, see M. Leeuwen (1994).

19   W. Sillem (1883), p. 561. It has been shown that of the Netherlanders who emigrated to London at more or less the same time, up to a third were "of no church." Of these only the relatively few Mennonites would have had any reason to conceal their faith; H. Schilling (1972), p. 21.

20 H. Geisenheimer (1912), p. 33. However, the claim that he converted has been repeatedly disputed.
21 G. Rückleben (1969), p. 39.
22 C. Lesger (2006), pp. 222, 245.
23 AHL, Nachlass Hagedorn, Packen 11–3, fl. 768 (StAHH, Reichskammergericht, H 127).
24 R. Hauschild-Thiessen (1974), pp. 35–37.
25 R. Hermes (1934), p. 19.
26 In 1648 the City Council declared to the senior elders that, "one need fear no seduction on the part of the Jews, while Calvinism always takes root"; cited in J. Whaley (1985), p. 116.
27 After 1640 Reformed religious services were sometimes held in the chapel of the embassy of the States General in Hamburg, although they were relatively small-scale. The clergy vehemently opposed these services, and they were not officially tolerated by the City Council; J. Whaley (1985), pp. 121–122; R. Hermes (1934), pp. 59–60.
28 H. Schilling (1972), p. 123; R. Hermes (1934), p. 27; StAHH, Deutsch-Evangelisch-Reformierte Gemeinde, II A b 1. Senior Pastor Bernhard Vaget went even further, demanding that the inhabitants should "neither house, foster, accommodate, support or promote, nor take into their service and employ or maintain" heretics [nicht hüsen, heegen, herbergen noch apholden edder vörderen, ock in synen Deenst unde Arbeit nicht nemen noch underholden]; cited in R. Hermes (1934), p. 28.
29 H. Schilling (1972), p. 39.
30 J. Whaley (1985), p. 121; R. Hermes (1934), pp. 33–34; S. Rau (2002), pp. 172–173.
31 H. Schilling (1972), pp. 20, 168–170; P. Benedict (2002), pp. 209–210, 287–288, 291; R. Hermes (1934), pp. 18, 43–45, 51.
32 R. Hermes (1934), p. 16; W. Sillem (1883), p. 564.
33 R. Hermes (1934), pp. 16–17; P. Benedict (2002), pp. 465–466; H. Schmidt (2009), p. 352.
34 R. Hermes (1934), p. 49.
35 Ibid., p. 37; see also P. Benedict (2002), p. 461.
36 In Le Mans and Amsterdam, respectively; P. Benedict (2002), pp. 463–464.
37 R. Hermes (1934), p. 16; see also P. Benedict (2002), pp. 463–464.
38 R. Hermes (1934), p. 39.
39 StAHH, Deutsch-Evangelisch-Reformierte Gemeinde, II A b 1 (February 11, 1605).
40 H. Schilling (1972), p. 124.
41 In Stade the Reformed cared for the poor even before the actual congregation was founded; R. v. Roosbroeck (1964), p. 66. Regarding the care of the poor, see also R. Hermes (1934), pp. 17, 19.
42 R. Hermes (1934), p. 27.
43 Ibid., pp. 40, 42, 49; P. Piper (1893), p. 11; StAHH, Deutsch-Evangelisch-Reformierte Gemeinde, II A b 1 (June 2, 1606).
44 J. Whaley (1985), pp. 123–124; S. Rau (2002), p. 177.
45 P. Benedict (2002), pp. 451–459.
46 W. Sillem (1883), pp. 593–598, quotation on p. 564.
47 R. Hermes (1934), p. 18.
48 E. Stols (1971); P. W. Gennrich (1936).
49 N. C. Borges (1986).
50 According to other works, Frankfurt and Augsburg as well.
51 ANTT, TSO, Inquisição de Lisboa, liv. 708–715 (see p. 117 of this book).
52 BNL, Manuscritos Reservados, cód. 11392.

53 J. D. TT, TSO, Conselho Geral, Habilitações, Diogo, mç. 2, doc. 83.

54 TT, TSO, Conselho Geral, Habilitações, João, mç. 11, doc. 338.

55 P. D. Hinsch (1888); M. Ehrhardt (1990); J. S. Ribeiro (1876), pp. 20–22.

56 P. W. Gennrich (1936), p. 21.

57 ANTT, TSO, Inquisição de Lisboa, liv. 212, fls. 19–28v.

58 "... gefähr- und hochprejudicierliche Kirchenschützung der teutschen Capelle S. Bartholomei"; P. W. Gennrich (1936), p. 28.

59 The Lübeck City Archive has a small portion of the brotherhood's accounts book; AHL, ASA, Externa Lusitanica 87.

60 R. Postel (1980), p. 74.

61 During the sixteenth century, the Brotherhood of St. Bartholomew was temporarily dominated by German artillerymen, which is why it was also referred to as the *Confraria dos bombardeiros alemães e flamengos*; during this time the merchants apparently met in the Brotherhood of St. Sebastian in another chapel of the Church of St. Julian. The two brotherhoods merged in the early seventeenth century under the name of St. Bartholomew, and the importance of the artillerymen decreased considerably; see P. W. Gennrich (1936), p. 15; E. Stols (1971), part 1, p. 81.

62 H. Dormeier (2009), p. 22.

63 For a time, the Brotherhood of the Soldiers of the German Guard (Irmandade dos soldados da guarda tudesca) was also housed there under the patronage of St. Hyacinth. The German Guard had been founded by Archduke Alberto VII of Austria when he became viceroy of Portugal under Felipe II. It existed until the middle of the seventeenth century; see Fr. L. de Sousa ([1623] 1977), part 1, pp. 344–365; V. Ribeiro (1917), pp. 17–20; P. W. Gennrich (1936), p. 15; E. Stols (1971), part 1, p. 81; E. de Lima (1958), p. 36.

64 V. Ribeiro (1917), p. 20.

65 "... ehrliche Begrebnüs in *St. Bartholomaei Capell* erhalten"; E. Merck (1856), p. 219.

66 Fr. L. de Sousa ([1623] 1977), part 1, pp. 362–363. See also E. Stols (1971), part 1, p. 83.

67 AHL, ASA, Externa, Lusitanica 87.

68 E. Merck (1856), p. 196.

69 "... so viel Ich von S[ieu]r Henr[ich] Buermeister vernemme, so werden die Unkostungen, welche Du dieser *charge* wegen thuen müßen, Sich woll bei 100 Rthlr betragen, welche Gott Dir anderwertß, mit seinem Segen, reichlich wiederumb ersetzen wolle"; "bedunckenß behöret Dein *Compagnon* die unkostungen zum Halben theil mit über Sich zu nemmen und daß also dieselbe auß der *Compagnie* musten guet gethan werden"; "Den Mittelsten Heil. tag wardt Johan Pell zum Geschwornen der Kirchen *Petri* erwehlet, Deine Fr. Mutter schertzte über der Mahlzeit wie die Kinder am selbigen tage bei Unß waren und sagte, Sie hette einen Sohn der hieß Johan der were auch ein Kirchgeschworner bei *St. Bartholomaei* Kirche in *Lissabon*, worüber wyr Unß lustig machten; E. Merck (1856), pp. 140–141.

70 "Sonsten habe ich in verlesung Deineß Schreibenß angemercket, daß Dier der ohrt Lißabon und die einwohner, so geist alß weltliche, noch nicht allerdingß anstendig und Du Dich in Deinem jetzigen Stande noch nicht recht finden könnest, dahero Ich den noch einige Ungeduldt von Dir verspüre. ... aber Du must wißen, daß Du in diesem *passu* aldorten und an andern ohrten gar viel vorgänger hast gehabt, denen eß also ergangen und denen die große verenderung in allen dingen auch in *religions* Sachen sehr befrembdet vorgekommen"; "Waß die *religion* betrifft, so wirstu vernünfftig, so viel immer thuen und müglich alle Heuchelei und alle *occasion* vermeiden und mit niemanden, auch nicht einß mit Deinem *Compagnon* von *religions* Sachen reden oder *discurs* führen, sondern für Dich zu rechter

Zeit lesen, auch Morgendt und abendtß Dein gebett zu Gott mit andacht thuen"; E. Merck (1856), pp. 19–20.

71 "... allbereitß einmahl auß Noht daselbst gesündiget, alß man die gesegnete *Hostie* daher getragen"; "arme [und] beine gebebet"; E. Merck (1856), p. 19, 22.

72 "... kein Banghase sein"; "Du meldest, daß in Lißabon viel pfaffen, auch viel Kirchen und Klöster sein. Woll! laß dar noch so viel sein, daß gehet Dich nicht an, laß nochmahl so viel Pfaffen da sein, Sie werden Dich nicht beißen, warte Du daß Deinige. In die Meße zu gehen und in die Kirche dazu nötigt man niemandt, und wen Du ümb die Oster Zeit ein Zettel von einem geistlichen kanst haben, alß ob du gebeichtet und *Communiciret* hettest, so hastu ümb die geistlichkeit Dich nicht mehr zu bekümmern, wan Dir auch von ferne die Pfaffen mit der gesegneten *Hostien* werden begegnen, wirstu alle vorsichtigkeit gebrauchen und einen ümbweg nehmen oder in ein Hauß gehen"; E. Merck (1856), pp. 19, 22. In addition, his son should look to others in a similar situation for cues about behavior upon catching sight of the host: "Daniel Dinschlag visited me recently ... and told me that his son Johann Caspar Dinschlag ... reported to him that no difficulties were to be encountered in Lisbon on account of religion, this Daniel also said that his same son had told him that when he encountered them carrying the consecrated host, and he saw it from afar, he often walked into another street; but if he could not do that he stood to the side and just doffed his hat" [Dieser tage war Daniel Dinschlag ... bei Mihr, der sagte Mihr, das sein Sohn Johan Caspar Dinschlag, ... Ihm bestendig berichtet, das es in Lisabon wegen der *religion* keine Beschwernus hette, Es sagte auch dieser Daniel, das bemelter sein Sohn Ihm gesaget, das wen Sie Ihm mit der *consecrirten Hostien* weren begegnet und er es von ferne gesehen, were er zwar offters in eine andere gase gegangen, wen er aber nicht hette gekont, were Er an der seite getreten und hette nur den Hudt abgenommen]; E. Merck (1856), pp. 16–17.

73 "... daß eß wegen der *religie* keine beschwernüß habe und daß Du Dich vor *dispüten* vorsehen und hüten und darin für Dich allein sein wollest, dieseß alleß gefelt Mihr sehr und wirstu woll thun wen Du dabei *continuiren* und von der Catholischen *religion* nichtß übelß oder verkleinlichß, auch nicht einß in Deinem hause oder gegen S[ieu]r Drinckherrn davon reden wirst, da die Leute so Lutherisch gewesen und zu der Catholischen *religion* Sich begeben, können oder mügen daß geringste nicht hören, wen man verächt oder kleinerlich von der Catholischen *religion* reden wollte"; E. Merck (1856), p. 33.

74 For the denunciation: ANTT, TSO, Inquisição de Lisboa, liv. 212, fls. 19–28v.

75 ANTT, TSO, Inquisição de Lisboa, liv. 713, fl. 280.

76 ANTT, TSO, Inquisição de Lisboa, proc. 10451.

77 ANTT, TSO, Inquisição de Lisboa, proc. 10442.

78 "Waß obgedacht Dein Schreiben anlangt, so wolte Ich woll, daß Du nicht so frey von der *Religion* schriebest, den eß möchte ohngefehr ein brieff aufgefangen werden und würdestu ungelegenheit haben"; E. Merck (1856), p. 89.

79 Ibid., pp. 135, 196.

80 "Im Fall Du der Meinung, daß Du in 2 à 3 Jahren im Handel also zu *avanciren* vermeinest, daß Du alßdan allhie in der Handlung auff Lißabon mit Deinem Nutzen werdest *continuiren* können so kanstu Mihr in künfftig alßdan wegen Deineß *repatrijrens* Deine Gemütß Meinung eröffnen und werden wyr Unß leicht darüber vereinigen können"; E. Merck (1856), p. 23.

81 For example, ANTT, TSO, Inquisição de Lisboa, liv. 708, fl. 184; liv. 710, fl. 7; liv. 710, fl. 66; liv. 711, fl. 351; liv. 711, fl. 359.

82 ANTT, TSO, Inquisição de Lisboa, liv. 711, fl. 194.

83 It is certain that Alexander Heusch was not of the Reformed denomination, as Kellenbenz and Baasch presumed; see H. Kellenbenz (1950), p. 32; E. Baasch (1895–1896), p. 165.

84 ANTT, Habilitação da Ordem de Christo, letra A, mç 45, doc. 72.

85 ANNTT, TSO, Conselho Geral, Habilitações, Diogo, mç. 2, doc. 83.

86 ANTT, TSO, Conselho Geral, Habilitações, João, mç. 11, doc. 338.

87 ANTT, TSO, Conselho Geral, Habilitações, Teodósio, mç. 1, doc. 10.

88 J. V. Torres (1994); F. Bethencourt (1996), p. 91.

Appendix

1 H. Kellenbenz (1954); M. Reißmann (1975).

2 StAHH, Niederländische Armenkasse, AI2, Stück 2 (1605); StAHH, Senat, Cl. VII Lit. Cc Nr. 2 Vol. 1 Fasc. 4, fl. 148–156v. (1615); StAHH, Niederländische Armenkasse, AI2, Stück 3 (1639). For a listing of the administrators of the Netherlandish Relief Fund, see appendix in R. Hauschild-Thiessen (1974).

3 W. Sillem (1883); see also H. Kellenbenz (1954).

4 StAHH, Senat, Cl. VII Eb Nr. 11 Vol. 6 (the Portuguese who paid *Werkzoll* between June 1608 and June 1610); A. Cassuto (1931); M. Grunwald (1902), pp. 35–36; M. Studemund-Halévy (2000); A. di L. Leoni and H. P. Salomon (2001).

5 StAHH, Deutsch-Evangelisch-Reformierte Gemeinde, I G 1 a; I G 2 a (alphabetical listing of congregation members); I G 2 b (membership listing of the congregation in Altona 1603–1621); I G 3 a (registry of the members and guests of the Eucharist in Stade 1588–1618); V D 1 (wedding registry of the congregation in Stade 1588–1618); W. Sillem (1883).

6 The information recorded during trials by the Inquisition were not considered, because it was based on the assumption that the indicted were Jews, while reliable self-information is lacking. The membership list of the congregation is published in A. di L. Leoni and H. P. Salomon (2001). All persons buried in the Portuguese-Jewish cemetery in Hamburg are listed in M. Studemund-Halévy (2000).

7 The attributes of the products resulted in differences in value in only a few exceptional cases. A *Fässchen* of sheet metal was taxed at 1, 1.5, or 4 shillings, depending on whether it was black, simple, or double. Unhackeled flax was taxed at 1 shilling per ship-pound, hackeled flax at 2 shillings (hackeled flax is clean and ready for spinning).

8 An exception was made, however, when contextual information (measurements and packaging, value, origin, naming in a previous entry) made it relatively safe to assume that raisins were being shipped.

9 E. Pitz (1961), p. 576.

10 Ibid., p. 338 (no. 271) and pp. 338–339 (no. 272); E.-C. Frentz (1985), p. 278.

11 A tariff scroll dating from before 1647 has survived that contains specified tariffs for a large number of goods; E. Pitz (1961), pp. 339–349 (no. 273).

12 A tariff list that has survived from 1671 values a crate of sugar at 140 marks; the difference of 10 marks seems sufficiently minor to justify the method; E. Pitz (1961), p. 348 (no. 274, §133).

13 Goods traded with non-Iberian countries, such as France and the Caribbean, were subject to a different basis of calculation and customs duties than were products in the Iberia trade. Sugar from the Caribbean, for instance, was transported in barrels, small barrels, tuns, and pipes, as opposed to the crates that were usual for sugar from Brazil or Portugal. As a result,

the customs duty on sugar from the Caribbean was calculated by the value, not by the crate. Likewise, wine from France was taxed according to its value, while wine from Spain according to the number of pipes, butts, hogsheads, or cardels it was transported in.

14 By this, as in the following, I mean the absolute error (difference) in relation to the size (arithmetic mean), in this case: (129,725 − 35,425) / ([129,725 + 35,425] / 2) = 114%.

15 Excluding the shipments in which the ports of destination were not noted.

16 That it was so much lower in 1647 is primarily because virtually no further remissions of customs duties were granted.

17 Differences of similar magnitude between the minimum and maximum value as seen in finished products, especially textiles, are also found for wax, indigo, cooperage, raisins, and tobacco. Indigo, cooperage, and tobacco were also taxed according to their value. The customs duty on wax, however, was calculated in ship-pounds, and raisins in pounds, *arrobas*, or baskets. Nonetheless, I had to do the calculations for wax and raisins similarly to those for goods taxed according to value, because for them, too, several items, each of them with different ports of destination or origin, were grouped into larger units. Other goods that were taxed according to their value, but had smaller differences between their minimum and maximum values, include dye woods, copper and iron products, leather, some spices, and fruits and nuts.

18 To this may be added collective terms such as *Kaufmannschaft* (general merchandise), which gave no indication about what they contained. For the two fiscal years under consideration, the turnovers for *Kaufmannschaft*, however, were barely 2 percent and 3 percent of the total turnover, respectively.

19 P. Jeannin (1964).

20 Brazilwood was used in Hamburg's textile dye works and is frequently mentioned in different sources. At the beginning of the century, Dominicus van Uffeln, a Netherlander living in Hamburg, imported brazilwood as part of a Portuguese crown contract; see E. Stols (1973), p. 41. In letters from the years 1668 and 1669 the Portuguese resident in Amsterdam, Jerónimo Nunes da Costa, wrote that large amounts of unsold brazilwood were warehoused in Hamburg. At that time it seems that Jerónimo together with the Nunes da Costas in Hamburg was organizing the brazilwood trade in northern Europe for the Portuguese king; BA, ms. av. 54–XI–29, ns. 189, 193.

References

Primary Sources: Manuscripts

Staatsarchiv Hamburg (StAHH)

Senat

Cl. VI Nr. 7 Vol. 4a Fasc. 1.
Cl. VII Eb Nr. 11 Vol. 6.
Cl. VII Lit. Cb Nr. 4 Vol. 1a Nr. 1b.
Cl. VII Lit. Cc Nr. 2 Vol. 1 Fasc 4b.
Cl. VII Lit. Cc Nr. 2 Vol. 1 Fasc. 4.
Cl. VII Lit. Cc Nr. 2 Vol. 2 Fasc. 1.
Cl. VII Lit. Hf Nr. 5 Vol. 3a Fasc. 1.
Cl. VII Lit. Hf Nr. 5 Vol. 3a Fasc. 4.
Cl. VII Lit. La Nr. 1 Vol. 4e.

Kämmerei I, Nr. 28, Bd. 1, 2 and 3.

Admiralitätskollegium
F3 Bd. 1 to 8.
F4 Bd. 1 to 15.

Jüdische Gemeinden 993, Bd. 1.

Deutsch-Evangelisch-Reformierte Gemeinde
I G 1 a.
I G 2 a.
I G 2 b.
I G 3 a.
II A b 1.
V D 1.

Niederländische Armenkasse, AI2.

Archiv der Hansestadt Lübeck (AHL)

Altes Senatsarchiv (ASA)
Externa, Hispanica 9.
Externa, Hispanica 17.
Externa, Hispanica 18.
Externa, Lusitanica 87.

Hansischer Geschichtsverein, Wissenschaftliche Sammlungen und Nachlässe, Nr. 9 Nachlass
Bernhard Hagedorn
Packen 9–1, Bl. 31–41 (StAHH, Senat, Cl. VIII, N. XXXI, Nr. 3a, pp. 123–125).
Packen 9–1, Bl. 163 (StAHH, Senat, Cl. VI Nr. 1a Vol. 1 Fasc. 10).
Packen 9–1, Bl. 205 (StAHH, Senat, Cl. VI Nr. 1a Vol. 1 Fasc. 10).
Packen 9–1, Bl. 405–407 (StAHH, Senat, Cl. VI Nr. 1a Fasc. 10).
Packen 9–1, Bl. 171 (StAHH, Senat, Cl. VI Nr. 1a Vol. 1 Fasc. 10).
Packen 9–1, Bl. 521 (StAHH, Senat, Cl. VI Nr. 1a Vol. 1 Fasc. 10).
Packen 9–1, Bl. 416–417 (StAHH, Senat, Cl. VI Nr. 6 Vol. 3b Fasc. 1).

https://doi.org/10.1515/9783110472103-021

Packen 9–1, Bl. 182–187 (StAHH, Senat, Cl. VI Nr. 7 Vol. 4a Fasc. 1).
Packen 9–1, Bl. 197 (StAHH, Senat, Cl. VI Nr. 7 Vol. 4a Fasc. 1).
Packen 9–1, Bl. 198–198v (StAHH, Senat, Cl. VI Nr. 7 Vol. 4a Fasc. 1).
Packen 9–1, Bl. 199v (StAHH, Senat, Cl. VI Nr. 7 Vol. 4a Fasc. 1).
Packen 9–1, Bl. 199v–200 (StAHH, Senat, Cl. VI Nr. 7 Vol. 4a Fasc. 1).
Packen 9–1, Bl. 204 (StAHH, Senat, Cl. VI Nr. 7 Vol. 4a Fasc. 1).
Packen 9–1, Bl. 419 (StAHH, Senat, Cl. VI Nr. 7 Vol. 4a Fasc. 1).
Packen 9–1, Bl. 350–375 (StAHH, Senat, Cl. VII, Lit. Ca, Nr. 2 Vol. 1b; Cl. VI Nr. 6, Vol. 5a Fasc. 1).
Packen 9–1, Bl. 885; 896 (StAHH, Senat, Cl. VII, Lit. Ca, Nr. 2 Vol. 1b; StAHH, Senat, Cl. VI Nr. 7 Vol. 4a Fasc. 1).
Packen 9–1, Bl. 688 (StAHH, Senat, Cl. VII, Lit. La, Nr. 3 Vol. 2c).
Packen 9–1, Bl. 857–860 (StAHH, Senat, Cl. VII, Lit. Ca, Nr. 1 Vol. 4a, pp. 171–173).
Packen 9–1, Bl. 134 (StAHH, Senat, Cl. VIII, N. XXXI, 4).
Packen 9–1, Bl. 557 (Blank, Mandatensammlung I, pp. 162, 163).
Packen 11–3 (StAHH, Reichskammergericht, B 93).
Packen 11–3 (StAHH, Reichskammergericht, B 96).
Packen 11–3 (StAHH, Reichskammergericht, D 11).
Packen 11–3 (StAHH, Reichskammergericht, F 34).
Packen 11–3 (StAHH, Reichskammergericht, H 127).
Packen 12–4 (StAHH, Reichskammergericht, K 5).
Packen 12–4 (StAHH, Reichskammergericht, T 7).

Arquivo Nacional da Torre do Tombo, Lisbon (ANTT)

Chancelaria de D. Afonso VI, liv. 31.
Chancelaria de D. Afonso VI, liv. 47.
Chancelaria de D. João IV, Doações, liv. 13.
Chancelaria de D. João IV, Doações, liv. 26.
Chancelaria, Próprios.
Corpo Cronológico, parte 1, mç. 118, doc. 165.
Corpo Cronológico, parte 2, mç. 307, docs. 101, 105, 106.
Freguesia de Santa Catarina do Monte Sinai, Lisboa, liv. 5B.

Registo Geral de Mercês (RGM)
D. Afonso VI, liv. 4.
D. João V, liv. 7.
D. Pedro II, liv. 7.
D. Pedro II, liv. 8.
D. Pedro II, liv. 10.
Ordens, liv. 5.

Habilitações da Ordem de Christo, letra A, mç. 45, doc. 72.

Tribunal do Santo Ofício (TSO)
Conselho Geral, Habilitações Incompletas, mç. 27, doc. 1131.
Conselho Geral, Habilitações, Andre, mç. 3, doc. 57.
Conselho Geral, Habilitações, Diogo, mç. 2, doc. 83.
Conselho Geral, Habilitações, Diogo, mç. 8, doc. 196.
Conselho Geral, Habilitações, João, mç. 1, doc. 36.
Conselho Geral, Habilitações, João, mç. 11, doc. 338.

Conselho Geral, Habilitações, Pedro, mç. 12, doc. 299.
Conselho Geral, Habilitações, Pedro, mç. 22, doc. 455.
Conselho Geral, Habilitações, Teodósio, mç. 1, doc. 10.
Inquisição de Lisboa, liv. 210 (9° Caderno do Promotor).
Inquisição de Lisboa, liv. 212 (11° Caderno do Promotor).
Inquisição de Lisboa, proc. 319 u. 319–1 (Manuel Cardoso).
Inquisição de Lisboa, proc. 3020 (Gaspar Bocarro).
Inquisição de Lisboa, proc. 3338 (Paulo de Milão).
Inquisição de Lisboa, proc. 3922 (Henrique de Lima).
Inquisição de Lisboa, proc. 4718 (Pedro Muller).
Inquisição de Lisboa, proc. 6677 (Henrique Dias Milão).
Inquisição de Lisboa, proc. 6707 (Manuel Rodrigues Isidro).
Inquisição de Lisboa, proc. 7119 (Luís Dias de Lemos).
Inquisição de Lisboa, proc. 7192 (Duarte Nunes da Costa).
Inquisição de Lisboa, proc. 7193 (Diogo Nunes Veiga).
Inquisição de Lisboa, proc. 7195 (Duarte de Lima).
Inquisição de Lisboa, proc. 7276 (Miguel Francês).
Inquisição de Lisboa, proc. 8089 (João Estrovée).
Inquisição de Lisboa, proc. 9173 (Miguel Francês).
Inquisição de Lisboa, proc. 9892 (Simão Gomes de Paz).
Inquisição de Lisboa, proc. 10295 (Luís Lamberto).
Inquisição de Lisboa, proc. 10442 (João Frique).
Inquisição de Lisboa, proc. 10449 (Julião da Maia).
Inquisição de Lisboa, proc. 10451 (João da Maia).
Inquisição de Lisboa, proc. 11362 (Gabriel Mendes).
Inquisição de Lisboa, proc. 11448 (Pedro Francês).
Inquisição de Lisboa, proc. 12212 (Rodrigo de Andrade).
Inquisição de Lisboa, proc. 12215 (João Francês).
Inquisição de Lisboa, proc. 12387 (Henrique Pit).
Inquisição de Lisboa, proc. 12493 (Heitor Mendes Bravo).
Inquisição de Lisboa, proc. 14409 and 16420 (Ana de Milão).
Inquisição de Coimbra, proc. 2425 (Jácome Becquer).
Inquisição de Lisboa, liv. 708 (Caderno [1] dos reduzidos).
Inquisição de Lisboa, liv. 709 (Caderno 2 dos reduzidos).
Inquisição de Lisboa, liv. 710 (Caderno 3 dos reduzidos).
Inquisição de Lisboa, liv. 711 (Caderno 4 dos reduzidos).
Inquisição de Lisboa, liv. 712 (Caderno 5 dos reduzidos).
Inquisição de Lisboa, liv. 713 (Caderno 6 dos reduzidos).
Inquisição de Lisboa, liv. 714 (Caderno 7 dos reduzidos).
Inquisição de Lisboa, liv. 715 (Caderno 8 dos reduzidos).
Inquisição de Coimbra, liv. 744 (Caderno dos herejes reduzidos).
Inquisição de Coimbra, liv. 613 (Caderno *).
Inquisição de Évora, liv. 562 (Caderno 1).

Biblioteca da Ajuda, Lissabon (BA)

Cód. 51–VIII–9, fl. 103.
Cód. 51–VIII–18, n. 326, fl. 141v.

Cód. 51–VIII–18, n. 341, fl. 147–148v.
Cód. 51–VIII–18, n. 547, fl. 220v–221.
Cód. 51–VIII–21, fls. 151, 159v.
Cód. 51–VIII–26, fl. 95.
Cód. 51–IX–4, fl. 135–136.
Cód. 51–IX–8, fl. 62–65v, 250–251v.
Cód. 51–IX–15, fl. 157v.
Cód. 51–X–4, fl. 227v–232v.
Cód. 51–X–16, fl. 202–203.
Ms. Av. 54–XI–29, ns. 162–162a, 193, 162, 171–172, 189, 191–199, 201–203, 206–210, 258.
Ms. Av. 54–XIII–7, n. 5.
Ms. Av. 54–XIII–8, ns. 244, 257.

Arquivo Histórico Ultramarino, Lisbon (AHU)

Códice do Conselho da Fazenda, n. 37.

Reino
Cx. 1, pasta 112.
Cx. 5, pasta 19, doc. 3.
Cx. 5, pasta 55, doc. 4.
Cx. 5, pasta 72, doc. 4.
Cx. 5A, pasta 2, doc. 5.
Cx. 8, pasta 22, doc. 5.
Cx. 8, pasta 26, doc. 4.
Cx. 8, pasta 26, doc. 5.
Cx. 11A, pasta 12, doc. 4.
Cx. 38, pasta 30, doc. 1.

Biblioteca Nacional de Portugal, Lisbon (BNL)

Manuscritos Reservados, Cód. 11392 (Carta de privilégio de Henrique Aires).

FelixArchief, Antwerp

Poortersboeken Inv. 029.

Gemeentearchief Amsterdam (GA)

Archief 5075, inv. no. 619X (Notariële acten van het Hamburgse notariaat van Peter Ruttens).
Not. Arch. 98/28; Not. Arch. 151; Not. Arch. 380; Not. Arch. 611A; Not. Arch. 628; Not. Arch. 629;
Not. Arch. 642; Not. Arch. 645; Not. Arch. 645B; Not. Arch. 646A; Not. Arch. 665 (20); Not.
Arch. 942/933.

Primary Sources: Printed

Abreu y Bertodano, Joseph Antonio, ed. 1740. *Colección de los Tratados de Paz, Alianza,*
Neutralidad …., Reynado de Felipe III, part 1. Madrid: D. Peralta, A. Marin y J. de Zuñiga.
Azevedo, Pedro A. d'. 1910. "O Bocarro Francês e os Judeus de Cochim e Hamburgo." In *Archivo*
Historico Portuguez 8, pp. 15–20, 185–198.

Blank, Johann Friedrich, ed. 1763–1774. *Sammlung der von E[inem] Hochedlen Rathe der Stadt Hamburg ... ausgegangenen allgemeinen Mandate, bestimmten Befehle und Bescheide ..., auch beliebten Aufträge und verkündigten Anordnungen,* 6 parts. Hamburg: Piscator.

Bolland, Jürgen, ed. 1960. *Hamburgische Burspraken 1346–1594, mit Nachträgen bis 1699,* 2 parts. Hamburg: Christians.

Brito, Bernardo de. 1609. *Monarquia Lusitana,* part 2. Lisbon: A. Crasbeck de Mello.

Cassel, Johann Philipp, ed. 1771. *Privilegia und Handlungsfreiheiten, welche die Könige von Portugal ehedem den deutschen Kaufleuten zu Lissabon ertheilet haben.* Bremen: H. C. Jani Witwe und Diedr. Meier.

Cassuto, Alfonso. 1931. "Neue Funde zur ältesten Geschichte der portugiesischen Juden in Hamburg." In *Zeitschrift für die Geschichte der Juden in Deutschland* 3, pp. 58–72.

Cassuto, Isaac, ed. 1908–1920. "Aus dem ältesten Protokollbuch der Portugiesisch-Jüdischen Gemeinde in Hamburg." In *Jahrbuch der Jüdisch-Literarischen Gesellschaft* 6 (1908), pp. 1–54; 7 (1909), pp. 159–210; 8 (1910), pp. 227–290; 9 (1911), pp. 318–366; 10 (1912), pp. 225–95; 11 (1916), pp. 1–76; 13 (1920), pp. 55–118.

Coelho, Possidonio Matheus Laranjo, ed. 1940. *Cartas de El-Rei D. João IV ao Conde da Vidigueira (Marquês de Niza), Embaixador em França,* vol. 1. Lisbon: Ática.

Davenport, Frances Gardiner, ed. (1917) 1967. *European Treaties Bearing on the History of the United States and its Dependencies to 1648,* vol. 1. Washington, D. C.: Carnegie Institution. Reprint, Gloucester, MA: Peter Smith.

Denucé, Jean. 1909. "Privilèges commerciaux accordés par les rois de Portugal aux Flamands et aux Allemands (XVe et XVIe siècles)." In *Archivo Historico Portuguez* 7, pp. 310–19, 377–92.

Dias, Enrico Gomes, ed. 2006. *Gazetas da Restauração, 1641–1648. Uma revisão das estratégias diplomático-militares portuguesas.* Lisbon: Ministério dos Negócios Estrangeiros.

Figueiredo, Jozé Anastasio de. 1790. *Synopsis chronologica de subsidios ainda os mais raros para a historia e estudo critico da legislação portugueza. Desde 1143 até 1603,* vol. 2. Lisbon: Academia Real das Sciencias.

Franco, José Eduardo. and Paulo de Assunção, eds. 2004. *As Metamorfoses de um Polvo. Religião e Política nos Regimentos da Inquisição Portuguesa* (secs. XVI–XIX). Lisbon: Prefácio.

Gallois, Johann Gustav. 1870. *Hamburgische Chronik von den ältesten Zeiten bis auf die Jetztzeit,* 5 vols., 2nd ed. Hamburg: Grüning.

Góis, Damião de. (1554) 1996. *Lisbon in the Renaissance. A New Translation of the Urbis Olisiponis Descriptio,* trans. Jeffrey S. Ruth. New York: Italica Press.

Gualdo Priorato, Galeazzo. 1674. *Relationi de'governi, e stati delle città imperiali, & ansiatiche di Colonia, Lubecca, Bremen, & Amburgo ...*. Bologna: Giacomo Monti.

Hamburger Stadtrecht (1605) 1978. *Der Stadt Hamburgk Gerichtsordnung und Statuta.* Hamburg: Frobenius. Reprint, Hamburg: Kötz.

Häpke, Rudolf, ed. 1923. *Niederländische Akten und Urkunden zur Geschichte der Hanse und zur deutschen Seegeschichte,* vol. 2. Lübeck: Duncker & Humblot.

Heskel, A. 1935. "Consilium politicum wegen der Stadt Hamburg. Eine Denkschrift des Dr. Michael von Mentzel aus dem Jahre 1628." In Heinrich Reincke, ed. *Hamburger geschichtliche Beiträge. Hans Nirrnheim zum siebzigsten Geburtstage,* pp. 40–58. Hamburg: Boysen & Maasch.

Hövelen, Kunrat von. 1668. *Der Uhr-alten Deutschen Grossen und des H. Röm. Reichs Freien An-See- und Handel-Stadt Hamburg Alt-vorige und noch Iz Zu-Nämende Hoheit.* Lübeck: Smalherz.

Klefeker, Johann, ed. 1765–1774. *Sammlung der Hamburgischen Gesetze und Verfassungen in Bürger- und Kirchlichen, auch Cammer- Handlungs- und übrigen Policey-Angelegenheiten und Geschäften samt historischen Einleitungen*, 13 parts. Hamburg: Piscator.

Koen, E. M., ed. 1967–2001. "Notarial Records in Amsterdam relating to the Portuguese Jews in that town up to 1639." In *Studia Rosenthaliana* 1, 1 (1967), pp. 109–15; "Amsterdam Notarial deeds pertaining to the Portuguese Jews in Amsterdam up to 1639." In *Studia Rosenthaliana* 1, 2 (1967), pp. 110–122; 2 (1968), pp. 111–126, 257–272; 3 (1969), pp. 113–125, 234–254; "Notarial Records Relating to the Portuguese Jews in Amsterdam up to 1639." In *Studia Rosenthaliana* 4, 1 (1970), pp. 115–126, 243–261; 5 (1971), pp. 106–124, 219–245; 6 (1972), pp. 107–123; 229–245; 7 (1973), pp. 116–127, 266–279; 8 (1974), pp. 138–145, 300–307; 10 (1976), pp. 96–104, 212–231; 11 (1977), pp. 81–96, 216–227; 12 (1978), pp. 158–179; 13 (1979), pp. 101–114, 220–240; 14 (1980), pp. 79–102; 15 (1981), pp. 143–154, 245–255; 16 (1982), pp. 61–84, 196–218; 17 (1983), pp. 66–79, 210–217; 18 (1984), pp. 61–73; 159–176; 19 (1985), pp. 79–90, 174–184; 20 (1986), pp. 109–130; 21 (1987), pp. 105–115, 198–203, 22 (1988), pp. 58–67, 189–196; 23 (1989), pp. 110–117, 203–209; 24 (1990), pp. 68–77, 216–225; 25 (1991), pp. 107–118, 176–189; 27 (1993), pp. 171–181; 28 (1994), pp. 204–215; 29 (1995), pp. 100–112, 214–230; 30 (1996), pp. 304–318; 31 (1997), pp. 139–151; 32 (1998), pp. 82–94, 210–216, 33 (1999), pp. 80–94; 34 (2000), pp. 74–88; 35 (2001), pp. 67–92.

Leoni, Aron di Leone, and Herman Prins Salomon. 2001. "La nation portugaise de Hambourg en 1617 d'après un document retrouvé." In Henry Méchoulan and Gerard Nahon, eds. *Mémorial I.-S. Révah. Études sur le marranisme, l'hétérodoxie juive et Spinoza*, pp. 263–93. Leuven: Peeters.

Lopes, Fernão. 1895–1896. *Chronica de el-rei D. Fernando*, 3 vols. Lisbon: Escriptorio.

Lünig, Johann Christian, ed. 1714. *Das Teutsche Reichs-Archiv*, vol. 14, 2, 2 (Pars Specialis Continuatio IV, part 2). Leipzig: Friedrich Lanckischens Erben.

Luz, Francisco Mendes da, ed. 1950. "Relação das rendas da coroa de Portugal feita em 1593 por Francisco Carneiro provedor de ementas da Casa dos Contos." In *Boletim da Biblioteca da Universidade de Coimbra* 19, pp. 45–108.

Menéndez Vives, Concepción, and Carmen Torroja Menéndez, eds. 1991. *Tratados internacionales suscritos por España y convenios de los reinos peninsulares (siglos XII al XVII)*. Madrid: Dirección de Archivos Estatales.

Merck, Ernst. 1856. *Briefe des Hamburgischen Bürgermeisters Johann Schulte Lt. an seinen in Lissabon etablierten Sohn Johann* Schulte, *geschrieben in den Jahren 1680–1685*. Hamburg: Perthes-Besser & Mauke.

Oliveira, Eduardo Freire de, ed. (1882–1911) 1982. *Elementos para a história do município de Lisboa*, part 1, 17 vols. Lisbon: Typographia Universal. Reprint, Lisbon: Câmara Municipal.

Oliveira, Nicolao d'. (1620) 1804. *Livro das grandezas de Lisboa*. Lisbon: Impressaõ Regia.

Ordenações Afonsinas (ca. 1448) 1792. *Ordenaçoens do Senhor Rey D. Affonso V*, 5 parts. Coimbra: Real Imprensa da Universidade.

Ordenações Manuelinas (ca. 1513) 1797. *Ordenações do Senhor Rey D. Manuel*, 5 parts. Coimbra: Real Imprensa da Universidade.

Ordenações Filipinas (1603) 1870, 1985. ed. Cândido Mendes de Almeida, 5 parts in 3 vols. Rio de Janeiro: Typ. do Instituto Philomathico. Reprint, Lisbon: Fundação Calouste Gulbenkian.

Pitz, Ernst, ed. 1961. *Die Zolltarife der Stadt Hamburg (Deutsche Zolltarife des Mittelalters und der Neuzeit*, part 2). Wiesbaden: Steiner.

Reils, P. D. H. 1847. "Beiträge zur ältesten Geschichte der Juden in Hamburg." In *Zeitschrift des Vereins für Hamburgische Geschichte* 2, pp. 357–424.

Reincke, Heinrich, ed. 1939. *Hamburgs Weg zum Reich und in die Welt. Urkunden zur 750-Jahr-Feier des Hamburger Hafens.* Hamburg: Petermann.

Révah, Israël Salvador. 1963. "Le premier règlement imprimé de la 'Santa Companhia de Dotar Orfans e Donzelas Pobres.'" In *Boletim Internacional de Bibliografia Luso-Brasileira* 4, pp. 650–91.

Ribeiro, Vitor, ed. 1917. *Privilégios de estrangeiros em Portugal (Ingleses, Franceses, Alemães, Flamengos e Italianos).* Coimbra: Imprensa da Universidade.

Roth, Cecil. 1930. "Neue Kunde von der Marranen-Gemeinde in Hamburg." In *Zeitschrift für die Geschichte der Juden in Deutschland* 2, pp. 228–36.

Salomon, Herman Prins. 1975. "The 'De Pinto' Manuscript. A 17th Century Marrano Family History." In *Studia Rosenthaliana* 9, pp. 1–62.

Santarém, 2º Visconde de [Manuel Francisco de Barros e Sousa da Mesquita de Macedo Leitão e Carvalhosa], ed. 1924. *Memórias e alguns documentos para a história e teoria das Côrtes Geraes*, part 2. Lisbon: Imprensa da Portugal-Brasil.

Schmidt, Michael. 1638. *Warhaffter und gruendlicher Bericht, Wie und welcher gestaldt Ich Michael Schmidt Von Hartich von Sprekelsen gantz unerhoerter unchristlicher und wider Rechtlicher weise auch grosser Gewalt wegen einmahl bezahlter Gelder Und Wucherlichen Interessen, sey beschimpffet ... .* Hamburg.

Schneider, Jürgen, Otto-Ernst Krawehl, and Frank Schulenburg, eds. 2001. *Statistik des Hamburger seewärtigen Einfuhrhandels im 18. Jahrhundert. Nach den Admiralitäts- und Convoygeld-Einnahmebüchern.* St. Katharinen: Scripta-Mercaturae.

Schudt, Johann Jacob. (1714) 1922. *Jüdische Merckwürdigkeiten*, part 1. Frankfurt am Main: Matthias Andreä. Reprint, Berlin: Lamm.

Silva, José Justino de Andrade e, ed. 1854–1859. *Collecção chronológica da legislação portugueza*, 8 vols. Lisbon: Imprensa de J.J.A. Silva.

Silveira, Luís, ed. 1958. *Privilégios concedidos a alemães em Portugal. A certidão de Duarte Fernandez, da Biblioteca de Évora e tradução em língua germânica.* Lisbon: Inspecção Superior das Bibliotecas e Arquivos.

Sousa, Fr. Luís de [Manuel de Sousa Coutinho]. (1623) 1977. *História de S. Domingos, ed. M. Lopes de Almeida*, 2 parts. Porto: Lello.

Sousa, José Roberto Monteiro de Campos Coelho e, ed. 1783. *Systema, ou Collecção dos Regimentos reaes*, vol. 2. Lisbon: Officina de Francisco Borges de Sousa.

Spinoza, Benedict de. (1670) 1883, 1951. *A Theologico-Political Treatise*, trans. Robert H. M. Elwes. London: George Bell & Sons. Reprint, New York: Dover Publications.

Studemund-Halévy, Michael, ed. 1994a. "Dokumentation Kahal Kadosh Bet Isreael." In Michael Studemund-Halévy, ed. *Die Sefarden in Hamburg*, part 1, pp. 37–62. Hamburg: Buske.

Taylor, John. 1888. *Early Prose and Poetical Works, the Water Poet 1580–1653.* London: Hamilton Adams & Co.

Teensma, Benjamin Nicolaas. 1976. "De levensgeschiedenis van Abraham Peregrino, alias Manuel Cardoso de Macedo." In *Studia Rosenthaliana* 10, pp. 1–36.

Vasconcelos, Luís Mendes de. (1608) 1990. *Do sítio de Lisboa. Diálogos.* Lisbon: Livros Horizonte.

Vieira, António. 1951. *Obras Escolhidas*, ed. António Sérgio and Hernâni Cidade, vol. 4 (Obras Várias 2, Os Judeus e a Inquisição). Lisbon: Sá da Costa.

Winkelman, Pieter H., ed. 1977–1983. *Amsterdamse bevrachtingscontracten, wisselprotesten en bodemerijen van de notarissen Jan Frans Bruyningh, Jacob Meerhout, 1593–1625*, 4 vols. 's-Gravenhage: Nijhoff.

Zedler, Johann Heinrich, ed. 1732–1754. *Grosses vollständiges Universal Lexicon Aller Wissenschafften und Künste*, 64 vols. and 4 supplements. Halle: Zedler.

Ziegra, Christian, ed. 1767. *Beyträge zur politischen hamburgischen Historie*, Stück 2. Hamburg: Christian Simon Schröder.

Secondary Sources

Agats, Arthur. 1904. *Der hansische Baienhandel*. Heidelberg: Carl Winter.

Ahrens, Gerhard. 1962. "Das Botenwesen der Hamburger Kaufmannschaft (1571–1821)." In *Archiv für deutsche Postgeschichte* 1, pp. 28–42.

Albrecht, Johannes. 1937. *Dom Duarte de Bragança. Ein Lebensschicksal aus dem Zeitalter des Dreißigjährigen Krieges*. Bremen: Geist.

Alcalá-Zamora y Queipo de Llano, José. 1970. "Velas y cañones en la política septentrional de Felipe II." In *Cuadernos de historia Jerónimo Zurita* 23/24, pp. 225–44.

—. 1975. *España, Flandes y el Mar del Norte (1618–1639). La última ofensiva europea de los Austrias madrileños*. Barcelona: Planeta.

Almeida, A. A. Marques de. 1986. "O perdão geral de 1605" In *Primeiras Jornadas de História Moderna. Actas*, vol. 2. Lisbon: Centro de História da Universidade de Lisboa, pp. 885–98.

Amaral, Maria Valentina Cotta do. 1965. *Privilégios de mercadores estrangeiros no reinado de D. João III*. Lisbon: Instituto de Alta Cultura.

Amsinck, Caesar. 1886 and 1891. *Die niederländische und hamburgische Familie Amsinck. Ein Versuch einer Familiengeschichte*, 2 parts. Hamburg: Lütcke & Wulff.

—. 1894. "Die ersten hamburgischen Assecuranz-Compagnien und der Actienhandel im Jahre 1720." In *Zeitschrift des Vereins für Hamburgische Geschichte* 9, pp. 465–94.

Antunes, Cátia. 2004. *Globalisation in the Early Modern Period. The economic relationship between Amsterdam and Lisbon, 1640–1705*. Amsterdam: Aksant.

Azevedo, João Lúcio de. 1931. *História de António Vieira*, 2 vols. Lisbon: Livraria Clássica.

—. 1978. *Épocas de Portugal económico. Esboços de história*, 4th ed. Lisbon: Livraria Clássica.

—. 1989. *História dos cristãos novos portugueses*, 3rd ed. Lisbon: Livraria Clássica.

Baasch, Ernst. 1893 "Erwiderung (auf die Ehrenbergsche Besprechung von Baasch, Hamburgs Seeschiffahrt und Waarenhandel)." In *Jahrbücher für Nationalökonomie und Statistik* 6 (3rd series), pp. 937–39.

—. 1894. "Hamburgs Seeschiffahrt und Waarenhandel vom Ende des 16. bis zur Mitte des 17. Jahrhunderts." In *Zeitschrift des Vereins für Hamburgische Geschichte* 9, pp. 295–420.

—. 1895/6. "Zur Geschichte des lutherischen Gottesdienstes in Lissabon." In *Hansische Geschichtsblätter* 23, pp. 165–72.

—. 1899. "Zur Geschichte des Ehrb. Kaufmanns in Hamburg." In *Festschrift für die Versammlung des Hansischen Geschichtsvereins und des Vereins für Niederdeutsche*

Sprachforschung am 23. und 24. Mai 1899 in Hamburg, pp. 1–66. Hamburg: Lütcke & Wulff.

—. 1902. "Handel und Öffentlichkeit der Presse in Hamburg." In *Preußische Jahrbücher* 110, pp. 121–42.

—. 1907. "Die 'Durchfuhr' in Lübeck. Ein Beitrag zur Geschichte der lübischen Handelspolitik im 17. und 18. Jahrhundert." In *Hansische Geschichtsblätter* 34, pp. 109–52.

—. 1915. *Die Handelskammer zu Hamburg 1665–1915*, 2 vols. Hamburg: Gräfe & Sillem.

—. 1929. "Zur Statistik des Ein- und Ausfuhrhandels Hamburgs Anfang des 18. Jahrhunderts." In *Hansische Geschichtsblätter* 54, pp. 89–144.

Bachmann, Sarah A. 2017. *Die kaiserliche Notariatspraxis im frühneuzeitlichen Hamburg*. Cologne: Böhlau.

Backmann, Sibylle, and Hans-Jörg Künast. 1998. "Einführung." In Sibylle Backmann, Hans-Jörg Künast, Sabine Ullmann, and B. Ann Tlusty, eds. *Ehrkonzepte in der Frühen Neuzeit. Identitäten und Abgrenzungen*, pp. 13–23. Berlin: Akademie Verlag.

Baetens, Roland. 1976. *De nazomer van Antwerpens welvaart. De diaspora en het handelshuis De Groote tijdens de eerste helft der 17de eeuw*, 2 parts. Brussels: Gemeentekrediet van België.

Bahrfeldt, Max von. 1917. "Über die älteren Hamburger Portugalöser." In *Zeitschrift des Vereins für Hamburgische Geschichte* 19, pp. 1–37.

Barros, Amândio Jorge Morais. 2003. "Irmandades do Mar (Marinheiros, mercadores e Inquisição no Porto dos séculos XV e XVI)." In Francisco Calo Lourido, ed. *Pontevedra e o Mar. Actas do Simposio de historia marítima do século XII ao XVI celebrado en Pontevedra o 29 e 30 de novembro e 1 de decembro de 2001*, pp. 73–93. Pontevedra: Concelho de Pontevedra.

Baumann, Wolf-Rüdiger. 1982. *The merchants adventurers and the continental cloth-trade (1560s–1620s)*. Florence: European University Institute.

Behringer, Wolfgang. 1990. *Thurn und Taxis. Die Geschichte ihrer Post und ihrer Unternehmen*. Munich: Piper.

—. 2003 *Im Zeichen des Merkur. Reichspost und Kommunikationsrevolution in der Frühen Neuzeit*. Göttingen: Vandenhoeck & Ruprecht.

Belo, André. 2001. *As Gazetas e os Livros: A Gazeta de Lisboa e a vulgarização do impresso (1715–1760)*. Lisbon: Instituto de Ciências Sociais da Universidade de Lisboa.

Benedict, Philip. 2001. *The faith and fortunes of France's Huguenots, 1600–85*. Aldershot: Ashgate.

—. 2002. *Christ's Churches Purely Reformed: A Social History of Calvinism*. New Haven: Yale University Press.

Beneke, Otto, ed. 1886. *Hamburgische Geschichten und Denkwürdigkeiten*, 2nd corr. and suppl. ed. Berlin: Hertz.

Beneke, Otto. 1875. "Zur Geschichte der nichtlutherischen Christen in Hamburg 1575 bis 1589." In *Zeitschrift des Vereins für Hamburgische Geschichte* 6, pp. 317–44.

Bethencourt, Francisco. 1993. "A Inquisição." In Yvette Kace Centeno, ed. *Portugal. Mitos Revisitados*, pp. 100–38. Lisbon: Salamandra.

—. 1996. *História das Inquisições. Portugal, Espanha e Itália*. Lisbon: Companhia das Letras.

—. 2000. "A Inquisição." In Carlos Moreira Azevedo, ed. *História religiosa de Portugal*, vol. 2, pp. 95–131. Lisbon: Círculo de Leitores.

—. 2009. *The Inquisition. A Global History, 1478–1834*. Cambridge: Cambridge University Press.

Beukemann, Ulrich. 1912. "Die Geschichte des Hamburger Mäklerrechts. Mit einem Anhang von z. T. ungedruckten Mäklerordnungen." In Konrad Beyerle, ed. *Deutschrechtliche Beiträge. Forschungen und Quellen zur Geschichte des Deutschen Rechts*, vol. 7, pp. 447–634. Heidelberg: Carl Winter.

Beutin, Ludwig. 1928. "Zur Entstehung des deutschen Konsulatswesens im 16. und 17. Jahrhundert." In *Vierteljahrschrift für Sozial- und Wirtschaftsgeschichte* 21, pp. 438–48.

—. 1929. *Hanse und Reich im handelspolitischen Endkampf gegen England*. Berlin: Curtius.

—. 1933. *Der deutsche Seehandel im Mittelmeergebiet bis zu den napoleonischen Kriegen*. Neumünster: Wachholtz.

Beutin, Wolfgang. 1994. "'Soll ein Land oder eine Stadt floriren ... / so muß man immer darinn kauffen und verkauffen ....' Johann Balthasar Schupp (1610–1661)." In Wolfgang Beutin, ed. *Vom Mittelalter zur Moderne*, vol. 1, pp. 143–66. Hamburg: von Bockel.

Bicalho, Maria Fernanda Baptista. 2003. "O que significava ser cidadão nos tempos coloniais." In Martha Abreu and Rachel Soihet, eds. *Ensino de História. Conceitos, temáticas e métodos*, pp. 139–51. Rio de Janeiro: Casa da Palavra.

Bleeck, Hans. 1985. *Lüneburgs Salzhandel im Zeitalter des Merkantilismus (16. bis 18. Jahrhundert)*. Lüneburg: H. Bleeck.

Bode, Hermann. 1908. *Die Anfänge wirtschaftlicher Berichterstattung in der Presse. Eine volkswirtschaftliche Studie als Beitrag zur Geschichte des Zeitungswesens*. Pforzheim: Bode.

Bodian, Miriam. 1987. "The 'Portuguese' dowry societies in Venice and Amsterdam. A case study in communal differentiation within the Marrano diaspora." In *Italia* 6, pp. 30–61.

—. 1997. *Hebrews of the Portuguese Nation. Conversos and Community in Early Modern Amsterdam*. Bloomington: Indiana University Press.

—. 2008. "Hebrews of the Portuguese Nation. The Ambiguous Boundaries of Self-Definition." In *Jewish Social Studies* 15, 1 (New Series), pp. 66–80.

Bog, Ingomar. 1959. *Der Reichsmerkantilismus. Studien zur Wirtschaftspolitik des Heiligen Römischen Reiches im 17. und 18. Jahrhundert*. Stuttgart: G. Fischer.

Böhm, Günter. 1994. "Antijüdische Ressentiments gegenüber den Hamburger Sefardim im 17. Jahrhundert." In Michael Studemund-Halévy, ed. *Die Sefarden in Hamburg*, part 1, pp. 89–102. Hamburg: Buske.

Bolland, Jürgen. 1951. "Die Gesellschaft der Flandernfahrer in Hamburg während des 15. Jahrhunderts." In *Zeitschrift des Vereins für Hamburgische Geschichte* 41, pp. 155–88.

—. 1977. *Senat und Bürgerschaft. Über das Verhältnis zwischen Bürger und Stadtregiment im alten Hamburg*, 2nd ed. Hamburg: Christians.

Bonacich, Edna. 1973. "A Theory of Middleman Minorities." In *American Sociological Review* 38, pp. 583–94.

Böning, Holger. 2007. "Hamburg als Vorreiter in der deutschen Pressegeschichte. Erste populärwissenschaftliche Zeitschriften im 17. Jahrhundert und die Anfänge des deutschen Zeitschriftenwesens." In Dirk Brietzke, Norbert Fischer, and Arno Herzig, eds. *Hamburg und sein norddeutsches Umland. Aspekte des Wandels seit der Frühen Neuzeit. Festschrift für Franklin Kopitzsch*. Hamburg: DOBU Verlag, pp. 123–36.

Borges, Nelson Correia. 1986. *A arte nas festas do casamento de D. Pedro II. Lisboa 1687*. Porto: Paisagem.

Boxer, Charles Ralph. 1949. "Padre António Vieira, S. J., and the Institution of the Brazil Company in 1649" In *Hispanic American Historical Review* 29, 4, pp. 474–97.

Boyajian, James Charles. 1993. *Portuguese Trade in Asia under the Habsburgs, 1580–1640*. Baltimore: Johns Hopkins University Press.

Braden, Jutta. 2001. *Hamburger Judenpolitik im Zeitalter lutherischer Orthodoxie 1590–1710*. Hamburg: Christians.

—. 2003. "Die Hamburger Judenpolitik und die lutherisch-orthodoxe Geistlichkeit im 17. Jahrhundert." In *Zeitschrift des Vereins für Hamburgische Geschichte* 89, pp. 1–40.

—. 2005. "Eine Probe aufs Exempel. Neue Forschungskonzepte am Beispiel Hamburger Konversionen von Juden zum Christentum (1600–1850)." In *Aschkenas* 15, 2, pp. 303–35.

—. 2016. *Konvertiten aus dem Judentum in Hamburg, 1603–1760. Esdras Edzardis Stiftung zur Bekehrung der Juden von 1667*. Göttingen: Wallstein.

Braga, Isabel M. R. Mendes Drumond. 1998. "A circulação e a distribuição dos produtos." In Joel Serrão and António Henrique de Oliveira Marques, eds. *Nova História de Portugal*, vol. 5, pp. 195–247. Lisbon: Presença.

—. 2002. *Os estrangeiros e a Inquisição portuguesa (Séculos XVI e XVII)*. Lisbon: Hugin.

Braga, Paulo Drumond. 2000. "Alemães na Lisboa seiscentista. As conversões ao catolicismo." In Helmut Siepmann, ed. *Portugal, Indien und Deutschland. Portugal, Índia e Alemanha. Akten der V. Deutsch-Portugiesischen Arbeitsgespräche. Actas do V Encontro Luso-Alemão*, pp. 421–33. Cologne: Zentrum Portugiesischsprachige Welt.

—. 2001. "Estrangeiros ao serviço da Inquisição portuguesa. Alguns contributos," In Luís A. de Oliveira Ramos et al. eds. *Estudos em homenagem a João Francisco Marques*, pp. 253–60. Porto: Faculdade das Letras da Universidade do Porto.

Brazão, Eduardo. 1979. *A Diplomacia Portuguesa nos Séculos XVII e XVIII*, vol. 1. Lisbon: Resistência.

Brentano, Lujo. 1916. *Die Anfänge des modernen Kapitalismus*. Munich: Verlag der K.B. Akademie der Wissenschaften.

Brulez, Wilfrid. 1959. *De firma Della Faille en de internationale handel van Vlaamse firma's in de 16e eeuw*. Brussels: Koninklijke Vlaamse Academie voor Wetenschappen.

—. 1960. "De diaspora der Antwerpse kooplui op het einde van de 16de eeuw." In *Bijdragen voor de Geschiedenis der Nederlanden* 15, pp. 279–306.

Brunner, Otto. 1963. "Souveränitätsproblem und Sozialstruktur in den deutschen Reichsstädten der früheren Neuzeit." In *Vierteljahrschrift für Sozial- und Wirtschaftsgeschichte* 50, pp. 329–60.

Buek, Friedrich Georg. 1840. *Genealogische und biographische Notizen über die seit der Reformation verstorbenen hamburgischen Bürgermeister*. Hamburg: Johann August Meißner.

—. 1857. *Die hamburgischen Oberalten, ihre bürgerliche Wirksamkeit und ihre Familien*. Hamburg: Perthes-Besser & Mauke.

Bulst, Neithard. 2008. "Les étrangers dans la ville. Perception de l' 'autre' et rapport avec 'autrui' selon le droit municipal allemand au Moyen Âge." In Pilar González-Bernaldo, Manuela Martini, and Marie-Louise Pelus-Kaplan, eds. *Étrangers et sociétés: Représentations, coexistences, interactions dans la longue durée*, pp. 45–62. Rennes: Presses universitaires de Rennes.

Burkhart, Dagmar. 2006. *Eine Geschichte der Ehre*. Darmstadt: Wissenschaftliche Buchgesellschaft.

Cardim, Pedro. 1998. "D. Filipe III (1621–1640): Do consenso à rebelião." In José Mattoso, ed. *História de Portugal*, vol. 4, pp. 401–04. Lisbon: Estampa.
—. 2002. "Embaixadores e representantes diplomáticos da coroa portuguesa no século XVII." In *Cultura* 15, pp. 47–86.
—. 2004. "O embaixador seiscentista segundo António da Silva e Sousa, autor de Instrucçam Politica de Legados (Hamburgo, 1656)." In Zília Osório de Castro, ed. *Diplomatas e Diplomacia. Retratos, Cerimónias e Práticas*, pp. 155–213. Lisbon: Livros Horizonte.
Cardoso, Eurico Carlos Esteves Lage. 1999. *História dos correios em Portugal em datas e ilustrada*. Lisbon: Edição do Autor.
Carlier, Myriam. 1994. "Migration Trends in the Towns of Flanders and Brabant (15th–18th Century)." In Simonetta Cavaciocchi, ed. *Le migrazioni in Europa. Secc. XIII–XVIII. Atti della "Venticinquesima Settimana di Studi,"* pp. 355–70. Florence: Le Monnier.
Cerrillo Cruz, Gonzalo. 2000. *Los familiares de la inquisición española*. Valladolid: Junta de Castilla y León.
Coelho, António Borges. 1987. *Inquisição de Évora. Dos primórdios a 1668*, 2 vols. Lisbon: Caminho.
—. 2001. "Política, dinheiro e fé. Cristãos-novos e judeus portugueses no tempo dos Filipes." In António Borges Coelho, *Política, Dinheiro e Fé. Questionar a História V*, pp. 109–52. Lisbon: Caminho.
Cohen, Abner. 1971. "Cultural Strategies in the Organization of Trading Diasporas." In Claude Meillassoux, ed. *The Development of Indigenous Trade and Markets in West Africa*, pp. 266–81. London: Oxford University Press.
Cohen, Robert. 1982. "Passage to a new world. The sephardi poor of eighteenth century Amsterdam." In Lea Dasberg and Jonathan N. Cohen, eds. *Neveh Ya'akov. Jubilee volume presented to Dr. Jaap Meijer on the occasion of his seventieth birthday*, pp. 31–42. Assen: Van Gorcum.
Costa, Leonor Freire. 2002. *O transporte no Atlântico e a Companhia Geral do Comércio do Brasil (1580–1663)*, 2 vols. Lisbon: Comissão Nacional para as Comemorações dos Descobrimentos Portugueses.
—. 2004. "Merchant groups in the 17th-century Brazilian sugar trade. Reappraising old topics with new research insights." In *e-Journal of Portuguese History* 2, 1 (2004), http://www.brown.edu/Departments/Portuguese_Brazilian_Studies/ejph/html/issue3/pdf/lfcosta.pdf.
—. 2005. "Elite mercantil na Restauração. Para uma releitura" In Nuno Gonçalo Monteiro, Pedro Cardim, and Mafalda Soares da Cunha, eds. *Optima Pars. Elites Ibero-Americanas do Antigo Regime*, pp. 99–131. Lisbon: Imprensa de Ciencias Sociais.
Crespo Solana Ana, ed. 2010. *Comunidades Transnacionales. Colonias de mercaderes extranjeros en el Mundo Atlántico (1500–1830)*. Madrid: Doce Calles.
Curtin, Philip D. 1984. *Crosscultural Trade in World History*. Cambridge: Cambridge University Press.
Daenell, Ernst. 1906. *Die Blütezeit der deutschen Hanse. Hansische Geschichte von der zweiten Hälfte des XIV. bis zum letzten Viertel des XV. Jahrhunderts*, vol. 2. Berlin: Reimer.
Dallmeier, Martin, ed. 1990. *500 Jahre Post – Thurn und Taxis. Fürstliches Marstallmuseum, Regensburg. Ausstellung anlässlich der 500jährigen Wiederkehr der Anfänge der Post in Mitteleuropa 1490–1990*. Regensburg: Fürst Thurn und Taxis Zentralarchiv.

Das, Gerrit. 1920. *Foppe van Aitzema. Bijdrage tot de kennis van de diplomatie betrekkingen der Nederlanden tot Denemarken, de Hanzesteden, den Nedersaksischen Kreits en den Keizer tijdens den dertig-jarigen oorlog*. Utrecht: den Boor.

Davis, Natalie Z. 1997. "Religion and capitalism once again? Jewish merchant culture in the seventeenth century." In *Representations* 59, pp. 56–84.

Detlefsen, Detlef. 1906. "Die städtische Entwicklung Glückstadts unter König Christian IV." In *Zeitschrift der Gesellschaft für Schleswig-Holsteinische Geschichte* 36, pp. 191–256.

Dias, A. M. Vaz. 1936. "Over den vermogenstoestand der Amsterdamsche Joden in de 17e en de 18e eeuw." In *Tijdschrift voor Geschiedenis* 51, pp. 165–76.

Dias, João José Alves. 1998. "A moeda." In Joel Serrão and António Henrique de Oliveira Marques, eds. *Nova História de Portugal*, vol. 5, pp. 254–76. Lisbon: Presença.

Dollinger, Philippe. 1970. *The German Hansa*, trans. and ed. D. S. Ault and S. H. Steinberg. Stanford: Stanford University Press.

Domingos, Manuela D. 1993. "Visitas do Santo Ofício às naus estrangeiras. Regimentos e quotidianos." In *Revista da Biblioteca Nacional*. 8, 1 (2nd Series), pp. 1–272.

Domínguez Ortiz, Antonio. 1963. "Guerra económica y comercio extranjero en el reinado de Felipe IV." In *Hispania* 23, pp. 71–110.

—. 1996. "Los extranjeros en la vida española durante el siglo XVII." In Antonio Domínguez Ortiz, *Los extranjeros en la vida española durante el siglo XVII y otros artículos*, pp. 17–181. Seville: Diputación de Sevilla, Area de Cultura y Ecología.

Dormeier, Heinrich. 2009. "Religiöse Bruderschaften der 'Oberschicht' in Lübeck im 15./16. Jahrhundert. Frömmigkeitsformen, soziale Beziehungen und wirtschaftliche Interessen," In Antjekathrin Graßmann, ed. *Der Kaufmann und der liebe Gott. Zu Kommerz und Kirche in Mittelalter und Früher Neuzeit*, pp. 21–44. Trier: Porta Alba.

Dreves, Lebrecht Blücher. 1850. *Geschichte der katholischen Gemeinden zu Hamburg und Altona*. Schaffhausen: Hurter.

Durrer, Ingrid. 1953. "As relações económicas entre Portugal e a liga hanseática desde os últimos anos do século XIV até 1640." Coimbra: Universidade de Coimbra (unpublished graduation thesis).

Duve, Thomas. 2008. *Sonderrecht in der Fühen Neuzeit. Studien zum ius singulare und den privilegia miserabilium personarum, senum und indorum in Alter und Neuer Welt*. Frankfurt am Main: Klostermann.

Ehrenberg, Richard. 1885. "Hamburger Handel und Handelspolitik im 16. Jahrhundert." In Karl Koppmann, ed. *Aus Hamburgs Vergangenheit. Kulturhistorische Bilder aus verschiedenen Jahrhunderten*, pp. 281–321. vol. 1. Hamburg: Leopold Voß.

—. 1889. "Zur Geschichte der Hamburger Handlung im 16. Jahrhundert." In *Zeitschrift des Vereins für Hamburgische Geschichte* 8, pp. 139–82.

—. 1893a. Review of: Ernst Baasch, Hamburgs Seeschiffahrt und Warenhandel vom Ende des 16. bis zur Mitte des 17. Jahrhunderts. In *Jahrbücher für Nationalökonomie und Statistik* 6 (3rd Seires), pp. 616–18.

—. 1893b. *Die Jesuiten-Mission in Altona* (Altona unter Schauenburgischer Herrschaft, vol. 7). Altona: Harder.

—. 1896. *Hamburg und England im Zeitalter der Königin Elisabeth*. Jena: G. Fischer.

—. 1899. "Vom Roden Tollen (Aus der Hamburgischen Handelsgeschichte 3)." In *Zeitschrift des Vereins für Hamburgische Geschichte* 10, pp. 29–40.

—. 1900 "Handelsgeschichtliches Allerlei." In *Mitteilungen des Vereins für Hamburgische Geschichte 7*, 19, pp. 120–21.

Ehrhardt, Marion. [1990]. *Die Bartholomäus-Brüderschaft der Deutschen in Lissabon. Ein Rückblick*. Lisbon: Bartholomäus-Brüderschaft.

Espinosa, Fernanda. 1972. "Bolsas Marítimas." In Fernanda Espinosa, ed. *Escritos Históricos*, pp. 174–76. Porto: Porto Editora.

Everaert, John. 1995. "Sur le balcon de l'Atlantique. La 'Nation Flamande' à Lisbonne au XVIIe siècle." In *Handelingen van het Genootschap voor Geschiedenis 132*, pp. 347–72.

Faria, Ana Maria Homem Leal de. 2005. *Duarte Ribeiro de Macedo. Um diplomata moderno (1618–1680)*. Lisbon: Ministério dos Negócios Estrangeiros.

Ferreira, Godofredo. 1964. *Algumas achegas para a história do correio em Portugal*. Lisbon: Administração Geral dos C. T. T.

Ferro, João Pedro. 1996. *Para a história da administração pública na Lisboa seiscentista. O Senado da Câmara (1671–1716)*. Lisbon: Planeta.

Fink, Georg. 1931. "Diplomatische Vertretungen der Hanse seit dem 17. Jahrhundert bis zur Auflösung der Hanseatischen Gesellschaft in Berlin 1920." In *Hansische Geschichtsblätter 56*, pp. 112–55.

Fonseca, Francisco Belard da. 1948/1949. "Arquivo Geral da Alfândega de Lisboa." In *Anais das Bibliotecas e Arquivos 20*, pp.50–77.

—. 1954. "Subsídios para a história das alfândegas em Portugal." In *Revista Aduaneira 1*.

Frade, Florbela Veiga. 2006. "As relações económicas e sociais das comunidades sefarditas portuguesas. O trato e a família, 1532–1632." Lisbon: Universidade de Lisboa (unpublished diss.).

Frentz, Eva-Christine. 1985. *Das Hamburgische Admiralitätsgericht (1623–1811). Prozeß und Rechtsprechung*. Frankfurt am Main: Lang.

Frevert, Ute. 2003. "Vertrauen. Eine historische Spurensuche." In Ute Frevert, ed. *Vertrauen. Historische Annäherungen*, pp. 7–66. Göttingen: Vandenhoeck & Ruprecht.

Friedland, Klaus. 1960. "Hamburger Englandfahrer 1512–1557." In *Zeitschrift des Vereins für Hamburgische Geschichte 46*, pp. 1–44.

Friedrichs, Christopher R. 2000. *Urban Politics in Early Modern Europe*. London: Routledge.

Fuchs, Arnold. 1921. "Aus dem Itinerarium des Christian Knorr von Rosenroth." In *Zeitschrift des Vereins für Hamburgische Geschichte 24*, pp. 87–139.

Gaedechens, Otto Christian. "Die Portugaleser." 1850. In Otto Christian Gaedechens, ed. *Hamburgische Münzen und Medaillen, Abt. 1 (Die Münzen und Medaillen seit dem Jahre 1753)*, pp. 2–9. Hamburg: Meissner.

—. 1880. *Die Niederländische Armen-Casse. Hamburgs stille Wohltäterin*, 3rd ed. Hamburg: Meissner.

Geisenheimer, H. 1912. "Der Bremer und Hamburger Aufenthalt des toskanischen Erbprinzen im Jahre 1668. Nach zwei Handschriften des Staatsarchivs zu Florenz." In *Zeitschrift des Vereins für Hamburgische Geschichte 17*, pp. 1–53.

Gelder, Ludwig, and Manfred F. Fischer, eds. 1991. *"Nutzen und Zierde zugleich bieten dem Auge sich dar." Hamburgs neue Börse 1841–1991*. Hamburg: Handelskammer Hamburg.

Gelder, Maartje van. 2009. *Trading Places. The Netherlandish Merchants in Early Modern Venice*. Leiden: Brill.

Gelderblom, Oscar. 2000. *Zuid-Nederlandse kooplieden en de opkomst van de Amsterdamse stapelmarkt (1578–1630)*. Hilversum: Verloren.

—. 2013. *Cities of commerce: the institutional foundations of international trade in the Low Countries, 1250–1650*. Princeton: Princeton University Press.

Gennrich, Paul Wilhelm. 1936. *Evangelium und Deutschtum in Portugal. Geschichte der Deutschen Evangelischen Gemeinde in Lissabon*. Berlin: De Gruyter.

Gindely, Anton. 1890. "Die maritimen Pläne der Habsburger und die Antheilnahme Kaiser Ferdinands II. am polnisch-schwedischen Kriege während der Jahre 1627–1628." In *Denkschriften der kaiserlichen Akademie der Wissenschaften in Wien. Philosophisch-Historische Classe* 39, 4.

Girard, Albert. 1932. *Le commerce français à Séville et Cadix au temps des Habsbourg. Contribution à l'étude du commerce étranger en Espagne aux XVIe et XVIIe siècles*. Paris: de Boccard.

Godinho, Vitorino Magalhães. 1968a. "1580 e a Restauração." In Vitorino Magalhães Godinho, *Ensaios II. Sobre História de Portugal*, pp. 255–91. Lisbon: Sá da Costa.

—. 1968b. "A divisão da história de Portugal em períodos." In Vitorino Magalhães Godinho, *Ensaios II. Sobre História de Portugal*, pp. 1–12. Lisbon: Sá da Costa.

—. 1968c. "A evolução dos complexos histórico-geográficos." In Vitorino Magalhães Godinho, *Ensaios II. Sobre História de Portugal*, pp. 13–23. Lisbon: Sá da Costa.

—. 1968d. "Finanças públicas e estrutura do Estado." In Vitorino Magalhães Godinho, *Ensaios II. Sobre História de Portugal*, pp. 25–63. Lisbon: Sá da Costa.

—. 1968e. "Flutuações económicas e devir estrutural do século XV ao século XVII." In Vitorino Magalhães Godinho, *Ensaios II. Sobre História de Portugal*, pp. 175–205. Lisbon: Sá da Costa.

—. 1968f. "Portugal, as frotas do açúcar e as frotas do ouro (1670–1770)." In Vitorino Magalhães Godinho, *Ensaios II. Sobre História de Portugal*, pp. 293–315. Lisbon: Sá da Costa.

—. 1978. "L'émigration portugaise (XVe–XXe siècles). Une constante structurale et les réponses aux changements du monde." In *Revista de História Económica e Social* 1, pp. 5–32.

Gomes, Saul António. 2005. "Percepções em torno da história do tabelionado medieval português." In *Revista de História da Sociedade e da Cultura* 5, pp. 81–100.

Gómez-Centurión Jiménez, Carlos. 1986. "Las relaciones hispano-hanseaticas durante el reinado de Felipe II." In *Revista de Historia Naval* 15, pp. 65–83.

Gönnenwein, Otto. 1939. *Das Stapel- und Niederlagsrecht*. Weimar: Böhlau.

Gorißen, Stefan. 2003. "Der Preis des Vertrauens. Unsicherheit, Institutionen und Rationalität im vorindustriellen Fernhandel." In Ute Frevert, ed. *Vertrauen. Historische Annäherungen*, pp. 90–118. Göttingen: Vandenhoeck & Ruprecht.

Gotzmann, Andreas, and Stephan Wendehorst. 2007. "Zwischen Kaiser, Landesherrschaft und Halacha. Zwischenräume als jüdische Rechts- und Handlungsspielräume." In Andreas Gotzmann and Stephan Wendehorst, eds. *Juden im Recht. Neue Zugänge zur Rechtsgeschichte der Juden im Alten Reich*. Berlin: Duncker & Humblot.

Graf, Friedrich Wilhelm. 2004. "Beeinflussen religiöse Weltbilder den ökonomischen Habitus?" In Hartmut Berghoff and Jakob Vogel, eds. *Wirtschaftsgeschichte als Kulturgeschichte. Dimensionen eines Perspektivenwechsels*, pp. 241–64. Frankfurt am Main: Campus Verlag.

—. 2009. "Vorherbestimmt zu Freiheitsaktivismus. Transformationen des globalen Calvinismus." In Ansgar Reiss and Sabine Witt, eds. *Calvinismus. Die Reformierten in Deutschland und Europa. Eine Ausstellung des Deutschen Historischen Museums Berlin und der Johannes-a-Lasco-Bibliothek Emden*, pp. 384–91. Dresden: Sandstein.

Grafe, Regina. 1998. *Der spanische Seehandel mit Nordwesteuropa von der Mitte des sechzehnten bis zur Mitte des siebzehnten Jahrhunderts. Ein Forschungsüberblick.* Saarbrücken: Verlag für Entwicklungspolitik.

Graizbord, David. 2004. *Souls in dispute. Converso identities in Iberia and the Jewish diaspora, 1580–1700.* Philadelphia: University of Pennsylvania Press.

Greif, Avner. 1993. "Contract Enforceability and Economic Institutions in Early Trade: The Maghribi Traders' Coalition." In *American Economic Review* 83, 3, pp. 525–48.

—. 2006. *Institutions and the Path to the Modern Economy. Lessons from Medieval Trade.* Cambridge: Cambridge University Press.

Greif, Avner, Paul Milgrom, and Barry R. Weingast. 1994. "Coordination, Commitment, and Enforcement. The Case of the Merchant Guild." In *Journal of Political Economy* 102, 4, pp. 745–76.

Grunwald, Max. 1902. *Portugiesengräber auf deutscher Erde. Beiträge zur Kultur- und Kunstgeschichte.* Hamburg: Alfred Janssen.

Guinnane, Timothy W. 2005. "Trust: A concept too many." In *Jahrbuch für Wirtschaftsgeschichte / Economic History Yearbook* 46, 1, pp. 77–92.

Häberlein, Mark. 2016. *Aufbruch ins globale Zeitalter. Die Handelswelt der Fugger und Welser.* Darmstadt: Theiss.

Hammel-Kiesow, Rolf. 2004. *Die Hanse*, 3rd updated ed. Munich: C. H. Beck.

Hancock, David. 2005. "The Trouble with Networks: Managing the Scots' Early-Modern Madeira Trade." In *The Business History Review* 79, 3, pp. 467–91.

Häpke, Rudolf. 1925a. "Die Erforschung der hansischen Spanienfahrt. Zugleich ein Gedenkblatt zu Bernhard Hagedorns zehnjährigem Todestag." In *Hansische Geschichtsblätter* 50, pp. 147–54.

—. 1925b. "Reichswirtschaftspolitik und Hanse nach den Wiener Reichsakten des 16. Jahrhunderts." In *Hansische Geschichtsblätter* 50, pp. 164–209.

Hardtwig, Wolfgang. *Genossenschaft, Sekte, Verein in Deutschland*, vol. 1. Munich: C. H. Beck, 1997.

Haupt, Heinz-Gerhard. 2007. "Comparative history. A contested method." In *Historisk Tijdskrift* 127, 4, pp. 697–716.

Hauschild-Thiessen, Renate. 1974. *Die Niederländische Armen-Casse. "Hamburgs stille Wohlthäterin." Ihre Geschichte von 1585 bis zur Gegenwart.* Hamburg: Christians.

Heckscher, Eli F. 1955. *Mercantilism*, trans. Mendel Shapiro, vol. 2. New York: Macmillan.

Heiber, Helmut. 1966. *Walter Frank und sein Reichsinstitut für Geschichte des neuen Deutschlands.* Stuttgart: Deutsche Verlags-Anstalt.

Henn, Volker. 1998. "Was war die Hanse?" In Jörgen Bracker, Volker Henn, and Rainer Postel, eds. *Die Hanse. Lebenswirklichkeit und Mythos. Textband zur Hamburger Hanse-Ausstellung von 1989*, pp. 14–23. Lübeck: Schmidt-Romhild.

Hermes, Rudolf. 1934. *Aus der Geschichte der Deutschen evangelisch-reformierten Gemeinde in Hamburg.* Hamburg: Christians.

Herzog, Tamar. 2003. *Defining Nations. Immigrants and Citizens in Early Modern Spain and Spanish America.* New Haven: Yale University Press.

Hespanha, António Manuel. 1986. *As Vésperas do Leviathan. Instituições e Poder Político. Portugal – Séc. XVII,* 2 vols. Lisbon: Rio de Mouro / Pedro Ferreira Artes Gráficas.

—. 1994. *As Vésperas do Leviathan. Instituições e Poder Político. Portugal, Séc. XVII.* Coimbra: Livraria Almedina.

—. 1998. "A Fazenda." In José Mattoso, ed. *História de Portugal*, vol. 4, pp. 181–213. Lisbon: Estampa.

—. 2005. "Porque é que foi 'portuguesa' a expansão portuguesa? ou O revisionismo nos trópicos." Unpublished presentation at the colloquium "O espaço atlântico de Antigo Regime. Poderes e sociedades," org. by CHAM-FCSH-UNL / IICT, Lisbon.

Hildebrandt, Reinhard. 1970/1971. "Wirtschaftsentwicklung und Konzentration im 16. Jahrhundert. Konrad Rot und die Finanzierungsprobleme seines interkontinentalen Handels." In *Scripta Mercaturae 1970/71*, pp. 25–50.

Hillen, Christian. 2007. "'Mit Gott.' Zum Verhältnis von Vertrauen und Wirtschaftsgeschichte." In Christian Hillen, ed. *"Mit Gott." Zum Verhältnis von Vertrauen und Wirtschaftsgeschichte*, pp. 7–16. Cologne: Stiftung Rheinisch-Westfälisches Wirtschaftsarchiv.

Hinsch, J. D. 1888. "Die Bartholomäusbrüderschaft der Deutschen in Lissabon." In *Hansische Geschichtsblätter* 6, 2, vol. 17, pp. 3–27.

Hitzigrath, Heinrich. 1907. *Die politischen Beziehungen zwischen Hamburg und England zur Zeit Jacobs I., Karls I. und der Republik 1611–1660*. Hamburg: Baumann.

Hoffmann, Christhard. 1995. "Juden und Judentum in der bundesdeutschen Geschichtswissenschaft." In *Zeitschrift für Geschichtswissenschaft* 43, 8, pp. 677–86.

Horch, Rosemarie Erika. 1983. "A missão de D. Miguel de Portugal e a prisão de D. Duarte de Bragança. Dois folhetos referentes à época da restauração de Portugal." In *Revista da Universidade de Coimbra* 30, pp. 575–90.

Irsigler, Franz. 2008. "Kreditgewährung und Formen der Kreditsicherung im Mittelalter." In Gabriele B. Clemens, ed. *Schuldenlast und Schuldenwert. Kreditnetzwerke in der europäischen Geschichte 1300–1900*, pp. 67–84. Trier: Kliomedia.

Israel, Jonathan I. 1978. "Spain and the Dutch Sephardim, 1609–1660." In *Studia Rosenthaliana* 12, pp. 1–61.

—. 1983. "The Economic Contribution of Dutch Sephardi Jewry to Holland's Golden Age, 1595–1713." In *Tijdschrift voor Geschiedenis* 96, pp. 505–35.

—. 1986. "The Politics of International Trade Rivalry during the Thirty Years War. Gabriel de Roy and Olivares' Mercantilist Projects, 1621–1645." In *The International History Review* 8, 4, pp. 517–49.

—. 1987. "Duarte Nunes da Costa (Jacob Curiel), of Hamburg, Sephardi Nobleman and Communal Leader (1585–1664)." In *Studia Rosenthaliana* 21, 1, pp. 14–34.

—. 1989. *European Jewry in the age of mercantilism 1550–1750*, 2nd ed. Oxford: Clarendon Press.

—. 1992. "The Sephardi Contribution to Economic Life and Colonization in Europe and the New World (16th-18th Centuries)." In Haim Beinart, ed. *Moreshet Sepharad. The Sephardi Legacy*, vol. 2, pp. 365–98. Jerusalem: Magnes Press.

—, ed. 2002. *Diasporas within a diaspora. Jews, Crypto-Jews and the World Maritime Empires, 1540–1740*. Leiden: Brill.

—. 2005. "Diasporas Jewish and non-Jewish and the World Maritime Empires." In Ina Baghdiantz McCabe, Gelina Harlaftis, and Ioanna Pepelasis Minoglou, eds. *Diaspora Entrepreneurial Networks. Four Centuries of History*, pp. 3–26. Oxford: Berg.

Jeannin, Pierre. 1964. "Les comptes du Sund comme source pour la construction d'indices généraux de l'activité économique en Europe (XVIe-XVIIIe siècle)." In *Revue Historique* 231, pp. 55–102, 307–340.

—. 1968. "Le marché du sel marin dans l'Europe du nord du XIVe au XVIIIe siècle." In Michel Mollat, ed. *Le rôle du sel dans l'histoire*, pp. 73–93. Paris: Presses universitaires de France.

—. 1975. "Die Rolle Lübecks in der hansischen Spanien- und Portugalfahrt des 16. Jahrhunderts." In *Zeitschrift des Vereins für Lübeckische Geschichte und Altertumskunde* 55, pp. 5–40.

Jenks, Stuart. 1996. "Zum hansischen Gästerecht." In *Hansische Geschichtsblätter* 114, pp. 3–60.

Jürgens, Henning P., and Thomas Weller, eds. 2020. *Religion und Mobilität. Zum Verhältnis von raumbezogener Mobilität und religiöser Identitätsbildung im frühneuzeitlichen Europa.* Göttingen: Vandenhoeck & Ruprecht.

Justino, David. 1994. *História da bolsa de Lisboa.* Lisbon: Bolsa de Valores de Lisboa.

Kaelble, Hartmut. 1990. "Historische Quantifizierung. Bemerkungen zu einem Dissens." In Peter Lösche, ed. *Göttinger Sozialwissenschaften heute. Fragestellungen, Methoden, Inhalte,* pp. 75–80. Göttingen: Vandenhoeck & Ruprecht.

Kagan, Richard L., and Philip D. Morgan, eds. 2009. *Atlantic Diasporas. Jews, Conversos, and Crypto-Jews in the Age of Mercantilism, 1500–1800.* Baltimore: Johns Hopkins University Press.

Kalus, Maximilian. 2010. *Pfeffer. Kupfer. Nachrichten. Kaufmannsnetzwerke und Handelsstrukturen im europäisch-asiatischen Handel am Ende des 16. Jahrhunderts.* Augsburg: Wißner.

Kaplan, Yosef. 1985. "The Travels of Portuguese Jews from Amsterdam to the 'Lands of Idolatry' (1644–1724)." In Yosef Kaplan, ed. *Jews and Conversos. Studies in Society and the Inquisition,* pp. 197–224. Jerusalem: Magnes Press.

—. 1989. *From Christianity to Judaism. The Story of Isaac Orobio de Castro.* Oxford University Press.

—. 1991. "Die portugiesischen Juden und die Modernisierung. Zur Veränderung jüdischen Lebens vor der Emanzipation." In Andreas Nachama, Julius H. Schoeps, and Edward van Voolen, eds. *Jüdische Lebenswelten. Essays,* pp. 303–17. Frankfurt am Main: Jüdischer Verlag, 1991.

—. 1992. "The Sephardim in North-Western Europe and the New World." In Haim Beinart, ed. *Moreshet Sepharad. The Sephardi Legacy,* vol. 2, pp. 240–87. Jerusalem: Magnes Press.

—. 1993. "Familia, Matrimonio y Sociedad. Los casamientos clandestinos en la Diáspora Sefaradí Occidental (siglos XVII–XVIII)." In *Espacio, tiempo y forma* 6 (4th Series), pp. 129–54.

—. 1997. "The Place of the Herem in the Sefardic Community of Hamburg during the Seventeenth Century." In Michael Studemund-Halévy, ed. *Die Sefarden in Hamburg,* part 2, pp. 63–87. Hamburg: Buske.

—, ed. 2000a. *An Alternative Path to Modernity. The Sephardi Diaspora in Western Europe.* Leiden: Brill.

—. 2000b. "The Self-Definition of the Sephardi Jews of Western Europe and their Relation to the Alien and the Stranger." In Yosef Kaplan, ed. *An Alternative Path to Modernity. The Sephardi Diaspora in Western Europe,* pp. 51–77. Leiden: Brill.

—. 2001. "Gente Política. The Portuguese Jews of Amsterdam vis-à-vis Dutch Society." In Chaya Brasz and Yosef Kaplan, eds. *Dutch Jews as Perceived by Themselves and by Others,* pp. 21–40. Leiden: Brill.

—. 2002. "Bom Judesmo: The Western Sephardic Diaspora." In David Biale, ed. *Cultures of the Jews. A New History,* pp. 638–69. New York: Schocken Books.

Karp, Jonathan. 2007. "Economic History and Jewish Modernity. Ideological Versus Structural Change." In *Jahrbuch des Simon-Dubnow-Instituts* 6, pp. 249–66.

—. 2008. *The Politics of Jewish Commerce. Economic Thought and Emancipation in Europe, 1638–1848.* Cambridge: Cambridge University Press.

—. 2009. "An 'Economic Turn' in Jewish Studies?" In *AJS Perspectives*, pp. 8–13.

—. 1966. *A participação da Companhia de Judeus na conquista holandesa de Pernambuco.* Paraíba: Universidade Federal de Paraíba.

Kellenbenz, Hermann. 1950. "Der lutherische Gottesdienst und die Niederlassung Hamburger Kaufleute in Lissabon im Anfang des achtzehnten Jahrhunderts." In *Hamburger Wirtschafts-Chronik* 1, pp. 31–40.

—. 1954. *Unternehmerkräfte im Hamburger Spanien- und Portugalhandel, 1590–1625.* Hamburg: Verlag der Hamburgischen Bücherei.

—. 1955. "Diogo und Manoel Teixeira und ihr Hamburger Unternehmen." In *Vierteljahrschrift für Sozial- und Wirtschaftsgeschichte* 42, pp. 289–352.

—. 1956a. "Der Pfeffermarkt um 1600 und die Hansestädte." In *Hansische Geschichtsblätter* 74, pp. 28–49.

—. 1956b. "Dr. Jakob Rosales." In *Zeitschrift für Religions- und Geistesgeschichte* 8, pp. 345–54.

—. 1956c. "Autour de 1600. Le commerce du poivre des Fugger et le marché international du poivre." In *Annales. E. S. C.* 11, pp. 1–28.

—. 1958. *Sephardim an der unteren Elbe. Ihre wirtschaftliche und politische Bedeutung vom Ende des 16. bis zum Beginn des 18. Jahrhunderts.* Wiesbaden: Steiner.

—. 1960. "Os mercadores alemães de Lisboa por volta de 1530." In *Revista Portuguesa de História* 9, pp. 125–40.

—. 1966. *A participação da Companhia de Judeus na conquista holandesa de Pernambuco,* Paraiba: Universidade Federal da Paraíba.

Kestner, Ernst. 1881. "Die Handelsverbindungen der Hansa, speciell Danzigs mit Spanien und Portugal seit 1583." In *Zeitschrift des Westpreußischen Geschichtsvereins* 5, pp. 1–22.

Kiecksee, Ernst Markus. 1952. "Die Handelspolitik der Gottorfer Herzöge im 17. Jahrhundert: Ein Beitrag zur schleswig-holsteinischen Landesgeschichte." Kiel: Universität Kiel (unpublished diss.).

Kiesselbach, Georg Arnold. 1901. *Die Wirtschafts- und Rechtsgeschichtliche Entwicklung der Seeversicherung in Hamburg.* Hamburg: Gräfe & Sillem.

Kirchenpauer, Gustav Heinrich. 1841. *Die alte Börse, ihre Gründer und Vorsteher. Ein Beitrag zur hamburgischen Handelsgeschichte.* Hamburg: Voigt.

Koch, Alfred. 1955. "Las primeras relaciones postales entre Alemania y la Península Ibérica." In *Boletin de la Academia Iberoamericana y Filipina de Historia Postal* 32, pp. 60–63.

Koch, Peter. 1998. *Geschichte der Versicherungswissenschaft in Deutschland.* Karlsruhe: VVW.

Koen, E. M. 1968. "Duarte Fernandes, koopman van de Portugese natie te Amsterdam." In *Studia Rosenthaliana* 2, 2, pp. 178–93.

—. 1970. "The earliest sources relating to the Portuguese Jews in the Municipal Archives of Amsterdam uo to 1620." In *Studia Rosenthaliana* 4, pp. 25–41.

Köhn, Gerhard. 1974. *Die Bevölkerung der Residenz, Festung und Exulantenstadt Glückstadt von der Gründung 1616 bis zum Endausbau 1652.* Neumünster: Wachholtz.

Kopitzsch, Franklin. 1981. "Hamburg zwischen Hauptrezess und Franzosenzeit. Bemerkungen zur Verfassung, Verwaltung und Sozialstruktur." In Wilhelm Rausch, ed. *Die Städte Mitteleuropas im 17. und 19. Jahrhundert,* pp. 181–210. Linz: Österreichischer Arbeitskreis für Stadtgeschichtsforschung.

Krawehl, Otto-Ernst. 2001. "Die Admiralitätszoll- und Convoygeld-Einnahmebücher als handelsstatistische Quelle." In Jürgen Schneider, Otto-Ernst Krawehl, and Frank Schulenburg, eds. *Statistik des Hamburger seewärtigen Einfuhrhandels im 18. Jahrhundert. Nach den Admiralitäts- und Convoygeld-Einnahmebüchern*, pp. 9–13. St. Katharinen: Scripta-Mercaturae.

Kriedte, Peter. 1996. "Trade." In Sheilagh Ogilvie, ed. *Germany. A New Social and Economic History*, vol. 2, pp. 100–33. London: Arnold.

Kunz, Andreas. 1997. "Historische Statistik von Deutschland. Ein Forschungsschwerpunkt der Deutschen Forschungsgemeinschaft 1981–1991." In *Historical Social Research* 22, pp. 236–49.

Labourdette, Jean-François. 1988. *La Nation Française à Lisbonne de 1669 à 1790. Entre Colbertisme et Liberalisme*. Paris: Fondation Calouste Gulbenkian.

Lammel, Siegbert. 1976. "Die Gesetzgebung des Handelsrechts." In Helmut Coing, ed. *Handbuch der Quellen und Literatur der neueren europäischen Privatrechtsgeschichte*, vol. 2, part 2, pp. 571–1083. Munich: C. H. Beck.

Lappenberg, Johann Martin. 1851. "Die Reisen des Herrn Johann Arnold von Uffele und dessen Anverwandte." In *Zeitschrift des Vereins für Hamburgische Geschichte* 3, pp. 272–80.

Leeuwen, Marco H. D. van. 1994. "Logic of Charitiy. Poor Relief in Preindustrial Europe." In *Journal of Interdisciplinary History* 24, 4, pp. 589–613.

Leptien, Heinz. 1933. *Stade als Hansestadt*. Stade: Stelzer.

Lesger, Clé. 2006. *The Rise of the Amsterdam Market and Information Exchange. Merchants, Commercial Expansion and Change in the Spatial Economy of the Low Countries, c. 1550–1630*. Aldershot: Routledge.

Lier, Hermann Arthur. 1896. "Vries, Hans Fredeman de." In Historische Commission bei der Königlichen Akademie der Wissenschaften, ed. *Allgemeine deutsche Biographie*, vol. 40, pp. 408–09. Leipzig: Duncker & Humblot.

Lifshitz, Yosef Yitzhak. 2004. "Foundations of a Jewish Economic Theory." In *Azure* 18, pp. 34–66.

Lima, Edgar de. 1958. *Ainda um Património Católico ... na Mão dos Protestantes*. Lisbon: Oficinas gráficas de Rádio Renascença.

Lindberg, Erik. 2008. "The Rise of Hamburg as a Global Marketplace in the Seventeenth Century. A Comparative Political Economy Perspective." In *Comparative Studies in Society and History* 50, pp. 641–62.

Lingelbach, William E. 1904. "The Merchant Adventurers at Hamburg." In *The American Historical Review* 9, pp. 265–87.

Linkemeyer, Carl. 1931. *Das katholische Hamburg in Vergangenheit und Gegenwart*. Hamburg: Lettenbauer.

Litten, Mirjam. 2003. *Bürgerrecht und Bekenntnis. Städtische Optionen zwischen Konfessionalisierung und Säkularisierung in Münster, Hildesheim und Hamburg*. Hildesheim: Olms.

Livermore, Harold V. 1954. "The 'Privileges of an Englishman in the Kingdoms and Dominions of Portugal.'" In *Atlante* 2, pp. 57–77.

Lobo, Eulália Maria Lahmeyer. 1963. "Aspectos da influência dos homens de negócio na política comercial ibero-americana, século XVII." Rio de Janeiro: Universidade do Estado da Guanabara (unpublished diss.).

—. 1965. "Alguns aspectos da história da mesa do bem comum dos mercadores. Séculos XVII e XVIII." In *Actas do V Colóquio Internacional de Estudos Luso-Brasileiros, vol. 2*, pp. 5–9. Coimbra: Gráfica de Coimbra.

Loose, Hans-Dieter. 1963. *Hamburg und Christian IV. von Dänemark während des Dreißigjährigen Krieges. Ein Beitrag zur Geschichte der hamburgischen Reichsunmittelbarkeit.* Hamburg: Christians.

—, ed. 1982. *Hamburg. Geschichte der Stadt und ihrer Bewohner*, vol. 1. Hamburg: Hoffmann und Campe.

—. 1968. "Ein Plan zur Verpfändung Islands an Hamburger Kaufleute vom Jahre 1645." In *Zeitschrift des Vereins für Hamburgische Geschichte* 54, pp. 143–50.

López Belinchón, Bernardo. 2000. "Olivares contra los Portugueses. Inquisición, conversos y guerra económica." In Joaquín Pérez Villanueva and Bartolomé Escandell Bonet, eds. *Historia de la inquisición en España y América*, part 3 (Temas y problemas), pp. 499–530. Madrid: Biblioteca de Autores Cristianos.

Lorenzen-Schmidt, Klaus-Joachim. 1979. "Umfang und Dynamik des Hamburger Rentenmarktes zwischen 1471 und 1570." In *Zeitschrift des Vereins für Hamburgische Geschichte* 65, pp. 21–52.

Luhmann, Niklas. 1968. *Vertrauen. Ein Mechanismus der Reduktion sozialer Komplexität.* Stuttgart: UTB.

Maack, E. 1935. "Die Anfänge hamburgischen Postwesens." In Verein für Briefmarkenkunde zu Hamburg von 1885, ed. *Hamburg, seine Postgeschichte, Postwertzeichen und Poststempel. Festschrift zur Erinnerung an die 50jährige Wiederkehr des Gründungstages des Vereins für Briefmarkenkunde zu Hamburg von 1885*, pp. 1–14. Hamburg: Völsch.

Macedo, Jorge Borges de. 1979. "Companhias Comerciais." In Joel Serrão, ed. *Dicionário de história de Portugal*, vol. 2. [Lisbon]: Iniciativas. pp. 122–30.

Magalhães, Joaquim Romero. 1981. "E assim se abriu Judaismo no Algarve." In *Revista da Universidade de Coimbra* 29, pp. 1–74.

—. 1987. "Em busca dos 'tempos' da Inquisição (1573–1615)." In *Revista de História das Ideias* 9, pp. 191–228.

—. 1993. *O Algarve Económico 1600–1773*. Lisbon: Estampa.

—. 1997a. "A Estrutura das Trocas." In José Mattoso, ed. *História de Portugal*, vol. 3, pp. 283–316. Lisbon: Círculo de Leitores.

—. 1997b. "Filipe II (I de Portugal)." In José Mattoso, ed. *História de Portugal*, vol. 3, pp. 475–81. Lisbon: Círculo de Leitores.

Marcocci, Giuseppe. 2011. "A fundação da Inquisição em Portugal. Um novo olhar." In *Lusitania Sacra* 23, pp. 69–92.

—. 2010. "Toward a History of the Portuguese Inquisition. Trends in Modern Historiography (1974–2009)." In *Revue de l'histoire des religions* 227, 3, pp. 355–93.

Mareš, Fr. 1880/1881. "Die maritime Politik der Habsburger in den Jahren 1625–1628." In *Mitteilungen des Instituts für Österreichische Geschichtsforschung* 1 (1880), pp. 541–78; 2 (1881) pp. 49–82.

Marques, António Henrique de Oliveira. *Hansa e Portugal na Idade Média*. Lisbon: Presença, 1959.

—. 1962. "Notas para a história da feitoria portuguesa na Flandres, no século XV." In [no editor noted]. *Studi in onore di Amintore Fanfani*, vol. 2, pp. 437–76. Milan: Gioffrè.

—. 1977. *Para a História dos Seguros em Portugal. Notas e Documentos*. Lisbon: Arcádia.

—. "Um preçário de mercadorias e de câmbios de Hamburgo do século XVI." In António Henrique de Oliveira Marques, *Portugal Quinhentista (Ensaios)*, pp. 71–77. Lisbon: Quetzal Editores, 1987.

Marques, José. 1993. "Filipe III de Espanha (II de Portugal) e a Inquisição Portuguesa face ao Projeto do 3º Perdão Geral para os Cristãos-Novos Portugueses." In *Revista da Faculdade de Letras. História* (Porto) 10 (2nd Series), pp. 177–203.

Mauersberg, Hans. 1960. *Wirtschafts- und Sozialgeschichte zentraleuropäischer Städte in neuerer Zeit, dargestellt an den Beispielen von Basel, Frankfurt am Main, Hamburg, Hannover und München*. Göttingen: Vandenhoeck & Ruprecht.

Mauro, Frédéric. 1958. "La bourgeoisie portugaise au XVIIe siècle." In *XVIIe Siècle* 40, 3, pp. 235–57.

—. 1960. *Le Portugal et l'Atlantique au XVIIe siècle (1570–1670), étude économique*. Paris: SEVPEN.

—. 1990. "Merchant Communities, 1350–1750." In James D. Tracy, ed. *The Rise of Merchant Empires*, pp. 255–86. Cambridge: Cambridge University Press.

McCabe, Ina Baghdiantz, Gelina Harlaftis, and Ioanna Pepelasis Minoglou, eds. 2005. *Diaspora Entrepreneurial Networks: Four Centuries of History*. Oxford: Berg.

McCusker, John J. 2002. "Information and Transaction Costs in Early Modern Europe." In Rainer Gömmel and Markus A. Denzel, eds. *Weltwirtschaft und Wirtschaftsordnung. Festschrift für Jürgen Schneider zum 65. Geburtstag*, pp. 69–83. Stuttgart: Steiner.

McCusker, John, and Cora Gravesteijn. 1991. *The Beginnings of Commercial and Financial Journalism: The Commodity Price Currents, Exchange Rate Currents, and Money Currents of Early Modern Europe*. Amsterdam: NEHA.

Mello, José Antônio Gonsalves de. 1996. *Gente da Nação. Cristãos-novos e Judeus em Pernambuco, 1542–1654*, 2nd rev. ed. Recife: Fundação Joaquim Nabuco.

—. 2000. *João Fernandes Vieira. Mestre-de-campo do terço de infantaria de Pernambuco*. Lisbon: CNCDP.

Meneses, Avelino de Freitas de. 2001. "A circulação." In Joel Serrão and António Henrique de Oliveira Marques, eds. *Nova História de Portugal*, vol. 7, pp. 302–48. Lisbon: Presença.

Messow, Hans-Christoph. 1935. *Die Hansestädte und die Habsburgische Ostseepolitik im 30jährigen Kriege (1627/28)*. Berlin: Junker & Dünnhaupt.

Miranda, Susana Münch. 2011. "António de Freitas Branco und die Verhandlungen über die Hochzeit von Maria Sophia Pfalzgräfin zu Rhein-Neuburg mit König Pedro II. von Portugal." In Alexandra Curvelo and Madalena Simões, eds. *Portugal und das Heilige Römische Reich (16.–18. Jahrhundert)*, pp. 65–82. Münster: Aschendorff.

Monteiro, Manuel G. 1969. "As Alfândegas no espaço português. Sua evolução." In *Ultramar* 37/38, pp. 41–76.

Moreira, Manuel António Fernandes. 1992. *A Alfândega de Viana e o Comércio de Importação de Panos no Século XVI*. Viana do Castelo: Câmara Municipal.

Morineau, Michel. 1985. *Incroyables gazettes et fabuleux métaux. Les retours des trésors américains d'après les gazettes Hollandises (16e–18e siècles)*. London: Cambridge University Press.

Muchnik, Natalia. 2007. "La re-judaïsation des judéoconvers espagnols par les négociants de passage au XVIIe siècle." In Albrecht Burkardt, Gilles Bertrand, and Yves Krumenacker, eds. *Commerce, voyage et expérience religieuse XVIe–XVIIIe siècles*, pp. 287–302. Rennes: Presses universitaires de Rennes.

Müller, Carl. 1940. *Der Stader Zoll. Vom Mittelalter bis zu seiner Ablösung. Eine wirtschaftsges-chichtliche Darstellung unter besonderer Berücksichtigung der hamburgischen Interessen*. Hamburg: Hansischer Gildenverlag.

Müller, Johannes. 2016. *Exile Memories and the Dutch Revolt. The Narrated Diaspora, 1550–1750*. Leiden: Brill.

Naudé, Wilhelm. 1889. *Deutsche städtische Getreidehandelspolitik vom 15.–17. Jahrhundert, mit besonderer Berücksichtigung Stettins und Hamburgs*. Leipzig: Duncker & Humblot.

Neumann, Max. 1863. *Geschichte des Wechsels im Hansagebiete bis zum 17. Jahrhundert nach archivalischen Urkunden*. Erlangen: Enke.

Newman, Karin. 1985. "Hamburg in the European Economy, 1660–1750." In *The Journal of European Economic History* 14, pp. 57–93.

Nikolajczyk, Alexander. 2006. "Integriert oder ausgegrenzt? Die Stellung der niederländischen Einwanderer im frühneuzeitlichen Hamburg." In *Hamburger Wirtschafts-Chronik* 6 (New Series), pp. 7–44.

North, Michael. 1991. "Einleitung." In Michael North, ed. *Kredit im spätmittelalterlichen und frühneuzeitlichen Europa*, pp. 1–8. Cologne: Böhlau.

—. 1996a. "Banking and credit in Northern Germany in the fifteenth and sixteenth centuries." In Michael North, ed. *From the North Sea to the Baltic. Essays in Commercial, Monetary and Agrarian History, 1500–1800*, pp. 811–26. Aldershot: Variorum.

—. 1996b. "Bullion Transfer from Western Europe to the Baltic and to Asia, 1550–1750. A Comparison." In Michael North, ed. *From the North Sea to the Baltic. Essays in Commercial, Monetary and Agrarian History, 1500–1800*, pp. 185–95. Aldershot: Variorum.

—. 1996c. "Introduction." In Michael North, ed. *From the North Sea to the Baltic. Essays in Commercial, Monetary and Agrarian History, 1500–1800*, pp. xi–xx. Aldershot: Variorum.

—. 2000. *Kommunikation, Handel, Geld und Banken in der frühen Neuzeit*. Munich: Oldenbourg.

—. 2005. "Von der atlantischen Handelsexpansion bis zu den Agrarreformen (1450–1815)." In Michael North, ed. *Deutsche Wirtschaftsgeschichte. Ein Jahrtausend im Überblick*, pp. 112–96. Munich: C. H. Beck.

Nowosadtko, Jutta. 1994. "Betrachtungen über den Erwerb von Unehre. Vom Widerspruch 'moderner' und 'tradionaler' Ehren- und Unehrenkonzepte in der frühneuzeitlichen Ständegesellschaft." In Ludgera Vogt and Arnold Zingerle, eds. *Ehre. Archaische Momente in der Moderne*, pp. 230–48. Frankfurt am Main: Suhrkamp.

Olival, Fernanda. 1991. "Para um estudo da nobilitação no antigo regime. Os cristãos- novos na ordem de Cristo." In Paulo Pacheco and Luís Pequito Antunes, eds. *As Ordens Militares em Portugal. Actas do I Encontro sobre Ordens Militares*, pp. 233–44. Palmela: Câmara Municipal de Palmela.

Ornan Pinkus, Ben-Zion. 1994. "Die Portugiesische Gemeinde in Hamburg und ihre Führung im 17. Jahrhundert." In Michael Studemund-Halévy, ed. *Die Sefarden in Hamburg*, part 1, pp. 3–36. Hamburg: Buske.

Pedreira, Jorge Miguel. 1995 "Os homens de negócio da praça de Lisboa de Pombal ao vintismo (1755–1822): Diferenciação, reprodução e identificação de um grupo social." Lisbon: Universidade Nova de Lisboa (unpublished diss.).

Pelus-Kaplan. 1981. *Wolter von Holsten marchand lubeckois dans la seconde moitié du seizième siècle. Contribution à l'étude des relations commerciales entre Lübeck et les villes livoniennes*. Cologne: Böhlau.

Penslar, Derek J. 2001. *Shylock's Children: Economics and Jewish Identity in Modern Europe.* Berkeley: University of California Press.

Penteado, Pedro. 1995. "Confrarias portuguesas da época moderna. Problemas, resultados e tendências da investigação." In *Lusitania Sacra 7* (2nd Series), pp. 15–52.

—. 2000a. "Confrarias." In Carlos Moreira Azevedo, ed. *Dicionário de História Religiosa de Portugal*, vol. 1, pp. 459–70. Lisbon: Círculo de Leitores.

—. 2000b. "Confrarias." In Carlos Moreira Azevedo, ed. *História Religiosa de Portugal*, vol. 2, pp. 323–34. Lisbon: Círculo de Leitores.

Pereira, João Cordeiro. 2003. "Organização e Administração Alfandegárias de Portugal no século XVI (1521–1557)." In João Cordeiro Pereira, ed. *Portugal na Era de Quinhentos. Estúdos vários*, pp. 1–117. Cascais: Câmara Municipal.

Peres, Damião. 1971. *História do Banco de Portugal.* Lisbon: Oficinas Gráficas da Neogravura.

Peters, Lambert F. 1994. *Der Handel Nürnbergs am Anfang des Dreißigjährigen Krieges. Strukturkomponenten, Unternehmen und Unternehmer: Eine quantitative Analyse.* Stuttgart: Steiner.

Pettegree, Andrew. 1994. "Protestant Migration during the Early Modern Period." In Simonetta Cavaciocchi, ed. *Le migrazioni in Europa. Secc. XIII–XVIII. Atti della "Venticinquesima Settimana di Studi,"* pp. 441–58. Florence: Le Monnier.

Pieper, Anton. 1886. *Die Propaganda-Congregation und die nordischen Missionen im siebenzehnten Jahrhundert.* Cologne: Bachem.

Piper, Paul. 1893. *Die Reformierten und die Mennoniten Altonas* (Altona unter Schauenburgischer Herrschaft, vol. 6). Altona: Harder.

Plaat, Gees van der. 2003. *Eendracht als opdracht. Lieuwe van Aitzema's bijdrage aan het publieke debat in de zeventiende-eeuwse Republiek.* Hilversum: Verloren.

Pohl, Hans. 1977. *Die Portugiesen in Antwerpen (1567–1648): Zur Geschichte einer Minderheit.* Wiesbaden: Steiner.

Pohle, Jürgen. 2000. *Deutschland und die überseeische Expansion Portugals im 15. und 16. Jahrhundert.* Münster: Lit.

Postel, Rainer. 1979. "Obrigkeitsdenken und Reformation in Hamburg." In *Archiv für Reformationsgeschichte 70*, pp. 169–201.

—. 1980. "Sozialgeschichtliche Folgewirkungen der Reformation in Hamburg." In Wenzel Lohff, ed. *450 Jahre Reformation in Hamburg. Eine Festschrift*, pp. 63–91. Hamburg: Agentur des Rauhen Hauses.

—. 1982. "Reformation und Gegenreformation 1517–1618." In Hans-Dieter Loose, ed. *Hamburg. Geschichte der Stadt und ihrer Bewohner*, vol. 1, pp. 191–258. Hamburg: Hoffmann und Campe.

—. 1992. *Kaufmännische Selbstverwaltung in Geschichte und Gegenwart.* Hamburg: Christians.

—. 1997. "Asyl und Emigration in der Frühen Neuzeit." In *Zeitschrift des Vereins für Hamburgische Geschichte 83*, pp. 201–23.

—. 1998. "Der Niedergang der Hanse." In Jörgen Bracker, Volker Henn, and Rainer Postel, eds. *Die Hanse. Lebenswirklichkeit und Mythos: Textband zur Hamburger Hanse-Ausstellung von 1989*, pp. 165–93. Lübeck: Schmidt-Römhild.

—. 2001. "Die Anfänge des hamburgischen Notariats." In Rainer Postel and Helmut Stubbe-da Luz, eds. *Die Notare. Johann Heinrich Hübbe, Eduard Schramm, Gabriel Riesser, Hans Harder Biermann-Ratjen*, pp. 9–15. Bremen: Edition Temmen.

—. 2006. "Reformation und bürgerliche Mitsprache in Hamburg" In Rainer Postel, *Beiträge zur hamburgischen Geschichte der Frühen Neuzeit. Ausgewählte Aufsätze zum 65. Geburtstag*, pp. 45–65. Hamburg: Lit.

Poussou, Jean-Pierre. 1994. "De l'intérêt et de l'étude historique des mouvements migratoires européens du milieu du Moyen Age à la fin du XIXe siècle." In Simonetta Cavaciocchi, ed. *Le migrazioni in Europa. Secc. XIII–XVIII. Atti della "Venticinquesima Settimana di Studi,"* pp. 21–43. Florence: Le Monnier.

Prange, Carsten. 1978. *Die Zeitungen und Zeitschriften des 17. Jahrhunderts in Hamburg und Altona. Ein Beitrag zur Publizistik der Frühaufklärung*. Hamburg: Christians.

Prestage, Edgar. 1925. *The Diplomatic Relations of Portugal with France, England, and Holland from 1640 to 1668*. Watford: Voss & Michael.

Pulido Serrano, Juan Ignacio. 2006a. "Hermandades portuguesas fuera de Portugal (siglos XVI–XVIII)." In Maria da Graça A. Mateus Ventura, ed. *O associativismo. Das confrarias e irmandades aos movimentos sociais contemporâneos*, pp. 29–49. Lisbon: Colibri.

—. 2006b. "Las negociaciones con los cristianos nuevos en tiempos de Felipe III a la luz de algunos documentos inéditos (1598–1607)." In *Sefarad* 66, 2, pp. 345–76.

—. 2007. *Os Judeus e a Inquisição no Tempo dos Filipes*. Lisbon: Campo da Comunicação.

Rachel, Hugo. 1910. "Die Handelsverfassung der norddeutschen Städte im 15. bis 18. Jahrhundert." In *Jahrbuch für Gesetzgebung, Verwaltung und Volkswirtschaft im Deutschen Reich* 34, 3, pp. 71–133.

Rau, Susanne. 2002. *Geschichte und Konfession. Städtische Geschichtsschreibung und Erinnerungskultur im Zeitalter von Reformation und Konfessionalisierung in Bremen, Breslau, Hamburg und Köln*. Hamburg: Dölling und Galitz.

Rau, Virgínia. 1954. "Subsídios para o estudo do movimento dos portos de Faro e Lissabon durante o século XVII." In *Anais* [Academia Portuguesa da História] 5 (2nd Series), pp. 197–277.

—. 1968a. "Les courants du trafic du sel portugais du XIVe au XVIIIe siècle." In Michel Mollat, ed. *Le rôle du sel dans l'histoire*, pp. 53–71. Paris: Presses universitaires de France.

—. 1968b. "Uma família de mercadores italianos em Portugal no século XV. Os Lomellini." In Virgínia Rau, ed. *Estudos de História. Mercadores, Mercadorias, Pensamento Económico*, pp. 13–57. Porto: Verbo.

—. 1984a. *Estudos sobre a história do sal português*. Lisbon: Presença.

—. 1984b. "Aspectos da legislação portuguesa sobre câmbios durante o século XVI." In Virgínia Rau, ed. *Estudos sobre História Económica e Social do Antigo Regime*, pp. 131–39. Lisbon: Presença, 1984.

—. 1984c. "Feitores e feitorias. 'Instrumentos' do comércio internacional português no século XVI." In Virginia Rau, ed. *Estudos sobre História Económica e Social do Antigo Regime*, pp. 141–99. Lisbon: Presença.

—. 1984d. "Privilégios e legislação portuguesa referentes a mercadores estrangeiros (séculos XV e XVI)." In Virgínia Rau, ed. *Estudos sobre História Económica e Social do Antigo Regime*, pp. 201–25. Lisbon: Presença.

Reichard, Konrad. 1867. *Die maritime Politik der Habsburger im 17. Jahrhundert*. Berlin: Hertz.

Reincke, Heinrich. 1951. "Hamburgs Bevölkerung." In Heinrich Reincke, ed. *Forschungen und Skizzen zur Hamburgischen Geschichte*, pp. 167–200. Hamburg: Hoffmann und Campe.

—. 1955. "Bergen, Sebastian von." In Historische Kommission bei der Bayerischen Akademie der Wissenschaften, ed. *Neue deutsche Biographie*, vol. 2, pp. 78–79. Berlin: Duncker & Humblot.

—. 1958. "Zur Vor- und Frühgeschichte des Hamburger Zeitungswesens." In *Zeitschrift des Vereins für Hamburgische Geschichte* 44, pp. 205–18.

—. 1961. "Hamburgs Aufstieg zur Reichsfreiheit, Vortrag am 25. Januar 1956." In *Zeitschrift des Vereins für Hamburgische Geschichte* 47, pp. 17–34.

Reißmann, Martin. 1975. *Die hamburgische Kaufmannschaft des 17. Jahrhunderts in sozialgeschichtlicher Sicht.* Hamburg: Christians.

Ressel, Magnus. 2013. *Zwischen Sklavenkassen und Türkenpässen. Nordeuropa und die Barbaresken in der Frühen Neuzeit.* Berlin: De Gruyter.

Révah, Israël Salvador. 1957. "Une famille de 'nouveaux-chrétiens': Les Bocarro Francês." In *Revue des Études Juives* 116, pp. 73–87.

—. 1959–1960. "Les marranes." In *Revue des Études Juives* 118, pp. 29–77.

—. 1975. "Les Jésuites portugais contre l'Inquisition: La campagne pour la création de la Compagnie générale du commerce du Brésil (1649)." In Israël Salvador Révah, ed. *Études portugaises*, pp. 155–84. Paris: Fondation Calouste Gulbenkian.

Ribeiro, José Silvestre. 1876. *Esboço Historico de D. Duarte de Bragança, irmão de el-rei D. João IV.* Lisbon: Imprensa Nacional.

Ródenas Vilar, Rafael. 1962. "Un gran proyecto anti-holandés en tiempo de Felipe IV. La destrucción del comercio rebelde en Europa." In *Hispania* 22, pp. 542–58.

—. 1967. *La política europea de España durante la guerra de treinta años (1624–1630).* Madrid: Consejo Superior de Investigaciones Científicas.

Roitman, Jessica Vance. 2009. "Us and Them. Inter-Cultural Trade and the Sephardim, 1595–1640." Leiden: Universiteit Leiden (unpublished diss.).

Roma Du Bocage, Carlos. 1916. *Subsídios para o estudo das relações exteriores de Portugal em seguida á Restauração (1640–1649)*, vol. 1. Lisbon: Academia de Sciencias de Lisboa.

Roosbroeck, Robert van. 1964. "Die Niederlassung von Flamen und Wallonen in Hamburg (1567–1605)." In *Zeitschrift des Vereins für Hamburgische Geschichte* 49/50, pp. 53–76.

—. 1974. *Brabanter Kaufleute im Exil.* Cologne: Forschungsinstitut für Sozial- und Wirtschaftsgeschichte an der Universität zu Köln.

Rowen, Herbert H. 1987. "Lieuwe van Aitzema. A soured but knowing eye." In Phyllis Mack and Margaret C. Jacob, eds. *Politics and Culture in Early Modern Europe: Essays in Honor of H. G. Koenigsberger*, pp. 169–82. Cambridge: Cambridge University Press.

Rückleben, Gisela. *Rat und Bürgerschaft in Hamburg 1595–1686: Innere Bindungen und Gegensätze.* Marburg an der Lahn: Impr. R. Rodenbusch, 1969.

Salomon, Herman Prins. 1971. "New Light on the Portuguese Inquisition: The Second Reply to the Archbishop of Cranganor." In *Studia Rosenthaliana* 5, 2, pp. 178–86.

—. 1982. *Portrait of a New Christian: Fernão Álvares Melo (1569–1632).* Paris: Fondation Calouste Gulbenkian.

Saraiva, António José. 1956. *Inquisição e Cristãos-Novos.* Lisbon: Publicações Europa-América.

—. 2011. *The Marrano Factory: The Portuguese Inquisition and Its New Christians, 1536–1765*, transl., rev., and augm. H. P. Salomon and I. S. D. Sassoon (Original: *Inquisição e Cristãos-Novos*). Leiden: Brill.

Schäfer, Dietrich. 1914. "Nachruf für Bernhard Hagedorn." In *Hansische Geschichtsblätter* 41, pp. III–XXXIV.

Schaub, Jean-Frédéric. 2001. *Le Portugal au temps du comte-duc d'Olivares (1621–1640): Le conflit de juridictions comme exercice de la politique.* Madrid: Casa de Velázquez.

Schildhauer, Johannes, Konrad Fritze, and Walter Stark. 1981. *Die Hanse*, 4th updated and augm. ed. Berlin: Deutscher Verlag der Wissenschaften.

Schilling, Heinz. 1972. *Niederländische Exulanten im 16. Jahrhundert: Ihre Stellung im Sozialgefüge und im religiösen Leben deutscher und englischer Städte.* Gütersloh: Mohn.

—. 1994. "Confessional Migration as a Distinct Type of Old European Longdistance Migration." In Simonetta Cavaciocchi, ed. *Le migrazioni in Europa Secc. XIII–XVIII: Atti della "Venticinquesima Settimana di Studi,"* pp. 175–89. Florence: Le Monnier.

—. 2009. "Christliche und jüdische Minderheitengemeinden im Vergleich. Calvinistische Exulanten und westliche Diaspora der Sephardim im 16. und 17. Jahrhundert." In *Zeitschrift für Historische Forschung* 36, pp. 407–44.

Schlimper, Jürgen. 1999. "Nachrichten für die Messestadt aus fernen Ländern. Zum Zusammhang von Leipziger Presse- und Stadtentwicklung zur Mitte des 17. Jahrhunderts." In Hartmut Zwahr, Thomas Topfstedt, and Günter Bentele, eds. *Leipzigs Messen 1497–1997*, vol. 1, pp. 167–82. Cologne: Böhlau.

Schmidt, Burghart. 2007. "'Unduldsames Betragen gegen Andersdenkende in der Religion ... gereicht jedem Staat zur unauslöschlichen Schande': Antijüdische Gewalttätigkeiten in Hamburg vom 17. bis zum 19. Jahrhundert." In Bernard Lachaise and Burghart Schmidt, eds. *Bordeaux – Hamburg. Zwei Städte und ihre Geschichte. Bordeaux – Hambourg. Deux villes dans l'histoire*, pp. 400–27. Hamburg: DOBU Verlag.

Schmidt, Georg. 2006. "Hanse, Hanseaten und Reich in der frühen Neuzeit." In Isabelle Richefort and Burghart Schmidt, eds. *Les relations entre la France et les villes hanséatiques de Hambourg, Brême et Lübeck. Moyen Âge – XIXe siècle*, pp. 229–59. Brussels: Lang.

Schmidt, Heinrich R. 2009. "Kirchenordnung und Kirchenzucht im reformierten Europa." In Ansgar Reiss and Sabine Witt, eds. *Calvinismus. Die Reformierten in Deutschland und Europa. Eine Ausstellung des Deutschen Historischen Museums Berlin und der Johannes-a-Lasco-Bibliothek Emden*, pp. 351–56. Dresden: Sandstein.

Schmidt-Eppendorf, Peter. 2004. "Die katholische Kirche in Hamburg von der Reformation bis zur Gegenwart." In *Hamburgische Kirchengeschichte in Aufsätzen*, part 2 (Reformation und konfessionelles Zeitalter), pp. 407–28. Hamburg: Verein für Hamburgische Geschichte.

Schmidt-Rimpler, Walter. *Geschichte des Kommissionsgeschäfts in Deutschland*, vol. 1 (Die Zeit bis zum Ende des 15. Jahrhunderts). Halle: Buchhandlung des Waisenhauses, 1915.

Schmitz, Otto. 1903. *Die maritime Politik der Habsburger in den Jahren 1625–1628.* Bonn: S. Foppen.

Schmoller, Gustav. 1884. "Die ältere Elbhandelspolitik, die Stapelrechte und -kämpfe von Magdeburg, Hamburg und Lüneburg (Studien über die wirthschaftliche Politik Friedrichs des Großen und Preußens überhaupt von 1680 bis 1786)." In *Jahrbuch für Gesetzgebung, Verwaltung und Volkswirtschaft im Deutschen Reich* 8, 4, pp. 23–50.

Schramm, Percy Ernst. 1969. "Hamburg und die Adelsfrage (bis 1806)." In *Zeitschrift des Vereins für Hamburgische Geschichte* 55, pp. 81–93.

Schuback, Arnold. 1820. *Chronologisches, bis auf die neuesten Zeiten fortgesetztes Verzeichniss der bisherigen Mitglieder eines Hochedlen und Hochweisen Raths, der Ehrbaren Oberalten und der Verordneten löblicher Cämmerey der Freyen Stadt Hamburg.* Hamburg: Meißner.

Schulte Beerbühl, Margrit. 2007. *Deutsche Kaufleute in London. Welthandel und Einbürgerung (1660–1818).* Munich: Oldenbourg.

Schultze, Alfred. 1908. "Über Gästerecht und Gastgericht in den deutschen Städten des Mittelalters." In *Historische Zeitschrift* 101, pp. 473–528.

Schultze-von Lasaulx, Hermann. 1961. *Geschichte des Hamburgischen Notariats seit dem Ausgang des 18. Jahrhunderts.* Hamburg: Hamburgische Notarkammer.

Schwartz, Stuart B. 2003. "The Contexts of Vieira's Toleration of Jews and New Christians." In *Luso-Brazilian Review* 40, pp. 33–44.

Schwindrazheim, Hildamarie. 1930. "Plastik in Hamburg aus der ersten Hälfte des siebzehnten Jahrhunderts III." In *Zeitschrift des Vereins für Hamburgische Geschichte* 31, pp. 123–60.

Selzer, Stephan, and Ulf-Christian Ewert. 2001. "Verhandeln und Verkaufen, Vernetzen und Vertrauen. Über die Netzwerkstruktur des hansischen Handels." In *Hansische Geschichtsblätter* 119, pp. 135–61.

Serrão, José Vicente. 1998. "O quadro económico. Configurações estruturais e tendências de evolução." In José Mattoso, ed. *História De Portugal*, vol. 4, pp. 71–117. Lisbon: Estampa.

Shaw, L. M. E. 1989. "The Inquisition and the Portuguese Economy." In *The Journal of European Economic History* 18, pp. 415–31.

Sieveking, Heinrich. 1933. "Die Hamburger Bank 1619–1875." In Universität Hamburg, ed. *Festschrift der Hamburgischen Universität ihrem Ehrenrektor Herrn Bürgermeister Werner von Melle*, pp. 21–110. Glückstadt: Augustin.

Sillem, Wilhelm. 1883. "Zur Geschichte der Niederländer in Hamburg von ihrer Ankunft bis zum Abschluß des Niederlänischen Contracts 1605." In *Zeitschrift des Vereins für Hamburgische Geschichte* 7, pp. 481–598.

Silva, Francisco Ribeiro da. 1988. *O Porto e o seu termo (1580–1640): Os homens, as instituções e o poder*, 2 vols. Porto: Arquivo Histórico da Câmara Municipal do Porto.

Smith, David Grant. 1974. "Old Christian Merchants and the Foundation of the Brazil Company, 1649." In *Hispanic American Historical Review* 54, 2, pp. 233–59.

—. 1975. "The Mercantile Class of Portugal and Brazil in the Seventeenth Century: A Socio-Economic Study of the Merchants of Lisbon and Bahia, 1620–1690." Austin: University of Texas at Austin (unpublished diss.).

Sombart, Werner. (1911) 1913. *The Jews and Modern Capitalism*, trans. M. Epstein. New York: E. P. Dutton.

Sprandel, Rolf. 1984. "Die Konkurrenzfähigkeit der Hanse im Spätmittelalter." In *Hansische Geschichtsblätter* 102, pp. 21–38.

Stock, Raimund. 1941. "Inhalt und Funktion der Reichspolizeiordnungen. Ein Beitrag zur Entwicklung des Polizeibegriffs." Leipzig: Universität Leipzig (unpublished diss.).

Stols, Eddy. 1970. "Les marchands flamands dans la Péninsule Ibérique à la fin du seizième siècle et pendant la première moitié du dix-septième siècle." In Hermann Kellenbenz, ed. *Fremde Kaufleute auf der Iberischen Halbinsel*, pp. 226–38. Cologne: Böhlau.

—. 1971. *De Spaanse Brabanders of de handelsbetrekkingen der Zuidelijke Nederlanden met de Iberische Wereld 1598–1648*, 2 vols. Brussels: Paleis der Academiën.

—. 1973. "Os mercadores flamengos em Portugal e no Brasil antes das conquistas holandesas." In *Anais de História* [Assis] 5, pp. 9–54.

—. 1988. "Dutch and Flemish Victims of the Inquisition in Brazil." In Jan Lechner, ed. *Essays on Cultural Identity in Colonial Latin America. Problems and Repercussions*, pp. 43–62. Leiden: TCLA.

—. 1997. "Convivências e conivências luso-flamengas na rota do açúcar brasileiro." In *Ler História* 32, pp. 119–47.

Stoob, Heinz. 1995. *Die Hanse*. Graz: Styria.

Straub, Eberhard. 1980. *Pax et Imperium. Spaniens Kampf um seine Friedensordnung in Europa zwischen 1617 und 1635*. Paderborn: Schöningh.

Stuczynski, Claude B. 2000. "Cristãos novos e judaísmo no início da época moderna. Identidade religiosa e 'razão de estado.'" In *Lusitania Sacra* 12 (2nd Series), pp. 355–66.

—. 2007. "New Christian Political Leadership in Times of Crisis: The Pardon Negotiations of 1605." In Moisés Orfali Levi, ed. *Leadership in Times of Crisis*, pp. 45–70. Ramat-Gan: Bar Ilan University Press.

Studemund-Halévy, Michael, ed. 1994b and 1997. *Die Sefarden in Hamburg*, 2 parts. Hamburg: Buske.

—. 2000. *Biographisches Lexikon der Hamburger Sefarden: Die Grabinschriften des Portugiesenfriedhofs an der Königstraße in Hamburg-Altona*. Hamburg: Christians.

—. 2002. "'Es residiren in Hamburg Minister fremder Mächte.' Sefardische Residenten in Hamburg." In Rotraud Ries and Johannes Friedrich Battenberg, eds. *Hofjuden: Ökonomie und Interkulturalität: Die jüdische Wirtschaftselite im 18. Jahrhundert*, pp. 154–76. Hamburg: Christians.

—. 2005. "Les aléas de la foi. Parcours d'un jeune Portugais entre église et synagogue." In Birgit E. Klein, ed. *Memoria. Wege jüdischen Erinnerns. Festschrift für Michael Brocke zum 65. Geburtstag*, pp. 363–82. Berlin: Metropol.

Studemund-Halévy, Michael, and Sandra Neves da Silva. 2004. "Tortured Memories. Jacob Rosales alias Imanuel Bocarro Francês: A Life from the Files of the Inquisition." In Stephan Wendehorst, ed. *The Roman Inquisition, the Index and the Jews. Contexts, Sources and Perspectives*, pp. 107–53. Leiden: Brill.

Studnicki-Gizbert, Daviken. 2007. *A Nation Upon the Ocean Sea: Portugal's Atlantic Diaspora and the Crisis of the Spanish Empire*. Oxford: Oxford University Press.

—. 2009. "La Nación among the Nations: Portuguese and Other Maritime Trading Diasporas in the Atlantic, Sixteenth to Eighteenth Centuries." In Richard L. Kagan and Philip D. Morgan, eds. *Atlantic Diasporas. Jews, Conversos, and Crypto-Jews in the Age of Mercantilism, 1500–1800*, pp. 75–98. Baltimore: Johns Hopkins University Press.

Subrahmanyam, Sanjay, ed. 1996. *Merchant Networks in the Early Modern World*. Aldershot: Variorum.

Sutcliffe, Adam. 2007. "Sephardic Amsterdam and the Myths of Jewish Modernity." In *The Jewish Quarterly Review* 97, 3, pp. 417–37.

—. 2009. "Jewish History in an Age of Atlanticism." In Richard L. Kagan and Philip D. Morgan, eds. *Atlantic Diasporas. Jews, Conversos, and Crypto-Jews in the Age of Mercantilism, 1500–1800*, pp. 18–30. Baltimore: Johns Hopkins University Press.

Swetschinski, Daniel M. 1975. "The Spanish Consul and the Jews of Amsterdam." In Michael A. Fishbane and Paul R. Flohr, eds. *Texts and Responses: Studies Presented to Nahum N. Glatzer on the Occasion of his Seventieth Birthday by His Students*, pp. 158–72. Leiden: Brill.

—. 1981. "Kinship and Commerce: The Foundations of Portuguese Jewish Life in Seventeenth-Century Holland." In *Studia Rosenthaliana* 15, pp. 52–74.

—. 2000. *Reluctant Cosmopolitans: The Portuguese Jews of Seventeenth-Century Amsterdam*. Oxford: Littman Library of Jewish Civilization.

Tavares, Maria José Ferro. 1982. *Os Judeus em Portugal no Século XV*. Lisbon: Universidade Nova de Lisboa.

Tavim, José Alberto Rodrigues da Silva. 2009. "Diásporas para o Reino e Império. Judeus conversos e sua mobilidade. Aproximações a um tema." In Andréa Doré and Antonio César de Almeida Santos, eds. *Temas Setecentistas. Governos e populações no império português*, pp. 369–88. Curitiba: UFPR/SCHLA.

Teensma, Benjamin Nicolaas. 1988. "Resentment in Recife: Jews and Public Opinion in 17th-Century Dutch Brazil." In Jan Lechner, ed. *Essays on Cultural Identity in Colonial Latin America. Problems and Repercussions*, pp. 63–78. Leiden: TCLA.

Thieme, Hans. 1958. "Die Rechtsstellung der Fremden in Deutschland vom 11. bis zum 18. Jahrhundert." In *Recueils de la Société Jean Bodin* 10, pp. 201–16.

Thomas, Werner. 2001a. *La represión del protestantismo en España 1517–1648*. Leuven: Leuven University Press.

—. 2001b. *Los protestantes y la inquisición en España en tiempos de reforma y contrareforma*. Leuven: Leuven University Press.

Torres, José Veiga. 1978. "Uma longa guerra social. Os ritmos da repressão inquisitorial em Portugal." In *Revista de História Económica e Social* 1, pp. 55–68.

—. 1986. "Uma longa guerra social. Novas perspectivas para o estudo da inquisição portuguesa. A inquisição de Coimbra." In *Revista de História das Ideias* 8, pp. 59–70.

—. 1994. "Da Repressão Religiosa para a Promoção Social. A Inquisição como instância legitimadora da promoção social da burguesia mercantil." In *Revista Crítica de Ciências Sociais* 40, pp. 109–35.

Treue, Wolfgang. 2000. "Aufsteiger oder Außenseiter? Jüdische Konvertiten im 16. und 17. Jahrhundert." In *Aschkenas* 10, 2, pp. 307–36.

Trivellato, Francesca. 2003. "Juifs de Livourne, Italiens de Lisbonne, hindous de Goa. Réseaux marchands et échanges interculturels à l'époque moderne." In *Annales. Histoire, Sciences Sociales* 58, pp. 581–603.

—. 2009a. *The Familiarity of Strangers. The Sephardic Diaspora, Livorno, and Cross-Cultural Trade in the Early Modern Period*. New Haven: Yale Universty Press.

—. 2009b. "Sephardic Merchants in the Early Modern Atlantic and Beyond. Toward a Comparative Historical Approach to Business Cooperation." In Richard L. Kagan and Philip D. Morgan, eds. *Atlantic diasporas. Jews, conversos, and crypto-Jews in the age of mercantilism, 1500–1800*, pp. 99–120. Baltimore: Johns Hopkins University Press.

Trivellato, Francesca, Leor Halevi, and Cátia Antunes, eds. 2014. *Religion and Trade. Cross-Cultural Exchanges in World History, 1000–1900*. Oxford: Oxford University Press.

Ulbert, Jörg. 2006. "La fonction consulaire à l'époque moderne. Définition, état des connaissances et perspectives de recherche." In Jörg Ulbert and Gérard Le Bouëdec, eds. *La fonction consulaire à l'époque moderne. L'Affirmation d'une institution économique et politique (1500–1800)*, pp. 9–20. Rennes: Presses universitaires de Rennes.

Verbeemen, J. 1957. "De buitenpoorterij in de Nederlanden." In *Bijdragen voor de Geschiedenis der Nederlanden* 12, pp. 81–97, 191–217.

Vlessing, Odette. 1995. "The Portuguese-Jewish Merchant Community in Seventeenth-Century Amsterdam." In Clé Lesger and L. Noordegraaf, eds. *Entrepreneurs and Entrepreneurship in Early Modern Times. Merchants and Industrialists within the Orbit of the Dutch Staple Market*, pp. 223–43. Den Haag: Stichting Hollandse Historische Reeks.

Vogel, Walther. 1928–1933. "Beiträge zur Statistik der deutschen Seeschiffahrt im 17. und 18. Jahrhundert." In *Hansische Geschichtsblätter* 33 (1928/1929), pp. 110–52, and *Hansische Geschichtsblätter* 57 (1932/1933), pp. 78–151.

—. 1956. "Handelskonjunkturen und Wirtschaftskrisen in ihrer Auswirkung auf den Seehandel der Hansestädte 1560–1806." In *Hansische Geschichtsblätter* 74, pp. 50–64.

Voigt, Johann Friedrich. 1892. "Einige Mittheilungen aus den ersten Jahrzehnten der Verwaltung der Hamburger Bank." In *Mitteilungen des Vereins für Hamburgische Geschichte* 5, 14, pp. 287–97.

—. 1912. "Die Anleihen der Stadt Hamburg während der Jahre 1601 bis 1650." In *Zeitschrift des Vereins für Hamburgische Geschichte* 17, pp. 129–253.

—. 1916. *Der Haushalt der Stadt Hamburg 1601 bis 1650.* Hamburg: Gräfe & Sillem.

Vries, Jan de, and Ad van der Woude. 1997. *The First Modern Economy: Success, Failure, and Perseverance of the Dutch Economy, 1500–1815.* Cambridge: Cambridge University Press.

Wagner, F. 1894. "Zur Geschichte der Jesuiten-Mission in Altona." In *Zeitschrift des Vereins für Hamburgische Geschichte* 9, pp. 633–38.

Wallenborn, Hiltrud. 2003. *Bekehrungseifer, Judenangst und Handelsinteresse. Amsterdam, Hamburg und London als Ziele sefardischer Migration im 17. Jahrhundert.* Hildesheim: Olms.

Wasserman, Stanley, and Katherin Faust. 1994. *Social Network Analysis: Methods and Applications.* Cambridge: Cambridge University Press.

Weber, Karl-Klaus. 2002. "Hamburg und die Generalstaaten. Von der Gründung der Republik 1579 bis zu den Anfängen des Dreißigjährigen Krieges aus Sicht niederländischer Quellen." In *Zeitschrift des Vereins für Hamburgische Geschichte* 88, pp. 43–88.

Weber, Klaus. 2000. "Die Admiralitätszoll- und Convoygeld-Einnahmebücher. Eine wichtige Quelle für Hamburgs Wirtschaftsgeschichte im 18. Jahrhundert." In *Hamburger Wirtschafts-Chronik* 1 (New Series), pp. 83–112.

—. 2004. *Deutsche Kaufleute im Atlantikhandel 1680–1830. Unternehmen und Familien in Hamburg, Cádiz und Bordeaux.* Munich: C. H. Beck.

Weber, Max. (1904/1905) 1958. *The Protestant Ethic and the Spirit of Capitalism,* trans. Talcott Parsons. New York: Scribner.

Weise, Erich. 1950. "Stader Fernhandelspläne seit den Zeiten der Merchant Adventurers und ihre Beziehungen zu Hamburg." In *Hamburger Wirtschafts-Chronik* 1, pp. 13–30.

Westphalen, Nikolaus Adolf. 1841. *Hamburgs Verfassung und Verwaltung in ihrer allmähligen Entwicklung bis auf die neueste Zeit,* 2 vols. Hamburg: Perthes-Besser & Mauke.

Whaley, Joachim. 1985. *Religious Toleration and Social Change in Hamburg, 1529–1819.* Cambridge: Cambridge University Press.

—. 1995. "Minorities and Tolerance in Hamburg, 16th–18th Centuries." In Hugo Soly and Alfons K. L. Thijs, eds. *Minderheden in Westeuropese steden (16de –20ste eeuw),* pp. 173–88. Brussels: Belgisch Historisch Instituut te Rome.

Wilke, Jürgen. 1984. *Nachrichtenauswahl und Medienrealität in vier Jahrhunderten. Eine Modellstudie zur Verbindung von historischer und empirischer Publizistikwissenschaft.* Berlin: De Gruyter.

Wiskemann, Erwin. 1929. *Hamburg und die Welthandelspolitik von den Anfängen bis zur Gegenwart.* Hamburg: Friederichsen, De Gruyter.

Wohlwill, Adolf. 1894. "Ein hamburgischer Auswanderungs- und Colonialpolitiker am Ausgange des 17. Jahrhunderts." In *Mitteilungen des Vereins für Hamburgische Geschichte* 6, 16, pp. 63–65.

Wubs-Mrozewicz, Justyna. 2013. "The Hanse in medieval and early modern Europe: An introduction." In Justyna Wubs-Mrozewicz and Stuart Jenks, eds. *The Hanse in Medieval and Early Modern Europe,* pp. 1–36. Leiden: Brill.

Wurm, Christian Friedrich. 1855. "Urkundliche Mittheilungen über die Schuld und die letzten Schicksale des Foppius van Aitzema. Nachtrag zum vorjährigen Osterprogramm." In K. W. M. Wiebel, ed. *Verzeichniss der Vorlesungen, welche am Hamburgischen akademischen und Real-Gymnasium von Ostern 1855 bis Ostern 1856 gehalten wurden,* pp. 43–57. Hamburg: Meissner.

Zeiger, Karl. 1936. *Hamburgs Finanzen von 1563–1650.* Rostock: Hinstorff.

Zunckel, Julia. 1997. *Rüstungsgeschäfte im Dreißigjährigen Krieg. Unternehmerkräfte, Militärgüter und Marktstrategien im Handel zwischen Genua, Amsterdam und Hamburg*. Berlin: Duncker & Humblot.

Zunkel, Friedrich. 1975. "Ehre, Reputation." In Otto Brunner, Werner Conze, and Reinhart Koselleck eds. *Geschichtliche Grundbegriffe. Historisches Lexikon zur politisch-sozialen Sprache*, vol. 2, pp. 1–64. Stuttgart: Klett-Cotta.

Index

https://doi.org/10.1515/9783110472103-022